Like a Bomb Going Off

LIKE A BOMB GOING OFF

*Leonid Yakobson and
Ballet as Resistance
in Soviet Russia*

Janice Ross

Foreword by Lynn Garafola

Yale UNIVERSITY PRESS   NEW HAVEN & LONDON

Yale University Press books may be purchased in quantity for educational,
business, or promotional use. For information, please e-mail sales.press@
yale.edu (U.S. office) or sales@yaleup.co.uk (U.K. office).

Printed in the United States of America.

Library of Congress Cataloging-in-Publication Data
Ross, Janice.
Like a bomb going off : Leonid Yakobson and ballet as resistance in
Soviet Russia / Janice Ross ; foreword by Lynn Garafola.
pages cm
Includes bibliographical references and index.
ISBN 978-0-300-20763-7 (hardback)
1. IAkobson, Leonid. 2. Choreographers—Soviet Union—Biography. 3. Dancers—
Soviet Union—Biography. 4. Ballet—Soviet Union—History. 5. Dance—Political
aspects—Soviet Union. I. Title.
GV1785.I17R67 2015
792.8'0947—dc23   2014022306

A catalogue record for this book is available from the British Library.
This paper meets the requirements of ANSI/NISO Z39.48–1992 (Permanence of Paper).

10 9 8 7 6 5 4 3 2 1

Frontispiece: Yakobson in rehearsal for *Troika* with dancers of his company,
Choreographic Miniatures, Leningrad, 1973. Photo: Anatoly Pronin.

Dedicated with love to the memories of Joshua Bartel and Keith Bartel

Contents

CONTENTS

Foreword

Lynn Garafola

SOVIET DANCE HISTORY is full of muted voices, artists who spent decades in creative silence while keeping inner faith with the modernist ideals of the 1920s. Among this courageous group was Leonid Yakobson. A choreographer as crotchety as he was resolute, Yakobson was an artist of contradictions, a modernist who shed his early proletarian skin but continued to make war on ballet and use unconventional movement, even as he worked with Russia's greatest ballet dancers. He made dances for the leading Soviet companies, but struggled for years to establish his own troupe, which became the first of its kind in the postwar Soviet Union. He was a Jew who created his first Jewish-themed dances in the late 1940s as Jews were being arrested as "rootless cosmopolitans" and "bourgeois nationalists," yet he refused to emigrate even when it became possible to do so. He was a man with a profound sense of irony who seemed unfazed when a work of his disappeared at a censor's pen stroke. He had an unquenchable desire to make dances. Denied a studio, he wrote libretti; even on his deathbed he awoke from a nap and told his wife that he had just made up a new ballet. He choreographed because he had to, and he believed that ballet mattered.

This contradictory and fascinating artist is the subject of *Like a Bomb Going Off: Leonid Yakobson and Ballet as Resistance in Soviet Russia*. Janice Ross, who teaches dance history at Stanford University, has already written two important books, both with an American twist. *Moving Lessons: Margaret H'Doubler and the Beginning of Dance in American Education* (2000) is about the educator who established the first U.S. college dance department, and *Anna Halprin: Experience as Dance* (2007) focuses on the experimental California choreographer who became a pioneer of the dance healing movement.

In her most recent book, Ross ventures far from these American modern dance subjects to explore the rich and complex history of twentieth-century ballet and the even more complex history of the expressive arts in the Soviet Union. A tightly focused and fascinating study of Yakobson's work, the biography presents its subject through the multiple ideologies of which he was both a product and a critic, offering a view of him as an artist, a citizen, and a man of high-minded principle. A "voice of dissent," as Ross calls him, Yakobson crossed swords with censors and cultural bureaucrats, "staging resistance from within the most public vocabulary of compliance."

Yakobson launched himself into the debates of the late 1920s as a prole-tarian artist, a maker in dance of the new Soviet present. As the 1920s turned into the 1930s, however, the ideological ground began to shift. Ballet after ballet was held up to a distorting mirror of ideologies. Soon, artists and intellectuals began disappearing. During these years, Yakobson staged relatively little for the professional stage. Much of his choreography was for students and hence scrutinized less for ideological correctness. He was also dispatched to the provinces to transplant ballet culture from the metropole, an example of the ethnographic populism that went hand in hand with Soviet cultural imperialism beginning in the 1930s.

Until the mid-1940s Yakobson behaved like an exemplary Soviet artist. True, he was Jewish, but this did not appear to alter the trajectory of his career; it was simply one aspect of his identity. As Jews became the target of anti-Semitic campaigns in the late 1940s, however, Yakobson's position grew increasingly tenuous. He was denounced as a "cosmopolitan" and in 1951, only weeks after winning the Stalin Prize for his ballet *Shurale*, dismissed from the Kirov Theater. Meanwhile, attacks on "formalism" were stepped up, and the screws on artistic expression tightened. After World War II only a fraction of Yakobson's ballets reached the stage. While others might have lost heart, Yakobson persisted. He became "increasingly adept," Ross tells us, "at playing with totalitarian discourse and challenging the idea that it was a completely suffocating ideological container for artists." His heroism was that of the *résistant*.

Despite the constraints, Yakobson kept up a steady stream of work. For a new Moldavian folk ensemble in Kishinev, whose Jewish population was decimated by the Nazis, he choreographed a suite of Jewish dances that sought to preserve "a vanishing culture" through performance. He created dances inspired by Isadora Duncan's technique, which was still taught in Moscow in the late 1940s. By far his most important project of the 1950s was *Spartacus*. With music by Aram Khachaturian, who dithered for more than a decade, and a libretto by Nikolai Volkov, the ballet was a plum assignment that came to Yakobson only when Fyodor Lopukhov became director of the Kirov after Stalin's death in 1953.

A success at home, *Spartacus* flopped abroad. Opening the Bolshoi's 1962 New York season, it became entangled in Cold War discourse, with Allan Hughes at the *New York Times* and Walter Terry at the *New York Herald-Tribune* taking potshots at the ballet's "dull" pageantry and "non-dancey" choreography. Yakobson was devastated. It was the first time he had been allowed out of the Soviet Union, his first time in New York since 1920, and he had counted on American plaudits to bolster his position at home. Now his "tormentors" had been handed a trump card. In ballerina Maya Plisetskaya's dressing room at the old Met, Yakobson wept.

The "Thaw" that followed Stalin's death allowed a modicum of artistic and intellectual freedom. Books like Solzhenitsyn's *One Day in the Life of Ivan Denisovich* (1962) were published, and the music of once-proscribed composers was heard in concert halls and on the ballet stage. As historians dug into modernism's forbidden past, Yakobson staged *The Bedbug* (1962), based on the 1929 satirical play by Vladimir Mayakovsky, a hero of Yakobson's youth. Two years later he returned to early Soviet subject matter in *The Twelve*, inspired by Alexander Blok's 1918 poem. In Yakobson's hands, both works acquired a critical sting, a raw emotionality, and a movement style that shattered the idea of ballet as an exemplary, academic practice. Both, moreover, were perceived as fiercely anti-Soviet, mocking the Revolution and attacking Soviet cultural arbiters and corrupt bureaucrats. *The Twelve* was pulled after its first performance, and it was only after endless sparring with censors that Yakobson was able to restage *The Bedbug* for his own company.

He received permission to organize this restaging only in 1969, by which time the Thaw had given way to the "Era of Stagnation." But Yakobson, now in his mid-sixties, was reinvigorated. His company, which he named "Choreographic Miniatures" because of its focus on short rather than full-evening works, was the first in Russia led by a choreographer since the 1920s. Over the next six years, all that remained of his life, he choreographed nearly two dozen works, in addition to restaging earlier ones. Had circumstances been different, his reputation, Ross speculates, might have been the equal of his early contemporary George Balanchine.

In some respects Yakobson remained an essentially Soviet artist, wed to the libretto, to characters rooted in time and place, to commissioned scores and lavish scenery. In others he refused to conform. In a system that exalted "objective reality," he insisted on following the promptings of his imagination, in creating ballets that looked at the world from a personal viewpoint. He peopled his most biting works with the flotsam and jetsam of Soviet society rather than socialist heroes, and in his Jewish cycle of works evoked the Yiddish folkways of the shtetl at a time when Soviet Jews were being aggressively persecuted. He was a throwback to the 1920s, when a Soviet artist could also be a nationalist artist, a time when modernism flourished and choreographers made some of the first plotless dances. It was also the decade when Yakobson walked into a ballet studio and found his calling. That studio and the innumerable ones that followed became his life. It was where he lived and worked, found family and friends, and created a singular body of memorable dances that spoke to the Soviet condition. In *Like a Bomb Going Off*, Ross brings to life the hidden history of this courageous artist, while revealing ballet as a medium of power that could challenge despotism and offer hope to those who dreamed of a better future.

Like a Bomb Going Off

Note on Transliteration

THE TRANSLITERATION SYSTEM used in this book generally follows the one devised by Gerald Abraham for *The New Grove Dictionary of Music and Musicians* (1980), with the modifications introduced by Richard Taruskin in *Mussorgsky: Eight Essays and an Epilogue* (1993). The principal exceptions to the system concern commonly accepted spellings of names and places (Stravinsky rather than Stravinskiy).

JOSEPH STALIN'S BOX in the Bolshoi Theater survived the bomb that heavily damaged the building during World War II. Shunning the majestic red-velvet-draped tsar's box that had been built as a stage within a stage for leaders when the grand theater was constructed in 1824, Stalin had restructured a more hidden side-stage box, with a complex of adjacent salons, to his specifications in 1936. He added a small office with a desk and chair in the gray salon, curtains, and, according to rumor, a dense window of bulletproof glass at the front of the box with surrounding reinforcements of concrete. This apocryphal story of bulletproof glass in Stalin's theater box led to its being nicknamed "Stalin's Glass," as if Comrade Stalin were a spectral reflection inside his own drinking glass. The more vivid metaphor this image evokes, however, is that of the need for a shield between spectator and performer in what could be the perilous enterprise of performing or viewing ballet during the Stalinist era. Even the customary ritual of tossing bouquets of flowers to dancers during the curtain call was suspended during Stalin's reign. Instead, floral tributes were restricted to large baskets that were inspected before being carried onstage by uniformed attendants.[1] It was well established that multiple committees of government officials vetted all ballets before they reached the stage, so restricting even the tossing of flowers to a single officially approved arrangement underscored just how controlled by the state the exchange between ballet artists and audiences had become.

This is the world that Leonid Yakobson inherited as a youthful artist. This is the world that shaped him, contained him, and alternately made possible and impossible his life as a rebellious artist. The Bolshoi Theater in particular was a place where the collusion of art and politics stretched back decades. After the Bolshevik Revolution of 1917, the Bolshoi stage was the platform that V. I. Lenin stood on to declare the birth of the Soviet Union. It has been dubbed "the public face of the Communist utopia."[2] These overlapping geographies of the stage and politics, heroism and art-making, only intensified and grew in complexity during the decades of Stalin's reign. Yakobson's resilient optimism enabled him to survive as a defiant artist in a climate that reduced others to blind despair.

Choreographers, particularly *ballet* choreographers, are rarely if ever valorized as heroic art makers, especially when confronting a totalitarian political state. In the Cold War lore it was the defecting Soviet *dancers* who were the heroes. The ones who made the dances, the choreographers, were rarely if ever mentioned as potential radicals. In contrast, during this same post–World War II period, choreographers in the West were heralded as expanding the boundaries of art and repudiating old traditions—innovations that Westerners, congratulating themselves, considered to be products unique to a democratic political system.

The story of Leonid Yakobson is a hidden yet monumental tale of an unruly native genius, and it brings with it the discovery that during the initial years of the Cold War, the West did not have an exclusive purchase on experimentation in dance, nor were the celebrated defectors from Soviet ballet companies the only ballet artists fleeing state-controlled art in the USSR. While American modernist choreographers and postmodern dance radicals were paring dance down to its spare, non-narrative essence, a parallel break with tradition was attempting to unfold in the USSR through many of the works that Yakobson created for the Kirov and Bolshoi ballets. This book restores his silenced voice from that era. It also invites a new understanding of the unique cultural work that dance—art built on the moving body—does in registering displacement and cultural exile, in this instance particularly for Soviet Jews. Yakobson never considered himself a political artist, but his most important ballets can be called political. They aroused strong sentiments, set Soviet authorities on edge, elicited prohibitions, sparked controversy, and drove the demand for tickets to levels that exceeded the capacity of theaters. Through careful and shrewd concessions and personal charm as well as rage, Yakobson managed to continue his work through most of the period of the Stalinist terrors by coding his dances so a portion of a repressed society understood what he was doing.

Yakobson's work reveals dance as the ultimate stealth art form—his ballets can appear complacent and docile on the surface while just below they display an aggressive aesthetic that challenges the status quo. This book traces why Yakobson was subjected to censorship for attempting to insert Jewish subjects into one of the most regulated Western ideals of the pure, culturally unmarked body—the Russian classical ballet dancer at the Kirov and Bolshoi theaters. It questions how his survival was possible in the USSR, while offering a sobering reminder of how political forces can reach deep into culture. It also reinforces an understanding that the intrigues of politics and ballet did not end with the French court of Louis XIV.

This book is the product of more than a decade of research undertaken in the United States, Russia, and Israel with the intent of discovering how it was that ballet could be so threatening to Soviet authorities as to incite repeated acts of censorship and suppression, and yet not be banned entirely or cause its author to be sent to the Gulag or murdered. My hope is that readers will come away from this book with a heightened sense of discovery about how ballet can be a vital forum for courage as well as beauty in times of danger, and about how artists who lack the freedom to choose subjects or styles still manage to produce important, even defiant, work.

"Like a bomb going off." This is the phrase that contemporary Russians often used when describing the impact of a new ballet by Yakobson during the Soviet era. A statement of surprise as well as danger, it captures the feeling of risk and exciting uncertainty that Yakobson's ballets aroused, even as his fraught relationship with Soviet political authority trapped many of his ambitions. His achievements as well as failures are put in historical, intellectual, and theatrical contexts here by a consideration of the varieties of subversive qualities that he inserted into Soviet ballet.

Yakobson's life was framed by momentous historical shifts, beginning with his early adolescence during the famine and depravations after the Russian Revolution of 1917 through to his emergence as a leading avant-garde choreographer during the 1930s and 1940s, the central years of Stalin's repression and terror. Yakobson continued working through the Khrushchev "Thaw" and until his death in 1975, during the retrenchment of Leonid Brezhnev's era of stagnation and just as he was realizing a company of his own after decades of entreaties to authorities.

That Yakobson continued to make bold, often culturally and socially provocative ballets throughout these tumultuous decades points to the uniquely powerful place that culture, and particularly ballet, occupied in the totalitarian Soviet state. Less directly, this examination of his life and work also allows a rare glimpse of the naked collusion between politics and the control of images in an autocratic system. The Yakobson ballets that were permitted on the stage, and especially those that were censored or prohibited, offer an interior glimpse of how dance could function simultaneously as a confirmation of, yet challenge to, authoritarian power.

Born in Saint Petersburg in 1904, Yakobson was the grandson of a famous Jewish violinist with the orchestra for the Imperial Ballet, employment that made it possible for the family to receive special permission to live in the city with its stringent restrictions on Jews as residents. Based there his entire life, Yakobson began his artistic path in the rich period of experimentation that flourished in the 1920s and then came to an abrupt halt with the rising conservatism of the anti-formalist campaign of the mid-1930s. Part of what lends his story its uniqueness is Yakobson's determination to keep alive the radical aesthetic impulses of this earlier period of artistic experimentation. That he succeeded in doing so within a Soviet cultural climate opposed to modernism—one mandating that art should be direct, uplifting, and with a clear narrative accessible to the broad masses—made his achievement all the more remarkable. While innovative Russian choreographers from the 1910s and 1920s who left before the borders closed, such as George Balanchine, Michel Fokine, Vaslav Nijinsky, and Bronislava Nijinska, carried forward the modernist impetus outside the USSR in a climate that welcomed ballet innovation, inside the Soviet Union the situation was dramatically different. There restrictions placed on Yakobson through party oversight committees forced a covert coding of both modernist and cultural inventions in his ballets as he worked to develop the movement vocabularies of *danse d'école*.[3] Other important innovators who stayed behind, Fyodor Lopukhov and Kasyan Goleizovsky foremost among them, effectively saw their careers terminated in the 1930s in the USSR by official prohibitions of their choreographic work.

Yakobson, however, persisted. He continued to explore and extend these early influences into the 1970s, creating numerous short-format works, called ballet miniatures, that often used grotesque, athletic, or pantomimic movements to address social, dramatic, or erotic subjects with narrative clarity and concision. He favored original music, often in a contemporary style, believing that distinctive forms of music elicited an individual choreographic response. Among his most notable works were his full-length *Spartacus* (1956 and 1962), which discarded the lifts and pointe work of traditional ballet language and featured characters who were fully developed psychologically, and *Exercise XX* (1972), a dance that verged on pure abstraction. In 1969 he founded Choreographic Miniatures, the first Soviet ballet company since the 1920s with a repertoire of original ballets by a single choreographer.

A latecomer to ballet, Yakobson began to study dance in 1921, at the age of seventeen, with the celebrated character dancer Aleksandr Chekrïgin. Despite Yakobson's advanced age to begin ballet training, Chekrïgin agreed to take him on and taught the teen in his Petrograd studio. After three years of accelerated study, Yakobson transferred to the former Imperial Ballet School, now renamed the Leningrad State Choreographic Institute. Here he studied first in the evening school and later in the regular school with Vladimir Ponomaryov and Viktor Semyonov. Upon graduating in 1926, Yakobson was accepted into the corps de ballet of the State Academic Theater for Opera and Ballet (GATOB), as the former Imperial Ballet and future Kirov Ballet was known in the 1920s and early 1930s. There he danced until 1933 and was promoted to soloist. Compact and muscular, with a big jump and a high degree of coordination, Yakobson excelled at grotesque and demi-character roles. From the start of his professional career, however, Yakobson was more interested in choreographing than in performing. He had particular admiration for Fokine and his pursuit of expressive naturalness, movement outside the danse d'école, and dramatic and stylistic unity.

In 1930 Yakobson choreographed his first major work, the second act of *The Golden Age,* to an original score by Dmitriy Shostakovich. In keeping with the revolutionary spirit of the times, and as a way of updating the language and subjects of ballet, Yakobson incorporated non-dance movements from athletics and acrobatics into his choreography. He returned to choreograph for the Kirov Ballet from 1942 to 1950 and from 1956 to 1975. Yakobson also served as a choreographer for Moscow's Bolshoi Ballet from 1933 to 1942. Immensely productive despite political and economic hardships, Yakobson over his lifetime choreographed 178 ballets, including scores of "miniatures"—movement portraits often no longer than three to five minutes—on a range of subjects. In all his works, Yakobson valorized a modernist aesthetic of uncertainty: he improvised in the rehearsal studio distinctive movement phrases crafted to the individuality of each dancer, and made artistic choices that resonated strongly as political statements.

Challenged rather than intimidated by the restrictions imposed by Soviet censors on his ballets, Yakobson offered Soviet dancers and audiences an experience quite different from the prevailing Soviet aesthetic. He was unwilling to cave in completely to the government's limitations on his artistic opportunities, so despite his fraught relationships with Soviet political authorities his ballets became important resistive cultural texts during the Stalinist decades and in the years following the cultural "Thaw" of the late 1950s and early 1960s. Yakobson's ballets featured both narrative as well as abstract qualities, and so offer a different lens on dance modernism as it originated in early twentieth-century Russia and was subsequently developed in the West. While questioning the form and content of ballet and repositioning its social relevance, Yakobson retained early twentieth-century movement innovations, such as turned-in and parallel-foot positions, oddly angled lifts, and floor work, all of which challenged Soviet ballet orthodoxies.

Yakobson viewed ballet as a form of political discourse that could be layered with social challenges. At the same time he used it to articulate individual and cultural subjectivities, particularly the suppressed identity of Soviet Jews. The majority of Yakobson's ballets celebrated reinvention and self-authorship—the freedom of the individual voice as subject and medium. Reaching beyond aesthetics, or Jewishness, and bolstered by his strong personal will, Yakobson's ballets challenged the role of the dancing body in the USSR during some of the most repressive decades of totalitarian control. He used performance to define prohibited cultural identities and resist propagandistic agendas while paving the way toward what would become a flowering of new dance in the post-Soviet 1990s.

Yakobson's work is little known outside Russia because it unfolded in a totalitarian state and there was little official effort to preserve his choreographic archive or export knowledge of him to the West—gaps that the publication of this book helps to redress. My introduction to Yakobson came in the 1970s, just as I was beginning my career as a dance critic. I began hearing brief cryptic references about a Jewish choreographer working in the USSR, someone—the only one—making interesting contemporary work. With the defections to the West in the early 1970s of the Kirov dancers Natalia Makarova and Mikhail Baryshnikov as well as Valery Panov's emigration to Israel in 1974, references to Yakobson in English-language publications increased. Then, in 1981, the name of Yakobson's widow, Irina, appeared on a list generated by the San Francisco Bay Area Council for Soviet Jewry that named prominent Soviet Jews who were being prevented from leaving the USSR.

The next reference came in 1985, when a friend, teaching at the San Francisco Ballet School, mentioned to me that a remarkable Russian woman had just started teaching in the school and company class. He described her as "the widow of some famous Russian choreographer" and the protégée of the legendary Russian ballet pedagogue Agrippina Vaganova. Once I discovered that this woman was Yakobson's widow, I promptly arranged to interview her. The first time I met with Irina Yakobson she had just finished a private coaching session at San Francisco Ballet with Makarova—who graciously helped with some impromptu translation during the interview. Thus an amazing story began to unfold. It continued across twenty-five years of conversations; scores of interviews with those who knew Yakobson or his work; observations of Irina teaching and rehearsing in the United States, Germany, Russia, and Israel; and extensive viewing of all the extant photographs and videos of her husband's ballets in her personal collection as well as his letters and unpublished writings. In 2010 Irina gave her archives to me, and I in turn donated them to the Stanford University Libraries.

Over the years, as I published articles about Yakobson, I received the same complaint from editors—why wasn't I citing contemporaneous accounts of his work by Russian critics, journalists, and other writers? As I attempted to write him into the history he had been denied, however, I confronted a double disappearance: many of his dances themselves were irretrievable, and the usual historical traces of critical reception and contemporaneous scholarship had also been suppressed. During Yakobson's lifetime, Soviet authorities had permitted essentially no major books, films, profiles, articles, or regular reviews of him and his work. His name was generally prohibited from mention in the major newspapers until and including his death in 1975, when no formal obituary ever appeared. But while the Soviet authorities may have done a systematic job of minimizing the recognition afforded him in his lifetime, they seem inadvertently to have inscribed him more indelibly in the memories of those who saw and experienced his dances. These were some of the same people who also whispered about his personal, artistic, and cultural courage in a historical moment that made standing up—or out—so dangerous. The path I trace through Yakobson's remarkable story frames the evolving role of ballet in the USSR against these complex political portraits of the nation, while highlighting the bizarreness mixed with generosity that marked life in the USSR under Communism.

ONE

Ballet and Power:
Leonid Yakobson in
Soviet Russia

From the very beginning [Leonid] Yakobson endeavored to vary, transform
and modify the movements of the classical dance with as much daring,
diversity and unconventionality as possible—as much as the genre would
tolerate. Yakobson's theatre became a declaration of freedom.
—Boris Lvov-Anokhin, *O balete,* 1962

THE BLACK-AND-WHITE FILM is only a fragment, yet its three-minute
length documents a remarkable, intimate exchange between two of the
most exceptional and beleaguered dance artists in the Soviet Union in the
late 1960s: the highly individualistic choreographer Leonid Yakobson and
the Kirov Ballet's young virtuoso Mikhail Baryshnikov. Seated side by side
as they face the mirror in a dressing room backstage at the Bolshoi Theater
in Moscow, the sixty-five-year-old Yakobson and the twenty-one-year-old

9

Baryshnikov are practicing a fleeting gesture from *Vestris,* a solo that Ya-kobson created for Baryshnikov in 1969. Repeatedly Yakobson unfurls the fingers of one hand, holding his palm close to his face, then snaps that hand into a fist, as if ripping off an imaginary mask. Each time he does this, his features instantly reconfigure, shifting from sobbing that shudders through his torso into sudden calm as his hand passes again in front of his face. In one action he wipes away an emotion and its residue in his body. Baryshnikov, sweating in his heavy stage makeup and the baroque jacket and breeches he is wearing for his role as the eighteenth-century danseur Auguste Vestris, watches Yakobson attentively.[1] He echoes the gestures of the older choreographer carefully, moving from sorrow to calm and then into drunken hilarity as his facial and bodily expressions careen from silent manic laughter, his head tipped back and his mouth open in a grimacing howl, to the swiftly reassembled expression of placid composure that ends each eruption of an emotion. In this part of the solo, Yakobson emphasizes the containment of emotions in *Vestris* just as readily as he does their demonstration. He suggests that being able to *close off* feeling is as valuable a skill as expression.

Mikhail Baryshnikov and Yakobson backstage at the 1969 Moscow International Ballet Competition, Bolshoi Theater. YouTube.

Jewish by birth, Yakobson held onto his Jewish identity culturally because religious observance was effectively prohibited. He was what Slavic Studies historian Yuri Slezkine has called "Jews in the Soviet sense . . . Jews by blood."[2] When other prominent Jewish artists or intellectuals were changing their surnames, he proudly maintained his unmistakably Jewish one. His facial features were also regarded as distinctly Jewish, particularly among non-Jewish Soviets. In later years, when the movement for the founding of a Jewish state in Palestine began, Yakobson clandestinely followed the Voice of America radio reports on the struggle, privately cheering for the Jewish fighters. Aesthetically he was more overt about demonstrating his Jewish background, pioneering pointedly Jewish-themed dances; incorporating gestures, characters, and mannerisms in these works drawn from conventions of Russian Yiddish theater; and collaborating with Jewish composers and visual artists. He also spoke out to family and friends about the importance of making a place for Jewish nationality in the USSR. Throughout the years of aggressive anti-Semitism, he created six ballets on Jewish themes—the first, *Jewish Dance,* was made in 1949 when Jews were being vigorously persecuted. Isolated from developments in the West, Yakobson's work angered Soviet authorities, who censored or at times forbade productions of his ballets. For those Soviet audiences who were allowed to view Yakobson's work, the choreographies offered a glimpse of dances that were modernist in their sensuality, subjectivity, and collaborative incorporation of music and decor by innovative artists in other media.

During the decades of repressive control of artists in Soviet Russia and the mandatory imposition of *narodnost* (the requirement that artists pay deliberate attention to the nation and its heritage as an ideological subject of their work), Yakobson reimagined classical ballet as a freshly pliant and contemporary medium. His project was to reshape ballet during the Soviet era into an artistic medium where modernist innovations in movement, choreographed individuality, and nondidactic meanings might be explored. For a brief four-year period, the final four years of his life, Yakobson directed his own company, the first individual solo-choreographer dance company in the USSR. Always Yakobson worked to shape ballet as a place of social multiplicity rather than of exclusion and uniformity, an arena for softer messages from the margins of daily existence.

Soviet authorities collided repeatedly and in a retaliatory way with Yakobson over his attempts to make and stage ballets centered on broadly inventive movement styles and subjects, sentiments, and individual voices. *Vestris,* a small but telling ballet created in the final years of Yakobson's life, was emblematic of the unique dialogue of resistance and the repositioning of the stage as a space for what might be called the new "detotalitarianized" body that he tried to configure through ballet. Pairings are unpredictable within it: a classically pure reference to baroque styling is followed by the fussy mannerisms of trembling hands and shuddering limbs that were trademarks of old and infirm characters from theater.

Yakobson's work interrupts the standard conception of ballet as politically neutral or collaborative in mainstream cultural values. Instead it offers a surprising demonstration of the cultural power of ballet and how it did important resistive work in a climate seemingly inimical to art modernism and the individual voice. While he certainly experienced difficulties and periods of being banned from working, Yakobson also succeeded in navigating cleverly around Stalinist politics much of the time that he was employed by two of the most prestigious cultural institutions in the USSR. His situation discloses the complex tensions involved: the Soviet state did value the arts, but even a renegade artist had to balance criticizing the state with supporting it in a de facto way.

Yakobson's ballets revealed narrative as well as abstract qualities, offering a different lens on dance modernism as it originated in early twentieth-century Russia and was subsequently developed in the West. With the exception of *Vestris,* which Mikhail Baryshnikov brought to the West, and five other ballets, the majority of Yakobson's work is little known outside Russia because it unfolded in a totalitarian state and was never considered worthy of cultural "display"; thus there was little official effort to preserve his repertoire.

Vestris

Filmed in 1969, the clip of Yakobson backstage coaching *Vestris* is a rare official recording of Yakobson's work. This footage was part of a documentary made by Soviet state television during the first Moscow International Ballet Competition held in the Soviet Union. Baryshnikov remembers Soviet television staging this moment of coaching specifically for the camera, and its artifice in regard to how he and Yakobson really worked.

"The backstage footage was not candid, but more 'staged' for the documentary about the dance competition," Baryshnikov said, noting that a dancer could not just mimic Yakobson. "He was very passionate, very detail-obsessed and required one hundred percent of attention every second of our work together," Baryshnikov said. "He was an extraordinarily gifted choreographer and a very freeminded and freespirited man."[3] This Moscow International Ballet Competition, the backdrop for the film, pitted the leading dance virtuosos of several nations against one another in a display of intense geopolitical competition on the ballet stage. It was not surprising that the young Baryshnikov won the gold medal among the male dancers—the Russian ballet training system at the time was known to produce the finest male dancers in the world. Yet even within that company, Baryshnikov's classical purity and technical prowess were fabled. Maya Plisetskaya, the leading Bolshoi ballerina and one of the judges, gave Baryshnikov a thirteen out of a maximum twelve points for his performance.[4] A protégé of the revered teacher Aleksandr Pushkin, Baryshnikov had been taken into the Kirov as a soloist in 1967, the same year he graduated from the Vaganova School, that is, he skipped the customary ascension through the corps de ballet.[5] The Russian ballet training system, however, was double-edged: it perfected excellence but within a narrow band of expectation of what a dancer could do.[6]

Baryshnikov was worried that his boyish looks, small stature, and lively personality would lock him into comic and more minor demi-caractère roles for his career rather than the danseur noble roles he desired.[7] Yakobson's ballet deliberately confounds the separation of these categories by demanding both genres from the same dancer. It highlights Baryshnikov's technical prowess, control, and elegance between his saturated and lusty demonstrations of sharply etched genre types. Initially Baryshnikov was shy about having to portray these extreme emotions and old and ugly characters of Yakobson's choreography. Yakobson's widow and rehearsal assistant, Irina Yakobson, reported that when her husband first started to work with Baryshnikov, she had the impression the young dancer was unhappy. "He thought he was only a very clean and very good classical dancer and he wanted to show his jumps, his pirouette, his beats—everything they do in classical ballet," she said. "Then they began to rehearse, and he found out how to speak with the body, not only with the face. He found out how to let the steps become movement that tells about the character," she explained. "And as he worked he began to love it."[8] Baryshnikov remembers being thrilled from the start, but nervous. "I was taken from the first rehearsal," he said. "This was a real, serious, meaty project. It was all very unusual and my first choreographic experience with a really great master. I knew instinctively he was really one of probably two choreographers of that originality (Goleizovsky was the other)."[9]

In *Vestris*, Yakobson, an admirer of the dance theorist Jean-Georges Noverre, was in part actualizing Noverre's critique of the Paris Opera Ballet's use of the mask in the eighteenth century, Auguste Vestris's era. Noverre saw the mask as restricting dancers from showing facial expressions that gave meaning to their characters. He devoted the whole of his Letter IX in his famous exposition of the theories and laws governing bal-

Mikhail Baryshnikov in *Vestris*, 1969 Moscow
International Ballet Competition, Bolshoi Theater.
Photographer unknown.

let and dance representation, *Les Lettres sur la danse et sur les ballets* (*Letters on dancing and ballets*), to the subject of facial expression. There he inveighs against the custom of wearing masks, writing, "All our movements are purely automatic and meaningless, if the face remain[s] speechless and do[es] not animate and invigorate them." Noverre ends this letter with a call for an aesthetic revolution, one in which Yakobson had also enlisted: "Let us destroy masks and gain a soul, and we shall be the best dancers in the world."[10] The dancer's face in *Vestris* is as elastic as his body.

Even Tatyana Bruni's early costume sketches for *Vestris* reflect how the character identity of the dancer was systematically carried through every element of this economically brief solo. One of Bruni's costume sketches for *Vestris* shows him in an embroidered velvet jacket and flashy garters as he props up his drooping form on a pair of inverted brooms like prickly oversized crutches. Bruni's sketch is a direct reference to one of the historic lithographs that Yakobson alludes to in this miniature, Eugène Delacroix's satirical portrait of the aged Vestris propelling himself into the air by hoisting himself up on a pair of brooms. In another drawing Vestris appears as something between an aged fop and a coquette, his doublet sporting so many layers of lace at the waist that it suggests a ruffled tutu. In the final finished version of the dance, the brooms and lace have disappeared but the body of Vestris has absorbed the tottering posture of decrepitude and foolish vanity that once emanated from these vanished props and costume details. Bruni, a celebrated painter, theater designer, and graphic artist who had been active in the early Russian constructivist art movement, would design costumes and decor for several Yakobson ballets, sharing his sensibility for the complex meanings that formalist structures could conceal.[11]

The biggest surprise of the Moscow competition, in fact, was that Baryshnikov earned his medal performing a competition repertoire that included this commissioned solo, because Yakobson's choreography so steadily challenged and incensed Soviet authorities. Helgi Tomasson, then a dancer with the Harkness Ballet and since 1985 the director of the San Francisco Ballet, was runner-up to Baryshnikov at the 1969 Moscow Competition, winning the silver medal to Baryshnikov's gold. Interviewed more than thirty years later, Tomasson still recalled *Vestris* as the standout work of choreography in the competition. "When I think back over the last thirty years there are very few dances I have seen that I can recall, but *Vestris* is one that I still see clearly. Its use of theatre and dance made a

Tatyana Bruni's sketch of the male costume
for *Vestris*. © A. A. Bakhrushin State Central
Theatre Museum, Moscow.

strong impression. It was so different from anything else the Russians were doing. It was so brave!"[12]

Not only did Yakobson reject the rigid Russian body-type casting of dancers, but he also often worked deliberately *against* expectation, fusing inventive steps with possibility and refusing to bow to the assigning of role, partners, and prominence based on how cooperative a dancer, and choreographer, were with party officials. Yakobson took particular pleasure in working with emerging young dancers who had not become hardened into derisiveness and cynicism about his often dramatically expressive ballets, and *Vestris* reflects these ideals.

Seven years earlier, in 1962, Yakobson had singled out another young Kirov dancer, Natalia Makarova, to dance the lead in his staging of *The*

Bedbug (*Klop*, 1962). This ballet is a satire of Soviet life based on the New Economic Policy (NEP) introduced by Lenin and depicted in a play by Vladimir Mayakovsky. Makarova, who in Yakobson's staging of Mayakovsky's work danced the role of Zoya Beryozkina, a young woman who hangs herself when her boyfriend betrays her, has credited her work with Yakobson as having initiated her understanding of dramatic portrayals in dance. "Most dancers did not like Yakobson," she observed. "Used to the standard classics, they felt uncomfortable in his contorted, expressively sharpened poses, which, in addition to everything else, Yakobson demanded they imbue with emotional content."[13] It is a statement as true for *Vestris* as for *The Bedbug*.

In the sphere of Soviet dance images there are no easy performance references for the deliberately grotesque. The most immediate sources for physical distortion imbued with emotional complexity are from not dance but Russian Yiddish theater. The shamed quality of the knotted, stooping, and sadly twisted postural and facial expressions that keep welling up in the midst of the elegant and mannered pirouette à la seconde and attitude turns that the character Vestris performs were in fact considered archetypically "Jewish," racially and culturally, by the Soviet population of this period. In the initial performances of *Vestris,* Baryshnikov remembers having to wear a soft latex nosepiece that added a bump to suggest the more prominent profile of Vestris's nose. (He discarded this in his subsequent performances of *Vestris* in the West.)[14] Curiously, the big or hooked nose is the physical feature of Jewish people that is most commonly caricatured.

Specifically Yakobson's depiction of the physically broken and emotionally labile evokes the work of the celebrated Russian Jewish actor Solomon Mikhoels and his Moscow State Yiddish Theater (GOSET), which was founded in 1919 and liquidated by the Soviet government in 1949. This tradition had been particularly visible in the period starting immediately after the Communist revolution, when the Jews had been declared a nationality with Yiddish as their national language and thus became eligible for the state support provided to artists and cultural institutions working in their native nationalities' languages. Consequently a range of amazingly rich theatrical experiments flourished in theaters led by Jewish actors and directors. Even though government support for Yiddish institutions and schools was subsequently withdrawn by the Soviets, theaters continued to receive state funding into the late 1930s, making theater the only arena where Yiddish remained in official use publicly. In addition to Mikhoels,

whose acting and directing style favored highly expressionistic stagings of
Yiddish dramas, there were a few other theater artists who were also actively challenging the dominant realism of Soviet theater. These included
Vsevolod Meyerhold, who made radical anti-naturalism work for the Moscow Art Theater; Alexander Tairov, founder and director of Moscow's
anti-naturalistic Kamerny Theater; and Yevgeny Vakhtangov, a Stanislavski protégé and champion of psychologically motivated characters in his
work for his Vakhtangov Theater.

Yakobson's widow, Irina, recalled that her husband had admired Mikhoels's work in particular among these experimental theater artists and
that he had certainly seen, live or on film, Mikhoels's most famous character portrayal, the title character in Shakespeare's King Lear from GOS-
ET's 1935 production.[15] Inspired by the style of the new realism of the
1930s, Mikhoels shaped his portrayal of Lear as a psychological study, one
that Jeffrey Veidlinger, a Mikhoels scholar, argues actually contained
veiled critiques of Stalin and covert assertions of Jewish national identity.
The resulting production became the most critically lauded performance
of Mikhoel's career. Edward Gordon Craig, an English theater practitioner
and Isadora Duncan's lover, saw Mikhoels performing Lear in Moscow and
wrote in 1935 that it stirred him more profoundly than any performance he
could recall.[16]

Although Mikhoels was brutally murdered in a staged "accident" by
Stalin's orders in 1941, a film of his performance from this 1935 production
of King Lear was in wide circulation, and it is this bank of images of extreme emotions that Yakobson seems to be referencing when shaping the
moments of rupture in Vestris. In the acclaimed final scene in Mikhoels's
King Lear, Yakobson portrays the king destroyed by remorse and tottering
on insanity, his emotions careening from sobbing to choking laughter as he
mourns over the dead Cordelia's body. With each emotional swing he
shields his face with his trembling hands before reemerging with his visage
in the sudden grip of a keening cry and then—literally swinging his torso to
the opposite side—a feeble giggle. Tucked into Yakobson's Vestris, this quotation through performance allowed for "cross-viewing spectatorship" as
well as recondite references to political hierarchies, since the vibrations of
the fingers and emotional excesses were a Mikhoels "Jewish" trademark.

Yakobson has taken one of the most revered symbols of Soviet-Russian
purity, the noble danseur, and grafted a Jew into it. Viewers who recog-

Solomon Mikhoels in *King Lear,* 1935 production
by Moscow State Yiddish Theater/GOSET.

nized Yakobson's choreography of Vestris's tragicomic character shifts
had the option of seeing them not only as ballet history but also as a covert reference to the more immediate history of Yiddish theater in Russia
and the virtuoso of that genre—Mikhoels. It has been noted that Mikhoels's stylization of Lear, with its long pauses and excessively dramatic
tone, itself references old Yiddish festival performances through its quality of a *Purim Shpiel,* a children's Purim play.[17] By 1949 the GOSET theater
had been dismantled, and Mikhoels and his Yiddish theater's style of acting, although lauded internationally, had effectively vanished, because
the actor-director had been falsely denounced as having promoted Jewish
nationalism and anti-Soviet behavior.

Commentators on Mikhoels's *Lear,* and the metaphoric bite of this production, have noted what a risky staging it was when it premiered in 1935.
It presented Lear as an egocentric and despotic king who denounces the
righteous, expels his one true daughter, and persecutes many of his original supporters—actions all with easy parallels as a critical portrait of Stalin
and his growing cult of personality.[18] Just as Mikhoels had inserted a Jewish accent, or even an entire physical language of Jewish verbal and body
vocabularies, into Shakespeare, Yakobson enacts the parallel strategy for
ballet. He takes the dancer literally hailed as "the Shakespeare of the

Dance" for the eighteenth century, Auguste Vestris, and inflects his pristine proto-classical vocabulary with physical (gestural) "Yiddishisms" while referencing Mikhoels's anti-Stalin performance barbs. Vestris was known as the greatest dramatic dancer-actor of his era, so *Vestris* cites the man who exemplified contemporary Russian performance theater—Mikhoels—and absorbs his signature gestures into this ballet. By 1969 this reference was still subversive, although no longer deadly. A month after Stalin's death, in an April 7, 1953, editorial, the party newspaper *Pravda* hinted at the lie, noting: "As a result of a careful examination, it was found out the public figure, People's Artist of the USSR Solomon Mikhoels, had been slandered."

THIS VERY IDEA of contorted poses, excessive and emotion-laden, is precisely the trademark of Russian literary scholar Mikhail Bakhtin's formulation of the carnivalesque. Bakhtin based his formulation on medieval narratives, but he was a direct contemporary of Yakobson, a Petersburgian as well, and, like Yakobson, shrewd about how systems of social commentary coexist with performance release. Both men decoded the historic past using insights that only surviving in the absurd horror of Stalinist Russia could have produced. Yakobson might have applied these obliquely Jewish references intuitively in order to make possible this highly visible work destined to be seen internationally as a secret "dispatch." Most importantly, political ideology was never the express focus of any of Yakobson's ballets—his battles were within the art form. In commissioning *Vestris* the director of the Kirov, Konstantin Sergeyev, had turned to Yakobson out of necessity, requesting that he make a solo specifically tailored to showcase the young dancer's virtuosity for the one contemporary portion of the competition. "Yakobson was chosen because he had become the most interesting choreographer working with the Kirov on a consistent basis," reflected Baryshnikov years later. "His great talent lay in the complexity and variety of movement styles he was able to develop; he had a special knack for creating steps and characterizations ideally suited to the dancers. In other words, his work did not imprison the performer, but always seemed able to reveal new, true aspects of his potential."[19]

This pairing of two of the most prominent, yet disaffected, Soviet dance artists of this time would provide a rare portal of possibility and public attention for both. Beginning in the late 1960s the Kirov had gone into a period of repression, due in part to a tightening of restrictions after the brief Khrushchev Thaw, and in part to the Soviets' crushing of the "Prague Spring" in 1968 in Czechoslovakia and their lingering anxieties from Rudolf Nureyev's 1961 defection. Adding to this climate was the presence of many informers and KGB associates within the Kirov and Bolshoi companies and staff.[20]

Histories of Ballet and Power

The ballet stage was a unique site in Soviet Russia. On the one hand the virtuosity of the dancers who performed on it was a testament to the legacy of discipline that the machinery of conservatory training had been producing since the late 1700s. On the other hand, this same attention to policing the narratives and genres of expression that could be performed produced a repertoire that turned against its art and opposed engaging with the world. Yakobson's work sought to navigate these regulations on artistic life and cultural production by exploring what was missing from views of the world in the thought and action of the mandatory socialist realist argument of *partiynost,* absolute allegiance to the party and Stalinist aesthetics. The party commissioners did not like *Vestris*.[21]

Socialist realism was formally established in 1934 as an artistic and literary style, the single legitimate one approved by the First All-Union Congress of Soviet Writers. As dance historian Christina Ezrahi has noted, "Socialist realism was not just an artistic style but a propagandistic ideology that promoted a view of Soviet life that had little to do with reality."[22] Unlike the aesthetic realism of the nineteenth century, which endeavored to depict life with as much immediacy as possible, the socialist brand of realism was a utopian project presenting a landscape of abundance, fellowship, and happiness. The essence of socialist realism, Miklós Haraszti, the Hungarian dissident writer, has noted, is that "artistic pleasure, once a private affair, is now the means for social insight, itself complicit in the transformation of society."[23] In this system each artist is "a state employee" and every artwork "must have an application in state culture."[24] Even art that refers to its own medium—as *Vestris* does through historical reference—can be accused of mere formalism and solipsism because it is denying the primacy of content. Left unstated here is that in the Soviet Union content too could be wrong if it wasn't tethered to a myth of state culture shaped by cultural policies such as "collective is beautiful."[25]

The realism in *Vestris* is pointedly of a different order. It too is ultimately aiming for social transformation, but away from, not toward, the
Soviet ideals of presenting unfailingly positive and optimistic images of
contemporary life and history. In his private handwritten notes for the
ballet, Yakobson described Vestris as a man whose "soul and heart are in
his feet," a statement that reflects his belief in dance's capacity to reveal a
moral core.[26] Commenting in 2011, dissident Soviet writer Vladimir Sorokin noted that during the Soviet period, art, and especially literature,
came to occupy the place of the church in Russian society—so the authority of the writer was enormous.[27] "Russians looked to literature for how to
live," he said in a statement that might also be applied to the ballet stage.[28]

Until the 1969 competition, both Yakobson's choreography and Baryshnikov's dancing had been seen outside the USSR only fleetingly. Yakobson's choreography was performed by the Kirov and Bolshoi on three of
their American tours—including his duet *A Couple in Love* (*Vlyublennïe,*
1958) on the Kirov's 1960 American tour; the miniatures *The Bird and the
Hunter* (*Ptitsa i okhotnik,* 1940), *The Gossips* (*Kumushki,* 1949), and *The Snow
Maiden* (*Snegurochka,* 1958) on the Bolshoi's 1959 American tour; and his
Spartacus (*Spartak,* 1956) on the Bolshoi's 1962 tour. Baryshnikov's international exposure prior to the competition had been limited to reports of his
dancing by the foreign press. But within months of Baryshnikov's winning the International Ballet Competition in Moscow, the public was insisting that they see more of the young prodigy. *Vestris* was hastily added
to the repertoire that he would be dancing on the Kirov's September 1970
tour to London.[29]

Vestris both ameliorated and exacerbated Baryshnikov's situation. Audiences in London wanted to see more of his unique possibilities as a
dancer, but in a repertory that also had aesthetic integrity—and apart
from the classics, *Vestris* was the only ballet in production around this
time that rose to this standard. Yet the tacit relationship between power
and ballet was also on display every time the Kirov toured, since Baryshnikov was an artist associated with service to the Soviet state, and this
made *Vestris* a more provocative dance choice.

Bonds between rules and art stretched back to the early 1700s when
Russian aristocrats, like other European nobility, organized their own
private theaters on their estates with their serfs requisitioned as singers,
dancers, and actors. Over time the theater in Russia evolved into an im-

portant state institution with recreational as well as educational functions. By the end of the eighteenth century, ballet troupes in the Bolshoi Theater in Moscow and the Mariinsky Theater in Saint Petersburg had been established and the court was encouraging the development of opera. The significant expenditures on culture that accompanied this state policy in turn served as proof of the wealth and power of the Russian empire. Many cultural institutions were subordinate to the Ministry of the Imperial Court and its departments, which were established in 1826.[30] This ministry had a special status—it was subordinate only to the emperor himself. The link between performance and the contemporary sovereign in Russia was sealed.

Thus in broad terms the dominant conception of the dance artist in the Soviet Union had undergone a shift in the late nineteenth century, from an earlier view founded on these aristocratic models of servitude in which serfs, children of servants, and orphans were among the classes trained into performers, into the post-revolutionary ethos of the early twentieth century, when young ballet students were selected based on their physical potential. In addition, because the prior class-conscious legacy troubled the new Communist aesthetic, there were attempts to remove the class element from Soviet ballet by making the style and subject more generally understandable and Soviet-related.

It is one of the paradoxes for dance artists in the Soviet system that the more they sought to navigate social and cultural change through the creation of new repertory and technical expertise, the more marginal their work was deemed and the more inaccessible their access to public exposure became. Fundamental to Yakobson's choreography in *Vestris,* with its complexity and variety of movement styles and characterizations, is the reflection of an ideological stance that located aesthetic meaning in an artwork's purity of impulse. Rejecting the ornamental or decorative in dance, he treated the body as a bearer of social meaning and a marker for cultural authenticity—a dangerous status in the Communist realm. In *Vestris* this emerges as a nine-minute solo that historicizes Yakobson's and Baryshnikov's disaffection for what was often the dull blandness and formulaic quality of party-regulated art. It delivers classicism—in a very pure and historical form—but as a frame for a center brimming with modernist emotion.

Yakobson, who was extremely well-read and self-educated in the arts and cultural history, researched sculptures and lithographs of Auguste

Vestris in the Hermitage collection and had read Noverre's 1803 essays on Vestris prior to beginning work on the ballet. In fact, Yakobson completed his *Letters to Noverre* (*Pisma Noverru*) within a year of beginning *Vestris*. In this manuscript, which was published only in 2001 when his widow financed its publication outside of Russia, Yakobson details his concerns about choreography in the form of a series of contemporary responses to the concerns that Noverre had had about ballet in his time. In his essays, Noverre had expressed alarm at what he saw as Vestris's corruption of the noble style by mixing it with the demi-caractère and comic, which violated not just his sense of ballet's hierarchy of bodies but also the social distinction that lay behind it.[31] In his choreographic treatment of Vestris, Yakobson posits the dance solo as a way to shift the stage character's locus of identity from his social niche to his political identity. Using the genre he pioneered as a choreographer—the dance miniature, a full narrative distilled into a dance of usually three to five minutes—Yakobson nests six mini character studies, none longer than a minute, inside *Vestris*. The ballet is like a choreographic matryoshka nesting doll depicting smaller and smaller caricatures of Soviet outcasts, until by the ballet's end, their forms seem to stretch metaphorically across the stage.

Just as Auguste Vestris had challenged the noble style of dance in the 1780s by deliberately exaggerating and showing the physical effort and labor of virtuosic dancing, Yakobson plays with the inner life of the dancer in the 1960s. He rejects the rigidity of the roles that the noble male danseur should perform and instead has him repeatedly cross age, gender, health, religious, and social boundaries to show a cast of social outliers—an old man, a coquette, a preacher, a praying woman, a drunkard, and a dying man.[32]

In *Vestris*, Yakobson invents a movement vocabulary that asks Baryshnikov to transition instantly into these extreme personalities, beginning and ending as the classically pristine Vestris. "The idea was to re-create several different personages who, we hoped, would demonstrate both the versatility of the dancer—that's me—and of the historical figure [Vestris]," Baryshnikov remarked about this dance several years later.[33] One of the things that made Yakobson's *Vestris* difficult for authorities was that it depicted aspects of reality so outside the sanctioned Soviet dance norm. The aged, the ill and dying, the penitent and prayerful are all shown in *Vestris* and in poses on their knees and prone on the ground, depictions that simply have no precedent in Soviet ballet.

The 1969 competition was thus a rare moment when Yakobson and Baryshnikov were glimpsed not only by the competitors, judges, and dance press from the West, but by the broader Soviet dance world as well. At one point during Baryshnikov's performance of *Vestris,* the camera cuts to backstage and reveals a crowd of Bolshoi theater staff and ballet coaches, all jockeying for viewing spots in the wings. So much about the immediate Soviet experience is signaled in this brief dance about revealing, concealing, and removing masks, feelings, genders, and identities.

Ballet and Political Power

Less immediately visible in the film materials documenting *Vestris,* but shaping it significantly, is the collision of the ideological agenda of the state and Communist Party bureaucracy with the autonomy of the individual artist. This twinning of political power and classical ballet has a long and unique alignment in Russia. Beginning with the inception of the Russian Federation after the October Revolution in 1917 and continuing through to Perestroika under Mikhail Gorbachev's leadership in the mid-1980s, ballet has negotiated a particularly charged relationship with Soviet authority. The story of this collision of power with ballet in the Soviet era brings an essential cultural complexity to any understanding of state-sponsored ballet and its tacit role in creating an illusion of civic and ethnic homogeneity in a totalitarian regime.

Classical ballet, particularly Russian ballet, is generally not examined for the way in which it functioned as a consciously constructed parable of social order, containment, and discipline during the Stalinist and Cold War eras. But it is only by beginning to understand what ballet signified in Soviet Russia that one can appreciate why Yakobson's works were so threatening to Soviet authorities and why they triggered such sustained efforts to keep them suppressed, silenced, and forgotten. The question of why he was not summarily liquidated as so many other artists and Jews were during the years of state terror is a fascinating one. Less apparent is how Yakobson persevered as a major force keeping the thread of ballet modernism alive through decades of restrictions and isolation, creating in the process the most significant body of modernist work in Russia. Yakobson negotiated this delicate balance of being regarded as both a dangerous force by party officials as well as a revered artist by the Russian cultural public from the 1930s until his death from cancer in 1975.

As has been discussed, *Vestris* afforded Yakobson a recondite post from which to comment within dance on Soviet aesthetics and the Soviet system of categorizing dancers and censoring dance memory. From 1932, the year Stalin abolished all independent artistic organizations in the USSR, until Stalin's death in 1953 (paralleling the first twenty years of Yakobson's choreographic life), the guiding principles since Lenin's articulation of socialist realism's theory were *partiynost,* party consciousness; *narodnost,* orientation toward the people; *ideynost,* ideological content; and *klassovost,* class content.[34] Taken together, these effectively precluded an individual voice in art. While Yakobson's strategy in *Vestris* of having a dialogue through choreography or literature with an earlier artist may sound like a benign practice to those in the West, it was still a perilously "cosmopolitan" undertaking during essentially all of his professional life. The composer Dmitriy Shostakovich, an artistic colleague and friend of Yakobson's, once spoke to these risks of looking to one's immediate personal or collective distant past, noting that "in the Soviet Union the rarest and most valuable thing is memory. It had been trampled down for decades; people knew better than to keep diaries or hold on to letters. When the 'great terror' began in the 1930s, frightened citizens destroyed their personal archives, and with them their memory."[35] Yakobson's *Vestris* serves as a collective memory for the genre of classical ballet. Moreover, many of Yakobson's actions were directed toward reviving and fixing memory through the physical and kinetic images of the body. *Vestris* both established a historical context and legitimacy for Baryshnikov's artistry and his artistic heritage and at the same time mapped future directions in which he might use his talents more broadly in new models of cultural production.

Swan Lake *and Power*

The depth of this link between ballet and power has been demonstrated outside the theater as well. When potentially tumultuous political events were about to unfold in the USSR, the state-controlled television station preempted all regular programming and began broadcasting *Swan Lake* in its full-length, four-act, three-hour expanse. That is, in 1982, 1984, 1985, and 1991, when the deaths of Leonid Brezhnev, then Yuri Andropov and Konstantin Chernenko were announced, and news broke of the failed coup against Mikhail Gorbachev, respectively, the events were heralded first by official silence and then by a TV broadcast of the work most emblematic of the purest form of classical ballet, *Swan Lake,* danced to a score by the echt Russian composer Pyotr Ilyich Tchaikovsky.[36] In a final ironic citation in 2011, long after the dissolution of the USSR, the twentieth anniversary of the 1991 putsch attempt was commemorated with documentaries and a rebroadcast of *Swan Lake* on Kultura, the Russian national television channel.[37] This time, however, columns of tanks were not grinding through Moscow streets as they had two decades earlier, when the ballet had been used, in part, to block the dissemination of real information and to soothe the masses through the use of squadrons of "tutus."

While the scale of these *Swan Lake* ballet broadcasts was unprecedented, the use of ballet with carefully orchestrated messages and deployed in moments of political frisson in Soviet Russia stretches back decades. Attendance at *Swan Lake* performances had routinely been a favored cultural field trip offered to dignitaries visiting the Soviet Union. In 1959, Vice President Richard Nixon and his wife attended a *Swan Lake* in what was then the fledgling industrial city of Novosibirsk. During intermission they strolled outside to greet a crowd in front of the theater in a "spontaneous" exchange between the Soviet people and a visiting American leader in the midst of consuming the quintessential Russian cultural product.[38] In 1963 when Fidel Castro visited the USSR and received the most lavish reception for a foreign leader up to that point, Nikita Khrushchev saw that it included an evening of *Swan Lake* at the Bolshoi Ballet. Khrushchev himself had once lamented, in a more confessional aside than he realized, that he had seen so many performances of *Swan Lake* "his dreams were haunted by 'white tutus and tanks all mixed up together.' "[39] It is revealing that in the 1950 Kirov production of *Swan Lake,* the artistic director and choreographer Konstantin Sergeyev rewrote the original tragic ending of *Swan Lake* into a compressed, happy conclusion in which Prince Siegfried slays the evil sorcerer Von Rothbart, tearing off his wings to the accompaniment of little more than three measures of Tchaikovsky's score, and Odette turns back into a woman and marries the prince.[40] This emphasis on optimistic art, especially ballets, is part of the socialist realism aesthetic, which underscored the need for performances to produce forced cheer as an antidote to the world outside the theater, where elation was in shorter supply.

State-mandated TV broadcasts of *Swan Lake* during Soviet power crises may seem puzzling to outsiders, but those who experienced it within the Soviet system say it rapidly came to trigger just what it was supposedly intended to defuse—that is, when Soviet citizens saw *Swan Lake* come over the airways, they became more anxious about an imminent political shift and suspected that someone (or something) had died. When seasoned lawmaker Sergey Filatov, a leader of a group defending the Russian White House from the August 1991 anti-Perestroika coup, turned on the TV while relaxing at the southern resort of Zheleznovodsk on August 19, 1991, he recounts his rising anxiety: "Saw the swans dancing. For five minutes, 10 minutes, for an hour. Then I realized that something had happened because we learned to read between the lines in Soviet times," he said.[41] Those looping swans made Filatov jump on the next plane to Moscow, where indeed an anti-Gorbachev coup was in progress.

The use of *Swan Lake* as a hedge against saying anything in a time of political emergency offers a unique window onto the dense calculus of ballet and power in Soviet Russia. Even highly placed political figures like Indulis Bērziņš, Latvia's former foreign minister, have spoken of remembering the sound of Tchaikovsky's score for the ballet as producing a more chilling effect and lasting memory than the tumult and Soviet tanks in the street. This was because once they had seized control of state television, Communist Party hardliners who were attempting to save the Soviet Union through that 1991 coup immediately aired the *Swan Lake* ballet. Vasiliy Starodubtsev, a coup organizer and former fighter pilot and governor in Russia's Tula region, told the *Washington Post* in 2011 that the coup's failure was that it misjudged the need for public relations. "Instead of broadcasting *Swan Lake,* we should have been explaining what we were doing," he said.[42]

To the astute dance observer, however, *Swan Lake* actually *did* offer an explanation. Through the medium of dance, a vision of idealized nationalism was being performed—dance became a trigger for sentiments of kinship given the inherent "Russianness" of *these* bodies on *that* stage, in *those* formations. Inherently those who promoted the use of *Swan Lake* in this way also seemed to understand that no socialist realist ballet did what real art did. Used as such, *Swan Lake* came to be saturated with the "ghostly national imaginings" that Benedict Anderson identifies as the triggers for the nationalistic sentiments that culture can evoke, or at least reinforce. It is useful to reflect on what was coded in those bodies for Soviet officials as a means of understanding why they expended such effort to permit and prohibit the parts and wholes of so many ballets.

Ballet and Imagined Communities

The ballet stage is always a platform for imagined communities—it is where the dreaming begins. There are few stronger visceral images of social harmony onstage than an ensemble of bodies rehearsed into that tight unison of the corps de ballet, and few more seductive illusions for the spectator that prompt the illusion of vicarious participation—the sensation of being invited to join in and complete a fluidly forming community—than the assembling and dispersing of circles, lines, and diagonals of identically costumed dancers moving with cohesion. The musical landscape of Tchaikovsky's score for Swan Lake is essential to this image. George Balanchine, who choreographed frequently to Tchaikovsky, once described the composer as "a great craftsman, a genius 'goldsmith' who worked on his compositions with diligence and care, while achieving an impression of artistic abandon and spontaneity."[43]

The televising of Swan Lake during a political crisis seemed to offer membership in the imagined fraternity of Soviet citizenship just when its cohesion needed bolstering and mobilizing for political ends.[44] Bodies moving to a musical score that sounds spontaneous but is in fact meticulously designed enhances the illusionistic charge of this image. Musicologist Roland John Wiley has noted how the relationship of choreography to Tchaikovsky's music in Swan Lake is an exemplary instance of simfonizm (the Russian term for the use of symphonic procedures in ballet), where the large-scale symphonic structure of the score is continually "responsive to the narrative and to the emotional states of the characters."[45] This relationship of movement to sound also echoes the social and militaristic order of faintly marching feet that reverberates visually through the choreography for the corps de ballet. As Wiley has noted in other Marius Petipa and Lev Ivanov ballets set to Tchaikovsky's music, the geometry of Ivanov's floor patterns illuminates the structure symmetries within the ballet and at the same time reveals a quality of volatility in the classical dances for the women of the corps de ballet.[46] Like Petipa, Ivanov invited the spectator to perceive the whole figure of a floor plan, with the difference that Ivanov's dancers were not set in a pose, but constantly in motion. (Many of the oblique lines and circles, serpentines and triangles in the lakeside dances in *Swan Lake* are similarly outlined in a constantly hovering or undulating movement of simple, repeated steps.) The incessant motion almost defies focus on a single point or dancer in favor of the totality. This focus on the totality of a large group as a unified but also animated and energized body suggests not just blunt militarism but also something even more kinesthetically appealing and subtle—a space for a flutter of individuality within the expressive gravity of the choreography.

It is tempting to try and parse the narrative of the Petipa and Ivanov 1895 choreography for *Swan Lake,* the basic core of the versions both the Kirov and Bolshoi ballets perform, to determine whether its symbolic meanings and potential value in regard to political displays and power shifts are uniquely suitable for Soviet political use or whether Soviet leaders are instead invoking ballets generally by using it on TV. In this way one might read Julius Reisinger's 1877 original setting of the folktale of a prince charged with discerning the real princess trapped in the form of a swan from a facsimile as a cautionary tale about the risks for a ruler of not seeing clearly.[47] This can lead to an understanding of what was perhaps so compelling to decades of aristocrats animated by a desire to use live performance as a means to instruct and discipline.

Much is encoded here kinesthetically as well as narratively. Certainly the preservation of hierarchy and order figures both metaphorically in the court depicted onstage in acts 1 and 3 of *Swan Lake* and literally in the highly disciplined and geometrically patterned ensemble dancing of the corps de ballet in Ivanov's choreography for acts 2 and 4. It is both a mirror of perfect control and perfect obedience and a display of the dialectic that challenges this stability. Petipa's choreography, which evokes autocratic power with its majestic verticality, hierarchy, and elegantly controlled physicality, is challenged by the contrasting easy geometry and sweeping gatherings of Ivanov's choreography for the rhythmic mass of swan women. The corps de ballet, in particular, comes into unique focus in *Swan Lake* as an ensemble that is coded as seductively feminine yet drilled into martial precision. As such its order in fact evokes another corps—that of the military.

It is fascinating that Russian ballet perfected the corps de ballet to new heights of discipline and ensemble precision during the same period when art and ideology in Russia were forced together more tightly. As the might of the military rose offstage, the complexity of its representation via the corps de ballet onstage intensified. Anatoly Lunacharsky, a literary critic and the first Soviet People's Commissar of Enlightenment, responsible for culture and education, noted the ideological utility of ballet's capacity to order masses to rally behind the Soviet state in his 1925 essay "Why Should We Save the Bolshoi Theater?" As Russian dance scholar Tim Scholl observed, "Lunacharsky was well aware of the ballet's potential; he wrote reviews of the Diaghilev ballet's European triumphs, yet his remarks acknowledge the myriad difficulties of defending the ballet in the Soviet Union in the 1920s. His essay ultimately justifies saving the Bolshoi Theatre for the creation of mass spectacles on appropriate (revolutionary) themes." He quotes Lunacharsky's politicized vision of ballet where "the harmony and precision of ballet movements, the complete mastery over one's body, the complete mastery over the moving mass—there is the promise of the enormous role the ballet could play in the organization of such spectacles."[48] Even the physical space of the theater and its stage held a special association with power at its moments of transformation. Prior to the Revolution, three tsars had held their coronations at the Bolshoi Theater, and in 1917 Lenin had declared the birth of the new regime from its stage.

As early as 1934, soon after the doctrine of socialist realism was proclaimed, Soviet critic Boris Asafyev wrote an essay about a revival of *Swan Lake* that had taken place the previous year. In the essay, he reinterprets the ballet though the political lens of the new doctrine, describing it as a document of protest by Tchaikovsky against the bourgeois society of his time and the main hero Siegfried's actions as exemplifying disobedience over narrow-mindedness. "This is not a fairy-tale utopian world, but a psychologically real one," he asserts.[49]

The Corps de Ballet and Militarism

The sources of this psychological realism that Asafyev identifies in *Swan Lake* are kinesthetic as well as dramatic, and the corps de ballet is an important medium through which this realism is refracted and amplified. A quality of visual and auditory, as well as sensate, rhythm unifies both the corps de ballet of the stage and the military corps on the parade grounds despite these groups' widely differing objectives. Both use the word "corps" (deriving from the Latin *corpus* and the French *corps,* or "body") to describe these disciplined groups of many marching and dancing bodies, which are drilled to move as a unified or synchronous corporeal entity—a massive single body or, as more customarily in the corps de ballet, a "flip-book" illusion as if one body were fractured into many identical echoes of itself across formations of lines, arcs, circles, or diagonals. These manipulations of the corps are customarily distinctly rhythmic, bound together visually and metrically in a manner that is seductive on multiple sensory levels at once. In fact, it might be argued, the centuries of appeal of both these kinds of corps—military and dance—which audiences have enjoyed since the baroque French courts of Louis XIII and Louis XIV, derive from the neat synesthesia offered by their union of visual motion and rhythm. The empathetic response provoked by the visual spectacle of a tight ensemble of dancers performing in a ballet is part of its appeal and a reason that it was formalized in the baroque courts of Louis XIV. Through ballet, the political could be shielded inside the spectacular—the echoes of marching soldiers could be disguised within the hushed steps of geometrical formations of dancers' ornate bodies.[50] Thus when large groups of dancers move in unison their collective "body" becomes a vehicle for aesthetic and social ideology.[51]

Equestrian ballet in particular was a ritualized form of military display and synchronized movement that was highly valued during the reign of Louis XIII in the early seventeenth century and where beauty and order paired as aesthetic virtues. This form of ballet—which celebrates noblemen riding together and directing their steeds to execute precise turns, leaps, and other difficult maneuvers—brought music to horsemanship, demonstrating both the ballet-like quality of dressage and the new unison work required of light cavalry in battle.[52]

The interlaced history of militarism and the rhythmic discipline of the corps de ballet become both more visible and more complex in the romantic era. As scholar Stephanie Schroedter has documented, the early nineteenth-century ballet master and choreographer Arthur Michel Saint-Léon made "numerous allusions to military formations" and even advocated for a separate *class de corps de ballet* whose organization should be *quasi militaire.*[53] Indeed, Saint-Léon invokes links between the military and musical in his 1856 treatise *On the Present State of Dance (De l'état actuel de la danse)* as he drafts recommendations for a corps de ballet trained and organized with militaristic discipline:

> The *corps de ballet* . . . must draw its whole charm from the *effect of a mass* and the precision it brings to its figurations, species of complicated maneuvers made up of *steps* and of *groups*. One cannot demand such strong execution of this *corps de ballet* if it does not know the duties of its profession.
>
> We must therefore establish rules for this part of the choreography, just as exist for military maneuvers, and join practice to this theory.[54]

This "charm" about which Saint-Léon writes refers to the heightened quality of fraternity that develops among participants, both dancers and soldiers, when a group moves together in time. Participating in a corps cultivates a tough and forceful presence, yet in both the military and dance it also demands that one be exquisitely sensitive to the other corps members. Military historian William McNeill has argued that as far back as the training of Spartan and Athenian warriors, discipline, morale, and emotional solidarity were cultivated through the collective, muscular work of marching and close-order drills.[55]

For the spectator there is the vicarious thrill of imagining oneself among those dancers or marchers. The effect of watching a well-drilled or rehearsed corps can feel like standing before a breaking wave or a swelling, round dance that will eventually fold one in as it sweeps past. The rhythm of those marching armies is now distilled into its visual index—the drilled body—a body that produces no actual sound other than the thrilling image of its orchestration as it navigates en masse through space.[56] In the late nineteenth century, to respond to demand for these kinds of perfectly orchestrated mass performances, the Kiralfy family in England and the United States and Luigi Manzotti in Italy produced vast popular ballet spectacles that employed 100 to 1,500 performers, including legions of marching women executing simple steps in extravaganzas so large that often they had to be staged outdoors.

The movements and gestures performed by a drilled ensemble can be an architectural and design spectacle as just described, but they can also uniquely trigger empathetic emotional responses in spectators and participants. It is known that art involving repetitive movement and chanting, particularly when performed in unison by many people, can set up resonance patterns in the brains of the participants. When McNeill was drafted into the U.S. Army in 1941, basic training required that he march for hundreds of hours on the drill field in close formation with a few dozen other men. At first McNeill thought the marching was just a way to pass the time because his base had no weapons with which to train. But after a few weeks of training, the marching began to induce in him an altered state of consciousness: "Words are inadequate to describe the emotion aroused by the prolonged movement in unison that drilling involved. A sense of pervasive well-being is what I recall; more specifically, a strange sense of personal enlargement; a sort of swelling out, becoming bigger than life, thanks to participation in collective ritual."[57]

Decades later, McNeill studied the role that synchronized movement—in dance, religious ritual, and military training—has played in history. He concludes that human societies since the beginning of recorded history have used synchronized movement to create harmony and cohesion within groups, sometimes in the service of preparing for hostilities with others. McNeill's discovery highlights how social possibilities can be rehearsed and performed in rhythmically unified mass movements.

One of the most sublime examples of this affective force of the corps de ballet occurs in *La Bayadère* (The Kingdom of the Shades scene), the 1877 ballet that Petipa made eight years prior to his 1895 production of *Swan Lake* (following Julius Reisinger's unsuccessful first staging of *Swan Lake*). Known as a remarkable vehicle for the corps de ballet, *La Bayadère*, with its score by Ludwig Minkus, uses the corps to frame the action and provide the weight and mass to complete the stage picture by having the dancers flow through sequence after sequence of lush patterns that dominate the floor space of the stage. Petipa's choreography here has been called by the critic Arlene Croce "the first expression of grand-scale symphonism in dance, predating by seventeen years Ivanov's masterly designs for the definitive *Swan Lake*."[58] It is the force of the corps de ballet that inspired Croce into rapturous description here, calling the works not only symphonic but also timeless. "Actually, the only word for this old-new choreography is 'immemorial.' *La Bayadère* (1877) looks like the first ballet ever made: like man's—or rather woman's—first imprint in space and time," she notes.[59] Writing about the famous entrance of the shades passage, Croce observed the physical source of its vicarious pleasure: "Motor impulse is basic to Petipa's exposition of movement [in *La Bayadère*] flowing clean from its source. It flows from the simple to the complex, but we are always aware of its source, deep in the dancer's back, and of its vibration as it carries in widening arcs around the auditorium. This is dancing to be felt as well as seen, and Petipa gives it a long time to creep under our skins."[60]

Croce's description of the corps in *La Bayadère* illuminates how the corps can be one of the most potent visual signs of sound in dance. It enacts simultaneously repetition and variation. All of these formulations point toward the complex sensory engagements that the unique pairing of music and movement offers, particularly through the kind of ensemble dancing that *Swan Lake* showcases so powerfully.

On a subconscious level the complex and metric militarism cloaked as artful discipline in *Swan Lake* may certainly have been a source of its appeal to political officials across both spectrums of Russian autocratic regimes—from the tsar through Stalin and his party successors. In particular, the ballet's surface of a folk-tale narrative muted what lay underneath. Tchaikovsky's orchestration, like the choreography, honors structure, hierarchy, and a racing ease as it alternately supports Petipa's aesthetic of balanced formality and drama and Ivanov's styling of fluent shifts and tenderness. The result is a kinesthetic portrait of a nationalist landscape that is dynamic yet reassuring in its musical order and visual balance.

For the dancers who were frequently pressed into cultural service for the fatherland by performing *Swan Lake*, the tedium was deadening. Plisetskaya, one of the Bolshoi Ballet's most famous interpreters of the leading female role of Odette/Odile in *Swan Lake*, is reported to have complained to a friend in the 1970s about *Swan Lake* that although she once adored it, she had danced it so often during the Soviet era that hearing the opening themes in the music now made her physically ill. "The most wonderful ballet music ever written. Maybe the best ballet ever created. And I want to pull my hair out and stuff it down the directorate's throat—that's what they've done to me."[61] "What would the Soviet government have done if Tchaikovsky hadn't written *Swan Lake?*" she asked caustically.[62]

Historic Intersections of Ballet and Power in Russia

It may seem ironic that the Soviet state adopted ballet while rejecting so much else from the cultural life of tsarist Russia, and that ballet could figure so prominently in both worlds. Yet it was this sense of its social expediency that made it appealing to such vastly different political moments. A companion concern about ballet's use by artists *not* purveying the party message would carry forward deep into the twentieth century. Peter the Great had been among the first to welcome ballet to Russia in the early years of the eighteenth century as part of his passion for Western European culture and particularly the aesthetic of Louis XIV. Peter I's reforms in the early eighteenth century, which included subordinating the church to the state and secularizing cultural life, are generally looked to as the moment when Russian culture became oriented toward European culture.[63] Like the French king and founder of the Académie Royale de Danse, the first dance academy, Peter simultaneously promoted ballet training while codifying the rules and manners of aristocratic comportment and court etiquette, effectively choreographing bodily actions as a way of shaping the performance of political obedience. Under Peter, and then Catherine II, the wealth and power of the Russian empire was displayed through the lavishness of its financing of culture, particularly the ballet companies at the Bolshoi Theater in Moscow and the Mariinsky Theater in Saint Petersburg, both founded at the end of the eighteenth century.

From its inception, ballet training was linked with military behavior and bearing in Russia. The state ballet school in Saint Petersburg (the descendant of the Imperial Theater School of the Mariinsky) began as the Saint Petersburg Cadet Corps, a military training program for young cadets, where the French ballet master Jean-Baptiste Landé was employed to drill the cadets. Peter's niece, Empress Anna, impressed with Landé's work with the cadet corps, hired him to teach in a formal ballet school, which she founded.[64] After a succession of French and Italian ballet teachers passed through the school, Marius Petipa arrived in Saint Petersburg from Paris in 1847. Within several years he would launch the great era of

Russian ballet that closed out the century with the 1895 premiere of his *Swan Lake,* which came to exemplify classical ballet with its adherence to the established framework of academic technique.

Ironically it was Lenin who is credited with indirectly bringing ballet forward into post-revolutionary Russia as early as 1917, the same year he was elected chairman of the Soviet Council of People's Commissars. Lenin believed that religion must be eliminated in the Soviet Union, and the major substitution for religion he saw was the arts. Yet rather than allow artists total freedom, he asserted that the Soviet leaders should decide the subjects and style of art and that early Soviet ballet, cinema, and theater were fully state-owned industries. (On August 27, 1919, Lenin gave his decree nationalizing the film industry in Soviet Russia.)[65] "As early as 1907 Lenin observed to a colleague that cinema could prove useful as an instrument of enlightenment if only it were controlled by proletarian forces rather than capitalists."[66] As much as Lenin may have distrusted avant-garde art, he considered film as well as ballet to have a unique legibility for the Russian masses, more than 60 percent of whom were illiterate at the time of the Revolution.[67] Committed to improving these working classes, Lenin once confided to Clara Zetkin, the German Communist, that personally he didn't enjoy modern art, preferring the older, more established styles. "We must preserve the beautiful, take it as a model, use it as a starting point, even if it is 'old.' Why must we turn away from the truly beautiful just because it is 'old'? Why must we bow low in front of the new, as if it were God, only because it is 'new'?" he asked.[68] Valuing film in particular for its capacity as a didactic medium, Lenin claimed cinema as "for us the most important of all the arts."[69] Ballet was similarly framed as an art form for a new visually based proletarian culture, beautiful and old but with the capacity to tell new stories.[70]

During the initial years of the Revolution, some criticized the Mariinsky and Bolshoi ballets for being elitist and incompatible with the revolutionary vision while others supported them as part of a Russian cultural past that needed to be preserved. Then in August 1919 the Council of People's Commissars nationalized all theatrical property of Russia and made all theaters subject to the jurisdiction of a Central Theater Committee, Tsentroteatr.[71] The word "academic" was added to the names of these ballet companies in 1920, and their importance to the Soviet cause was secured. Lenin reportedly defended his protection of resources for ballet theaters when there were fuel shortages for serious essential services like hospitals and trains by arguing to Aleksandr Vladimirovich Galkin, who urged that the theaters be closed, "It seems to me that Comrade Galkin has a somewhat naive idea of the role of the significance of theaters. A theater is necessary not so much for propaganda, as to rest hard workers after their daily work. And it is still early to file away in the archives our heritage from bourgeois art." The Council of People's Commissars voted to stand with him.[72] Not surprisingly the art that those theaters performed was decreed to be "utilized for communistic propaganda directly."[73] Lenin agreed, declaring that the regime, not the artist, should and would determine the outcome in the arts.[74]

In 1917 the Russian ballet became the Soviet Ballet, formalizing this rise in linking the agenda of the state to arts institutions in Russia and the consolidation of new ties between powerful state institutions and ballet. The Mariinsky's name also was changed—to the State Academic Theater of Opera and Ballet (GATOB) in 1920 and then to the Kirov Ballet after Stalin had the prominent Bolshevik leader Sergey Kirov assassinated in 1934. The Bolshoi ("big" in Russian) retained its name throughout.

Since the medium of ballet was movement, not text, the ballet was seen as particularly accessible for the sizable illiterate post-revolutionary audience in the Soviet Union. "Understood by the millions" was the idealized future goal for literature stated in the 1925 resolution of the Central Committee of the Russian Communist Party: "Concerning the Policy of the Party in the Realm of Literature."[75] In contrast ballet literacy was thought to be more immediate. The State Academic Theater of Opera and Ballet and the Bolshoi both remained open with performances scheduled during the Russian Revolution and civil war. The dancers did their part as well, performing in unheated but packed theaters in a gesture of solidarity with the masses.

Lenin's decree that theater should "provide rest for workers" was an injunction antithetical to that of the ballet experimentalists, who wanted to bring the tensions and clash of visions onstage as a means of animating, not anesthetizing, viewers. As Russian dance historian Elizabeth Souritz explains,

> The art of the first postrevolutionary years leaned toward abstraction, hyperbole, and extreme feelings, situations, and characters.

The image could be raised to a symbol, or it could be lowered to the limits of naturalism where it seemed no longer to be art. . . . There was no time for psychological analysis, for weighing the pros and cons, just as there was no time for meditating about whether the accused was totally guilty and whether the accuser was totally correct.[76]

Souritz explains because the general populace had little experience with art, the expectation was that they would first listen to the masterpieces of the past, then use that experience as a basis for beginning to understand modern, innovative works. The slogan "learn from the classics" became popular starting in literature in the late 1920s and then was extended to theater and eventually dance.[77]

In Russia the ruling powers' use of classical ballet as a means for rest from labor and strife varied surprisingly little from Lenin to Stalin, Khrushchev, and up to Gorbachev. By the late 1930s Soviet authorities, and Yakobson, saw dance as an important medium of social expression—but they had very different views on where the control of that expression should reside. Russian historian Robert Conquest's phrase "the heritage of terror" to describe Stalin's reign suggests the depth of the layers of control and scripting of behavior that permeated it. Just as Yakobson saw the stage as a space to offer complex, restive images as a subtle commentary on doctrinaire state art, Soviet authorities considered it another forum where the social effectiveness of "the cult of personality" and its pyramidal structure of "many little Stalins" was asserted. "The population had become habituated to silence and obedience, to fear and submission," notes Conquest, describing these first decades of Communist leadership. "The machine has been started up, and could now be kept rolling without extraordinary efforts." In regard to the intensity of the purges of 1936 to 1938, he writes, "In one vast operation, the country had been silenced and broken, and from then on more selective terror was sufficed."[78]

Ballet performances figured in this calculus of control through fear in curious ways. Khrushchev in his memoirs recounts how whenever the top men at the Kremlin would turn up at the Bolshoi Theater in a group it meant that a crisis of some kind was brewing. Khrushchev wrote in his memoirs how in one instance the ruling leadership of the Kremlin was about to renounce and eliminate a senior comrade, Lavrentiy Beria:

I remember a period of six or seven days when the danger was particularly acute. Seeking to take the heat off the situation somehow, I suggested to the other members of the government: "Comrades, let's go to the Bolshoi Theatre this evening. Our own people as well as foreign eyes will notice, and perhaps it will calm them down. They'll say to themselves, 'If Khrushchev and our other leaders are able to go to the opera at a time like this, then at least tonight we can sleep peacefully.'" We were trying to disguise our anxiety, which was intense.[79]

Thus even the act of attending the ballet carried special symbolic meaning. As Orlando Figes writes, "In the early days of the revolution, Leon Trotsky had forecast that the cinema would compete with the tavern and the church: it would appeal to a young society, whose character was formed, like a child's, through play."[80] The theater in Russia, then, was used as a place for signaling normality and for performing images of a comfort that did not really exist. This also suggests the stage as a potent site for these messages. But art was a far less manageable, ludic activity than organized play, and would not prove easy to overwrite—even if, like play, its performance had a deep social value.

Defectors

At the opposite extreme of the challenge of what was permitted *on* the Soviet stage were deep anxieties surrounding any attempts by the Kirov and Bolshoi ballet stars to leave that stage for performing opportunities in the West. Once the stage had been shaped as a cultural centerpiece of the totalitarian state, any action away from it also became an action away from the state. As difficult as things were for him, Yakobson never expressed a desire to leave the Soviet Union. Instead he worked to make ballets that revealed, as Kenyan scholar Ngũgĩ wa Thiong'o called it in another context, "a decolonized mind." In Yakobson's instance he worked to detotalitarianize the body and make the stage a zone of aesthetic and cultural possibility. He alternately succeeded and failed in this enterprise—succeeded because his ballets had the effect of temporarily opening a space for Soviet dancers and spectators to finally sample serious new statements in dance, and failed because his breakthroughs were often partial and temporary. Yakobson was not alone in being an outsider to Soviet ballet. There were others who stood apart because of social difference, including the Georgian dancer and choreographer Vakhtang Chabukiani and Konstantin Sergeyev (who, like Yakobson, began his training late and whom Igor Belsky also derided as a formalist), but no one resisted through his art as strenuously or relentlessly as did Yakobson. His works were all subject to review by functionaries and committees reporting to the *khudsovet* (artistic council or Khudozhestvennyi sovet that existed in every theater) and this process of gaining approval to perform and use the costumes, score, and decor, as well as the choreography he desired, had to be repeated, argued, and negotiated with each new dance he made.

Yakobson's *Vestris,* after it helped Baryshnikov win the Moscow Ballet Competition, was the one ballet that Baryshnikov carried with him to the West when he defected in Toronto in 1974.[81] Like choreographic samizdat, Baryshnikov had the steps for *Vestris* in his memory, but the commissioned score for this solo was locked back in the USSR. A few months later, when he joined American Ballet Theatre and wanted to perform *Vestris,* the dance critic Patricia Barnes finally located the only recording of the music made outside of the USSR—a pirated recording that a British balletomane had secretly made during one of Baryshnikov's performances of *Vestris* on the Kirov Ballet's 1970 tour to London.[82] So *Vestris* was revived and not only became Baryshnikov's introductory solo in the West, but also allowed Yakobson's choreography to be seen outside the Iron Curtain, although the choreographer remained behind. "A lot of people said, 'Who is this choreographer? Why don't we know anything about him?'" Baryshnikov recalled about the enthusiastic public responses to his performances of *Vestris* in the West.[83]

Although it was little noted at the time, the Soviets were also protective of their choreography. When Yakobson's widow applied to leave the USSR in the late 1980s, one reason that was given for her being turned down was concern that she would be taking with her, in her memory, Soviet choreography that she could then restage. The collateral damage from a defection extended to the *stukach* (slang for informant) as well as to handlers entrusted with guarding specific dancers against defecting.[84]

Punishment when a dancer defected was swift. The defector was barred from any contact with those left behind. This insured that the loss would be avenged—punishing the one who left and the ones who remained behind.

An exploration of the politics and language around defecting USSR dancers during the Cold War offers additional insights into the symbolic and effective power of ballet bodies. Of the hundreds of defectors who fled the USSR, none were so celebrated by Western media—and so censored in the Soviet's crafting of its contemporary history—as the handful of dancers who defected from the Kirov and Bolshoi ballets. The word "defector" technically refers to someone who disowns his or her country, but defecting dancers' departures were customarily referred to in the West primarily by the name of the Soviet ballet company they had left— "Baryshnikov defected from the Kirov"—as if fleeing the Kirov and Bolshoi ballets was the more serious offense given the limitations of life in the Communist state. More ideologically driven than just desertion, the idea of forsaking one's nation of origin for another is foregrounded in this formulation of the dancers' defections and reveals how strongly performing classical ballet was read as embodying the public display of nationalistic allegiance to the Soviet state. The dancer's body was a government body just as much as the soldier in his military corps belonged to the country and ruler he defended. To step out of this role in the midst of a dance's equivalent to a battle—a performance—made the rejection very public and embarrassing for the home nation. The clear hierarchical order of ascension within a ballet company reinforces this image of all the dancers being in service to the state, since the corps de ballet is technically the beginning point for each dancer no matter whether he rises rapidly to the status of soloist and principal as Baryshnikov did or, alternatively, spends years or even his or her entire career in the corps.

The concept of defection is essentially a twentieth-century phenomenon inherent in totalitarian regimes. The word came into common usage only in the postwar period when it served to describe Soviet soldiers who slipped into the West. As Vladislav Krasnov, himself a defector, argues, "Those who coined the word apparently sought to suggest that if these soldiers were not quite traitors, there was still something defective about them." He cites Charles Fenyvesi writing in the *New Republic* as noting that the etymology of the word "defector" implies damage, deficiency, and defect.[85]

The way that Soviet ballet defectors' actions became synonymous with anti-Soviet Cold War rhetoric and triggered tensions demonstrates the nationalistic pride attached to these dancers and the international humiliation their departures caused for Soviet officials. Beginning with the defection of Rudolf Nureyev from the Kirov in 1961, followed by Natalia Makarova in 1970 and then Baryshnikov in 1974, minimizing the risk of defection became a paramount concern. Cultural historian David Caute has remarked that the anxiety over possible defections was so great during their peak in the Cold War period that dancers *remaining* with their touring Soviet ballet company became a cause for relief. From the early 1960s to the late 1980s the absence of a defection during a tour to the United States "took on the public relations force of a military victory," Caute observed.

> Every Soviet ballet company returning from America to triumphant acclaim and without suffering the defection of a prima ballerina . . . was worth a Red Army division on the Elbe. The Soviet press eagerly recorded every word of praise for Soviet cultural achievements uttered in the capitals of bourgeois decadence, New York, London, and Paris. . . . There is no precedent or parallel for the cultural Cold War between the Soviet and American world-systems.[86]

While in reality hundreds of Russians in professions ranging from fishermen to nuclear scientists defected in the 1960s and 1970s, none generated the degree of media and public interest as the ballet dancers. They were cultural soldiers, and joining the other side—an American ballet company—was tantamount to artistic treason. The stage is a site of labor for the ballet dancer and a space of leisure for the spectator, and during this period one of the products of that labor was a demonstration of the essential attributes of a good citizen. Increasingly physical discipline and avoidance of prohibited art "isms" were associated with social discipline and good self-regulation. At the same time, self-expression became increasingly perilous territory to explore on the Soviet stage.

As sociologist Henri Lefebvre has observed, for modern society to have meaning and to convey a sense of coherence, it must convey a purpose beyond consumption. Lefebvre argues that one of its purposes ought to be the production of autonomous, thinking, feeling individuals able to experience their own desires and develop their own styles. While this was impossible in a totalitarian state, the ballet stage was ironically a space in which both the illusion of obedience and the illusion of this utopian delight of play that Lefebvre identifies can coexist. In Lefebvre's formulation he considered the great contribution of industrialism to urban society the proliferation in, and access to, art for the working masses. Lefebvre argues that art is a harbinger of an alternative world because it confronts us with opposition to what is.[87] As heavily policed as the Soviet stage was, practically and ideologically, each defection was a reminder that the only real hope of alternative worlds for artists lay outside the USSR's borders, beyond "what was." Yakobson spent his career in Soviet Russia as an architect of many of these alternative worlds, which he created not only through the physicality of his choreographed movements but through his own defiant personal style of fearlessness as well. The personality of Yakobson was inextricably linked with his choreography.

Makarova and Baryshnikov both credited their work with Yakobson as providing them a first taste of what it might be like to dance modernist ballets in the repertoires of ballet companies in the West. It's not known when Soviet authorities knew about these disclosures since they were contained in biographical self-portraits that each dancer published years after their defections and well after Yakobson's death in 1975.[88] Yakobson's widow, Irina, says he was never questioned about any of the defecting dancers, though their close friends were. Soviet authorities certainly didn't need additional justification to become more aggressive in assigning KGB tails to any dancer whom they were worried might defect on tour or even converse with a Western visitor to a Russian theater. Cold War historians have noted the extreme anxiety over all aspects of cultural contact between the USSR and the West, but few examples are as visible as the preoccupation with and repercussions over the defection of ballet dancers.

There were repercussions at the Kirov Ballet immediately after Baryshnikov defected during the company's tour to Canada in 1974. As soon as the rest of the dancers returned, the Soviet army, in what some considered a transparently retaliatory move, reportedly drafted several young males from the Kirov Ballet, even though dancers were customarily exempt from the military because an interruption of two or three years would mean the end of their careers. Russian ballet photographer Nina Alovert recounts that when one of the Kirov dancers who was being suddenly drafted asked an official why, he retorted, so "you won't be running off like Baryshnikov!" After the story received media attention in Russia, Alovert said, the dancers were quickly allowed to return to the Kirov.[89]

It took considerably longer, until 1988, before the names and images of the defectors Baryshnikov, Makarova, and Nureyev were returned to public view in the Kirov Theater and Vaganova School, although dance professionals and knowledgeable members had continued to follow their careers through books and other materials smuggled from the West.[90] This gesture of erasing defectors from the history of the Kirov (and Bolshoi) carried with it the implication that in acknowledging a great dancer, anything he did, including defect, was automatically valorized as well. Like the quality of militarism that shadows the training and disciplined display of bodies in ballet, the axiom that a dancer who defected from a Soviet ballet company had to be metaphorically liquidated from the culture's memory illustrates the ways in which a sensibility of the Cold War abroad transmuted into a war against Russia's own artists on the ballet stage—their bodies were that exquisitely, and dangerously, emblematic. Once Russian dancers had been shaped as a medium for the manufacture and display of a standardized national culture, they had little if any say in the ideological demands of what they were used to symbolize. A defection from the Kirov was de facto a defection from the Soviet state. The metaphoric power that had been built into these bodies had to be quickly silenced through retroactive erasure and collateral punishment of anyone who might have known of their plans to defect.

Balletomanes like Alovert, however, suggest how memories of the dance defectors could linger although replacements took over their roles in ballets. One might enjoy a moment of unspoken nostalgia for a vanished defector even as film footage and group photos were cut up to excise his image. In her scholarship historicizing the spectatorship of dance in the United States during the Cold War era, dance historian Susan Manning has identified the prevalence of what she calls a capacity for "cross viewing" among dance audiences, that is, the same audience could identify in multiple ways with the dance formations they saw.[91] Thus some in the audience at Yakobson's performances could view the technical prowess of the dancers in his works as Soviet but his choreography as dangerously erotic, formalist, and modern.

Yakobson's identity as a Jew in Stalinist Russia was in some ways analogous to the status of black and queer artists and audiences in the United States, in that his work allowed audiences to perceive dance differently from the unitary model that Soviet standardization policy assumed, permitting them to watch from the vantage point of the periphery and thereby to view their social place in relation to it. There were major differences, however, since the Jews were a recognized minority but disproportionately represented in state and cultural professions. According to those who watched Yakobson's ballets in the USSR, his dances were rich with cross-viewing possibilities for spectators. It was in this space that he was able to begin to individualize the mass, inserting cultural asides, gestures that viewers familiar with Jewish or contemporary cultural images would have known to read as "Jewish," "modernist," and other embargoed references.

Contrary to the official emphasis of party officials on standardizing a new national Soviet culture through the arts, recent scholarship on Soviet nationality politics, and on how their intersection with cultural practices shaped national consciousness, suggests that diverse Soviet experiences existed even within this frame of strict central state control of arts consumption.[92] Michael Rouland's case study of music in Kazakhstan in the 1936 Festival of Kazakh Arts, for example, details how aspects of Kazakh national music and native culture survived inside the official early Soviet nationality culture.[93] "National music underwent a struggle parallel to the repression of the arts and to the attacks on 'formalism' in Moscow," Rouland writes, in an observation that could extend to Leningrad's dance theaters as well. "With the growing ideological demands of 'high' (intensified) Stalinism, a greater effort was made to standardize Socialist artistic creation and make it more accessible to the masses."[94] Part of the strategy in making this effort was to fold in elements of various republics' and ethnicities' folk melodies, costumes, and imagery. So while to the party officials this may have seemed a successful recipe for homogenized, unified nationalism, viewers with deeper experience in reading these cultural elements individually could recognize the sources of who and what had been submerged.

Ballet against Power: Rediscovering Yakobson

In the daily world of Soviet ideological control of the arts, choreographers, like composers, could be subject to comparatively more intense levels of oversight than dancers or musicians because they created the content and the form, effectively the "messages," that others performed. From Yakobson's perspective he approached each new dance he made with openness and a belief that all might be possible even though experience had proved repeatedly that it rarely was. Still he resisted self-censoring in the studio, preferring to make his ballets and then take his chances through the many layers of vetting that each new ballet had to undergo. "The chief question occupying Yakobson's thoughts during his entire creative life was: What is dance?" Russian dance scholar Valeriy Zvezdochkin has observed in distilling the impulse that animated Yakobson.[95] Yakobson worked and lived with a deep focus on aesthetic objectives over political ones, and this is what enabled him to survive the terror of the 1930s, 1940s, and early 1950s. While this focus did little to lessen his friction with Soviet authorities, it strengthened his determination to continue his project of bringing modernity into Soviet ballet.

Eventually, as the stifling climate of the Stalin era began to ease slightly in the post-Stalin years of Nikita Khrushchev's "Thaw," the open dialogue around Yakobson's work and the public regard of him as a brave idealist grew. In the first decades following the collapse of the USSR, when this author interviewed middle-aged and older Russian intellectuals from the former Soviet Union, the majority of them, whether in New York, Jerusalem, San Francisco, Saint Petersburg, or Moscow, immediately knew of Yakobson and spoke about his "moral bravery" as twinned with his "artistic genius." For them the combination of resistance and invention that his works championed represented a distant horizon of intellectual courage as he persevered in making art to his own dictates. He served as a beacon of moral strength in those bleak times. "In the theater world it was known that he was one of the great artists of ballet," reminisced Olga Levitan, now a professor of Russian Theater at Hebrew University in Israel, who in the 1970s was a teenager in Leningrad and saw several performances of Yakobson's works. "In the 1970s Yakobson was known by those who were the cultural public in Leningrad. They were always interested to see his works and ballets. It was also known he had problems with the authorities."[96]

Indeed, the artist's personal situation of having "problems with the authorities" over his art heartened many who shared the same level of official criticism. Valery Panov, a principal dancer with the Kirov who danced in Yakobson's ballets before being dismissed and shunned as a "refusenik" for two years as he sought to emigrate to Israel, said that witnessing Yakobson's personal courage was inspirational to his summoning his own: "Whenever I thought of acceding, I remembered Leonid Yakobson, who should have been another Balanchine. His love of ballet somehow sustained him through thirty years of persuading, pleading and reworking to the instructions of Party secretaries."[97] Culturally Yakobson's artistic stature occupied an inverse relationship to Soviet power: as the officially forbidden arts practices and subjects became fewer in the post-Stalin decades, the scale of Yakobson's achievements in having worked separate from party dictates was remarked on more frequently and with greater approval.

But the in-between years were not easy. After being fired from the Kirov in 1951 because he was Jewish, Yakobson was unemployed for several years until he formally reemerged with the premiere of his evening-length epic, *Spartacus,* late in 1956. This was a ballet made at the invitation of Kirov director Fyodor Lopukhov. The date is auspicious because it followed by several months Khrushchev's "secret speech" at the Twentieth Party Congress in February 1956, when Khrushchev critiqued Stalin and his cult of personality, opening the first crack in the wall of party silence around the terror of the Stalin era. Soviet historian W. Bruce Lincoln has noted that this initial questioning of Stalinist orthodoxy eventually inaugurated other critiques of the narrowed vision of socialist realism that Stalin had championed.[98]

When the Soviet Union moved toward dissolution in the early 1990s, the interest in rediscovering Yakobson's ballets lost in the fifteen years since his death accelerated. Russians were drawn not only to his aesthetic achievements but also to the independent aesthetic vision and steady personal courage that he embodied. "They wanted to find out what they had lost," was his widow's explanation.[99]

The profile of courage that Yakobson's story offered was unique, and uniquely attractive, in the world of mid-twentieth-century Russian ballet. In contrast to the artists in the Soviet literary underground whose visual and literary art often used satire as a conduit for rage, Yakobson rarely posed deliberate political asides to party functionaries in his ballets; instead he chose to operate, at least in his studio, as if the climate of invention of the 1920s had never ended and modernist innovations were still desired and urgently necessary. Askold Makarov, who performed Yakobson's works while a principal with the Kirov and who subsequently directed Yakobson's Choreographic Miniatures company after he died, described Yakobson as a particularly enigmatic subject for dance historians. He was "an opponent of classical dance," Makarov said. But "Yakobson nevertheless outshines many other classical ballet masters, who combine ready-made forms. . . . Seeking to reform ballet, Yakobson has appealed to the expressiveness of sculpture, painting, and sport. He has turned plastic expression inside out, producing forms that for all intents and purposes are precluded in ballet and while he has oftentimes paid dearly for this, sometimes he has hit the jackpot as well. For him, a choreographer has unlimited rights."[100] These unlimited rights for Yakobson included the possibility of being both a critical voice against rote ballet classicism as well as an advocate for new forms that used what he called the classist vocabulary as their springboard.

An artist who envisioned himself with "unlimited rights" and defied the government's system of external censorship was a daring construct for Soviet Russia. More typically, artists who wished to continue working during this period distilled the model of external censorship into internal censorship of their own works.[101] Yakobson did not expend energy on trying to negotiate social change. Instead of lamenting or hardening into disappointment, he focused on the next work he wanted to get onstage before the public. "Yakobson was constantly reprimanded," his widow, Irina, said. "But in questions of art he was not ready for any compromise, nor did he ever give up any of his artistic agendas. He had to fight for almost all his programs, but sooner or later he invariably came out the winner. It is no wonder the authorities disliked him. They realized that he was not afraid of them. He never deferred or pandered to them—he was a free man in the full sense of this word—a position that was not typical for those times, as is well known."[102]

For the artist in Soviet Russia, avoiding this first layer of self-censorship already constituted a small victory, and particularly for Yakobson it became and remained an important part of the dialogue of ego and courage surrounding his work in the rehearsal room as well. According to Makarova, who performed in several of Yakobson's ballets in the Kirov: "His self confidence never abandoned him. No criticism could sway him—no matter how severe or just; no disappointment—however bitter; no failure—however obvious. . . . What was the source of his appeal? It's as simple as that he was possessed, inspired and immensely talented—maybe even a genius."[103]

Despite the fact that he was not deliberately political, Yakobson's work always troubled Soviet authorities. In his lifetime, and even after, Yakobson's work was repeatedly subjected to erasure, a conscious "forgetting" by Soviet authorities through restrictions about printing his name or reviewing his ballets in Soviet journals and especially in the two major newspapers of historical record, *Izvestia* and *Pravda*. His situation showed that an artist could remain on Russian soil and still be eclipsed from the nationalist narrative. While the dancers who defected moved out into a global world of increased possibility, Yakobson's sphere of visibility was always subject to the whims of the Soviet authorities who controlled access to the dancers, stages, and audiences where his ideas achieved visibility.

Commencing in the late 1980s, with the increased emphasis on remembering that was finally permitted through the new openness of *glasnost* and Perestroika—which included freer dissemination of news, discussion, and criticism of government officials—the legacy of Yakobson's work was gradually rediscovered. His personal courage as an artist also achieved a new recognition. Along with the celebration surrounding revivals of his major ballets, including *Spartacus, Shurale,* and *The Bedbug,* came mourning for what had been lost through censorship as well as for the wasted effort and time he had had to expend for the incremental permissions he was granted. Reflecting on this in a 1991 posthumous tribute to Yakobson in the Kirov Theater, Oleg Vinogradov, then director of the

Kirov Ballet, noted, "The sense of loss of Yakobson is immense because we realize how much is gone. On this stage Yakobson started here and led an extremely complicated life. They would not let him work—whatever he did was banned. I don't know anyone with the same lot. If he had had a normal life like that of George Balanchine, his place in the history of choreography would be no less."[104] Critic Boris Lvov-Anokhin, in a Russian monograph on Yakobson, echoes these twinned sentiments of loss and discovery: "It's hard to come to terms with the fact that a lot of his work has been lost," he wrote long after his death. "But even so Yakobson will live forever as a prophet of the new. That he was the harbinger of the new in ballet was discovered in the 1930s by his good friend and mate in combat, [Dmitriy] Shostakovich."[105]

Shostakovich and Yakobson were not only "mates in combat" but also, on several occasions, collaborators. They both died in the autumn of 1975 a few weeks apart. Unlike the scores that Shostakovich left behind of his prohibited compositions, however, few choreographers' dances survive independently of the dancers who were trained to perform them. This was particularly true of Yakobson's works, and this gap adds to the challenges and at times disappointments in restaging these dances. As Tatyana Kvasova, a leading dancer for many years with Choreographic Miniatures and a restager of his ballets, observed, "It is [often] said that Yakobson destroyed tradition, that he rejected classical ballet on principle. Nothing of the kind actually happened. He developed the classical tradition and perfected its language. Yakobson had perfect and profound knowledge of the classical dance and all its rules, and this knowledge gave him the tools and the right to experiment."[106] Kvasova's comments reflect how complicated the layers of memory, adulation, and resentment are that linger around Yakobson's legacy. Without the primary evidence of the actual dances, his innovations might retrospectively be read as an attempt to destroy the classical art of ballet.

Soviet officials expended enormous resources and attached great importance to ballet because of their belief in its mass reach and appeal. So while representatives of the Minister of Culture's office harassed Yakobson repeatedly, for all but a few years he was able to find ways to keep working. Yet working always came with supervision, as party representatives previewed Yakobson's ballets and demanded title, costume, music, choreographic, and other changes—demands that he usually answered by making small token adjustments and then reporting that he had complied. Like a star dancer who might defect, Yakobson was too talented, and his work too vital for audiences and dancers, for officials to silence him completely or permanently. He occupied a valued but problematic role in the demand and supply chain of socialist realist ballets because his work engaged very successfully with Soviet themes without embracing a socialist realist aesthetic. For Soviet spectators, Yakobson and his work represented a pathway to covertly negotiate difference in a country where cultural production and its reception were under totalitarian control.

The Swan

Two of the major formations that have historically stood for Russianness and power in ballet—the fragile Swan in *Swan Lake* and the synchronized corps de ballet of women in identical costumes—were two tropes that Yakobson never used. In 1970 Yakobson choreographed *The Swan,* his first and only dance in which a ballerina portrays a swan. Rather than using *Swan Lake* as his reference point, Yakobson chose a score and narrative even more succinctly emblematic of Russian ballet, from what some consider the most famous solo for a ballerina ever created, *The Dying Swan (Umirayushchiy lebed).* Created by Michel Fokine in 1907 for Anna Pavlova's appearance in a charity gala, this dance was reportedly shaped in a thirty-minute rehearsal with the legendary Russian ballerina. Fokine's *The Dying Swan* is a tragic four-minute portrait of a swan's futile struggle to take to the air one last time.[107] At the time of its premiere it stood as a mini-summation of Fokine's ambitions for changing ballet. Dance historian Jennifer Homans describes Fokine's innovations in the historic 1925 film footage of Pavlova dancing his *The Dying Swan* as "improvisatory and astonishingly simple, without a single bravura step."[108] Costumed like Odette, the white swan ballerina in *Swan Lake* who wears a feather-adorned white tutu and feather-covered headband, the ballerina in Fokine's *The Dying Swan* skims the surface of the stage in a stream of tiny purring toe steps (bourrées) while her arms and torso gesture poetically upward, trying to lift her into flight.[109] In the final moments of the dance the defeated swan descends to one knee and then folds softly to the floor, her head and arms draping over her leg in a last flutter as she expires.

Yakobson's *The Swan (Lebed)* is set to the same music as Fokine's "Le Cygne" section from Camille Saint-Saëns's *Le Carnaval des animaux*, in which a tremulous solo violin mirrors the struggling swan. Qualitatively the resemblance ends there. The swan in Yakobson's ballet usually wears the all-black costume of the white swan's menacing double from *Swan Lake*, Odile, and her resistance is staged as a defiant and dangerous battle against a force that doesn't permit survival or gentle deaths. As she navigates the stage, her full body arcs, curving in space with a forcefulness that suggests how strongly the air offers resistance and how urgently she is striving to avoid having gravity hurl her downward. The action of her arms starts deep in her back and stretches her chest wide as she strokes her arms backward in a gesture suggesting massively weighted wings fighting to pull her from peril. The task Yakobson sets for himself here is formidable—using the pairing of score and plot most emblematic of ballet shorthand for bird in the classical ballet archive, and then discarding all the customary woman-as-bird choreography and inventing a new raw movement syntax driven by nerve and emotion. Technically challenging and not always pretty to watch, Yakobson's Swan uses her whole body expressively. She makes small frantic nibbling actions with her head stretched forward on her neck as she bourrées unevenly in place, then her feet, legs, and finally her whole body buckle and crumple jerkily to the floor. It is as if some force had bludgeoned her down. Yakobson's choreography for the Swan feels urgent and painful and by the accounts of the dancers who performed it, this was true physically as well. This knowledge raises the level of the struggle the ballet depicts to an even higher pitch, eclipsing the poignancy of a beautiful death by fierce resistance.

Igor Kuzmin, formerly a soloist in Yakobson's Choreographic Miniatures ballet company, noted how the originality of Yakobson's *The Swan* begins with the different possibilities that Yakobson heard in the Saint-Saëns score. "Yakobson perceived not only its lyricism and the character's fatalistic hopelessness and submission to fate, but also its tragic tone and the motif of struggle against one's destiny," he explained.[110] Valentina Klimova, the ballerina who worked with Yakobson as he created *The Swan*,

recalled how the choreography literally seemed impossible during rehearsals.

> Sometimes what he wanted to achieve seemed unrealistic. An ex-
> ample is *The Swan,* which I was the first to perform, dressed in a
> white tutu (later on [Alla] Osipenko, [Elena] Volïnina and [Lyudmila]
> Shilova wore a black one). The choreography of *The Swan* is com-
> plicated and awkward. The difficulty, however, does nothing to en-
> hance its impact on the viewer: it is completely lost on a layman,
> but the dancer has a very hard time of it. The first part of *The Swan*
> is danced slowly, with an emphasis on maintaining postures. At
> one point, Yakobson demanded that, while standing on one foot
> and waving my arms, I gradually lower myself in a *plié* until my
> right "wing" touched the floor, and then as gradually stretch to
> my full height. This would have required leg-muscle strength im-
> possible for a woman! I was rescued by the coaches, who managed
> to convince him to give up this "vision": "Leonid Veniaminovich,
> she cannot jump from such a [deep] *plié* directly on her toes!" The
> position in the finale was no less difficult: I had to turn around
> twice while gradually lowering myself down on the pointes, and
> then continue turning on half-pointes into a maximally low *plié*. . . .
> For the staging of *The Swan* Yakobson assigned ten rehearsals—
> which testifies to the complexity of the choreography he was plan-
> ning to realize.[111]

Although Yakobson was a generation younger than Fokine, Yakobson
admired him greatly. He particularly respected Fokine's early efforts to
draft a set of principles for making Russian ballet less stiff and more expressive. Fokine's works made in the early years of the twentieth century
insisted on an evocative dancing body and choreography that treated each
subject individually, with less reliance on premade steps or phrases. In
Yakobson's *The Swan,* one senses the dancer is in the midst of staging an
epic battle with a force more pervasive and menacing than the end of life.
It is clear there is urgency to the movement language being used as the
ballerina heaves her arms in great forward arcs, pumping the air like a
swimmer slamming the waves in a butterfly stroke. She arches her neck
forward and to the side, pulling with her entire body to rise up and away

as if indifferent to the look of her actions, only concentrating on the effort. Echoing one of Fokine's principals for the "New Ballet," Yakobson makes the dancer's upper and lower body in *The Swan* equally evocative. Her struggle is both moving and unrelenting through to the final moments when she shudders to the ground, her feet and legs caving under her in an oddly broken and soulful end. Kuzmin called Yakobson's *The Swan* "a motif of struggling against one's destiny."[112] It is homage and also elegy, and more than a little sad. A coded message where he identifies with Fokine as an earlier fellow apostate from ballet classicism, Yakobson's *The Swan* feels autobiographical in its quality of suffering. Its final image depicts the iconic figure of Russian classicism, the swan ballerina, as one whose supplications are futile as she strives to escape, stumbles, and expires.

VESTRIS AND *THE* Swan were created just a year apart, at a point in Yakobson's life when his premonitions that he had a serious undiagnosed illness may have begun. Certainly both ballets can be read as mini-valedictories to Yakobson's life of creative experimentation. They were purified disquisitions on his own approach to "going against the current," his favorite Fokine motto. The premise in each ballet is a dialogue with a summative moment in ballet's history, which Yakobson then comments on choreographically, breaking open a styling of the ballet dancer from a past era and then playing it forward. Not movement translations but rather danced commentaries, *Vestris* and *The Swan* show what lies alongside and beyond the formal movements of classical ballet. They frame new possibilities for what contemporary bodies, shaped by years of deep historical training, can convey about the Soviet Union.

The bodies of the solo dancers in both *Vestris* and *The Swan* show ruptures in the official ideal—the strains on an idealized image and the physical and emotional realities that tear at it beneath the surface. This is the Soviet experience, the Soviet presence, Yakobson seems to be saying. Russian audiences understood and at *The Swan's* premiere in 1971, on the opening concert that inaugurated Yakobson's final triumph of being permitted his own company, Choreographic Miniatures, the audience greeted it enthusiastically. Predictably, the Soviet officials felt differently and they expressed their displeasure to Yakobson. "They were upset and said that *The Swan* did not look like our Russian ballet inheritance," Irina Yakobson recalled.[113] In fact it did chart a new facet of the Russian ballet inheritance—one that was still decades away from acceptance. *Vestris* and *The Swan* made possible different ways of moving through the dance's narrative while depicting nuanced portraits of gender for the male and female dancers, portraits that collided with stock socialist realist gender ideals. The heroic male danseur of *Vestris* is Russian—with ambivalence and sorrow inside. The heroic swan of *The Swan* is a staunch Soviet female, not a fragile bird like Pavlova's swan, but a massive force. She is a woman who doesn't softly expire so much as rage until—broken, bent, and defeated—she dies.

Vestris provided Baryshnikov with a virtuoso showpiece for his exquisite classical purity—his easy suspension in a sustained pirouette à la seconde and his racing chain of floor-skimming split runs across the stage are all citations from antique lithographs of Auguste Vestris's signature

Yakobson rehearsing a dancer in *The Swan* (1971).
Photo: V. Nikitin.

virtuosity. But it gave equal play to the subtler edges of how *Vestris* expanded classical ballet technique by extending and hybridizing the styles of ballet dancing into a genre for a single dancer who both ranged freely across the genre of demi-caractère, with its technical innovation and pantomimic expression, as well as captured the sophistication and elegance of the danse noble. Dance historian John Chapman said about Auguste Vestris's paradigm-shifting work, in an observation that might also describe Yakobson: "He was not bringing new technical material to the noble dance. Instead, he was uniting the genres and in so doing, rendered noble dance obsolete. Previous innovations took place within the traditional system. Vestris changed the system."[114]

These works chart loss and mourning for Yakobson—loss for the art form he was so passionate about and mourning for the impossibility of changing it sufficiently to bring it back to life. He wanted to resuscitate ballet in the open and full way he desired and the art form needed, but doing so was extremely problematic during his lifetime. Both *Vestris* and *The Swan* breathed new life into Soviet ballet by looking back to the eighteenth and early twentieth centuries, respectively, as if corresponding with history were not still forbidden and everyday life did not still demand deceptions. Judith Butler has suggested that mourning loss is about "agreeing to undergo a transformation the full result of which one cannot know in advance."[115] *The Swan* and *Vestris* are signature works of Yakobson's modernist style because they reveal his knowledge of classicism and display his efforts to refute and radicalize it as he strives for transformation in a climate of loss. Yakobson opened up classicism in both dances and recast the Swan's power—metaphorically ballet's power—as a way to make this signifying possible.

Both *Vestris* and *The Swan* are quintessential Yakobson miniatures—dense and complete little dance nuggets that were his trademark genre and into which he breathlessly packed more than most censors could take in quickly enough to forbid. Reaching beyond aesthetics, or Jewishness, and bolstered by his strong personal will, Yakobson's ballets challenged the role of the dancing body in defining prohibited cultural identities and by defying propagandistic agendas. Ballet and power had long been aligned in Russian ballet, but leaders—the tsar, Lenin, Stalin, Khrushchev—strengthened their connection and wielded the combined power in new ways. Yakobson, however, an uncommon artist, claimed

The Swan (1971), Elena Volïnina, Choreographic Miniatures, Leningrad. Photo:
Vladimir Zenzinov.

the ballet stage as a space of dignity and expression for, and about, the common person.

The consequences of totalitarian authority are more ambiguous, and for the artist more urgent, in dance than in other art forms or media. Due to the needs of dance as a sentient medium and the aesthetic and intellectual demands of Soviet dancers to be steadily challenged and engaged as artists, Yakobson fulfilled an important but risky function for Soviet officials. He and his art were needed but feared. Functionaries could try and shape his dances from outside, command, forbid—but when he began building his dances in the rehearsal room, these officials could not control Yakobson's hand. Shostakovich could compose and then keep a score hidden; Aleksandr Solzhenitsyn could smuggle a secret a copy of his manuscript to the West until he determined the right moment to publish. For the ballet choreographer Yakobson, it was a different game. He was staging resistance from within the most public vocabulary of compliance by inventing a new syntax in full view of the Soviet-controlled world. As the interests of the individual in the USSR were dissolved in ideological and artistic programs imposed by the state, the stakes of Yakobson's achievement rose. The moral, aesthetic, and political implications of each ballet that Yakobson made represented lifelines of hope that he was creating, and extending to others, through dance.

TWO

Beginnings: Learning to Be an Outsider

It was partly the war, the revolution did the rest. The war was an
artificial break in life—as if life could be put off for a time—what nonsense!
The revolution broke out willy-nilly like a sigh suppressed too long.
Everyone was revived, reborn, changed, transformed.
—Boris Pasternak, *Doctor Zhivago*, 1957

NO PHOTO EXISTS of the iron knuckles that the teen-aged Leonid Yakobson obtained in the autumn of 1918. He acquired the knuckles to protect
his two younger brothers from older children stealing their warm coats
while the three Yakobson boys—Leonid, fourteen; Sergey, thirteen; and
Konstantin, twelve—were part of the Petrograd Children's Colony, a sto-
ried encampment of eight hundred orphaned children trapped in the Ural
Mountains near western Siberia during the Bolshevik Revolution.[1] Yakob-

son kept these iron knuckles in his pocket for most of his life, explaining that they offered him a sense of security while returning from work late at night. "It's not always safe in the Soviet Union," he said.[2]

Nearly thirty years later, from 1948 to 1953, Joseph Stalin's campaign to liquidate what remained of Soviet Jewish culture accelerated. His actions included removing Jewish literature from bookshops and libraries; closing the last two Jewish schools; dissolving Jewish theaters, choirs, and both amateur and professional drama groups; arresting hundreds of Jewish authors, artists, actors, and journalists; and systematically dismissing Jews from leading positions in the government, the military, the press, the universities, and the legal system.[3] It was at this moment that Irina Yakobson took her husband's iron knuckles and hurled them into the Fontanka River, which runs through Saint Petersburg.[4] She was nervous that discovery of a weapon on a Jewish artist during a time of increasing terror against Jews could be deadly, particularly since a new law had been passed that would punish, with ten years in prison, anyone carrying a weapon. Even so he was annoyed. "How could you!" he reportedly remonstrated with her. "That was my only means of self-defense."[5]

Yakobson himself was never fearful of detainment or reticent about disclosing himself as a Jew despite institutionalized anti-Semitism. When others changed their names, he kept his identifiably Jewish one, and he choreographed ballets that not only addressed Jewish themes, but also included Jewish characters, incorporated Jewish gestures, and used music by Jewish composers and visual designs by Jewish painters. Nonetheless, in mid-career Yakobson was denounced as a "rootless cosmopolitan" (a derogatory euphemism for Jewish intellectuals).[6] The slur appeared in an article in the Kirov theater newsletter in 1951 titled "Kosmopolit v balete" (A cosmopolitan in ballet) written by the conservative choreographer Aleksey Andreyev.[7] Immediately fired as a choreographer from the Kirov Ballet as a consequence, Yakobson was unable to work for the next four years.[8] His talents were sorely missed by dancers and audiences, and soon after Stalin's death, Fyodor Lopukhov, who succeeded Konstantin Sergeyev (under whose watch Yakobson had been fired), rehired Yakobson.

Like many Jews in Russia, Yakobson conceived of his Jewishness as essentially a matter of biology and sentiment—heredity and sensibility. He did not know if any of his family members were observant Jews, but his widow, Irina, recalled that Leonid would sometimes sit in a chair at home and lightly rock or sway his body in the pattern of Jewish prayer, or *davening*. When she asked him why he was moving in such a strange way, he replied that evidently this came from his grandparents. When friends visiting their apartment noticed this also and asked him about his movements, he replied, "Because I am a Jew."[9]

Officially Yakobson's identity appeared as an assigned category in the fifth line of his passport, known as the *pyatïy punkt* (fifth line), where for Soviet Jews their nationality was automatically registered as "Jewish" instead of "Russian."[10] One of the paradoxes of Soviet policies was that Soviet Jews were both pressured to forget their Jewish heritage and simultaneously categorized as Jewish. Yakobson was culturally Jewish— assimilated rather than a Zionist, an Orthodox believer, or a Bundist. Two of the leading historians of Russian Jewry, Steven Zipperstein and Zvi Gitelman, have both noted that since all religious observation and the learning of the Hebrew language were forbidden for Jews in Soviet Russia, the primary ways they demonstrated that they were Jewish were marriage to another Jew and secular identification—that is, the citation of cultural memory. "Most Jews in Russia and Ukraine conceive of their Jewishness as a matter of descent" and hold "subjective feelings of belonging to a group," Gitelman has argued. "Jewish identity is understood in the way the Soviet state defined it, as membership in an ethnic group (a 'nationality')."[11] He explains that the contradiction inherent in these policies, which officially negated nationalism while at the same time constraining assimilation, resulted in Soviet Jews being treated as lesser citizens from the 1930s to the 1980s.[12] When Lopukhov rehired Yakobson as a choreographer for the Kirov Ballet, Yakobson pointedly made the first new work he staged—after his return from exile for being Jewish—a duet for two overtly Jewish characters called *A Couple in Love*. He cast his wife, who was Jewish, because she was the only Kirov female who would play a Jewish role. Aleksey Mironov, a non-Jewish member of the Kirov, agreed to be her partner.

The Petrograd Children's Colony

It is likely that Yakobson's introduction to the possibility of consciously negotiating a relationship outside of a Russian identity started in early adolescence with his nearly three years as part of a colony of orphaned

Petrograd children. Yakobson and his brothers' odyssey began in May 1918 during the famine that swept Petrograd after Tsar Nicholas II's reign collapsed and a disorganized provisional government took over. Of the big Russian cities, Petrograd was hit the hardest by the combination of famine, a significant breakdown of much of the public transportation within the city, and approaching anarchy. Most of the schools were shut down since it was not safe for children to be on the streets. There were chronic shortages of food and fuel, which would become so severe over the coming months that the population of Petrograd would be reduced by half as people died or fled the city. Russian historian Orlando Figes describes a city where "trees and wooden houses were chopped down for firewood; horses lay dead in the middle of the road; the waters of the Moyka and Fontanka were filled with rubbish; vermin and diseases spread; and the daily life of the Tsars' capital appeared to return to the prehistoric age."[13]

Figes notes that for the old intelligentsia in Petrograd conditions were especially difficult. In the new hierarchy of the "dictatorship of the prole-tariat" they were put at the bottom of the social pile, where they were given third-class rations of food and offered few if any jobs and then usu-ally only on labor teams.[14] In response, some parents from the middle class and intelligentsia, with the aid of school administrators and a civil-ian organization called the Union of Towns, organized an evacuation of 850 of their children between the ages of three and fifteen.[15]

Yakobson's mother, Vera Mikhaylovna Torina, had been struggling as a widowed homemaker since the death in September 1915 of her husband, Veniamin Samoylovich Yakobson, an employee in the advertisements sec-tion of a commercial-industrial newspaper. Little more is known about Yakobson's parents or his siblings. The family resided in Petrograd be-cause the young Yakobson's grandfather (no one remembers if it was his paternal or maternal grandparent) had been allowed to move with his wife and children into Saint Petersburg in the mid-nineteenth century to take up a post as first violinist of the Mariinsky Theater Orchestra. It was his renown as a young violin virtuoso that made it possible for him to obtain this special permission as a Jew to leave the distant shtetl of his birth and live in the Russian capital while serving as concertmaster of the distinguished orchestra for the Mariinsky opera and ballet. To arrive at such a position, Yakobson's grandfather had negotiated the maze of legal and occupational divisions of tsarist Russia to transform his outsider status as a Jew into a different kind of freedom as a musician. As Russian musicologist James Loeffler has shown, becoming a musician could give Jews tangible benefits such as the right to live outside the Pale of Settlement—and in major cities like Saint Petersburg, potential exemption from military service, the ability to study at a university, and as a result more professional opportunities than the lower-status jobs to which Jews were usually restricted.[16] Access to civil rights like these led many Jews, including Yakobson's grandfather, to turn toward music as a profession in nineteenth-century Russia.

In the months following the Bolshevik takeover of the October Revolution and its collapse into the tumult of the proletariat dictatorship of early 1918, Vera Yakobson found herself unable to feed and clothe her five children. She decided to keep her two older daughters with her but take her three sons to Petrograd's Finland Station, where she put them on one of the three train caravans filled with children whose parents were similarly sending them to a safer location with more available food.[17] The expectation was that they would spend the summer regaining their health and enjoying the outdoors under the close supervision of a group of teachers, medical personnel, and staff, and return home by train in a couple of months once things had returned to normal.

From the start, however, the journey did not go as anticipated. What should have been a two-day trip to the town of Miass in the southern Urals, the original destination, stretched into a four-week ordeal because of the chaos of the railroad system. There were repeated delays due to mined bridges, threats to security, and daylong stops when the children would leave the train to search for food. Finally in July the transport arrived at a former summer resort on the Miass River and the children began a two-month period of taking classes, swimming, and rejuvenating their malnourished bodies. But by August the tensions between the Bolsheviks and other parties had deteriorated into a full-scale Russian civil war, an army of eighty thousand Czech troops was trying to cross the breadth of Russia, and the Poles had invaded.

Piecing together what happened from a series of unpublished archival reports from the field made by members of the American Red Cross, it seems that the spreading famine, currency devaluations, and social chaos cut off the children from their families and made it impossible to even send them money, food, and clothing. With the chill of the Siberian fall beginning and the food supplies the colony had brought with them exhausted, the Russian teachers and staff overseeing hundreds of hungry children in worn summer clothes panicked. As food for the children diminished to watery soup made from rotten vegetables, the frightened teachers divided the children into seven groups and sent them out in different directions, hoping that townspeople and villagers might take them in. Most of the Russian teachers and staff then fled, taking with them all of the remaining money and abandoning the hundreds of children. Just a couple of dedicated teachers remained to help them survive through the Siberian winter.[18]

Initially the children secured what little food they could by begging. Then, when the townspeople's food also dissipated, they resorted to stealing, sharing whatever they could get with their groups, and, as a last resort, eating roots and berries from the forest—a practice that resulted in the death of at least two of the younger children when they unknowingly ate poisonous berries. Sparring factions of the Red and White armies also passed directly through their encampments, with soldiers stealing provisions from the starving children. Eventually stories began to circulate about these groups of dirty, hungry, abandoned children wearing rags and living in derelict stockades and trash-filled, unheated buildings. An Englishman and his Russian wife, Alfred and Katya Swan, who were also fleeing east by train, heard about these "wild children of the Urals" and circled back to try to locate them and bring some aid. Their efforts eventually led them to the newly arrived American Red Cross (ARC), which had landed in Vladivostok to begin humanitarian aid programs for individuals needing assistance regardless of their political stance.[19]

The ARC promptly undertook the project of rescuing the children. Over the next several months all but the few children who had died were gathered from the seven different villages scattered across hundreds of miles of Siberia where they had been sent. They were then transported four thousand miles to Vladivostok, the largest Russian port city on the Pacific Ocean. En route the train was attacked by raiding bands working under General Semyonov, and it passed through villages that had nothing left but the ruins of buildings burned to the ground and hanged corpses dangling from the trees. The individual children's voices don't emerge from the archival narratives, just the institutional cataloguing of the massive scale of humanitarian rescue efforts required to reassemble them in one big colony in Vladivostok, played out against landscapes of death, ruin, and suffering. It is also unknown what Yakobson's personal experiences were apart from a few anecdotes one of the leading American Red Cross volunteers, Burle Bramhall, who helped shepherd the Soviet children around the world from 1918 to 1920, recounted decades later. The following passage from a Red Cross site report of the time gives some sense of the logistical challenges of getting the children to Vladivostok and hints at the physical hardships that being rescued entailed for them—suggesting how rapidly the experience swung between adventure and ordeal.

> The first train load with the group from Turgoyak arrived on August 19th, after a journey of some five thousand miles covering a period of thirty-seven days. This train was followed by two others arriving respectively on September 3rd and 20th, after journeys of equally long duration and even greater hardship as one group was compelled to make part of the trip by water in open barges which exposed then to merciless Siberian sunshine and thunder storms. Immediately upon arrival in Vladivostok, the children were subjected to a period of precautionary quarantine, bathing and delousing.[20]

For the next ten months, beginning in September 1919, the 780 surviving children, Leonid and his two brothers among them, lived in derelict stone barracks that had once housed the men of the tsar's fleet. Situated on a rocky outcropping in the Golden Horn Bay called Russian Island, the barracks had been hastily repaired and sanitized by the Red Cross, which decided that the strategically placed rock was a safer place to keep the children than the chaos of the city.[21] Initially life became ordered again: reports indicate that school was reestablished, there were dances on Saturday nights, and once a month plays and recitations were presented. The older boys (perhaps Leonid was one, since he was now fifteen) staged Anton Chekhov's one-act The Wedding (Svadba, 1889), reportedly to great applause. It was apparently during this period that the only surviving letter from Leonid home to his mother was written. It survives in an awkward English translation published in Floyd Miller's 1965 book, and its source is not indicated. After briefly assuring his mother that he and his two brothers are well fed and have blankets and warm trousers and linens, Yakobson mentions dance in the context of affirming how far the comforts of his situation in the colony extend: "We have our own club, are making up dancing literary evenings and in general living very merry. We are kissing strongly, very strongly you, Nadya and grandmother," he writes, signing it from himself and his two brothers.[22] There is no record if Yakobson received a reply, but one child who wrote to his family at the same time, Pyotr Azarov, did receive a letter back—a grim reminder of the conditions in the city at the time. The boy's father wrote that in Petrograd they were spending "5,000 rubles a month to buy grain and dried herring; even then the quantity is so small that we are starving. . . . Every month we lose more weight. Many of our friends have died."[23]

This juxtaposition of realities is remarkable and must have produced conflicting emotions for the children who understood that while their families were starving in a major city of Russia, they themselves were comparatively comfortable because of resources made available from a foreign country. Perhaps this early experience of being a cultural outsider within one's home country (albeit at the geographic margins of that country) helps to explain Yakobson's comfort with the outsider status he would occupy as a Jewish artist in his future adult life. Fittingly, Yakobson chose a career—choreographer—that is in some respects about "world making." However excluded he felt because of his Jewishness, inside the studio and rehearsal room Yakobson could make the world he wanted, one quite separate from the difficult, unwelcoming one he found outside those walls.

Given the state of chaos across Russia, the very possibility of this letter exchange by mail was a remarkable feat accomplished by extra-national support. The posting of letters between the colony's children and their parents, which began after eighteen months of no communication, was facilitated by the Red Cross worker and Honolulu-based American journalist Riley H. Allen, who with Burle Bramhall orchestrated the repeated rescuing of the children. By late 1919 the Trans-Siberian Railway had been blown up so often and in so many places that it was less a railroad than sections of track littered with rusting equipment—transport of people and mail was impossible. Allen, however, felt that for the children's sake contact with their families was essential and he now also realized it would be many more months until they would be returned home. Bramhall persisted and finally succeeded in arranging for the children's letters to be sent continuously eastward until they had circumvented Eastern Russia to reach Petrograd from the West, avoiding the chaos of the civil war and literally circling the globe in a path that prefigured nearly the identical route the children would eventually have to follow in order to reach home.[24]

So it was that American consular officials shipped the Petrograd Children's Colony mail across the Atlantic to America and then across the North Sea to Stockholm, where the neutral Swedish government shipped it to the International Red Cross in Tallinn, Estonia, and from there to Petrograd. Reportedly as news of the children's good care by the American Red Cross circulated through this correspondence, it created an awkward situation for the new Bolshevik government because food shortages for Russians at home continued. The commissar of enlightenment, Anatoly Lunacharsky, responded by publishing a telegram in *Izvestia* claiming, disingenuously, that the children in the Petrograd Children's Colony were living under disgraceful conditions, physically and morally, and that they were being cruelly mistreated.[25] It's not clear if the children knew that their situation was being used as propagandistic ammunition between the Americans and the Soviets, but it added a new front of moral tension to the civil and social catastrophe of war and its consequences that were unfolding around them.

As it became apparent that it would be impossible to return the children to Petrograd by land, Bramhall determined that returning the children by sea—effectively taking them around the world in the same eastward circulation as their mail—was the only possible option. He first tried repeatedly to secure a Russian ship. But each one was promptly taken over by the new Bolshevik government, which announced that it belonged to the people and not a private shipping firm—and which meant that soon all privately owned Russian vessels stopped coming to Vladivostok to avoid the same fate. Thus over the next several months Bramhall pursued another option: he raised funds to lease and outfit the *Yomei Maru*, a small Japanese freighter owned by the Katsuda Steamship Company, which had just made her maiden voyage. The freighter was built to accommodate only a crew of sixty, but Bramhall packed a thousand people onto the ship, including the 780 children, a Japanese captain and crew, Red Cross staff doctors, nurses, a dentist, teachers, a cook, and several German POWs destined for Berlin.

Yakobson (*standing, sixth from left*), age sixteen, aboard the *Yomei Maru*
with the Petrograd Children's Colony. Collection of Jane Swan.

During the months that Bramhall was securing and then refitting the
Yomei Maru, the children's lives again became more difficult as food supplies fell and the ennui of daily life with little to do affected the older boys
like Yakobson and his brothers especially hard. Among Yakobson's personal possessions when he died were two notebooks from these months
on Russian Island off of Vladivostok, Russia. "I advise you not to get mad
and not to fight when they call you pretty boy," reads a March 2, 1920, entry signed Vlad. "Memory to a future poet," a March 3, 1920, entry is titled, in which another colonist forecasts that young Yakobson will do
something creative. "It is only the strong ones who go through the storm.
Limitless is the kingdom of thought. Here is your calling—a good deed in
your motherland. Your way will not be easy," it cautions. These entries
have the usual bravado of yearbook epigrams—but also something more.
They document an adolescent boy who took pleasure in preserving, and
orchestrating, people's reactions to him and who seems to have been a
favorite of the group. At the outset his notebooks caution the signers to

write in ink and not to use the backside of the pages. "I am asking my friends to write in my album and in their lives to remember me often," he writes on the title page. Numerous boys as well as girls register affectionate and at times intense emotional responses to him. If there were an officer's school for cultural heroes, this might be what it looked like.[26]

In contrast, the adult view chronicles the social chaos. A hand-typed letter in the Hoover Institution Archives for War, Revolution, and Peace dated June 21, 1920, and written by a new Red Cross staff member, Sister Kurguzova, details her first impression of the squalor of the older boys' Barrack No. 4, where 120 of them lived in a poorly provisioned and crowded dormitory. "The children did not bathe as there was no water. Sometimes, in the middle of the day a barrel of water was brought for 120 people and all jumped on it and fought for their water. . . . The big boys are very apathetic, lazy and don't seem to take any interest in life whatsoever. The little ones are satisfied with their little work in the Barrack, the big boys, naturally, need regular work and mental development—and these two factors don't exist in the Colony."[27]

Sister Kurguzova's account continues to suggest indirectly that even on land the children frequently enjoyed practicing for and putting on shows of various kinds—a practice she regarded as detrimental. "I consider *too frequent* dances and cinema shows a great evil for the Colony. Children don't get enough sleep, don't feel like working the next day, and small, nervous and weak children certainly are affected by the excitement caused by this kind of recreation."[28] The experience of general disenfranchisement during what would be nearly three years of homelessness for the children must have been profound. At the same time the popularity of performance, drama, dancing, and choral groups suggests that art played an immediate and valuable role in their lives. The performing arts may well have provided not so much an escape as a forum where collective organization did function and order was obeyed because the products were tangible and gratifying. The children's lingering excitement as well as their fatigue afterward attest to these having been consuming experiences. By the time the colony is on the waters, Yakobson, who had no training in dance or the performing arts before this odyssey began, has consolidated his title as the best dancer in the group.[29] On board the performances also continued with the older boys and girls performing in orchestras, bands, and choruses that entertained the entire ship, particularly on Sunday evenings.[30] Other entries in Yakobson's colony notebooks hint at budding romances between Yakobson and some of the female colonists. "Think kindly from time to time of me. Only the morning of love is beautiful," someone wrote in an undated note. And another, from October 30, 1921, as the colony is nearing the end of its journey in Finland, cautions, "Unrequited love is hotter than fire but don't be sad. It is much harder to live without loving anyone."[31]

Finally in July of 1920, more than two years since that short summer trip to the Urals began, the children began a final fifteen-thousand-mile journey homeward.[32] Photos taken of the children, the boys shirtless and all in worn baggy clothing, lying tightly packed side by side on bedding rolls on the crowded deck of the *Yomei Maru* with their clothes bundled next to them, prefigure another boatload of disenfranchised people navigating international waters looking for a safe port—the Holocaust refugees on *Exodus 1947*, which at midcentury would symbolize the human toll of another international crisis, World War II. The children do look like refugees, not revelers. Accounts from the ship's log reveal how arduous the trip was—on the first length from the Japanese port city of Muroran to San Francisco there were turbulent seas and an incident of one of the Japanese crew members molesting a Russian girl, and when they traveled through the Panama Canal to New York scores of children suffered from the stifling tropical heat and insect-born illnesses. Here Yakobson's name surfaces a second time. Forty years later Bramhall and a former colonist vividly remembered Yakobson as the boy "who was determined, emotional and very enthusiastic. He put his nose in everywhere."[33] Insatiably curious, he once secretly stole into the machinery room of the ship and stuck his hand into a piece of moving equipment, accidentally cutting off the tip of his thumb.[34]

Most importantly, it was on board the ship that Yakobson distinguished himself for the first time by his dancing ability. The only boy who joined the girls in exhibition dancing on deck, Yakobson was dancing and performing, even if only recreationally. By September 1920 the *Yomei Maru* had arrived on the coast of the United States, docking in San Francisco Bay. The children were brought ashore and escorted around the city for three days—including a welcoming concert at the Civic Auditorium that included singers, acrobatic acts, and Cossack and folk dances, as well as reciprocal performances by the colony's orchestra and girls' chorus. The city's hospitality was labeled "extraordinary" in staff reports. The days were filled with different entertainments each day, including trips to Golden Gate Park, a visit to the zoo, and lunches of American hot dogs and ice cream. One gets the impression that the children were celebrated not only as survivors but also as symbols of how humanitarian values can transcend political agendas, even in a time fraught with international conflict.

A month later the children arrived in New York, the only other American city they visited, and there Bolshevik versus anti-Communist sentiments ignited around their presence. A grand welcome for the children with musicians, dancers, church choirs, and an audience of sixteen thousand Russians, Ukrainians, Armenians, Georgians, and Moldavians was scheduled for Madison Square Garden. Alexander Brailowsky, a Russian pianist living in New York who was also a pro-Bolshevik and anarchist activist and (as the White Russian opposition pointed out) a Jew, delivered a welcoming speech that suddenly deviated radically from the advance text he had supplied the event officials into a tirade against the American Red Cross as an imperialist organ of the State Department. He claimed that the ARC was imprisoning the Petrograd children, mistreating them, and holding them hostage. The Red and White factions in the Madison Square Garden audience began shouting down one another and two of the children, an eighteen-year-old boy and sixteen-year-old girl unnamed in the accounts, walked onto the stage to explain that in fact the American Red Cross had saved their lives. The children then reportedly exited up the aisle in pairs and with the ARC staff, to warm applause. The political tensions continued when the following day U.S. Justice Department agents came on board the *Yomei Maru* searching the ship for Communist literature. The agents, who did not read Russian, burned the only books they found, mistaking for subversive literature a collection of leather-bound Russian literary classics that had just been given to the children by expatriot Russians.[35] It is hard to imagine the forceful drama and pageantry of these events not having had a profound influence on the young Yakobson. It's one thing to live through a war, but another to have been part of a village-sized contingent of refugee children whose lives were saved because of the kindness of a contested adversary—and for whom art played such a central role.

From New York the ship departed on the final leg of the journey across the Atlantic Ocean. Unable to land in Brest, France, the ARC's first choice, because of political tensions on both sides, the group continued cautiously through the Kiel Canal, which had been heavily mined, and into the Baltic Sea, arriving in Finland in November 1920. The ship anchored in the harbor of Helsingfors, Finland, and the Red Cross officials interviewed Finnish authorities who, after a five-day delay, refused to permit so many Russians to land. Eventually the Red Cross received permission for the children to land at Viborg and be taken thirty kilometers by train. They then walked an additional eleven kilometers through the forest to the Halila Sanatorium in Finland, a vast complex of buildings built by Tsar Nicholas II just before the Revolution to accommodate Russian elites with tuberculosis. Because of a change in the border between Russia and Finland, the complex had never been used.[36]

The children were housed in the sanatorium while the Red Cross staff printed thousands of flyers about the colony that they distributed in an effort to reconnect them with their families. Many parents wrote letters in response, and the repatriation of the children proceeded in small groups as the ARC handed them off to Soviet soldiers on the other side of a small bridge linking Finland and Russia. On January 26, 1921, the final group of children to receive word that someone would meet them in Petrograd was escorted across the border into Russia. The city to which they returned was vastly changed. No public transportation functioned and most of the buildings and shops were boarded up. The children walked the final stretch home from the border escorted by the soldiers, who reportedly stole their possessions, including the farewell Red Cross gifts of food and medicine.[37] Some of the children and their parents had trouble recognizing each other. One mother looked for a specific birthmark in order to confirm that a healthier and taller boy really was her son. Another girl initially refused to accept that an emaciated woman was, in fact, her mother.[38] Yakobson's mother was still alive but we do not know if she met him and his brothers upon their return, or if the boys were greeted by their older sisters who were caring for them by the time their mother died in 1931. He continued his independence and resourcefulness after his return, earning money through small jobs to help the family and discovering the city as he wandered through it during the day.

Once they were back in Russia, a climate of total secrecy rapidly closed over these survivors of the Petrograd Children's Colony. An adventure so remarkable it should have made them instant legends instead had to be

hidden as a dangerous secret. The children were welcomed home and immediately warned not to speak of their travels, trials, or triumphs for fear
of reprisals for having been in contact with the capitalist enemy and cosmopolitan West. A few children did mention their travels and suffered
professional sanctions. The vast majority, however, Yakobson among
them, obediently buried any mention or reference to those extraordinary
three years, understanding the risks. In Soviet Russia even having relatives outside of the country could have serious consequences. While there
were a couple of brief general references to the Petrograd Children's Colony in children's magazines in the 1930s, as the lockdown of Stalinist terror began, even these benign references ceased.[39] Reportedly several of
the children who did speak about their experience were later arrested and
subsequently vanished—presumably because of this time in the West.

In 1978, as if opening a time capsule, a Leningrad sailor and journalist,
Vladimir Kuperman (who wrote under the pen name Lipovetsky), learned
about the colony when he was on a ship that docked in Seattle, Washington, and happened upon an obituary about Bramhall.[40] In the article,
Bramhall was eulogized for having saved hundreds of orphaned Russian
children. Intrigued, Lipovetsky began to research the story; over the next
several years he interviewed former colonists and visited archives in the
Soviet Union and the United States. He eventually self-published a Russian monograph on the colony in 2004. The survivors told him various
memories, including one about Dmitriy Erokin, a descendant of an old
aristocratic family who was ten years old when he was taken into the colony and later became a leading astrophysicist in the Soviet space program.
The KGB arrested him in 1936 after discovering his personal archive with
photos and information about the colony, and sentenced him to death. He
was shot in 1938 and "rehabilitated" posthumously.[41] "They were afraid to
mention it and many of these children eventually suffered in some way or
another," said Lyubov Krokhalyova, daughter of Leonid Danilov, who
had also been one of the colony children. "Some of them just weren't
trusted because of this exposure to Western life, [and] some were denied
the right to get higher education."[42]

Yakobson never told anyone, except his future wife, Irina, about his
time in the colony, and then in strictest secrecy as he was filling out the
required biographical form while applying for a job with the Kirov Ballet
during World War II. He did secretly preserve two school notebooks with

poems and notes from other colonists written during the second year of their odyssey. In 1953, he was required to write an official autobiographical statement falsely crediting the Russians for the rescue, and he described the journey this way:

> In 1918, due to the famine in Petrograd, school children were evacuated to Siberia. When the Civil War broke out, perhaps a thousand children were moved month after month from one Siberian city to the other. For almost a year, I lived in Vladivostok, where I continued my studies. Finally, when the time came to return to Petrograd, because of the destruction of the Trans-Siberian Railway, the government sent us by steamship across the Pacific and the Atlantic Oceans.[43]

He revealed the full story only in 1973, when Bramhall visited Leningrad for the first time since the rescue.[44] "It was a big secret that Yakobson had been on the ship," Irina confirmed. "He never wrote that he had been out of the country. No one who was abroad wrote about it." In advance of Bramhall's visit there were announcements in the newspapers and radio asking all the surviving colonists to return for a celebration with Bramhall, who was being awarded the Medal of Honor by the Russian Red Cross Society.[45] Two hundred surviving colonists turned out and Bramhall reminisced with them. He specifically asked for Leonid Yakobson by name, remembering his devotion to caring for his younger brothers but primarily his eager curiosity and dancing skill. In a gesture of expansive reciprocity Yakobson impulsively invited all two hundred people at the reunion gathering to reconvene later that evening at a performance of his company at the Leningrad Conservatory. Afterward, his wife anxiously reminded him that the concert was already sold out. That evening, when a hundred former colonists arrived at the theater, Yakobson took to the stage. Standing there he told the audience about the remarkable Bramhall and his rescue of the Petrograd Children's Colony. "If it were not for the American Red Cross, of which Mr. Bramhall was a part, I would not be on this stage tonight," Yakobson concluded. He promised ticket holders seats for another evening if a hundred of them would please relinquish their seats—which they graciously did. As Bramhall walked down to his seat the entire audience gave him a standing ovation, and at the conclusion of the evening he joined Yakobson's company on-stage for the final curtain call.[46] Neither Yakobson nor Bramhall ever suggested there might be a link between his salvation through the colony and his subsequent career in dance where he effectively remade his own safe colony—on the ballet stage—but the possibility seems strong.

From his ordeal with this colony of orphaned Russian children, Yakobson seemed to have learned fortitude in the face of isolation, how social order can be circumvented or challenged by nonverbal behavior, and how real beliefs can be revealed through involuntary expressive behaviors. Yakobson's childhood experience of displacement and itinerancy may have honed essential skills that helped sustain him for his life as an artist, and later an overtly Jewish artist, in Soviet Russia. Yakobson's loss of family, school, home, and country as a consequence of the Bolshevik Revolution, and the chaos that ensued as Russia was reshaped, uprooted him from the earlier forms of social organization in his life and likely set the stage for his eventual embracing of dance as his new nation.

It might be argued that Yakobson turned to dance as the metaphoric language of his loss. Within weeks of his return to Petrograd in the early months of 1921, the dance studio would become the site of Yakobson's greatest allegiance. It was where physicality was rewarded with a clear system for attaining goals and with a path into a possible future for a seventeen-year-old who had missed most of his formal high school education because of war. Although his mother lived until February 1931, ballet would effectively become his family. It could be a parallel place from the world outside, one where he might shape his social resistance and invite Soviet audiences to share his vision within the relative safety of the theater. Later the ballet stage would also serve as a proxy for politics, a way to negotiate the complex dangers of the cultural category of being Jewish in Soviet Russia.

The years that Yakobson spent as an orphan in the Petrograd Children's Colony are most significant for helping him become comfortable as an outsider while giving him insight into his own capacity to survive. In the process some realities about political myths related to the Soviet's proclaimed superiority and the West's supposed capitalist greed were likely also disclosed. These experiences would become the foundation of Yakobson's new vision for Russian ballet as a performance medium that could harbor social difference and hold this fragile cultural dissonance through physicality.

Petrograd, 1921—Discovering Ballet

Yakobson's own account of how he discovered ballet was framed as pure chance. Soon after his return to Petrograd, as he walked the streets of the city one evening selling spices from a tray to earn money, Yakobson turned onto Nekrasov Street and glimpsed through a lighted window a room full of young people jumping and turning. "I was a well-built, lightweight lad," he recounted, "and I thought, 'Why not drop in?' I went up and looked around. At that moment my attraction to ballet began."[47] Irina suggests that it was Yakobson's determination as much as his physique that earned him a place in this class, which happened to be taught by the distinguished ballet pedagogue Aleksandr Chekrïgin. "He was very bold and he went in and told the instructor he would like to do this," Irina said. Chekrïgin explained that it was too late—one needed to start by age eight in order to become a dancer. But Yakobson was persistent, and Chekrïgin let him begin studying ballet.[48] He was seventeen years old, well past the customary age for beginning training, yet being a male gave him a certain advantage since men are underrepresented in ballet. His proportions were good, although at 5 feet 6 inches and 154 pounds he was muscular but too short to partner most women on pointe. It is also probable that the same natural grace that Yakobson displayed dancing aboard the ship with the colony helped persuade the instructor to let him join the class. Up to this point Yakobson had never even seen a ballet performance, so he wasn't drawn to ballet class because of any fully formed idea of its endpoint. Rather it is likely that when he looked in that window it offered a vision of the most important pedagogy he had experienced to date—the safe and structured community of the colony with its dances and amateur theater performances. It had been a world that literally floated free of national borders and where ethnic identities were not the primary standard by which one was defined; instead performance was the cohesive glue of belonging.

Chekrïgin was a respected teacher of classical dance, a dance notator, and distinguished character dancer with the Mariinsky Theater. He was known for the musical and dramatic richness of his portrayals of the ballet genre of character figures known as the grotesque. Chekrïgin was also drawn toward sharp and dramatically saturated portraits of comical old women in particular, and his signature role was as the echt evil fairy Carabosse in *Sleeping Beauty*.[49] Lopukhov, who was the leading Russian ballet theorist and choreographer of the time, once said that of all the distinguished interpreters, including the original Carabosse, Enrico Cecchetti, "only Chekrïgin observed the differing themes and made an attempt to treat this section in the way Tchaikovsky intended." Lopukhov explains that rather than filling out the musical phrases, Chekrïgin interpreted their musical color and emotional range, from spiteful rage at his entrance to increasingly stormy flashes and finally explosive anger as his malice grows at being slighted at Aurora's christening.[50]

In Chekrïgin, Yakobson found an ideal early mentor. Not only was Chekrïgin teaching evening classes tailored for those starting too late for the traditional ballet conservatory, but the spirit of Chekrïgin's highly dramatic and musical performances suggested a professional path for Yakobson, whose stature and late start meant he could likely never aspire to leading danseur noble roles. Chekrïgin agreed to take Yakobson on as a student; he also permitted him to enroll simultaneously in levels one and three of the beginning classes. Indeed after three years of this privately accelerated study with Chekrïgin, Yakobson had progressed so rapidly that he advanced to the Petrograd (later Leningrad) Choreographic Institute. Yakobson's acceptance into the former Imperial Ballet School, despite his late start and his having studied previously in a private ballet academy, was another incidence of fortuitous timing, since in the post-revolutionary climate there was a new effort to democratize and diversify the school, many of whose students came from theatrical families. In the school Yakobson studied first in the evening and later in the regular school with Vladimir Ponomaryov and Viktor Semyonov, who would graduate in 1926. Both teachers imparted to him essential training techniques for the male dancer. Ponomaryov was known for the strong system of his classes for men, distinguished by its logic and efficiency of progression and its challenging jump combinations.[51] From Viktor Semyonov, Yakobson would have been prompted to develop great endurance and strength from exercises that began, even at the starting point of the barre, with difficult steps that progressed through long and hard center-floor adagios and ingenious big jumping combinations. These two masters of male dance preparation outfitted Yakobson with strength, endurance, and breadth of technique—all foundational for the innovations he would soon begin making in classical ballet.[52]

Although Yakobson concluded his formal study with Chekrïgin fairly rapidly, he could not have had a better initial guide for his budding choreographic sensibility, where Yakobson would define himself far more than as a performer. In particular, Chekrïgin understood how to take a small role and made it a satisfying and full portrait, a talent that may have inspired Yakobson to his trademark genre: dance miniatures. A photograph in the Vaganova Museum in Saint Petersburg showing Chekrïgin in full costume and makeup for Carabosse hints at how dramatically and weirdly intense he must have been as a performer, and how fully and physically he made his portrayal of the fearsome fairy. Wearing a full-length dark satin gown and robe, he stands menacingly hunched over his cane, one hand peeking out from a sleeve like an arthritic claw as his head

Yakobson's teacher Aleksandr
Chekrïgin as Carabosse in *The
Sleeping Beauty,* ca. 1936. Vaganova
Ballet Academy Museum,
Saint Petersburg.

hangs forward on his neck and his face folds in a deep and angry scowl. His lower lip juts forward in a terse frown that looks as if it has been permanently set by a lifetime of disappointments. It is a remarkable image, radically different from the restrained older matron portrayal that the role's originator, Enrico Cecchetti, gave his Carabosse just a few years earlier. Chekrïgin looks fearless in his embrace of a character type so distorted from the frame of classical ballet that he seems more like an actor playing a Jewish folk hero than a dancer in *Sleeping Beauty*. In fact he looks like Solomon Mikhoels as Tevye in the Moscow State Yiddish Theater's 1938 production of Sholem Aleichem's *Tevye the Dairyman*—a caricature of a Jew playing a Jew. Perhaps Yakobson sensed this too in Chekrïgin, who opened a new door of coded ethnic images that Yakobson would eventually bring onto the stage as a focus of his own ballets. At the same time Chekrïgin gave the developing dancer the kind of close observation and structured encouragement crucial to ballet mentorship.

UPON GRADUATING IN 1926, Yakobson was immediately taken into the corps de ballet of the Leningrad State Academic Theater for Opera and Ballet (which became the Kirov Ballet in 1935). Chekrïgin, impressed with Yakobson's talent and determination, had gone to the State Academic Theater and lobbied for them to accept Yakobson with this compressed preparation. Having developed his big jump and extraordinary coordination, he had more than compensated for his late start. During the next seven years, while he danced with the State Academic Ballet, Yakobson advanced to soloist, performing several character roles including Puss in Boots in *The Sleeping Beauty* (*Spyashchaya krasavitsa*, late 1920s), the Acrobat in *The Red Poppy* (*Krasnïy mak*, 1928), and the Guest Dressed as a Bat in Fyodor Lopukhov's new version of *The Nutcracker* (*Shchelkunchik*, 1929). While he excelled at grotesque and character roles, from the start he was always more interested in choreographing than in performing.

The leading Bolshoi ballerina, Maya Plisetskaya, a fan of Yakobson's choreography, remembered that when she saw him dancing in the early 1940s she felt that "Yakobson the choreographer was anointed by God. But as a dancer, he was just the opposite—quite average. I saw him when I was a teenager on the Bolshoi stage in a few episodic roles. My memory retains only one small part as a fellow with a balalaika, where the dancer was distinguished not by his leaps but by his humor."[53] At school Yakob-

Leningrad State Choreographic Institute dancers. (*Left to right*) Galina
Ulanova, Mikhail Shpalyutin, Leonid Yakobson, Yu. Reinke, and
Tatyana Vecheslova. Central State Archive of Cinema, Photographic
and Phonographic Documents in Saint Petersburg.

son studied alongside several dancers who would become leading performers with the Kirov and dance in his ballets, including Galina Ulanova,
the most celebrated Soviet ballerina of her generation. In recalling Yakobson's dancing from the 1930s, Ulanova said, "From an early age, I remember Yakobson always fantasizing, inventing, designing. He was constantly
arguing, proving, convincing, constantly burning with choreographic ideas,
intentions, plans. . . . At a very young age, a demon of choreographic innovation entered his being—he was possessed with choreographic [inven-
tiveness]."[54]

Yakobson began making his first ballets in the late 1920s for his fellow
students. Askold Makarov, who danced leading roles in Yakobson's subsequent ballets at the Kirov and later wrote essays about him, remarked
about these early works:

As is characteristic of very few, Yakobson had a genuine feeling for
contemporaneity. In the first years of his activity, the Leningrad
Choreographic Institute became his workplace. The School at that
time lacked the means to pay its budding choreographers, but

Yakobson in turn lacked the time to wait until funds appeared. He wanted to stage ballet numbers, to gather his creative energies, to give free play to his imagination, and he could not wait for the propitious moment to present itself. So, once, taking a look at the work of his contemporaries working in other art forms, he mounted the anti-religious number *Little Priests (Popiki)* in 1926, and the socially biting number *They About Us (Oni o nas,* 1926), in addition to staging physical culture studies and marches. For the Kronstadt Fleet Folk Ensemble, he even created the ambitious *Maritime Suite (Morskaya syuita)* in 1931.[55]

Yakobson also staged pieces to music by Chopin and Grieg for the pupils of Agrippina Vaganova, including Tatyana Vecheslova and Natalia Dudinskaya, while citing as his choreographic idol Fokine and Fokine's choreographic dictum to "go against the current." Being a choreographer allowed Yakobson to orchestrate and populate a world of his own making. His introduction to dance by a master of the grotesque, and his subsequent launch into the field of professional ballet as a dancer of grotesque and sharply etched characters, all combined to make what is sometimes thought of as a side category of dance, one that someone might retire into, the young Yakobson's primary point of entrance instead. Character dance and character acting in fact were valued aspects of the repertory of late Imperial Russian ballet, and as the *drambalet* of the 1930s developed, the richly expressive characterizations and clear narratives it demanded boosted the importance of character dance and acting as well.

The grotesque-character dancer training attuned Yakobson to bodily gesture in a unique way. Indeed, character dancing is a curious wing of classical ballet. It is the space at the margins where ethnic, cultural, class, and age differences are most vividly inscribed. It is a vestige of when ballet was intertwined with opera and theater—and it is what allowed ballet to offer veiled social and political commentary in those historical eras when certain topics were deemed too risky for the central content of a dance. "Until Yakobson came along no one thought that ballet could be political and dangerous," said Nataliya Zozulina, a Saint Petersburg dance critic and writer in 2011, when asked to name Yakobson's major achievements.[56] Certainly Yakobson himself never realized how dangerous it would become.

THREE

What Is to Be Done with Ballet?

Today no artistic genre is steeped in stagnation so deeply as choreography. The classical tradition that is suspended doom-like over contemporary
choreography and prevails over all other movements within it has lost the
last vestige of artistic value. The classical dance is no more than a combination of French airs and coquetry—which we unaccountably misrepresent as
gracefulness—and soulless Italian virtuosity. It does not contain a drop of
human feeling or carry the slightest promise of progress. How can
anything so totally unnatural possibly be deemed beautiful?
—Leonid Yakobson, "The New Ballet Association," 1928

THE USE OF ballet as a way of commenting on the Soviet state and its political ordering of the individual ironically began at the moment of its dis-
mantling at the end of the Bolshevik Revolution. Yakobson was one of

ballet's most outspoken early critics—in editorials in the 1920s and 1930s he called for its destruction—but then he became one of its most passionate defenders.[1] He never abandoned either impulse, the revolution or the rebuilding; instead he continued to champion both to the end of his days, carrying the experimental impulse of these early years deep into the twentieth century. He endeavored to do this against the background of Stalin's purges, which historian Robert Conquest once described thus: "In one vast operation, the country had been silenced and broken, and from then on more selective terror sufficed."[2] Recently some scholars have begun to conceptualize the Soviet period under Stalin as an era that also included dynamic changes and consolidations as subcurrents within these larger constraints.[3] It was within these constraints that Yakobson emerged as an artist.

In 1928 Leonid Yakobson began his first published article, an essay for *Zhizn iskusstva*, with an opening blast at dance classicism, a prelude to what was effectively an obituary for the Russian Imperial Ballet. He was twenty-four years old, a budding choreographer who just two years earlier had joined the State Academic Theater for Opera and Ballet (Russian abbreviation GATOB, and previously the Mariinsky) as a member of the corps de ballet.[4] Almost immediately he had launched himself with high visibility in all three roles: dancer, choreographer, and now cultural polemicist. Yakobson's essay echoes familiar Soviet themes of liberating the proletariat from effete bourgeois soullessness and into a radiant new future under Communism. He argues for discarding classical ballet's superficial repertoire and the former Imperial Ballet School, renamed the State Theater Ballet School of the RSFSR's National Education Kommissariat's Governance of Academic Theaters in 1921, as outdated remnants of this oppressive tsarist extravagance.[5] His sentiments echo the perspective of another document released that same year—Joseph Stalin's First Five-Year Plan for the USSR. Stalin's document outlines a series of military and economic goals designed to rapidly, and aggressively, remake the Soviet Union into an industrial power, transforming it from an old stratified social system into a new futuristic collective one—a leap analogous to what Yakobson argues for in ballet.

The year 1928 also marked the beginning of what historian Sheila Fitzpatrick has called a "cultural revolution" in the consolidating Soviet state.

Zhizn iskusstva (The life of art), the journal where Yakobson's article appeared, was one of several publications encouraging members of the ballet world to participate in serious debate about the future of ballet in the new socialist state. Yakobson's essay, "The New Ballet Association," calls for a radical overhaul of ballet choreography and its schools of professional training, which, he wrote, exemplify the "artistic stagnation" and "anti-creative quagmire" of ballet choreography and the mechanistically repetitive classical vocabulary.[6] He saw these as inimical to the new role of culture in the Soviet state.

Yakobson's essay was published as a response to a series of questions that the leading arts critic, Ivan Sollertinsky, had posed to various dancers, choreographers, and critics, inviting them into public dialogue about what he identified as five essential questions for the future of Soviet ballet. Lurking within these questions are innuendos about the problematic past and uncertain future of culture itself in the Soviet Union. These questions would prove deeply heuristic because, as dance historian Tim Scholl has noted, they "accurately forecast the main theoretical and ideological concerns of the Soviet ballet for decades to come."[7] Most critically, they reveal the intersection of ballet with the propagandistic machinery.

Reading Yakobson's essay side by side with Sollertinsky's questions recontextualizes his text as the response of an artist who is being gently coaxed into answering proscriptive questions formulated by a savvy critic.[8] Sollertinsky's device is consciously pedagogic, and for many years he served as a close friend and demanding intellectual provocateur to the composer Dmitriy Shostakovich in much the same spirit. His life intersected Yakobson's at this start of his career and indirectly his death would as well (when the memorial trio that Shostakovich wrote to commemorate him was used by Yakobson as the score for one of his bravest ballets, *Jewish Wedding*). Sollertinsky's 1928 queries stimulated bold, if not nuanced, thinking on the part of young Yakobson. It is possible to read Yakobson here, even in the limited mode of respondent, as a dancer awakening to the realization that the structures that built him as an artist are mutable. One can sense his exhilaration at the potential power of scripting change. Equally significant, several of these idealized plans were eventually carried out in practice—and important public space was being devoted to impassioned dialogues about art and its potential role in drafting the new Communist order.

Within the space of six paragraphs Yakobson effectively throws into question the entire art form of Russian ballet as it then existed. He calls for the elimination of the tsarist model of ballet as a decadent and bourgeois amusement and the creation of a new model for a dance performance group, a new repertoire, a new movement vocabulary, even a new model for training in the ballet academy. Yakobson's tone in responding to Sollertinsky's queries has a quality that is as much about discovery as pronouncement. Sollertinsky posed the following questions in that summer of 1928:

1. What themes could be used in contemporary ballets?
2. Can a contemporary choreographic spectacle be built on the basis of classic dance?
3. Can acrobatics be used?
4. How can ballet pantomime be renewed?
5. Would an experimental studio help solve the current problem?[9]

For a young choreographer just beginning on his path of a life in art, it is difficult to imagine a more charged environment orienting one toward innovation. For Yakobson, Sollertinsky's questions would prove to be an equally useful blueprint for his own life's direction in dance. He had found himself launched as a dance artist in the midst of one of the most fraught periods of exchange between culture and political systems that any people in the twentieth century would experience.

The Soviet state began the period after the Bolshevik coup, which coincided with the final years of the creative brilliance of the Silver Age, by encouraging vanguard formations in ballet. While it would soon turn to impeding them, this memory of possibility seems to be something that Yakobson never forgot despite the decades of suppression that eventually followed. In these early years of his career Yakobson had already been witness to the artistic borrowings between disparate vanguard elements of the Soviet arts, including the symbolist experiments of Vsevolod Meyerhold's biomechanical stage movement and Konstantin Stanislavski's realist theater innovations. He saw art as a separate sphere from politics, and he had witnessed the arbitrary manner in which artistic or cultural initiatives by the Soviet leadership were suddenly withdrawn as the government varied its tactics for shaping public attitudes. The one constant was the Soviets' interest in using ballet to generate images about the new social order and to promulgate the belief that a utopian future lay ahead.

Many leading Mariinsky artists—dancers, choreographers, composers, and visual artists—would leave for Western Europe during the initial years after the Revolution and on through to Stalin's early rise to power, joining those who had already departed. Initially things did not seem so bad at home; in 1925 when Balanchine wrote to former members of his Young Ballet company trying to recruit them to join Sergei Diaghilev's Ballets Russes, they all turned him down.[10] As Russian ballet became more Sovietized, however, it became clear that those who had left Saint Petersburg to join the Ballets Russes in Europe a few years earlier were not going to return. Scholl quipped wryly that Diaghilev could boast the leading dancers, choreographers, visual artists, and composers because "he managed to take everything that was not tied down" when he left Russia. In addition, "though his strategy revealed long-term weaknesses, innovation remained on his side even as the Soviets actively strove for modernity and relevance."[11] While the departure to the West of such illustrious choreographers as Michel Fokine, Léonide Massine, Vaslav Nijinsky, Bronislava Nijinska, and George Balanchine was an enormous loss for Russia, it did offer Yakobson a less crowded field as a young choreographer at GATOB. Yakobson had precedents, contemporaries, and mentors among the early Soviet choreographic avant-garde, which in addition to those who left included Fyodor Lopukhov and Kasyan Yaroslavich Goleizovsky, who remained and had their careers ruined in the 1930s. So while Yakobson had not been alone initially, his path of both remaining in the USSR and continuing to work quickly became a uniquely solitary one.

Yakobson and Fyodor Lopukhov

For those like Yakobson who remained, the two strongest models of innovative ballet choreographers trying to accommodate to changing party demands were Fyodor Vasilyevich Lopukhov and Kasyan Yaroslavich Goleizovsky. Yakobson was familiar with the work of both men. Lopukhov, based in Leningrad, a former prominent experimental dance artist, modified his avant-garde approach to choreography and produced works that attempted to address the demands of the new political objectives.

Lopukhov had been the artistic director of GATOB since the fall of 1922 and so was also Yakobson's immediate boss. Eighteen years older than Yakobson, Lopukhov would become an important mentor to him—the younger choreographer watched Lopukhov's intermittent public and critical success as he tried to bend revolutionary ideals into ballet allegories that would satisfy Communist Party officials. Although Lopukhov was regarded as a leader of the formalist movement in ballet, he never lost his respect for danse d'école, the pure academic style of classical ballet founded on the principles laid down by Pierre Beauchamps, Carlo Blasis, and subsequent teachers. He worked in the lacunae, extending this inherited language and modernizing it as a few other adventuresome Russian choreographers—including Fokine, Nijinsky, Nijinska, Balanchine, Romanov, and Goleizovsky—had done. Lopukhov at times reformulated classic works like *The Nutcracker* (*Shchelkunchik*) with updates such as constructivist decor, allusions to sport and physical culture, and acrobatic movements—presuming that the non-dance vocabulary would make them more accessible for new proletarian viewers.[12] Lopukhov had premiered several works like this that aimed to revitalize ballet while both conforming to Soviet ideology and retaining aspects of ballet's past.

Among the most successful of these ballets was *The Red Poppy* (*Krasnïy mak*), a full-length work about Chinese revolutionaries pointedly conceived as a dance on the theme of imperialism vanquished by socialism. The ballet premiered at the Bolshoi in June 1927 and the first year alone it was given sixty-nine performances, far beyond that of any of the other ballets in the company's repertoire. *The Red Poppy* remained in the repertoire for the next eleven years with various characters and their nationalities adjusted as diplomatic tensions in the real world shifted, so that its pointed contemporary and anti-imperialist message, as well as the identity of those hostile nations holding different values, would remain easily legible.[13] In addition to its reputation as the first Soviet ballet with a modern revolutionary theme, *The Red Poppy* is also regarded as having initiated the heroic theme or dramatic ballet (drambalet) as a new genre of Soviet ballet, one focused on themes of noble passions and heroic deeds described through a unified vocabulary of gesture and movement rather than nineteenth-century pantomime.[14] It was this extended form of a full-length, plot-driven ballet with clear characterizations that would ultimately edge out the shorter modernist works.

In January 1929 *The Red Poppy* was also staged in the old Mariinsky Theater in Leningrad and it was here that Yakobson was cast in the role of the Ribbon Dancer, one of the solos requiring the most virtuosity among the ballet's fantasy pageant of Chinese acrobats and others who appear to the heroine in an opium delirium. Galina Ulanova, the leading Soviet ballerina and teacher who performed with GATOB from 1928 to 1944, saw Yakobson dance for the first time when he was performing this solo. In a tribute essay to him thirty years later, she recalled how even in this three-minute role he was so determined to challenge himself that he doubled the number of long ribbon props he was supposed to snake through the air as he danced. "I remember how Yakobson himself performed the ribbon dance from *The Red Poppy*," Ulanova said. "Usually, dancers have executed this number with only one ribbon, but Yakobson decided to dance it with two, and doggedly rehearsing it, he persisted, until he attained precisely the effect that he sought."[15]

A brief film clip of Bolshoi soloist Asaf Messerer performing the Ribbon Dancer in 1940, with one ribbon, reveals just how exposed the virtuosity in this solo is as he executes two double-air turns in succession while his right arm gracefully rotates a fifteen-foot length of ribbon in a huge arc around his orbiting body. The challenge of doing this with two ribbons, something apparently only Yakobson ever performed, seems daunting, but also in keeping with the personality of the young dancer whom Ulanova describes. "From my earliest years, I knew Yakobson as an incessantly improvising, inventive, imaginative artist. It seemed to me that he was constantly composing a work, resolving an idea, testing in his imagination new movements and compositions. He always seems to be arguing with someone about something, proving his point, persuading the dubious interlocutor. He was always the dreamer, afire with his thoughts and ideas," Ulanova wrote.[16]

The impulse behind Yakobson's remaking of the ribbon solo in *The Red Poppy* suggests an experimental sensibility eager to stretch formal challenges. It also speaks to his interest in adding more detail to the plot, since virtuosity that extreme could only occur as fantasy—and opium deliriums should conjure spectacles on a scale beyond reality. While there is no report of Yakobson having been criticized for his embellishment with the extra ribbon, Lopukhov did receive criticism for other aspects of the production, including for presenting an opium dream. The Soviet committee's approach to art had become so literal that this familiar conceit of a dream as a portal to a new vista of expression was instead taken literally as advocating substance abuse as a social escape (and so was considered an affront to the Soviet's Chinese comrades, who were working to eradicate their opium problem at the time). The name of the ballet was thus changed to *The Red Flower* (*Krasnïy tsvetok*) to mute the opium association. Soviet critiques might be framed as based on aesthetic considerations, but at their core they were political and ideological.

While Lopukhov's troubles with party oversight unfolded in Leningrad, his formalist colleague Goleizovsky was dealing with similar problems in Moscow. The classically trained Goleizovsky had performed as a dancer in the Bolshoi from 1909 to 1918, when he began doing his own work. When, like Lopukhov, he was forced to turn his aesthetic to the service of the Soviet message, his 1925 ballet *Joseph the Beautiful* (*Iosif Prekrasnïy*), with its constructivist-influenced scenery, dancers in bare feet and scanty costumes, and a plot based on the biblical tale of Joseph, was criticized for not aligning more closely with the political interests of Soviet audiences.[17] Two years later, Goleizovsky presented a consciously allegorical ballet, *The Whirlwind* (*Smerch*), with "fox-trotting capitalists opposing the world of the proletariat, dancing in light blue working clothes and displaying hammers and sickles." The preview audience reportedly walked out on the ballet, and it was considered a failure both ideologically and artistically.[18]

In December 1927, less than six months after the premiere of *The Red Poppy* in Moscow, however, the pressure on all of the arts, and the theater and ballet in particular, increased yet again. The result was an even more stringent system of lay oversight of artistic productions. This system, once instituted, eventually would attend and frustrate Yakobson for the rest of his career. Furthermore, as Stalin consolidated his political power, he announced details for a new campaign for the state control and development of the economic life of the country under the banner of the Five-Year Plan. To help script popular support for this campaign, he enlisted the arts, but especially ballet, which was seen as being particularly persuasive because of its use of body images and legibility. Special assemblies for artists were called where artists in dance and theater, in particular, were prompted to create works promulgating myths about the socialist state and its new social order.

The People's Commissariat for Enlightenment (Narodnïy komissariat prosveshcheniya, abbreviated as Narkompros) had been created by the Bolsheviks soon after the October Revolution to oversee the fundamental role of art and culture in the new society being created. Russian historian James Loeffler suggests that although Narkompros's function was pragmatically to be "a mechanism to employ education and culture in the revolutionary reconstruction of Russian society," it progressed slowly "as elements of the old and new regimes jostled incongruously against one another."[19] The Narkompros director, the literary critic Anatoly Lunacharsky, a longtime supporter of ballet and a man who was savvy about the nuances of cultural expression, negotiated these contradictions as he tried to carve out a middle ground. He responded to proletariat activists' demands for censorship power over the repertories of the theaters as they tried to ensure that the political ideology was served. "Theatre must become a real weapon of agitation and propaganda," Lunacharsky had conceded at a conference a few months earlier in 1927. He followed this statement quickly with another, this time attempting to mitigate their power: "The censor must have a definite place. [But i]ts interference must be minimal," he asserted.[20] As a result, the following year a classification system for ballets was created with five levels of ranking based on the ideological acceptability of the ballet's narrative. This rubric was particularly useful for the repertory commissions that had previously been formed "to oversee the repertoire of the State theatres in Moscow and Leningrad whose members included the Party historian V. I. Nevsky, Lunacharsky, and Voronsky; also, senior representatives of the Party, trade unions, and proletarian writers' organizations."[21]

At this point Yakobson was still an outspoken advocate of refocusing ballet toward the proletariat and eliminating most of the classical works. He, like so many others at the time, embraced this path toward change without questioning what the costs might be. In retrospect many of the post-revolution cultural projects of the Bolsheviks, like the demands for political content in art, might now be seen in part as shrewd marketing strategies for selling their product of Communism. As the grip of Stalin's control tightened, the demands on ballet as a means of state propaganda became more extreme. The situation was not unique to dance. Loeffler traces a parallel constricting of liberal possibilities for Jewish musicians at this same period, noting, "By the late 1920s however, treading the tightrope had become increasingly difficult. The Soviet regime began to roll back much of its support for Jewish national culture. After 1927, following a spate of Stalinist directives, Soviet society lurched toward a new radical phase of cultural revolution."[22]

In 1928 Yakobson witnessed the beginning of the painful fall of Lopukhov. Although Lopukhov initially had been encouraged by the state, his efforts to incorporate Soviet political themes and the acrobatic and gymnastic vocabularies backfired severely in his restaging of *The Nutcracker* at GATOB, which reworked such beloved staples of the ballet as Lev Ivanov's "Waltz of the Snowflakes" into a Western chorus line with Snowflakes doing splits.[23] The failure of the ballet as either innovation or a respectful homage to classicism earned Lopukhov the enmity of effectively everyone: critics, dancers, and especially the then director of the ballet academy, Agrippina Vaganova. In her biography of Vaganova, Vera Krasovskaya paraphrases the distinguished ballet pedagogue's response to watching her students trying to execute the "acrobatic tricks" of Lopukhov's *The Nutcracker* choreography: "Some of them were unable to make a complete split. Others could not sustain a cartwheel with their weak arms when their bodies rotated upside down. . . . But what connection could there possibly be between such circus tricks and the spaciousness of Tchaikovsky's adagio?"[24]

Krasovskaya uses the phrase "polluting the purity of classical ballet" when discussing the way Lopukhov interpolated "acrobatic tricks" into the revered duo of Tchaikovsky's score and E. T. A. Hoffmann's libretto for *The Nutcracker*. It seems to have been the arbitrary pairing of disparate aesthetics and styles that she found most troubling. The affront was compounded because Lopukhov staged this at the State Academic Theater for Opera and Ballet, which, as Russian dance historian Elizabeth Souritz has noted, was the place that Soviet Russia looked to as the guardian of the legacy of Russian ballet. The power to stage ballets in the former Mariinsky Theater was concentrated solely in the hands of Lopukhov, she observed.[25] Vaganova's concern over policing the purity of the classical ballet body and its lexicon is a reminder of how the ballet dancer came to symbolize the Soviet "body" in so many Soviet party cultural debates and policies.

Lopukhov was excoriated for *The Nutcracker* in the organ of the party, *Worker and Theatre* (*Rabochiy i teatr*), as much for his representation of socialist ideologies as for embracing formalism. His offense was that he showed an "absolute lack of understanding of the tasks facing the Soviet theatre"—a lack demonstrated, in part, by his incorporation in the choreography of popular dance forms from the West, including chorus girls.[26]

In keeping with the increasingly doctrinaire style of the Stalinist Central Committee, this artistic "error" required a special kind of scripted performance of a formal apology—the public ritual of "criticism/self-criticism" (*kritika/samokritika*). As historian J. Arch Getty has noted, beginning about the early 1930s, this ritual of *samokritika* replaced the more relaxed forums of policy debate and discussion. "In the 1930s, when open opposition was no longer tolerated, these [*samokritika*] meetings seem at first glance to have been pointless scenes where policies already decided above were dictated to the assembled members, where challenges to and debates about those policies were prohibited, and where those decisions were approved unanimously," Getty writes, but "these rituals were not frozen set-pieces. They were contingent and unpredictable performances in which outcomes and punishments depended more on how well the subject complied with the symbolic transaction than on the nature of the offense itself."[27]

It's easy to see how the opaqueness of all of this could easily set up a constant state of anxiety since what triggered a violation seemed so unpredictable and unavoidable. The text of Lopukhov's declaration of self-criticism is cut through with corresponding ambivalence and uncertainty so that the boundary between his volitional offenses and the basic nature of how the art form of ballet is practiced becomes unclear. The choreographer is faulted if people do not come to the performance or, rather, if the wrong people come—so that two of Lopukhov's ten points of apology relate to audiences: "It is necessary to draw the worker to the choreographic performances," he wrote in his "Declaration," and immediately before that, "[It is necessary] to reveal and categorically to put an end to the balletomania which went underground after the revolution." So it needs to be popular, but not too popular, and only with the right people. Lopukhov also offers the expected mea culpa for displaying "enthusiasm for acrobatics" as an end in itself. In addition, he promises to "search specifically and in detail for a new language of choreographic expression of the new social, political mode."[28] Lopukhov seems desperate to appease, and indeed he must have been, for within a few months he was forced out of his position as artistic director of the Leningrad State Academic Theater for Opera and Ballet.

Vaganova would replace Lopukhov from 1931 to 1937, bringing with her a heightened emphasis on brilliant, clean technique combined with an amplitude of movement and a suppleness of the upper body. Yet her artistic tastes remained fundamentally conservative and her stagings of *Esmeralda* in 1934, followed by a *Swan Lake,* though they introduced some revisions, ultimately reinforced both ballets as gems of the classical repertory.[29] Lopukhov's attempts at innovation to please multiple audiences finally pleased almost no one. As Souritz observed about Lopukhov's next staged ballet after *The Nutcracker*—that is, *Bolt,* his 1931 satirical ballet about industrial espionage set to a score by Dmitriy Shostakovich: "Who knows what the attitude toward such a ballet might have been if it had appeared not in the early 1930s but a decade earlier. Lopukhov's *The Nutcracker,* an eccentric ballet, had something in common with Eisenstein's *The Wise Man* and Meyerhold's *The Forest,* but it was not staged until 1929. . . . The pace of events was so sweeping that a gap of several years already seemed immeasurably great."[30] *Bolt* was regarded as another failure and Lopukhov was asked to resign from the company (which would be renamed the Kirov in 1934).[31]

In 1935 Lopukhov choreographed *The Bright Stream* (*Svetlïy ruchey*), also to a Shostakovich score and with a libretto that he and the writer Adrian Piotrovsky co-authored, for a troupe he had formed at Leningrad's Maly Opera House. Lopukhov turned this troupe into a forum for experimentation, but again he found that his work displeased Soviet authorities, especially Stalin, and he was forced to resign a final time, never again choreographing any major ballets. Although *The Bright Stream* had been given a warm reception at the Maly Theater in Leningrad, when it was subsequently restaged at the Bolshoi in Moscow it was attacked in a prominent, unsigned article in the February 6, 1936, edition of *Pravda* under the headline "Baletnaya Falsh" (Ballet fraud). That the article was unsigned meant that it came from the highest echelons of the party, Stalin. Deriding the work as "doll art of its time," the author decries the choreography for its false portrayal of the "people of our country" and their "true clothes and folk dance forms." "Ballet foolishness in the worst sense of the word rules on the stage," the article complained. "Under the form of a *kolkhoz* [collective farm] ballet there is presented a mixture, contrary to nature, of

false *plyaski* [peasant dances] along with numbers by dancers in tutus."
Lopukhov's attempt to adhere kolkhoz realism on the ballet idiom backfired dangerously in this instance and Shostakovich's music was similarly
sharply criticized for its indifference to kolkhoz literalism. "The composer
has the same devil-may-care attitude toward the folk songs of the Kuban
(a region of Southern Russia) as the librettists and producers have toward
its folk dances," the *Pravda* article continues.[32] As ballet music scholar Stephanie Jordan notes, this effectively concluded Lopukhov's career as a choreographer.[33] Although he returned as director to lead the Kirov from
1944 to 1946 and from 1951 to 1956, the creative part of Lopukhov was broken by the humiliation and irrationality of trying to appease party doctrine. The public shaming of Shostakovich for his scores for *Bolt* and *The
Bright Stream* must also have been intensely dispiriting to witness.

The Soviet political leadership also found itself in an increasingly complicated relationship with the authority of cultural institutions, particularly the prerevolutionary ones like the Kirov and Bolshoi ballets, which,
although they were subject to censorship, were also permitted modest
apolitical license—such as not having to force all the members of the
company to become Communists in order to continue working. As Fitzpatrick has noted in her argument for a more fluid interpretation of the
exchange of influence between Soviet leaders and Soviet artists, "Certainly the political leadership was determined to prevent the arts from
posing a political or philosophical challenge, or from depicting reality so
starkly that a challenge might be provoked. Yet at the same time, the leadership's attitude toward many established cultural values was more often
deferential than destructive. As party values penetrated culture, the cultural values of the old intelligentsia were penetrating the party."[34]

Yakobson's Early Choreography

For Yakobson, Lopukhov's experience would eventually become an object lesson in the treachery of accommodation and the fickleness of party
judgment, but for the time being he continued trying to craft rhetoric for
a new genre of ballet compatible with party norms and political culture.
No leading artists who worked in the Soviet Union throughout these decades, particularly in the performing arts, ever found a sure formula for
doing this. Getty suggests that the frequently shifting rules revealed the

Communist Party members' underlying sense of the entire system's weakness and vulnerability. "Insecurity and anxiety were strong components of the regime's worldview. The Stalinists feared foreign encirclement, peasant discontent, economic sabotage, unauthorized social groupings (including even stamp collectors and Esperantists), and even such mundane things as unauthorized jokes and anecdotes. The Bolsheviks, even into the 1930s, never felt secure and constantly feared for the safety of their regime."[35]

Yakobson made his first ballets in 1925, one year after Balanchine and his small troupe of touring dancers had left Russia for a short tour of Western Europe that turned into lifelong voluntary exile. In fact, Balanchine later said it was Goleizovsky's work that had inspired him to found his own Young Ballet (Molodoy Balet) troupe in 1923 for which he created several experimental works. But the authorities threatened the dancers with dismissal from GATOB and so the company disbanded. The following summer Balanchine again formed a performance ensemble, and this time he and fellow members Tamara Geva (Tamara Zheva), Alexandra Danilova, and Nikolay Efimov were allowed out of the Soviet Union for a brief tour to Western Europe. They never returned. The fourth member of the troupe, Lidiya Ivanova, who was to have joined them, died in a mysterious boating accident shortly before they received their visas.[36] Balanchine would spend the next sixty years advancing Russian imperial ballet into the plotless, neoclassical grandeur of modernist ballet while also creating several important story ballets. Yakobson, who would emerge with his own first work of choreography one year later, in 1925—a waltz for the students of the academy—would live his artistic life within the erratic and capricious restrictions of the Soviet state. In contrast to Balanchine, who found his steady inspiration in music, classical technique, and pointe work, Yakobson treated classical technique as more malleable and philosophical, and literary ideas as much as music were the basis of his inspiration. Despite similarities in their early histories, the two choreographers' later aesthetic sensibilities would diverge in these important ways. Their closest correspondence was in their early years. In 1923 Balanchine created *Étude* and *Enigma,* the latter a pas de deux he danced with Geva that has dramatic experimental lifts and cascades of the ballerina across her partner similar to those that Yakobson would use four years later in his *Sports March* and *Sports Étude.* Balanchine's unconventional forms in these 1923 works were called, ironically, "infamous distortions of the *danse d'école*" by historian Juliet Bellow because their radical break with the classical ideal of a balanced and symmetrical body so distressed certain vocal viewers.[37] Yakobson's pursuit of his own "distortions" would also lead him into the uncharted territory of invented lifts and partnering—as if improvising a forbidden romance. The element of acrobatism in post-revolutionary dance aesthetics that had been such a rich site of experimentation for both choreographers in the 1920s would continue in subtler ways for Yakobson in his work of the subsequent decades.

From the summer of 1924 onward Balanchine, Danilova, Geva, and Efimov stayed permanently in the West, having left before the full impact of Soviet political demands on the content and style of ballet and before restrictions on leaving had been implemented. Balanchine also left Russia early enough to take with him inspiring memories of the possibilities of the formalistic innovations of Goleizovsky and Lopukhov, before these artists were compelled to concede their aesthetics and careers to Soviet agendas. Yakobson, however, remained through it all and saw not just the work of both choreographers compromised, but their reputations and professional affiliations as well. After the failure of *The Whirlwind*, Goleizovsky's work was absent from the main Bolshoi Theater for the next few years.[38] During this interval he worked primarily in music halls and vaudeville productions, occasionally choreographing for the young dancers of the Bolshoi.[39] Forty years later, when Balanchine returned to Russia with the company he had built, the New York City Ballet, and showed his repertory for the first time, Yakobson was interested that it was this formalist path he had stayed with most consistently. "I found a formula that is golden," he reportedly said to Yakobson. When Yakobson later recounted this comment to Irina, they interpreted it to mean that Balanchine had found a way to ensure his work would receive financial and critical support. This observation, however, also speaks to Yakobson's personal aesthetic restlessness and begs the question of whether his practice of rarely repeating an artistic style was perhaps not simply his intense curiosity but also in part an accommodation to avoid censorship.

Throughout his career Yakobson would at different points measure his life against Balanchine's, and considered Balanchine a model for what a contemporary choreographer's life outside the USSR might have been.

This was not only because both men were influential choreographers during the same era in their respective nations. Balanchine began his training at the Imperial School and graduated from its successor, the Leningrad State Choreographic Institute in 1921, a year before Yakobson began studying privately.[40] So their initial training was closely parallel and their divergence a case study of how global circumstances influenced their aesthetic development. Although their time at the Leningrad State Choreographic Institute did not overlap, both choreographers not only trained there but also shared the same birth month and year: January 1904 (Yakobson was seven days older than Balanchine). While Balanchine left Russia in the summer of 1924 and spent his career shaping his aesthetic as a choreographer in Europe and America, the confines of totalitarianism framed Yakobson's work after this brief initial period of relative freedom in the late 1920s and early 1930. Yet he found a way to turn resistance into stimulus. Beginning in the late 1920s and into the next decades—until Stalin's launching of the anti-Jewish and anti-cosmopolitian campaign—Yakobson adjusted with relative ease to the changing aesthetics governing ballet production. The first ballets that Yakobson made were for himself and for his fellow students at the Leningrad State Theater Ballet School of the Russian Soviet Federative Republic's National Education Kommissariat's Governance of Academic Theaters, and what we know about them from photos and accounts from dance artists who were there is that his talent was evident early.

There are no descriptions of the first work that Yakobson choreographed, *Waltz (Vals)*, created in 1925 for students of the Leningrad Choreographic Institute and set to music by Frédéric Chopin. He made twelve short ballets over the next three years, including his first work for the Kirov Ballet—a short dance study that he called a "dance miniature," *Brazilian Dances (Brazilskie tantsï)*, choreographed to the work of the French composer Darius Milhaud in 1928.[41] Photographs exist for only two of three of these early ballets, *Fantasy (Fantaziya,* 1926) and *Sports March (Fizkulturnïy marsh,* 1926), but not *Sports Étude (Fizkulturnïy etyud,* 1927). The images for both ballets depict couples in bracingly athletic poses; in the first one in *Fantasy,* the man, Yakobson, stands behind the woman (Tatyana Vecheslova). With Yakobson's arm holding her at the waist, she leans away from him, arcing backward so far that her head is upside down as she gazes out evenly at the camera.

In the second image Yakobson is gently holding the wrist of Vecheslova's lifted arm and with his other hand, hidden behind the arch of her extended foot, he helps to hold her right leg in a waist-high supported arabesque. Both young dancers look like they are concentrating hard on the task. Yakobson studies Vecheslova as she glances back toward him, helping to hold her own extended leg at the knee while waiting for the photographer to snap the shutter. Perhaps unintentionally, we see simultaneously the arabesque image and the effort of this achievement—that is, Yakobson's hand and her arm both helping to keep her leg aloft. Their attire is 1920s ballet modest—white tights for both, ballet shoes, sleeveless tops, and puffy bloomer-like shorts so that no contours of either the male or female anatomy of the pelvis is visible. The mood is considerably different in a second photo labeled *Physical Étude*, choreographed by Yakobson in 1927. Here Vecheslova has looped herself across Yakobson's left shoulder, knotting herself across his chest like a sash as she arches backward to grab one foot with her hands. This pose is reminiscent of an acrobatic movement done by the Siren in Balanchine's *Prodigal Son,* which will premiere in Paris two years later, in 1929. In Balanchine's work the Siren, while seducing her partner, forms herself into the letter "O" and slides like a belt down the partner's upright body. In contrast, Yakobson's use of a similar image in *Physical Étude* is delivered with what appears to be a deliberate emotional neutrality, like a very beautifully shaped gymnastic feat performed by a pair of athletes with masterful control. There doesn't appear to have been any story or characters in *Physical Étude,* just the direct simplicity of a pair of skillful dancers performing partnering maneuvers with a look of utter ease.

Although *Sports March,* choreographed in 1931 to the music of the then popular but soon forgotten music of Grigoriy Lobachyov, dates from only a year later, 1931, the impression it imparts is far bolder and more futuristic. Here a young man, Vladimir Fidler, faces the camera squarely, kneeling on one leg with his other bent forward in a lunge as he supports fifteen-year-old Natalia Dudinskaya on one shoulder. Both dancers smile broadly as Dudinskaya balances confidently on Fidler, her legs stretched tautly together in midair behind her and her arms extending out from her shoulders in a "T" as if she were a passing bird he had just grasped out of the air in mid-flight. Dudinskaya's line already hints toward classical purity, which will become a trademark of her technique as a prima ballerina with

Physical Étude (1927), Yakobson and Tatyana
Vecheslova. Central State Archive of Cinema,
Photographic and Phonographic Documents
in Saint Petersburg.

the Kirov Ballet in later years. The dark scarf that Dudinskaya wears tied
around her head resembles that worn by a laboring female factory worker
and replaces a ballerina's tiara and its allusion to the court. In the photograph she dispenses this moment of virtuosity with the ease of an acrobatic feat, a quality complemented by the dancers' costumes of athletic
shirts, shorts, and rolled socks above their soft shoes.

Read against the iconic man-holding-airborne-woman pose of classical
ballet, like the poisson or "fish dive" lift, this *Sports March* moment looks
aeronautical, as if it might be a passing homage to the newly developed
Tupolev I-4, the first Soviet single-seat, all-metal fighter airplane newly designed and deployed in 1927. Yakobson's use of this acrobatic pose in *Sports
March* and the dancers' costumes of worker-like attire honor the Bolsheviks' exhortations for the use of acrobatics in the arts on two levels—
Yakobson is appending a physical culture vocabulary onto ballet, and more
subtly, by using these athletic gestures from the world outside the stage he
is alluding to the physical preparedness needed to defend the homeland.

Yakobson working with dancers at the Bolshoi Theater,
Moscow, 1930s. Photographer unknown.

Vaganova reportedly played a distinct role in commissioning *Sports
March* from Yakobson with the specific intent that it showcase the contemporary side of her prize pupil of ballet classicism, Dudinskaya. An anonymous May 2011 web posting said of the origins of *Sports March*:

Seeker of new forms, Leonid Yakobson, heard in the banal optimism of the march its impudent plastic equivalent. The sports costume snuggly fitted a thin teenager—Dudinskaya, with her arms
straightening in a deliberately sharp manner. Thrown by one partner towards the other, with every new impulse of the music the
dancer drew in the air a dotted contour of the arabesque: the lines
stretched, crossed and overlapped each other, in an impudent inter-
change of acrobatic holds. To all appearances everything here denied
tradition. At the same time everything spoke of the boundless opportunities of tradition. The more clearly Vaganova understood her
duties, the more confidently she pursued both short- and long-term
objectives. In Leningrad she took care of the balletic Saint Peters-

burg the same way architectural landmarks of a city get saved while it is changing shape.[42]

In the USSR of the 1920s, this emphasis on the physical education of the younger generation was an essential element in the overall system of Communism. Practice in gymnastics and acrobatics was considered a good way to prepare youth for both labor and defense by developing attentiveness, mental preparation, and muscular grace and strength. Yet while the title and photo from Yakobson's *Sports March* suggests that he is hewing to this Soviet belief, he also seems to have tweaked the athleticism toward art, to have borrowed qualities from gymnastic poses but rendered them on the clean, open line of ballet bodies. This step inaugurates a practice of movement sampling that Yakobson will continue in his choreography, using athletic movements as a neutral vocabulary rather than part of a Marxist-Leninist cultural framework. Outside of Soviet Russia several of Yakobson's former compatriots, including Massine, Nijinska, and Balanchine, were all playing with the inclusion of movements from athletic and acrobatic vocabularies in parts of some of their 1920s ballets as well—but in *Parade* (1917), *Les Noces* (1923), *Le Train Bleu* (1924), and *Prodigal Son* (1929), respectively, they had the license to make these references ironic or satiric commentaries, something that Yakobson's *Sports March* can only hint at fleetingly.

Yakobson continued to explore his ideas for a new Soviet ballet in print as well as on the stage. His next two essays called for a new model of ballet and were published in the 1929 and 1931 issues of *Rabochiy i teatr* (Worker and theater), a new Leningrad journal that had been launched in September 1924 and whose focus was the establishment of the new culture. It was in particular competing with *Zhizn iskusstva* (The life of art), the journal in which Yakobson had published his previous essay.[43] In this new, more actively proletariat journal, Yakobson's tone changes correspondingly. His arguments for advancing ballet into alignment with the socialist agenda now include a critique expanded to include the elite Leningrad State Choreographic Institute, the associate school of the Kirov Ballet that previously had been known as the Imperial Ballet School and from which he himself had just graduated three years earlier. Yakobson's personal archives, now at the Bakhrushin Museum in Moscow, contain a well-worn copy of Akim Lvovich Volïnskiy's *The Book of Exaltations,* an important manual of the period published by Leningrad's Choreographic Techni-kum in 1925.[44] In the margins, Yakobson has penned several comments to Volïnskiy's text, including an observation that two hours in the contem-porary period is too long for a ballet. And in a subsection of Volïnskiy's book titled "Erotica in Classical Dance," Yakobson wrote in the margins of his copy, "Oh!—I am not alone!" adding, "Without a doubt classical bal-let is erotic." He gathered support from both the present and the past as he shaped his credo.

In his 1929 essay "For a New Generation in Choreography," Yakobson argued that the ideological preparation of ballet dancers as class-conscious socialists was lacking and needed attention because "inculcating the idea that art is subject to class distinctions" was as vital as the content of what they will be dancing.[45] Strategically this soon proves to be unwise, for the director of the school, the renowned pedagogue Vaganova, clearly understood that she and her training system were the object of Yakob-son's critique. While she came to respect Yakobson as a choreographer, she never forgot this youthful and foolish class-based attack on her work and on her dedication to classical ballet. In 1931, out of necessity because there were not enough choreographers who could create ballets in the classical style, Vaganova invited Yakobson to serve as chief choreogra-pher in the GATOB academy. Personally, however, she did not like Yakob-son, and after two years he left for Moscow to work with the Bolshoi Ballet.[46]

Written in the period immediately following the government's adop-tion of the first Five-Year Plan of 1928, "For a New Generation in Choreog-raphy" reveals a preoccupation with hierarchies of class that is in step with the tone and political sentiments of the time. Yakobson argues that "socialist upbringing should be assigned uppermost importance" within the ballet academy. Although he himself is just a few years out of the bal-let academy, Yakobson's focus on educating youth in ballet according to Marxist ideology neatly aligns him with what Russian historian Katerina Clark calls the socially obligatory rules of the cultural ideology game in Leningrad in the late 1920s—attention to Marxism, sociology, and work-ers. "Hardly new, they were now *de rigueur* and every player in the game of establishing a new culture had to invoke them and justify his or her position in terms of them," Clark notes about this ideological game.[47] Ya-kobson calls for a promotion policy for choreographers and a bigger voice for young dancers, particularly those of the proletariat. He doesn't am-plify this further in his essay; instead he returns to what finally concerns him most—the task of creating a meritocracy for young choreographers. He suggests that the rapid industrial development mandated for industry can evolve in parallel in ballet through the training of socialist dancers. But it is the inherited choreography of the classical tradition that Yakob-son singles out for his harshest criticism—labeling the classics "decaying tatters of the canon":

> No new form of choreographic performance has so far been found—and without it, choreographic performance cannot become genuinely Soviet. Our young people should champion physical culture—replacing the decrepit classical tradition with the bracing tempos of physical culture. They should study diligently, fight for the class-specific proletarian art, and search for new forms of dance. Give us the opportunity to work! Provide us with class orientation, and the resulting socialist reorganization of the theatre will follow without delay. Give way to the young generation of choreogra-phers, to young cadres who will build a new choreographic perfor-mance.[48]

The respected ballet critic Yuriy Brodersen responds to this young Ya-kobson, the proletarian activist, a few issues later, in his essay "Reply to Comrade L. Yakobson." There Brodersen notes that Yakobson accurately diagnosed the situation of ballet's choreographic illness, but then he faults Yakobson for naively and peremptorily suggesting that the best remedy is to throw out all of the old ballets (except *Sleeping Beauty* and *Swan Lake*) and replace ballet technique with pantomime. "He does not realize he is cutting off the branch on which he is perched," Brodersen admon-ishes. "Calvary attacks by Comrade Yakobson will help very little to forming this new choreographic art," he chides further, dismissing Ya-kobson for the naïveté of his solutions. Brodersen concludes with his own grand cure for "sovieticizing ballet theater": "Critical learning of the legacy of the past, class differentiation and the widest artistic dis-cussion and competition in the theater on the basis of which the new artistic method will crystallize—those are the ways that ballet should follow," he asserts.[49]

The Golden Age

Brodersen's phrase about deciding how to make ballet worthy of the Soviet state by opening it out to "the widest artistic discussion and competition" proved prescient, as Soviet cultural officials announced a ballet libretto competition. The winner would receive a large cash award and the distinction of having his libretto produced as an evening-long ballet. Although the idea for a competition had originally been proposed at a 1927 meeting of theatrical workers, the decision to implement it now, two years later, was apparently in response to the dearth of Soviet ballets. The announcement of the competition, which appeared as a full-page notice in the January 13, 1929, issue of *Zhizn iskusstva,* carried with it a list of eight necessary characteristics of a winning libretto, which can be read as a position statement of the values of the new Soviet ballet theater.

The way the Soviets cast a wide public net to solicit submissions for a new ballet libretto seems egalitarian on the surface. In reality, however, it was disingenuous because the number of possible librettists, choreographers, and composers in Leningrad was not legion but rather a small, well-known pool of people. The prizes were listed at 300, 200, and 100 rubles, presumably a first, second, and third place, although no mention is ever made of any runners-up. Based on the value of the ruble in 1929 the size of these prizes is remarkable—300 rubles is the amount that the USSR government defined in May 1929 as the annual income for an average industrial worker or well-off kulak farmer—and a testament to the extraordinarily high value placed on the competition. The winning work would be produced on the former Mariinsky stage, the major venue for ballet in Leningrad.

The framing of this search for a new Soviet ballet librettist offers a glimpse into the tightly scripted ideological constraints shaping artistic productions during this New Economic Policy (NEP) period, which had formally begun in 1921 and ended in 1928, although its impact was felt earlier in the disappearance of several of the private ballet studios that had supported innovative work. Ideology was supposed to infuse the very genesis of a ballet and be expressed in the ballet's text-based scenario, its libretto, before the choreography or even the musical score was developed.

This approach extended the reach of party oversight into the actual act of ballet creation—so that the party's desires and standards dictated even the conceptualization of a ballet. *Ideas* about ballets were now being vetted—thoughts were being policed before one even entered the ballet studio. The call also announced that the winning work would premiere at the State Academic Theater of Opera and Ballet, the company that Lopukhov was still actively directing. (He would be fired the following year, in part for failing to produce successful "Soviet" ballets, revealing the extent to which the party had rewritten his role from director—someone who decided about the repertoire—to someone who matched choreographers to projects.)[50]

The competition's call for submissions is a recipe for what the committee considers an ideologically correct ballet:

Stipulations of the Competition on the Creation of a Libretto for Soviet Ballet

Having announced a contest on the composition of librettos for Soviet ballet, the State Academic Theatre of Opera and Ballet is directed by the following considerations:

Choreography, until recent times an art preeminently of the court aristocracy, now must become, thematically and formally, Soviet art. The old ballets have outlived themselves and have ceased to satisfy the mass of spectators. The new spectator demands that the choreographic theatre bring meaning to scenic activity taken from events near to us. The libretto of contemporary ballet is not just an accidental frame for the display of dance which lacks inner cohesion and does not issue from the basic activity—but the libretto is a choreographic drama, obligated to satisfy all the demands laid upon Soviet dramaturgy in general.

To write a really contemporary scenario for ballet is to take a first step along the way in the path of creating a Soviet choreographic theatre.

A libretto presented to the contest must satisfy the following demands:

1.) Revolutionary theme. . . .

2.) Themes must be developed on the level of a concrete perception of reality, and not by constructing abstract dance forms loaded with symbolic or allegorical meaning. . . .

3.) It is desirable to build a spectacle on mass movements. . . .

4.) It is necessary that intrigue in the scenario be sufficiently un-complicated for it to be understood as a whole from pantomime. . . .

5.) It is necessary that the librettist take into account the achieve-ments of contemporary theatrical technique. . . .

6.) Not presenting any kind of categorical demands concerning genre of the scenario, the State Academic Theatre of Opera and Ballet points to the possibilities of use of the following genres: con-temporary reviews (Soviet revue, lyric-heroic poems, choreo-graphic comedies and satires, contemporary fairy-plays).

7.) It is desirable that the scenario of the ballet give the balletmaster material for pantomime . . . , but also new forms of dance: acrobat-ics, physical culture and others—and new pantomime gestures.

8.) The scenario of the ballet must be calculated as a whole evening performance (two or three hours of pure activity).[51]

In this call the word "dancer" is curiously missing. In its place is *balet-meyster,* the Russian word for choreographer, that is, the individual who choreographs, rehearses, and thus drills bodies to telegraph unequivo-cal meanings. The choice of verbs also suggests militaristic command—"must," "it is necessary," "it is desirable." There is no gray here—everything is focused with the deliberateness of factory production. And the last item in the list signals the return of the full-length ballet, to replace the short miniature or étude associated with the earlier modernism.[52]

The libretto selected as the winner was written by Aleksandr Viktoro-vich Ivanovsky, a forty-eight-year-old film and musical theater director employed by the state-controlled film industry in Leningrad. Ivanovsky seems to have checked off all the boxes as he drafted his libretto, resulting in a narrative so crammed with ideological clichés that it reads like a spoof of Soviet art. Recruiting a writer from dramatic theater to strengthen the plot of a ballet libretto was common practice at this time. The libretto that Ivanovsky submitted was daunting as a plan for dance, since the scale and density of images and narrative that film, and for that matter musical theater, employ are very different from those in ballet. Ivanovsky's li-bretto is set in a capitalist city where an industrial exhibit, *The Golden Age* (*Zolotoy vek,* 1930), the ballet's title, is taking place. Approaching the guide-lines like a shopping list, Ivanovsky scripted a plot across three acts about the fictional adventures of an actual Soviet soccer team, Dinamo, when they visit an industrial exhibition and have a series of altercations, both ethical and physical, with a delegation from a capitalist country called Fashlandiya.[53] The number of characters and events depicted in the first act alone is huge—African American boxers, corrupt fascist boxing referees, Soviet citizens, soccer captains, fascist cabaret dancers, and a diva argue, fight, and flee. In the second act a Soviet Komsomol woman and an African American man walk around the city and then are framed and arrested by the fascist police. The third and final act happens in a music hall near the exhibition where a series of popular dances—a tango, tap dance, and polka—are performed along with the screening of film footage of the Red Front rescuing prisoners. The ballet culminates with a grand dance symbolizing the cooperation of workers experiencing the joy of labor.[54]

Once Ivanovsky was announced as the winner in the spring, Lopukhov was delegated to select the choreographers to realize his libretto. Deciding to divide the choreography among three choreographers—one for each long act—Lopukhov picked two better-known choreographers, Vasili Vainonen and Vladimir Chesnakov, for acts 1 and 3, and then, surprisingly, he assigned act 2, the one with the most direct sports and acrobatic references, to the unknown ballet activist and youngest of the group, Yakobson. The gifted composer Dmitriy Shostakovich, in a period of rising success and fame, was commissioned to create the score. It would be the first of the three ballets he would compose in the period 1929–1935.

Shostakovich made rapid progress on the score. On September 17, 1929, he demonstrated the first completed act—fifty-five minutes of music—for the theater's artistic council, which responded "with unanimous admiration."[55] He then submitted the completed score to the State Academic Theater for Opera and Ballet in late October 1929. The challenge of writing his first music for ballet absorbed Shostakovich, who worked to shape his score as a soundscape that would interact with the dancers rather than merely accompany them. For the scenes in the cabaret he took popular music from the West—can-cans, polkas, waltzes, and even a musical quotation of the popular tune "Tea for Two" that he had written on a bet in 1928—and packed this all into the score.[56] Shostakovich's score masterfully and ironically animates the libretto, sectioning it into thirty-seven numbers each marked by rich melodic and harmonic invention.[57] The score is witty and densely rhythmic, and gave the choreographers a musical platform to dig into that was far more kinesthetically suggestive than the libretto. The music unfolds with a lively expansiveness, taking the listener on a tour of physical rhythms linked to sport and art with just enough dissonance and musical quotations to suggest the composer's ironic detachment from the political subject at hand. Russian cultural historian Harlow Robinson has noted that in writing the music, Shostakovich said he was striving musically to illustrate "the juxtaposition of two cultures. . . . The Western European dances have left the sort of unhealthy eroticism so characteristic of contemporary bourgeois culture, while the Soviet dances must be saturated with elements of healthy calisthenics and sports. I cannot envision the development of Soviet dance in any other way."[58]

This concept of a Soviet dance "saturated with elements of healthy calisthenics and sports" is precisely the quality around which Yakobson focuses much of his dance invention in *The Golden Age*. Certainly it was the vogue of the times to draw from these types of athletic movement disciplines, but the rationales for doing so varied dramatically. The Soviets regarded acrobatics, gymnastics, and sport as classless and neutral body practices, free of cultural legacies and also more accessible to those who had seldom or never seen live artistic performances. For Yakobson there was also an aesthetic heritage to these forms—the clean modernism of Nikolay Foregger's machine dances as well as Goleizovsky's and Lopukhov's experiments with movement abstraction and elemental forces.

What makes Yakobson's use of these non-dance vocabularies different is the manner in which he works to integrate the shapes and dynamics of non-dance gestures into the bodily form of classical ballet. It is not a clean sweep. Rather Yakobson, in choreographing act 2 of *The Golden Age*, is taking the first steps toward what will become his signature—the creation of a classically based yet eclectic movement vocabulary.

In his score for *The Golden Age*, Shostakovich samples various musical genres from the popular to the prosaic, from music hall and cabaret performances to pompous marches and grand entrances. This task of writing his first dance score so engrossed Shostakovich, according to Robinson, that he reflected deeply on how to make the interaction between music and live performance most productive. "Music for the theater must provide not only accompaniment, but interaction," Shostakovich said in an interview published at the time of the premiere of *The Golden Age*. "A failure to observe this principle will relegate music to the background and forfeit its enormous power of interaction. . . . I have found it necessary to write not only the sort of music that one can dance to but also to dramatize the musical substance itself, to lend the music a real symphonic intensity and dramatic development."[59] Those involved with *The Golden Age* production reported that once Yakobson, Vainonen, and Chesnakov began work it became clear that Ivanovsky's libretto was "sketchy and involved" (that is, complex), and offered little support for the choreographers.[60] Thus Shostakovich's insightful score became all the more important.[61]

Shostakovich's score effectively made audible the dramatic pulse of the ballet, by employing dance melodies to tell social tales in tandem with the libretto's narrative themes.[62] Many of the predictable scenes of political, racial, and class conflict in *The Golden Age* were filtered through the medium of movement itself—especially the vocabularies of sports and popular dances of the 1920s. These were augmented with milling crowds at the industrial exhibition, police, detectives, young people dancing the tango and foxtrot, athletes posturing, and even a Josephine Baker–styled Diva character dancing an erotic adagio. Shostakovich made the libretto danceable and he gave the choreographers a dramatic and sonic floor on which to visualize these complex movement battles. Shostakovich's only immediate experience with movement prior to composing for *The Golden Age* was his well-documented personal passion for soccer, which he dubbed "the ballet of the masses." Shostakovich was a passionate fan of the two home teams of Leningrad, the Dinamo and Zenit; in fact, one of the Dinamo stars, Pyotr Dementyev, was known affectionately as "the Ballerina," presumably because of his grace in play.

The *Golden Age* score percolates with melody, harmonic invention, and a gentle sarcasm. In the "Overture," scurrying musical lines seem to rush in from all directions at once, like the overload of themes in the plot. Shostakovich's use of popular dance and music hall melodies in *The Golden Age* sound to contemporary ears like parodies. This consciousness was important for the composer at the time, and a critical distinction, since any other use of these "decadent" forms could be read as an embrace of them. Early in 1930 Shostakovich's sentiments about this appeared in print in the journal *Proletarskiy muzïkant* (Proletarian musician). On composers who wrote "light music" like foxtrots, he used the term "wrecking activity" to signify the danger of publishing and performing this kind of popular music.[63] Fitzpatrick, who summarizes the major interpretive paradigm of the Soviet Cultural Revolution as an assault on the old Russian intelligentsia, suggests that *Proletarskiy muzïkant,* like many others, was the vehicle of a newly emerged cadre of Communist specialists during the first Five-Year Plan—specialists who effectively conducted class warfare in the pages of journals like this during its brief life from 1929 to 1932. Shostakovich's remarks against light music were published a few months before the premiere of *The Golden Age,* and they underline how carefully he used "light music," that is, dance references, in his score.[64]

The Golden Age occupies a curious place in Soviet cultural lore. It was born out of a moment of enthusiasm for what ideology and art conjoined might produce and a stellar cast of young artists assembled to realize that dream, yet it disappeared after only a few performances.[65] Reportedly it was a failure—certainly the Soviet leadership lashed out at it—and all of its various components were essentially lost. The choreography vanished and what remained were scattered accounts and a couple of Valentina Khodasevich's sketches for her remarkable costumes. Shostakovich's score, too, was put away and remained unpublished in his archives for thirty-four years until 1994, when conductor Gennady Rozhdestvensky's recording of the ballet's score, played by the Royal Stockholm Philharmonic Orchestra, reappeared.[66]

What has not been recovered is just how monumental a dance event the premiere of *The Golden Age* was and what a remarkable act of experimentation and artistry from deep within Soviet and Russian culture it represented. It has been called the first anti-fascist ballet because of its plot details, but it is also, despite some modernist elements, the first major ballet in the emerging form of "neotraditionalism."[67] *The Golden Age* maps a future for ballet, wrapped inside a Soviet skin. Both its influence and the hastiness of its burial explain, at least in part, the way that Yakobson would shield modernism inside his ballets over the next several decades. Ballet modernism could hibernate in Yakobson's works because the Soviets, even though they wanted to have as much control as possible over the ballets that were created, still needed enough new works to keep ballet alive.

The question of how *The Golden Age* passed into Soviet history as a failure when it was initially a popular success with audiences suggests the power of the Soviet censorship apparatus to designate success and failure retrospectively. *The Golden Age* premiered on October 26, 1930, to enthusiastic audiences, though the assessments of proletarian critics were much more negative. As part of the 1930–1931 season at the Mariinsky Theater it was performed eighteen times, almost every other week for the length of the season, that is, from October to June.[68] As Manashir Abramovich Yakubov, president of Russia's Dmitriy Shostakovich Society, has noted, this extended run of many performances over several months is generally what happens to a ballet that is an artistic and popular *success*.[69] The ballet was given ten performances in 1930 and eight in 1931 with subsequent performances mounted in Kiev in 1930 and Odessa in 1931.[70] Yet the official cultural memory that was constructed around *The Golden Age* labeled it a flop, a stigma that remained attached to it for the next sixty-five years.

What this remarkable team of artists had done was take a seemingly impossible set of constraints, and while honoring every limitation, come up with a witty, moving, sophisticated, and successful work of art. The surface message may have hewed to the party line, but its medium, tone, aesthetic, and style, at least in its best sections, were wonderfully disobedient. Much more dangerous to the Soviet position than a short-term success, *The Golden Age* was a true hit. That it was overwritten as a failure revealed the essential problem of making art to please the Soviet state, showing that even the mildest messages could seem subversive and frightening to the regime.

Although he was young, Yakobson was a logical choice for Lopukhov when he selected the choreographer to stage the second act of *The Golden Age*. Yakobson had been advocating for the use of more athletic vocabularies in his published writings, and had promoted the use of more pantomime and acrobatics to increase ballet's accessibility to the general public through his own choreography like his *Sports March*. At this point in his career he believed sincerely that both could be possible and that a dance work of serious artistry that also adhered to party lines and guidelines could be achieved. An almost antic physicality is suggested by the titles of the scenes in the second act of *The Golden Age,* the portion Yakobson was designated to choreograph. This second act of Shostakovich's score included the following scenes with the mini plots of each one spelled out: scene 3, "Mime of the Agents Provocateurs, Provocation and Arrest (Gallop)," scene 4, "Procession of the Workers to the Stadium—Dance of the Young Pioneers—Sports Games," and scene 4, "Dance of the Western

Komsomol Girl and Four Sportsmen." Those subtitles are so specific they might be stage directions.

One dancer who had danced in the "Sports Games" scene of *The Golden Age,* Natalya Sheremetyevskaya, then a thirteen-year-old student in the Leningrad Choreographic Institute, recalled how minutely detailed Yakobson's shaping of each individual's actions in the sports sequences had been. He structured his staging so that all of the athletes for the various sports were in motion simultaneously in different parts of the stadium, just as in a real warm-up for a sports event—possibly in a nod to V. E. Meyerhold's stagings.[71]

In her memoirs written at the age of ninety, Sheremetyevskaya recalled vividly the meticulous care that Yakobson took to construct what looked spontaneous in the sports and games sequence of the ballet. "We had to recreate precisely the moves of a volleyball game, the teams were next to each other and there was an imaginary net separating them. After the ball was put in play, it was hit back either with a high jump or at the level of the floor and we had to keep constantly moving from place to place. All this was put together with a spritely rhythm and so it looked very good and was effective and attractive," she wrote. "But it was not satisfying because the rehearsals were as a rule very painful and torturous. Portraying a live game made you want to improvise, but instead Yakobson demanded we reproduce exactly each movement staged by him."[72] As Sheremetyevskaya recalls, Yakobson also saw that the effect was stilted, but rather than back off he kept inserting revisions until the young dancers were lost, at which point he grew even more impatient and shouted his disapproval at them.

Two small black and white rehearsal photos of *The Golden Age* in the Saint Petersburg State Museum of Theater and Music reproduced in Soviet ballet critic Galina Dobrovolskaya's 1968 Russian monograph on Yakobson, *Baletmeyster Leonid Yakobson,* provide a rare glimpse of how Yakobson's choreography for the ballet might have appeared. The first thing one notices is that these photos document labor. In each a quintet of dancers, four men and one woman, are captured in a moment of work and the momentum from what they have just done or will do next. This hint of their being in a snapshot of an action makes their formation feel not so much static as temporarily arrested. In the more dramatic of the two, a twenty-year-old Galina Ulanova stands on the stomach of a man

(Konstantin Sergeyev) who lies stretched on the floor. He holds his right arm and right leg with rigid straightness at 45-degree angles. With one foot balancing on Sergeyev's abdomen, Ulanova curves backward in a deep and beautifully arched backbend. Ulanova's hands walk along Sergeyev's uplifted leg as if any moment she might kick her legs over her head and do a complete 360-degree backflip onto her feet.

Only two years into the Leningrad State Academic Theater and Ballet at this point, Ulanova already projects the elegance, lightness, and pliant ease that will become her signature qualities as she ascends to the role of a leading ballerina of her generation. For a classically trained female ballet dancer her action looks like an unusual assignment and a stretch for her as a ballerina, but the character she portrays is not. In *The Golden Age* Ulanova plays a Soviet Komsomol woman, the "good" female who offsets the "Diva"—the dangerous and seductive evil female lead representing the capitalists. It is not likely that at this early stage of both of their careers Yakobson knew enough about Ulanova's evolving politics to be consciously making an inside political joke, but casting her as a Komsomol—a junior member of the Communist Party in his or her teens or early twenties— was neatly apt. Since 1922 the focus of the Komsomol had shifted toward a new emphasis on the physical, specifically to engage members in health activities and sports among other industrial and service projects. Ulanova herself would within a few years be the ballerina most emblematic of the party. Recalling her role in Yakobson's choreography for *The Golden Age* in a memorial essay she wrote nearly fifty years later, in 1977, for a collection of essays titled *The Music and Choreography of the Contemporary Ballet*, Ulanova noted, "I remember as well, how he had been assigned to stage one act of the ballet, *The Golden Age*, in which, it turned out, my four partners and I danced the sportsmen number. [But] alas, informally at work, I met Yakobson only once. He was one of the three choreographers who staged the ballet *The Golden Age*, to the music of Dmitriy Shostakovich. I danced the role of the Komsomol Sportswoman, the so-called positive heroine of the ballet. To me, the physical culture scene remains the best in the ballet. In it Yakobson elicited from us not a replica of gymnastic movement, but the figurative sensation of athletic lightness, the beauty of the human body in action."[73]

The second rehearsal photo, like the first with Ulanova, appears to represent labor performed by athletic bodies arranged aesthetically—a curious hybrid that looks consciously, and provocatively, experimental—as if Yakobson were taking the proletariat vocabulary of daily actions, done by real people, and grafting them onto a classically trained cast. This is the figurative sensation of athletic lightness that Ulanova mentions. In this second photo Yakobson himself stands in a deep squat in the center of a semicircle of three men, each frozen in the pose of a herculean sports-man hurling a discus or a spear or shooting a bow. Yakobson's "sport" in which he poses, however, is anomalous, or perhaps prophetic. He grasps the hands and ankles of Olga Mungalova, a dancer with exquisitely long legs (and about whom the young George Balanchine once said, "Ev-ery acrobatic trick was a snap for her," when she had performed as a student in Balanchine's 1920 work *La Nuit*.)[74] Mungalova's expression here as she rehearses with Yakobson is calm while her body is held in a bowed backward curving shape as if she were a human projectile he were about to scoot along the floor and then hurl into space.

What makes Yakobson's use of these non-dance vocabularies different is the manner in which he works to integrate the shapes and dynamics of non-dance gestures into the bodily form of classical ballet. It is not a total clean sweep like the birth and refinement of dance modernism in Amer-ica in the 1920s and 1930s or the theatrical inventions of Meyerhold and Stanislavski in pre- and immediate post-revolution Russia. Rather Yakob-son is taking the first steps in *The Golden Age* toward what will become his credo "I do what the music tells me" and toward the creation of a classi-cally based, yet eclectic, movement vocabulary. His non-literal and less presentational form of movement is an accommodation from the sensibil-ity and vocabulary of classical ballet. Askold Makarov, a leading dancer with the Kirov Ballet who danced the leads in several later Yakobson bal-lets including *Spartacus (Spartak)* and *Ali-Batïr* in the 1950 and 1955 Kirov productions, commented about the interior experience of this style from his years of performing Yakobson's work. His reflections apply equally well to *The Golden Age*:

Leonid Yakobson was obsessed by a quest for new ways in the ballet art. Eschewing the classical dance, he staged his works, both in large or small genres, on principles of physical culture. He grasped the gymnastic acrobatic style as one expressive of his times. Power, youth, the beauty of the human body, a heartiness of spirit, energy—should these not be the attributes of a new idiom in choreographic art?[75]

Beyond the daring physical postures that Yakobson assigns to both Ulanova and Mungalova in these athletic sequences, these two leading women in *The Golden Age*'s second act were costumed by Khodasevich, the adventuresome modernist visual artist who designed the costumes for the entire production. Photographs of two of the surviving costume sketches in the Saint Petersburg State Museum of Theatre and Music, both for female dancers, suggest how Khodasevich's costumes and visual designs must have extended this aesthetic of athleticism and symbolic political commentary. One of the sketches is labeled "Soviet Dance," a reference to the allegiance of the character. Khodasevich's costume for a sports woman is dynamic and functionally fashionable, depicting a female dancer in a short skirt and blouse. The texture of the costumes has a sleek, shiny quality, and Khodasevich writes on the sketch specifying silk, leather, or oilcloth as less expensive alternatives for the fabrics. The colors she chooses are intense and pure with red, black, or white sections appliquéd onto the skirts and blouses. The realism of Khodasevich's costume carries through to the little accoutrements of a red kerchief knotted functionally around the female dancer's hair, fashionable red and black sports shoes, and a black wristwatch with a red band. Khodasevich has also noted that this woman in her sketch is one of four female soloists in *The Golden Age* and that her energy quality is "impetuous and wild" and her dance style "folkish and not at all classical." A second sketch for a much more sparsely costumed female, identified as being in "Dance of the World [Based] on Class [System]" is for a woman in a brightly striped hard hat who stands on her full pointes, her body bare except for a narrow bandeau across her breasts and a tennis skirt of red and white stripes with a starred blue cloth over the crotch. The narrow bandeau she wears over her breasts and the wristbands are both in the colors and designs of the French flag, with pockets and points in the Italian and other nationalities' colors. Despite these allegiances, she is left essentially uncovered. The impression is that every element of the production is working overtime to pack in the details of its cultural references and to shape without ambiguity its political message.

Valentina Khodasevich's costume sketch for
the second act of *The Golden Age* (1930).
© The St. Petersburg State Museum
of Theatre and Music.

Khodasevich was already a respected theatrical designer when she joined *The Golden Age* team. Her pedigree as an artistic radical stretched back to the early 1920s when, influenced by Kazimir Malevich's sets and figures for *Victory over the Sun* (*Pobeda nad solntsem*, 1913), she had designed the violently asymmetric and angular sets and costumes for the 1922 constructivist theater production of *Archangel Michael* (*Arkhangel Mikhail*). Prior to beginning work on *The Golden Age*, her work had been featured in the big exhibition titled *Russian Stage Designs, 1917–1927* (*Vïstavka teatralno-dekoratsionnogo iskusstva 1917–1927*), held at the Academy of Arts in Leningrad in 1927.[76] So when she was selected for *The Golden Age* the producers were picking a serious and adventuresome artist. Khodasevich was a theater designer who in the spirit of the earlier cubo-futurist artists Mikhail Larionov and Natalia Goncharova was boldly applying an overall design concept that included performers' costumes as well as their makeup and hair, so that the effect was of a tightly unified yet radical aesthetic. Khodasevich's costume designs appear simultaneously dynamic yet logical, and their lines are clean and sharp. The way she plays boldly with geometrical elements and ornamental patterns in her costumes references both everyday clothing and traditional theatrical costumes. Khodasevich's designs, like Yakobson's choreography and Shostakovich's score, merge everyday elements. In this instance the modernist hybrid of the costumes parallels the choreography and decor, which also play with historical clothing and traditional theatrical costumes.[77]

The myth that *The Golden Age* was an artistic failure lingered until 1995, when the Shostakovich scholar Manashir Abramovich Yakubov made the first in-depth investigation of its reception. He discovered that officials in 1930, anxious about what their competition had yielded, sought to bury *The Golden Age* retrospectively. The journals *Proletarskiy muzïkant* and *Rabochiy i teatr* both published withering ideological critiques.[78] *Proletarskiy muzïkant* described the ballet as "such a coarse alloy of nauseating fox-trots and other decadent dances" and "insufferable on the academic stage," warning that "the ideological harm of such productions is evident."[79] Ten days following the premiere of *The Golden Age*, *Rabochiy i teatr* published a lengthy, scathing assessment of the ballet by Yuriy Brodersen. "How could it happen that the ideology of the bourgeois music hall, that urbanist mongrel, that ideology so hostile to the Soviet theatre—how could it penetrate to the stage of the state ballet theatre, and what is more, in such an excessive dose?" he asked. "Instead of using every means to prevent elements of bourgeois art from penetrating to the Soviet stage; instead of completely exposing the producers who insinuated the ideology of the western pigsty on to the stage under the guise of satirical interpretation, the Arts Political Council did everything it could to justify the staging of this unfortunate performance."[80]

Brodersen, who had sparred with Yakobson in print, tempered his remarks about the young choreographer's work in *The Golden Age*, giving him the highest praise for being the choreographer among the three who resisted most effectively the libretto's inducements to formalism. He praises Yakobson as an undoubtedly talented choreographer while cautioning that individual formalist successes cannot justify the cultivation of a subject-less dance.[81]

In contrast to the party-dominated media, the arts press responded to the aesthetic dimensions of the performance itself. The musical director of the production, Aleksandr Gauk, noted in his memoirs that the adagio Vainonen choreographed for Olga Iordan, who danced the seductive role of the Diva (which involved virtuoso turns to tango and foxtrot rhythms mixed with classical ballet gestures), generally resulted in demands for an encore from her mid-performance. Gauk also recalled that even the orchestral entr'acte to the third act was received with enthusiastic applause and demands for an encore.[82] Ballet critic Boris Lvov-Anokhin, too, reflecting on Yakobson's career, noted that it was in *The Golden Age* that he developed a new "plastic language in keeping with the present time and based on springy, strong, athletic movements."[83]

Shostakovich, a man who could be deeply self-critical, gave a series of measured and extended assessments of the production, beginning two days after the premiere when he wrote the following letter to the director of the Leningrad state theaters, Zakhar Lyubinskiy, who had been out of town for the opening performance.

> Dear Zakhar Isaakovich, the première of *The Golden Age* took place the day before yesterday. . . . In short, the performance went well. All of us who were responsible for writing it were very successful. There have not been any notices, but that is of little importance. What is important is that yesterday and the day before the audience judged our work. . . . The performance was so successful that on 6 November it will be performed . . . at a gala session of the Leningrad City Soviet. It was the second and third acts which were the most successful. For some reason the first act left the audience unmoved. I put this down to the dance numbers being somewhat refined. So come along and see for yourself.[84]

Shostakovich thought highly of the music he had written for the ballet, calling the score "unusually successful compared to many that I have done." He arranged a short four-part ("Introduction," "Adagio," "Polka," and "Dance") orchestral suite from it even before the stage premiere, as a sampler. His most extended analysis of *The Golden Age* came in his later essay "My Artistic Association with Leonid Yakobson," where he recalled the visually arresting images that Yakobson created. He described these images as encompassing both broad political humor as well as a subtler playfulness through the construction of cinematic images that comment on both the quality of theatrical time as well as its genres:

> Pupils of the famous Leningrad Choreographic Institute partici-
> pated in this ballet, depicting a game in which one dancer repre-
> sented a capitalist. Dressed in tails and a top hat, the Capitalist
> suddenly disappeared into the general crowd where, unexpectedly
> and unnoticeably, his costume was ripped off and before the spec-
> tators, lo and behold, stood a Pioneer. The chuckle emanating from
> the auditorium was the reward for this clever gimmick. Especially
> memorable was the mass-sporting scene, with its yellow décor that
> so resembled patches of sunlight, and matching costumes by Val-
> entina Khodasevich. In this scene all types of sports were repre-
> sented, transformed by Yakobson into choreographic statements.
> The entire presentation had been so harmonically unified into one
> whole, that when after an extraordinarily dynamic action, the en-
> tire ensemble abruptly stopped and slowly floated as in a slow mo-
> tion film, I no longer heard the music, because of the ovation from
> the auditorium acclaiming this choreographic device.
>
> An unforgettable evening! It seemed to me that Yakobson and I
> were being born into art, and that through his choreographic inter-
> pretation, my music began to resonate in a new way. From that
> time on, Yakobson's artistic path never ceased to interest me.[85]

The Golden Age's Legacy

Shostakovich's score for *The Golden Age* has in retrospect been called the next stage in the development of Russian ballet music after Tchaikovsky and Stravinsky. Yakobson provided choreography that endeavored to move Russian ballet forward in that same way. But as the revolutionary ideology of the new Soviet state shifted again, ballet found itself answering questions that had been asked in one ideological moment and were now being answered in a far different and more hostile one.[86]

For choreographers the accusation of formalism was particularly damaging and reflected the shift in preferred aesthetic categories and qualities that had begun in 1929 under Stalin.[87] Formalism in this sense was shorthand for overindulgent abstraction and a disconnection from history. By definition, Russian formalism was a school of literary theory and analysis that had emerged in Russia around 1915 and was devoted to the study of literariness. It had begun as a reaction against the vagueness of previous styles of literary analysis, and attempted instead a scientific description of art that deliberately disregarded the contents. Marxist critics were unhappy with this, so for them "formalism" became a term of reproach. With the consolidation of Stalin's dictatorship in the period of 1929, formalism in art was declared a heresy in the Soviet Union. As Fitzpatrick has noted, in music the "great retreat" from the revolutionary cultural values of the 1930s and its dovetailing into the new anti-formalist campaign were marked by a dramatic intervention of the party leadership into cultural matters—specifically the denunciation in the January 28, 1936, editorial in *Pravda* of Shostakovich's *Lady Macbeth* opera. "The 'formalist' label was applied to art that was stylized, modernist, and pessimistic, and took its inspiration from the West," Fitzpatrick writes. "The antithesis of formalism—that is, the art that *Pravda* endorsed and sought to encourage—was realistic, traditional, and optimistic, and took its inspiration from folk art."[88]

From the early 1930s onward, Soviet ballet found itself increasingly in service of objectives outside of the aesthetic, or often in place of it. Yakobson had a combative spirit that sustained him—that and his determination to persevere in building a contemporary repertoire of Russian ballets. The vanguard artists and party officials like Lunacharsky had affirmed that ballet served a social purpose—and Yakobson continued to believe that—but he differed with the Soviets regarding who defined that purpose and determined how it was used. He turned this social purpose approach to art back onto the Soviets themselves—harnessing it at times as a way of bringing to the stage a style steeped with Jewish-authored idealism and independence. He subverted not only modernity and abstraction, but also the deeply subjective experience of being an outsider. Yakobson continued his role as one of ballet's harshest "inside" proletarian critics by arguing against much of classical ballet into the early 1930s. At the same time he was working through parallel arguments physically in the studio with student and company dancers.

Yakobson published his last disputatious essay from this transitional period in 1931. In the essay, published in *Rabochiy i teatr*, he decries that classical ballet is "obsolete and pointless" with a training system that only "produces young performers who seek oblivion in the sterility of technical skills."[89] The article is obviously written in the aftermath of strongly negative comments about *The Golden Age* made in the same journal just a few issues earlier. Yakobson seems supportive of this pro-proletariat perspective. He mentions *The Golden Age* only once by name, chiding the production's "young artists" (of which he is the youngest on the creative team) who attempted to solve the problem of choreography by introducing innovation into the dance form without understanding that choreography is "an ideational system." Yakobson opens his essay with a lament for ballet's resistance to change, noting that all theatrical arts have to become attuned to modernity, and that ballet is still contentedly sticking to its two-hundred-year-old traditions. He singles out Lopukhov for particularly pointed criticism, chiding him in language that closely echoes the anti-formalist rhetoric of 1930s socialism. Yakobson faults Lopukhov specifically for his unexamined devotion to classical ballet conventions, his mistaken belief that content will emerge out of form, and his use of acrobatic stunts that are not integrated into the content of the ballet.[90] This complaint earns him the enmity of Vaganova, who read these comments as a personal affront on her work in the institute, which they were.[91] Yakobson also accused Lopukhov of "strangling classical ballet through meaningless acrobatic stunts borrowed from the circus."[92] Unlike Vaganova, who took some time to forgive Yakobson for his slights, Lopukhov appears to have been very forgiving indeed. In later years he was one of Yakobson's major supporters.

Despite Yakobson's vitriol for the stuffy conventions of classical ballet, in 1931 it is apparent that he did not know precisely how to replace them. Toward the end of his lengthy critique of ballet he mentioned one artist by name whom he regards as a model of artistic innovation—Vsevolod Meyerhold. It is a reference with tragic irony because Meyerhold, who had been one of the most enthusiastic activists of the new Soviet theater, was soon fated to fall from favor because of Stalin's repression of experimental arts and Meyerhold's own outspoken antipathy to socialist realism. In less than seven years after Yakobson's essay was published, Meyerhold's theater was shut down, and by early 1940 he had been arrested and executed.

This is the blunt reality that lay just around the corner from the optimism that Meyerhold, Yakobson, and other Soviet artists were feeling, however briefly, as late as 1931. "Either we embark on a vast experimental enterprise or we doom ourselves to a life-long confinement within the bounds of prettiness and estheticism," Yakobson wrote. "Thus the restructuring of choreography pivots on the affirmation of pantomime as a genre—which, in turn, can be accomplished only by revolutionary means: by resolutely severing all ties with the dance systems of the past."[93]

While it sounds like Yakobson might be merely echoing the prevalent anti-popular-culture rhetoric of Soviet critics, he was sincere. By 1931 he had already choreographed at least two short works and an act of a full-evening ballet that incorporated movements drawn from sports and acrobatics, *Sports Étude*, *Sports March,* and *The Golden Age.* He was endeavoring to apply sports movements as a physical vernacular that could be performed with the same rigor as the classical vocabulary and thus extend ballet, making it more accessible and contemporary. From the start of his career Yakobson had regarded classical ballet as an art form in need of revision—his vanguard impulse was constant. As the ruling regime behind it shifted from socialist idealism to the totalitarian stultification of socialist realism, however, the target of his critique also changed.

The shift toward art as a medium of politics that led to the doctrine of socialist realism would begin in the 1930s, and it played out with unique complexity in ballet into the immediate postwar period. As Slavic dance historian Christina Ezrahi has noted, socialist realism as a propagandistic ideology had promoted a view of life in the USSR that was far from realistic; instead an idealized view of a nation was presented in which all classes and nationalities were joined in harmonious comradeship.[94] Offering up this mandated realism presented a special challenge for ballet because of its nineteenth-century origins as a spectacle for the aristocrats of Russia's former imperial courts and the inherent unrealism of classical ballet's vocabulary of metaphor and artifice. "A fear of virtuoso classical dance began to take hold over the ballet stage," Ezrahi notes. "In the wake of the anti-formalism campaign, ballet became an apprentice of drama," hence the drambalet became the only genre of ballet that was acceptable.[95] But this too was short-lived. "By the last Stalinist period," she writes, "the preoccupation of drambalet with narrative plausibility ran the risk of negating the essence of ballet as a unique artistic medium relying on complex classical dance as its main means of artistic expression. The path of drambalet turned out to be a blind alley."[96]

After he had experienced the chill of party censorship firsthand in the reception of his first major work, *The Golden Age,* and witnessed the liquidation of the proletarian organizations in literature and art by the Communist Party in 1932, Yakobson's allegiance shifted permanently. He moved toward becoming one of ballet's most passionate defenders. Yakobson may have entered the field of dance at a moment when a great deal of change seemed possible, but this window of opportunity would shrink as the Communist Party under Stalin began exercising increasing control over the content and form of culture through this imposition of anti-formalist and socialist realist aesthetics. Ballet would become what Scholl once called "a ward of the Stalinist state in the 1930s."[97] Over the next fifty years, the opening and then rapid shrinking, and at times disappearance, of creative possibilities was the rhythm in which Yakobson became accustomed to working in the art form he had initially sought to discard. What did vanish was the possibility of pairing open invention in Soviet ballet with free expression.

Certain vanguard radicalisms of the 1920s would go forward in the new Soviet state, most importantly the belief in ballet as a vital medium for conveying social knowledge. What would be left behind in the repeated expansions and contractions of official regulations and Communist Party oversight was the cultural oxygen necessary for intellectually challenging art to survive. Lunacharsky, like Lopukhov, found himself increasingly in conflict with the Stalinist political system. In 1929 Lunacharsky was fired as commissar of enlightenment, yet he continued to fight for the preservation of ballet and its heritage. The following excerpt comes from one of Lunacharsky's most often quoted, and eloquent, final speeches, delivered on May 12, 1930, at the Bolshoi Theater in Moscow in defense of ballet:

> If Russian classical dance would be killed, standing at such an unusual height, against which no one in the world dares compete, then not only the lovers of ballet will weep bitter tears, but, perhaps, proletarian youth, when he begins to build the palace of his life, will ask: "Where do you have it?"—and then we will say to him "That is something imperial; we annihilated it," and they will

stigmatize us with a black word. For that reason I prefer now to make a mistake, not in the opinion of the proletarian mass, but of those who are prepared to break the porcelain in our museums, because aristocrats drank from those cups.[98]

Reading Lunacharsky's defense it's easy to picture the unruly and vengeful proletarian mass in 1930s Soviet Russia, determined to end classical ballet as well as modernist performance, that is the object of his pleading. At issue was who should control ballet's authors and message. Lunacharsky would be dead within three years of making these declarations, succumbing to a heart attack in 1933 as he was being demoted in the wake of Stalin's rising power. His rise and then fall from grace as an influential figure reflects the lurching revolt against the old and embrace of the new that marked the initial years after the October 1917 Revolution, when the new—like jazz, conductor-less orchestras, dissonant music, and machine dances—was enthusiastically embraced. In ballet this impulse toward the radically new found a counterpart in the work of choreographers like Goleizovsky, the former Bolshoi Theater dancer turned choreographer. Goleizovsky was interested in portraying the new individualism and emotionalism of post-revolutionary freedom through a ballet vocabulary that incorporated acrobatic and gymnastic poses and actions designed to bring the art of ballet closer to the broad democratic masses.[99] In 1933–1934 Goleizovsky returned briefly to the Bolshoi after his earlier ballets, including *The Whirlwind,* had been allowed very limited performances and then dropped from the repertoire.

The complicated exchanges between cultures and political systems in the Soviet Union swung wildly from acceptance to rejection in the late 1920s through the 1930s, with the new revolutionary tenor contributing to and then impeding evolving art modernisms. The world that Yakobson was born into as a choreographer turned out to be a rare moment. How did he navigate its changes—what happened during this lurch into invention and then the retreat from it for those, like him, who stayed?

Yakobson's initially negative comments about formalism were genuine. He personally found a way to partially sustain the original bright optimism of the 1920s cultural revolution and use it as he turned political party directives into aesthetic challenges.[100] His article for *Rabochiy i teatr,* for example, was sincere—he didn't just drop acrobatics in, he found a way to fuse this style of movement with the ballet vocabulary and so revitalize the form. That was indeed his one true mission as he learned how to take each negative prohibition and turn it into a possibility.

Ethnographic Knowledge

Even though he was only a few years older than the young students in the Choreographic Institute with whom he began working in the late 1920s, Yakobson slipped easily into the role of cultural mentor, dazzling them with his adventurousness and teaching them not just how to perform his choreography but also how to become informed witnesses to the rich performance world beyond ballet. Sheremetyevskaya and her fellow Choreographic Institute students who performed Yakobson's ballets in the early 1930s, in the post–*Golden Age* period, were captivated by him and the boldness of his experimentation. Sheremetyevskaya along with Boris Fenster, Vladimir Varkovitskiy, and others were dubbed "Yakobson's Brigade," perhaps an ironic borrowing of the term for workforces on collective farms in the 1930s who were clustered in small groups, or brigades, to maximize productivity.[101]

As Sheremetyevskaya describes the students' interactions with Yakobson, it is evident that even at this early stage of his career, he had a strong sense of how to catalyze broader awareness in the students. "He talked to us in the manner someone would use when talking to adults," she recalled. Yakobson enthusiastically described to the young dancers his plans for new stagings that would address serious and deep topics. "We did not try to understand his goal," Sheremetyevskaya said. "It was just interesting for us to see something different in ballet. Working with him introduced us to new ideas culturally." Indeed Yakobson took his young dancers to see a performance by the Chinese performer Mei Lanfang and to Meyerhold's theater to see Vishnevsky's 1931 work *The Last Decisive Battle (Posledniy reshitelnïy)*. Sheremetyevskaya speaks for Yakobson's Brigade when she says that this exposure to innovative culture left an indelible impression on them. Yakobson was grappling with how to include pantomime in ballet as a way of both meeting the Soviet demands to make ballet accessible to wide audiences and continuing to push forward with new paths of movement investigation that interested him personally. Sheremetyevskaya remembers Yakobson claiming that one way to achieve this dual purpose was to increase the portion of pantomime so that the meaning was carried clearly. "At the same time he did not really believe in the old ballet pantomime," she said.[102]

Arkady Raikin, the most famous Soviet comic of his time and a brilliant satirist during the Stalin years (when satire was nearly unthinkable), was then a student of the theater institute and he would often come as a guest to the Yakobson's Brigade social gatherings. At these gatherings Raikin would offer inspired parodies of ballet pantomime to the delight of the ballet dancers who, like Yakobson, understood the staleness of traditional ballet mime. Sheremetyevskaya recounts that at one of these gatherings Raikin coined a new mime phrase, rewriting the established "I love you" mime gestures with a substitution of his hand circling an oval around his face and then clenching the calf of his leg in place of the final finger pointing toward the beloved to signify the much more practical "I love blinis with caviar (calf-iar)!"[103]

A few months after *The Golden Age* closed, Yakobson began staging a new musical pantomime called *Chavdarcho*, or *The Young Pioneers* (*Pioneriya*, 1932), for his hardy group of Yakobson's Brigade dancers. "All of us in the activist brigade started getting very tired," Sheremetyevskaya wrote about rehearsals for this production. "Why they called us *The Young Pioneers* we don't know because the scenes that Yakobson did manage to stage took place at a female nunnery prison. And we of course were portraying the prisoner nuns. In this scene we sat bent over and doing something weaving or embroidery, doing all these movements that would follow the music. To tell you the truth all this did not interest us so much. After a few rehearsals the enthusiasm ran out, we started getting very tired until soon dancers were just going through the motions." Yakobson responded by yelling at the dancers and thereafter Sheremetyevskaya says it became his normal manner at work. "He especially yelled at those activists, members of that brigade whom he considered responsible for maintaining the discipline at the rehearsal. So the staging of *The Young Pioneers* was going very slowly."[104] By the time *The Young Pioneers* was to be performed at the Maly Opera Theater, Yakobson had managed to complete only three or four scenes of the ballet.

Sheremetyevskaya recalls the most memorable event of the program being a discussion that happened on stage following the concert. In the middle of an otherwise empty stage Yakobson sat at the table wearing a t-shirt and very casual pants, clothing that Sheremetyevskaya says pointed to his disdain and disregard for the formality of the occasion. His words were just as provocative as the comments from the audience. "We observed this from behind the curtain and we went 'Ah!'" she said. "Then we gasped when Vaganova, sitting in a box in the theater, said that she did not understand anything in Yakobson's *The Young Pioneers* ballet. Yakobson responded disdainfully, 'You, Agrippina, you wouldn't understand this.'"[105] Given that Vaganova was among the first people to appreciate his talent as a young choreographer and invite young Yakobson to work at the school, the affront was doubled.

The young dancers were shocked at Yakobson's daring. "Who else could have replied to Vaganova, the same Vaganova in front of whom everyone trembled?" Sheremetyevskaya asked rhetorically. To Vaganova's credit, there were no consequences for Yakobson's affront. He continued working at the school, although Vaganova could have put an end to it. The next work Yakobson did with the students went faster. He now understood that using pantomime exclusively was a dead end and started searching for what Sheremetyevskaya referred to as the "bearer of the foundation of meaning."[106] Like many others during those times Yakobson turned toward sports, which was associated with the new dynamism and changes of the idealized Soviet life.

In 1933 Yakobson choreographed *Till Eulenspiegel* (*Til Eylenshpigel*) to Richard Strauss's tone poem, as a graduation production of the Leningrad Choreographic Institute. Yakobson's choice of the legendary comic anti-hero Till, a prankster who holds up the mirror to man's foolishness, seems perhaps an autobiographical reference given Yakobson's own reputation at this point as a young artist who was not shy about charging in with his own opinions. *Till Eulenspiegel*, Yakobson's third ballet, involved a smoother rehearsal process for the dancers. Sheremetyevskaya credits Yevgeny Aleksandrovich Mravinsky, who was just beginning his career as a conductor, with getting Yakobson interested in staging *Till*.[107] She recounted that working with someone who was so organized and correct helped contain Yakobson's temperament. In addition, the clear borders of the script were hinted at by the music itself, which permitted him to focus on a clearly defined task. "The staging was moving fairly quickly and without any incidents," Sheremetyevskaya noted. "The performance was listed as the graduation but I do not remember that any of the graduates took part in it in 1933. Vladimir Fidler, a recent graduate of the school, was invited to do the main role of Till Eulenspiegel. The rest of the roles were given out to the members of Yakobson's brigade." Sheremetyevskaya recalled that she was cast as the mother and that every dancer in the crowd scene was given his or her own fully developed character even though the parts were minor.

"I had to create a chicken who sits on her eggs and guards them and tries to safeguard her chicks. That's why I had to look wide and short and I was moving my arms like wings and I would walk around in a humorous way," she recalled. The bride wore a costume with numerous wide skirts and she helped me with this. I have to say that in the performance there was an interesting contrast between the styles of costumes—bright, catching your attention—and the set design that only hinted at the time long gone."[108]

In her memoirs Sheremetyevskaya describes the set for the ballet as a complex metaphoric frame, explaining that upstage on a small raised platform there was a frame in the shape of a trapeze surrounding a picturesque landscape in the Renaissance style. The curtain rose on an empty stage and then suddenly the performers would come tumbling out of the frame, filling up the stage with the bustle of an instant bazaar. In the midst of it was a burst of energy that was the character of Till. His appearances were accompanied by a musical phrase that sounded like "cock-a-doodle-do." "Fidler really looked like the part given his features, short with a nice face and playful eyes as well as professional features, his temperament, his high jump and he was a good turner," she noted. "His role was built on the technical elements of always being chased after. He would slip away from his pursuers teasing them with things that he did. Fidler was fluid and that would infect everyone with this card gambling spirit. However *Till* was played only once unfortunately, because it could have helped Yakobson become established in Leningrad. Without that opportunity he left for Moscow," she concluded, in one of the very few descriptions of this long-lost ballet.[109]

During this time, Yakobson completed three courses at the Leningrad Institute of Scenic Arts, renamed the Technicum of Scenic Arts in 1933. That year, he also received an invitation to the State Academic Bolshoi Theater and its affiliated training academy.[110] The aftermath of *The Golden Age* had been difficult for all the artists involved, so in late 1933 Yakobson gladly left Leningrad and moved to Moscow, where he joined the Bolshoi Theater as a dancer and choreographer. Since the Communist Party attacks on *The Golden Age* three years earlier, several in the creative team for that ballet had found GATOB unwelcoming to further work. Shostakovich, who had been disparaged for his *Golden Age* score, found the criticism against him increasing. It would reach a crescendo on January 28, 1936, with the publication of what is sometimes called the Historic Document—an unsigned editorial on the third page of *Pravda* titled "Muddle Instead of Music" about *Lady Macbeth of the Mtsensk District.* The author, widely believed to have been Stalin, excoriated the opera's subject and style after attending a performance in Moscow by the Maly Opera Theater of Leningrad group. The *Pravda* article accused Shostakovich simultaneously of formalism and naturalism, as well as crude primitiveness and vulgarity for the bleak horror of the plot of Katerina Izmailova, a merchant's wife who murders her husband, father-in-law, and ultimately her lover's girlfriend, after a musical passage suggesting sex between Katerina and her lover.[111] The impact on Shostakovich was devastating and the collateral chill on other brave artists was profound.[112]

Meanwhile, in his new job at the Bolshoi, Yakobson's production of dances continued at an ambitious pace—and before leaving Leningrad he had choreographed two one-act ballets and eleven miniatures, almost all for students in the Leningrad Choreographic Institute.[113] He did this in part because of the post–*Golden Age* restrictions on his access to the main company.[114] While with the Bolshoi he created several dances for the State Moscow Choreographic Technicum, the school that since 1920 had been affiliated with the Bolshoi Ballet, as well as the Sverdlovsk Academic Theater for Opera and Ballet in the city of Sverdlovsk (now Yekaterinburg), near the Northern Urals.[115] In place of the more formalist and athletic-focused works he had made earlier and through to *The Golden Age,* many of the miniatures he now made in the period immediately after used themes drawn from Russian and ethnic myths and fairy tales.

It was while at the Bolshoi that Yakobson met a beautiful young Russian corps de ballet dancer fifteen years his junior, Nataliya Spasovskaya, who effectively became his first wife. Although they did not marry officially, they lived as domestic partners in a communal apartment in Moscow with several members of her family for more than ten years, until the start of World War II. Spasovskaya never progressed beyond the corps and occasional soloist parts. Although it is likely that Yakobson fashioned a character piece or two for her, there is no record of which of his small ballets she might have performed. More than her dancing ability, she was remembered by those who knew her as a witty, charming, and lively conversationalist.

It was during this period that leading Bolshoi ballerina Maya Plisetskaya, who was then a young ballet student, met Yakobson for the first time and was cast in her initial ballets with him as student work. "Leonid Veniaminovich took me for his number *Disarmament Conference* [*Konferentsiya po razoruzheniyu*]," she wrote in her autobiography, referring to his 1932 work from the Leningrad Choreographic Institute, which he restaged on the Moscow students, including Plisetskaya, in 1934. The music was by Mikhail Glinka and the cast of ten or twelve dancers each represented a different country. "I got the part of a Chinaman [*sic*]," she recalled. "I was shorter than the others. I came out from the wings in a pointy straw hat in a series of Yakobson's glissades. I was afraid all the time, swiveling my head and narrowing my eyes. I ended up hiding under a chair. This was supposed to depict the useless ruler of China, Generalissimo Chiang Kai-shek. How small and ridiculous he was."[116] Perhaps something of an agit-prop theater piece, *Disarmament Conference* points to Yakobson's steady engagement with topical issues during this period. He continued to make dances that did the ideological work demanded of culture in Soviet society—moving the populace toward party understanding—but he was doing it through an evolving, inventive choreographic vocabulary.

On June 21, 1941, on the occasion of the graduation of Plisetskaya and her class from the Moscow Choreographic Institute, Yakobson's choreography again intersected with politics, although not intentionally. He restaged his 1938 pas de trois, *Impromptu: The Nymph and the Two Satyrs* (*Ekspromt: Nimfa i dva satira*), with music by Tchaikovsky, for Plisetskaya, Leonid Shvachkin, and Gleb Evdokimov. The dance, like most of Yakobson's work, was never preserved and all Plisetskaya remembers are moments: "It was all Yakobsonian. Classical and yet not. Shvachkin and Evdokimov were satyrs and I was the nymph. The satyrs moved on imaginary hooves. They carried equally imaginary panpipes. They played them, barely touching their lips. That was the dance. The nymph was naughty, tugging at the satyrs' beards, slipping out of their grasp, swaying in fragile bends. . . . It was a poetic number," she concluded. It must have been at least that, for Plisetskaya records that both the final rehearsal and performance audiences were wildly enthusiastic. Years later Goleizovsky's wife, Vera Vasilyeva, who had been present at the run-through of the concert, remarked to the adult Plisetskaya: "The best dancing you did in your life was Yakobson's *Impromptu* at school. I never liked you better."[117] This was a comment Plisetskaya recounted with pleasure. At the formal concert on the stage of the Bolshoi's Second Stage the following day, Plisetskaya and her partners took repeated bows in response to the audience's excitement. "In Yakobson's *Impromptu* I tasted for the first time the love of an audience and joy of success, the intoxicating roar of clapping hands, the thrill of the first reading," she wrote.[118] This traditional plot device of a trio of dancers called *Nymph and Two Satyrs* gave Yakobson license to make a playful pas de trois with a superficially mythological theme to assuage any worries about modernism. As with *Disarmament Conference*, he clearly understood the rules he had to abide by in order to continue working, yet he also seemed to be learning how to balance idealism, ideology, and trying to keep open a space for the expression of a personal rather than a state voice—that is, for a flicker of modernism.

Race, Nationality, and Culture

As Yakobson continued developing his art, a new set of ideological challenges facing the Soviet regime in regard to its official position on race, nationality, and culture emerged that would stretch his modernist ballet aesthetic in new directions. The rise of National Socialism in Germany and the spread of race theories in the international scientific community during the early 1930s prompted Soviet ethnographers to define these concepts for themselves.[119] Soviet historian Francine Hirsch argues that the Soviets defined all three concepts—race, nationality, and culture—in sociohistorical terms, in deliberate opposition to the Nazis, who saw race as a determining and immutable status. More critically, she asserts that through the ways in which the Soviet Union negotiated race and ethnicity, it became a modernizing empire, a new type of state that created nations and for which questions of nationality were of central importance. As European ideas about the concept of "nation" and "empire" flowed into Russia, they changed through contact with the dominant Marxist vision of historical development. Following a November 1936 speech by Stalin about the new Soviet constitution, during which he announced that socialism had been established in the USSR, an accelerated program to bring about "evolutionism" or the rapid consolidation of clans, tribes, and diverse nationalities into Soviet socialist nations commenced. Hirsch notes that "by 1936, the Nazi propaganda machine was in full gear and German anthropologists were pronouncing their findings that the peoples of the USSR were of inferior racial stock and destined to degeneration. Against this backdrop, the Soviet regime became ever more intent on showing the world the successes of Soviet-sponsored development."[120]

Dance was rapidly recruited to be part of this effort, providing a visual affirmation of patriotic culture and the racial health that had resulted from this consolidation. Thus in 1936 Vyacheslav Molotov, a Soviet politician, diplomat, and close associate of Stalin, recruited Igor Moiseyev, a dancer at the Bolshoi with Yakobson, to organize the USSR's first festival of national dance. Moiseyev's first work of choreography had been a sports-themed work, *The Footballer* (*Futbolist*), made for the Bolshoi in 1930. Meanwhile his free time had been devoted to roaming the Russian provinces. Traveling on foot or on horseback across the country, he had observed dances in locales including Pamir, Belarus, Ukraine, and the Caucasus. In the early 1930s Moiseyev had been the first choreographer to stage acrobatic parades on the Red Square, garnering notice by Stalin for a seven-minute piece he had created for a sports-training college and later for staging another parade for the team favored by Lavrentiy Beria, whom Stalin had brought to Moscow as deputy head of the People's Commissariat for Internal Affairs (NKVD) in August 1938. In early 1937, supported by Soviet funding, Moiseyev gathered a group of amateur and professional ballet dancers in a Moscow studio to teach them folk dances from some of the Soviet nationalities he had seen, dances that he wanted to restage. On August 29, 1937, this nascent Moiseyev Dance Company gave its first performance in the Moscow theater Hermitage to great public acclaim, marketing a vision of harmonious race partnership across clan, tribal, and geographical divides. This was an idealized and glossy vision of assimilation where categories of difference in nationality were marked by variations in not just dances but also costumes, rhythms, and choreography, all performed by an upbeat troupe of classically trained professional dancers. Years later Yakobson's widow, Irina, commented that although Moiseyev was Jewish, it was not until the late 1980s that this ethnicity was represented by a Jewish-themed dance in the Moiseyev Dance Company.[121] This underlines not only the cultural and political work of articulating nationality categories, which the showcasing of folkloric dance was seen as accomplishing, but also its selectivity when faced with complicated nationalities such as being Soviet and Jewish.

The dancer, and particularly the ballet dancer, functioned as a virtual screen onto which Soviets projected central questions about art, nation, identity, and cultural superiority, and this symbolic significance was not lost on Yakobson. He had been present in Moscow when artistic performance was announced as a way to advance the national agenda by offering ethnographic representations of the Soviet republics through dance and other cultural forms. Beginning in 1936, as Yakobson stayed in step with this broader trend, his short ballets reflect his own turn toward ethnic folk tales as the basis for new dance narratives .

Baga Yaga

In 1939 Yakobson made a brief miniature, *Baba Yaga,* a two-minute solo for a male dancer dressed as the ragged old woman in the well-known Slavic folk legend of Baba Yaga. According to legend, Baba Yaga is a witch who flies through the air in a huge mortar. Looking for small children to eat, she uses her pestle as a rudder and a silver birch broom to sweep away the tracks behind her. A mythical bogey from folklore, Baba Yaga is a curious choice of subject in the midst of the Soviet regime's new emphasis on nationalities (although she does come from folk material, which was a source artists were encouraged to use), because she is a monstrous, superhuman figure whose appearance confuses gender categories.

One explanation for why Yakobson chose this character may be the dance's original audience: children. Yakobson created *Baba Yaga* for a performance at Artek, a camp for young people located in the Crimean resort of Gurzuf, in Ukraine. Founded in 1925 as one of the earliest and most elite summer camps for the Young Pioneers on the Black Sea, Artek's audience presumably included children, who would have enjoyed the terror and delight of the dance and the figure's agitated scouring of the horizon as if searching for a child to grab. The score is an excerpt from Modest Mussorgsky's *Night on Bald Mountain (Noch na Lïsoy gore,* 1867), which was rarely heard in the Soviet Union at the time, but which made for a charged thematic accompaniment. Mussorgsky similarly borrowed from Russian folk traditions for both the melody and tonal coloring of his score, which also celebrates witches (in his tonal narrative, however, they gather atop a bare mountain to await Satan). Yakobson's presence at Artek also suggests his de facto conscription into the task of cultural Russification of areas like Crimea.

Visually *Baba Yaga* works on another level of sophistication as well. It extends the quality of playing with new cinematic devices that Yakobson had sampled in *The Golden Age,* in this instance by using an offstage strobe light. As a result, when Baba Yaga mounts her broom to fly through the night sky by bounding up and down in place in the center of the stage, the stroboscopic effect gives the illusion that she is flying by illuminating only every other moment when she is airborne and leaving her in darkness when her feet touch the ground. Yakobson's use of the strobe to freeze time in this dance reflected his continuing modernist impulse to insert new technologies into dance. In 1939 strobe lights were just a few years old, having been invented at the Massachusetts Institute of Technology in 1931. *Baba Yaga,* while referencing folklore and ethnicities, thus goes

Baba Yaga, V. Lebedev, Choreographic Miniatures, Leningrad, 1973. Photographer unknown.

beyond the usual benign images for depicting a Marxist-Leninist empire of nationalities. In fact its imagery has shadings of the category of the monstrous from Nazi race theory, a darkness in Yakobson's *Baba Yaga* that might also be seen as a commentary on the Soviets' marking for elimination members of "aberrant" cultural groups like the Jews.

The Bird and the Hunter

The following year, in 1940, Yakobson made another miniature on a mythological theme, *The Bird and the Hunter* (*Ptitsa i okhotnik*). This is a duet that takes the soft intimacy of classical partnering and combines it with the myth of captured women/birds who reform the men who hunt them. But Yakobson takes this ballet trope of redemptive love and turns it inside out. In his telling, accompanied by music by Edvard Grieg, the ballerina portraying the injured bird expresses her wound by broken-off flutterings of her hands while the hunter looks on mournfully—then infuses her expansive leaps and swooning balances with a quality of gradual weakening that is as integral to the choreography as the virtuosity. In *The Bird and the Hunter*, Yakobson takes a favorite tale from Russian classical ballet—a woman as a majestic bird—and the Russian style of dancing, where the projection of both movement and feeling are grandly scaled, and mutes them to a level of whispered subtlety. *The Bird and the Hunter* is a dark tale of sorrow and death, all told in less than five minutes. But the movement is fresh, racing, full of invention, so that each phrase of dancing deepens the tragic story. The Bird uses her legs like a second set of massive wings, slicing them through the air in desperate split leaps as she tries to return to the air. Then, in the ballet's final moments, she folds to her knees in the Hunter's grasp and gives a final surge outward as her arms drop stiffly down and her body falls limply across his arms. It is a poignant miniature about regret and loss but without the idealized and transcendent soulmate discovery that colors the great White Swan adagio in act 2 of *Swan Lake*. Yakobson's miniature has the emotional and dramatic impact of a much longer work. Indeed *The Bird and the Hunter* is one of the few dances from these early years, and *Baba Yaga* is another, that Yakobson continued to stage over the next several decades, transferring his emerging ideas about narrative, the miniature, and his modernist extension of traditional classical ballet onto the bodies of professional dancers.[122]

Yakobson was participating at least indirectly in the new Soviet project of the late 1930s by creating both *Baba Yaga* and *The Bird and the Hunter*. In these works he illuminated mythic tales from Crimean folkloric culture by positioning them through what was de facto the borderless Soviet national dance, ballet. Ethnographic collections in museums had been exhibiting cultural artifacts from Soviet lands and peoples and re-presenting them in exhibits and lectures since the 1930s in an effort to celebrate how diverse religious and cultural beliefs might be enlisted in the project of transforming these cultures from exotic to modernized. Now Yakobson was opening ballet to the same revolution and cultural display, but doing so by showing indigenous peoples' folklore, in this instance from Crimea, as a living text performed by professional dancers—as if ballet were as neutral a medium as an empty vitrine in a museum.

Shurale

Since the mid-1930s the Soviet government had been scaling up the role of the arts of different nationalities in an effort to show the high level they were achieving under socialism as part of its policy of modernization and the promotion of nationalism. The guiding motto for art was that it was "national in form and socialist in content." A popular vehicle for displaying this dual allegiance was through the staging of large festivals of the performing arts and culture from the various republics in the Soviet capital of Moscow. On the surface these were grand demonstrations of national identity, but in practice they at times revealed the deliberate linking of a "refined" cultural nationality and consciousness with the idealized Soviet citizen under construction. National culture de facto became a path to Soviet culture, and the higher the development of the different republics' art under socialism, the stronger the proof that the social transformation under way through Communism was succeeding. At times, a dissenting voice arose, like that of Shostakovich, who argued in 1936 against the transparent falsity that could result from this desire to showcase greatness in all Soviet cultural arenas. In commenting on the 1936 Festival of Kazakh Arts, Shostakovich pointed out that it had led to the manufacture of artist heroes and the Soviet press's glorification of minor figures as cultural icons.[123] With daring sarcasm, Shostakovich said about Jambyl Jabayev, a minor poet elevated into a Soviet hero: "The great leader of all the peoples needed inspired singers from all the peoples, and it was the state's function to seek out these singers. If they couldn't find them, they created them, as they did with Jambyl."[124]

In 1940 Yakobson found himself formally linked to this new Soviet ethnographic directive. Beginning with the 1935–1936 theatrical season, Yakobson had been working in the Soviet republics. Initially he was sent by the Committee on the Arts to Sverdlovsk to found a ballet school and to stage *Lost Illusions* (*Utrachennïe illyuzii*, 1936) to the music of Boris Asafyev at the Sverdlovsk Theater of Opera and Drama. In 1939–1940, he was sent on assignment to Ashkhabad to found a ballet school.[125] Then in 1940 the Tatars, who were one of the major ethnic groups in the USSR, were selected as the subject of a major ten-day festival scheduled for Moscow in the autumn of 1941. The whole cultural life of the Tatar Republic was to be the focus, with music and dance events as an important element. In late 1939 the republic had just opened its new Tatar State Opera Theater in the capital of Kazan, two years after the founding of the Tatar Orchestra, which immediately moved into these new premises. It would be another two years before the theater would expand into ballet, becoming the Tatar State Theater for Opera and Ballet. That 1941 expansion came as a result of this forthcoming Tatar festival. Elizabeth Souritz has noted that Soviet festivals displayed a certain hypocrisy, however: "It was necessary to show that, during the years of Soviet power, opera and ballet in each republic had reached a high cultural level. Performances in the national traditions would not satisfy this, only real European ballet, if possible with classical dances."[126]

A group was thus assembled by Soviet authorities to create this first "Tatar ballet." The title and plot of the ballet came from a poem about an old folkloric tale of a mythical forest creature, Shurale, who sadistically likes to painfully tickle humans who lose their way in his black forest. The revered literary version of the Shurale myth was written by the most famous Tatar poet, Gabdulla Tukay, and for the purposes of moving it into a stage production the Tatar writer Akhmet Fayzi was engaged to adapt it into a libretto. A twenty-six-year-old Tatar composer, Farid Yarullin, writing his first music for ballet, composed the score in 1940. Yakobson, the only non-Tatar among the production team, was hired to create the choreography.

This was to be Yakobson's first full-length ballet choreographed alone, yet he would be in part a cultural ventriloquist—expressing themes, movement qualities, and cultural and aesthetic insights about the Tatars, an ethnic group to which he did not himself belong. Yakobson began shaping the ballet's action by personally editing the libretto. This was an important process that allowed him to prepare himself conceptually for when the real work of choreography began, in the studio with the dancers before him. He had also learned from *The Golden Age* experience that working from a clear written plot could help assuage anxieties of the various party oversight committees in regard to the dance containing anything potentially subversive. Yakobson's strategy was obedient, but also a bit sly, because what happened in the moment of the live performance could, and as time went by more frequently did, vary from what he sketched out on the printed page. In the actual studio he created through charged improvisation, often moving about so rapidly and with such spontaneous invention that he could not repeat what he had just shown the dancers— they had to learn how to grab onto his movement directions quickly, as they spilled from him.

Yakobson found Fayzi's libretto inadequate and rejected it, creating instead his own more dramatically cohesive plot (he later would claim that one really needs to be a choreographer in order to craft a libretto for ballet). The result was a detailed twenty-page essay that provided extensive scenic particulars about the three-act ballet. With ethnographic care Yakobson adapted the great Russian ballet trope of women as swans into a regionally specific recasting of the lead woman in *Shurale* as an elegant crane, like the stately Demoiselle Cranes native to the grass steppes of the Crimea.[127] Then, in the same spirit with which he had inserted Jewish-inflected gestures in *Vestris,* Yakobson inflected the mythical Shurale, originally a mischievous animal creature with a horn in the middle of its forehead, with the overscale and brooding terror of what seems a Jewish bogeyman, one reminiscent of the Golem of Prague.[128] In an unpublished manuscript Yakobson wrote in 1941 about his theoretical ambitions in the making of *Shurale,* he explains why he found Fayzi's libretto unusable and offers insights about his evolving modernist aesthetic as well as his standards:

> The characters Fayzi traced did not offer a plot or the dramatic basis for theatrical tension. . . . It is not a coincidence that ballet masters are often authors of libretti. Clearly knowing ballet dramaturgy

and the ability to see the logically developing dance act is not something most writers know. . . . Stories and dramatic development are not one and the same. In the libretto there are a lot of incidents. But it lacks the single big overall conflict. Ballet theatre requires the conflict to be clearly visible and specific, to have distinct motives, a plot that is expressed in actions. *It is a progression and culmination that takes place in front of the audience.* That's the natural condition without which you cannot do something. That does not need the aid of speech or words. But in Fayzi's libretto he only hints at the possible struggles of the hero.[129]

The idea of a clear aesthetic progression and culmination that takes place in front of the audience is an important critical formulation for both socialist realist art and the new realism of modernism, and while these two categories are not customarily thought of as contingent, this was a direction toward which Yakobson was stretching ballet classicism in *Shurale*. Yakobson also took as a central theme in *Shurale* the common modernist objective of advancement toward a utopian ideal. Here the monster and his forest friends represent the primeval past that has to be subdued through the epic environmental destruction of setting the forest on fire. The future lies with the evolved species—and Syuimbike joins them when she voluntarily discards her link with the animal world, her wings, to marry her rescuer, the woodcutter. Yakobson plays with movement genres here as if they were proxies for character as well as evolutionary stages of life. The Russian dance critic Boris Lvov-Anokhin remarked on what he called "the angular, prehensile" and abrupt gestures of the wood goblin Shurale, who moves as if his limbs were intertwined with roots, branches, or twigs, and Yakobson's skillful alternation of this movement styling with folkloristic Tatar steps and classical ballet.[130]

Yakobson's widow recounted the intensity of the offstage tensions that surrounded the project, noting that Fayzi sued Yakobson when, without asking, he rejected his libretto and substituted his own.[131] "He also had a friendly but complicated relationship with Yarullin the composer," she said. "My husband told stories about how he would lock Yarullin up in a hotel room demanding that he change a certain section in the music and keep him there until he did."[132] Yarullin was a conservatory graduate and his score is richly symphonic with Tatar melodies skillfully woven through it, but he was inexperienced with composing for ballet.[133] Yakobson's personal notes for the ballet contain a detailed minute-by-minute list of what is happening with the dancers in each act and scene—so his need for a score that was danceable and corresponded to his plan was indeed very exacting.

As if it were a window into his unfolding ideas about the ballet, Yakobson's libretto doesn't describe steps, tempi, or choreographic design; rather it focuses on the dramatic tenor and look of his detail-filled narrative. The use of libretti in Soviet ballet was generally quite different from in the West. Writing about Soviet drambalet in the mid-1950s, dance writer Hélène Bellew remarked on this difference: "In the Western world the libretto is generally merely a starting point—an inspiration—for the choreographer who does with it what he will. In the USSR it completely dominates him. He must arrange his choreography so that no detail, however small, shall be omitted or not fully understood by his audience. Costumes and décor must be equally detailed."[134]

The plot is simple. A flock of cranes stop to bathe in the forest lake and the most beautiful of them, Syuimbike, who is a bird/woman in the tradition of swan queens, removes her wings and slips into the water to bathe. As she is bathing, Shurale steals her wings and her struggle to regain them unites her with a brave hunter, Ali-Batïr, whom she eventually weds. There is little, if any, mention of actual dance steps in Yakobson's libretto; rather he traces the flow of action across the stage. Yakobson conceptualizes the stage architecturally. The actions flow across it as if they were driven purely by the dramatic imperatives of the narrative myth. The characters and their gestures are closely linked, as if Yakobson were actually recording a scene rather than scripting it. An example is the following from the initial page of Yakobson's libretto describing the first sighting of Shurale and Ali-Batïr:

> Suddenly the woods start agitating, the trees are moving and a wind kicks up. Then the hunter is twisted to one side and then hurled across the stage. He gets up and again is twisted and flies to the side. Suddenly the tornado quiets down and then the hunter gets up and then again there is this burst of tornado and it hurls him towards Shurale's abode.
>
> The tornado calms down and then suddenly again there is a very strong wind that picks up and throws the young man toward

Shurale's abode. Looking around he suddenly sees a huge hand coming up from the crevice where Shurale, who is just waking up[,] lives. The hunter[,] terrified[,] climbs up another tree. Suddenly the crevice opens up and Shurale jumps out[;] a sound is heard and Shurale jumps out and the trees are bowing to show homage to their master as he jumps onto a branch.

Shurale is a fairytale monster[;] by looking at it makes you think of a wood demon and satyr—half demon half satyr. He is thin but tall, hirsute with fur and he has claws, his hands are like a male equivalent of Baba-Yaga. His eyes are deep and they shine like burning coals. His awful, terrible glance is like fire and his hands are constantly moving looking for the next victim. Shurale jumps from tree to tree, then falls on the grass and scratches his back. He is happy and he is playful. The woods['] magical light changes and the woods change the way they look as the light shifts.[135]

Yakobson animates not just characters but also the actual scenic elements in *Shurale*—beginning with the opening scene where he plays with the idea of choreographing the air and set as if reveling in the scale and resources that come with a commission to create a three-act ballet. Here the lurking danger in the forest is conveyed through the surprise of what moves and the play of unseen forces that toss characters about the stage as if the wind itself were in the service of Shurale, which in fact it is. Everything animates movement and action in this description. Its visual richness extends into details of costuming, set, and lighting, and includes an image of the forest and its characters, which possess a kinesthetic perspective at their core. We don't hear what the characters think—rather we see how they move—Ali-Batïr buffeted about by angry invisible forces, Shurale's restless hands, his cat-like frolicking and rubbing his back on the grass. There may be a nascent modernist sensibility here in the way Yakobson's ballet can also be read as acknowledging the unconscious fears of a darker humanity and the realization that the individual scale of resistance is finally what really matters.

Askold Makarov recalled his experience of learning the role of Ali-Batïr and simultaneously discovering the sophisticated beauty of its play with classical structure:

A storm swoops down upon Ali-Batïr, he fights back its swirling vortex and finally falls beneath the mysterious tree. In this episode the winds rise up and knock him down. To depict the storm, Yakobson introduces the *renversé*. The winds throw back and toss the hero who *chaînés*, in various directions, while the *pas de bourrée* in all of its variants (Yakobson's favorite step) transmits the tempest's force that has been hurled forth at the hunter. With his arms, Ali-Batïr fights off the storm, lending the classical ballet combinations a notable naturalness and expression. After ceding to this initial onslaught of Nature, like many a brave fairy-tale hero, Ali-Batïr jumps to his feet. The storm abates, he pulls an arrow from his quiver, and in full views of the birds about him, makes ready to bring down his quarry.[136]

In *Shurale*, Yakobson reworks technical as well as narrative conventions of classical ballet beginning with the trope of woman as a bird and extending through forms of classical partnering and corps de ballet patterns. Before he explores the particulars of Syuimbike's animal/human duality, Yakobson introduces several trios of flocking birds, cranes like Syuimbike, whose coverage of space is grandly scaled from the moment they enter from the stage's wings in running, unison grand jetés. Their extended arms stroke forcefully upward, fingers held tightly closed so that the hand assumes the line of wingtip ending in a point. These trios of cranes enter with a naturalistic irregularity and when they assemble onstage their cluster suddenly settles into the huge "V" formation of a flock in migratory flight. Their "birdness" carries through in smaller ways too, like the open and upward stretching of their chests, which suggests the proud curve of a grand bird in midair, and the stretched impulse of their jetés, which evoke the attenuated legs of a streamlined crane body moving through the air.

In this act 1 section of *Shurale*, Yakobson presents a visual disruption of the classic symmetry of Lev Ivanov's bird/women formations from act 2 of *Swan Lake*, a clear reference here. The flocks of cranes enter at irregular intervals from both sides of the stage in briefly poised low arabesques on pointe that suggest the alert tentativeness of birds, an image that is reinforced as they rapidly flutter their hands like trembling wings with a tensile energy. Makarov recounts that this movement was difficult, taking considerable rehearsals to learn and forcing the dancers to coordinate their rapid upper body movements with the much slower leaps of their legs. "The triangular formation of the *corps de ballet,* with the ballerina as its peak, was a superb strategy on the part of the choreographer. The triangle rearranges itself, rushing first to one side, then to another, creating the impression of a flock of birds soaring in the sky. Syuimbike's variation also conveys the image of a bird, circling in one place, then freely hovering in the air until she descends to the earth."[137]

There is no record of what the choreography was for these portions of the ballet in the original version created in Kazan, but its technical challenges must have been considerably easier given the pool of dancers Yakobson had to work with. Indeed once Yakobson had prepared his libretto, it became apparent that the Tatar State Theater for Opera and Ballet did not have sufficient dancers to cast a full-length dance, nor did they have dancers with strong enough training to dance the leads in a classical ballet, particularly with the date of the Tatar festival in Moscow looming barely a year away. Nayma Baltacheyeva and Abdurakhman Kumïsnikov, two Tatars dancing in Leningrad, were brought in to learn the leads, but Yakobson still needed a large group of trained dancers for the ensembles of forest creatures and villagers. Pyotr Gusev, a former member of the Young Ballet in the 1920s and former colleague of Yakobson from GATOB in Leningrad, was hired to assist Yakobson and to coach the dancers as they prepared for the festival. Next the search began for a group of young dancers to perform the rest of the roles.

The Island of Dance Company

Since 1933 the Moscow Communist Party Organization had sponsored a school of the arts on an island in Golitsyn Pond in Moscow's Gorky Park, which came to be called Island of Dance because of the prominence of dance teaching and performing there. It was here that Yakobson found his instant ballet ensemble. Souritz has documented how in the autumn of 1940 the Island of Dance Company, which was composed of more than sixty dancers, was invited to go to Kazan to work with Yakobson and Gusev in preparation for the festival. When the dancers from the Island of Dance arrived, however, they found that they had to do much more: they were charged with helping organize a ballet group and a school for the

Tatar State Opera House. Everything was being assembled hastily and in some instances in reverse order to support the accelerated creation of a troupe of ballet dancers strong enough to carry off a high-visibility, full-evening performance of native Tatar culture. About two hundred students in the second, third, and fourth years of the Island of Dance school, as well as the head of the musical division, a designer, and a number of technicians, all moved to Kazan. The dancers, like Yakobson, had been classically trained, and they needed to project their "Tatarness" through Russian classical ballet.

Yakobson initially made *Shurale* using a cast of these young Island of Dance dancers and the few imported Kirov soloists for the leading roles. The ballet works much of its meaning through the juxtaposition of ensemble crowd patterns and the emotional rapport between dancers in duets and pas de deux. In each of these groupings Yakobson pushes the parameters of a classical ballet vocabulary and the patterns of Tatar folk idioms by shaping steps and hand gestures from Tatar folk dance. He includes wrists and arms that spiral upward and raised, fluttering hands. Yarullin creates similar hybrids in his orchestration, which is lushly pictorial in its adaptations of Tatar folk melodies and their pentatonic scales. These were stylizations the cast had to learn in place of the usual regal postures and movements of classical ballet.

In *The Golden Age* Yakobson had experimented with the high virtuosity of acrobatic flips and tricks, and in nesting these in a ballet he had also consciously acknowledged and used their neutral register and direct manner of delivery. In *Shurale,* the Tatar culture is the context, with the dancing undergirded by the simple nobility of the ethnic Soviet body of the republics. In *Shurale* Yakobson seamlessly incorporated nontraditional dance movements into the classical matrix he had inherited, bringing a sensitive understanding of the partnership of dance and music. Fokine had also looked toward Tatar culture as ethnic embellishment when he re-choreographed Ivanov's fiery *Polovtsian Dances* (*Polovetskie plyaski*— from Borodin's opera *Prince Igor* [*Knyaz Igor*]) for Diaghilev's first Paris season in 1909. Yakobson explores subtler sides of the folk dance spectrum in *Shurale,* clustering performers in the Crimean Tatar "Horan" circle dance that he varies by inserting advancing and retreating—contracting and swelling—circles of dancers.

The several pas de deux in *Shurale* are propelled by emotions that dictate the fluctuations in tone. In Ali-Batïr's first meeting with Syuimbike after he challenges Shurale, it is only after Syuimbike enlists him to help her find her missing wings that he notices her beauty and steps back in astonishment. Their encounter is filled with wonder told through tentative lifts where Syuimbike perches briefly on Ali-Batïr's shoulder, her legs tucked under her, before springing to the ground and dashing off as she presses her arms behind her torso signaling her yearning to fly away. This first-act duet ends tenderly, with Syuimbike falling asleep on a rock and Ali-Batïr gently lifting her up and ferrying her away to safety in the same elongated horizontal pose in which he found her. "There are no dancers' arabesque . . . no renowned 'little chairs,' in which the danseur catches his partner in mid-air, who seats herself in his arms," Makarov remarked in surprise as he learned this pas de deux. "Rather Ali-Batïr strives to protect Syuimbike from the wood goblin, and every pose, every movement, develops the poetic image of the theme in the intermeshing of the steps, in the tense, accelerated tempi unfamiliar to the eyes of ballet goers. Everything is headlong but consistent."[138] To dance his character, Makarov said he had to break through his own ideas about his physical limitations as a dancer until gradually his body became accustomed to the exceptional demands of the role and he realized something about his own psychology as well as that of the figure of the male dancer. "I came to understand various sides of the male temperament—a powerful indestructible spirit, a tenderness and a thirst for the unknown, for perfection." These testimonies from Yakobson's dancers suggest that despite his volatile temper Yakobson's dancers loved him and worked hard for him—allowing him, in turn, to elicit new responses and fresh material from them.

A tension between choreographic symmetry and the symmetry of emotions shapes the structure of *Shurale*. The darkness and atmosphere of unease and uncertainty in the act 1 forest scene give way to act 2 and the brightness of daylight in a Tatar village in the midst of wedding festivities for Syuimbike and Ali-Batïr. Yakobson keeps the narrative moving while tucking in various cultural signs that add a dense cultural specificity to the narrative. The bride enters act 2 carried in on a carpet, followed by the bridegroom, who drives up in a carriage. Syuimbike's disappearance in the final moments of this act is foreshadowed by the villagers teasingly making Ali-Batïr hunt for his bride, who is hidden in the midst of a cluster of villagers. This search echoes the final lakeside scene in *Swan Lake*, when Prince Siegfried unfolds clusters of swans looking for his one among

Shurale/Ali-Batïr, Vladimir Levashov as Shurale,
Maya Plisetskaya as Syuimbike, and Yuriy
Kondratov as Ali-Batïr, Bolshoi Ballet,
Moscow, 1955. Photographer unknown.

the many, and thus also makes a subtle reference to Syuimbike now in her
human form as still being dangerously connected to the animal. Yet it
also borrows from Tatar wedding rituals. Yakobson's game in *Shurale* is
not about facsimiles, but falsity. Each time Ali-Batïr peels open a cluster of
villagers he is mocked when a bearded man or matronly woman pops up
instead of his slender and beautiful young bride.

Next the stage yields to a series of divertissements, the first of which is
danced by nine pairs of children who carefully imitate the adults' wedding circles. The boys wear the traditional *tyubeteyki* (Tatar skull caps). A
women's dance with quivering veils and a jesting dance by Ali-Batïr with
a group of eight men who play hunters attacking him also resonate both

Shurale/Ali-Batïr, Lyubov Voyshnis as Syuimbike
and Boris Bregvadze as Ali-Batïr, Kirov Ballet,
Leningrad, 1950. Photographer unknown.

forward and backward in time, referencing the conflicts between Shurale
and Ali-Batïr that open and close the ballet. Everyone except the wedding
couple is getting drunk and happy at this wedding, which Yakobson discloses in a rich and raucous series of dances for various clusters of tipsy
revelers who stumble out of the wedding hall. This is a village wedding
reminiscent of the tragic gaiety of Nijinska's *Les Noces.* Here, as in that celebration, the couple getting married are the only people not sharing in the
wild fun.

Act 3 brings Ali-Batïr back to the forest to rescue Syuimbike again, after Shurale has lured her into the woods by returning her wings to her at
the wedding. The moment she puts them on, a flock of black crows, de-
lightfully portrayed by an ensemble of children in all black costumes with

WHAT IS TO BE DONE WITH BALLET?

big feathery black wings, race on stage and surround Syuimbike. With the dark silhouettes of their forms they force her to fly with them to Shurale's lair in the woods. Ali-Batïr follows Syuimbike and as she vanishes in the sky he grabs a lighted torch and rushes back into the woods. He struggles with Shurale across the forest floor. At one point Ali-Batïr trips and the wood goblins and spirits pile on him while Shurale scrambles to the top to sit as if on a throne of bodies. This time Ali-Batïr destroys not just Shurale but the entire forest that he sets on fire, leveling the landscape because apparently the evil is so deep it can only be eradicated from nature by destroying it.

Nora Nemchenko, who was part of the initial cast of dancers on whom Yakobson built *Shurale* in Kazan, recalled the challenges of working with him as he drilled the cast of dancers in a frenzy of on-the-spot creation:

> All of the performers in the ballet were divided into two groups: birds and evil spirits. I was a bird. I remember my first appearance— flying all over the stage with grand jetés. And the strokes of my hand/wings. When Leonid Veniaminovich [Yakobson] staged the dances of the evil spirits, his fantasy was unlimited. He was generally ingenious in all kinds of movement, poses, and here he excelled himself in turns, like those of a screw, jumps, and jerks. A pyramid built of coiled bodies. A wonderful dragon, opening its mouth and sticking out its tongue, with long body and swishing tail—all these made of people, their backs, arms, legs. . . . The poor performer at the end of the "tail"! He was flung from side to side. . . . Yakobson compelled [us] to lie about the floor and to stand endlessly in very uncomfortable poses, imitating tree trunks (which then revived). He required the corps de ballet to dance on pointe in Tatarian dances, wanting the small "tapping movements" which are so painful on the toes. Leonid Veniaminovich was unpredictable in his work . . . always excited. As inspiration overtook him, he invented new and newer unusual combinations. We couldn't master them at once and became worried too—afraid of him and afraid to be shamed.[139]

Eventually Gusev, who was accustomed to Yakobson's temperament and style of improvisatory invention in rehearsals from their days together as dancers in the Kirov, reassured Yakobson, and the dancers, that he would lead follow-up rehearsals to Yakobson's, helping to make repeatable the splashes of choreography that spilled out of Yakobson as he responded to Yarullin's music in the studio. "He [Gusev] began to rehearse us and soon everything was in order, comfortable and joyful as everything began to become clear," Nemchenko recalled.[140] A sizable portion of the *Shurale* cast were children from the Island School, and Yakobson worked with them with the same seriousness he used for professional adults. As Makarov recalled from rehearsing with Yakobson and performing in *Shurale* at the Kirov in 1950:

> Yakobson had a special flair for children's ballet. His numerous pieces staged for young people are distinctive in the seriousness with which they take into account the psychology of the young. An experienced pedagogue who loves children, he "converses" with them not in a saccharine condescending discourse, but seriously as with equals. So Yakobson staged his young people's works, not coyly admiring the little darlings, but proposing to young artists that they consciously become attracted by these artistic solutions, based on situations from the experiences of young people. Then the orientation of the dance became authentic and convincing as if it were an original piece for a young people's theater.[141]

In *Shurale* there are transcendent images that are accessed through violations of classical form. "The action developed like the free movements of a song without words," wrote Soviet ballet historian Vera Krasovskaya. "Were it to be translated into the language of conventional drama, it would require a different mise-en-scène, a different development."[142] Doubt, hesitation, and finally free will guide Syuimbike's decision to stay with Ali-Batïr, in much the mode of a new Soviet woman whose force and physical presence do not need a male proxy to be effective in the world. Gone are the references to class hierarchy that are so prevalent in the nineteenth-century ballet classics; instead the village is marked by lightness, teasing gaiety, and comical drunks while the woods are reduced to a plane of darkness and the danger of things that cannot be seen.

In shaping the ballet, Yakobson combined distinctly different dance elements. Although he included many of the traditional forms that were also used in drambalet—detailed narratives and characterizations, folk-derived movements, and structural elements like divertissements—there is a qualitative difference in where these theatrical devices lead the viewer emotionally. In act 1 the winged, mysterious maidens with their magic powers dance a classical vocabulary, which Syuimbike as the most impetuous and curious among them imbues with a dreamy languor that sets her apart. Yakobson's skill for grotesque movement offers a cross-species counterpoint and the main vocabulary of the half-animal, half-vegetable forms along with the various demonic wood spirits that attend the puckish Shurale. Ali-Batïr moves between these styles, embodying Yakobson's new image of the ballet dancer who is both a product of and an antagonist of this form. Character and folk-dance idioms dominate act 2, which unfolds in the bright sun of the Tatar countryside. Set against this background, the individualized dances of Ali-Batïr and Syuimbike, as they try to connect at their wedding, suggest a hybrid of classical ballet and local folk forms. These reach their richest fusion in act 3, where the menacing grotesque movements of Shurale and his forest creatures are vanquished by the force of these two dance traditions drawn together in a fresh stylistic fusion. Some of his elements may be recognizable, but the emotional frontier into which they lead the viewer is far from the predictability of the dramballet.

In describing his first rehearsals with Yakobson, Makarov recalled how after his entrance as Ali-Batïr in the opening moments of the ballet Yakobson suddenly turned his attention to Shurale. As Makarov and the cast watched, he seemed to draw that figure into being from three casts of his Shurale—Igor Belsky, Robert Gerbek, and Yury Grigorovich (who sprained his ankle in rehearsal and missed the first performances with the Kirov).[143] "In dancing the role of Shurale, a dancer not only could sprain his ankle but break his neck as well, so difficult did the *plastique* become, so original was it, without any models like it whatsoever in our ballet repertoire," Makarov recalled. "At one moment, Belsky winds himself into a tuber, at another, he swings about with his bent and his branchy arms, then he jumps supple as a lynx, only to stiffen up in a threatening pose." Makarov thought that Belsky, a fine character dancer, had the best understanding of the difficult *plastique* of Yakobson's choreography. The movement patterns showed the mercurial quality of Shurale's temperament through "an emotional and physical range so original that there were no models in the existing ballet repertoire with which to compare it," Makarov said.[144]

Makarov explains that although Shurale is present on stage from the beginning of the action, neither Ali-Batïr nor the audience must suspect this. He sleeps on the bough of the enchanted tree, having every appearance of a rough, dried-up branch. "Early on, the very manner in which Shurale awakens makes evident the choreographer's delicate penetration into the essence of folk poetry, apportioning, endowing the fantastic images in nature with truly human qualities," Makarov said, describing the shock of Shurale's awakening as the evil spirit of the forest. Shurale rouses on his tree branch early in the ballet. Stretching himself out lazily, he rocks back and forth, then swings down to the ground in an entrance that establishes immediately his otherworldly nature.[145]

In *Shurale* the thirty-seven-year-old Yakobson sought to displace the hegemony of classical forms because they were not representative of the range of possibilities he wanted to express. Instead of employing standard forms whereby corps de ballet are arranged decoratively as a frame for the technical feats of the soloists and principals, Yakobson ceded his stage formations to the classical ballet forms he believed in: Fokine's animation of the corps as a crowd of distinctive individuals, the pas de deux as a conduit of emotional development, and ethnic cultural forms as sources of reworked choreography, not decorative artifice. Yakobson built transcendent images by translating folk culture into the classical vocabulary and shading the actual expressive form of what dance could express about Soviet nationality categories. At the same time he offered challenges to the Soviet regime and its approach to nationalities and cultural transformation—showing an accommodation on stage that upset the classical idiom as he worked to transform it.

But the world outside Kazan, in the Tatar Autonomous Soviet Socialist Republic, was moving too fast to make possible *Shurale*'s opening as scheduled. On the evening of June 21, 1941, Yakobson and his entire cast assembled in the Tatar State Academic Theater for Opera and Ballet for the final full dress rehearsal of *Shurale* before the official opening that was scheduled for the next evening. The following day, however, on Sunday June 22, 1941, as dawn broke over Europe, Adolf Hitler began an attack against Soviet Russia on a massive front extending from the Arctic regions of Finland to the Romanian borders of the Black Sea. In a proclamation he read that morning to the German people, Hitler boasted that this military action was the largest in the history of the world.[146]

The Kazan premiere of *Shurale* was immediately cancelled and the young male dancers in the company were ordered to report immediately to military stations. Within a few weeks most of them would be sent to the front. A key objective of this campaign would be Nazi Germany's siege of Leningrad. For nine hundred days the armies of Germany surrounded the city, bombing, shelling, and starving this city that for two-and-a-half centuries had stood as the moral and intellectual heart of Russia.[147] The Soviet intelligence had warned that Germany was about to attack the Soviet Union, but Stalin had refused to believe that Hitler would break their nonaggression treaty.

The final scene in *Shurale* presages a landscape of destruction as Shurale and his woods are engulfed in flames by the fleeing Ali-Batïr, who believes that burning this forest is the only way to free Syuimbike from Shurale. As Ali-Batïr urges her to fly to safety and save herself, with the roaring red flames lighting up the darkness of the forest around her, Syuimbike instead throws her wings into the fire, choosing to die in her new freedom and stay with Ali-Batïr. In the ballet this act of selfless love overwhelms evil and the fire magically subsides. While this vista of a burning landscape might be seen to eerily presage the ruin that the German invasion would inflict on the Soviet Union on its own soil, ending the real-world conflict would not be nearly as easy. Within one month, more than 2.5 million Russians would be killed, wounded, or captured. The young composer Yarullin would die in combat in 1943, at the age of twenty-nine, without ever seeing his only ballet score produced.

With the German invasion Yakobson was immediately summoned back to Moscow, where he awaited word as to whether he would be sent to the front as well. Eventually it was decided that no one from the Bolshoi Theater—singers, dancers, or musicians—would be sent into military action. As additional protection, the director of the Bolshoi Ballet petitioned for an exemption for the choreographers, including Yakobson, protesting their importance to the company, and the nation's cultural heritage by extension. The situation at the Bolshoi was chaotic because of the announcement of war, and it would be several months before the government finally made the decision to begin evacuating the entire Bolshoi to Kuybyshev (formerly Samara) in late 1941. The other leading Soviet cultural organizations, theaters, orchestras, and film studios—along with airplane factories and industrial plants—were also evacuated to safer distant cities.[148] In early 1942 Yakobson was summoned back to Moscow to join the affiliate of the Bolshoi Theater in the capacity of choreographer, while the main company remained in Kuybyshev (Samara) until July 1943. While in Moscow, in addition to staging a ballet, Yakobson presented an evening concert of Bolshoi soloists featuring Olga Lepeshinskaya, Mikhail Gabovich, Gusev, and Olga Preobrajenska.

Yakobson, greatly influenced by the reports of Hitler's army's invasion of western Russia, started sketching out the scenario of a new full-length ballet about the war, *The Land of Miracles (Strana chudes)*. This would become a common work pattern for him—especially in the final years of Stalin's Terror when he was prohibited from working, he would instead visualize his ballets, scripting them on paper for a time until the situation changed and he could work again in the theater with live dancers. So Yakobson worked on *The Land of Miracles* steadily until late 1942, when he was invited by the director of the Kirov Ballet to come to Molotov, formerly Perm, in the Western Urals, the city to which the Kirov had been evacuated. The creation and performance of ballets were considered valuable tools for maintaining national morale. In Molotov he staged a series of concert numbers and two ballets that were performed by graduates of the Leningrad Choreographic Institute—*Romeo and Juliet (Romeo i Dzhulyetta,* 1944), which was set to the music of Tchaikovsky, and *Capriccio Espagnol (Ispanskoe kaprichchio,* 1944), which was scored by Rimsky-Korsakov. When the ballet company returned to Leningrad after the siege ended, these Yakobson ballets were given their premieres at the Kirov Theater in 1944. By this time Yakobson had developed new personal ties to the company that would draw him permanently back to Leningrad.

The opening night that was to have followed the dress rehearsal of *Shurale* by one day would be delayed nine years. The intervening years of war were followed by Stalin's own mass terror on his own citizens so that by the time of his death in 1953, a shocking 20 million people were dead and 40 million repressed through torture and imprisonment. Yet in the moment of its creation *Shurale* presented a remarkable vision of the possible accommodation between the Soviet medium of ballet and the ancient folk practices and legends of Tatar and other republics' cultures. It succeeded beyond anyone's expectations in hewing to the new demands for performing works inflected with distinctive national themes, and it did so with such respect for both subtle values of ethnic representation and fidelity to the imperatives of ballet modernism that it advanced both significantly.

Shurale *at the Kirov*

When *Shurale* was finally premiered on May 28, 1950, almost exactly nine years to the day of its postponement, it was at the Kirov Ballet, in a re-staged production. The influence of World War II as well as the fact that the Kirov dancers were technically much stronger than the Kazan dancers meant that Yakobson significantly revised the ballet before it opened. It premiered under a new title mandated by Soviet officials, *Ali-Batïr,* as befitted the proper Soviet emphasis on an iconic hero. In its initial version the ballet had concluded on a note of sadness, depicting the heroine, the girl/bird, tearfully leaving her bird friends in order to live her life with people instead. In the 1950 staging, under orders from the Soviet Ministry of Culture to display "historical optimism" in all art, the ending showed the heroine happy at her forced departure from her friends.[149] Yakobson was mindful of the terrible price that Russia had paid during the war, with 20 million dead, but the Soviet censors accused him of giving prefer-ence to "the fascist evil" in the original sad ending of *Shurale.* They did not want to remind the Russian people of how difficult it had been to win the war, and they were fearful that Yakobson's ballet would trigger these memories. Yakobson was by now accustomed to the heavy hand of Soviet censorship and the meddling of censorship committees as they attempted to control not just the narrative but even the associations that an audience member might draw from the images in the ballet.

The Kirov rehearsals had their own special drama, since even nearly a decade after its creation the demands of the choreography stretched the limits of what many of the classically trained Kirov dancers considered ballet. Makarov, who danced the lead of Ali-Batïr in the ballet's opening night at the Kirov on June 28, 1950, opposite Igor Belsky as Shurale, wrote about his initial impressions working with Yakobson, which grew from skepticism to admiration: "Arriving at Yakobson's rehearsals, at first I could not feel comfortable with the plan of the choreographer's demonstration. It was all so new to me. Only some time later, did I understand that so regulated an outline of the movements would not shackle my perfor-mance but rather open it up to the shaping of an image in its unbroken correlation with the music. Then I became fascinated with the transition from the simplest of expositions to the *plastique* itself, to its developing dance expressivity."[150]

Yakobson's method of leading dancers into new physical territory often taxed them emotionally as well. "He was extremely demanding," Irina agreed. "He made the dancers miserable because it was so difficult for them to do the new steps he was inventing." Finally the Kirov dancers held a meeting and said it was not possible to do Yakobson's choreography; it was too difficult and too unclassical. Pyotr Gusev, who was serving as Yakobson's rehearsal assistant for *Shurale,* stopped the incipient revolt and told the dancers to get back to work. A few days later the men in the corps, along with the conductor of the orchestra, Pavel Emilyevich Feldt, drafted a rejoinder—a satirical and scatological poem. They posted it backstage in the Kirov Theater, where the staff and dancers could see it when they arrived for work. It described the men of the corps de ballet tumbled in the huge heap that Shurale scrambles atop in the ballet's final act.[151] Dubbing this passage the *grand pas sur derrière,* the men in the company expressed their affectionate irritation at Yakobson's penchant for nonclassical movement with the following text:

> A terrible moan is heard on the stage,
> Yakobson is staging his new ballet.
> Arms, legs, faces are gleaming,
> A grand pas on buttocks is being performed.
> All the devils have burned up in the fire.
> The stage was left full of shit
> And in the center of the biggest heap
> Our mighty Yakobson is standing.[152]

Yakobson was so amused by the poem that he preserved it among his personal papers.

The production was such a success with audiences and dance professionals that five years later, Yakobson set *Shurale* on the Bolshoi Ballet, where it opened on January 29, 1955, to acclaim, with a cast that included Vladimir Levashov as Shurale, Yuriy Kondratov as Ali-Batïr, and Plisetskaya as Syuimbike. In June of 1956 the chief dance critic of the *New York Times,* John Martin, visited the USSR and reviewed the Bolshoi production of *Shurale*. His prose reveals the sharply polarized tone of what might be called Cold War dance criticism, a conscious "us and them" tone of measuring the art of the "enemy" nation against the superior art of home. Even so, and seemingly almost despite himself, Martin is both surprised and charmed by the ballet. "One foreign visitor, while realizing the short-comings of the ballet itself, found the entire production full of interest and even of revelation," he wrote. "Here, for one thing, were evident many of the roots from which Fokine's repertoire stemmed however much he [Yakobson] grafted new stock upon them."[153] Martin cites specifically Fo-kine's *The Firebird* (*Zhar-ptisa*, 1910) and the Polovtsian dances from *Prince Igor*. "The style is far from subtle, and the choreography by L. V. Yakobson is sometimes frankly corny, but there are magnificent passages of acro-batic adagio that leave one breathless," Martin continues. He mentions specifically "stunning lifts by four men and when the excitement gets go-ing it is really something, but these exhibitions of strength under control of skill are apparently an integral part of ballet practice hereabouts. And don't think for a minute they are not wonderful." He concludes his review by suggesting that the narrative heft of *Shurale* can instruct the future of ballet in America: "One beauty of these full-evening ballets is the essential leisureliness of their construction. Though they are not in any sense slow they undertake a theme and develop it until there is not another drop of juice in it. But everybody involved, both on stage and in the orchestra pit, is vital and vigorous and authoritative, and there are no empty spots to allow for a single yawn. How anemic ballet in America suddenly looks in retrospect!"[154]

Shurale was subsequently performed in Odessa, Riga, Saransk, Saratov, Tartu, Kiev, and Alma-Ata, as well as Bulgaria, Mongolia, and Poland. Lopukhov, who was reinstated in his post as director of the Kirov from 1951 to 1956, praised *Shurale,* saying that finally a real ballet master had re-placed those who just directed or staged pantomime.[155] The Soviet dance world was taking note of what Lopukhov called Yakobson's gifts, which included "imagination and originality." He had "an inborn command of dance structure; a remarkable ability to make movement express emo-tion, narrative and atmosphere; and a dance vocabulary that bonds classi-cal and folk techniques in a way that seems natural, not dutiful or just plain awkward," Lopukhov wrote about Yakobson.[156] He had negotiated choreographically the "friendship of peoples" ethos that the Soviet Union was promoting about itself. That is, the Soviets were seeking to project an image of the USSR as a multiethnic state with different ethnic groups whose cultural level was being raised through the civilizing mission of what Fitzpatrick has called an "elder brother, Soviet Russia."[157]

In 1951, the year following the Kirov premiere, Yakobson and his cast were awarded the USSR State Prize for *Shurale*. *Shurale* actually straddled two conflicting aesthetics, depending on what one looked for in the ballet. While Soviet officials might have considered *Shurale* on the surface a drambalet because of the nobility of the passions and clarity of the drama it conveyed—hallmarks of the type of ballet that dominated Soviet dance in the 1930s and 1940s—Yakobson actively disliked this genre. He regarded drambalets as usually empty, pompous works on contemporary themes.[158] When he made them they were different because he infused them with personal content and an expressive, individual use of movement.

The more illicit form he is flirting with in *Shurale* is its opposite—formalism. Russian formalist Vladimir Propp's *Morphology of the Folktale* (*Morfologiya skazki*), published in Russian in 1928, was an influential and important text theorizing folklore at the time when Yakobson was creating *Shurale*. In his book, Propp distills the elemental building blocks that form the narrative structure of Russian folklore and fairy tales, breaking them down into a generalizable list of eight character types and thirty-one situations that are present in all folktales and fairy tales. Yakobson's retelling of the Shurale legend incorporates many of these and it plays with another key formalist device—Shklovsky's "ostranenie." This quality of defamiliarization or "making strange" is a way of opening oneself to the sensation of things as if viewed for the first time, and it saturates the plot of *Shurale* with its forest of living trees, dancing toadstools, duets of wind and fire, and the fantasy creature of Shurale himself, a villainous tree branch.

The ultimate testament to *Shurale*'s success at negotiating the inclusion of various cultural elements and at eluding Soviet censors' discovery of its revisionist and formalist secrets, however, may be that more than seventy years after its premiere it remains a cherished symbol of Tatar culture. It is frequently included in the annual ballet seasons performed by the ballet troupe of the Tatar Academic State Theater as a statement of Tatar nationalist pride. In some references Yakobson's name is clearly stated as the choreographer, but more often his name is the one member of the original all-Tatar creative team that is omitted. The following excerpt from a Tatar website in 2012 is an example:

> The "Shurale" ballet is a first national ballet that is the main pride of the Tatar musical theatre nowadays. A twenty-six-year-old talented Tatar composer Farid Yarullin wrote the ballet in 1940. The same name tale of Gabdulla Tukay, a great Tatar poet, became a base for the ballet plot enriched by the Tatar folklore motifs and images. Real and fabulous characters exist in the ballet as well as truth and fiction are interwoven with each other. . . . The qualities of whole-souled Tatar people are shown in the character of Byltyr, a noble, courageous and ready-witted peasant. . . ."Shurale" became world-known with the end of the War. Bulgaria, Holland, Rumania, Poland, Germany, Egypt, Albania applauded it. Nowadays the "Shurale" ballet is honoured and loved by the house and is a part of the golden fund of the M. Jalil Opera and Ballet Tatar Academic State Theatre.[159]

It is possible to consider Yakobson's success at scripting a Tatar national identity into Soviet ballet as related to his own sensitivity toward how Soviet politics alternately made visible and invisible the culture of minority groups.

Irina Pevzner, in 1943 a nineteen-year-old corps dancer with the Kirov who had just graduated from Vaganova's class in the school, recalled Yakobson's wartime visit to Molotov, which was followed in a few months by performances there of several of his ballets by a small troupe of Bolshoi dancers. "When we saw this evening, this performance, everyone was in shock," she said. "I remember for me it was like something coming from God. And I thought if this person can create this kind of art he should be unbelievable. I thought no matter what he is like, handsome or not, I will love him." Irina, the top student in her class, performed a Hungarian dance and the entire grand pas from the last act of *Raymonda,* as well as the lead in Makovets's *The Magic Flute* at the student graduation concert that evening. Vaganova favored Irina for her musicality and analytic intelligence and thus had cast her prominently in the concert.[160]

The chance meeting between Irina and Yakobson following the concert proved to be critical to Yakobson's personal as well as professional life. Pevzner would become his dancer, rehearsal assistant, choreographic

Leonid and Irina Yakobson on holiday at Artek,
in Crimea, ca. 1949. Photographer unknown.

memory bank, and life partner. By using Irina's classical training as a protégée of Vaganova as well as her talent as a teacher and skilled character
dancer, Yakobson was able to support his own work in important ways.
Pevzner, who eventually became Mrs. Yakobson, danced with her future
husband for the first and only time of the thirty years they were together
during the night of their first meeting in 1943. They danced foxtrots,
waltzes, and tangos at a party given in honor of the graduating ballet students. Irina remembers Yakobson as a wonderful social dancer and says
she was immediately smitten, despite his being twenty years her senior.
"There were a lot of women around him because he was very famous at
this time," she said, acknowledging that it took him longer to commit to
the relationship. (She was also apparently unaware that Yakobson was
married at the time to Nataliya Spasovskaya, a non-Jewish corps de ballet

dancer in the Bolshoi who would eventually become close friends with Irina and her sister, Anna Klimentenko.) Because most of the men were at war, Yakobson was even more attractive to women, Irina recalled. When the war ended Yakobson returned to Leningrad and eventually began to work as resident choreographer with the Kirov. Irina continued living in Molotov with her mother, sister, and another dancer from Irina's ballet class whom the Pevzner family took in after the woman's father had been shot and her mother had been sent to the Gulag. These four people lived crowded into one small room where Pevzner and her sister slept on the kitchen table at night. She recalls their being hungry all the time and using the ration of Vaseline they were given to remove their makeup as cooking oil to fry potatoes.[161] Finally, two years later, Irina, with her family, also returned to Leningrad, to the Kirov, and to Yakobson.

Yakobson never recorded his memories of that first meeting with Irina, but a note he wrote few months after meeting her survives in his archives at the Bakhrushin Theatre Museum in Moscow. Dated November 7, 1943, it is written as a humorously formal contract between Yakobson and the Pevzner family, with Irina's father, David, as one signatory and Yakobson as the other. It reads as follows:

> I, Leonid Veniaminovich Yakobson, the ballet master of the State Academic Bolshoi Theater of the USSR, the theater that has been awarded the Lenin Prize, promise to invite to my first performance of *Shurale* at the Kirov Theater in Leningrad: To reserve a Box in the theater for the Pevzner family and its members. The Pevzner family in turn promises to invite me over for supper with champagne. Here we sign our names:
>
> L. V. Yakobson and David Pevzner, representative for family Pevzner. November 7, 1943, Molotov Oblast[162]

Yakobson's title was *baletmeyster* (choreographer) as he notes in this "contract," but the job he was doing was considerably more complex. He was taking the layered, ideologically contradictory, and culturally overdetermined ways that national identities take form and rewriting them through dance. As Joseph Roach has argued about performance in another context in his theory of surrogation, people will find ways to perform their culture in order to "retain their identity within larger hegemonic

Leonid Yakobson in a playful pose with Irina on the shore
at Artek, Crimea, ca. 1949. Photographer unknown.

societies." In describing this complicated genealogy of performance that he calls surrogation, or substitution, as being a process whereby one generation honors the preceding one by quoting and revising through performance, Roach notes how performance takes memories, as well as the accommodations that cultures undergo to persist, and renders them visible rituals.[163] Yakobson was approaching ballet with the same determination to make it a vital cultural form and repository of cultural memories of ethnicity, invention, modernism, and resistance, all of which were at risk of being actively erased. Jewish identity would now be at the forefront of his thinking in a different way than it had been in the 1920s and 1930s. He was prepared to use ballet as a way of theorizing memory and infusing a Jewish sensibility and content into his future work.

In the winter of 1943, in the midst of World War II and under evacuation in Molotov, Yakobson had no proof that he, or his yet-to-be-premiered ballet *Shurale,* would survive, much less be transferred from Kazan to Leningrad to be performed by the Kirov Ballet. Yet it is in this moment, and under these circumstances, that he offers a grandiose invitation in the guise of a contract for the entire Pevzner family, currently living in one borrowed room: they are to be his guests in box seats in the Mariinsky Theater for the premiere of his ballet.

Yakobson certainly had great self-confidence, but rather than a gesture of hubris, this "contract" can be seen as revealing his assurance about the value of what he is doing in building a dance that speaks from and to basic human emotions and social exigencies. In the decade between *The Golden Age* and *Shurale,* Yakobson found his own voice as a choreographer. More critically, he discovered a negotiated balance between the constantly shifting rules about making and *unmaking* art under the Soviet regime. What became clear was his growing determination that this would be his platform for modernizing the empire of twentieth-century ballet and for supporting contradictory formations of identity, nationality, and ethnicity through performance. Soviet nationalism was once described by scholar Benedict Anderson as "stretching the short tight skin of the nation over the gigantic body of the empire."[164] A short tight skin also describes a dancer's unitard, and in the case of Yakobson that skin now sheathed the lithe body of a prototype for a different kind of empire.

FOUR

Chilling and Thawing: Cold War Ballet and the Anti-Jewish Campaign

What is socialist realism? What is the meaning of this strange and jarring
phrase? Can there be a socialist, capitalist, Christian, or Mohammedan realism?
Does this irrational concept have a natural existence? Perhaps it does not exist
at all; perhaps it is only the nightmare of a terrified intellectual during the dark
and magical night of Stalin's dictatorship.
—Andrei Sinyavsky, *On Socialist Realism*, 1959

COLD WAR TOTALITARIANISM invigorated Yakobson. Rather than being
completely suffocated by it, he played with totalitarian discourse in his
ballets, shaping counter viewpoints that could be perceived alongside
the dominant messages. In the wake of the massive losses sustained
by the USSR during World War II, hope rose and then faded for an end to
the Soviet terror against its own citizens as well as for a stop to the treachery

toward national minorities, especially the Jews. Dangerously, and defiantly, Yakobson choreographed his first Jewish works at this time, just as Jewish identity was under intensified attack by Soviet authorities. He shaped ballet into a medium that allowed politics, and his lifelong project of using ballet to assert his identity, to hide in plain sight. Ironically, in this process the Cold War created the conditions for him to continue. He was allowed to address topical issues, even as he suggested that there was not a single doctrine but rather many socialist realisms, and even as he pressed the idea that ballet could be uniquely situated to act in the gap among them.

The Cultural Front

In the Soviet Union, the "Great Patriotic War" was the preferred name for World War II, a title that in retrospect references not only the patriotism of defense but also an increasingly narrow definition of the ethnic boundaries of Soviet nationalism. This shift grew more apparent as early as August 1942, when this wartime Russian chauvinism and false accounts of Jewish treachery met Nazi anti-Semitic propaganda. Georgy Aleksandrov, director of the party's agitprop division, instituted specific anti-Jewish measures during this period. He was especially concerned about what he called excessive representation of "non-Russian persons" in Soviet cultural institutions. Singling out the Bolshoi Theater and the Moscow and Leningrad state conservatories, he claimed that Jews were overrepresented in the arts and recommended that Russians be promoted instead.[1] By the time the war ended, and the Soviet Union had tallied its catastrophic losses, there was new hope that those Soviet national minorities, and especially Jews, who had shared in the defense of the nation during the war might expect to share the postwar benefits. This was not to be. Instead Soviet Jews soon found themselves the target of a new campaign involving the "purification" of artistic institutions, in particular in the Bolshoi Theater, the Moscow and Leningrad state conservatories, and the Moscow Philharmonic. It was not just artists; repatriated prisoners of war also were sent to the Siberian camps of the Gulag because they were considered "tainted" by having seen the West.[2] A Jewish identity became an added burden, the marker of subversive bourgeois leanings. "Being Jewish became a crime," historian Yuri Slezkine asserts. "Those who claimed a separate Yiddish culture were 'bourgeois nationalists'; those [Jews] who identified with Russian culture were 'rootless cosmopolitans.'"[3]

Thus the end of the "hot" war and the commencement of a chill new ideological battle began internally in the Soviet arts before it spread outward through postwar cultural diplomacy. The Cold War is often cited as having formally begun with Winston Churchill's March 5, 1946, speech about the Iron Curtain descending across the Continent. Within five months, in August 1946, Andrei Zhdanov, the architect of socialist realism as the dominant Soviet aesthetic (and the author of the Zhdanov doctrine proclaiming that "good and best" were the only acceptable tensions in Soviet art), made that a blackout curtain, with his intensification of the campaign to rid Soviet culture of "foreign" (non-Russian) influences.

Soviet culture, and especially ballet, had been a touchstone of national cohesion during the war and an illusionistic way to suggest that at least cultural achievement would endure when so much else did not. Indeed, the wartime devastation in the Soviet Union had been massive—more than 20 million men, women, and children, a significant number of them civilians, were dead. Many of the military dead had reportedly carried with them a chaste talisman: a photograph of the USSR's reigning ballerina, Galina Ulanova, who sometimes performed for the troops. Such photographs of the lyrically graceful Ulanova in her famous roles as an imperiled but courageous heroine in *Romeo and Juliet* or the lone compassionate member of the female militia in *Giselle* suggest how ballet's pedagogical imagery circulated during the war. The state's continued circulation of this imagery after the war was marked by a cultural inclusiveness that reached from the intelligentsia to the foot soldier, while ballet's importance to the state intensified and its achievements became sealed against outside change.

Stalin's oversight of the arts, especially performance, inserted him into a state of vulnerability and potential danger from enemies and ideas—and ideas as enemies. At the same time, however, it demonstrates his enjoyment of the status of belonging to the cultured elite and the necessity of being seen watching. The act of "consuming" culture was also a facet of controlling it. The position of spectatorship took on a new and intensified resonance in a totalitarian state where informants were actively working in every theater and performing arts company.

This historical context is important for understanding Yakobson's seemingly contradictory situation of having his work subject to frequent censorship while still being allowed to continue working as a resident choreographer, or at least as someone who proposed choreography, for the Kirov and Bolshoi ballets. Ballets during the Soviet era, even if the Soviets invited their production, were subject to preliminary censorship through the requirement that a written plan, or libretto, for each one be submitted to the various party officials in charge. Even if the libretto was approved, a range of various modifications and additional committee reviews would usually be required and could occur as late as the dress rehearsal, when an entire production could be peremptorily cancelled for any one of a number of reasons, including anti-Soviet sentiments, eroticism, formalism, revelations of Western influences, and on and on.

The Soviet audiences who filled the theaters to see Yakobson's work by all accounts took pleasure in sensing the covert aesthetic challenges it offered, since overt political rebuffs to the ruling authorities were impossible. Even Yakobson's retaining his Jewish name in public had become a nationalist act.[4] Yakobson's main agenda was to expand and contemporize classical ballet's vocabulary, range of expression, and subject matter. Since an abstract ballet crossed into the forbidden categories of formalism and Western influence, Yakobson's works were almost exclusively narrative by necessity—yet within this constraint he repeatedly risked what could be said, or how much could not. He played with the limitations on narrative freedom imposed by government officials as if they were instead a new open door. "In creating mostly narrative ballets Yakobson is unequalled," the choreographer and Kirov Ballet director Fyodor Lopukhov wrote. "He is the number one author of original, varied, choreographic narratives."[5] Artur Romanenko, a dancer with the Kirov and with Yakobson's company, once called the ideological effect of these narratives the "unstoppable genius of Yakobson," explaining that, even curbed, "Yakobson broke away the ideological blinders of the party."[6]

Yakobson's widow recalled how in the years immediately after the war, when Yakobson's job title was choreographer for the Kirov Ballet, only a fraction of the ballets he proffered were permitted to be realized. The usual reasons for the rejections were that the dances he suggested, at times through detailed libretti about the subjects, were "not in line with academic ballet" or "not traditional."[7] (These continued rejections brought with them financial hardship because if Yakobson wasn't working, he wasn't being paid. So Irina, who was dancing with the Kirov, did odd jobs including knitting sweaters to bring in extra money during the leanest years.)

On occasion, when Yakobson received clearance to make a ballet, he could also be a victim of the collateral damage of a collaborator's work being censored. This happened in 1947 when Yakobson put forward a request to create a ballet for the Kirov based on the eighteenth-century Russian fabulist Ivan Krylov's popular fable of *The Dragonfly and the Ant* (*Strekoza i muravey*). A retelling of Aesop's *The Grasshopper and the Ant,* Krylov's work was popular because of its often-satirical portraits of incompetent bureaucracy. Other artists had also been drawn to his fables. In 1913 a famous animated stop-action film of staged action scenes between real (dead) dragonflies, ants, and beetles was made by the Russian-Polish animator Vladislav Starevich (Władysław Starewicz), and in 1922, Dmitriy Shostakovich had composed a song on the same fable for mezzo soprano and orchestra. Shostakovich had played with the satire of Krylov's fable to make the Dragonfly's folly that she sang and made music when she should have been working. In Yakobson's version, called just *The Dragonfly,* his Dragonfly spends the summer playing with friends and dancing until she finds herself cold and hungry with the coming of winter. She begs food from her industrious neighbor, Ant, who has been diligently storing provisions and building a shelter all summer, but Ant refuses. The Dragonfly then dies a pitiful, suffering death in the snow.

As a parable the plot has been analyzed for presenting two negative heroes, with some interpreters arguing that Ant, in choosing to let the Dragonfly suffer, becomes as negative a hero as the lazy dragonfly.[8] The Russian educational psychologist Lev Vygotsky, writing in 1926, also found Krylov's fable filled with the wrong messages: "The child's sympathies are aroused by the carefree and lyrical dragon fly who, all summer long, is always singing. . . . Again, the bite of mockery is pointed in the wrong direction, and instead of instilling children with respect for business-like efficiency and for work, the story suggests the joy and charm of an easy and carefree existence."[9] It is not hard to imagine the party censors at the Kirov parsing these kinds of ideological dangers as well, but they did permit Yakobson to begin staging his ballet in 1947 on the graduating students of the Leningrad Choreographic Institute. He progressed fairly far when he was prevented from completing the ballet for the Kirov school.

It happened, however, that Olga Lepeshinskaya, one of the Bolshoi Ballet's prima ballerinas in the 1930s and 1940s, and Joseph Stalin's favorite performer (rumored to be his lover), had been in Leningrad with a group of people from the Bolshoi who watched a rehearsal of *The Dragonfly*. The Bolshoi group, especially Lepeshinskaya, liked what they saw of Yakobson's unfinished ballet, and she decided it would be a good vehicle for her talents. Using her influence, she persuaded the Bolshoi to bring Yakobson to Moscow to stage it with her in the title role. In addition to her friendship with Stalin, Lepeshinskaya was married to another power figure, General Leonid Raykhman, chief interrogator of the NKVD and a friend of Lavrentiy Beria. This powerful line-up of associates secured the production of the ballet—up to a point.

In the autumn of 1947, when *The Dragonfly* was close to completion at the Bolshoi with its commissioned costumes and sets completed for the large cast, including a corps of at least fifty dancers, it became collateral damage in an explosive reaction between Zhdanov and composer Vano Muradeli's new opera *The Great Friendship* (*Velikaya druzhba*, 1947). Muradeli, one of the first recipients of the Stalin Prize and a popular, if not very distinguished, Georgian composer, had created this opera for the celebration of the thirtieth anniversary of the October Revolution, and performances were staged in multiple Soviet theaters, including an especially spectacular one held in Moscow's Bolshoi Theater on November 7, 1947.[10] Shortly after this premiere a performance, closed to the public, was held and attended by Zhdanov and very likely Stalin himself. The authorities' response was extremely negative.[11] A scathing denunciation of *The Great Friendship* was subsequently published through the Central Committee of the Central Party, which pronounced it "a faulty, inartistic production, both in its music and plot." Muradeli was reprimanded for "having taken the path of formalism [emphasizing the structure and technique of an artwork over its content], which is a false path and fatal to the creative work of the Soviet composer."

Muradeli and the acting director of the Bolshoi at the time, Yakov Leontyevich Leontyev (1889–1948), met with Andrei Zhdanov after the opera had its last premiere, in the Soviet city Alma-Ata. Reportedly "Muradeli repented" for his errors in the production, and Leontyev died several days later of a heart attack.[12] The director of the Bolshoi Theater, too, was promptly fired for having brought *The Great Friendship* to the Bolshoi stage. Everything he had scheduled for the coming opera and ballet season was also immediately cancelled, including Yakobson's *The Dragonfly*, which was just a few days away from its Bolshoi premiere. Some have speculated that it was the inclusion of the lezginka, the melody for a Georgian folk dance that Muradeli had tweaked in his opera, that angered Zhdanov and Stalin, but whatever the trigger, the reaction was swift and the pronouncement effectively blacklisted Muradeli for a couple of years. More broadly it heralded a sustained campaign of criticism and persecution of the Soviet Union's leading composers, including Shostakovich, Sergei Prokofiev, and Aram Khachaturian, for alleged "formalism" in their music. *The Dragonfly*, having twice come close to opening, would never be performed. Back in Leningrad, Irina learned of the last-minute cancellation. Concerned that Yakobson would be upset at so much wasted work, she and her mother prepared a meal of Leonid's favorite foods to comfort him. They were shocked when he arrived home in fine spirits and skipped dinner in order to rush to a soccer match being played that evening by his favorite team. Confident about his own creative talents, which allowed him to generate new ballets with astonishing speed, and possessed of a profound sense of irony, Yakobson was able to rise above the bipolar cultural climate that threatened to overwhelm one's sanity.

Solomon Mikhoels

The year 1948 was a dangerously problematic time to be a visible Jewish artist in the Soviet Union, particularly one who resisted official controls. Yakobson would have been keenly aware of this. On January 15 of that year, the broken body of the great Yiddish actor Solomon Mikhoels lay in state in Moscow's auditorium on Malaya Bronnaya Street from four in the afternoon until midnight and again the following day. More than ten thousand people filed past to pay their respects to the artist who had been murdered by Stalin in a staged car accident two days earlier in the Minsk country house of Lavrentiy Tsanava, who was later discovered to be a high-ranking Belorussian NKVD member.

Just a few years earlier, in early 1942, Mikhoels had been embraced by Soviet authorities, recruited by the Soviet Bureau of Information to be the Soviet Union's public face of the special Jewish Anti-Fascist Committee (JAFC). JAFC was an organization formed by the Soviets specifically to raise funds from Jews around the world by appealing to their anti-Nazi sentiments. In the summer and fall of 1943 Mikhoels and Itzik Feffer, a Yiddish writer and Soviet secret police informer, made an extremely successful fundraising tour of North America, raising a considerable part of the $45 million that Jewish organizations gave the JAFC for the Soviet war effort. Within a few years, however, with the founding of a Jewish state in Palestine on the horizon and the launching of the Cold War, Jews in the Soviet Union were coming to be regarded as an ethnic diaspora with potentially dangerous loyalties to a foreign state—Israel. As Slezkine notes, "The official assault on the Jews would be a belated application of the ethnic component of the Great Terror to an ethnic group that had escaped it (as an ethnic group) in 1937–38." After the creation of Israel and the launching of the Cold War, Soviet Jews "had become analogous to the Germans, Greeks, Finns, Poles, and other 'nonnative' nationalities presumed to be beholden to an external homeland."[13]

Shortly before his death, in speaking before a Soviet audience, Mikhoels had become increasingly outspoken in his support for the United Nations' plan to establish a Jewish state in Palestine, and so seemed to the Soviets to endorse Jewish nationalism (Zionism). Jewish Studies scholar Jeffrey Veidlinger's archival research suggests that Mikhoels's statement of support for the partition plan was the first time that any Soviet Jew had publicly endorsed the establishment of the Jewish state, and that the intense emotional chord this struck with the Jewish population that heard Mikhoels led Soviet authorities to decide to silence Mikhoels swiftly by assassinating him.[14]

Mikhoels's murder was part of the intensification of the *zhdanovshchina*, Zhdanov's anti-Semitic campaign, which was accelerating toward its goal of the eventual destruction of Jewish culture in the Soviet Union. Veidlinger has established that at the same time this anti-Semitic campaign against "rootless cosmopolitans" was intensifying—with the Ministry of State Security starting its preparations for the total destruction of Jewish culture in the Soviet Union—officials were concealing their complicity in the murder by publicly deifying Mikhoels after his death, thereby perpetuating the myth that Stalin's nationality policy celebrated every national culture.[15]

The Isadora Duncan School in Moscow

With the erasure of his new ballet and the Bolshoi season, and the increasing risks of being visible as a Jewish artist, Yakobson turned to an unusual forum for a ballet choreographer. In 1948 he accepted an offer from Ilya Ilyich Shneyder, a longtime Jewish friend and director of the now-struggling Isadora Duncan School in Moscow, to create several dances for the dancers in the school's performing group. The Duncan school had opened in 1921 at a moment of high optimism about the importance to the Russian proletariat of the American dancer Isadora Duncan's new aesthetic of natural dance. Shneyder had been a theatrical journalist working in the press department of the Commissariat for Foreign Affairs when Lunacharsky recruited him to assist and translate for the American dancer and her protégée Irma Duncan during their July 1921 visit to Moscow at the invitation of government officials. Nikolai Podvoisky, president of the Military Revolutionary Committee and the officer who oversaw the storming of the Winter Palace, shared Lunacharsky's interest in Duncan's methods of dance as a resource for the new society.[16]

Podvoisky, in keeping with the emphasis on improving the physical fitness of workers, regarded Duncan's movement and approach to dance as a useful way of linking physical and aesthetic education. Vladimir Lenin had also supported Duncan's visit to the new Soviet state in this unsettled transitional period as the civil war strife continued. The officials hoped that assisting her in opening a school in Moscow would create an institution that could serve the children of industrial workers. Isadora was presented with 150 children, from whom she selected forty to attend her school. Wasting no time in stating her views about classical ballet, Duncan published an article in the November 23, 1921, issue of *Izvestia* titled "The Art for the Mass," in which she claimed that her earlier visits to Russia, and the subsequent circulation of her ideas, had caused the "unnatural" Russian ballet to undergo reforms. Her statement riled Vasiliy Tikhomirov, master at the Bolshoi Ballet school. "Ballet plots are by no means suited to the pace and the mood of our life: the presence of eroticism, the absence of heroism," Duncan wrote. "My influence on the art of dance in the last twenty years has penetrated into all types of choreography, and I can boldly say there is not a dancer nowadays who would unconsciously but quite noticeably (gladly) bring my ideas to his dancing. And hasn't the Russian ballet in recent years experienced a period of big reforms that turned out to be the result of my ideas? And is it not right that I should be the head of the new school of dance, school in a wide meaning of that word?"[17]

Duncan was given the Balashova mansion, formerly the home of the ballerina Aleksandra Balashova at 20 Prechistenka Street. It was a two-story palace with rosewood columns, gold molding, and marble staircases, and to support Duncan's school the staff grew to nearly sixty, including a doctor, a cook, a typist, and even a plumber.[18] Shneyder gradually expanded his role from interpreter for Isadora into director of the school. When Isadora and Irma eventually left the Soviet Union and Isadora died in a freak automobile accident in 1927, he became its permanent steward.

By the time Yakobson arrived in 1948, Shneyder had been extending invitations to a range of guest artists including Vladimir Burmeyster, the main choreographer at the Stanislavski and Nemirovich-Danchenko Moscow Academic Music Theater, as he looked for ways to expand the group's repertoire and keep the school and its students current with work beyond the original dances left by Isadora before her death. Immediately after accepting Shneyder's invitation to create works by using the Duncan School dancers, Yakobson asked that the school perform for him all of the Duncan dances in the repertoire. "He wanted to see them in order to know what kind of material he had to work with," Irina said, suggesting that it was both the ability of the dancers and the Duncan repertoire that he was interested in reviewing.[19] With his typical bountifulness Yakobson created at least six new dances for the school, none of which were filmed or preserved but all of which, according to eyewitness accounts, seem to have responded to various facets of Duncan's style of movement. Russian dance writer Natalia Roslavleva, who saw the performances, recounted in a monograph on the Duncan School in Moscow that of all the guest choreographers only Yakobson created dances with independent integrity and yet remarkable fidelity to the Duncan style: "It was Leonid Yakobson who penetrated with the deepest insight into the style needed by the Duncan Studio. His *Parade Finale,* to Chopin's *Valse Brillante,* cleverly made use of movements taken from Isadora's Chopin pieces. He also created many completely new dances: *Podvig* ('Heroic Deed') to a prelude of Chopin, *Mother* to Scriabin and *Zoya*."[20]

Russian ballet and Duncan's style of easy athleticism, drawn freely from her impressions of the naturalism of the Greek arts, had already proved fruitful inspiration for an earlier generation of Russian ballet artists when Michel Fokine, Sergei Diaghilev, and Anna Pavlova saw the American dancer on her initial triumphal visit to Russia in late 1904 and early 1905. The experience prompted them to incorporate a more naturalistic use of the upper body and a vocabulary of unhurried runs, skips, and jumps into their ballet. Now Yakobson, a devotee of Fokine, was closing the circle—arriving as a ballet choreographer to make work for the Duncan-trained dancers in the school.

Yakobson was the only Soviet ballet choreographer to make this reverse migration and create dances for the Isadora Duncan School. His larger project of developing ballet as a modernist form in the USSR both allowed and benefited from this exchange. It was as if he needed to go back to the same fountainhead of Duncan that had inspired the first modern dancers in America. Roslavleva's observation that the success of Yakobson's work with the Duncan dancers came from his "penetrating with the deepest insight into the style needed by the Duncan Studio" refers to his capacity to draw from a dancer's distinctive abilities in creating movements for that particular dancer. The fact that he could do this so readily with a genre outside of ballet—in this case, modern dance—suggests how complete his absorption was in discovering what it was possible for a dancer to do, rather than how to make that dancer fit an abstract ideal.

The only dance that Roslavleva describes of those Yakobson choreographed for the school is *Zoya*. The title and description clearly suggest this dance was made to commemorate the Soviet war heroine Zoya Kosmodemyanskaya, a seventeen-year-old partisan who reportedly carried out acts of brave resistance against the German occupation until she was captured, tortured, and hanged in 1941. Shostakovich composed music for a 1944 film about her, *Zoya*, directed by Leo Arnshtam. The story of this young woman's brave defiance up until the moment of death became a legendary point of national pride in what may well have been an apocryphal story. Roslavleva declared Yakobson's solo for Elena Terentyeva, as *Zoya*, "a revelation." Terentyeva, who by 1948 had been a Duncan dancer for twenty years (she had joined the school as a young child), portrayed this character by simply walking across the stage alone, her arms held behind her back as if bound together and her posture and carriage as much as her walking movements conveying the suffering of her torture. "Later, the girls as peasants carried her tiny body high up with their own arms and hands," Roslavleva wrote in her description of how Yakobson used a cluster of dancers, rather than any props, to show the gallows on which Zoya was hanged. "The audience was deeply moved by the eerie impression of the body swaying on the scaffold, but they were moved, not only by memories of their own experiences of war, but by the art of the choreographer and the dancer," she concluded.[21]

The Duncan dancers performed Yakobson's works, along with several of their repertory dances on the subject of war, during their 1948–1949 season at the Tchaikovsky Concert Hall in Moscow. They gave their final concert on April 7, 1949, a program that included only one remaining dance by Isadora. Roslavleva, whose account of the school was published in 1976, makes no mention of Shneyder's fate; instead she focuses on the happy ending of Duncan's continuing influence within the "artistic gymnastic" wing of Soviet gymnastics. There is, however, a darker story.

The fate of the school had likely been sealed six months earlier, when Shneyder, who was Jewish, is believed to have turned out to see Golda Meyerson (later Meir), who served as Israel's first ambassador to the USSR. Her arrival in Moscow in early September 1948 had sparked a series of spontaneous political rallies wherever she appeared in public. On October 4, 1948, on Rosh Hashanah, the holiday marking the celebrations for the Jewish New Year, Meir, who served as ambassador from September 1948 to March 1949, attended religious services at Moscow's Choral Synagogue, where a crowd of nearly fifty thousand gathered outside to see her and mark the founding of the State of Israel.[22] Nine days later, on October 14, 1948, following her attendance at Yom Kippur services, a large crowd followed her from the synagogue to the Metropole Hotel.[23] Within a few months Shneyder had been arrested and imprisoned, and in 1949 the Isadora Duncan Moscow School was officially closed. Shneyder contacted Yakobson and asked if, as a prominent artist, he might write letters on his behalf to help get him released from prison. Yakobson wrote but his efforts did not earn Shneyder's release. Many Jews who turned out to see Meir were subsequently arrested and the Yakobsons believed this was also the cause of Shneyder's arrest. (Yakobson too had joined the crowd assembled to glimpse Meir, but he refrained from any active participation in the demonstrations simply because the focus of his protests was always artistic and his battleground the stage.)

Shneyder's arrest was part of a sweeping roundup of the most promi-nent remaining representatives of Soviet Jewish culture undertaken by the Ministry of State Security in the months after Meir's arrival.[24] They saw the Jewish support of Meir as evidence of a "fifth column"—Jews who allegedly would betray the Soviet motherland for the Zionist homeland.[25] During the period of Meir's appointment as Israeli ambassador in Mos-cow, the shutting down of Jewish cultural organizations continued with the closure of the Jewish Anti-Fascist Committee chaired by Solomon Mikhoels, the Yiddish language journal *Eynikeyt* and publishing house *Der Emes,* as well as the arrest of important Jewish cultural workers whose books were also confiscated from libraries.

Yakobson's work with the Duncan dancers in fact did not end with the closure of the Moscow school. A decade later, in 1958, working in the Kirov Ballet, he created an emotional solo, *Mother,* for a female dancer as part of a series of miniatures he choreographed on the theme of the hu-man tragedy of war. Less than three minutes in length, *Mother* is not only a portrait of a mother's anguish over her lost child in the midst of war, but also a remarkable study of what Duncan scholar Ann Daly once defined as the essence of Duncan's solos: "a single body struggling against, shrink-ing from, floating on, and thrusting into space."[26] The soloist in Yakob-son's ballet, Mother (*Mat'*), dances to the same Scriabin piano étude as Duncan had used for her dramatic solo tribute to the Bolshevik fighters—the *Revolutionary Étude*—which she performed in Russia in 1923 after re-turning from a yearlong trip to Europe and the United Sates with the Russian poet Sergey Yesenin.[27] Dancing with fiercely upraised fists and with her arms flung open from the shoulder as if she were trailing sorrow from her fingertips, the dancer Olga Moiseyeva in Yakobson's *Mother* moves majestically across the stage. With her hair loose, legs and feet uncharac-teristically bare, and her ripped and torn dress rippling in the fierce wind of an offstage fan, her costume flutters like a Duncan Grecian tunic but one that has been Russianized into the faded dress of a peasant woman. The body of the dancer in *Mother* is animated by a quiet urgency as she moves with the defragmented fullness reflective of Duncan's dictum of strength at the core, lightness at the edges.[28]

The anguished mother was one of Duncan's great autobiographical tropes, and she used it in not only solos but also the metaphorical Mother Russia of *Revolutionary* (1924) and the more intimate sorrow of *Marche Slave* (1917). Both of these dances by Duncan appear as reference points for Yakobson's 1958 *Mother*. In addition to sharing the title of one of Duncan's works from the 1920s, Yakobson's choreography for the Duncan dancers in his *Mother* ballet reveals how effectively he recognized the attributes of Duncan's dancers and styling and how readily he molded them onto a Kirov-trained body. In *Mother*, Yakobson takes the organizational efficiency of the classically trained body and pushes it through a range of drifting descents to the floor and beseeching gestures that begin with high-reaching steps in bare feet and end with yearning arms and an upward thrust of the chest. Yakobson's *Mother* could have comfortably appeared on a concert of works by second-generation American modern dancers like Anna Sokolow, so faithfully does it capture the terse and penetrating feelings of despair that animated Sokolow's American modern dance in the 1950s.

In another miniature he also created in 1958 on a similar theme of desperation in wartime, *Stronger than Death (Silneye smerti)*, Yakobson transports some of the qualities of Duncan's grounded aesthetic onto male bodies. For Yakobson the miniature was a form of autobiography, a vehicle for his personal voice and a way to register diaristic images of how he saw the world. Costuming three Kirov men as sweaty, shirtless, dirt-streaked survivors hurled into a prison cell, he gives them very simple repeating movement phrases based on falling, rising, supporting, and defiantly challenging body postures. The effect is to perceive the singular as universal, as if the replacements for these brave souls were legion. This is not happy heroism Yakobson is portraying; it is unequivocally tragic and endless. The score by Isaak Shvarts (Isaac Schwartz), who in 1954 had just graduated from the Leningrad Conservatory of Music and who would become a well-known composer for popular Soviet movies, adds to the heavy narrative tone of the work. The aesthetic feels decidedly socialist realist on the surface, and Shvarts's simple, melodious score, which underlines each emotional swing with a shift in musical color, reinforces this quality.

The men's physical actions are sculptural with the legibility of spoken text, but the identity and nature of their unseen oppressor are shrouded and ambiguous. By 1958 Yakobson had become a master of *apparent* accommodation in his dances while delivering a message of highly negotiable meaning within them. There is a churning rhythm to the men's discovery of their captivity, their courage, and their solidarity up to the moment when they are fatally shot and one by one recoil but still do not collapse. With his trademark dramatic concision and literalism, Yakobson shows us the men's courage as if it were as renewable as a deck of cards being shuffled. Repeatedly they swing a leg just ahead of the man in front of them, thrusting their shirtless chests forward and planting their legs wide apart in a literal gesture that says "Here, shoot me instead." Like *Mother* this dance lasts a mere three minutes, and the characters have a singular dimension, but the efficiency of the narrative is compelling even when one knows it will end with the men's deaths. True to the title, in the final moments the men break into mocking laughter at their tormenter, then one by one contract their abdomens in time to a drum roll representing gunshots. They buckle and crouch, but do not collapse, dropping into a final sculptural pose as if moving directly from death into being eulogized in art. Looked at as a male companion piece to *Mother,* *Stronger than Death* suggests what Duncan's dance might have looked like had she worked with Russian men and made gravity the default. The trio is predictable, yet also surprising in the way that the men in *Stronger than Death* rebuff the external world with a very narrow range of actual movements, not one of them recognizable as ballet.

Like a rhythmic round punctuated by abuse from offstage tormenters, the three men who perform *Stronger than Death* revolve through their actions with a repetitiveness and in a confined space that make clear the futility of their efforts from the start. Yet as with *Mother,* we see Yakobson reaching outside of ballet to expand it. The heavy theme of the heroic Soviet, reassuring in its literalness, at the same time deceives the viewer into thinking this might be just an empty propagandistic party ballet. But it is not. Neither of these dances looks like a ballet, nor do the performers look only classically trained. Instead of mime they communicate through the Soviet movement style of dance pantomime. Here too they are animated by realistic gestures, but without the literal flatness or roar of stock socialist realism, and certainly without its mandated plot of a cheerful finish. Think of both these works as souvenirs from Yakobson's 1948 trip to Moscow, snapshots of what he saw in those studios of the Balashova mansion before the Isadora Duncan School at 20 Prechistenka Street vanished and before its director was swept into a cell not unlike that which the men in *Stronger than Death* share.

Hiding in Plain Sight

Yakobson was becoming increasingly adept at playing with totalitarian discourse and challenging the idea that it was a completely suffocating ideological container for artists. Although the experimentation of the 1920s was a distant and forbidden memory, he continued to sow what he could of modernist seeds—such as Duncan's plasticity. As part of this effort, he quietly continued experimenting with the new forms of pantomime he had begun with his initial works in the 1930s. Fyodor Lopukhov, in a 1966 essay describing Yakobson's innovations as a dance maker, uses the metaphor of an opera composer who plays with the various tonalities of the voice to describe the originality of his manipulation of what could be said with the dancing body (while staying within the strict boundaries of narrative demanded by the Soviet aesthetic). "Yakobson's dance is a half-dance . . . it's a quarter-dance. It's not a choreographic dance or a movement aria for a soloist but something developed to a new limit—it is choreographic narrative."[29] In the overview of sixty years of Russian ballet from which this essay comes, Lopukhov praises Yakobson for "forcing out archaic forms of conversational recitative and instead inventing forms of dancing recitative."[30] In an interview in 1950 with the Kirov Theater's in-house newspaper *Za sovetskoe iskusstvo* (For Soviet art), Yakobson explained that he was striving to eliminate ballet pantomime and to relate a story line and images through dance that is full of action. "The story line will resonate with our epoch," he promises. "Because the major themes of the ballet are the struggle of a man for his happiness, victory of the good, good over evil and bright over dark forces."[31]

In 1950 Yakobson revisited the influence of World War II on his own work as a choreographer when, after a nearly ten-year delay, his Tatar ballet created in Kazan on the eve of the German World War II invasion, *Shurale* (now titled *Ali-Batïr* at officials' request so that it honored the hero rather than the villain), finally had its premiere—at the Kirov Ballet. The production, which subsequently moved to the Bolshoi Ballet for the 1955 season, was such a huge hit that *Pravda* and *Izvestia* broke their customary silence about Yakobson's work.[32] They heralded the ballet as a story of "the victory of humanity with mighty heroes who represent the force of the people and the capacity of true love to triumph over evil." The writer of the *Izvestia* review, Dolgopolov, praised what he called Yakobson's "juxtaposition of the fairy tale and everyday" as well as the dances by Shurale and the forest creatures, which he called "filled with craziness" because of their being built on "very sharp, broken lines that help to relate the tensions of the struggle between the hero and his foe."[33] This review offers an interesting inside view of Soviet ballet criticism of the time: note the way in which parsing the plot for its literalness is the major concern of the writer, as if he were responding to a text on paper. Critics, like the artists working in the postwar climate of state control of art and its reception, wrote with deliberateness about the concrete aspects of the ballet, being careful to make observations within the range of acceptable reactions and about unequivocal parts of the performance, all of which could easily be confirmed by others.

Minutes from two separate party meetings at the Kirov Ballet offer an interesting glimpse of how during the Cold War administrative oversight could continue through the life of a major ballet like *Shurale* and even into its restagings. In the discussion about the ballet's aesthetic and ideological content documented in a report dated April 1, 1949, some of the changes mandated were "to make the role of the people and the heroine fighting for their happiness more active. . . . The ending of the show should look like a celebration of this victory." One member, V. Adekhterev, raises a question about the metaphor of Syuimbike as a bird woman who falls under a spell. "This is not a ballet between good and evil but about the struggle for real life and living among good people and their dreams," he is quoted as declaring. The second set of minutes come from an April 11, 1950, meeting, held a few weeks before the ballet's June premiere. These comments are more proscriptive still:

What should be done:
1.) Shorten the name of the ballet.
2.) Change the dance of the fire witch.
3.) Do not include the monsters in the Act One finale. End the act with Syuimbike being carried away by the hunter, but show it in

such a way that the members of the audience will understand that Shurale did not die but will take revenge on the hunter.

4.) Restage the entrance of the main bird.

5.) The dance of the maidens after Syuimbike leaves gives it the sense of a conspiracy.

6.) Shorten the looking for bride. Search musically and choreographically to make it look like a play and not something you do in following tradition.

7.) Shorten the children's dance.

8.) Lessen the image of the drunkards.

9.) Hunters must leave after Ali-Batïr and appear in the woods to help Ali-Batïr.

10.) Give more power and force to Belsky's Shurale.

11.) Try to give one more dance characteristic to Ali-Batïr.

12.) To end the finale of the ballet the scene should show the people's power and wisdom triumphing over the evil spells of Shurale and its elements.

13.) Change the melody of the finale.[34]

This "oversight" directive reads like notes from uninvited collaborators. Ironically, Yakobson's most laudatory viewer of *Shurale,* symbolically at least, was Joseph Stalin. In March 1951 Yakobson learned that *Shurale* had been awarded the 1950 Stalin Prize in Literature and Arts.[35] One of the USSR's highest civilian honors mirroring the Soviet military's decorations, the Stalin Prizes had been created by Stalin in 1939 as a Soviet version of the Nobel Prize. Given annually in recognition of a single outstanding work of art in genres including literature, music, ballet, opera, and the visual arts, the prize reflected an additional leverage point in the government's agenda for the arts and culture. The way a work was fashioned was often secondary to its theme. Yakobson understood well this content-over-style inversion as well as the way the prize fed into the cult of personality around Stalin, and he always cited this great honor with ironic disdain. In Yakobson's official biography, which he was obliged to maintain, he noted that he was a Stalin Prize winner in the very last line, like an afterthought, because the distinction was so insignificant to him. Yet the very fact that *Shurale* entered into the Stalin Prize canon was proof of how well Yakobson could finesse being a laureate even while staying a renegade at heart.

Within a few weeks of Yakobson's return to Leningrad and the Kirov Theater after the elaborate ceremony at the Maxim Gorky Art Theater in Moscow, where Stalin Prize certificates and medals had been presented to him along with the other new laureates, he found himself suddenly relegated from celebrity to pariah. One morning when he arrived at the Kirov Theater to begin work, he was shocked to discover in the newest issue of *Za sovetskoe iskusstvo,* the internal Kirov theater newspaper posted in a glass case in the backstage entrance hallway, an anonymous denunciation with the headline "We Have a Cosmopolitan in Our Midst." The brief article described a choreographer working in the Kirov who was never named, but could clearly not be anyone except Leonid Yakobson.[36]

Two years earlier a parallel denunciation, in this instance of theater and ballet critics, had appeared in similar fashion in the March 31, 1949, issue of *Za sovetskoe iskusstvo* under the headline "Annihilate Completely Bourgeois Cosmopolitism." The rhetoric was searing, defining cosmopolitism ideology as "a reactionary ideology, sermonizing and nihilistic feeling denying national pride and self esteem. Cosmopolitism ideology goes against Soviet patriotism, it is a radical enemy," this report from a party meeting by N. L. Badkhan asserts as it systematically enumerates by name the theater critics, many of them with Jewish surnames, who had praised the wrong works and disparaged ideologically appropriate ones like *The Red Poppy,* enumerating these and other dangerous behaviors under the category of "cosmopolitanism." "This group of rootless cosmopolitans does not value the interests of the motherland and the Soviet people. Bowing down to being a slave to anything foreign they poisoned Soviet art with their deadly spirit of bourgeoisie cosmopolitanism and aesthetics. The extremely important and timely task before us is to push forward and raise new critics from the creative workers at the theatre whose adherence to the party line and principles would [qualify them to] evaluate every work by the theatre." The article concludes with a statement revealing how instrumental critics are viewed as part of the system of art production and reception over which the party wants to exert ideological control. "Our task is to completely annihilate cosmopolitan critics and clear the way to allow the Soviet art to flower," concludes this cynical view of art criticism as a handmaiden to state ideology.[37]

Being called out as a cosmopolitan was a serious and, on occasion, even deadly accusation. In this postwar period, Stalin's anti-Semitism unfolded in a series of public denunciations against Soviet Jews as being weak patriots, or worse, traitors with a stronger allegiance toward their cultural identity than for the Soviet Union. The code word for Jews thus became "rootless cosmopolitans." Mikhoels's murder, Ilya Shneyder's arrest, and now Yakobson's denunciation were all artifacts of this same racist paranoia.

Soviet culture was closing its door to Jews, and Yakobson understood immediately from the wording of the backstage denunciation that he was its object. He had effectively been fired from the Kirov Theater, and within a few days it became official. It would be nearly four years until he would work again as a member of the Kirov artistic staff. All around him Stalin's descent into the darkness of his final years of deepening paranoia against the Jews and intellectuals accelerated. Indeed, right up until Stalin's death his treachery increased with a series of major, although unpublicized, purges including the "Leningrad Case" of 1949–1950, which, as Robert Conquest details, led to the arrest and brutalization of three thousand senior party members. Following this tragedy were the 1952 and 1953 liquidations of hundreds of leading Jewish intellectuals, the 1952 Crimean Affair that involved the execution of important Yiddish writers, and a wave of arrests culminating in the (Jewish) "Doctors' Plot."[38] Yakobson's family believed that he survived Stalin's liquidation of Jewish culture only because Stalin died first.

On June 25, 1953, Yakobson and Irina formalized their long-term relationship with an official marriage license: she took his last name, and three months later, in September 1953, their son Nicholas was born. Having lost his salary at the Kirov, Yakobson took whatever choreography jobs he could find. Over the next few years, Yakobson made works for the Leningrad Choreographic Institute in 1951 and 1953; the Leningrad Musical Comedy Theater; and the Leningrad Academic Maly Opera Theater (MALEGOT), where Yakobson staged *Solveig* and *Spanish Capriccio* in 1952. The Labor Reserves sport society and the Leningrad Concert Organization—both in Leningrad—accepted small works from him. And early in 1953 he made a duet for Irina and a fellow dancer from the Kirov—*Alborada*, set to the music of Ravel. They worked on it quietly in one of the studios of the Kirov school but once it was finished there was no possibility of showing it anywhere and so it joined the list of Yakobson's dances that were never performed. For much of the time during these six years Yakobson worked in the small corner study of his Leningrad apartment, researching and writing libretti for ballets that he hoped someday to have the opportunity to create.

Despite his avowed apoliticalness, Yakobson certainly knew of the tightening noose around the necks of the Jewish intelligentsia in the USSR during Stalin's 1948 to 1953 "anti-cosmopolitanism" campaign. The same political crime that his denunciation implicitly accused him of, supporting Jewish nationalism, was reverberating through every art discipline and institution. To take just one example, in 1950 Soviet authorities attempted to close down the composition department of the Gnesin Institute, of which the prominent Jewish composer Mikhail Gnesin was the director. To save the department, Gnesin agreed to a forced retirement and handed his position over to one of his leading students, Aram Khachaturian, a composer who would eventually cross paths with Yakobson. Khachaturian helped shield Gnesin, but many prominent Jews in the Yiddish and Russian literary and theater intelligentsia were arrested and secretly executed.[39]

As historian Conquest has noted, probably the most chilling indication of the thoroughness of Stalin's Great Terror was that when he died on March 5, 1953, and his successors appealed against "panic and disarray," their caution was unneeded. "Although the single will of the creator of the new State had now gone, the machinery he had created remained in existence. And aspirations among the citizenry toward a different order of things had no possible means of expression and organization," Conquest explains.[40] Living through the nearly thirty years of Stalin's reign had pushed censorship to such a deeply internal point that the very act of creative thought was placed in jeopardy. According to Yakobson's widow, she and her family were quietly happy when they learned of Stalin's death. Yakobson, however, although he went to Moscow to watch the ceremonial procession of Stalin's coffin, appeared indifferent. "He said the death of one person cannot change things. They will find another one. The system is rotten and within the system different forces will fight for power."[41] While outwardly Yakobson reacted with neutrality to the news of Stalin's death, inwardly his imaginative life registered the change. He called it *Vienna Waltz*. "The Return of Breathing and Consciousness" is what the writer Aleksandr Solzhenitsyn called the period after Stalin's death.[42] Ya-kobson's *Vienna Waltz* shows us what that might have looked like.

Vienna Waltz

Indisputably the most resolutely joyous of all Yakobson's dances and the first work he made after Stalin's death, the 1954 duet *Vienna Waltz* (*Venskiy vals*) is an exuberate explosion of romantic joy. Set to a waltz from Richard Strauss's opera *Der Rosenkavalier,* Yakobson's duet is a moment of danced euphoria and the celebration of a return to civility. Yakobson made this duet in response to a commission from the Soviet zone of Vienna for the city's new Vienna Festival. Begun in Austria in 1951, the festival was in-tended as a way to help the country de-Nazify its image and reintroduce itself culturally and politically to the international world. To do this the festival was looking to showcase the non-fascist aspects of Viennese cul-ture. It included cultural representations from the four nations occupy-ing it—Britain, America, France, and the USSR. Yakobson accepted the assignment to do the choreography for the Soviet sector, appreciative for the work since it would be another two years until he was rehired and fully employed at the Kirov. Yakobson's personal library, now housed at the A. A. Bakhrushin State Central Theatre Museum and Archives in Moscow, contains a book that he likely consulted in the preparation of *Vienna Waltz.* It is a worn 1948 text about sixteenth- through nineteenth-century ballroom dance in which Yakobson made several notes comment-ing on the various styles of bows worn and hat-tipping done depending on people's occupations; the proper placement of a woman's hands on her dress; and the ceremoniousness and smoothness of the dancers' foot paths on the floor.[43] Yakobson's notes suggest that he was trying to identify the bodily gestures that signal social standing, gender, and character, gestures that he might tuck into his choreography.

Vienna Waltz survives in black and white footage from a 1960 perfor-mance, one of the few films made of Yakobson's early dance miniatures. For the film the dance was set on a promenade on a luxurious balus-trade overlooking what appears to be the Neva River with Leningrad on the far shore. Two dancers from the Kirov, Ninel Kurgapkina and Boris Bregvadze, perform this brief duet. As the ballet begins, Bregvadze, looking like a nineteenth-century dapper dandy in tails, walking stick, and top hat, is lounging on the balustrade. Kurgapkina, a young woman in a full-length frilly white ball gown, races in, her darting steps and fluttering fan suggesting flirtatious chatter as she feigns disinterest in Bregvadze.

Vienna Waltz taps into a sensibility of abandon and innocence—a welcome antidote to the postwar gloom. The duet is Viennese in flavor but pure Russian in its ballet virtuosity, with its athletic, technical feats. Surprisingly, Yakobson uses music by Richard Strauss rather than Johann Strauss for this waltz. This was a particularly provocative choice because beginning with the rise to power of Adolf Hitler in 1933, it had been forbidden to perform most of the music by Richard Strauss and his modern German composer colleagues.[44] So while Yakobson's choice may have been pushing the Soviets toward accommodation, for the Austrians who were aware of this history, his use of Richard Strauss's music was a subtle gesture of rapprochement. Yakobson uses choreography in *Vienna Waltz* to parry with Strauss's symphonic score—showing masculine and feminine modes of amorous teasing that intensify into climaxes of passion—and all of it measured against the lilting $\frac{3}{4}$ rhythm of the waltz. The mood is sensuous and tender—as if an entire Fred Astaire and Ginger Rogers film were compressed into 180 seconds.

The ballet begins chastely, with the first waltz rhythm arriving as the young woman hurriedly crosses the terrace on her entrance and the man interrupts her. Within moments she is swooning backward across his chest. He keeps the momentum of the tempo by waltzing while circling backward like a dancing chaise lounge on which she just happens to have reclined. It's a perfect Viennese waltz rhythm and the lyricism of their tender contact pulls us along as the intimacies and music accelerate. At the same time Yakobson is also giving us a mini-tutorial on the Russian versus Viennese waltz. The Russian waltz is generally a more staid and melancholy dance, darker in feeling and with a rhythmic structure that is played perfectly steadily, without the surging anticipation of the second beat that gives the Viennese waltz its vitality. Soon the woman begins to launch into flight, as the man holds her by the waist and swings her up and around with her skirt and legs arcing upward in circles of frothy tulle. When he sets her down, she even swoons momentarily in waltz time as she seems to get her dizzy bearings before their dancing takes off again and she is tossed high in the air. This is Yakobson at his easiest and most showily inventive. He took the limitations of the assignment—two dancers, a tribute to Vienna—and made it anything but a routine and dutiful effort.

Yakobson's vision, which the dancers set in motion, feels like a man bursting free. First the floor, then the air near it, and finally the sky are the backdrops against which Kurgapkina and Bregvadze ride. Instead of keeping the waltz tempo just in the steps, Yakobson plays with it as a diminuendo and then crescendo in the dancers' full bodies. In a moment of quiet teasing Bregvadze tries to kiss Kurgapkina, then the action accelerates, getting wilder and wilder. Soon she happily takes his cane in one hand and her fan in the other and allows him to hurl her into the air so that her body does a complete 360-degree rotation laterally—a rivoltade in waltz time with her full skirt following like a falling cloud. She never stops smiling, and with none of the strain or effort of this amazing feat evident, he catches her, pivots, and then tosses her in the air twice more. It's like watching the release of a huge captive bird replayed three times,

Vienna Waltz, with Tatyana Kvasova and
Eduard Paley, Choreographic Miniatures,
1973. Photographer unknown.

187

as if Kurgapkina were a stunning creature that should be airborne and is being set free back into flight.

There is not a single routine waltz step in *Vienna Waltz*. Instead, this miniature is a deft portrait of love from the moment of its casual meeting to the swelling excitement of its flirtation and ending with a chase offstage where there is the suggestion that it continues in perpetuity. Set on an outdoor balustrade overlooking a city vista that might be Vienna or Leningrad, the dance succeeds in being both Viennese and Russian—Viennese in the direct sensuality of Kurgapkina and Bregvadze as the teasing young woman and dapper courtly man who encounter each other just as the opening strains of Strauss's rhythm begins, and Russian in its choreographic daring and flair. At first they partner traditionally, but as the music accelerates so too does the risk-taking of their encounter, until within a matter of moments she is holding her fan and his walking cane as he hurls her into the air in the full 360-degree revolution in midair above his head. You don't believe it the first time it happens, and as they repeat it, with a slow ease and rapturous look of delight on their faces, you feel as if this somersault in the sky were as simple as a skipping run around the dance floor.

Yakobson's rhythmic bite and theatrical surprise are flawless, and free of heavy calculation or build. They waltz, she becomes airborne, and they reunite on the ground. Then with his passion building, Bregvadze does a curious thing. It's so quick one might miss it, but very deliberately he stands close to Kurgapkina and tries to turn her attention toward him as if he has something to say. She pauses and watches as rather than reaching for a kiss he makes a more intimate disclosure: with his heels held softly together he pulses and twists his upper body softly side to side—his arms upraised and fingers silently snapping in the bobbing pulse of the man's variation from a Russian Jewish wedding dance. He is a man in love and he wants to reveal who he is to her. Perhaps autobiographically, Yakobson was doing the same to the Austrian audience. *Vienna Waltz* is an irrepressibly happy dance, and within this happy dance Yakobson has nested this other tiny, and quite personal, dance of Jewish elation. Finally the dancers share a private kiss, hiding their faces from the audience with a bit of mime fanfare. Afterward they separate, and with the swell of the final waltz she rushes toward him—pausing to be tossed into the air in a final froth of ruffled petticoats as if flight were the most natural next stage of courtship.

The Jewish mini-dance inside *Vienna Waltz* was slipped in with a covert slyness similar to that achieved in *Vestris*. But it also has another reference. During the 1950s and 1960s the Israeli government had been utilizing its agricultural attachés in the Moscow embassy to travel around the Soviet Union, distributing tiny Israeli mementos like miniature Jewish calendars and Star of David pendants. These little symbols of Jewishness were usually handed off surreptitiously in a handshake. Given the strongly negative associations for being Jewish or expressing it in the USSR, little bibelots like these were reportedly weighted with special meaning for the Soviet Jews who received one. Yakobson's Jewish bagatelle in *Vienna Waltz* signifies as a Jewish aside with the same brevity, but one communicated through the medium of dance.

In 1951, three years before Yakobson made his *Vienna Waltz*, the waltz was the same dance form that George Balanchine, working in America, used for his exploration of a cultural moment in postwar Europe. Using Maurice Ravel's *La Valse* as well as his *Valses nobles et sentimentales*, Balanchine's *La Valse* makes the waltz a medium for presenting the climate of romanticism tinged with decay and futility that marked Europe in the late 1920s and early 1930s.[45] The theme of death appeared in earlier Balanchine's "party" ballets *Le Bal* (1929) and *Cotillon* (1932), both of which he choreographed before he settled in the United States and both consciously referenced by *La Valse*. Instead of the waltz as a springboard to joy, as was true of Yakobson's treatment, Balanchine's ballet offers a far darker vision—a view now from America, where death in the form of a dancer literally stalks the Viennese waltzers like a predator circling its unknowing prey. This marked difference in each choreographer's treatment of the power-driven romanticism of the waltz suggests how radically disparate their art-making contexts had become. For Yakobson the Viennese waltz was colored more with possibility than sorrow, given the context of what he had just survived in the USSR. Balanchine, in contrast, used the waltz to reflect on the season of death that he had narrowly escaped by coming to the United States in 1933. Yet it is interesting how both men reached for this seemingly innocuous social dance, with its sometimes overflowing emotions and rushing rhythms, as the ideal medium for telling two very different political stories.

As a testament to the universality of the emotional dance language in Yakobson's *Vienna Waltz*, it had a life far longer than that of an occasion piece for a long-ago postwar festival. The 1960 film clip resurfaced in the second decade of the twenty-first century, nearly sixty years after the ballet's premiere, this time as a popular YouTube clip. Posted and reposted, it garnered thousands of hits from viewers who chatted in online amazement at the rare virtuosity of this 1950s-era dance and wondered from where it might possibly have come. Yakobson's name was rarely attached to these clips, but his invention and courage were written on each frame.

Choreographing Jewishness

One of the most problematic topics that Yakobson addressed during his career as a choreographer was the depiction of Jewish identity through a dancing Jewish body. Ann Pellegrini's analysis of Jewishness as gender, and her tracing of how in nineteenth-century Europe categories of religious difference—Christian and Jew—were transformed into categories of "racial" science (Aryan and Jew, respectively), offer a useful lens for viewing how Yakobson negotiated similar territory in Soviet Russia, using ballet to frame the physical stereotypes of the Jew in a landscape where its religious identifiers had been stripped away. In her argument Pellegrini extends the concepts of performativity and citationality to the experiences and idea of "race" and she gives as an example how "the Jewish male's putative effeminacy came to signal 'the' Jewish people's 'racial' difference." She observes that this was accomplished through "eliding differences between Jewish men and Jewish women."[46]

This collision of categories of ethnicity with gender was particularly freighted with political meanings in Soviet Russia, where the socialist realist aesthetic in the visual arts, ballet, and folk dance tended to homogenize ethnicity and essentialize gender. In the visual arts under Stalin a physical type emblematic of the New Soviet Man and the New Soviet Woman evolved in the 1930s as a personification of the Communist ideals of athleticism and robust, broad-shouldered vigorousness. Both the New Man and the New Woman were inflated into muscular human monoliths. Ideal Russian womanhood, in particular, was depicted as a broad-shouldered, broad-hipped, big-boned female laborer, exemplified by the *Woman Metro-Builder with a Pneumatic Drill* painting of Aleksandr Samokhvalov.[47] In ballet, particularly at the Bolshoi, just blocks from the Kremlin, the dance counterpart to these visual images of essentialized masculinity was cultivated. Its trademarks for the men were high jumps as well as racing, space-eating leaps and one-armed lifts of their female partners.

"The rhetoric of 'race' secularized the difference of the Jewish body from the Christian body," Pellegrini explains, in an argument that can also be applied to Soviet Jews. Pellegrini connects Homi Bhabha's description of the stereotype together with Judith Butler's theorizing of gender as performative to make a claim for race, and Jewishness within it, as a mode of differentiation in which the body represents boundary, fixity, and surface. Certainly Yakobson was negotiating multiple imprints of performance on the body created by Russian ballet training as he worked to make grotesque and caractère roles a richer category for social commentary on ethnic difference than they historically had been in this dance genre. In the process the implicit "whiteness" and "Russianness" of Soviet ballet became clear along with the tacit racial boundaries that circumscribe it. "Jews were conceptualized as exceeding the norm," Pellegrini writes of the conversation around their stereotyping. "They were a 'people' with too much of extremes."[48] Most prominently the Jewish male was characterized as sickly, scrawny, and meek. "The caricatured signs of his [the Jewish male's] effeminacy were visible in his stumbling gait and effete mannerisms," writes Pellegrini, describing how these myths of the fragile Jewish male effectively ungendered him as a man in anti-Semitic literature and cartoons. At the same time, he was racialized through medical narratives and biologistic discourses. She notes that this "feminization of the Jewish male body took on special significance for the health of the body politic, which was identified with masculine vigor."[49]

Nowhere was the vigorous masculine body politic more sharply defined than in socialist realist Soviet art, and ballet was one of the most aesthetically charged of these art forms. Socialist realism was established at the First All-Union Congress of Soviet Writers in 1934, where it was framed as the only acceptable literary and artistic style for all Soviet art. This imposed art movement, an aesthetic dictated from above, pushed for men in public images to be portrayed as extremely masculine. Yet late twentieth-century Western scholars of ballet have theorized that the male dancer is compromised by the gendered frame of spectatorship even before he begins to move. That is, as Ramsay Burt and other theorists have argued, the male dancer performing on stage is de facto in a position of having to resist the feminization of his role that occurs simply because he is performing—and to do so he has to assume ever more extreme exaggerations to challenge the conventional circulation of power between the one who watches and the one who is gazed upon.[50] Yakobson's efforts to create a nuanced portrait of the Jewish male and female were therefore doubly problematic. In addition to navigating the stereotypes of Jewish people as "off-white" racial "half-breeds," as Pelligrini describes, Yakobson, when he wanted to portray a Jewish male character, had to delineate its identity through movements that showed just enough of the stereotype so that the character was recognizable and then shift that portrayal into one that fleshed out a more fully dimensioned character with whom one might respond more sympathetically. As an ironic testament to his general success in creating portraits that resist the clichés about the Jewish male as racially impure and feminized, Yakobson found that the sanctions leveled against him were swift and harsh for all of his Jewish-themed dances and the male figure was often the target of heightened outrage.

The Jew in Soviet ballet is thus a layered set of stereotype references—beginning with the softness of the feminized male—conveyed by necessity through a highly disciplined physicality. Within a few years after Yakobson began working to inscribe Jewishness in ballet as a choreographer, the leading American Jewish choreographer in ballet, Jerome Robbins, was getting his start in the United States on a similar trajectory. Like Yakobson, Robbins initially found dramatic works most receptive to his choreographic style, while as a performer he personally excelled in grotesque and caractère roles such as the tragic puppet Petrushka in Michel Fokine's ballet by the same name. There is an ironic aptness in this, for as Russian culture scholar Catriona Kelly has suggested in another context, the character of the beak-nosed Petrushka in Russian fables might also be seen as a caricature of the Jew.[51] While Robbins could experiment in performance forms that did not exist in Soviet Russia, like musical theater and burlesque, he, like Yakobson, stretched the expressive capacity and vocabulary of ballet, making it a contemporary medium for dark, topical, difficult truths. Robbins's explicitly Jewish-themed works *Fiddler on the Roof* (1964) and *The Dybbuk* (1974) offer an interesting counterpoint to what Jewishness in the postwar period looked like filtered through a Jewish American ballet choreographer's sensibility as opposed to Yakobson's Russian one.

Robbins, akin to Yakobson, made the stage a place to probe, express, and reconcile his feelings about being a Jew through empathetic physical constructions. Like many second-generation American Jews of the era, Robbins also flirted with the political Left. Between 1943 and 1947 he was a member of the Communist Party—an affiliation that he later renounced infamously when in 1952 he was summoned to appear in a public hearing before the House Un-American Activities Committee (HUAC). Robbins named the person who had recruited him into the Communist Party, and gave up the names of various actors, playwrights, and critics who were party members. From what we know now, it seems that he was caving in to the fear that he would be revealed in the category he wanted to keep hidden even more than his ethnicity and politics: that of his sexual prefer-ence, his homosexuality.

"I didn't want to be a Jew. I didn't want to be like my father, the Jew—or any of his friends those Jews," Robbins once said, personal sentiments that differed strongly from those of Yakobson.[52] According to the cultural his-torian Nicholas Fox Weber, "Even when he was working for the Yiddish theater as a young man" his stage names included *un*-Jewish fictions like "Robin Gerald, Gerald Robbins, Gerald Robins and Jerry Robyns"—that is, he enlisted multiple ways to mask his identity even while performing it.[53] Perhaps Robbins felt that explicit Jewishness in his dances would keep general audiences from identifying with his work's other themes. In his *The Dybbuk*, Robbins adds gender to these personal questions that he is using ballet to explore, creating a supportive community of essentially all men whose bodies are eroticized by an intense spirituality. It is as if their fearful obedience to external religious force also carries a binding and sexual charge. Robbins once said that his affinity for ballet had "some-thing to do with the 'civilizationing' of my Jewishness."[54] This comment echoes this sense of Jewishness being an identity that is primal, socially risky, and marked by a set of behaviors that can perhaps be undone or re-paired through re-performing.

In Russia genres like modern dance, jazz, or Broadway musical theater were impossible, so Yakobson was forced to make his alternatives to ballet within the genre of ballet itself. (There were so-called Soviet tractor musicals, which involved robust communal peasants cheerfully sing-ing as they hurled bushels of wheat from a massive harvest, but this genre was so completely the creation of Soviet propaganda that a subversive messenger like Yakobson had no hope of adding anything to it.) Indeed, he often said his mission was to bring Russian ballet forward, not to abandon it, underlining his determination to reinvigorate Soviet culture and the iconic body at its center. For American audiences, however, the Broadway musical may well have been similar to Soviet ballet in terms of its cultural accessibility and prominence. Andrea Most, in writing about Jews and the Broadway musical, identified this uniquely American song and dance form as a forum that permitted Jewish Americans in particular to reinvent themselves on stage. "First- and second-generation American Jewish writers, composers, and performers used the theater to fashion their own identities as Americans," she writes. "In the musical, they discovered a theatrical form particularly well suited to representing the complexity of assimilation in America."[55]

Yakobson was endeavoring to represent the Soviet Jews' paradoxical condition of being both unable to assimilate yet also unable to be fully separate from the mainstream culture. He does it through the medium of ballet, whose vocabulary and style were similarly exclusionary and inflected with racial and ethnic overtones. The imagined ideal Russian body on which Soviet ballet was constituted was unlike the stereotypical Jewish body in almost every way. Andrea Most identified themes in musicals by American Jews that address this subject of alienation, but these composers and writers did not have to live it as vividly offstage as Russian Jews of Yakobson's era were forced to do. She notes, "First each [musical plot] tells a story about difference and community . . . the experience of being an outsider." She then goes on to assert that the American public has "learned how to 'see' Jews by seeing musical theater" and that "the musical theater exists because of the unique historical situation of the Jews who created it. The social reality of being a Jew in America is fundamentally inscribed in the form of the American musical theater."[56]

In several respects Yakobson was engaged in a parallel project, demonstrating in a far less hospitable location the social reality of being a Jew and even just an "Other" in the Soviet Union. He made the stage, in this instance the ballet stage, a place where it was possible to see Jews in Soviet Russia through the powerful language of dance. It is remarkable how hard he fought to achieve what so many Jewish artists in America were doing at about the same time but with far less resistance. "Jews self-consciously used performance, in all of its manifestations, to negotiate their emergence into modern, cosmopolitan, non-Jewish societies," Most asserts. "Musical comedies . . . were narratives of a desperate Jewish desire to resist essentialized (or racialized) identity through the powerful language of theatricality."[57] Andrea Most sees musical theater in particular as "an arena in which Jews and non-Jews alike could experiment with the shifting identity boundaries so characteristic of the modern world." She asserts that this exploration of Jewish identity through cultural forms was historically often paired with its expression through performance. "In early modern Europe, the emergence of Jewish culture outside a religious context was nearly always accompanied by significant Jewish production of theater," she writes.[58] This observation supports the idea that Yakobson embraced the Russian ballet stage as a space to capture parts of Jewish culture that were vanishing outside. He consciously essentialized and racialized these images to set them apart from the hypothetical viewer who was always conceptualized as Soviet.

Jewish and Black Identities in Ballet

In comparing Soviet Russia and the United States in terms of their emerging incorporations of cultural difference in dance, the challenges that black ballet dancers in the United States encountered in gaining acceptance and a space to articulate their narratives offer a useful context. Dance studies scholar Thomas DeFrantz has framed the dynamic between race and power by arguing that racial identities have historically foregrounded power dynamics between groups of people, so that we see racial identities first and the social or political condition that attaches to them second.[59]

While other Soviet ballet choreographers who survived the 1930s and 1940s also created ballets using national folkloric materials, often as an aesthetic decorative motif, Yakobson's work with Soviet minority ethnic groups like the Tatars and Jews focused primarily on stretching the *subject matter* of ballet to open a space for inclusion—a space where the viewer discovers cultural and political connections along with the viewed. In the United States, by contrast, initial efforts to include blacks in ballet generally focused more on the integration of their bodies into the dominant whiteness of ballet; changes to the actual narrative content of those ballets came later. Scholar Brenda Dixon Gottschild has commented on how this "visual value of skin color" in American ballet, particularly in regard to the work of George Balanchine, played a part in several of his ballets in which he cast black dancers, particularly his *Agon*.[60] The image of a black male and white female together in the *Agon* pas de deux made the ballet stage a site of racial challenge in the segregated United States of the 1950s.[61] This strategy has parallels with Yakobson's pushing the boundaries of which ethnic identities could be represented on the ballet stage in Soviet Russia. There was not such a developed inventory nor distinctly physical vocabulary of aesthetic politics defining Jewish performance in ballet when Yakobson began; his work, then, inaugurated this project in the USSR.

In late 1970, as Yakobson was struggling to get his most ambitious ballet about Jewish identity on stage with his company, the Alvin Ailey American Dance Theater visited Leningrad for the first time. Yakobson and his company were among the crowds who turned out to see the company, the first American modern dance company to visit the USSR. After their Leningrad performance Yakobson went backstage and spoke with Ailey through an interpreter and under the eye of the watchful KGB. He was enthusiastic about the company and particularly the dancers.

With his customary exuberance Yakobson spontaneously invited Ailey and his dancers to come see his new company in the midst of rehearsals for their first season. "My husband showed everything that was ready for the first program—*Rodin, Exercise XX* and also his Stravinsky ballet, *Ebony Concerto*," Irina said, miming an exaggerated minstrelsy-like stance with her hands stretched open and her derrière extended behind her to suggest how the *Ebony Concerto* ballet included steps caricaturizing blackface stereotypes. Ailey laughed when the ballet was performed for him, Irina said, adding that he enjoyed it.[62] Vladimir Zenzinov, a dancer in the company at the time, has a different memory of this meeting with the Ailey company. Zenzinov said that although Ailey appreciated the dance as a fellow choreographer, the dancers of Ailey's company looked shocked by the blatant racist stereotyping of Yakobson's choreographic styling. "Their faces were like this," he gestured with his neck forward and his eyes wide in disbelief. "Yakobson was like a child and he didn't realize how he had offended the dancers with this work." Zenzinov then demonstrated, just as Irina had, the work's racialized postures of hyperextended buttocks, hands held in open splayed-fingers jazz hands, and lips pursed outward.[63]

Tatyana Bruni, costume sketch for *Ebony Concerto* (1971).
© A. A. Bakhrushin State Central Theatre Museum, Moscow.

Ailey never recorded what his private reaction had been. But a note he sent to Yakobson that was recently discovered in the personal archives of Anatoly Pronin, a Soviet photographer who captured Yakobson's work from 1971 to 1975, records his polite and carefully worded response: "For Mr. Yakobson—Whose 'Ebony Concerto' with music by Igor Stravinsky and choreographed by himself I found to be interesting, creative, amusing and in every way very good theater. Alvin Ailey, Leningrad, October 30, 1970."[64]

Zenzinov took several photographs memorializing this union of the Ailey and Yakobson companies as they gathered together in Yakobson's Leningrad studio. In these images the Ailey dancers are in street clothes and the Yakobson dancers are in rehearsal attire as the two groups, smiling, crowd into the camera's frame. They cluster around a program that one of the dancers holds, a sketch of a jauntily posed dancer from *Ebony Concerto*. In the foreground Ailey and Yakobson crouch down, smiling broadly around this little figure whose fingers stretch in jazz hands as he juts out his hip to one side. For both this memorializes a pinnacle period in their pioneering efforts to open dance in their respective nations to a broader range of individuals—Ailey as the founder and director of the first black American dance company, and Yakobson as his Jewish counterpart in the Soviet Union. The cultural faux pas of Yakobson's stereotyping of the black body in his *Ebony Concert* ballet, now lost, may well have been his attempt to stylize the black body much as he did the Jewish body without realizing the dangers of cultural and racial appropriation outside one's immediate world.

For several decades Yakobson worked to integrate the ethnically different—Jews—in a way that highlighted a difference that was often invisible or only subtly apparent visually. Using dancers who rarely were Jewish, since few in the Kirov were, Yakobson signified Jewishness through

Dancers of Choreographic Miniatures and Alvin Ailey American Dance Theater
with Yakobson and Ailey at the Choreographic Miniatures studio,
Leningrad, 1970. Photo: Vladimir Zenzinov.

postural and gestural shaping as well as narrative content. Yakobson's focus was on drawing attention to ethnic difference by emphatically staging it on his own company as he had selectively tried to do in the Kirov Ballet.

By contrast, for choreographers of black ballet dancers in American companies, the thrust was on attempting to *ignore* a visual difference, something that could not be "unperformed." Since trying to integrate existing ballet companies in the United States was problematic, some American dance directors simply created autonomous all-black ballet companies, such as the American Negro Ballet and the Dance Theater of Harlem. Yet despite their obvious differences, there is more than a coincidental relationship here between the strategies of making visible certain aspects of cultural identity while trying to make invisible others. Both the American and Soviet efforts revealed how ethnic identities and social conditions from outside the theater always impinge on the created, staged world of the gesturing body and its social values.

Shaping Ballet and Outsider Status in Soviet Russia

One of the implicit questions that Yakobson's Jewish-themed dances asked was how could dance—and specifically ballet—in Soviet Russia serve as practice and metaphor for these relationships with an ethnic outsider. Certainly the larger theme of fortitude in the face of being a cultural outsider is a constant, but Yakobson's images of Jews rarely lingered on victimhood. Instead he approached choreography as an act of what dance theorist Susan Foster called in another context "theorizing about what a body can be and do."[65] He was bold to bring such images into the Soviet-era ballet world, and bolder still to ask such open-ended questions. As Ailey and Arthur Mitchell were doing in American dance, Yakobson's ballets invite the spectator to reflect on various aspects of social order by viewing the nonverbal expressions of dance. The best of Yakobson's 180 ballets attempt, and oftentimes realize, a display of the freedom of re-invention and self-authorship—the individual voice as subject, practice, and medium. His use of ballet to express the conditions of a persecuted ethnic minority in the USSR was risky. It was made possible in part through his capacity to display via choreography the affinities between movement and culture as shaped through the musculature of a dancer's body.

These insights developed over time. Spanning a period of twenty-one years, from 1949 to 1970, the Jewish-themed dances that Yakobson created included three miniatures and one extended ballet on Jewish themes. He also began planning two major Jewish-themed dances in the early 1970s but they were never realized. The arena he had in mind for this challenge initially was the stage of the Kirov Ballet. When Stalin's attacks on modernist artists and Jews intensified and his situation as a resident choreographer in the Kirov became increasingly problematic, however, Yakobson found himself drafting this message about Jewish identity from outside the Kirov Ballet.

Neither coincidental nor purely a reaction, Yakobson's turn to his first Jewish-themed dance in 1949, as the political situation within the Kirov deteriorated, was a consequence of practicality and possibility in equal measure. Needing work, he had been offered a position as the head of a new Moldavian folk ensemble that the Soviets had decided to create in Kishinev, capital of the Soviet republic of Moldavia, and the site of what had previously been one of the oldest Jewish communities in the Soviet Union. Yakobson arrived in 1949, just a few years after the Jewish community of Kishinev had been devastated by the Nazi invasion during the Holocaust. During the invasion 53,000 of the 65,000 Jewish inhabitants of the city had been killed, with some complicity from Moldavian townspeople.

During the postwar period, the Soviets continued their exclusionary policies against the remaining Jews of Kishinev by imposing increasingly difficult restrictions on them. Yakobson had no particular knowledge of Moldavian culture or dance, so he began by immersing himself in the surrounding villages' practices as a self-styled cultural ethnographer. Specifically he was hired to make work for the Kishinev Dance Company, a folk dance troupe that was being assembled with Yakobson as the ghost director and choreographer and a Moldavian as the titular head. A leading Bolshoi ballerina, Maya Plisetskaya, in a passage in her autobiography about Yakobson, noted the financial pressures on him when he undertook this assignment and how he had no choice but to remain anonymous as the real choreographer behind the Moldavian troupe's folk dances. "His wife, Irina, drew a salary as a dancer at the Mariinsky. But the magic wand to save them when things got very tight was folk dance: Yakobson would set off for Moldavia, to Kishinev. To work with Zhok, the famous folk ensemble. The audiences loved the flavor and authenticity of the

Moldavian folk dances, and no one ever suspected that they were all choreographed by Leonid Yakobson. He was a virtuoso stylist. The Moldavians paid generously, with only one condition—anonymity. Yakobson agreed without a murmur. Even a genius needs to feed his family," Plisetskaya concluded.[66]

Yakobson was always intent on discovering rather than manufacturing culture, so he began to create several works for this new Moldavian dance company on what he was finding in the local folk culture. Yakobson's wife recalled that soon after he arrived in Kishinev he began visits to several of the surrounding villages where traditional weddings were still being practiced. "He took it very, very seriously," she said of his expeditions. "He wanted to know exactly how weddings were done there. For him it was very important to understand through feeling how these happened."[67] Indeed, while Yakobson's original impulse might have been ethnographic curiosity, his observational skills swept in both the picturesque and the poignant as he watched the customs of these village marriages. The immediacy of the Jewish community's loss there, including being a site of Russian anti-Jewish pogroms stretching back to the beginning of the twentieth century, coupled with Yakobson's own de facto exile from Soviet hierarchy by virtue of being Jewish, may have helped inform his decision to make Jewish culture the subject of at least one of the dances he made for the company in Kishinev.

The suite of Kishinev dances Yakobson made—*The Gossips (Kumushki;* music by Shiko Aranov), *Jewish Dance (Evreyskiy tanets;* folk music), and *The Bridal One (Svadebnaya;* folk music)—together with the additional two Jewish-themed dances he would eventually choreograph back in Leningrad, all perform and preserve a vanishing culture. Being geographically removed from Leningrad, Yakobson found himself reaching for a very different kind of realism in Kishinev than the perennially optimistic gloss of socialist realism. At the same time his ballets frame the live artistic encounter of the ballet theater as a place where new experiences and theories of social interaction coexist. This is where social order and its regulation through nonverbal behavior are described through enduring cultural motifs—motifs of movement.[68]

The cultural practices that Yakobson witnessed in Moldavia in 1949, particularly in the Kishinev Jewish community, may have had a unique quality of sorrow that would have tinged even joyful occasions. Like an ethnographic palimpsest, the rubbed and scraped-away portions of the earlier history of the Jews and other cultural types he encountered around Kishinev seem still partially visible in the folk-styled dances Yakobson made there. His only surviving intact work from this period is *The Gossips,* a rollicking miniature for five frantically chattering and gap-toothed babushkas who lurch wildly around the stage propelled by the urgent need to spread and collect gossip. Droll, witty, and farcical, it is a deft study of village types, not necessarily Jewish but abundantly peasant figures who converse in a physical language of spilling emotions. All of their exchanges are conveyed through racing movement phrases of skittering runs, eager listening postures, and comical collisions as each woman dashes off to spread the newest bit of hearsay she has just received.

The grotesque body and its parodic behaviors of excess, qualities that the Russian philosopher and critic Mikhail Bakhtin labeled "carnivalesque," shape the dancers' behaviors in *The Gossips.* In barely three minutes' time, Yakobson delivers a saturated portrait of the pleasures of gossip. It moves like a wild current racing through the bodies of this quartet of female senders and receivers. Padded out in comically garish patterned skirts, striped aprons, and frilly blouses, and with short pigtails peeking out from the scarves that cover their heads, the women's bodies are in continual motion, animated and agitated by forbidden conversations. All of the dancers' bodies in *The Gossips* buckle delightedly as they trade juicy slander and innuendo. They are lumpy, old, socially unregulated—the antithesis of traditional images of the female in ballet. They really don't dance in the sense of performing recognizable ballet movements, and they wear heeled boots, scarves on their heads, and heavy layered clothing—costumes more typical for the theater than for dance. They are a reminder of how folk laughter and culture can provide a safe way to champion creativity and a defiant consciousness in the face of oppression, to carve out a second hidden life in the midst of a conservative society.

In his generative 1930s text *Rabelais and His World,* Bakhtin argues that festive folk culture evolved to combat the dread of a late medieval world filled with strict hierarchies of power and rules, a society "poised on the brink of cosmic destruction." This sounds much like the moment in Soviet history and ballet that Yakobson was inhabiting. Bakhtin posited that through folk laughter and the symbolic degradation of carnival performances, "the abstract terror of the unknown was 'made flesh,' transformed

The Gossips (1949). Photo: V. Nikitin.

into a 'grotesque monster' that was to be laughed at and overcome."[69] In Bakhtin's model, carnival also broke down the formalities of the inherited differences between social classes, ages, and life stations, championing a refusal to accept the present social system, all within the safe frame of performance. At the time Bakhtin was developing his idea of this oppositional utopia of carnival, the first of more than twenty years of Stalin's oppression had barely begun. But Bakhtin clearly noted the striking parallel between the omnipresent cosmic terror of the medieval age and that of the Russia around him. In a similar fashion Yakobson's choreographic strategies reveal the circumstances of their production at the same historical moment.

A Couple in Love

The only other dance that survived from Yakobson's Kishinev period, although in a revised format, is a version of *Jewish Dance* (*Evreyskiy tanets*), restaged in 1958 for the Kirov Ballet under the new title of *A Couple in Love* (*Vlyublennïe*). Within the four minutes of this duet miniature, Yakobson effectively shows how the language of performance can be useful for shaping critical models of social relations. In the opening seconds of the dance the young couple, danced by Yakobson's wife and her fellow Kirov dancer Aleksey Mironov, spill onstage in a cascade of flirtatiously tripping little footsteps. The impulse and effect are as if the sparkling pointe work of classical ballet were being danced in mud-caked work boots. The attack is there but the daintiness is weighted and rounded. The choreography quickly begins unfolding a sequence of tableaux as if displaying movement snapshots of the couple's life to come: the flirtation, the commitment, the parental blessing, the wedding, and the arrival of the firstborn all pour from Irina and Mironov like photographs from the memories of Kishinev's Jews. The physicality of Yakobson's choreography invites an easy visual identification of these kinesthetic portraits through the unique communication that comes from live bodies watching other live bodies perform. Much of the technical virtuosity is hidden, allowing spectators to develop their own understanding and memory from the encounter, depending on the range of viewpoints in the audience.

No photographs or film of either of these original dances that Yakobson made for the Kishinev Dance Ensemble survive. But there is an old black-and-white film of Mironov and Irina Yakobson dancing the reworked version of this duet on an empty stage, costumed in the finery of poor Jewish peasants from the early twentieth century. The 1958 *A Couple In Love* displays a more complicated relationship between its characters than the title suggests. Bounding onstage to Simon Kagan's upbeat score of sections of several old Moldavian folk melodies, the woman strikes the floor in precise heel and toe footwork that relates to traditional Jewish line dancing, while holding her arms in the lifted casual embrace of folk dancing. Every action of the dancers is tightly correlated to the music, and the economy of their narrative is breathless. The dancers are in constant bounding motion from the moment Simon Kagan's plaintive Yiddish folktune orchestrations begin. Wearing low-heeled character shoes, they attack the score with insistent ball, heel, and toe taps on the floor, echoing the soulful fancy footwork of wedding celebrants. Both performers use highly animated facial expressions and mime to describe the rapid evolution of their relationship from flirtation to passion and its consummation in the domestic union of parenthood.

All of the details in the dance are framed as revealing cultural artifacts—from the overly fancy ruffles on the woman's white blouse and skirt to the small jacket and too-short pants the lanky man wears. *A Couple in Love* seems almost overeager in the density of its packed references to Jewish culture, from its shtetl couture to klezmer rhythms and animated facial gestures of hope, then despair. Jewish culture encrusts these two flirtatious yet shy characters as they keep up a pattern of heel-tapping slides and skips, a rhythmic foot conversation that makes clear that there is a language of romance being spoken through the body. Their posture often includes the hunched shoulders with upward palms and shortened neck that is a movement cliché of a Jew conversing with God and asking "Why me?" Several other identifiably "Jewish" gestures are included. For example, the woman shields her eyes and gazes downward as if uttering the Sabbath prayer over lighted candles. Seconds later both dancers stand side by side, their arms outstretched and palms open upward as if receiving a blessing, or a benediction. Indeed at times the religiosity of the references is more constant than their affiliation—at one point the man and woman lightly touch their fingers to their forehead, nose, and chin as if gesturing in a Muslim prayer or crossing oneself before a Christian prayer. What is important is that we know the gestures connote religiosity; it apparently was less important to Yakobson which religion was referenced. The dance requires highly trained dancers but the vocabulary that Yakobson invents in *A Couple in Love* is a new dance vernacular. It is no longer pure classical ballet since there is no pointe work, partnering, or elevation in the traditional sense. In its place Yakobson offers characters saturated with emotions, sorrows, and dreams. The ballet virtuosity in the dancers' bodies is transposed into the vernacular of folk culture— but retains the speed, attack, and lifted and taut movements of trained Kirov dancers.

In Yakobson's duet what we see and what we hear seem to be fused by the setting of the dancers' actions to the score step for note. While maintaining a bounding, doll-like gaiety, the two dancers begin by suggesting a very modest courtship in a community with strict social rules about the limits on romance between young people, as was true of the Orthodox

Jewish communities. Gradually the dancers, whose footfalls make no sound, persuade the viewer that they're entranced with each other and they dash forward in time—ready to imagine the blessings of their parents, their marriage, and the birth of their first child in a society that retains its own communal rituals. The couple flirts and shyly gets to know one another in a dance of little advancing and retreating steps, pivots, and turns. Yet instead of being about joyous rhythmic expression, these actions are all small and tentative, replete with details of emotions, although self-conscious about not expressing too freely or boldly the inner life of each character. Irina recalled this duet as growing out of a long-standing interest Yakobson had in creating a ballet on a Jewish theme, a desire that was ignited by the events of late 1948 when Golda Meir came to Russia. "My husband watched all this and he kept thinking how he could do something in dance about Jewish Culture," Irina said.[70]

A Couple in Love (1949), Irina Pevzner (Yakobson)
and Aleksey Mironov, Kirov Ballet, Leningrad.
Photographer unknown.

As modest as its scale and ambitions may have been, *A Couple in Love* became a subject of controversy for Yakobson almost immediately. Irina says that in the late 1950s, a year or so after he first reconstructed the Kishinev duet for the Kirov, the distinguished Russian-American impresario Sol Hurok came to the Kirov Theater to select repertoire for the company's forthcoming 1961 first American tour. The full company and choreographers were present as each work the troupe was prepared to tour was performed for Hurok. The front row in the Kirov Theater was filled with Kirov officials and Yakobson was also present. As the run-through of the officially chosen company works from the repertoire ended, Yakobson stepped forward and said, "Now, I would like to show Mr. Hurok one more piece." Konstantin Sergeyev, artistic director of the Kirov, quickly said, "No, we're finished." Hurok, however, interrupted and said to Yakobson: "No, I would like to see what else you have."[71]

So Yakobson gave a sign to his wife and Mironov, who had been waiting in the wings. Immediately they launched into *A Couple in Love*. Hurok, who had been born in a small Jewish village in Ukraine and emigrated alone to the United States when he was eighteen, certainly understood the shtetl references in Yakobson's duet, and the companion dangers that came with a Jewish subject for any Soviet artwork. Yet he was also shrewd about marketing Russian culture outside of Russia, especially in the United States, so he promptly announced that he wanted this duet to be included in the tour. "We will take it. It's wonderful! We will take it," Irina remembers Hurok announcing excitedly. When Sergeyev and the other Communist Party officials protested that it was not on their approved program, Irina reports that Hurok replied, "Well, put it in the program. I don't want to do the American Gala without this piece."[72]

A Couple in Love was consequently performed in the United States on the Kirov Ballet's 1959 tour and was greeted with enthusiasm by audiences. Irina recalled how after one performance on the tour she and Mironov were invited to a lunch hosted by the local Jewish community and she watched the surprise and then disappointment on their hosts' faces when they stepped from the car and it was immediately evident that Mironov was not Jewish. "Why he is a goy," she recounts the host remarking, using the Yiddish word for a non-Jew. She later relayed this comment to Yakobson as an affirmation for how convincing his choreographic portrayal of a shtetl Jewish male had been. Decades later she still remembered being the focus of pointed questions by her Jewish hosts about the conditions for Jews in the Soviet Union. She was diplomatic in her responses because the KGB representatives in the company stood close by, saying simply that the situation was fine—didn't they see that half the Kirov orchestra was Jewish?[73]

Arguably the most sympathetic audience that ever viewed *A Couple in Love* was composed of former members of Solomon Mikhoels's Moscow State Yiddish Theater, whom Irina chanced to meet in a labor camp in the Eastern Urals in 1964. She and Mironov were completing a tour and happened to perform there, deciding at the last minute to show this work. Afterward a huddle of worn and broken people approached, the survivors of Mikhoels's Moscow State Yiddish Theater. Irina recalled how thin and exhausted their bodies looked and how blackened from labor their hands were as they thanked her for the opportunity to see this dance. "It is pure Sholem Aleichem," they said appreciatively. The irony was tragic, for Aleichem's Jewish tales were the inspiration for productions that had ended careers for the members of Mikhoels's troupe.[74]

The next Jewish-themed ballet Yakobson created was, like this first one, a study of a young Jewish couple, but this time the couple was newly married. No visual record exists of this ballet, *The Newlyweds,* which was created in 1969, because it was set on the only group of dancers Yakobson had access to then and on whom he could build the ballet: Irina's advanced students at the Vaganova School who were especially good at character dance. Initially it was performed in a closed studio, and, then, when Kirov officials saw it, they reluctantly agreed to an additional showing at the performance of the graduating students. It proved very popular, however, and so Lenkontsert (the Leningrad Concert Organization), which formed small groups of dancers and sent them to outlying regions to perform, arranged for the ballet to be performed by these dancers on the programs they were doing in small towns throughout the Soviet Union. This arrangement was designed to give performing experience to dancers who had not made it into the Kirov or Bolshoi ballets but who had trained for years and wanted to perform. "They received diplomas, but they were not so talented," Irina said of this troupe. "Yet they needed to be used so they could earn a bit of money.[75] This format proved a useful alternative to the Kirov for Yakobson so that when he made a ballet that the Kirov would not allow the company to perform he could offer it to the Leningrad Concert Organization, where the dancers may not have been as adept but the layers of oversight from various theater union and party representatives were fewer.

Yakobson's use of ballet to express the conditions of an ethnic minority in the USSR—the Jews—was daring. In the process he had negotiated ballet as a tacit but effective medium of national re-identification. Although Jewish-themed dances were not the only, or even the most frequent, subject that Yakobson addressed in his choreography, the fact that he explored it at all, and did so repeatedly over a twenty-year period, already shatters precedents for Soviet ballet. His actions augmented ballet as more of a contemporary *political* medium than generally recognized and thus enhanced its use as a means to glimpse the corporeal practices through which communities create and sustain themselves.

Jewish Wedding

Among the major works of Yakobson's choreographic legacy is the third and final Jewish-themed ballet he made, *Jewish Wedding,* or as the Soviet authorities insisted it be retitled (since the word "Jewish" was objectionable), *Wedding Cortège (Svadebniy kortezh).* Although he created and set all the ballet's movement in the single month of January 1970, *Jewish Wedding* in many respects looks back to the initial cultural investigations that Yakobson began in Kishinev in the late 1940s. Metaphorically it can be scaled up to the level of an autobiographical reflection, since he finalized it during the last year of his life and its content stands as a valedictory to so many of his working methods and cultural values. It also represents a statement of new possibilities since the immediate postwar years of the late 1940s, when Yakobson had first approached the possibility of having a Jewish subject in his dance. That postwar period has been called a period of terror unmatched in the history of Soviet rule for its effectiveness in demoralizing the individual, particularly the Jew. This was accomplished through "state-encouraged anti-Semitism" and "the destruction of every social structure" so that Soviet society was effectively transformed into an amorphous mass and "the citizen had become a slave of the state," as scholar Shimon Markish asserts.[76] In an observation that resonates in particular with Yakobson, Markish notes, "The particularly cruel persecution of the Jew, the special derision aimed at him, were not only a function of traditional Russian or Stalin's personal anti-Semitism, nor merely an instructive example or a safety valve. They amounted to a recognition that the Jew possesses a particular ability to resist total leveling, a particularly stubborn individualism (both on the personal and on the national level)."[77]

The importance of *Jewish Wedding* is the clarity with which it asserts that a kinesthetic expression of culture through stylized movement can impart a national feel to art. Yakobson's development as a choreographer in defining this territory in the intervening years between *A Couple in Love* and *Jewish Wedding* is profound. In *Jewish Wedding* his rumination on the sensations and physical and psychological manifestations of living one's life in a state of exclusion has grown into a deeply physical experience for the viewer with every dimension—musical, thematic, visual, spatial, and choreographic—woven so tightly together that it's impossible to imagine changing one without a chain reaction tearing through the others. Irrationality is the one constant, he seems to warn, and our bodies register and hold it all inside. Dance is one of the few public spaces where these sensations can be shared. *Jewish Wedding* amplifies the brief sketch of Jewish nostalgia that *A Couple in Love* exhibits into a twenty-five-minute work of modernist experimentation that becomes a sharp polemic on the experience of Jews as an oppressed minority in the Soviet Union.

On the surface the plot is a simple story about an arranged Jewish shtetl marriage between a poor girl forced to forsake her impoverished true love for the rich but doltish groom in an arranged marriage. Unlike the Yiddish folk tales of Sholem Aleichem from which this narrative is drawn, there is no wry humor here to undercut the sadness, just unrelenting pathos leading up to the final tragic ending. The pleasures and meanings in *Jewish Wedding* are nuanced and the effect is layered in such a way that we sense the richness of the cultural life that struggles to express itself and experience the loss that accompanies its exclusion—something several of the artistic collaborators sharing the stage with Yakobson in this work had also experienced.

In 1960, long before he set out to make *Jewish Wedding*, Yakobson and his wife had visited the last remaining synagogue in Leningrad to observe how Jews gestured when they conversed and prayed, as material for a future ballet. Like many of Leningrad's 300,000 Jews, neither he nor his wife had ever been inside a synagogue because of the tacit understanding that doing so could be construed as expressing religious practice or affiliation and thus was dangerous. The historian Shmuel Ettinger describes how in this era "an enlightened Jew who wished to make a way for himself in Russian society had to stress his aversion to Judaism, either by religious conversion or by taking part in the criticism of Judaism for its 'deficiencies.'"[78]

Jewish Wedding represents the antithesis of this stance and it does so by acknowledging the work of three artists whose aesthetic was censored in various ways in their respective media: the composer Dmitriy Shostakovich, the painter Marc Chagall, and the writer Sholem Aleichem. At first glance *Jewish Wedding*'s style of overt emotionalism and exaggerated gesturing might seem melodramatic, but it is more a device by Yakobson to create through choreography what he must have sensed as the fragile sorrow in these other artists' works on Jewish themes. Melodrama, like irony, opens a gap between the subject and the artwork so that the author could be said to ironize rather than proselytize his ideas. Yakobson, a pragmatist, knew how to use exaggeration as a distancing device so that the artwork would not be so overt a social critique that it might be banned outright. Still, *Jewish Wedding* is an unfailingly brave work. The specific gesture and dance vocabulary Yakobson creates in this ballet are drawn from shtetl mannerisms and gestures blended with folk and classical dance steps. It is enhanced by Valery Levental's decor, which is styled deliberately in the spirit of the prohibited painter Marc Chagall's surrealist phantasmagorias of Jewish life in outlying villages in Russia. In *Jewish Wedding,* Yakobson creates the choreographic equivalent of pictorial flatness as transcendence, distorting stage space in a manner that echoes the visual techniques of the anti-naturalist symbolist painters Vincent van Gogh and Paul Gauguin, who had also influenced Chagall.[79] The ballet suggests Yakobson's personal identification with religion and ritual as forces that code movement. His slipping in of the Yiddish culture of the shtetl—a vanishing culture of a small world—is effective in part because it is so non-didactic; it is a part of the Jewish folk culture imaginary that he introduced to the Soviet ballet stage.

Chagall's scenic designs influenced other leading Jewish artists in Soviet Russia, providing a visual model for how the everyday shtetl life of Sholem Aleichem's stories could become what Igor Golomstock called

Jewish Wedding (1971), the Bride and Poor Groom duet,
Elena Selivanova and Aleksandr Stepin, Choreographic Miniatures,
Leningrad. Photo: Daniil Savelyev.

Jewish Wedding (1971), Elena Selivanova (the Bride) and Dmitriy
Vovk (the Rich Groom), Choreographic Miniatures, Leningrad.
Photo: Daniil Savelyev.

metaphysical realism and a means to give expression to "age-old inner-most meaning." It is possible to see an implicit choreography in Chagall's images; for the Jewish actor Solomon Mikhoels, for instance, "acquaintance with Chagall's sketches changed all his own creative individuality, the rhythmic quality of his body, of his speech and movements."[80]

Dmitriy Shostakovich's equally risky Piano Trio No. 2 in E minor, Op. 67, composed in the style of a shtetl trio of klezmorim, gives the work its sound environment, with the music's mournfulness suggesting the sadness that tinges gaiety in Aleichem's Yiddish tales of shtetl life.[81] Shostakovich's score also makes the *sound* of Jewish folk motifs present in the ballet. Musicologist James Loeffler, in writing about Jewish identity in Russian music, has commented on the long-standing dualities framing the figure of the Jewish musician in Soviet Russia. "From the mid-nineteenth century onward, the figure of the Jewish musician functioned as a virtual screen onto which Russians projected a larger set of elemental questions about art, nation, and identity. As a minority concentrated on the empire's Western border yet with cultural origins in the East, the Jews were perfectly suited to stand in for modern Russia's own dualistic identity as a civilization caught between Europe and Asia, East and West. The Jewish musician proved particularly irresistible as a useful symbolic double for the Russian intelligentsia."[82] Yakobson casts three dancers as slightly comical onstage musicians, adding a teasing note to this reference to the intelligentsia.

The ballet opens on a note of extreme musical dissonance as the wild rushing dance of cello, piano, and violin that begins Shostakovich's Piano Trio, effectively a requiem, unfolds. Shostakovich's score, written in 1944, in the midst of World War II and dedicated to his close friend Ivan Sollertinsky, the Russian critic, musician, and Jew who had died recently at age forty-one, surges with mad fugues, frenzied dances, and Jewish-styled klezmer melodic lines so that the impression is of a whole village of chaotic and distressed sound—making it a perfect companion to the cast of twelve characters in the ballet. Indeed the choreography maps so tightly onto the score that there is a music-box neatness to the way the characters match the musical motifs. At times even gestures are synchronized to match a musical passage note for note.

The score is the base of the work's layers of thematic polyphony, the phenomenon of multiple voices speaking through one utterance that

Bakhtin called heteroglossia. Shostakovich had developed a musical equivalent of this—what Orlando Figes calls "double-speak in his musical language"—to negotiate delivering a message in one idiom to please the officials, and another, beneath this triumphant voice, that was "the carefully concealed voice of satire and dissent only audible to those who had felt the suffering his music expressed."[83] Whether Shostakovich intended this association or not it is particularly fitting since the man to whom the trio is dedicated, Sollertinsky, was an active participant in the philosopher Mikhail Bakhtin's circles, even going so far in his student days as to follow him from seminar to seminar to hear his lectures in Petrograd's intelligentsia circles during the years 1924–1929. This multi-voicedness theory of Bakhtin to describe a grouping of phenomena sharing a common trait is also a strategy Yakobson uses by layering various cultural references inside formal dance structures. The whole ballet is a vivid portrait of a past moment and, metaphorically, a moment of pain that feels very present. All of the performers in *Jewish Wedding* dance with a doll-like tightness. Their limbs and torsos move as if they were wooden parts with no range beyond stiff angular actions propelled, or even controlled, by outside forces. Yakobson's choreography captures the nuances of how puppet limbs jump with a sudden start and then fall limply back once the tension on the string is released—a realistic touch that gives a tactile quality to the air of hopelessness that shrouds the ballet.

Conceptually the design of *Jewish Wedding* began with Yakobson's readings of Aleichem's shtetl tales and his viewing of Chagall's paintings, which were banned in Russia at that time but available privately to Yakobson through the generosity of a curator at the Hermitage Museum in Leningrad. There were significant risks for even this kind of virtual collaboration with Chagall. Chagall's work had been labeled formalist and he had been so thoroughly purged from the history of Russian art by the caretakers of socialist realism that in 1967, when a collection of Anatoly Lunacharsky's essays was published that included mention of Chagall from the 1910s, the Soviet intelligentsia was surprised to learn he was still alive. In 1973, after decades of living in Paris, Chagall received an invitation from the Soviet Ministry of Culture to visit Moscow and Leningrad, where an exhibition of his work had been organized in the Tretyakov Gallery. Throughout Chagall's visit to the USSR the KGB carefully monitored his movements, to the extent of overseeing his reunion with his sister and her children in their private apartment in Leningrad and forbidding others access to him.[84] He was aware of Yakobson and wanted to meet him—Yakobson too was eager to see Chagall—but the authorities kept Yakobson confined to his hotel in Moscow, where he was touring with his company. Thus a meeting between the two never took place.

The former Kirov director and choreographer Fyodor Lopukhov, although not a fan of Jewish subject matter, shared his enthusiasm for *Jewish Wedding* with Yakobson privately in a report he wrote about the Choreographic Miniatures repertoire. Since Lopukhov's wife, Klara Lopukhova, worked for Yakobson as a coach, Lopukhov often attended rehearsals and was very interested in the troupe.[85] Lopukhov wrote about *Jewish Wedding* among other Yakobson ballets, but never published his essay because of the risks.[86] The following excerpt from Lopukhov's unpublished 1971 report offers a remarkable glimpse into the convoluted ideological justification he employed as he tried to refute Soviet censorship of Yakobson:

> Now I am going to speak about some of Yakobson's choreographic miniatures that had been prohibited to show to the public: *Wedding Cortège* and *Negro Concert*. I am not going to disprove the decision to prohibit them; nonetheless, I am going to share my vision on those miniatures. In my view, they were quite bright miniatures. Today my analysis probably will not be published, but if the situation changes tomorrow, it can become possible. . . .
>
> Some misunderstanding took place with the Yakobson's *Wedding Cortège*. During rehearsals Yakobson mentioned some Chagall who ostensibly had betrayed his Motherland and escaped abroad. I am not going to justify him at all. One's attempts to plead thirst of new art for his escape abroad are ridiculous, since it is obviously not true. Moreover, the most advanced masters of choreography are Soviet ones; because the most advanced (Soviet) ideology, which does not exist abroad, serves as a basis of their art. Lenin's vision opened new horizons for the art of choreography and provided understanding of the essence of real life not embellished with ideological lie.
>
> I state that this Chagall did not influence Yakobson with his choreo-novel *Wedding Cortège* at all. It was purely Yakobson's art

and had nothing to do with notorious "Zionism." Moreover, it had nothing to do with Jewish issue, it just portrayed the story about working Jews, which was a mixture of humor and sadness. Yakobson's creation showed how these people kept their obsolete traditions, about which they themselves told each other humorous anecdotes. . . .

Wedding Cortège was a genre scene of Jewish wedding with all typical attributes. It humorously presented how a poor rite seemed to be a luxurious cortège to those people. This act was performed as a choreographic anecdote expressed through poses and movements of the dance conveying the color of that society.

By that time Yakobson had already had experience in creating performances based on Jewish themes, which was called *A Couple In Love* and was in full color performed by performers of the Kirov Theater of Opera and Ballet, Irina Pevzner (Irina Yakobson) and Mironov. . . .

In his *Wedding Cortège* Yakobson showed real color of Jewish life-style without a retrospect to ancient Judaism, because modern Jews live rather different lives. Thus, their life-style with obsolete traditions was shown truthfully with no figment. Yakobson resolutely portrayed them in a satiric way.

A performer Kuznetsova played a role of the bride very naturally that again indicated high level of Russian choreography.

The performance truthfully conveyed the way of life of poor working Jews who had always evoked feeling of compassion. Possibly, some hidden Zionists did not like this truth of our time, because they might have wanted a recreation of "Zion" and liked to see characters like Raquel and her father from Feuchtwanger's *The Spanish Ballad* or *The Jewish War* on the stage. However, this all is just a past.

I talk about Yakobson's creation according to what others talk about it. . . . Anyway, Yakobson staged *Wedding Cortège* brilliantly, complying with the sense of beauty and, thus, beating "Zionism." Significance of this creation for our time is huge and I think that its prohibition was a mistake caused by some misunderstanding. . . . In my view, there was nothing harmful for Soviet ideology in the performance.[87]

In this excerpt Lopukhov repeatedly attempts to separate Yakobson from Chagall, Zionist sentiments, and non-Russian values, issues about the ballet that Soviet censors had identified as particularly irksome. Instead Lopukhov tried to convince them that the tone of Yakobson's portrait of Jews was "satiric," and as such might even irritate "hidden Zionists" rather than please them because what is depicted is so far from a laudatory portrait of *"The Jewish War"* that *Jewish Wedding* actually ends up "beating Zionism." It is a brave essay, and also in its own way tragic, as one senses Lopukhov's desperation to open a possibility for this ballet to be seen.

As if offering something in exchange that the officials *can* censor, Lopukhov continues, suggesting that he does support the prohibition of another new Yakobson ballet, *Negro Concert (Negrityanskiy kontsert,* 1971). Lopukhov is clever, because by way of discussing why *Negro Concerto* (or *Ebony Concerto*) should be banned, he opens up a space to in fact praise it,

(*Left to right*) V. Bogdanov, Anatoliy Gridin, Yakobson (*kneeling*), Fyodor Lopukhov, Klara Lopukhova, and Irina Yakobson at the Choreographic Miniatures studio, Leningrad, ca. 1972. Photo: Vladimir Zenzinov.

specifying its original presentation of tap dance references and its caution in not oversimplifying "Negro" dance. Finally he concludes that it is the use of the word "concert" in the title that is the censurable issue since the ballet does not fit the structural definition of a concert as used in music, that is, a work that "contains different parts expressing cohesive content." Lopukhov writes: "*Negro Concert,* although very professionally staged, was not a concert meaning a big performance like a symphony or sonata. I would call this creation 'capriccio' (a short performance not encompassing the whole essence of black peoples) rather than 'concert.' *African Capriccio* could have been a good name for it," he concludes.[88]

The choreographic action of *Jewish Wedding* unfolds along a snaking processional path, with each character, costumed in Levental's interpretations of Chagall's colorful and fantastical clothing and face-painted makeup, making an entrance along the front apron of the stage. As they enter, each of these characters, or set of characters—in the instance of the parents of the groom, parents of the bride, and trio of musicians—dances a brief opening soliloquy that establishes who they are and their temperament and perspectives. After these brief physical introductions the dancers exit on the opposite side of the stage only to reappear farther upstage seconds later. An evocative physicalization of Chagall's similar use of space as little narrative compartments, this choreographic and staging device allowed painter and choreographer simultaneously to present events from different times and places in the same manner that stories are depicted visually in Russian icon paintings.[89] Strategically it also removes the narrative from the literal, and thus more dangerous, realm of realism. Perhaps this is a final riposte from Yakobson to Stalin's false utopianism, particularly its manifestation in Soviet cinema musicals of the 1930s and 1940s, which depicted models of utopian worlds with "life not as it [was], but as it will be."[90] Here is Jewish life as it was and will not be again.

In the late 1930s Bakhtin had coined the theory of the "chronotope," a formulation that insisted on the appropriateness of a specific conception of space to each historical era.[91] *Jewish Wedding* is marked by a radical conception of space, a dividing of the imaginary expanse of the stage into small, boxcar-like units of rolling spaces. The two extremes of space the Soviet era is known for are the cramped quarters of forced communal apartments and the huge rural expanse of massively collectivized farms. Both these extremes of space are conceptually present in Yakobson's ballet as an unsettling aspect of the characters' lives. His use of both space and time in *Jewish Wedding* is consciously anti-realistic and highly illusionistic, an original chronotope. Even though all twelve of the performers are on stage for the entire ballet, none except the bride and her beloved seem to be able to see or emotionally connect with one another. Levental's painted scrims and his restricting of the dancers' actions to the narrow serpentine path they trace one by one leave large expanses of the stage empty of any dancing much of the time. These are bodies that have learned how to act out their dramas in tight domestic quarters with the suggestion of a massive expanse of the Soviet land around them.

Jewish Wedding opens with seven separate processional entrances along this narrow path—one for each of the characters or groups of characters, as in the case of the three musicians and the parents of the bride and groom. The friend of the bride is the first to enter the stage and embark on the snaking path to the offstage synagogue. She is spirited, breathlessly miming her news with a young woman's excitement reminiscent of Lise's daydreaming about becoming a wife and mother in Sir Frederick Ashton's *La Fille mal gardée*. Traveling solo, she conveys through a gestural vocabulary of bouncing little arm and torso gestures a hyper-gaiety and a sense of delivering deliciously secret news to the audience in the movement equivalent of a conspiratorial whisper. She jubilantly shares her secret that her friend is getting married with hands that flutter back and forth near her ears as if she were also hearing the news she is spreading. Next her hands swiftly describe the bulging curve of a pregnant abdomen and she tilts backward, all the while her feet pivot inward and out in an excited counterpoint. Snapping back upright she leans forward, greeting imaginary wedding guests with encircling arms as she moves toward the wings. The rabbi enters next and the spotlight shifts to his brief gestural monologue as the bride's friend freezes on her path upstage. The rabbi, too, chatters away in a physical language of busy hand gestures and bucking leaps with his legs and arms shooting forward as if he were both the rider and the racing horse on which he is seated. "The boy is rich and everything should be okay," he signs. "It is all arranged just as it should be, just so," he signals as his hands straighten up imaginary piles of documents around him, stamping seals and imposing official order as he pats the air and his head nods excitedly to the repeated motif of the piano with a note-for-action symmetry so literal it almost seems satiric.

Irony and satire hover at the margins of all the affectionately grotesque distortions of character types the dancers portray. It is as if Yakobson were mockingly imitating the ethnicity of "Jewish" gesticulations by having the dancers echo each metrical accent in the music. Three dancers portraying the musicians enter, miming playing on their invisible violin, flute, and piano—although the actual Shostakovich trio we hear is scored for violin, cello, and piano. Their actions are rhythmic and tightly mechanistic as they joyously mime bows sliding across strings and fingers pounding out notes on the keyboard, all the while staying in a tightly arranged little cluster like a real klezmer combo. Then the parents of the couple enter separately. First come the wealthy and aloof parents of the groom, holding hands formally as if in a quadrille, tilting back pompously as they gesture haughtily to the audience that they imagine staring enviously at them. Next the poor parents of the bride enter in their faded and fraying clothing that hangs loosely on their thin frames, their shoulders hunched and their hands gesturing beseechingly upward as they skitter toward the wings—where the bride's mother hops onto her husband's back to be carried off, signaling that their poverty makes a carriage or even a horse impossible.

The sense of alienating unfamiliarity that attaches to every visual element in the ballet carries through to the exaggerated makeup the dancers wear, their features skewed by the heavy black outlining of their eyes, a white square over one eye, or a jagged red slash across a forehead. Just as Shostakovich's violent articulations rumble through the dancers' bodies, animated by Yakobson's choreography, facial features are also skewed toward a fascination with violence and chaos that parallels those of figures in Chagall's paintings. The final two dancers to enter are the bride and groom and it is immediately evident that there is no love in this relationship for her, only an opportunistic business arrangement for both sets of parents. Costumed all in white, with her face a ghostly gray, she scales the air struggling to escape the grasp of the infantile groom who lunges at her, one finger pressed into his mouth like a pacifier. Accompanied by the ascending cries of the violin, she claws the air, her actions darting and agitated, suggesting the desperation of a half-animal, half-human creature like the hybrid human-with-cow-head figures in a Chagall painting.

Lastly, the impoverished lover who cherishes the bride, and who in turn is loved by her, enters alone in halting steps, his body caved inward

Jewish Wedding, Klezmorim, Choreographic Miniatures,
Leningrad, 1973. Photo: Daniil Savelyev.

as if an essential organ had already been removed. To tremulous bowing on the cello he shudders, sobs, and keeps folding himself inward. He advances, staggering forward with the halting hopelessness of someone dancing his own requiem, or just proceeding directly to the grave. He is the most tragic figure in the ballet and the only character with two extended dance passages—one a dream sequence with the bride and the other a final soliloquy of remorse as he loses her. He begins the duet with his body animated with passion, embracing his love as he moves in synchronicity with her. This dance and its attendant happiness, however, are only wishful dreaming. After a brief fantasy interlude of dancing with the bride, this groom collapses in misery at the front of the stage, his dream shattered. This despondent figure, the ballet's central protagonist, is not only a Jew, but also a failed hero and thus was a double affront to the socialist aesthetic. Jewish studies scholar Harriet Murav has identified one of the goals of socialist construction as "the construction of a new Jew. . . . The stoop-shouldered, anemic, sickly Jewish male, the *shtetl luftmentsh*, was to be transformed into an able-bodied, muscled, heroic worker."[92] In *Jewish Wedding* this transformation never takes place. Just when he had been disappearing from Jewish life and cultural depictions in literature in Soviet Russia, Yakobson made not only the *shtetl luftmentsh* visible again, but also his physical and emotional collapse a featured event on the ballet stage. As if in direct opposition to the USSR's project of remaking the human being, he was unmaking the new Jewish male.

The entire ballet lasts just under half an hour, and in that time it swiftly folds together its story of personal anguish, a village's tensions, ethnic insularity, class friction, the collapse of space, and Jewish despair bordering

Jewish Wedding (1971), the Bride and Poor
Groom duet, Vakhrusheva and Igor Khokhlov,
Choreographic Miniatures, Leningrad.
Photographer unknown.

on insanity against a background of beautiful yet grotesque distortion and a re-inscription of the reality behind the Soviet ideal. Shostakovich's score in *Jewish Wedding* is replete with the musical grotesque—tuneful melodies of frenzied dances intersect Jewish klezmer tunes and parodies of Jewish wedding music—so that taken together all the visual, sonic, and choreographic elements evoke a quality of existential irony.

Visually, Chagall's paintings also pair images of suffering with themes of love. These are tempered with kabalistic mysticism; the figures, many of them brides and grooms, often fly suspended in the air over the shtetl town of Vitebsk. Yakobson echoes this image in a poignant duet between the bride and her true love where he embraces her in a series of cascading falls that have her spilling headfirst across his body, each time closer and closer to the floor as if both were suddenly freed from gravity and the weight of their sorrows. They steal this moment before the repetition of the march to the chuppah resumes and he and the bride recede back into their separate paths winding upstage. As the obsessive repetitions in the music grow, so does the scale of doom and menace that hangs over all. This danger is suggested visually through the garish colors and precipitous angles of the painted scenery of houses and a floating table, as well as through the asymmetry of the dancers' violently mismatched lapels, color patches, and make-up. Their postures, too, seem abstractions of real-life actions, like the hunched and drooping shoulders of the poor suitor amplified for the stage.

These are images of beauty under siege, of emotions struggling out of containment, metaphors for artists whose struggle to be honest was also a struggle for free expression. "The Hassidic Jew must free himself from his sadness to make contact with God," Chagall once said, explaining, "If I weren't a Jew I wouldn't have become an artist."[93] Indeed, if Yakobson also were not a Jew and had not endured the dangers of being a social outsider under Stalin, he would likely have been a very different kind of artist. Certainly he would not have been as steeled for the challenges of being a Soviet-era modernist choreographer with an interest in articulating ethnic difference.

Yakobson tried for four years to get approval to show *Jewish Wedding* to the public, beginning in early 1971, when he completed choreographing it. His wife remembers that each year there was a viewing, and each year the prohibition on it was renewed. Finally in 1975, with Yakobson's reputation growing internationally after his choreography for a Luigi Nono opera at La Scala, he decided to show the ballet. The director of Lenkontsert,

Kirill Sadovnikov, heard about the plan and begged Irina to persuade him to wait for the next commission's review. "Foolishly, I persuaded him not to show *Wedding Cortège (Jewish Wedding)*," she recalled. "He was very upset. However, the commission did arrive: they saw the ballet, heard all arguments in its favor advanced by Leningrad's critics, and left without saying yes or no. Leonid waited impatiently for the officials' call, not leaving the apartment. Finally, the phone rang," Irina said. The caller was Tamara Andreyevna Petrova, from the local committee, who informed him that they authorized the release of the ballet, provided that he change the ending. "What utter disrespect for human dignity—to make a protagonist scramble on his knees!" she chastised him. "This infuriated Yakobson," his widow said. "Have I ever tried to teach you how to carry out ideological campaigns?" he retorted. "Your job is to tell me why you object to this ballet on ideological grounds. Whether my character scrambles on his knees, slithers on his stomach, or hops on one foot is my business, not yours—since in choreography you are ignorant!" Petrova hung up. But someone else called and informed Yakobson that *"Wedding Cortège* could be performed on stage—this happened just a few months before Yakobson's death," Irina said.[94]

Gestures and Embodiment

With the completion of *Jewish Wedding* in 1971, Yakobson radically expanded the style, tone, and subject matter of Soviet ballet. Yakobson's wife, who assisted him in the staging of *Jewish Wedding,* recalled how Yakobson established a behavioral code that he insisted every dancer follow for this and all subsequent works he choreographed. From the first day of rehearsals, as he set about inventing the choreography, Yakobson demanded that the full company, even dancers who specialized in classical roles and who would probably never dance a genre piece like *Jewish Wedding,* be present in the studio for the entire process. "Everyone had to learn the part of the bride, both boys and girls, big and small. All other roles as well," Irina said. "This is not to say that the dancers were merely standing by watching: they had to dance every pas. Sometimes he would turn to the dancers on the margins of the room and ask them to repeat a phrase he had just taught one in the center," she recalled. "One would ask, to what end?"

she asked rhetorically. "They would never perform this role on stage anyway. True, the aim was not for the dancers to memorize the movements per se, although in the future that, too, might prove useful. Rather, L. V. felt that it was essential for the dancers' bodies to become acculturated to his *plastique* with all its stylistic nuances, to learn to express themselves in a wide range of dance vernaculars, and to be transformed into multifunctional instruments capable of articulating his ideas. 'I am offering you expressive form, and it is your job to imbue it with meaning,' he often said."[95]

To have the entire Choreographic Miniatures company effectively become a village, the village of *Jewish Wedding,* is an interesting inclusionary strategy. It eliminated a divide between spectators and dancers initially within the company and contributed to a stylistic cohesion that flows from one character to the next. It also made all the dancers working with Yakobson complicit in this preservation of Jewish culture. Their work became a collective action of memory retrieval and reinvention, which was significant on another level: Yakobson's choreography was the last stage of his project of archiving Jewish gestures, which he had begun with that first visit to the old villages of Kishinev in 1949. Scholar Carrie Noland has theorized on the significance of gesture as a means of identifying, preserving, and inculcating values and images into a culture. In *Agency and Embodiment* she suggests ways in which culture is both embodied and challenged though corporeal performance, an act of agency that she calls "kinetic acts as they contingently reiterate learned behaviors." In her formulation, gestures are seen as a type of inscription, a way to "pars[e] the body into signifying . . . units" so that it can reveal human anatomy disciplined through a set of bodily practices that are specific to a culture.[96] In time, and through repetition, like that of performance, these gestures that were once shaped by culture eventually come to be representative of it. Applying this credo of Noland's allows us to consider how the dancers in the studio learning all the roles in *Jewish Wedding* are undergoing a cultural conditioning. In this instance the process is twofold: first they are acclimatized to Yakobson's style of working, a variation on the Russian system of ballet training in which they had been formed, and then, even more importantly, they learn the cultural forms of a Jewish body by practicing the distinctive gestures of *Jewish Wedding*'s choreography that Yakobson has "found" and archived as dance.

In Noland's formulation, "gestures literally transform the bodies that perform them." As a result meanings in a gesture become embodied on their practitioners. "It is by gesturing that bodies become inscribed with meanings in cultural environments," Noland explains. Yakobson's decision to insist all dancers learn all the roles in *Jewish Wedding* was, on one level, a practical way to inscribe this meaning into his dancers. The dancers in the company he created in 1970, and who performed *Jewish Wedding,* were drawn from many different training backgrounds. Their skill level was more uneven than that of company members in the Kirov, where he was accustomed to having the most technically brilliant dancers in the Soviet Union available to him. Acclimatizating a new company of dancers to his working process by having them "try on" the gestural forms of shtetl Jews vividly marked his dances as a cultural production challenging the dynamic between dance and Soviet society. Can "the body that performs the routine" eventually "[perform] culture itself?" Noland inquires, wondering about how gesture eventually shapes the culture that initially had shaped it.[97]

This faith in the capacity of bodily techniques, movements, and gestures to preserve and even influence culture echoes French sociologist Marcel Mauss's belief that "the human body becomes a classed, gendered body—to wit, a *social fact*—through the act of gesturing."[98] Certainly this is a key premise of how dance works to invent a language of kinesthetic experience on the stage. Noland extends Mauss's argument that "there simply may not be a 'natural way' for adults to do things"—that "culture divorce[s] the meaning of gestures from the way they make the body feel" by acknowledging that the body, a priori, speaks through cultural frames.[99] What this meant for the spectators of *Jewish Wedding* at the time of its premiere, when the Soviet Union was still a closed society, was that the authorities indeed had reason to fear Yakobson's dances. The same act of empathy that he was inspiring from his dancers by making them learn each other's roles could extend to audiences, inspiring spectators to "resonate to dance and other movement performances in acts of empathy that may have an ethical, socializing function in human communities."[100] In fact, *Jewish Wedding* is almost all gesture with very little action in it that looks like traditional ballet. This is still true more than forty years after its premiere and was certainly the case when it was created. The dancers in the ballet move with a doleful wooden quality, but they are not cute and hollow like puppets; instead they have the affect of numbed avatars, the detritus of a failed social experiment.

Yakobson also rethinks the way ballet uses the body in *Jewish Wedding* so that it becomes a desolate yet socially recognizable repository of experiences. For Jews the body already has a complicated history as the locus of religious rules rendered as physical prohibitions, and in *Jewish Wedding* the companion emotional dimension of each character is added to this portrait. Practices ranging from circumcision to sexual and dietary laws all inscribe on the body affiliations of community and social regulation.[101] For the most part these are rarely seen, internal modifications, visible generally through behavioral choices. If, as anthropologist Mary Douglas contends, the body is one of the places in which social concerns are symbolically enacted, and threats to the body politic are mirrored in the care and treatment of the physical body, then Yakobson's choreography on Jewish themes could be read as performing allegorical truths about constraints on life for Jews in the USSR.[102]

In *Jewish Wedding* the use of turned-in, toe-to-toe body stances; heads held oddly tilted off to one side; and arms that move of a piece from the shoulders as if the ribcage were frozen, reference deeper knowledge of the forms that cultural anguish can assume. Many of the positions that the spurned groom and bride's poor parents move through are deliberately grotesque—knotted postures that feel like raw grief. While inside Russia earlier choreographers like Michel Fokine, Vaslav Nijinsky, and Kasyan Goleizovsky had experimented with postures that challenged the idea of turnout, they did so as a choreographic innovation rather than as a training tool (as Yakobson did). One dance referent to Yakobson's use of inward foot and body positions to depict emotional pain is Bronislava Nijinska's constructivist snapped-parallel-feet poses in her *Les Noces*. In this 1923 ballet she too depicts a Russian wedding as a sorrowful ritual, particularly for the bride.[103] Indeed, in the final moments of Yakobson's ballet the abandoned suitor piteously crawls slowly downstage on his knees if his stature had suddenly been halved. With each drag of a knee forward he pauses to collect his falling tears from one eye and then the other. Finally he drops to the floor at the front of the stage and, slowing, mimes swirling them in his cupped hand and gulping them down as if they were a poisonous brew. As the violinist plays slowly descending tones, the groom folds inward. A last pleading reach upward with his hand still

Jewish Wedding, final scene, Aleksandr Stepin (Poor Groom),
Choreographic Miniatures, Leningrad, 1973. Photographer unknown.

receives nothing in return so he hugs one knee to his chest; knots his hand underneath; and resting his cheek against his leg, consoles himself by closing his limbs into his body. The solo violin that had been his musical companion until this point thins and then vanishes. The groom's swallowing of his tears could be viewed as a reference to the ritual of tasting salt water to remember the bitterness of slavery during the Passover Seder, yet even without this religious frame, its sorrow feels softly, pitifully, absolute.

The Russian ballet critic Valeriy Zvezdochkin has commented on how Yakobson was asked by party authorities to change these final minutes of *Jewish Wedding* (which he refers to below by its de-ethnicized Soviet title):

When attempting to obtain approval for the production of *Svadeb-niy kortezh* ten years later, Yakobson was asked to change the plastic [features] of the finale. Those who have seen this ballet will surely remember the concluding scene, where the pitiable bridegroom, having lost all hope of being reunited with his beloved and crushed by this misfortune, scrambles across the floor writhing in agony, and then, grief-stricken, crouching even lower, collects his tears

into the palm of his hand and gulps them down. This highly evocative mise-en-scène was judged by the Leningrad artistic committee
too pessimistic, and [therefore] ideologically flawed.[104]

Zvezdochkin wrote this statement in 1989, voicing, from the safety of
many years post-Stalin, his indignation at the absurdity of the officials'
censorship demands for it to be re-choreographed. Equally evident is the
depth of sorrow he sees in the ballet's final image, years after initially having viewed it. Both responses—those of the officials and the dance critic—
attest to the impact of Yakobson's work on the Soviet cultural leadership.
What Yakobson did mattered so much because the conversation that
framed his work stretched well beyond ballet.

Jewish Wedding exists spiritually at the crossroads of what political sci-
entist Zvi Gitelman has characterized in another context as an active and
passive cultural identity. He argues that especially in the case of the Russian Jews, it is useful to distinguish between two types of culture and two
types of identity. The first of these—active and passive culture—has to
do with the creation and consumption of cultural artifacts, and one can
imagine ballets fitting neatly into the cultural artifact category of visual
performance culture as part of this. Gitelman defines passive culture as
"patterns of thought and behavior which are not necessarily consciously
ethnic" but "are derived from or are typical of the ethnic group," and here
as well is material Yakobson mined in shaping each character that appears
in one of his Jewish-themed ballets.[105] Dance invention exists in this territory of thought and behavior reconceived and amplified into a graspable
stage image ready for perception and understanding by others.

While the Soviet system successfully discouraged most active Jewish
identification, Gitelman asserts that it was paradoxically maintained through
what he calls the category of passive Jewish identity, that official identification rules and anti-Semitic policies in fact helped define and reinforce
the boundaries of Jewishness. Yakobson's ballets with Jewish references
negotiated a space of public display between these cultural categories,
playing between the inclusion of active and passive references and disclosing them within the frame of ballets. The balance of literal and hidden
references was shaped by external constraints so that a cute folktale or
genre study ballet on the surface might have a passive, subversive Jewish
content nested inside.[106]

Along with passive culture and identity content, other strategies of conveying meaning were also operating in Yakobson's ballets. What probably resonated most profoundly for his Soviet audiences, the majority of whom were not Jewish and knew little if anything about Jewish practices, were their choreographic daring and dramatic intensity. The multivocality of his ballets, their layering of different narrative interpretations, also allowed non-Jewish responses just as the parodic intrinsic elements of Shostakovich's Jewish music references in his scores relayed compound meanings to a range of Soviet viewers.[107] Gitelman claims that active and passive culture are always being negotiated in differing ratios, and always in response to the surrounding political and social context. In regard to the situation for Jews in the USSR, he notes that "in times of great pressure, such as 1948–53, the proportion of active identifiers, and the amount of overt cultural activity, decline. In times of relative relaxation, such as the mid-1970s, active identity and culture grow, especially if external forces feed them."[108]

These two time periods correspond precisely to the first and the last Jewish-themed ballets Yakobson made—with the 1949 *Jewish Dance* (subsequently *A Couple in Love*) being marked by light and passive references to Jewishness and the 1970 *Jewish Wedding* being a far bolder, more overt work that makes it subject and its political position more obvious. So the shifting social climate in regard to Soviet Jews does map with surprising fidelity onto not only what Yakobson attempted with these Jewish-themed ballets, but also the relative ease and difficulty with which he succeeded in getting them out into the world in different political periods. He was always adamant, however, that these were not political statements but artworks arrived at through his impressions from life around him. He too was a consumer of passive and active Jewish culture during the Soviet era, as well as the author of some of its most transcendent performance images. In a 1971 interview soon after he had finished *Jewish Wedding,* Yakobson said about the sources of his dance inspiration:

> My choreography, I'd say, arises out of my observations—out of the impressions that I ceaselessly accumulate and store away. They comprise what I have seen, what I see, and what I experience. Whether I am sun-tanning on the beach, whether I am watching kids scuffling on the street, whether I am viewing a film, all the

while I am squirreling away impressions. But this doesn't mean that I use my observations "raw," that what I see, I stage. No! From a street fight I may take one movement and use it in a ballet miniature that describes, shall we say, a passionate kiss, or I may put the movement for the episode of the kiss into the ballet scene of a street fight. This gestural translation from one situation to another lends depth and three-dimensionality to each fragment.[109]

This statement about his working method and how he manipulates the visual inspirations that flowed through him into his choreography is particularly revealing for what it says about Yakobson as a collagist—a choreographer who captures seconds of human action glimpsed in the world and then reorders them with an eye toward the impression he wants them to convey in the theater. Life is not the constant here as much as his vision and the narrative he wants to unfold with these gestures no matter what the context of their original source.

Although *Jewish Wedding* was finished in January 1970, and shown to local Communist Party officials and Ministry of Culture representatives in January, the initial response was to ban it as ideologically unacceptable. A rising young Russian professional then, who was interviewed in 2003 and subsequently requested anonymity, remembered being present at the initial showing of *Jewish Wedding* for party officials. He recalled how shocked the officials were when they discovered Yakobson intended this ballet to be part of the opening program of new works to launch his company, Choreographic Miniatures, which he began rehearsing in March of 1970. "It was like a test," he recalled. "Leonid Yakobson was very strong and he decided now is a good moment for me to fight the bureaucracy. He said, 'No, I will never cancel this ballet. I am determined to show this performance to an audience.'"[110]

It would be four years before *Jewish Wedding* would be permitted a performance in Leningrad. In the interim Yakobson's ballet would have an unusual path into acceptance via Akademgorodok, a massive scientific research complex in distant Siberia located south of Novosibirsk and Chelyabinsk, a city created during World War II when Stalin moved weapons production to the isolated region. (In fact Chelyabinsk would eventually produce most of the Soviet Union's tanks, a distinction that earned it the nickname "Tank City.") These seem unlikely places in which to present

Yakobson's unusual and contemporary ballet works. What distinguished them was their populations' interest in being spectators of dance with meaningful content. This was particularly important given that Yakobson was being watched closely by party officials to see if he could indeed attract full theaters of average Soviet audiences to programs of his own company dancing his works. The minister of culture was one official, and there were numerous others, who expected, and hoped, that he would fail, particularly in these government-created towns where, by design, the populations were made up of mostly scientific or industrial workers.

Novosibirsk had been built during Stalin's industrialization push and it rapidly became one of the largest industrial centers in Siberia. The scientific research complex of Akademgorodok was constructed several miles south of the city center in 1957 and it was home to several distinguished scientific research centers, including the Siberian branch of the Academy of Sciences and several research institutions and universities. It was in this setting in 1970 that Yakobson's supporter, a young Soviet social innovator who had founded a ballet club, organized performances of Soviet cultural stars in these remote Siberian locations. He was familiar with not only Yakobson's work but also the difficulties he was facing in obtaining permission to perform *Jewish Wedding*. He had discovered Yakobson while in his early twenties, and had been immediately excited by his work. "I observed what was going on in the Kirov Theater and at the Bolshoi and I discovered for myself that Leonid Yakobson was a genius," he recalled in an interview in Saint Petersburg in 2003.

"For professionals, amateurs and dance lovers of course, Yakobson's history was not a secret," he explained in regard to how well-known the choreographer and his difficulties with suppression were by the early 1970s. "It was very difficult to read some articles about Yakobson, but there were many rumors in the dance community and in the dance network about him. . . . I thought it would be wonderful for us to bring Leonid Yakobson's dance company to perform in Siberia, especially in this scientific town with a population of 40,000. It was a very intellectual place," he said, having trained in geophysics at Novosibirsk State University. He understood that this was a dangerous undertaking, but he also realized that bringing Yakobson's new company, Choreographic Miniatures, to a town far from Leningrad might help it break through the prohibition that forbade performances of *Jewish Wedding* in Leningrad.

So Yakobson's supporter met with Yakobson in Leningrad in early 1973, when Yakobson was at an impasse in his attempts to gain permission to show *Jewish Wedding*. Yakobson surprised him by asking directly if he could arrange an invitation through Terpsichore for him to tour with his company to Akademgorodok. Yekaterina Furtseva, the fearsome Soviet minister of culture and a longtime antagonist of Yakobson and his work, seemed determined to force the closure of his new company by prohibiting his performing and touring. "It became impossible for Yakobson because he created *Jewish Wedding*," the supporter said. "I thought it was a masterpiece. There was no doubt." "But according to Furtseva, it was too ideological, because of the Jewish question. With its use of Chagall, Shostakovich, it was a very unusual combination. She recommended Yakobson cancel this ballet and not to show it to any audience. But he said, 'No, it is my work. I want to show it to audiences.'"

The supporter began by contacting Mikhail Lavrentyev, the distinguished Soviet mathematician, chair of the Siberian branch of the USSR Academy of Sciences, a recipient of the Soviet Union's highest awards, and the founder of Akademgorodok, under the direct authorization of Nikita Khrushchev. "Mr. Lavrentyev was a very great man and very famous," he said. "I asked him to invite Leonid Yakobson to perform in Akademgorodok. I explained how wonderful it would be for the scientific town to see this very non-traditional performance and how it would also help Yakobson to survive since he needed to show his work outside Leningrad. I also mentioned the political situation about this program having a Jewish ballet on it," the supporter said. "To my surprise Lavrentyev said, 'Yes, I've heard of Leonid Yakobson. I will invite him.'" Lavrentyev's authority was such that he had a direct telephone line to the high-level Communist Party officials. He called Furtseva, the minister of culture, and requested Yakobson and his company. Surprised, and cornered, she gave her consent saying, "You know, I never contradict the Academy of Sciences."

"For a Jewish man to create a very unusual art work like *Jewish Wedding* it was a double obstacle," he acknowledged. "It was very, very dangerous, especially in the former Soviet Union time, to be a fighter, and with the bureaucracy from the Ministry of Culture and with the local bureaucrats. Yakobson was a fighter. The Communist Party very much controlled the artistic activity. It was impossible to be truly independent; but he had the ability to be very independent. He found a special place in the

Soviet Union to continue to be independent and to demonstrate un-believable artistic results. Leonid Yakobson made a breakthrough," the supporter said, describing the political influence of his steady but un-flinching determination to make and show a ballet on a Jewish theme.

Yakobson's supporter then searched for a second Siberian sponsor be-cause after Furtseva agreed to let Yakobson tour his company to Siberia in response to Lavrentyev's invitation, Communist Party officials quickly added a new condition—that he could not perform in the scientific town for only an audience of scientists, but instead must show his ballets to or-dinary workers. The officials seemed to think that an audience from the scientific town might be "too elite" and thus respond favorably to Yakob-son's ballets. The supporter imagined that the officials were hoping the "ordinary workers will immediately start to criticize Yakobson." The pro-cess stretched on for several more months as he searched for another sponsor and venue that would address this mandate to reach Soviet work-ers. Then the supporter chanced upon an interview in *Sovetskaya Kultura,* the leading Moscow-based newspaper covering cultural events in Russia, featuring Yakov Osadchiy, the director of the Chelyabinsk Tube Rolling Plant, a large industrial factory that manufactured oil pipes and was lo-cated in Chelyabinsk, east of the Ural Mountains. Noting that Osadchiy was a supporter of cultural events, he traveled to Chelyabinsk to meet with him. A close friend of Soviet Prime Minister Aleksei Kosygin, and a graduate of the same Ukrainian polytechnic institute as Leonid Brezhnev, Osadchiy liked the project, saying he found it a very interesting prospect for the 100,000 workers in his factory.

"These ordinary industrial workers immediately understood," the sup-porter recalled of that first performance in the three-thousand-seat Palace of Sports in Chelyabinsk. Initially Yakobson's company had been sched-uled for only two performances because of uncertainties about how an audience of scientists and industrial workers would respond to his ballets. The first night a fairly modest audience turned up, but the next day word about the company began to spread. The second night the performance sold out and each subsequent day, as word of the performance circulated, the lines of people trying to get tickets grew until 3,300 people were crowd-ing into the theater and the performances, which had been extended for a full week, were sold out. "It was big. It was unbelievable," the supporter said. "The audiences kept spreading the news and they kept growing. It was very emotional for people. People understood immediately about *Jew-ish Wedding*. They had never seen a performance like Yakobson created," he said. "People were whispering what an unbelievable experience it was. The company ended up performing for an entire week, and every night the theatre was full."[111]

This enthusiastic reaction by an audience of workers and the Soviet scientific elite from Siberia caught the party leaders back in Leningrad by surprise. "It was a great reaction and it was impossible to stop," the supporter said. "Of course they were hoping that the public's reaction would be bad, that the ordinary workers will never support this work. That it would be a good example that Leonid Yakobson's art was pro-bourgeois and held no interest for the average Soviet citizen." But after the reaction of the audience it was impossible for the local bureaucracy in Leningrad and the Ministry of Culture to stop the performances. "It was a great success, with many good articles in the newspapers," he continued, enumerating the triumph of the performances of *Jewish Wedding* as if the ballet had been a weapon in a pitched ideological battle, which in fact it was. A diverse sample of Soviet people had embraced Yakobson's ballet, and their enthusiasm and its success could not be erased. "It was a very big event for the Ural Mountains area. It was possible because we combined the powerful positions of Yakov Osadchiy and Academician Lavrentyev. Just imagine an industrial leader and a scientific leader. It was a very powerful combination and a good strategy. We developed this strategy with Leonid Yakobson to break the bureaucracy, to overcome the bureaucracy, the Minister of Culture, the local Communist Party bureaucracy. After that Leonid Yakobson began to travel."

It is interesting to consider how *Jewish Wedding* might have looked to these new audiences in distant Soviet cities. Reflecting back on the influence of the ballet during these initial performance years, Igor Kuzmin, one of the original dancers with Yakobson's company, wrote:

Every one of the characters in *Wedding Cortège* [the Soviet title for *Jewish Wedding*] is so distinctly shaped in terms of plasticity and movement that time and again the spectator is amazed by the choreographer's perspicacity, wit and humanity. The plot is almost banal in its simplicity: a poor couple is marrying off their daughter to a rich bridegroom, while her lover assumes the role of the unwanted third party in the love triangle. However, with a strong hand, Yakobson pushes back the boundaries of the genre scene, rendering it both profoundly earnest and generic. In all fairness, we must admit that the performers fully rose to the challenge presented by the dance score. For Yakobson, dance was a mode of human cognition that used images.[112]

Kuzmin's comments speak directly to Yakobson's achievement in *Jewish Wedding:* he took one of Sholem Aleichem's localized tales of fin-de-siècle shtetl life and expanded it into a much larger parable about suffering and loss that resonated for a population without a prior affinity for either ballet or Jewish issues. Kuzmin credits Yakobson for the originality of his treatment of a plot about a semi-tragic Jewish wedding—a plot that is similar to the narrative in Jerome Robbins's *Fiddler on the Roof,* which also takes its name from the title and image of a Chagall painting and its story line from Sholem Aleichem's tales. Although Robbins directed and choreographed *Fiddler* in 1964, six years before *Jewish Wedding,* Yakobson never had the opportunity to see the Robbins production and there is no evidence that he even knew about it.

It is interesting to consider how within this space of just a few years the leading Jewish choreographer in the United States and the leading one in the USSR were both using ballet as a medium to consider cultural difference. Both looked back to the Yiddish tales of Sholem Aleichem about shtetl life in tsarist Russia as narratives to frame this dance portrait. For Robbins the plot was ringed with a generally pleasant nostalgia, but for Yakobson the reality was much closer and the dissolution of the myth of a happy ending more vivid. Even so, the danger around addressing this subject in Soviet Russia extended even to Robbins's much lighter treatment of the subject in *Fiddler.*

Reportedly American producers were anxious prior to *Fiddler's* opening that *Fiddler* would be "too Jewish" for American audiences.[113] The fear was even more pronounced in the USSR, where no one dared stage *Fiddler on the Roof* until the mid-1980s. Even then, although it was staged in the remote and specifically designated Jewish city of Birobidzhan, in the Jewish Autonomous region near the Chinese border, Yuriy Sherling, the man who directed *Fiddler* and played the lead in his little theater's 1984 production of it, was arrested and imprisoned for staging the musical. He was charged under the Soviet penal code with "aiding a Zionist conspiracy to undermine Soviet authority," for which he spent a year in prison.[114]

Whereas Robbins's treatment of Aleichem's writings preserves their quality of humor and folksy nostalgia for a fading way of life while looking toward the future, Yakobson senses something much darker in Aleichem's short stories. His work is somber both in content, medium, and prognosis. In *Jewish Wedding* there is no singing and no dancing, in the slick and showy sense of the Broadway musical, just the relentless pulse of tragic fate and the destiny for the protagonist of being left shunned and alone.

At the very end of Yakobson's life *Jewish Wedding* was finally permitted a total of thirty performances in Leningrad and Moscow, where it was received enthusiastically by the Soviet public. It was about more than an anachronistic little shtetl wedding, and the public understood. Yet the Soviet authorities persisted in trying to reduce the ballet's influence. After giving their grudging approval to *Jewish Wedding,* they requested that an upbeat work always follow it on the program—it should never conclude an evening since it was such a "somber" work.[115] Soviet authorities also controlled media coverage of Yakobson's ballets and they saw to it that no reviews of the Leningrad or Moscow performances were published. In fact, the only published article about *Jewish Wedding* was an advance article written by the prima ballerina Maya Plisetskaya for *Soviet Culture* magazine. "You must see it by all means!" Plisetskaya wrote enthusiastically.[116] The Russian art critic Natalya Sheremetyevskaya reported that in *Sovetskaya Kultura,* the text reviewing *Jewish Wedding* was removed from the newspaper before publication.[117]

The moment of *Jewish Wedding*'s creation also aligned with the launch of a new global initiative by UNESCO to designate nonmaterial forms of cultural heritage as valuable but neglected modes of cultural transmission in need of protection. As early as 1954 The Hague Convention had voiced concern about preventing "damage to cultural property belonging to any people whatsoever" as "damag[ing] the cultural heritage of all mankind."[118] But now in the 1970s rising interest in folkloric traditions had prompted a discussion about the need to expand initiatives of cultural preservation into a new category of "intangible cultural heritage," including stories, designs, musical forms, and dance.[119] Yakobson's ballets about vanishing cultural traditions of tsarist-era Jews were doing parallel work by inserting citations of this intangible cultural heritage into classical ballet, itself long an intangible cultural heritage of a lost world.

EXAMINING YAKOBSON'S JEWISH-THEMED dances offers a new lens on the subject of ethnicity in ballet. This exploration also suggests how the creation of government-sanctioned ballets during the Soviet era worked to provide tangible symbols of control for Soviet leadership, a way to script the ideal comrade racially and behaviorally. No matter how tenuous their identity as "Jewish," Jews in the Soviet Union felt threatened whenever Jewishness was associated with a disruption of the social system.

Despite his renown and achievement, Yakobson's career consistently jostled conventional notions of assimilation and the Soviet system's domestication of ethnic minorities. The protean nature of his ballet style and the new vocabularies he was creating can be read as mercurial signifiers of Jewish identity in the USSR in the face of the official absence yet presence of this identity. Yakobson was forced to live his artistic life between these two poles—as a Jew but also as an experimental Soviet artist. Through his ballets he nested this first forbidden nation inside the shell of the second official one, displacing the Soviet ideal through ballet.

It was more than just the message of an alternative nation that gave Yakobson's work, particularly the Jewish-themed ballets, such an emotional charge for audiences. He was, to borrow Susan Foster's phrase, "choreographing empathy," by allowing spectators to cultivate a connection with others' feelings through the witnessing of choreography.[120] It is this capacity for inviting a connection with the experience of alienation in Soviet Russia that his ballet conveyed most profoundly. The source of their popularity was also the source of the prohibitions they triggered as Yakobson's movement design and staging, his whole conception, offered connectivity between dancer and viewer. "To 'choreograph empathy,'" Foster summarizes, "entails the construction and cultivation of a specific physicality whose kinesthetic experience guides our perception of and connection to what another is feeling."[121] On an intuitive level Yakobson understood this use of physicality to guide and link as he worked to generate his alternative visions from a key site where civic obedience was modeled in the Soviet nation. Performing in the remote stretches of the USSR to audiences of workers and scientists—which officials decided would be stand-ins for the Soviet nation at large—he touched a responsive chord.

Jewish Wedding animated kinesthetic empathy in viewers, an injunction to remember and witness. Employing Russian folk material, Yakobson was also able to hold up "a sobering mirror" and frame of irony to Soviet citizens' lives. As philosopher Jonathan Lear has argued about the deeper value of irony, "It reaffirm[s] to us our passions and beliefs. It shows how exactly we measure up to our professed ideals, all in an effort to strive for excellence—to become better at whatever it is we devote our lives to. Irony asks us, in a fundamental way, 'Am I really who I say I am?'" Lear said. "In its primary use, irony is a sign of how much things can matter and ought to matter and what they really ought to be like."[122]

Lear's formulation of irony as a way of signifying how much things count, while argued based on literary and philosophical examples, also might be extended to help explain the aura of rueful beauty that haunts much of Yakobson's choreography, and particularly these folk portraits of a vanished Jewish life. He fought to have his works seen not only because he understood they were important, but also because they might *give importance,* triggering insight, perhaps even empathy or ironic recognition, and thus alter the social equation about who and what mattered.

Forty years later, in 2008, when the successor company to Choreographic Miniatures visited New York City with a repertory of three Yakobson ballets including *Jewish Wedding,* the theater was packed with expatriate Russians. Many of them were Jewish, and all it seemed had a vivid memory of the story of Yakobson's struggle and determination. With the passage of time the contextual details of his struggles had become bonded to his work. All of his dances on the program were greeted with warm applause, but for *Jewish Wedding,* theater-goers at each of the three performances held a special moment of silence at the performance's conclusion—and then joined together in the rolling thunder of unison applause. The intensity of the audiences' response suggests the success of his ballets in communicating two messages—one to Jewish members of the audience, another to everyone else.

Olga Levitan, who was part of the diasporic community of Russian Jews (subsequently residing in Jerusalem) and who followed Yakobson's work in Russia, said: "Yakobson gave us the opportunity to open something that was forbidden. This was true for a lot of people and for the entire theatre public in Leningrad."[123] Scholar Henry Bial has called this capacity for a work of art to speak at once to different constituencies at once "double coding," basing it on the late performance theorist Dwight Conquergood's formulation that "subordinate people do not have the privilege of explicitness, the luxury of transparency, the presumptive norm of clear and direct communication, free and open debate on a level playing field that the privileged classes take for granted."[124] The double coding in Yakobson's works like *Jewish Wedding* allowed the experience of the Jews in Soviet Russia to be spoken through his ballets, through iconography, kinesthetic images, gestures, rhythms, mise-en-scène.[125] In childhood he had discovered what it was to feel an outsider. Now as a choreographer he had learned how to stage those marks of difference on others.

FIVE

Spartacus

If the actors do not walk on stage with the red flag and do not sing *The Internationale,* and if there are no slogans to accompany the performance throughout, people say: *The Inspector General* is not revolutionary.
—Vsevolod Meyerhold, *Stati pisma rechi besedï,* 1968

THERE IS NO ballet among the 180 works that Yakobson made over his lifetime that is more autobiographical, personally and professionally, than *Spartacus.* The subject matter and circumstances of its performances would come to be freighted with meanings for him—beginning with the chance to create an original full-length work for the Kirov Ballet using a new approach to classical ballet and through to the content itself, the heroic courage of the leader of a slave revolt who bravely challenges a despot for liberty. *Spartacus* is Yakobson's manifesto for the future of ballet. In it he maps a way of dealing with a heroic theme in which the social is infused with both an individual and a subjective voice that harkens back to the early post-revolutionary era of experimentation. *Spartacus* was its own revolution, and its story is one of conflict and the toll of chasing an ideal. The Soviet arts critic Valeriy A. Zvezdochkin, in writing about the ballet looking back from the 1980s, called it a watershed work for Russian art. Expansively, he suggested it should be regarded as the defining ballet for an era and the inspiration from which all attempts at reworking Soviet ballet would spring for the next four decades after its appearance.[1]

Much about the ballet *Spartacus* originally seemed shaped to advance propagandistic goals. Although it did not reach its full form until fifteen years later, it was conceived as part of a wartime Soviet project to arouse citizens to a heightened state of optimism and determination in the uncertain days of December 1941. During that period, as part of a government project to excite nationalist loyalty and build confidence that the USSR would triumph over the Nazis as the invading German army advanced across the Soviet Union, Soviet newspapers began publishing interviews with leading artists describing ambitious new artworks they would be making. "For a Soviet composer it's an enormous joy when his work is heard in a theater like the Bolshoi, which is considered, with a reason, one of the best theaters of the world. . . . My major task was to reveal through the music the tragedy of Spartacus in the time of slavery, his burst forward, his historic exploit in the name of the oppressed," wrote the Soviet Armenian composer Aram Khachaturian, who is considered, along with Sergei Prokofiev and Dmitriy Shostakovich, one of the three "titans" of Soviet music, for a 1958 issue of *Moskovskiy komsomolets*. "And if the contemporary audience, while watching the performance, is reminded of the heroic battle led nowadays by the peoples of Africa, Asia, and their often unknown heroes—that will be the best reward for me as the composer," Khachaturian explained.[2] The experienced librettist Nikolay Volkov was commissioned to write the libretto for a planned production at the Bolshoi Theater. Volkov had worked successfully on other major ballets, including writing the libretti for choreographer, dancer, and opera director Rostislav Zakharov's *The Fountain of Bakhchisarai* (1934, with music by Boris Asafyev), as well as Zakharov's *Cinderella* (1945, with music by Sergei Prokofiev).[3] Volkov's inclusion suggests the importance assigned to the *Spartacus* project.

The tale of the slave Spartacus, leader of a famous Roman slave uprising against oppression in the years 74–71 BCE, has a history intertwined
for decades with Communist politics as well as with authors sympathetic
to those politics outside of the USSR. As classics scholar Martin Winkler
has noted, the linking of Spartacus and Communism began with the Russian Revolution:

> The ruling classes in Britain and America had no interest in mak-
> ing Spartacus a heroic model. Besides, he was a slave—someone
> who had no business being an epic-style hero—and too low-class
> and dangerous an opponent to be dignified with heroic status. He
> was not brought into the center of Roman history until Karl Marx
> and his followers put him there and until somewhere there was a
> society which established itself, at least in theory, by bringing about
> the revolution that Spartacus failed to accomplish (and probably
> did not try to bring about).[4]

Winkler argues that it was the Bolshevik Revolution that moved
Spartacus up to the status of a mythic hero for Russia. Indeed both
Lenin and Marx had praised Spartacus in their works as a forerunner of
twentieth-century revolutionaries. Marx described Spartacus as "the most
magnificent figure in all of ancient history," and Lenin called him "one of
the most outstanding heroes of one of the most important slave rebel-
lions."[5] In addition to political and ideological documents, Soviet athletic
teams also evoked Spartacus's name. Indeed the name of the Spartak Moscow Sports Society, which included the ice hockey, basketball, and football
teams, was so named in 1935 from the Russian version, "Spartak," and inspired by the eponymous leader of the rebellion immortalized through Italian author Raffaello Giovagnoli's popular fictionalized historical novel.
Spartacus as the mascot for Soviet sports teams seemed a fitting choice
since, as Winkler notes, the slave leader had started out his rebellious career as an ancient sportsman, a gladiator in public arenas.[6]

   In the initial months of the war, after Germany's invasion of Russia in
1941, Yakobson had immediately conceived two pointedly anti-Nazi dances,
Friendship Hitler Style (*Druzhba po-gitlerovski*) and *Four Gs* (*Chetïre "G,"* for
Goebbels, Göring, G[H]ess and G[H]itler), so he was no stranger to shaping anti-fascist statements through dance. He never was permitted to

present these to the public after they were suppressed following a preview showing to one of the official oversight committees. Even so, the outbreak of war in the USSR had resulted in an outpouring of songs, musical scores, and other works of art glorifying the Soviet spirit. Partly the result of nationalism and partly the consequence of the government being distracted from its customary close censorship because of the war, during the period 1941–1945 there was a brief flowering of artistic work, and for some artists, more possibilities.

Giovagnoli, who had been a participant in the nineteenth-century Italian movement for unification, the Risorgimento, was one of the earliest widely read writers in the USSR on fictionalized treatments about overcoming tyranny. In Giovagnoli's 1874 novel *Spartacus* (*Spartaco*), translated

Dress rehearsal of *Four Gs*, Aleksandr Stepin as Hitler,
Choreographic Miniatures, Leningrad, 1970.
Photo: Vladimir Zenzinov.

into Russian in 1881, the hero was an ancient revolutionary who rose against a tyrant in an adventure story designed to appeal to the broad masses. A few years later another popular Spartacus author emerged—the Hungarian-British author, journalist, and Communist Party member Arthur Koestler. Koestler also used the story of Spartacus and the slave revolt in his 1939 novel *The Gladiators* as a parable for examining the situation for the European political Left in regard to the solidification of Communist rule in the USSR. In Koestler's treatment, published soon after he became disillusioned over Stalin's atrocities and left the Communist Party, Spartacus's revolt becomes a parable for exploring "the inevitable compromises of revolution, the conflict of ends and means, the question of whether and when it is justifiable to sacrifice lives for an abstract ideal."[7]

The most widely read of all Spartacus novels, however, was that by American Communist Party activist Howard Fast. Fast published his novel himself in the United States in 1951 during the McCarthy era. He had begun writing it as a reaction to having been imprisoned for his earlier involvement in the Communist Party and his refusal to disclose to Congress the names of contributors to a related fund. Within a few years Fast's *Spartacus* had been translated into several languages, including Russian; it was quite popular in the USSR. Fast was once quoted as saying, "I don't boast about it but I am the most widely read author of the century." His claim could well be true. Indeed *Spartacus* not only was a strong Communist parable—one reason why it was such a success in the USSR—but also entered the marketplace at a time when the effects of a decade of Stalin's suppression of new publications by Soviet authors were reportedly being felt.

Spartacus had been envisioned by the composer Aram Khachaturian as a potential topic for a ballet as early as 1941, when the only permissible enemy subject was one outside the USSR—Adolf Hitler.[8] A letter in the Bakhrushin Museum from Khachaturian to Yakobson dated May 19, 1946, documents that as far back as this date, nearly a decade before he received the commission to make *Spartacus*, Yakobson was already in conversation with Khachaturian about it:

I have a contract with Bolshoi theatre for *Spartacus* but they are still silent and afraid of ancient Rome. Fearful that this may be contemporary Italy.

If in the end I were to write *Spartacus,* as you understand, it won't be before the fall of 1947 and then we will see. If I were not to write it then I need to start thinking about the libretto for the ballet because I have plans for 1946 and 1947. If you can work out platonically in the meantime for the sake of art then work it out and send me the results of your work, the libretto. If not, and you are interested in the business side of the deal, then let's wait. In any case I am very thankful to you for the attention that you have shown me and I wish you health and great success in your artistic endeavors. Respectfully yours,
Aram Khachaturian[9]

Khachaturian's first connection to Spartacus as the subject of a musical score for a ballet occurred when the choreographer Igor Moiseyev suggested it to him. (Moiseyev would in 1958 finally choreograph his own short-lived and unsuccessful ballet on *Spartacus* for the Bolshoi.) After Khachaturian's *Pravda* announcement, Soviet authorities were supportive of a ballet on the theme of the revolt and heroic death of the legendary slave leader, but Khachaturian was so delayed with other projects that it was nearly a decade later, 1951, before he finally began writing the score. This was a very tense moment in Khachaturian's career because just three years earlier, in the same February 10, 1948, resolution (of the Politburo of the Central Committee of the Communist Party of the Soviet Union) that had been published in *Pravda* and that had attacked Muradeli for his opera *The Big Friendship,* Khachaturian, along with L. Atomvyan, had been suspended from the leadership of the Soviet Union of Composers. Soon thereafter the persecution of the "formalist composers" continued at the First All-Union Congress of the Union of Composers, when one of the primary targets of the attacks was Shostakovich. Khachaturian reportedly fell into a deep personal and creative depression as a result of these attacks. He needed to find an ideologically appropriate project with which to rehabilitate himself, and *Spartacus* appeared to be a solution.[10] In an interview on the project published in *Sovetskoe iskusstvo* in June 1953, Khachaturian emphasized the ballet's ideological relevance in the Cold War era. "*Spartacus,*" he said, "was a symbol of the struggle of oppressed peoples for their freedom, against greedy masters," he continued. "It seems to me that the theme of *Spartacus* is resonant and near to our era, when the freedom-loving peoples of Korea and Vietnam are shedding blood for freedom and independence, when all of progressive humanity is struggling for peace against imperialists and their greedy plans for the enslavement of peoples. . . . The theme of Spartacus is especially relevant today when colonialism is in its death throes," Khachaturian concluded, deliberately contemporizing the theme in a reference to the Korean War and the First Indochinese War, which ended with Vietnam gaining its independence from France.[11]

Spartacus would also prove career-changing for Yakobson. He chronicled extensively the process of his work on *Spartacus*, which would bring him the broadest success of his career. As with much of Yakobson's choreography, however, it seemed that the higher the stakes, the bigger the controversy. This was particularly true with *Spartacus*, which sparked conflicts starting long before the work ever reached the stage. It was just prior to his blacklisting as a "cosmopolitan" that Yakobson began writing his extended aesthetic tract outlining his viewpoints on choreography, the book-length manuscript *Letters to Noverre*.[12] Sometime in 1947 Yakobson had discovered, in an antiquarian bookshop in Leningrad that he frequented, a Russian translation of the famous treatise *Les Lettres sur la danse et sur les ballets* (1760) by the great eighteenth-century ballet choreographer and theorist Jean-Georges Noverre. Intrigued, he purchased it and as he began reading realized the parallels with his own situation and Noverre's efforts to revolutionize ballet by insisting that ballets have dramatic motivation and coherence rather than just technical virtuosity. Yakobson's excitement grew as he began writing his own responses along the margins of *Les Lettres*, and soon he developed these marginalia into his own letters about the changes needed in Soviet ballet and his attempts to initiate them.

Yakobson's manuscript begins with a series of these letters on the subject of the ballet *Shurale* and then *Spartacus*. Writing as if Jean-Georges Noverre were a colleague with whom he maintained an active two-way correspondence, Yakobson commences this intimate conversation across the centuries by commiserating with Noverre over such difficult issues as how to choreograph on topics from antiquity and how to balance "expressive mime-dance" with classical ballet. Both of these subjects are issues that informed his work on *Spartacus*.

As Yakobson writes about the preamble to his involvement with *Spartacus*, the project seems at once alluring and daunting. Volkov had already completed the libretto for the ballet based on Giovagnoli's novel, having been commissioned by the Bolshoi in early 1941, when they had also asked Khachaturian to prepare the score. After Moiseyev began and then stopped his own plans to choreograph the ballet for the Bolshoi in early 1953, Volkov's *Spartacus* libretto languished in the library of the Bolshoi Theater until the Kirov expressed interest in doing a production. Then the project again stalled and the libretto remained in the Kirov's literary department despite repeated announcements that it was in preparation for a forthcoming season. The Georgian dancer and choreographer Vakhtang Chabukiani, famed for his heroic and romantic roles in the Kirov, also expressed interest, but he delayed so long thinking about making the ballet that eventually another choreographer was sought.[13]

In 1955 Lopukhov, newly reappointed as director of the Kirov Ballet following Stalin's death in what would be his third and final tenure in this capacity, suggested Yakobson as the best choreographer for *Spartacus*. As he describes in his book *Sixty Years in Ballet* (*Shestdesyat let v balete*, 1966), his suggestion was initially met with strong administrative resistance for several reasons, including Yakobson's temperament, work process, and artistic style. He was known to be a man who disobeyed political or institutional rules he deemed unnecessary. Lopukhov, however, who had been following Yakobson's work with admiration since his Kirov debut with *The Golden Age* in 1930, insisted that Yakobson be given the commission, arguing that he was the best suited of all Leningrad choreographers to create the ballet:

Yakobson thinks about the dance in the plastique. And this is the only way to create *Spartacus* as something that you believe in, artistically valid, real. . . . For the artistic committee of the theater Yakobson's name did not elicit enthusiasm. The opposite; a lot of people were against it. Some were put off by his difficult temper and personality and others disliked the painfully long and difficult nature of his work process. A third reason was his choreographic style, a fourth difficult relationships with the authors of the ballet—[Khachaturian and Volkov—]and a fifth reason was the unwillingness of the choreographer to take into account the wishes of the ballerinas, and what the principal dancers dictate as their wishes.[14]

Lopukhov's defense of Yakobson is frank yet insistent. He writes in a tone that suggests he understands all the objections—including that Yakobson's intensity exacerbates his own difficulties—and still believes that Yakobson is worth the trouble. Finally, in December 1955, Yakobson at last was signed on to begin work on *Spartacus*. As Yakobson writes in *Letters to Noverre,* he was so eager to take on the production that "even before getting acquainted with the score and libretto, in my imagination there appeared a grandiose performance—monumental, sculpture-like and on a grand scale, with a strong Spartacus in the lead."[15] Nowhere in any of Yakobson's excitement about the ballet is there mention of it as a political, pro-Communist, or even anti-Stalinist statement.

In fact, the sources Yakobson names as his inspiration are, with the exception of Giovagnoli's novel, primary sources from antiquity, including Plutarch and Appian of Alexandria, as well as "everything that could be found in literature, prints in the public library and the Hermitage." This last reference to the Hermitage is deliberately cryptic because at the time Yakobson wrote this it was dangerous to be more specific. In fact the "things that could be found in the Hermitage" in 1955 were the precious Greek and Roman antiquities that the retreating Soviet Army had taken from Berlin in 1945 at the close of World War II. Most famously these included the massive Pergamon Altar from 180–160 BCE. The Russians had acquired the altar as war booty when in the final days of World War II the Red Army had found pieces of it that the Germans had placed in an air-raid shelter near the Berlin Zoo. The army took these pieces back to the Soviet Union as war trophies, where they were stored in the depot of the Hermitage Museum in Leningrad until 1958. By 1959 most of the altar fragments had been returned to what was now Soviet-controlled East Berlin, where the gigantic structure became the centerpiece of the Pergamon Museum on Berlin's Museum Island.

The Saint Petersburg State Art and Industry Academy, located in a huge former mansion near the center of town, at some point acquired full-scale plaster castings of the altar's bas-relief. In 2012 it could be viewed on permanent display in an open second-floor-corridor gallery in the repurposed mansion. Even in this less than ideal setting the choreographic monumentality of the struggling figures is remarkable. It is easy to imagine Yakobson standing before his dancers and offering this work as a stylistic primer for the ballet he has started to make.

According to Yakobson's widow, a curator at the Hermitage allowed him to view the original altar in 1955 in the Hermitage's storage area. That is also where Yakobson's dancers first saw it when he asked them to study the ancient bas-reliefs as primary texts of the images he would use in his ballet. One of those dancers, Tatyana Legat, who was a young dancer at the time, recounted that experience more than fifty years later, referring to the visit to the Pergamon Altar under Yakobson's tutelage as a "creative school." "It's so fortunate to go through this kind of creative school," she said. "Yakobson wanted us to understand the arts of ancient Rome. At that time the USSR had not returned the Pergamon Altar to Germany so it was in the cellars of the Hermitage. Yakobson did whatever it took . . . so that they allowed soloists of the Kirov theatre to go look at these famous ruins. We looked at the fragments of the struggles of the titans with gods that were taken down from the famous temple. That's how he developed us."[16] Yakobson was fortunate that the window of possibility for viewing the Pergamon Altar panels in the USSR coincided with this brief period during which he was preparing *Spartacus*.

By including the altar in his research for his *Spartacus* ballet, Yakobson made struggle rather than an uprising the central focus. It is a more physically kinetic and politically ambiguous allegory. Yakobson had selected an extraordinary work as his visual inspiration for *Spartacus*. The Pergamon Altar is one of the most intense, indeed choreographic, scenes of conflict from antiquity. It depicts a battle between gods and giants in scenes filled with tension and ferocious twisting limbs and with stone figures spilling across the panels. The goddesses seem to move with an elevated floating ease while the giants are twisted in pain as they are being destroyed—an agony depicted with the sharp realism of bulging eyes and straining necks. Using these panels as a main point of inspiration for a ballet about a hero fighting oppression adds a complicated layer of contemporary politics to the story that Yakobson is recounting in *Spartacus*. The references grow thicker if one considers that he is telling a tale of resistance, through an art medium in which he is staging a kind of aesthetic revolt by creating a new movement style and vocabulary.

Although Yakobson was deliberately apolitical when it came to government politics, he was intensely political in regard to his art. In *Spartacus* the two intertwine with remarkable subtlety. In all of his statements and writings about *Spartacus* Yakobson focuses on the aesthetic rebellion sparked by his ballet, which opens up the classical vocabulary to a new freedom of expressiveness. His symbolic oppressors as a choreographer are the authoritarian rules of ballet classicism as defined by the Soviets in the 1930s and 1940s. Refuting these by virtue of his approach to choreography, his goal is to extend the doctrines of Jean-Georges Noverre and Michel Fokine into an expressive naturalness outside the lines of *danse d'école.*

Lopukhov understood clearly the originality of what Yakobson was doing and saw the criticism that greeted Yakobson's *Spartacus* as confirmation of its significance historically for Russian ballet. "The premiere of the ballet brought him success which he had not known before," Lopukhov noted of the ballet's reception. "It's interesting that in the intermissions I heard the phrase more than once, 'this is not ballet'—oh, familiar words, I heard them, believe it or not, at *Evnika, Armida's Pavilion, Carnaval, Petrushka, Scheherazade*—at most of Fokine's works. I heard practically the same words when my *Ice Maiden* (1927) premiered and 13 years later during a performance of [Leonid Lavrovsky's] *Romeo and Juliet*. Of course, . . . *Petrushka* is not a ballet compared to *The Little Humpbacked Horse*," Lopukhov concluded.[17] Here he juxtaposes innovative ballets against a blandly traditional one as he makes his point that the novelty of Yakobson's *Spartacus* exceeds the perceptual tools of most audiences and that it belongs in the pantheon of Russian ballet masterworks.[18] "The words 'this is not a ballet,' when applied to new stagings, are praise," Lopukhov continues. "I would like to say a little bit about it. The problem with a lot of stagings of the 1930s and 1940s is that they were not ballets but moldings of dramatic plays and operas without the text and vocals. There is nothing worse than that for our art. . . . You cannot say the same thing about Yakobson—he is attractive because he refuses to create 'not a ballet.' "[19]

Despite the grandeur and scale of the *Spartacus* narrative, and the heft of Yakobson's cast and props as well as Khachaturian's orchestration, the real story his ballet tells is one of remarkable intimacy and emotional privacy. Within the images of massive authoritarian power, he shows us the personal scale of suffering. The ballet is set as a series of kinetic tableaux alternately animated and still, with scenery and costumes designed by the modernist artist Valentina Khodasevich. The effect of Yakobson's playing with extremes of emotional scale in *Spartacus* in this way serves as a vivid reminder that this is how history impinges on the present and how all seemingly free actions in the contemporary moment have ripples connecting them to the past. The scenes of intimacy are set in interior spaces and are bracketed by sweeping public displays of violent confrontation, usually in exterior civic locations. Viewed both live in a 2012 revival production at the Mariinsky Theater in Saint Petersburg and also in archival footage from an earlier Kirov production in the 1970s in his widow's personal archive, this juxtaposition has a powerful impact on the viewer.

The ballet opens with a series of crisp marching squadrons of military battalions, their lines starched, their tempos brisk, and their pivoting maneuvers crisp as they enter the city center like human antecedents to the tradition of Soviet war tanks advancing in huge spectacles of power. One of the few times when Yakobson choreographed for a corps, *Spartacus* offers nearly the real thing with a corps de ballet performing as a Roman military army: male squadrons trot in, stepping as smartly as trained horses to Khachaturian's triumphal fanfare, which evokes the sweep of the triumphal march from Giuseppe Verdi's *Aida*. Each group of military forces has its own distinctive rhythm, step, and weapon, as if their bodies were musically primed specifically for their role in battle. "A dramatic director would have been proud to have staged the first scene of *Spartacus,* the Triumph of Rome, as expressively as Yakobson did," Lopukhov wrote admiringly. "But to do this he would have needed a choreographer. Yakobson's staging was [pure] ballet imagery and it requires choreographic thinking."[20]

Next the human cost of this grandeur is shown: staggering through the stone archway of the city, the enslaved captives of Crassus are driven to market like human chattel. The final person to enter is Spartacus, who lumbers slowly forward with his fellow slave Harmodius, as both men wear harnesses, yoking them to pull the massive chariot on which stands the Roman oppressor Crassus. Yakobson doesn't belabor big-scale imagery of enslavement, however; instead the next scene exemplifies the "choreographic thinking" about which Lopukhov spoke by disclosing a large subject through the small moment of two women inside the slave market. There is only a short solo in this scene—the dance of a young Egyptian woman who is being sold by slave traders and who pleads to have her

Spartacus (1956), act 1: The Triumph of Rome,
Askold Makarov (c.), Kirov Ballet, Leningrad.
Photographer unknown.

aged mother purchased with her. "Both the script writer and composer were against this scene," Lopukhov said, explaining that they wanted a big market with lots of divertissement of slaves of all different ethnicities being sold. "Yakobson thought it was out of the question and I supported him. The choreographer was correct in thinking that there is no reason to look back at the mise-en-scène of the old ballet when you are staging *Spartacus*. These debates went for a long time," he wrote, but finally Yakobson prevailed. All they needed was one dance depicting the marketplace with all its diverse attributes. "Without really forcing it on you and showing you too much, the [solo slave woman's] dance talks about the cruelty of slavery and later helps us understand Spartacus' and his friends' spirit of revolt. . . . This Egyptian dance touches the audience and prepares it to see the tragedy of Spartacus," Lopukhov continued in support of Ya-kobson.[21]

On several levels *Spartacus* tries to pick up the threads of innovation from the decade of the 1920s, to remember a modernism suppressed by socialist realism and the drambalet. Specifically Yakobson also quotes from his own work in *The Golden Age* a quarter century earlier, pulling these artifacts of dance innovation into the 1950s Soviet experience. These included the use of the cinematic technique of slow motion, the expression of subjectivity through a personal dance language, and a dance vocabulary that stretches outside of classicism to embrace gymnastics and athletics. Cinematic effects include the grand opening of *Spartacus*, which is frozen in midaction by a blackout and followed immediately by a scene that opens on the tableaux of the captured slaves being handed off with a cash transfer to their owners. Repeatedly throughout the ballet Yakobson uses frieze action and *tableaux vivants* so that action quiets into stillness and then animates back into full movement. One of the most arresting uses of this device occurs in the battle scenes of the slave revolt, where the dancers assume the attenuated drama of the actual scenes from the Pergamon Altar, freezing as the curtain falls and then rearranging themselves in a newly advanced stage of the conflict, which we glimpse like a stop-action snapshot when the curtain rises again a moment later.

Some of the Soviet dance critics of the time who reviewed *Spartacus* were both pleased and puzzled by its innovations, particularly the man-

Spartacus (1956), living bas-relief interlude, Kirov Ballet, Leningrad.
Photographer unknown.

ner in which Yakobson offered a modernist reworking of the classical vocabulary. Ballet historian and critic Vera Krasovskaya, who followed Yakobson's work closely over many years, wrote at length about *Spartacus,* noting respectfully in a passage he quotes in his own *Letters to Noverre* that "the choreography of *Spartacus* is based on the devices just contrary to those of the classical style."[22] She continues, explaining that there is no pointe work in the entire ballet, something that had historically been attempted only in short ballets like Nijinsky's *Afternoon of a Faun* (1912), never a full-length work.[23] Yet she is displeased with the lack of "leaps, extended movements and particularly spins," all of which, including the obligatory fouetté turns for the female dancer and multiple pirouettes for the male, Yakobson deliberately left out of his ballet. Yakobson "escapes the temptations of drama directing," Krasovskaya observes, "usually regarding the libretto as the starting point for his composing some huge canvases which comment on the plot through different aspects of figurative plasticity. . . . Yakobson undoubtedly has music in his heart and soul. But he excels Fokine and Goleizovsky in regarding music as a servant to his imagination."[24] Yakobson quotes Krasovskaya's comments about *Spartacus* at length in his *Letters to Noverre* monograph, puzzling with irritation how she could agree that a new vocabulary is needed and then fault him for not including the staple show-off steps of classical ballet. "It is evident that *Spartacus,* deprived of pointe work, classicism, the usual arabesques, turns, pirouettes, supported partnering and spins is not a ballet to Krasovskaya," Yakobson grumbles. "Is she longing for antiquity drawn by the graceful slender tips of stretched out toes?" he inquires sarcastically about what would be a false and anachronistic pairing for him.[25]

Phrygia, Spartacus's faithful wife, has the ballet's most extended and least conventional solos and they are all dances of sorrow and loss. Her actions are shaped with the sinuous melting quality and relaxed musculature that evoke Isadora Duncan's style of dissolving from one moment into the next without any sense of arrest or posing. These culminate in her final dance of anguish and mourning performed in soft sandals and without any virtuoso movements. This solo, the most often excerpted section of the ballet for galas and mixed repertory programs, reveals Phrygia's desperate farewell to Spartacus as he heads into a battle she already knows he will lose. It is best preserved in a documentary film clip made in 1962 of the staging that Yakobson created for the Bolshoi Ballet. This clip was subsequently broadcast on a Soviet television program called *About Ballet,* with narration by the critic Boris Lvov-Anokhin.[26] Here Maya Plisetskaya as Phrygia dances in bare legs, soft sandals with small heels, and a sheer tunic as she performs Yakobson's beautifully spare choreography. Her partner, Spartacus, danced by Dmitriy Begak, is monumental and solid as she winds about him like a tendril, loving, containing, and trying to restrain his quiet yet fierce determination to go forward into battle.

Together the two dancers channel their feelings through a poetic series of bas-relief-like compressed postures that both frame their emotions and sequence their advancing desperation. There is no divide between acting and dancing; all of the action is naturalistically in character as one senses their devotion to each other but simultaneously his pull toward leadership and change and her foreboding that she has already lost him. Yakobson uses, and then disrupts, conventions of ballet aesthetics to tell this story. He puts *Spartacus* in the signature stance of the heroic Soviet male—a solid legs-apart pose—but then he extends it into muscular stillness to suggest the more nuanced emotions of contemplation and reflection. This use of stillness and quiet were uncommon postures and emotions on the Soviet dance stage, particularly for male dancers. In Plisetskaya's signature interpretation for the Bolshoi staging of Yakobson's *Spartacus,* the constraint of the two-dimensional linearity becomes a stylization that adds emotional depth to the historic specificity of this pas de deux. When Plisetskaya's Phrygia alights repeatedly in a soft, parallel, bent-kneed stance, it is as if the crush of oppression and sorrow from the hostilities surrounding them allow only these small, emotionally furtive steps. The postures are beautifully shaped, antique without being static, as if the movement captured inside a Roman wall relief or mosaic were temporarily released. The rhythm of inner emotion that Plisetskaya conveys and the quality of pushing through space in three dimensions all echo the Isadora-like sensibility that Yakobson captures here. "I think this was my most complicated work with Leonid Yakobson," said Plisetskaya, who revered him and danced in several of his ballets.

Here he really did demand that each movement, each turn, each pose, each gesture should be repeated a hundred times over. The position of the arms, hands and feet were new for us. Dancing without hard ballet shoes in ancient Roman sandals!

What is more, all the customary positions of the feet were changed. They had to be "heels up," not "turned-out," whereas we had always been taught to keep our "heels down" and feet "turned-out." Our feet adopted that position automatically, but Yakobson stopped us and forced us to alter it. And when I, like the others, gradually grew accustomed to these new positions of feet, arms, hands and body, work began on the part proper. . . .

To combine everything, think of everything, but dance as if you were improvising—it was extremely complicated and did not come easily. To say nothing of the fact that it seemed impossible at first to remember such a vast number of movements. Unlike other choreographers Yakobson gives a *pas* for almost every note. So in one minute you have to do as many as fifty, and they have to be executed accurately but look quite natural. Your feet are dancing one thing, your arms and hands another and your head a third, yet everything is in the same style, everything fits in, and the dancing expresses Phrygia's spiritual state, her emotions, her tragedy.[27]

Plisetskaya has said that she would have danced the entire *Spartacus* ballet just for the opportunity to dance this remarkable duet, so singular

Spartacus, Spartacus and Phrygia duet. Photographer unknown.

was its condensation of the flickering emotions of grief, resolve, and the anguish of parting.[28] What became the most famous passage in Khachaturian's score for *Spartacus,* the "Adagio of Spartacus and Phrygia," accompanies this final farewell duet that Plisetskaya describes here. This passage highlights the musical achievements of the score, which broke new territory for Soviet ballet music, as Russian music scholar Harlow Robinson has noted in writing about Yury Grigorovich's 1967 *Spartacus* for the Bolshoi—a different choreography created to the same score: "Taken on tour abroad by the Bolshoi Ballet in a revised version, *Spartacus* also became one of the most internationally successful ballets written by a Soviet composer. . . . Because of his proletarian origins, non-Russian ethnic origins and Soviet training, Khachaturian became a powerful symbol within the Soviet musical establishment of the ideal of a multinational Soviet cultural identity, an identity which the composer enthusiastically embraced and exploited both at home and abroad."[29]

This Grigorovich version of *Spartacus* is the one best known in the West, but it differs significantly from that of Yakobson, replacing the nuance and subtlety of his characterizations with more predictable and one-dimensional ones. The central adagio for Spartacus and Phrygia exemplifies this. In Grigorovich's version their exchanges are studded with familiar dramatic poses, one-handed lifts where Spartacus hoists Phrygia into the air and ferries her about the stage. While Yakobson's approach used movement to prompt empathetic connection here, the narrative—a poignant adagio of farewell—falls away in the face of self-conscious display. The various rings of the corrupting power are shown through other small dances in Yakobson's *Spartacus,* especially those of Aegina, wife of the wealthy Roman slave owner Crassus. In her teasing flirtation with Harmodius, the coolly beautiful Aegina repeatedly offers her body with the calculated salesmanship of someone marketing a new luxury item, hands gently outlining her breasts and gesturing down the length of her leg as she arches her head back in a finely etched silhouette of temptation.

By keeping all of the romance here chastely within the boundaries of Soviet censors, Yakobson achieves the reverse, a heightened eroticism. We never see the consummation or even foreplay, just the intensity of longing building on itself between these two couples, one passionate and noble, the other hedonistic with an appetite for carnal pleasures and raw

Spartacus (1956), act 3: Etruscan Dance at Crassus's
Feast, Yuriy Umrikhin, Tatyana Legat, and
M. Gulyaev, Kirov Ballet, Leningrad.
Photographer unknown.

power. The sex scenes in Yakobson's *Spartacus* are so effective in this
regard that even 1950s Hollywood, under the thumb of the Hollywood
decency code, would have marveled at how far Yakobson went with innuendo in *Spartacus*. In one of the tenderest moments between Phrygia
and Spartacus, they pivot in a tight two-dimensional unit, staying in profile as they come closer in their passion, ending in a series of stunning yet
subtle lifts. In the first, Spartacus lifts Phrygia onto a perch on his chest,
and she raises her arms in a lifted circle and presses her flexed wrists
against the sky three times as if knocking on a celestial door for release
for them both. Then, on the ground again, she takes several steps backward

before rushing toward Spartacus and letting him run his hand lovingly along the length of her body. He pauses near her feet and she folds herself to her knees as he scoops her up, carrying her in profile like a figure on an urn before letting her slowly descend in a trembling arabesque to the lyrical cry of a violin.

The very final moments of the ballet are reserved for the most tragic and also emotionally exposed scene in the ballet, Spartacus and Phrygia's final duet. But this time Phrygia dances alone a solo of despair over the dead body of Spartacus. Rippling through a series of images of mourning women taken from ancient Greek urns, Phrygia flails her hair, then throws herself atop Spartacus, her whole body seeming to heave with sobs and cries. Then, as if understanding the finality of the loss, she adjusts his shield and sword and raising her arms above her head, she gently sprinkles earth from her fingertips over his body. She has turned the battlefield into a grave. Straightening her own posture into one of cold determination to take up the struggle, she stands quietly as the curtain falls.

Yakobson and Khachaturian had many heated conflicts over the score, at one point coming to accidental blows on Nevsky Prospect when the composer and choreographer encountered one another. Yakobson insisted that Khachaturian trim the score from four acts to three and make other adjustments to render it both more danceable and dramatically legible. When Khachaturian refused to cut the repetitious music for the battle scene despite Yakobson's entreaties, Yakobson responded by devising a series of sharply etched battle tableaux that reconfigured each time the curtain rose and fell until all the battle music had been exhausted. Lopukhov tried to help, but he also found Khachaturian intractable. "After he wrote interesting music, Khachaturian refused to meet half way the choreographer, thinking that all the choreographer has to do is read the music. But the choreographer is not a performer of the music, nor even its interpreter," Lopukhov said.[30]

In his *Letters to Noverre* Yakobson describes how he filled Khachaturian's extended passages of battle music by inventing the sequence of stop-action battle scenes that has become one of the ballet's most distinctive elements. The effect was of a slowly shifting panorama of an epic struggle, arranged linearly as if one were slowly circumnavigating the Pergamon Altar—and it filled out the music. This stage solution, however, did not fix their personal relationship. By the time of the ballet's premiere, Yakobson and Khachaturian were not speaking to each other. Despite Yakobson's masterful choreographic contribution to Khachaturian's score, the composer deliberately excluded Yakobson from the opening night post-performance celebration and pointedly referred to him as "Citizen" Yakobson whenever his name came up, using the appellation reserved for Soviet criminals. It would be at least three years before this rift was mended.[31]

Khachaturian had his own personal and artistic agendas. Denounced in 1948 for a "formalist, antinational tendency in contemporary music," and dismissed from the Organizing Committee of the Union of Soviet Composers, he was working to reinstate himself and his status as both an Armenian and Soviet musician.[32] Nationality thus plays a role in the *Spartacus* score. As Robinson has observed, Khachaturian himself claimed that Rome in the time of Spartacus had been multinational: "One of the organizing principles of the score is the contrast made behind the musical world of the Roman masters (military fanfares, marches, decadent waltzes and bacchanals) and the musical world of the slaves (Oriental, lyrical, folk inspired). Since most of the slaves in the Roman Empire were non-Roman members of conquered ethnic and national groups, the music that accompanies their appearance on stage is strongly 'ethnic'—Ethiopian, Egyptian, Thracian, Gallic, German, Syrian, Nubian."[33]

When the Kirov presented a revival of *Spartacus* in 2010, one Russian critic writing in the *Moscow Times* dubbed it "the Soviet *Cleopatra*." Indeed, sex is another of the major socialist aesthetic taboos that Yakobson contests through *Spartacus*. He does this by using a physical vocabulary that departs from the Soviet pas de deux's conventional expression of heterosexuality, instead giving the full body an expressiveness that puts technique in the background. He shows us the noble and ignoble dimensions of love as if they were the flip sides of the same coin of human desire. Particularly in the bedroom scene of act 3, where Aegina treacherously leads Harmodius through a breathless seduction, she is a perfidious Black Swan to Phrygia's innocent White Swan, yet both women are depicted as being more independent than female protagonists in Soviet classics like *Swan Lake* or *The Fountain of Bakhchisarai*. It almost seems as if each moment of tenderness in Spartacus and Phrygia's love duet from the second act is turned inside out in this other couple's anti-pas-de-deux, where allure repeatedly yields to entrapment.

Yakobson uses the Spartacus legend as a means to depict vividly the personal cost of living under a brutal authoritarian ruler. In scenes where the gladiators are goaded into fighting their compatriots, they perform a dance of darting footwork that neatly suggests the edgy anxiousness of their mental states as they realize they must kill a friend to live. Yakobson thus suggests how political systems eat into the souls of their citizens, replacing humanity with savagery. Although this strategy is enormously risky, he is able to pull it off because the surface story seems so transparently about the oppressed that the deliberate ambiguity of just who the oppressor is doesn't register. Yakobson shows us bags of money being tossed to the slaves' handlers in the ballet's early scenes as the newly arrived male and female slaves are examined and purchased, their commodification bluntly apparent. We then see their humanity being steadily erased through the blood-sport gladiatorial games that serve Crassus's sadistic power displays.

By the time *Spartacus*'s heroically scaled portrait of villainy was at last realized, in the post-Stalin USSR, the greatest tyrant was finally acknowledged to have been inside the USSR all along—Joseph Stalin. In creating *Spartacus,* Yakobson tested the ways in which the contemporary body interacts with historical texts. He made the meeting an occasion for inverting the customary hegemony of dance history so that the voice of the narrator is not that of the dominant power but that of the one tearing at it from inside. Instead of the alternative forms of narration being silenced, Yakobson configures history in *Spartacus* as a way to make the voice of the individual rise up out of history and point the way toward social change through art. He does this through the medium of ballet itself, questioning the archival function of the stage so that the premium is on how bodies instruct us more vividly in preparation for the present rather than to memorialize the past. It was a delicate negotiation that ballet was uniquely situated to handle in his hands.

Yakobson's *Spartacus* is a brave work on several levels. One is this slipping in of a counter-narrative of the personal cost of living within an authoritarian system. and another is the use of the cloak of antiquity and historical realism as ways to finally crack open ballet classicism on the huge scale of a full-length production. But there is yet another level of covert daring to Yakobson's *Spartacus.* When he began working on his vision for the ballet in late 1955, there were no well-known modern accounts of Spartacus in Russian; rather Howard Fast and Arthur Koestler, both Jewish authors with Central European backgrounds, brought *Spartacus* forward for English readers. Their implicit context was the public persecution of cultural and literary members of the American Communist Party, via Joseph McCarthy and the "show" hearings of the U.S. House Un-American Activities Committee (HUAC).

Thus the only contemporary source that Yakobson cites in his personal writings about the making of *Spartacus* is the officially approved one—Giovagnoli's 1874 historical novel *Spartacus*. But Fast's *Spartacus* novel was also available in Russian in the Soviet Union, and since Yakobson researched so extensively in preparation for making his ballets, and especially *Spartacus,* he may have been aware of Fast's treatment as well.[34] Even without this direct link, Yakobson's *Spartacus,* with its deliberate ambiguity about which oppressor Crassus is a proxy for, leaves open the possibility that this ballet *Spartacus* is, like the Spartacus novels and the 1960 Stanley Kubrick *Spartacus* film, a reference to the plight of the Jews as a community apart—slave labor under the Nazis. Yakobson knew another reality for many Jews his ballet could reference—that of social disenfranchisement in the Soviet Union. Depending on the spectator position, there were at least two narrative possibilities for where the oppression was located and for whom the slaves are proxies.

Spartacus is one of the strongest examples of how Yakobson keeps these multiple points in view in a ballet that is neither purely historical nor only morally prescriptive, but a combination of both. It is a sensorium of his dreams of what ballet beyond classicism could be, realized within the tight aesthetic confines of the Soviet state. The *Spartacus* choreography, like its score, carried forward the wartime faith in the arts' capability to inspire the masses to nationalistic good, even though it was premiering a decade after the end of active conflict. It in fact debuted in the midst of the new conflict that had opened since the end of the Cold War. Yakobson understood the *Spartacus* commission was a unique opportunity and he was determined to use it to realize his vision, even though his other major collaborators had differing ideas. The Soviet model of artistic creations being an institutional rather than an individual's endeavor seemed unfortunately to have fostered a climate of nonproductive competition. In the nearly two hundred pages he wrote in his *Letters to Noverre* about *Spartacus,* Yakobson rails against both Volkov and Khachaturian in language that hints at the daily tension among these three men. Here is Yakobson on the Volkov libretto: "The drawbacks of Volkov's libretto predetermined the lack of continuity and fragmentariness of Khachaturian's score. Khachaturian is totally devoid of a gift for dramaturgy. . . . A talented composer, he is not gifted as a dramatist—ballet music and dramaturgy are two different genres. Many composers combined these two qualities, but quite a number of them had no gift for scenic vision and Khachaturian is one of them. That is why our endless arguments came to nothing, the co-operation was nervous and tense."[35]

Yakobson concluded that if no changes were possible with the librettist and composer, particularly revisions as drastic as he wanted, he would simply edit the score and revise the libretto himself. Although he never received credit for reworking Volkov's libretto, his version was the one that was used by Moiseyev and Yury Grigorovich for their *Spartacus* ballets. Lopukhov and the three assistant directors, Igor Belsky, Yuriy Druzhinin, and Takhir Baltacheyev, as well as many of the Kirov dancers, supported Yakobson's request for changes. But it was only after Yakobson presented the first sections of his choreography in a closed showing at the Kirov that tensions cooled. In a letter that Khachaturian and Volkov sent Lopukhov after that showing, they praise Yakobson as a "talented choreographer" of those "brilliant fragments from *Spartacus*."[36]

Finally Yakobson exhales. "Life became easier from this moment," he writes. "I was able to make some alternations but failed in carrying out cardinal changes. In the final analysis the production was a compromise."[37] It's a confession that echoes through much of Yakobson's life, and while his diaristic entries about the back and forth surrounding the creation of *Spartacus* are among the most detailed accounts he left of his work process, the situation is not unique. What is rare is the opportunity he affords to glimpse into the interior working process of a ballet moving from conception to the stage during the Soviet period, and how clotted with artistic, political, and personal agendas collaborative art-making had become.

One of Yakobson's most comprehensive letters to Noverre is an extensive defense of what he calls "one more front" that he had to fight in creating *Spartacus*. This battle was over his abandonment of pointe work and many of the recognizable steps and hallmarks of classical ballet. Indeed, this is one of the more daring features of the ballet, since while there is a long tradition of ballet narratives that dispense with pointe, beginning with Fokine, until *Spartacus* ballet modernists had not made three-act ballets (although in the West the modern dancers Doris Humphrey and Martha Graham were experimenting with full evening works). When the Kirov (now the Mariinsky) mounted a revival of *Spartacus* in 2010 in Saint Petersburg, the dancers still marveled at the technical challenges of Yakobson's nonclassical vocabulary. Viktoriya Teryoshkina, who danced the female lead of Phrygia in the 2010 Mariinsky revival observed, "It would appear that there is nothing special here, but in fact it is insanely difficult to rehearse. Your legs get very sore because all these poses are unfamiliar to us. And the most important thing is that in no circumstance at all can you turn your legs outward. You have to cover all your turnout up," she remarked. This emphasis, Teryoshkina notes, is the opposite of traditional ballet, where the line of the outwardly rotated leg, the turnout, is a prized feature of the years of a dancer's training. "To start we didn't even understand," she confesses. "It was very hard, but now we like it. We like it a great deal."[38]

If more than fifty years after its premiere Yakobson's ballet still presents this level of challenge to principal dancers in the Mariinsky Theater, then one gets a sense of how radical its movement innovations must have been for the dancers to learn in 1956. Tatyana Legat, who danced in the original 1956 production, speaks of the same physical challenges of the choreography that Teryoshkina does in 2010. As *Spartacus* neared the date of its premiere, murmurs predicting its failure, its probable short life, and the impossibility of asking spectators to sit through a four-act work without classical dance began to build, calling into question whether what Yakobson had created in *Spartacus* should even be called a ballet.

As was his style, Yakobson faced the skepticism directly. Legat recounts how he invited dancers and other choreographers to watch portions of the ballet and then listened as each one would offer his comments. Yakobson was continually revising his work, she said, and his openness and lack of pretense were rare for the usual "big personalities" of Soviet ballet. "In 1956 I was barely out of the Kirov school and Yakobson staged an Etruscan dance for me and allowed me to dance at the premiere," she recalled. "The dance was very difficult on demi-pointe and included elements of belly dance. Yakobson used poses drawn from Etruscan vases at the Hermitage. After this rehearsal our legs and feet were collapsing, we couldn't stand up we were so tired," Legat continued. "Then he said to me, 'Tatyana, tonight we are getting together at my house, we are going to change the libretto, something isn't working.' I go to his house on 30 Marat Street, and there are a lot of people there. Librettist, choreographer, soloists, I am just sitting on the side of the couch and I can't say anything and Yakobson asks how I do this scene and this one—that's the kind of atmosphere he created." Equally surprising was his lack of favoritism in casting, even in regard to his wife, Irina. "His wife danced with the second cast," Legat said. "All choreographers' wives always dance in the first cast. But Yakobson had integrity, he had a creative artistic conscience unlike anyone else," she said.[39]

The Marat apartment, in which the Yakobsons lived with their son and both of Irina's parents, was a cramped communal home whose few rooms, including one bathroom and a kitchen, were shared by fourteen people from four different families. To at least relieve the crush in the summer, Irina received permission to have her father build a small dacha for the family in an old resort area of Estonia where several dancers from the Kirov had summer cottages. It took one year to build and when it was completed it was a five-room, two-story house with large verandas near the woods and sea. Yakobson went when he could to rest, walk in the woods, and swim.

Finally in 1960 Yakobson's entreaties to officials that it was impossible for him to work in the communal Leningrad apartment resulted in the couple being given a larger three-bedroom apartment at 11 Vosstaniya Street, no. 7, which Yakobson insisted Irina's parents, for whom he had a deep affection, share with them as well. This remained his home for the rest of his life. They also obtained a car sometime earlier, which Irina usually drove because Yakobson was always "dreaming." That arrangement was made permanent one day when the car was parked in front of a wall, facing the street, and Yakobson, who was sitting behind the wheel, accidentally put the car in reverse rather than forward. Irina was in back washing the rear window and the car lurched back, shattering her leg and forcing her to spend nearly a year in a cast healing. "What shall I do?" the

Leonid, Nicholas, and Irina Yakobson at their
dacha, 1965. Photographer unknown.

stricken Yakobson asked her. "Never drive a car again," was her reply. He
never drove again.[40]

The Reception of Spartacus

The success of Yakobson's *Spartacus* was by all accounts extraordinary—
crowds queued for tickets hours in advance of sales and the Kirov Theater
played to sold-out houses night after night. "I managed to save from failure and somewhat improve the plot of the ballet, the development of action and the general composition; otherwise a fiasco would have been
inevitable," Yacobson wrote. *Spartacus* was a movement treatise about resistance and the election of freedom over slavery, and it was also a danced
treatise *of* that resistance and an election of an alternative. After these

debates over his modernism Yakobson called classical ballet a "cult," a "fetish," and "a religion that has conquered all the spectators in the world." By contrast, he described himself as an "artistic dissident." "Though they are not numerous, I belong to them. I am a firm antagonist of this obsolete, decrepit, self-repeating system which proved its inability to survive in contemporary life," he said. "If art does not move forward, it moves backwards and becomes history, it turns into a museum piece. As a museum piece I greatly appreciate the art of classical dance. I see the reasons of its popularity, though this art is so far removed from the burning problems of today. Classicist dance cannot tell the story of *Spartacus*," he concluded.[41]

Spartacus would remain in the Kirov's active repertoire continuously for the next eighteen years, and it enjoyed popular revivals well into the second decade of the twenty-first century. To capitalize on its unprecedented success, the Kirov management made purchasing a ticket for *Spartacus* conditional on also buying one for the least popular opera in the Kirov's season.[42] In recounting the influence and significance of *Spartacus* on Soviet ballet, Valeriy Zvezdochkin, a leading Russian dance critic, writing in a 1974 article noted:

> In *Spartacus,* Yakobson for the first time breaks away from the canons of dramatic ballet with its esthetically inflexible dance forms. In this monumental four-act piece, Yakobson emphatically rejects all attributes of the classical tradition, helmets and turnout included—an unprecedented occurrence in academia. Today, this Yakobson-inspired helmet-free choreography has taken root on the professional stage. At the time, however, [Yakobson's innovative approach] raised a storm of protest. While the production was being prepared, as well as after the premiere, Yakobson was accused of abandoning [cherished] traditions, replacing dance with pantomime and undermining the foundations of academic choreography.
>
> Certain episodes that occurred during the rehearsals of *Spartacus* are worth mentioning here. Even the troupe leader, F. Lopukhov—an innovator in his own right who had paid a heavy price for his [unconventional] opinions—had misgivings regarding Yakobson's choreography, which was [he feared] excessively "anti-classical." He started a diary where he recorded comments and opinions

made by artists about working and rehearsing with Yakobson. To the dancers' credit, all of the entries are highly laudatory. Representatives of the Cultural Bureau, however, proved somewhat less amenable. During the rehearsals they wondered: What sort of ballet is this if girls are hopping around the stage without pointe shoes? They were assured that this was done solely in order to spare the ballerinas' feet, and that during the premiere, the women would wear pointe shoes and every man would be sure to appear in a helmet. These explanations appeased [the functionaries].[43]

Yakobson, of course, never did add pointe shoes or helmets to the ballet. In addition to discarding pointe work, helmets, and turnout, Yakobson reworks in *Spartacus* other cardinal attributes of heroic classical ballet: the corps de ballet, or ensemble passages, and the pas de deux—both foundational structures of ballet classicism. With its cast of nearly two hundred performers one would expect that *Spartacus* would use synchronized masses of dancers to convey the crowds of Roman spectators, gladiatorial combatants, and slave rebels. But in *Spartacus,* Yakobson deliberately disrupts this signifier of not only ballet classicism but also imperial order by inventing what he called "choreographic recitatives" or "speaking polyphony," a musical device borrowed from formal opera whereby multiple characters stand onstage and declaim simultaneously their independent texts and vocal lines. It is difficult, but when it is done well the effect is thrilling, like looking into a crowd and being able to discern the individual thoughts of each character. When this happens in dance, metaphorically it enacts the plurality of a republic in action—a particularly radical image to insert in the midst of the performance genre entrusted with ordering the status quo of unison militaristic obedience.

Many in those crowds that filled the Kirov Theater to see *Spartacus* must have sensed, or known viscerally, that the daring in this ballet was happening on several levels. This recitative effect gives a vivid realism to the battle scenes as well as to the orgiastic bacchanalia attended by Crassus's soldiers and the maidens. The duet danced by Aegina as she seduces Harmodius also elicited official criticism, with party representatives labeling it pornographic. In reflecting on the distinction between the sensual and the pornographic, Yakobson wrote about this passage in an essay that was later reprinted in 1991 in a special edition about erotic art in the Soviet journal *Iskusstvo Leningrada* (*The art of Leningrad*). "In the Etrus-can dance the incredibly beautiful music gave me the possibility to com-pose an original deeply sensual dance, one that was completely devoid of sexuality. It was danced in order to please and excite the Patricians. It con-tained in itself the eroticism that is contained internally, that is isolated, and kept inside itself. It is one that does not go outside," Yakobson ex-plained about his conception of "the purity and modesty" of the dancing, which spread from the upraised hands to the undulating hips.[44]

The opportunity to work with Yakobson appealed not only to dancers but also to nondancing extras who were eager to fill out crowd scenes. One such man was twenty-one-year-old Mikhail Bresler, who as an engi-neer in his late seventies still recalled with delight how he and his wife, Natasha, had served as extras in the original *Spartacus*. Observing first-hand how Yakobson's vision unfolded from day to day, Bresler wrote:

> I have to tell you it made me speechless then. He strayed from the classical aesthetic, which had become so frozen. The music for *Spartacus* was magnificent, juicy, and emotive. He choreographed his ballet with scenes that were simply, according to the Soviet view, very erotic. And that was so unexpected. Before that in ballet eroticism just didn't exist anywhere. He made it very high-class. But as soon as he started working on it at the Kirov problems started arising. There were visits from Party organs, commissions, the regional committee, the city committee, from every depart-ment, commissions were coming in. The people who were there in the committees were lower class, not educated. And every one of them felt it was his duty to make his views known, to make com-ments, to force changes. And they cut. I think they changed all of the scenes about five times each. He had to redo it all about five times. And in the end the workers of the theatre were upset, be-cause you know, it was this talented production and it was being slashed. But no one could do anything. And so in the end, this cut-apart version of *Spartacus* was shown to the public and it cre-ated such a strong impression on the intelligentsia. It generated a lot of debate and discussion even when it was seen in this cut up version.[45]

Bresler became so eager to see what the full ballet looked like that one evening he arrived at the theater early, checked in as an extra as usual, and then slipped out into the house rather than going backstage and getting into his costume. At the end of the evening he was discovered and fired, but he did get to enjoy *Spartacus* with the audience and to experience the ballet's effect on the public. "In Russia at that time there was a particular public, it was mainly the intelligentsia that attended his ballets. And everyone was blown away; everyone really liked it. They liked the same things I did: the innovation, the talent. From the point of view of the public the relationship with Yakobson's work was always very positive."[46]

Yakobson's treatment of eroticism in *Spartacus* was a particularly difficult subject for his censors. Even so, Bresler notes that in Yakobson's work the presentation was always tasteful; "he was just showing that a sphere of relating to others physically exists. In Yakobson's work, a male ballet dancer could pet and touch his partner and it wasn't at all inappropriate but the authorities did not understand. They just didn't like free people in the Soviet Union and Yakobson was a free spirit."[47]

Indeed sex also acquired a new freedom and vividness of feeling in Yakobson's *Spartacus*. This was particularly true in the duet between Crassus's wife, Aegina, and the handsome slave Harmodius. Pushing the narrow Soviet boundaries of decorum and continuing to challenge ballet classicism by discarding what he called the "senseless" adagio of classical ballet, Yakobson gave the love duet for the slave and Crassus's wife a saturated passion. This propelled them into risky postures and a state of heightened erotic suspense. In both instances Yakobson's choreography has the fresh realism of improvisation, although nothing is improvised. He took Michel Fokine's aspirations for a more realistic treatment of crowds and passions in *Petrushka* and *Scheherazade,* respectively, and stretched them to large scale in the saturnalia orgy scene. Neither Fokine ballet was seen in its original form in the USSR during Yakobson's viewing lifetime and thus was known to him only through Fokine's early writings about his ambitions for ballet and two secondhand versions done by Soviet choreographers in the 1960s.[48] Yakobson, in fact, quotes Fokine as also having commented on the limitations of the artifice of turnout and its absence in masterpieces of antiquity as a way to bolster his own decision to discard it in favor of Roman realism in *Spartacus*.

By freeing the female dancers in *Spartacus* from not just turnout but also toe shoes (he placed them instead in sandals with small heels), Yakobson has created the impression that the women's legs are continuously stretching to give the elongated line and lift of a dancer in pointe shoes. Yet the effect is all the more dramatic because it is achieved through the sheer muscular effort of a forcefully pointed toe, without the caged support of a toe shoe. For this reason it's one of the consistently most beautiful images of the women's dancing in *Spartacus*. One young dancer who found this image particularly inspirational was Rudolf Nureyev. Then an eighteen-year-old student in the Leningrad State Choreographic Institute, the Kirov's training ground, Nureyev was drawn to Yakobson's *Spartacus* because of its technical innovations. "Male dancing was very rough in Russia at the time," Nureyev recalled. "They did not believe in lyrical passages, they did not believe that man could execute woman's steps, and that's what I was doing. They could not believe it, they could not be emotional; they could not really find that negative feeling which men are never permitted there; it was always positive."[49] Where Nureyev did find a model for male lyricism in this quest to redraw some of the gender boundaries of Russian ballet was in Yakobson's *Spartacus*. Nureyev biographer Julie Kavanagh calls it "his most audacious plagiarism of all"—specifically Nureyev's appropriation of the high relevé from the women's dances in soft slippers in *Spartacus*.[50] Adopted by a man, this lifted, stretched line of dancing high on the ball of the foot in sandals that Yakobson had devised as a modernist gave the distinct impression that Nureyev wanted for his own performing—the effect that as a man he was also dancing as high and lifted as if he were en pointe.

In the early months of 1956, as Yakobson began preparations for staging his *Spartacus* at the Kirov, the world outside began to shift. On February 25, 1956, Nikita Khrushchev delivered his infamous "Secret Speech" to the Twentieth Congress of the Communist Party of the Soviet Union in which he denounced Stalin's authoritarian rule and the cases he had falsified against innocent victims based on torture. It was a major breakthrough marking the beginning of the slow process of de-Stalinization.[51] Although Khrushchev's speech was not formally published in the USSR until 1989, his official acknowledgment that Stalin had been ruling through terror and lies had been registered.

It was in this slowly changing climate of possibility that Yakobson's *Spartacus* took shape. In the months ahead, additional shifts in the global political terrain would affect, for better and worse, the fate of Yakobson's ballet. In October 1956, the Bolshoi, as the first Soviet ballet company to tour outside the Soviet Union with a full-evening ballet, traveled to London, where the troupe performed at the Covent Garden Royal Opera House, Britain's new national home for ballet and opera.[52] (Prior to that, in 1954, a group of selected dancers from both the Bolshoi and Kirov went to Paris and Berlin to perform a mixed repertory concert. Although the Paris performances at the Grand Opera were cancelled due to tensions with the USSR over the First Indochina war, the Berlin performances were performed as scheduled.)[53] Western critics attributed what they saw as the Bolshoi's lack of inventive choreography on this tour to their having missed out seeing the innovations of the Ballets Russes that unfolded in the West.

Soviet ballet's participation in Cold War dance diplomacy had begun. The Bolshoi Ballet made additional tours to Paris, Hamburg, Munich, and Brussels in 1958—preludes, it appeared in retrospect, to the company's long-awaited first tour to the United States in 1959. The Igor Moiseyev Ballet Company also toured to the United States for the first time in 1958 under Hurok, and audiences packed the Met to see them.[54] Hurok quipped that he had been working for thirty years to get the Bolshoi to America, reflecting the company's status as an ultimate symbol of Soviet pride.

The reputed preeminence of Soviet ballet was a particular point of pride for Khrushchev. When the Soviet premier visited a Hollywood sound stage on his first trip to the United States in September 1959, he watched the filming of a B-movie scene with lackluster can-can dancing. In response, he infamously took the microphone and threw down a Cold War gauntlet to his hosts by proclaiming: "Which country has the best ballet? Yours? You do not even have a permanent opera and ballet theater. Your theaters thrive on what is given to them by rich people. In our country, it is the state that gives the money. And the best ballet is in the Soviet Union. It is our pride."[55]

A few months earlier, in the summer of 1959, Yakobson had engaged in a small act of private cultural diplomacy when he encountered U.S. Vice-President Richard Nixon on a visit to Leningrad that included attending a performance at the Kirov Ballet. Nixon reportedly had been told that Yakobson's work was worth seeing, possibly by conductor Eugene Ormandy, who had praised it the previous year when on tour to the USSR with the Philadelphia Orchestra. After the Kirov performance, Nixon came backstage to personally tell a surprised Yakobson how much he had enjoyed his ballets. In an effort to reciprocate, Yakobson then arranged for a small book published about him in Russian to be mailed to Nixon through someone he knew who was going to the United States. Nixon received the book, and sent a book about American ballet to Yakobson in return, along with a thank you note offering his assistance should Yakobson ever need it. Yakobson was subsequently called before the party bureau of the Kirov Theater to explain this gift from a man who had become the U.S. Republican presidential nominee, but in the end he was permitted to keep Nixon's book.[56]

Yakobson's personal files in the Central State Archive of Literature and the Arts of Saint Petersburg offer a rare glimpse into the internal workings of this process of constriction and expansion of controls. There we can see various redactions in committee reports made in late 1958 and into 1959 about a program of his ballets at the Kirov, *Choreographic Miniatures*. After a December 25, 1958, showing of several Yakobson works, the committee reported that "having discussed the new stagings of the work *Choreographic Miniatures* by Yakobson this meeting of the people points out that the concert program *Choreographic Miniatures* is an 'extraordinary event'" (this is crossed out and replaced with the phrase "considerable appearance"). The initial report praises Yakobson's importance for Soviet ballet, noting: "In the Soviet Choreographic arts this area of artistic work has been neglected, run down and not a single ballet theatre in the USSR has produced a similar program." Initially his dances are lauded for their "high professional quality and interesting, creative, conditions for the dancers." This is revised to a more muted acknowledgment of their "variety, different genres and topics." Word by word throughout the report each passage of enthusiasm and praise is diluted and Yakobson is chastised for details like not using the music of well-known composers. The tone is prescriptive and patronizing and the watering down of each element of enthusiasm in the officials' report gives a taste of how even minor affirmative responses to Yakobson's work were considered threatening.

The relationship between the arts and repressive political systems is complicated. Cultural historian Peter Jelavich, in writing about the early days of National Socialism and Berlin cabarets in prewar Germany, identified what he considers a beneficial effect of arts censorship. In tracing how the performing arts and specifically cabaret functioned in a climate of censorship, Jelavich found a concentric process where what gets shut down externally may well open up new imaginative possibilities internally in spectators and artists. This is a social model that likely could also have been operating in the Stalin era for Soviet artists like Yakobson. (Indeed, Jelavich suggests that artists working under a social system of censorship in Nazi Germany, and who pushed the limits of what was possible, may have inadvertently helped sustain the status quo because their work "spoke to people's repressions, but did not call for a major restructuring of thought or action.")[57] Jelavich builds this reading on Freud's model of how jokes work cognitively as a form of thought emancipation. Freud has suggested that jokes and satire can help us retrieve what was lost—such as the freedom of thinking, speaking, or acting.[58] For Jelavich this was a major aspect of cabaret culture too. Parts of this model apply to Yakobson's work, which could similarly hover at the border of the permissible and the impossible. Indeed Yakobson walked this tightrope of trying to get his ballets by the censors with the suspended calm of someone about to deliver a risqué joke that he knows might offend but which will also surely delight.

More by necessity than choice, Yakobson gave voice to people's repressions, especially during this Cold War period. But he did so without directly calling for a major restructuring of thought or action, since to do so would have risked the total cancellation of his work and possibly career. It may well be that what this stretching-of-the-boundaries-of-the-permissible that Yakobson's ballets achieved was a little piece of free real estate inside the public's head. This internal territory was the true battleground, as Jelavich describes it (here referencing Berlin cabaret culture): "The most effective censor sat, in fact, in the public's head. Often prevailing norms had been internalized so successfully that audiences were unwilling to hear performers who challenged their political or moral values."[59]

Spartacus *at the Bolshoi*

Included in feedback the Bolshoi had received about its 1956 London season were critics' observations that the dancing was impressive but the repertoire outdated. In 1958 Igor Moiseyev had tried, and failed, to stage his own *Spartacus* for the Bolshoi Ballet using Khachaturian's score and Volkov's libretto. A February 1959 feature in *Life* magazine on the Bolshoi

Ballet and Moiseyev's *Spartacus* discusses the production in a tone that suggests it will be part of a forthcoming American tour by the Bolshoi that spring. Clearly efforts were being made to assemble a repertoire that could showcase a more contemporary side of the Bolshoi, and a new full-length ballet seemed destined to be part of it. The *Life* photos of Moiseyev's production depict a courtesan in a saggy beige body stocking doing a striptease with a crowd of Romans grabbing at her feet. Despite its enormously expensive costumes and decor, Moiseyev's *Spartacus* was a failure with Soviet audiences and critics. It lasted just two performances before it was permanently erased from the season and the Bolshoi repertoire.

Ironically, that 1959 tour by the Bolshoi was also to have included a full evening of Yakobson miniatures performed by Bolshoi dancer Olga Vasilyevna Lepeshinskaya with Pyotr Gusev as her partner. While on tour with the Bolshoi to Brussels several months prior to the American tour, however, Lepeshinskaya was arrested and taken to jail. According to the Reuters news report, "Olga Lepeshinskaya, 41-year-old star of the Soviet Bolshoi Ballet who was known as Stalin's favorite ballerina, was detained on Friday for alleged shoplifting in a Brussels department store. Police said today the Soviet dancer was released yesterday evening, after questioning. The articles concerned were an umbrella, cuff links, gloves and a roll of adhesive paper. Police added that unless the department store brought the matter to court there would be no sequel. A spokesman for the department store said no final decision had yet been made."[60] Lepeshinskaya avoided prosecution, but she was not permitted to join the Bolshoi on their next tour, the one to America, so the evening of Yakobson's choreography featuring her was eliminated from the tour as well.

Mindful that the company needed a fresh full-length ballet for its tour to the United States, the Bolshoi turned to Yakobson and invited him to Moscow in early 1962 to stage a revised version of his *Spartacus* for the company. The Bolshoi dancer he selected to dance the role of Harmodius was Vladimir Vasiliev. Vasiliev had met Yakobson three years earlier when the dancer was in his first season with the Bolshoi and Yakobson had come to Moscow to set three of his Rodin-inspired miniatures, including *The Eternal Idol* (*Vechnïy idol*, 1958), on Vasiliev and Galina Ulanova. The *Rodin Triptych* had premiered the previous year, in 1958, in Leningrad, and *Eter-*

nal Idol (Vechnïy idol) was danced on that occasion by Alla Shelest and Igor Chernïshov.

In a confidential report in Yakobson's personnel file dated April 18, 1959, four days after the Moscow premiere of the *Rodin Triptych (Triptikh na temï Rodena)*, Comrade P. Abolimov summarizes *Rodin* as involving "excessive looking at semi-naked bodies and erotic movements," creating "ecstatic views for one part of the audience and arousing indignation and protest in the other half."[61] The Kirov, however, continued to program *Rodin*, but with what may have been an added note of caution. The poster advertising an evening of Yakobson's miniatures at the Kirov later that year, on December 31, 1959, contains an explicit disclaimer printed along with the usual date, time, and casting information: "No one under sixteen allowed."[62] While at the time it was customary to exclude children under the age of sixteen from evening performances of the Bolshoi and Kirov, this was an implicit understanding.[63] Spelling it out on the official poster for the concert was tantamount to suggesting the contents would be too explicitly sexual for a child to watch. Here is Vasiliev on the cancellation of *Rodin*:

> There was one more chance for me to dance with Ulanova. It was in Leonid Yakobson's choreography for the famous triptych of *Rodin*. The Bolshoi was preparing a program with three pieces by Yakobson made on Rodin's sculptures especially for the Bolshoi's first tour of the USA in 1959. Our piece was called *Eternal Idol*. We rehearsed a lot but had to show our piece to a special commission to get approval to perform it. Yakobson wanted to use new costumes just coming into fashion in the theatre, which would outline our figures. But because these costumes were knitted (not made of lycra, as nowadays), they were thick and made our bodies wider, which was unacceptable to the commission, and they declared the work unfit for performance. So, alas, it didn't happen.[64]

When Yakobson returned to the Bolshoi in 1962 to stage his *Spartacus*, it was the imposing young Vasiliev whom he selected to dance the title role of the statuesque hero's friend, Harmodius. Impressed with Vasiliev's abilities and potential, Yakobson approached Khachaturian for some additional music so that he might create a new slave variation solo specifically for Vasiliev. Natalya Arkina, writing for the *Culture and Life (Kultura i zhizn)* newspaper, which was founded in 1946 as a journalistic facet of Cold War diplomacy, described the ballet in sweepingly grandiose terms out of scale with the modest, unhistrionic tone of Yakobson's ballet: "*Spartacus* projects a visual image of a man inspired by great love and a great idea. . . . The world of his dance is the world of a hero who is ready to sacrifice himself for the sake of mankind." The final image of him crucified by a cluster of spears appeared as "a monument to all the heroes who gave their lives for humanity and humaneness."[65] During the rehearsal and the premiere, Vasiliev drew a sketch of himself dancing this solo and presented it to Yakobson with the inscription "From a slave, and, hopefully, in the future also participant, in your performances. With cordial love and respect, Volodya Vasiliev." Twelve years later, this time on the occasion of Yakobson's seventieth birthday and a year before his death, Vasiliev wrote to the choreographer, again expressing his gratitude for the profound effect that encountering Yakobson and his work so early in his career had had on him:

> Now I appreciate how important it is for a young dancer to cross paths with interesting choreographers at the beginning of his creative trajectory, when he has not yet become set in his ways and opinions, but is only confident in his own powers; when the critic's voice inside him is still silent, and when you only absorb everything that those around you have to offer you, without discriminating between the good and the bad. It is to you that I am grateful for this, for you are the one who has made a significant contribution to my art.
>
> Strangely enough, I have never pondered what exactly I have gained from you as a choreographer. Indeed, during the thirteen years of our acquaintance, we have met very seldom. I cannot boast having seen all your works, although every new performance interests me. Probably, the influence of such a great master, whether acknowledged or not, to some extent leaves a mark on all subsequent art of a dancer. I cannot recall now what you said during our first rehearsal or the words you used to express your vision of the character. . . .

I only remember the plastic expression of the music, your sparkling eyes, your brows drawn together, your protruding lower
lip—which made your face look even more severe [than usual, and]
a flitting smile that lit it only once, I think. I remember unusual
musical phrasing of the movements, which seemed somewhat odd,
possibly due to a certain angularity. . . . At times, your look seemed
to turn inwards, concentrating on some inner point, to which your
thoughts [seemed] to rush, jostling one another along the way. You
would ask the conductor to repeat a passage over and over again,
and when something didn't come out as you wished, you assumed
the look of a miffed child. . . . I don't remember ever seeing you
tired. You were always burning with creativity, and this unquenchable thirst was transmitted to me, the performer.[66]

Vasiliev's affectionate reminiscence highlights how much of Yakobson's presence as an individual was tied up with the spirit of his invention
in the studio. Hurok, who had always been a supporter of Yakobson's
work, began enthusiastically spreading the word about his spectacular
new Soviet *Spartacus* ballet almost as soon as it was announced. In a June
5, 1962, article in the *New York Times* about the Bolshoi's impending autumn tour to the United States, Hurok is quoted as promising three new
ballets—the full-length Yakobson *Spartacus,* and two one-acts, including
Asaf Messerer's *Ballet School,* a grand défilé in which every Kirov School
student performs a set of classroom exercises on stage, restaged on American ballet students for the tour. Yakobson thus began commuting between Leningrad and Moscow as he raced to prepare a *Spartacus* for the
Bolshoi that would meet the demands of all the oversight committees and
still do justice to his vision. At the same time he was about to begin another major work for the Kirov, his two-act *The Bedbug (Klop,* 1962).

A few weeks after Yakobson started the Leningrad to Moscow com-
mute to restage *Spartacus* on the Bolshoi, a cartoon about him appeared
one day in the *Newspaper of the Bolshoi Theater.* Drawn by Bolshoi soloist
Aleksandr Radunsky and titled "A Friendly Cartoon—to L. Yakobson,"
the sketch depicted a breathless Yakobson wearing a sports tank top and
gym shorts—a middle-aged, modern-day Spartan combatant sprinting
along a running track, his muscular legs windmilling underneath him.
The track he is on circles back on itself, and its path is marked by statues

of historical Russian and Soviet cultural figures—Leningrad's statue to Peter the Great and the Admiralty are at the top of the track, and Moscow's Mosfilm and the Bolshoi Theater are equidistant on either side. Yakobson was indeed linking and making history at this moment in his career, an artist working like an athlete to tie history, culture, and the contemporary image of Soviet ballet together for the Bolshoi's debut in America. A limerick at the bottom completes this teasing tribute: "How hard it is for poor Yakobson; he has lost all rest and sleep; *Spartacus,* Mosfilm, Leningrad; he would be glad to embrace them all; and our advice to you Yakobson is to finish your marathon well."[67] Yakobson hardly needed reminding about the opportunity before him—to have the major work of

"A friendly cartoon—to L. Yakobson," drawn by Bolshoi soloist
Aleksandr Radunsky for the *Newspaper of the Bolshoi Theater,*
ca. 1962. The cartoon satirizes Yakobson's frenzied circling as he set
works on both the Kirov and Bolshoi simultaneously.

his career, the one ballet in which he had worked out most thoroughly his new ideas of a modernist plastique mode of expression, shown on the Bolshoi tour to the United States, was indeed the chance of a lifetime.

Maya Plisetskaya, who danced Phrygia in the Bolshoi Ballet production of *Spartacus*, recalled that at the April 4, 1962, opening night in the USSR, "all of theatrical Moscow was in the audience and divided into two groups—pro-Yakobson and anti-Yakobson." "At one pole were his admirers, at the other those who rejected him and could not accept his work," Plisetskaya wrote. "The ones who were outraged were the bosses, the commission-givers, the commanders of art. They tormented and berated Yakobson mightily. . . . He was considered leftist, a formalist. His talent was obvious; his innovations, endless; but his intentions?" she asked, mimicking their rhetorical accusations. "In my opinion nobody suffered so much from Soviet power as Yakobson. Whatever he did, offered, created, the answer was inevitably, 'No!' accompanied by mockery," she explained.[68]

Hurok, in marketing the Bolshoi's upcoming tour to *Times* readers, remarked that with the inclusion of *Spartacus* in the repertory, American audiences would see "one of the world's greatest spectacles in ballet." Hurok stressed the scale of it above all else, noting that two hundred people would appear on stage and that Yakobson was creating a new version of the ballet for the United States tour.[69] Among the American press the pairing of the two words "spectacle" and "ballet" was problematic, and indeed the word "spectacle" would come back to haunt *Spartacus* as a blistering term of denigration used by American journalists to suggest that it was not real art, but a danced variety of Soviet kitsch. *Time* magazine circulated one such quip reporting that at the Moscow premiere "a Hollywood producer took one stunned look at *Spartacus* and remarked that if Cecil B. DeMille had been 'alive to see this, he would drop dead.'"[70] Inexplicably this flip comment was immortalized in English journalist Ralph Parker's program essay for the Bolshoi's souvenir program for the tour, where he also states that *Spartacus*'s raison d'être is "to show the Bolshoi Company's mastery of stagecraft."[71]

The priming of the American audiences' excitement continued when the *New York Times* sent correspondent Seymour Topping to cover the premiere of Yakobson's *Spartacus* at the Bolshoi Theater on April 4, 1962. Topping filed an overnight review, calling the ballet a "sensual extravaganza" and noting that the premiere was greeted with cheers from the audience. He also wrote that there were foreign critics in the first-night audience who expressed some doubts about the portability of the ballet to Western audiences, and he wondered himself how a "richly costumed tale of Roman violence and lust, danced on half points, would be received by American audiences who look to the Bolshoi for a more traditional approach."[72] Curiously, this take was quite different from that of the British critics who had found the Bolshoi repertory too traditional just a couple of years earlier.[73]

Spartacus *in America*

As eager as the Bolshoi had been to secure Yakobson's *Spartacus* for its American tour, and indeed as the opening ballet for its engagement in New York, a sequence of events, many of them out of the company's control, systematically undermined it. To begin with, Yakobson, who never restaged a ballet without reworking parts of it, revised *Spartacus* extensively for the Bolshoi. "Yakobson has created a new version: he has rewritten the plan and composition," Boris Lvov-Anokhin wrote in an explanatory essay for the souvenir program. "The scenes follow each other without attempting to convey the sequence of historical events, but giving a plastic picture of life in ancient Rome."[74] In an attempt to frame Yakobson as a fashionable rebel, Lvov-Anokhin labels him "one of the most restless of our modern choreographers." Sounding as if he is describing the bad boy of Soviet Ballet to appeal to Western audiences' tastes for outlaws, Lvov-Anokhin also mentions the "almost improvised" impression of Yakobson's choreography. "His road to art has been far from smooth. . . . Yakobson argues boldly and sharply about art himself and evokes violent arguments around him. He is a real 'controversial' artist in the most direct and best sense of the term," Lvov-Anokhin wrote.[75]

Yakobson's widow, Irina, recalled Yakobson explaining that once the Kirov had arrived in America, the company had insufficient in-theater rehearsal time for *Spartacus*. Certainly the company had arrived sufficiently in advance of the September 13 opening; on September 2 the *New York Times* published a feature with photographs of the company rehearsing in preparation for the opening night *Swan Lake* performance the following week. Yakobson reported to Irina afterward that the three dozen or so "supers" (extras) hired from local ballet schools also had not rehearsed fully with the company and that their integration with the company on stage was therefore not as smooth as it should have been. A lack of preparation for the *Spartacus* performers, particularly with choreography that was already uniquely challenging and outside of their normal movement vocabulary, could certainly have contributed to an uneven opening night performance. Some, like Kirov ballerina Natalia Makarova, contend that the Bolshoi version of *Spartacus* was considerably weaker than the Kirov production had been, contributing to the uneven reception in America.[76]

One of the American student "supers" for *Spartacus* was Rosemary Novellino-Mearns, a sixteen-year-old ballet student from New Jersey who studied in a local ballet school with a niece of Michel Fokine. She recalled how the performances looked from the stage, remembering that she had been told to dash onstage at the opening of the first act, carrying a large urn on her head. Novellino-Mearns and the other nine extras with her were then to rush to the edge of the stage and lie down by the footlights to watch the various grand entrances of the military regiments and Crassus on his chariot being pulled by a chained Spartacus. Novellino-Mearns recounted that opening night: "As I was lying there on the Met stage right in front of the footlights, all of a sudden I heard booing. Yes, loud, rude, shocking BOOING. The audience hated what they were watching. There was not one pointe shoe and not one tutu to be found in *Spartacus* and this made them mad. I think they thought that they were going to see Swans and Princes, but they got sandals and swords. This was shocking for us, and I can't even imagine what the Bolshoi was feeling."[77]

A fellow ballet student and super with Novellino-Mearns, Wendy Perron, who became a professional dancer and dance writer, kept a detailed diary of her experience as a super in *Spartacus*. She confirms that the preparation was indeed compressed, beginning with the initial audition on Sunday, September 9. She recalled only two rehearsals, including the dress rehearsal, before the ballet opened. In an interview, Perron could not remember ever rehearsing with the Bolshoi dancers in *Spartacus*, only going through the supers' directions about their places on stage. What she does remember vividly as a fifteen-year-old super in *Spartacus*, however, is the orgy scene, where her instructions were to make the performed love-making as realistic as possible.[78] "I froze," she said. Perron's experience, beginning with the audition, suggests how vital verisimilitude was in both casting and onstage actions for what Yakobson wanted from the extras. Her friends padded out Perron's slender figure with wads of paper towels, trying to make her match the request for the extras to look "womanly." "In the orgy scene we had to be making out, eating grapes and writhing all over each other," Perron said, adding that, as a teenaged girl, being instructed to kiss someone onstage made her really nervous. "I remember the movement being so sinuous and the whole ballet seemed very, very dramatic," Perron recalled.[79]

Without a proper context for the radicalism of Yakobson's choreography, and with tensions heightened by the themes of geopolitical competition echoing through *Spartacus*, two of the critics for the major New York newspapers, Allen Hughes at the *New York Times* and Walter Terry at the *New York Herald Tribune*, took aim at Yakobson's *Spartacus* with sharply polarized Cold War prose. The most knowledgeable daily dance critic in New York, John Martin with the *New York Times*, was absent. Martin was about to retire and he was making his exit by accompanying the New York City Ballet on their eight-week tour to the USSR, scheduled to begin soon after the Bolshoi's arrival in New York. So the job of covering the Bolshoi's opening fell to Allen Hughes, the second-string dance writer for the *Times*. (Hughes would subsequently serve as interim dance critic for two years, between Martin's departure at the end of 1962 and the arrival of Clive Barnes as chief dance critic in 1965.) Although Hughes's main beat was music, when it came to dance, he was a self-declared partisan of modern dance. In 1963 he would earn the enmity of the ballet world by protesting in print the Ford Foundation's magnanimous $7.7 million grant to stabilize ballet in America, particularly the New York City Ballet.

The morning after the Bolshoi premiered *Spartacus* at the Metropolitan Opera House in New York, the *New York Times* published Hughes's review, a catalogue of unfulfilled expectations. His article opens with the statement that "the Bolshoi Ballet's much-heralded *Spartacus* was given its first American performance last night, and this reviewer feels it is only fair to preface his remarks with the admission that he found the spectacle to be one of the most preposterous theatrical exercises he has ever seen." Hughes proceeded to deride *Spartacus* in caustic prose designed to display the wit of the writer more than the attributes or problems of the production. "There is so much that is unbelievable about it that it is difficult to know what to mention first." Hughes wrote. "But, for example, the fact that one of the greatest ballet companies in the world would invest so much talent, time, money and, presumably, belief in the staging of a dull pageant is simply beyond understanding." Hughes repeated his contention that the ballet "contains very little dancing of any kind" and is "conspicuously lacking [in taste]." One of the sections of the ballet that he actually described was the gladiators' fight scene, which he found objectionable because the number of corpses on the ground did not equal the number of fighting sequences depicted. Khachaturian's score was dismissed in the same deprecating tone; it was "in the style of Hollywood sound tracks," Hughes wrote. "The work as a whole represents a sadly disappointing attempt to do something that Hollywood manages better."[80]

Terry's review in the *New York Herald Tribune* adapted a similar tone of personal affront. "You have to see it to believe it," was his opening sentence. "*Spartacus* is not as non-dancy as the comment overheard at the end of the first act would lead one to believe: 'Look Ma, no dancing!' There is dancing, pseudo-Roman, pseudo-Oriental, pseudo-Isadora Duncan and pseudo quite a few other things. . . . The truth is that the dancing gets lost in the bigness of it all. Only the unrestrainedly emotional acting manages to hold its own with the massive towers and statues and with costumes that knock you senseless."[81] In a tone that suggests an adult admonishing a child that what he thought was good is in fact awful, Terry compares the ballet to "the eye-battings, lurchings and gesticulations of silent movies," and "an extravagant extravaganza" that suggests if one can "combine your sense of humor with a nostalgia for the fanciful improbabilities of the old screen spectacles, you will have a whirl."[82] The essence of Terry's summation is that whatever Yakobson's *Spartacus* is, it is not dance, much less serious art.

Edwin Denby, the most sophisticated viewer of ballet among the New York dance critics of this period, wrote an essay for the *Hudson Review* about the Bolshoi's first visit to the United States in 1959. In this article three years before the 1962 tour, Denby reflected on the technical differences between the Bolshoi and American ballet companies. His prose also has a certain condescension and pedantic quality that suggests he is taking his reader by the hand and patiently pointing out the shortcomings in this exotic and inferior dance artifact known as Soviet ballet. In his essay,

Denby compares the Russian choreographers and dancers with those of the New York City Ballet by way of answering Khrushchev's rhetorical question from Hollywood about which nation's ballet is better. "The fact is, the Bolshoi choreographers couldn't have imagined dances like *Agon, Episodes,* or *Divertimento 15.* Bolshoi dancers couldn't have danced them, or the conductors played the scores so straight. It may be that the New York ballet public is the only one quick enough of eye and ear to enjoy these pleasures. Does that prove our ballet is better?" Denby asks, concluding that American ballet is different in a way that will set the standard internationally far into the future.[83] He continues, citing differences in both nations' style of ballet, such as the momentum and physical quality of accenting given the movements. His conclusion is that the Bolshoi is lacking if measured against "Western Standards." "Bolshoi technique stresses big jumps more than quick toes; it stresses mobility of shoulder and upper spine, and acrobatics like those of a vaudeville adagio-team. Western ballerina technique requires a sharply versatile, high-speed exactitude of step and of ear and a high tension stamina—which are not Bolshoi characteristics."[84] Denby concludes his assessment of the shortcomings of the Bolshoi by enumerating many of those attributes that Yakobson's *Spartacus* worked so hard to redress, yet which remained invisible to the majority of the American dance press:

> The Bolshoi has formalized its style and it does what it does on principle. It covers up with care the brilliantly unreasonable resources of expression which are the glory of ballet dancing. It does so to stress instead an acted mime meaning. . . . Nor has the choreography a gift for narration. . . . The Bolshoi means to uncover its dance power in the next few years. When it does, it will add to the literal meaning of pantomime the metaphorical meaning of dancing. As of now, Western ballet—and even our own part of it— offers more fun, a fiercer luster, more grace of irony, and much more imaginative excitement and poetic courage, though it isn't stronger and is ever so much less secure.[85]

Denby's remarks, although written well in advance of the Bolshoi's New York premiere of *Spartacus,* anticipate the same tone of the reviews that will tear apart that production. The similarities are not accidental, although the medium of a dance review might be unexpected. This is the rhetoric of Cold War dance criticism. A war was being waged through rhetoric and Yakobson's *Spartacus* had become target practice. Rhetorician Martin Medhurst argues that the art of rhetoric became the central feature of the Cold War as political and rhetorical exchanges took the place of physical combat. "Rhetoric was not something added on or peripheral to or substituting for the 'real' issue," Medhurst asserts. "No, rhetoric was *the* issue; it constituted the central substance that required serious attention if the Cold War was to remain cold."[86] Ballet performances by touring companies from the "enemy" country made easy targets for prose saturated with cool superiority, and the reviews of the Bolshoi by Hughes and Terry are written in this spirit. Hughes's criticism of *Spartacus* focused on sharp-edged rhetoric more than any real assessment of the dancing or choreography.

On September 23, 1962, Hughes wrote again about *Spartacus,* this time as a Sunday feature. Under the headline "About *Spartacus:* Can It Be Understood Though Disliked?" Hughes commences a half-hearted reassessment that reveals the angry responses that his flip initial review must have generated from *New York Times* readers. "Now that the general astonishment created by the Bolshoi Ballet's unveiling of its 'Spartacus' has abated somewhat, it might be worth while to think more calmly about this work, its reason for being, and its lack of significance for us." Hughes editorializes: "Let us begin by reminding ourselves that for all the universality it is supposed to possess, art—even the best of it—does not invariably travel well. . . . Just now, the New York City Ballet is headed for its first tour of the Soviet Union, and it will be surprising if the Soviet press and public do not find at least a part of the company's repertory and dancing style incomprehensible and, therefore, valueless," he writes, suggesting that his reviews might be peremptory attacks on Soviet audiences and any responses by their press to the New York City Ballet.[87]

In an effort to justify his earlier critique of *Spartacus,* however, Hughes suggests that perhaps the ballet was not really as popular in the USSR as was reported, or if it was, the interest was short-lived. "We have not been told how the Muscovites felt the morning after, nor how they have responded since," he offers. Then he tries a second justification, suggesting that if in fact the Soviets did like the ballet (and it would have taken little effort to confirm its extraordinary popularity at the Kirov and Bolshoi), then that was either because it had "a special patriotic or ideological appeal for Russians it does not have for us" or because "Soviet concepts of staging and costuming [that] seem markedly old-fashioned to us . . . do not seem so to the Soviets." Perhaps even the absence of classical dancing for audiences accustomed to ballet classics, Hughes writes, may seem quite refreshing or strike the Russian people as being genuinely modern. He then resumes his defensive stance, concluding in the same lofty tone with which he began: "That *Spartacus* is not for us we know for sure, and it is probably safe to assume that the work is of no artistic significance whatsoever." Then in his next sentence, Hughes contradicts himself, ending with a final statement that is the closest he comes to an honest assessment in either article: "The possibility exists, however, that it represents a necessary if faltering forward step of Russian dance on a winding path to real modernism. Let us hope so."[88]

The public that Hughes suggests he speaks for with his frequent invocation of "us" finally has its own say in a column adjacent to this Sunday piece, where three letters from readers commenting on the Bolshoi reviews appear. The most notable one, titled "Spartacus Praised," reads as follows:

I found Leonid Yakobson's choreography for "Spartacus" to be one of the most beautiful expressions in plastic terms of feeling, or drama, that I have ever seen in dancing.

I don't know what decided [*sic*] the Bolshoi to do "Spartacus," but having chosen, they have done it without the cynicism that often pervades the work of dancers other than Russians. In my opinion, the remarkable thing in the concept of the choreography is that within its framework of grandeur, everything that is done is considered and refined to the last detail, and is constantly surprising and unexpected in its variation.[89]

The author of these remarks is James Waring, a respected dancer and choreographer who was considered one of the most influential figures in the New York dance avant-garde in the late 1950s and early 1960s. As knowledgeable about ballet as modern dance, and with substantial training in both, Waring used his knowledge and insight of dance in his assessment. This was the voice of an informed American dance-audience member responding positively to *Spartacus*, but it was too late. By the time Waring's letter to the *New York Times* appeared in print, *Spartacus* had been precipitously erased from the Bolshoi's entire tour. Yakobson would never tour the United States again.

On September 18, five days after Hughes's vitriolic opening-night review, a notice appeared in the *Times* announcing that the "three scheduled showings of 'Spartacus' [at the Metropolitan Opera House, would] be replaced by other works."[90] Five days after that, it was announced that *Spartacus* would not be staged in Los Angeles: the *Los Angeles Times* gave notice in an article with the headline "*Spartacus* Taken Out of Ballet Repertoire." The non-byline article cites as the reason: "Because of the difficulties of transporting huge settings [*sic*] and other complicated trapping by air to the west coast for the presentation of 'Spartacus,' word has been received from New York that the ballet has been taken out of the repertoire of the Bolshoi Ballet." As if this issue had not been considered and resolved long before the tour ever began.[91]

The Bolshoi's American tour had been made possible in part by the efforts of not only Hurok but also Yekaterina Furtseva, the Soviet minister of culture. Thus the decision to terminate Yakobson's ballet came out of concern for further negative reviews. There were in fact rules of engagement for dance criticism in the Cold War, and Hughes, Terry, and those who booed in the audience at the Met had violated them. The Soviets must have felt deeply humiliated by the Americans' rudeness, doubly so since what they were providing as a centerpiece of the Bolshoi's major tour was the riskiest and most experimental full-length ballet, or for that matter ballet in any category, that they had created. Putting forth Yakobson on such a grand venue was a bold gesture designed not only to please but also to ask: "Was Yakobson's strange, experimental ballet really good?" Hughes, Terry, and the others had become so swept up by a different agenda that they had, with tragic irony, fallen in step with Yakobson's Soviet detractors. Yakobson's *Spartacus* was effectively the seed of a popular uprising from deep within the Soviet system, and the Americans had failed to recognize it or send aid. Even those who should have known better failed to see the real politics beneath the superficial. Sol Hurok's Russian-born wife, Emma, who rarely came to her husband's presentations, attended the opening night of *Spartacus* in New York but left after the first act. She theatrically displayed her annoyance, muttering audibly as she departed that Hurok kept "bringing those goddamn Communists."[92]

All we know of Yakobson's response to the critics and the cancellation comes from Maya Plisetskaya, who said she talked with him after the fifth and final *Spartacus* performance in New York. She remembered:

> When we finally performed *Spartacus* in America, with Yakobson there—the first time he had ever been allowed out of the Soviet Union—it was the bitterest experience for me to hear how cruelly and devastatingly the American press attacked him. And not for essential things but over trifles. . . . I worried, seeing how Yakobson suffered and agonized, and how the ministry hacks who accompanied us gloated—so, Mr. Yakobson, your Western innovations got what they deserved. Yakobson tried to not show how dispirited and burdened he felt. His animated, mobile face was hidden behind a mask of indifference. Only after the last performance of *Spartacus* in New York (the ballet was quickly replaced for the rest of the cities on the tour), did Yakobson sit down on the metal stool in my dressing room at the Met and break out into silent weeping. Large, heavy tears dropped from his blue eyes.
>
> "Mayka, you were brilliant today. Your weeping scene was so powerful, that I . . ."
>
> "Leonid Veniaminovich, don't pay attention to the critics. You saw how the audience applauded, how they didn't want to leave."
>
> "I'm afraid my tormentors in Moscow and Leningrad have been given a big trump card."[93]

In this paraphrased, remembered conversation, Plisetskaya also recalled Yakobson's despair over the critics having written that there wasn't enough dance when he saw his ballet as being *all* dance. "There isn't a single nondance movement, not a single pantomime," he countered. "This is the most danceable of all my ballets!"[94] Yakobson's widow said that he in fact continued on the tour with the Kirov, even though the last three performances were cancelled. He stayed out of the public eye and purchased a camera and books on the works of Chagall and Picasso, which he brought back with him. Soon after his return, the New York City Ballet arrived to commence its Soviet tour, a performance experience that Soviet critics and audiences reacted to with significantly more respect and decorum than the Americans had afforded Yakobson. The American company had enough time and resources, and their performances were thoroughly well prepared; in fact, John Martin remarked in one of his reviews that the company had never danced better. He also recorded that Soviet audiences at first greeted the non-narrative ballets with quiet puzzlement but gradually warmed to them over the course of an evening or, in the instance of the larger cities, a two-week string of performances.[95]

Yakobson saw the company when they came to Leningrad, and he chatted with Balanchine briefly in a meeting in a room adjoining the little museum in the Leningrad Choreographic Institute. This meeting had been arranged between Balanchine and fourteen Soviet choreographers, including Yakobson as the oldest, Igor Belsky as the youngest, and twelve student choreographers. Martin mentioned this meeting in his review of the Leningrad performances, calling it "perhaps the most important event in the entire Soviet tour." According to Martin, "at [the choreographers'] request, [Balanchine] told them of the underlying principles of an art that differs widely from their own." In a tone of reverence, suggesting that Balanchine conversing with Soviet choreographers was like bringing bronze to the Stone Age, Martin continues: "It is fair to believe that choreography in Leningrad will never be quite the same again although there is strong official opposition to new ideas."[96] So taken with his own authority and power was Martin that his reporting of the New York City Ballet in the USSR was in fact as propagandistic as what the Soviets were accused of doing through ballet. Martin's sentiments in this review also reflect the significant shift he had made from just a few years earlier in his regard for ballet. As dance scholar Gay Morris has also noted, in the early 1950s Martin's enthusiasm for Balanchine was increasing and his attacks on ballet formalism were softening and shifting. "Balanchine's work was difficult; it did not court audiences, which indicated that it was more than easy entertainment. The difficulty of his work also put Balanchine on the side of innovation and experiment. According to Martin, Balanchine had replaced the flair of the old Russian ballet with substance."[97]

A photograph of Yakobson and Balanchine chatting in the hallway outside this meeting room in the choreographic institute documents the moment of reunion, a metaphorical healing of a separation that was more historical than personal. Most significantly it was about art opportunities found in one instance and lost in another. Irina remembers *The Prodigal Son* (1928–1929) being in the repertoire that the New York City Ballet had brought to Leningrad. Yakobson, who had seen all of the tour's performances, asked Balanchine why he had made *The Prodigal Son,* a ballet with big emotions and a big story, when most of the other ballets he presented were non-narrative. According to Irina, who heard it from Yakobson, Balanchine replied that he had continued in this vein of abstraction because he had found a way to be successful in the United States with the non-story ballets. "Russian people like to have some emotion or cry or be sad or happy, a bit naïve maybe, but maybe also a little more sensitive," Yakobson's widow said, reflecting on her and her husband's reactions.[98]

This anecdote also rehearses what was for the Soviets an exaggerated conception of capitalism, where the eagerness to make money drives even artistic creation. On the Western side, that the hero Spartacus was the subject of Yakobson's ballet seems to have excited and irritated Western journalists, since the USSR and United States had both embraced this mythic figure as emblematic of their own nationalist politics. Yakobson's *Spartacus* was more about personal introspection and quiet nobility, whereas

George Balanchine and Leonid Yakobson backstage at the
Kirov Theater, Leningrad, 1962. Photo: Daniil Savelyev.

the U.S. version was more about militaristic and Christian-inflected heroism. So although this 1962 cultural exchange between the Bolshoi and New York City Ballet was supposed to help foster international understanding, the Cold War politics unfolding around it made the proposition tenuous.

None of the advance press in the United States for Yakobson's *Spartacus* tried to prepare audiences for the aesthetic novelty of the ballet, nor its radical interventions in the face of Soviet restrictions. Rather it is repeatedly represented as a spectacle, a performance implicitly complicit with Soviet politics. The assumption was that all Soviet art was a mouthpiece for the government. American audiences were not expecting to have to read between the lines or look inside the steps of Yakobson's *Spartacus,* so they missed his text within the text. They, like the Soviet censors who had reluctantly let it pass at the Kirov and Bolshoi showings, only saw and reacted to the outer layer of its meanings.

A range of U.S. cultural and political influences also complicated even the very subject of *Spartacus.* Some of the American audiences were likely familiar with Howard Fast and the tensions of the U.S. House Un-American Activities Committee around his 1951 pro-Soviet novel *Spartacus.* More immediately, however, the young director Stanley Kubrick had just begun his film career with the enormously successful release of his *Spartacus* film, which featured Kirk Douglas as the Christ-like gladiator leader. Dubbed "the thinking man's epic," Kubrick's *Spartacus* film, with its cinematic grandeur, sweat, and gore—reportedly 70,000 fans at a college football game were recorded shouting "Hail Crassus" for one of the sound effects in a gladiator fight scene—would be a difficult act for any live performance to follow, particularly a ballet hobbled by Soviet limitations on theatricality, religious symbolism, narrative openness, and eroticism, or basically everything a Soviet ballet *Spartacus* would need if it were even to begin to offer a compelling alternative to the American *Spartacus* film.

By the time the Bolshoi arrived at the Metropolitan Opera House for its opening on September 13, 1962, the lore around the *Spartacus* film was turning it into a celebrated anti-fascist statement rivaling the original gladiator's story. Instead of Crassus, the foe was Senator Joseph McCarthy, the self-appointed eliminator of democracy's leftists. The screenwriter for Kubrick's film was Dalton Trumbo, a writer blacklisted by McCarthy.

Defying the ban on employing him, Kubrick and Douglas had publicly announced that Trumbo was the screenwriter of their *Spartacus* film and had deliberately displayed his name on the film in the Spartacus spirit of resisting HUAC's inquisition into the film industry. Even President Kennedy made a public show of defiance against the intimidation of the blacklist by crossing anti-Communist picket lines to attend the opening screening of the *Spartacus* film, a gesture that in retrospect is credited with having helped to end blacklisting.

Not only was the hero Spartacus a political mascot of radically different sorts for each nation, but the ballet *Spartacus* was seen as resisting socialism and the film *Spartacus* was perceived as defying capitalism. Kubrick explained that the climactic scene in his film—where recaptured slaves are asked to identify Spartacus in exchange for leniency and instead each slave proclaims himself to be Spartacus, thus sharing his fate—came from a story he had heard about the Holocaust. "The S.S. had paraded all the English prisoners and ordered any Jews to take one step forward. One or two did so. The S.S. officer yelled out that if there were any others, they had better admit it by the time he had counted to three. The menace in his voice somehow alerted the prisoners to what might happen to the few Jews who were being singled out. One, two . . . at the shout of three, *all* the prisoners stepped forward. Pretty good scene," Kubrick said admiringly.[99] Yakobson did not have the freedom to be explicit about any specific cultural groups in his *Spartacus,* but his audiences could bring their own narratives in their minds.

The Soviets sent KGB agents with their dancers, whereas the Americans carried two of the most influential dance writers of the period with them. Not surprisingly these writers chronicled the Bolshoi–New York City Ballet exchange of 1962 as an encounter where one company and country would emerge the creative victor and the other would be a vanquished second. Yakobson and his *Spartacus* were a casualty of these intellectual skirmishes. The ballet touring exchanges may have been ostensibly about Cold War diplomacy, but in 1962 they became a Cold War front themselves. National allegiances and competition were displaced onto the ballet troupes and dance criticism reinforced polarized outlooks. Dance critics hurled rhetorical barbs, with one company—the New York City Ballet—seen as free, modernist, and socially daring about race, and the other, the Bolshoi, perceived as reinforcing the status quo.

The New York City Ballet opened its eight-week tour in Moscow on October 9, 1962. John Martin, writing in the *New York Times,* raved about the performances and disparaged Soviet audiences' response as ranging from "perplexed and fairly indifferent" to the non-narrative dances to "delight" with the clear storyline of *Western Symphony* (1954). The tone of Martin's as well as Lincoln Kirstein's reports, which he subsequently published, is similarly disdainful, with the authors remarking on the astonishment of the audiences and ridiculing Soviet dance critics' far less enthusiastic reactions. Kirstein paraphrased the Soviet's thoughts about the New York City Ballet: "Our spareness in decoration and costume was hapless formalism; our androgynous lack of polarization between musculated [*sic*] males and bosomy females was the result of a fatal absence of Socialist health and psyche."[100]

Martin, who filed stories from nearly every city the New York City Ballet visited, wrote at considerable length about the Soviet audiences, ascribing intellectual and emotional responses to their applause as if divining meanings from silence. His first review was filed the night after the company's opening in Moscow on October 9. Here he wrote with grandiosity about how transforming and enlightening this contact with Balanchine's genius will be for "Russian culture." Noting that the company is the first American ballet troupe to appear at the Bolshoi Theater, he editorialized: "What is more important, it introduced a completely new style of ballet to its great stage. . . . A genuine victory had been won." After using this metaphor of combat, he commended the "highly experienced ballet audience" for having recognized the excellence of Balanchine's art.[101] The most consistent observations Martin makes, however, are about the "cordial," "thoughtful," "warm," "fresh and welcoming," "understanding and keen expressions of appreciation" that typified Soviet reactions to the company's performances throughout the two months of their USSR tour. It is a more civil response by far than that given the Bolshoi and Yakobson in New York. Elizabeth Souritz, who saw the 1962 New York City Ballet performances in the Soviet Union, remembered that the rules of decorum set by Soviet authorities were very clear: "While the Americans danced in Russia, the Bolshoi dancers performed in America. For this reason, the press had to abide by certain rules. You could not write anything . . . insulting . . . , abusive; you had to remember they were official guests. At the same time there was the Soviet ideology to be taken into consideration. You had to impress upon the reader that here was something not as good as our own product, but also that any good part was the result of past Russian influence."[102]

Khachaturian wrote one of the celebrity artists' responses to the New York City Ballet performances. In the complaint about the lack of plot in Balanchine's ballets, essentially the obligatory statement against formalism, Khachaturian, or his editor at *Izvestia,* similarly exempted from his review any mention of *Agon,* which was arguably the most purely formalist work performed. A tone of diplomacy pervades Khachaturian's review, which is open and complimentary about Balanchine's dancers' technique even as Khachaturian noted the Russian origins of Balanchine's training:

> The first impression from the performance by our American guests is the flawless classical technique, which the artists are in beautiful control of. Probably this is the result of a serious school of classical dance brought here by the artist of the American ballet by George Balanchine—by the way, he is a graduate of a Russian school of classical ballet and graduated from Leningrad Choreographic Institute.
>
> These positive traits especially are felt in the ballet *Serenade* choreographed to Tchaikovsky's music in the tradition of classical recitative. *Serenade* is a beautiful spectacle that has a fresh choreographic handwriting and original choreographic lexicon; the creative imagination of Balanchine shows itself with great force. . . .
>
> Balanchine is against pulling out stars in his group and that is why we do not evaluate the individual dancers. . . . This idea, in my opinion as a conductor, deserves attention. . . . But Balanchine in his artistic practice takes the side of the principle of plotlessness. This looks strange to Soviet artists and audiences. Without ideas [and] without plot, not a single emotional art can exist.
>
> Moscow audiences also were happy to greet the first performance by our guests from the USA as much and as warmly as American audiences are greeting the Bolshoi Ballet right now.[103]

Souritz, who also wrote about the New York City Ballet tour for the Soviet magazine *Teatr,* noticed the heavy oversight under which Khachaturian's *Pravda* review appeared. The rules of critical engagement for writers guaranteed that the official ideology—which deemed nothing as good as the Soviet product and success elsewhere to be attributable to past Russian influence—would always prevail. "Of course, *Pravda* was the first to give a signal to every other newspaper and critic, so that they would know what they should write," Souritz noted.[104] Khachaturian did deviate from the script a short while later, when he was quoted in *Time* magazine in an exchange with George Balanchine. Venting his continuing anger against Yakobson for having edited his *Spartacus* score, Khachaturian suggested that if Balanchine had created the choreography for *Spartacus* it would not have been so unsuccessful. Balanchine reportedly countered that *Spartacus,* like much of Soviet contemporary ballet, excessively emphasized plot and decoration at the expense of mime and music, and was therefore hopeless from the beginning.[105]

Meanwhile, outside the theaters where the New York and Soviet ballet companies were performing on tour, the Cold War approached active engagement. On October 14, 1962, a U.S. Air Force U-2 plane flew over Cuba. The plane was on a photoreconnaissance mission and it captured photographic evidence of Soviet missile bases under construction in Cuba and within easy striking range of the United States. While the building of the missiles in Cuba had begun long before the ballet tour exchange, the discovery of the missiles precipitated a showdown between Khrushchev and Kennedy that came dangerously close to escalating. In retrospect the affront to Soviet courtesy and ego that the mistreatment of *Spartacus* occasioned was unfortunate in both spirit and timing. It's not clear how aware of the missile crisis the Soviet dancers might have been (reportedly none of them were), since the only one among them who was fluent in English was Anastasia Stevens, the daughter of Edmund Stevens, Moscow correspondent for *Time* and *Life.* In contrast, the New York City Ballet dancers on tour in the USSR were all on high alert during the Cuban missile crisis and were well aware that their status as cultural ambassadors offered a feeble immunity when it came to real conflict. Dance scholar Naima Prevots recounts that despite Lincoln Kirstein's saying that awareness of the conflict "hardly percolated down to the dancers," Allegra Kent, one of the New York City Ballet dancers on tour, remembered it differently: "The world looked as if it might blow up, but I couldn't miss a beat with my preparations for dancing or else I'd fall behind. . . . My muscles, mind, and shoes had to be ready because, despite the crisis, the audience didn't stay home."[106]

Anastasia Stevens might not have been the most neutral source to dispense information about American and Soviet politics to the Bolshoi dancers. The American media idolized her during the early 1960s as a living symbol of cultural rapprochement because of her acceptance into the Bolshoi Ballet as their first and only American member. Beginning in 1960, when at the age of eighteen she joined the Bolshoi, Anastasia had been the subject of photo essays in American publications.[107] During the Bolshoi's 1962 tour she was even the subject of a short film made by American filmmakers David and Albert Maysles. Yet in the *Life* blurb about her, the unidentified writer (likely her father) is careful to mention that she nearly flunked Russian grammar while excelling in the Bolshoi School. It is as if to prove she can match Soviet cultural standards but she is still an American at heart. This was an emblem of national loyalty that Edmund Stevens might well have wanted to advertise. The elder Stevens was rumored to be a Soviet, and even a KGB, collaborator for years.[108] In 2009, after a major Soviet informer defected and Stevens had already passed away, it was confirmed that Stevens had indeed been on the Soviet payroll, thus suggesting that his daughter's job in the corps de ballet was likely more political than artistic. Wendy Perron remembers Anastasia Stevens as being the translator for the *Spartacus* supers and an idol for the young American ballet dancers because of her dual status as one of "us" yet also one of "them."[109]

There was a certain painful irony to the entire arc from start to endpoint for Yakobson's *Spartacus* ballet. Conceived in the midst of an active war to spur patriotic zeal, it was realized in the changed world of the Cold War, when the rhetorical posture of defiance was a new arena for combat. Yakobson's experience with his *Spartacus* in America was a reminder that not just bullets but also language could deliver a fatal wound. Despite the pronouncements of American critics, Yakobson's *Spartacus* continued in the Soviet Union as one of the most successful productions in the Kirov repertoire for twenty years. In 1968 Yury Grigorovich, who had danced in Yakobson's original *Spartacus* at the Kirov, created his own version for the Bolshoi, using the same Khachaturian score and Volkov-Yakobson libretto as well as other aspects of Yakobson's ballet. Grigorovich, however, added pointe work; huge ensembles of dancers in unison; and all the bravura ballet lifts, pirouettes and fouettés, and technical fireworks that Yakobson had so scrupulously avoided. This was the version of the *Spartacus* ballet for which the Bolshoi became known on its subsequent tours to the West. It fell neatly into the aesthetic polarization of heroic and overstated bravura, a dance in which Stakhanovite laborers were framed as descendents from antiquity.

Spartacus was Yakobson's grandest manifesto as an artistic dissident. It was also his most public international humiliation. In many ways it came to symbolize the shadow side of Cold War cultural diplomacy, in part due to Yakobson's path crossing once again with Balanchine's even as the gulf between their two experiences continued to widen. Here was Yakobson with the heavily redacted remnants of a once grand ballet, suddenly the target of American critics' anti-Soviet ire when in fact he was one of Soviet culture's staunchest dance dissidents. In contrast, Balanchine's aesthetic, with its embrace of the much touted evil of formalism, had a unique cachet in the USSR. He was also touring with an entourage that included two of the most influential dance writers of the time, Kirstein and Martin, both of whom had written informed critical and historical analy-

Yakobson in his study at home in Leningrad, ca. 1971. Photographer unknown.

ses of Balanchine's work at home and abroad, something that Yakobson was never allowed to do. These two choreographers' experiences during the 1962 tour reveal much about the very different paths that cultural expression took in the twentieth century as it diverged from the fertile innovations of the 1920s and 1930s in Russia into the polarized landscape of postwar U.S.-Soviet geopolitics.

SIX

Dismantling the Hero

Blind or paralyzed, limping, one-legged, or wearing prostheses—the world
of the Stalinist novel and Stalinist film is filled with damaged male bodies.
Their sacrifices to the Soviet cause make them worthy of elevation to
the status of "hero'" yet their extreme forms of physical disability reveal
what might be called an ideological and cultural fantasy of Stalinism:
the radical dismemberment of its male subjects.
—Lilya Kaganovsky, *How the Soviet Man Was Unmade,* 2008

THE BALLETS THAT Yakobson made after *Spartacus* had a different sort of
strength. Increasingly they chipped away at the myth of the indestructible Stalinist-era male by presenting images of broken, abnormal dancing
bodies. These were ballets with forms and movements that allowed anti-
heroic postures to be seen underneath the stolid hero image. In Soviet

film and literature of the late 1950s, the fantasy Stalin hero was also being rewritten as the heroic wounded invalid, or what Soviet scholar Lilya Kaganovsky has dubbed "the second version of Stalin's New Man."[1] But the images that Yakobson was producing resisted being tucked back into any category of Stalin-era hero, their deconstruction of the Stalinist-era male was so absolute.

Overall, the assertively modern vocabulary that Yakobson had been moving toward continued to develop, but he added another register—a more satiric and brutally emotional one. Implicit in his major works from the mid-1960s—*The Bedbug* (1962), *The Twelve* (1964), and *The Land of Miracles* (1967)—was a shift in the kinds of questions he was asking, and answering, through ballet. Increasingly he focused on the conflicting conceptions of what a good life is and how to understand and organize human lives.[2] He used choreography to generate ideas about leadership and bravery, and shaped his art to quietly explore the ambiguities around these issues in everyday Soviet life. *The Bedbug* and *The Twelve* were both choreographed during the period known as Khrushchev's "Thaw," the period from the mid-1950s to the early 1960s when, under Nikita Khrushchev's de-Stalinization policies, repression and censorship in the Soviet Union were eased, millions of political prisoners were released from Gulag labor campus, and it was possible for the first time in decades to access material of the modernist 1910s and 1920s. During this period of transformation for Soviet society, not only was Yakobson's sense of himself as an artist undiminished by the harsh reception of *Spartacus* abroad, but also his resolve to inhabit uncertainties in ballet while he pushed the classical lexicon toward a contemporary narrative intensified. In all three of these ballets he deliberately confuses one's sense about the heroes of modern times and about Soviet culture's imposed beliefs about the social world, its problems, and solutions. These were big subjects for ballet. In the USSR they were dangerous ones as well.

Spartacus had been based in part stylistically on inspiration and influence from other dance artists and styles Yakobson admired—specifically Michel Fokine and, to a far lesser degree, the Isadora Duncan style of dance naturalism. In Fokine he saw a choreographer who drew the main impetus for his work from artistic realms outside ballet. He also admired how Fokine pursued a unity of expression with his ballets, tying together their subjects, styling, and vocabularies of movement. Certainly in *Sparta-*

cus, too, Yakobson's simple tunic costumes for the women, soft shoes, and statuesque poses (for example, Phrygia's pose with Spartacus in which she stands with her neck arched back like an undulating Greek column) suggest the postures of near repose so emblematic of Isadora Duncan, though he reimagines this movement quality for bodies trained in classical ballet.

In *The Bedbug,* which the Kirov premiered in its first version on June 24, 1962, three months before the ill-fated Bolshoi tour to the United States, Yakobson reached for a more immediate personal past—the artistic hero of his youth, Vladimir Mayakovsky. A leading futurist poet and playwright from the 1920s, Mayakovsky, like his contemporary the poet Alexander Blok, had helped *un*make the young Yakobson's world.[3] Now Yakobson had begun using their writings to remake the world of Russian ballet. In *The Bedbug,* Yakobson turns Mayakovsky's 1929 poem by the same title into a freely interpreted two-act, fifty-minute ballet in which Mayakovsky appears as a working artist, interlocutor, and hero, shaping the dance as it unfolds before the audience. The ballet begins with the character Mayakovsky the poet standing on the stage as he muses and imagines, conjuring into life his characters and the various dancers portraying them. In the original performances Askold Makarov, the dancer on whom Yakobson specifically created the role of Mayakovsky, was a captivating and theatrically swaggering figure who danced this role to great acclaim.

"I created the role, counting on him, on his individuality and temperamental qualities," Yakobson once remarked. "In this role we saw a new Makarov, one who discovered in himself those dramatic qualities that he had not the opportunity to display earlier. . . . Beginning with his physical attributes he was a hero, an imposing figure of broad, free gestures, of a largesse of movement."[4] His description of how the stage character was tailored to the dancer and also how the choreography led the dancer deeper into himself has another layer of reference. Mayakovsky, who is onstage throughout the ballet inventing the dancers' actions and showing them their steps as they perform, also emerges as a proxy for Yakobson himself, the choreographer making his ballet from inside the dance. In both layers Yakobson is working for a deliberate confusion of the staged and the lived—but it is a conscious confusion arrived at by reaching into the subjective experience of what it is to inhabit a stage role for the dancer, and also to shape a role on the real-life proclivities of a performer.

In an extensive interview he gave about *The Bedbug* the year before his death, Yakobson explains that he turned to Mayakovsky's play because of his continual search for what he called his central concern: "finding a living, contemporary dance language."[5] His choice of the verb "find" is interesting for it suggests how Yakobson let his subjects shape the supporting elements of movement vocabulary, scenery, and costumes—a contemporary echoing of Fokine's dicta about historical consistency and stylistic unity as the foundation of modern ballet. "I searched a long time for stage designers," Yakobson said in regard to the scenery and costumes for *The Bedbug*. "Finally, I turned to the stage designer Andrey Goncharov. He called together a group that included Boris Messerer, Tatyana Selvinskaya, and Lev Zbarsky. Dividing up the functions, each designer took on a given section of the work."[6] In the end it was what he called "the satiric element, the grotesque," that pleased Yakobson the most about the scenery and costume's evocation of the spirit of his ballet. Although Dmitriy Shostakovich had composed the incidental music for the original production of *The Bedbug* play, that score was lost, so Yakobson commissioned Oleg Karavaychuk to compose improvisations to Mayakovsky's themes.[7] As Yakobson reported, that turned out to be difficult: "For a long time, we rehearsed without a precisely established musical foundation. The score changed at virtually every rehearsal." It was only as the work neared completion that Yakobson brought in the composer Georgiy Firtich, who orchestrated Karavaychuk's selections, supplying him with a workable musical text for this first version of *The Bedbug*. Yakobson once remarked that he considered *The Bedbug* a pioneering work and one of his two favorite ballets (the other was *The Twelve*). "The subject matter of Mayakovsky's play attracted me, it gave scope to my quests," he said.[8]

Yakobson's quest was both social and aesthetic. He based his ballet broadly on Mayakovsky's text, emphasizing the play's ironic exploration of the crass "NEP men," who by the mid- and late 1920s were being portrayed as grasping, corrupt bourgeois entrepreneurs only concerned with making money. The New Economic Policy (NEP), which had begun in 1921, ended with Stalin's first Five-Year Plan in 1928. Yakobson turns Mayakovsky's narrative into a means to acerbically mock the Communist Party bosses of the 1960s who seemed to him as cockroach-like as the NEP men Mayakovsky had parodied forty years earlier. To do this he ironizes their movement vocabulary, eliminating rounded-off lines and rendering the forms of the dancers, as well as their rhythms and transitions from one movement to the next, disjointed and broken. The ballet has been called a "choreographic poster in two acts" because of its visual designs based on the posters of the Russian Telegraphic Agency (ROSTA), the legendary Soviet state news organization that used writers and poets to contribute to the government's propaganda program. "Windows," one of its most successful projects, used six hundred cartoons with little phrases created by artists, including Mayakovsky, and it is these images that adorn the backdrop in Yakobson's ballet as well as dictate the style of the props, the dancers' costumes, and the mannerisms of *The Bedbug*. "It is a dazzling, loud, satirical and sometimes histrionic poster, where movements, dances and postures display an affinity to the outlines of the Windows of ROSTA," is how the critic Lvov-Anokhin described the ballet.[9] Yakobson works his movement radicalisms through the choreography of *The Bedbug*, eliminating traditional lifts, turnout, vertical alignment, and naturalistic action, and instead truncating the reach of the dancers' movements so that their interactions assume the two-dimensional quality of cartoons. He is moving further and further away from socialist realism, and doing it surreptitiously, in the spirit of historical evocation. What he is really presenting is modernism in disguise.

Yakobson streamlines the narrative in Mayakovsky's play into what is in some ways the ballet staple of a marriage plot, but with an acid twist; the groom is Ivan Prisïpkin, a vulgar and smug conformist, a professional "philistine," and the villainous bug of the title, and his bride is the promiscuous daughter of a coarse but rich couple. Prisïpkin makes his entrance by scuttling across a huge mattress onstage, and then, glimpsing Zoya Beryozkina, a pure and fair "worker girl," he fussily pretends to become a man. His ruse works and she falls in love with him—until Mayakovsky arrives and interrupts the seduction by slapping Prisïpkin, who scrambles away and onto a park bench behind which the attempted seduction had taken place. Yakobson designed Prisïpkin as the archetypal NEP man, who from his initial entrance moves in an evasive, furtive, and anxious rhythm. Prisïpkin's next prey is his future bride, Elzevira Renesans (for the Russian word "Renaissance"), the unrefined, buxom daughter of a vulgar rich couple, whom Yakobson once described as "an unsparing mockery of an acquisitive social class." (Yakobson's wife said these roles were intended to be caricatures of a bourgeois Jewish family.) Their wedding

ceremony is etched with vitriolic humor and looks like a satirical baccha-
nalian parody of the sculptural saturnalia in *Spartacus*. Yakobson's ruptur-
ing of the classical style in this way to insert this character portrayal was
particularly irritating to the dancer Dmitriy Vovk, who was one of a small
group of dancers playing onstage musicians. Yakobson wanted them to
dance in what Irina calls "a Jewish manner," a request that meant repeating the specific detailed gestures of this Jewish dance. Seeing Vovk's frustration, Yakobson offered to show the young dancer the movements again,
at which point the nervous and irritated dancer whispered under his
breath, "I refuse to pull these Kike stunts!"[10] Irina heard this but she says
fortunately her husband did not. It's a revealing moment suggesting the
ethnic vividness of Yakobson's satiric dance snapshots—and the tensions
these could produce even among dancers in his company.

The Bedbug and his Jewish bride consummate their nuptials on the
oversized blood-red bed in the midst of the stage as she is metaphorically undressed with the removal of two large, pompom-like flowers
stuck over the portion of her leotard covering her breasts. Yuriy Gromov,
a Saint Petersburg professor and choreographer, called this duet on the bed
a work of genius. "He had Nonna Yastrebova wear three roses, which Konstantin Rassadin tried to appropriate. When the latter managed to remove
two roses and was reaching for the third, Mayakovsky—Askold Makarov—
grabbed him and flung the whole lot of dancers—all of the vermin—on
the bed, setting them alight with a cigar, so they all went up in flames.
The entire scene was executed with astounding perspicacity, precision
and acumen—it couldn't have been better."[11]

The poet is on stage throughout the entire ballet, composing and orchestrating the dancing and drama by stirring his hands and pivoting his
body as if he were a demonic puppeteer or a magician conjuring his characters out of the dancers' bodies. Writing about *The Bedbug* the Russian
dance critic Viktor Vanslov praised it for its daring, originality, and path-
breaking boldness. "Leonid Yakobson, it can be claimed, effected a scenic
turning point in the staging of a theme that was entirely outside the prov-
ince of ballet," Vanslov wrote in commendation of the dance's importance for Russian ballet.[12] In the daring of its depiction of raw animalistic
passion, *The Bedbug* also evoked memories of Shostakovich's 1936 collision with Stalin and his censors over his opera *Lady Macbeth,* which had
been criticized in *Pravda* for displaying a "vulgar form of love" because of

The Bedbug (1974), the duet at the wedding of Elzevira Renesans and Prisïpkin, with Elena Selivanova, Igor Khokhlov, and Dmitriy Vovk (*standing*), Choreographic Miniatures, Leningrad. Photo: Vladimir Zenzinov.

the merchant's double bed that occupied the central place in the stage design.[13]

Eighteen-year-old Natalia Makarova, a young new member of the Kirov Ballet who was selected by Yakobson to dance the female lead of Zoya Beryozkina, agreed that its focus was Soviet culture through modernism. She noted how radical Yakobson's *The Bedbug* was in staging the act of artistic invention as the ballet's subject. The character of Mayakovsky is shown conjuring each character and then scripting their actions with a self-reflexiveness that was risky to put on the Soviet Union stage at the time. "Most dancers did not like Yakobson," Makarova noted in her autobiography. "Used to the standard classics, they felt uncomfortable in his contorted, expressively sharpened poses, which, in addition to everything else, Yakobson demanded they imbue with emotional content. Beautiful but sluggish bodies capable only of serving as props on stage made him furious." Makarova recounts that the first time he saw her, he reportedly whispered behind her back, "What a sex bomb has turned up." Makarova said this remark stunned her as a naive young woman who was already being typed for chaste, romantic ballerina roles.

Yakobson inverted that type-casting of Makarova in *The Bedbug*, suggesting to her that she perform Zoya like a contemporary Giselle. Instead of a romantic tutu and on pointe he costumed her in low heels; a faded, ill-fitting little dress; and a short, boyish wig. "I appeared on stage shaking my shoulders and swinging my hips, and I simply reveled in it—I loved both Zoya's brazenness and her shy vulnerability," Makarova said. She confided, "At the time, I was not very unlike my heroine and, basically, I danced as myself."[14] Makarova's experience of self-discovery through working with Yakobson was something he was able to do with many dancers, by tapping into their personalities and hidden potential. "All my life I have been lucky with dancers," he said about the dancers in *The Bedbug*. This is an observation that extends to all his work. "Perhaps I appreciate them fully, perhaps I am able to perceive their potential and try to tap their hidden reserves, my ballets have given a head start to many dancers."[15]

Yakobson quoted a variety of popular Western social dances in *The Bedbug*, and for Makarova these included the twist. Yet his contouring of the dancer's character and the choreographic image were so gently pressed together that Makarova insists she did not *play* a part in dancing Zoya. "I felt no discomfort at being a romantic ballerina who was dancing on heels, with knees knocking, a springy step, awkward lines, and crossed arms."[16] Her friends however, cautioned her against what they called "distort[ing] her beautiful body in those ugly poses." The most chilling of these is her final wild dance, not unlike an updated acerbic version of Giselle's mad scene and death at the end of the first act of *Giselle*. In *The Bedbug* the artistry is muted and the futile emptiness heightened as Zoya, in Makarova's words, "run[s] about, unaware, as if borne along by unbearable pain, tossing my legs back, knees giving way, dropping, writhing, and clutching with my hands in the air." She then staggers to a standstill. Sidling up to her, Mayakovsky reaches up with his hand for an imaginary rope, placing it around his neck and jerking the cord to break his neck. Zoya follows him numbly, her neck snapping to the side with the last gesture, her body seeming to buckle and give way although she remains standing.[17] The image is shaped so perfectly that it reads with the sharp narrative clarity of a storyboard as she obediently hangs herself. It is a deftly shaped movement metaphor about breaking down the boundaries between art and life—which was also a goal of Mayakovsky and his fellow avant-gardists.

The Bedbug, Askold Makarov and Natalia Makarova. Photo: © Nina Alovert, 1962.

The Bedbug, Askold Makarov and Natalia Makarova. Photo: © Nina Alovert, 1962.

The Bedbug, Askold Makarov and Natalia Makarova. Photo: © Nina Alovert, 1962.

The experience of working with Yakobson on *The Bedbug* changed Makarova profoundly as a dance artist. "In *The Bedbug*, I sensed for the first time just how constrained I had felt in the romantic vein," she admitted. "I am eternally grateful to Yakobson for believing in me and, little by little, as it were incidentally, drawing out my nature and my self. Thereafter, I did not have to coax it out of myself. I was possessed by power. I wanted to try everything, to empty myself into the dance. . . . Yakobson simply gave me the chance to get free of constraints and a kind of inexplicable shame that had been preventing me from opening up."[18]

As much as Yakobson opened up Makarova to herself and expanded her horizons as a ballerina in *The Bedbug*, so too did he go right to the edge of the permissible in revealing the Soviet party bosses and cultural arbiters as the models for the decadent and culturally ignorant human insects who crawl through the narrative. "Essentially, [these] were the ones," Makarova wrote, "who had forced their retrograde tastes on him and interfered with his realizing his precious talent. He set his satirical sights on them in his *Bedbug*—and without restraint; it took real daring to drag out a huge nuptial bed with a satin blanket onto the puritanical stage at the Kirov and then have my unfaithful love and his new lady squirming about in it, like two gigantic insects, in a love duet. The same is true for the scene of the wedding, with its bottles, cigarette butts, flowers, the fat rear ends wiggling to the chirring of the fox trot and the greasy wedding cortege."[19] This is Yakobson's portrait of the NEP, played out as flashing lights upstage illuminate the vulgar songs and decadent foxtrotting couples downstage.

This wedding scene in the ballet was themed as a Revolutionary Red wedding, according to critic Galina Dobrovolskaya. She describes a march of Philistines across the stage carrying huge chunks of ham and wine bottles, framed by scenes from the Russian Revolution and civil war behind them, as well as the murder of a Red Army soldier and Communist.[20] As with *Spartacus,* the grand scale of social conflict distills into smaller and smaller personal narratives until finally a husband and wife find themselves alienated through politics, as if it was the raw conflict and not the political resolution that was the most durable part of revolutions.

On one level *The Bedbug* seems an after-the-fall inversion of *Spartacus,* particularly in its opening, which swells with marching crowds of landowners, merchants, mill owners, and priests juxtaposed with detachments of Baltic sailors, marines, and workers marching against them, with the Poet in their midst. In *Spartacus* the sexual flirtation between Aegina and Harmodius was played out with the dancers perching decorously on settees, but in *The Bedbug* Yakobson places a hugely overscaled king-sized bed in the midst of the stage for the wedding night scene. Gromov describes a curious moment of comradeship over the first appearance of the bed that occurred between the Kirov's artistic director, Konstantin Sergeyev, and leading Georgian dancer and choreographer (and former Kirov dancer) Vakhtang Chabukiani. "Yakobson placed an enormous bed on the stage and announced that he was going to stage the wedding night scene. Chabukiani and Sergeyev, who had hated one another since childhood, suddenly struck a friendship and attacked Yakobson together, contending that putting a bed on the Kirov stage was tantamount to the toppling of Petipa's academic tradition. . . . I still remember them standing side by side, a hand across each other's shoulder, and ranting in indignation," Gromov recalled. "At the time this surprised me, but now it seems utterly appalling."[21]

In the final moments of *The Bedbug* Yakobson breaks the theatrical fourth wall, after having Mayakovsky set fire to the vermin-infested kingdom of Philistia that houses the Bedbug. Inspired by Mayakovsky's 1920 poem "An Extraordinary Adventure that Happened to Vladimir

Mayakovsky One Summer at a Dacha," he turns the stage lights onto the audience, flooding the theater with light in a direct reference from the poem. Yakobson's libretto for the ballet next describes how, "full of disgust, Poet lights his cigarette and sets fires to some clothes. Everything breaks out. Bugs writhe in the flame. Everything burns down. The land is clean."[22] Slowly he walks down to the edge of the stage to peer into the hall at the audience, turning his gaze outward and silently suggesting that the social detritus onstage—its excesses, conflict, and anger—spills into Soviet life at large.

Twelve years later, in 1974, soon after Yakobson was at last granted permission to found his own company, Choreographic Miniatures, he mounted a revised version of *The Bedbug*, this time to music by Shostakovich arranged from several of his early works composed in the 1920s and 1930s. "Shostakovich and Mayakovsky suited each other perfectly," Yakobson said about having these artists as collaborators in a ballet for his company, seeing their spirit as emblematic of the company's emphasis on contemporary themes.[23] Yakobson quickly found that the various committees of Soviet and Communist Party officials did not agree. "For many people, the very idea of putting Mayakovsky into a ballet seemed a sort of blasphemy," he explained.[24] The power circulating through his abandonment of ballet conventions was becoming evident to those vested with censorship authority.

Irina Yakobson recounts a Kafkaesque tale of the extremes to which Yakobson had to go to get *The Bedbug* onstage with his own company, particularly in its second staging in 1974, which coincided with the era of Brezhnevian Stagnation that had begun in 1973. This frustrating process shows how deeply unsettling modernism, eroticism, and sharp satire were for Soviet functionaries. That *The Bedbug* had made it onto the stage at all, in 1962, had been a matter of timing and opportunity. Nikita Khrushchev's "Thaw" had begun in 1962, with Solzhenitsyn publishing his *One Day in the Life of Ivan Denisovich* (*Odin den Ivana Denisovicha*) in November, and had lasted until Khrushchev's ouster in October 1964. Solzhenitsyn's book had become the de facto anthem of the disclosure of Stalinist repression and with its opening two sentences had ushered in the literary genre known as the "camp theme" and the two-year window when one could write about such things in Soviet newspapers and magazines.[25] As Yakobson set to work to recreate the two-act *The Bedbug* into a one-act *The Bedbug* for Choreographic Miniatures in the mid-1970s, however, it was impossible for him even to study the 1962 Kirov Theater version because nothing had been recorded. "Certain movements were remembered by the body," recalled Irina, who assisted him with rehearsals for the 1974 restaging, "but for the main parts he improvised, as usual. No sooner did Yakobson stage *The Bedbug* than the party functionaries banned it. Then a Commission arrived for another viewing, and banned it again," she said, describing the scene of its vetting by the khudsovet (the Soviet censorship organ mentioned earlier).[26]

"Naturally, they wanted the hall to be empty of people (the viewing took place at the Maly Opera Theater). But when they entered the premises they found that the hall was filled to capacity. People had come from everywhere. The commission members were all sitting in the front row, waiting for the performance to begin. And all of a sudden Leonid Yakobson came onto the stage and addressed the audience: 'I am very grateful to you for coming here today. I greatly appreciate your support. However, you will benefit as well—for half of what you are about to see today, no one will be able to see ever again.' Needless to say, the discussion after the performance opened with the question, 'Leonid Veniaminovich, who gave you permission to address the public?' This was followed by a round of accusations," Irina recalled.[27] At this point in his life, Yakobson was a master at the tactical pas de deux, the gesture that could be at once a provocation and a means of surreptitiously garnering permission to display his ballets whenever and wherever possible.

Point by prohibited point, Yakobson sparred with the authorities as he tried to narrow the gap between their desire to close down *The Bedbug* and his insistence on getting it before the public. The oversight committee claimed that Yakobson had made Mayakovsky into a laughable figure and not the patriotic one he should have been. Yakobson explained that it would be inconceivable to expect *The Bedbug* to convey the spirit of heroism; his ballet had followed the style of Mayakovsky's Windows for ROSTA and thus demanded a satirical choreographic treatment. "Even the great poet's muse, Lilya Yuryevna Brik, who saw Yakobson's *The Bedbug,* came to his defense, saying that in this ballet Yakobson had captured the Mayakovsky she knew in real life, and that no portraits or statues conveyed the essence of his personality so vividly," Irina recalled. "But no one paid any attention to his words: the functionaries kept talking as if they were deaf."[28]

Yakobson's art was doing what obedient Soviet art was *not* supposed to do—posing a political or philosophical challenge and depicting reality so starkly that it might be construed as a call to challenge the system. He had the guise of an earlier epoch to shield him, but he was also registering a moral protest on just how absolutely the regime could guide the artist's hand. At the next viewing several musicologists were invited, "and afterwards the conversation turned to music. Music and ballet critic Leonid Arnoldovich Entelis inquired what right Yakobson had to appropriate the music of the great Shostakovich and mingle it with songs by Pyotr Leshchenko. Yakobson, he contended, had insulted the composer, who would never have permitted his music to be used in such a way. Therefore *The Bedbug* could not be released."[29]

Yakobson had learned over the years of back and forth with party officials how to strategize like a chess player toward the true endgame. Entelis did not know that Yakobson had a long-standing friendship with Shostakovich, dating back to the staging of *The Golden Age* in the 1930s. "They had great respect for each other's art," Irina said of the composer and choreographer. "Shostakovich wrote that Yakobson's choreography made him see his own music in a new light," she continued, describing a visit Yakobson had made to Shostakovich in preparation for one of these meetings with the commission. "So Yakobson set out to visit Shostakovich at the House of Writers' Creation," she said.[30] "Yakobson wanted Dmitriy Dmitriyevich to come to Leningrad and see *The Bedbug*. But by that time, Shostakovich was already very ill: his heart [was rapidly failing]. Yakobson, equipped with a tape recorder and the [*Bedbug*] score, traveled to see Shostakovich. He relayed his problems with the censors and their contention that his use of Russian folk songs between passages of Shostakovich's music was an offense to the composer. He may even have danced some parts of the ballet," Irina said. "Shostakovich responded by giving him a letter saying that not only was he granting Veniaminovich permission to use his music as he wished, but that he was both proud and happy that a choreographer of Yakobson's caliber had chosen his music for his ballets."[31]

"As we were about to attend the fourth—or was it the fifth?—discussion of *The Bedbug,* Leonid put this letter in his pocket," Irina recalled. "The local and district committee members had already arrived, along with numerous functionaries from other committees."[32] Once again their attacks were directed mainly against the music. With remarkable composure, Yakobson produced Shostakovich's letter and placed it on the table before a woman from the local committee who headed the commission, saying: "Read this." She did and turned green with rage. Then she replied, not even bothering to address him as "comrade Yakobson" but simply as "Yakobson": "Yakobson, what you did is illicit—it is a blow below the belt!" whereupon she got up and headed for the door. Everyone else followed. Leonid then started yelling as he had never before yelled at anyone: "Chameleons! Giftless nonentities!" and so on. "He yelled and I restrained him, so as to keep him from running after them. . . . The result was that we finally received the permission to present *The Bedbug*."[33]

The Twelve

One year after *The Bedbug* premiered at the Kirov, Yakobson, still intent on razing the Soviet hero, found inspiration in another early Soviet modernist and the other leading poet of the Bolshevik revolutionary period, Alexander Blok. Taking Blok's famously enigmatic 1918 poem *The Twelve* (*Dvenadtsat*) as the subject of his next major ballet, Yakobson created a dance that is so far removed from classical ballet in form as well as content that, were it not being danced by the Kirov Ballet in 1960s Soviet Russia, one might defensibly call it modern dance. Since that genre was an impossibility for the time and place, however, Yakobson nestled his increasingly radical dance experiments within the pinnacle of ballet purity, chipping away from inside. Like Blok's extended poem, which in the words of one of its defenders, the theorist Viktor Shklovsky, is filled with "mood-creating sounds, polyphonic rhythms, and harsh, slangy language," the physical vocabulary in Yakobson's dance is emotionally raw and weighted, shaped more for its dramatic punch than its visual design.[34] "In *The Twelve,* Yakobson succeeded in discovering plastic means that correspond to the images and rhythms of Blok's poem," the Russian critic Lvov-Anokhin said, noting that the stormy winds in the poem, "symbolizing tribulations and catastrophes of the 1917 Revolution, are tamed and controlled by the will of the revolutionary masses," a metaphor that becomes a vivid reenactment in Yakobson's choreography.[35] The poem of Yakobson's fellow revolutionary across time describes the march of twelve Bolshevik soldiers (likened to the Twelve Apostles of Christ) through the streets of revolutionary-era Petrograd, while a fierce winter blizzard rages around them. When the poem was first published, the Russian intelligentsia and even former admirers, friends, and colleagues who objected to Blok's portrayal of Petrograd as peopled by criminal revolutionaries, attacked the poet, accusing him of a lack of artistry. Shklovsky came to the defense of Blok's poem, likening it to Pushkin's *The Bronze Horseman* (*Mednïy vsadnik,* 1833), but with a rudely realistic vision of contemporary Petrograd in place of Pushkin's mythologized history of the city. Shklovsky also noted that the poem was written in the street slang of 1918 criminals. Yakobson matches this verbal vernacular with filaments of vernacular dances and dramatically realistic non-dance gestures at different points in the ballet.

In creating his ballet, Yakobson enlisted as his music collaborator a brilliant young composer protégé of Shostakovich, Boris Ivanovich Tishchenko. Tishchenko, who was in the midst of three years of postgraduate composition study with Shostakovich when Yakobson approached him with the idea to set Blok's subject to music for his ballet, produced a fifty-minute ballet score for Yakobson that became one of Tishchenko's most famous works of modernist composition for the stage. Extremely influenced by Shostakovich, Tishchenko tried some experimental and modernist musical ideas, including twelve-tone and aleatoric techniques. Judging from a grainy twenty-five-minute film fragment of the first half of the dance in Irina Yakobson's archive, the only video recording of the choreography that survives, Tishchenko's score teamed with Yakobson's choreography is striking and theatrical, with accents of wind and brass instruments punctuating the pulsing, contemporary, inventive feel of the dancers' actions. The movement of the dancers, who wear a theatricalized version of street clothes, is edgy and restless. Like figures in an expressionistic film noir, they pace the dark and bleak urban environment of the set, recoiling from or advancing into tragedy. Their bodily postures have the canted urgency of figures walking into a raging storm, as they tuck their heads and shoulders down as if to deflect a fierce wind.

Tatyana Bruni, an acclaimed visual artist working in opera, ballet, and theater since the 1920s, provided Yakobson with a remarkable set of costume sketches, including some for characters who were never realized, such as a badly wounded man limping on crutches and a ragged double amputee who propels himself across the stage with his hands in a low wooden cart. Bruni was a member of a famous artistic dynasty and designed dozens of performances, including those for ballets staged by Goleizovsky and Lopukhov as well as Yakobson. For *The Twelve,* she created costume sketches that suggest the depth of Yakobson's bitter reflection on human suffering and war.[36] One of her sketches depicts two different images of the double amputee in a crude low four-wheeled cart that has to be propelled by pulling himself along the ground with his hands. In one of the images, a ragged man crouches in the cart and stretches his head and face upward imploringly. Through this sketch Yakobson has drawn a large "X" of rejection. He indicates his approval of the second image by initialing it and noting that the dancer portraying the legless man must hide his own legs by folding them under a black velvet cloth in the cart. In this sketch the man hangs his head in forlorn and hopeless sadness.

The image of a legless man in a ballet drawn from a poem about Bolshevik revolutionaries was a problematic reference for both Yakobson and Bruni to make, and it is not one that survives in the available film footage of the ballet. This figure belongs more to the idealization of the Soviet man after World War II through masculine images of virility, strength, and superhuman drive than to Blok's allegorical poem of an earlier era. Among the mythically scaled great Soviet heroes of World War II the famous fighter pilot Alexey Petrovich Maresyev, who had to have both his lower legs amputated following the crash of his plane in 1942, seems an obvious reference in Bruni's costume sketch for this character for Yakobson's ballet. Soviet scholar Lilya Kaganovsky has noted that in 1948 Maresyev had been immortalized in a popular film by Aleksandr Stolper, *A Story about a Real Man,* which depicted Maresyev's aggressive fitness regimen that allowed him to retrain as a fighter pilot and fly more missions before the war ended, which he did successfully. In Soviet accounts Maresyev is larger than life, but in Yakobson's ballet the human suffering of war is instead projected as an unremitting tragedy; Maresyev's disfigurement is not disguised by the prosthetics he used to retrain himself as a fighter pilot. Kaganovsky describes how in one of the scenes of the film exemplifying Maresyev's bravery it is his missing legs and feet that become symbols of his courage. "Maresyev's flight instructor scolds him for wearing thin boots that won't protect his feet in the frigid air. 'I have no feet,' says Maresyev proudly. The instructor doesn't understand. 'I have no feet, Comrade Lieutenant,' Maresyev replies, with a grin spreading all over his face. After insisting on seeing Maresyev's prostheses, the instructor embraces Maresyev and tells him ecstatically, "You don't realize . . . the sort of man you are!' "[37] In staging the mutilation of Maresyev's body so bluntly Yakobson is suggesting that the New Soviet Man valorized by socialist realism is more accurately a body that has been grotesquely damaged and transformed.

It's easy to see why Yakobson considered *The Twelve* one of his favorite ballets. The emotion and stories are so densely packed into each character; the bodies telegraph such sharply etched characterizations; and yet from the opening moments, the dancing flows with the ease of an improvisation. The curtain rises on twelve individual characters on stage—a priest, a prostitute, a sailor in love with her, and so on. As they are tossed in the storm, lurching from one side to the other, they clasp their hands tightly together to prevent anyone from being torn away by the fierce winds that their stumbling falls convey. Eventually the coming storm chases everyone from the stage and the dancers return one by one to unfold their private stories. This is the side of the socialist social experiment we weren't supposed to see.

Natalia Makarova, the Kirov ballerina who worked with Yakobson during this period before defecting to the West in 1970, and who saw the preview of *The Twelve* (the premiere of which took place on December 31, 1964), called it "unbelievably audacious" and "the most daring" work by Yakobson. The ballet includes a bar scene where the patrons, indifferent to the approaching revolution, prefer to get drunk. An officer despoils Katka, the bride-turned-prostitute of rebel leader Petrukha, and both collapse in a drunken haze across the table from each other in the bar. As Katka sprawls backward in her chair and tumbles out, a succession of identical blonde-wigged prostitutes roll through her exact pose in the chair, in a vision that suggests an endless supply of commodified women or Katka's ruin replaying itself to the point of insanity in her mind.[38]

The Twelve (1964), Katka's Death, Igor Chernïshov, Kirov Ballet, Leningrad. Photographer unknown.

At the preview the party officials viewing the ballet were incensed by the way the Red Army soldiers of the Revolution moved into the future, not boldly but with what Makarova remembered as the creeping movements of "Red bedbugs scrambling up a ramp from beyond which blinding scarlet light poured, the glow from the world conflagration. Standing with their backs to the audience, they looked meekly into this future." As Makarova recalled, the party censors took this metaphoric slight literally, reading the dancers' apparent plunge into an abyss as desecrating "the creative force that inspired the Russian Revolution."[39]

"Yakobson tried to justify himself before the censors by saying that the future is known to no one and that it is possible only to look into it furtively. 'Ah, so you still are unfamiliar with the future of our Revolution?'" Makarova recounts they asked him threateningly. "'*We* are familiar with it.'" Rather than trying to appease the censors, many of whom Makarova speculates never read Blok's poem, Yakobson stood his ground and refused to change this ending. One year later he did finally design a new conclusion to the ballet. He decided to bring on Blok's Jesus Christ carrying a red banner so that it was clear whose religious messengers these were. At this point in the ballet, now retrievable only through spectator's accounts since the only existing film fragment stops well before the end of the performance, all twelve characters have finished gradually stripping off their torn and ragged vests, jackets, and cloaks, revealing themselves as Red guardsmen. In his revised ending Yakobson wanted Christ to appear from the wings and then disappear as if he were a mirage in front of the Red Army guardsmen. Makarova reports that "Yakobson's idea was met in the new [khudsovet] with confusion and caustic laughter" and a feeling that the choreographer was mocking the party officials through the red under costumes. *The Twelve* was never again permitted to be shown to the public.[40]

As with *The Bedbug*, Yakobson was playing with the devices of artistic expression, metaphor, imagery, and symbolism in full view of his audience, disclosing the Soviet message and the means of its manufacture. Those twelve disparate and lost individuals at the start of *The Twelve* who metamorphose into Red Army guardsmen are casting about for direction, leadership, a future, and a cause. Yakobson is suggesting that none of this can be found in the current Soviet world of 1964, and to have believed the path to it was there in 1917 was a delusion. Here Yakobson grapples with the meatiest issues of his era, using them as subjects but also levers through which the body might speak. Many of these narratives express an urgency to speak with a frankness that was not allowed in live performance.

Yakobson's means into these issues was through a reconception of the human form in classical dance; he understood implicitly that one could not tell new stories through old forms. Makarova, like other dancers, found his rewriting of the movements of classical ballet—like dancing with the feet turned in, the torso curved forward in a deep contraction, or the body moving in tight parallel positions instead of an open turned-out posture—revelatory. She expressed her disappointment in not having worked on more ballets with Yakobson before defecting to the West. "Today, I am very sorry that I did not share with Yakobson the fate of his fallen ballet and dance Katka, the slut and whore, the lost soul swept to nowhere by the merciless Revolutionary turmoil," Makarova noted remorsefully. "Moreover, I couldn't give myself over entirely into Yakobson's hands. To dance constantly with the feet turned in was physically—stylistically dangerous. . . . Yakobson demanded too much involvement and energy from me," she lamented of

The Bedbug (1974), Mayakovsky, Prisïpkin, and Zoya Beryozkina.
Photo: Vladimir Zenzinov.

her decision to not dance the role of the seductive Katka which he had begun to create on her.[41]

Yakobson was not the only experimentalist choreographer drawn to Blok's poem. In 1924, shortly before he left Russia, George Balanchine choreographed *The Twelve* as a ballet performed to the rhythmic vocal chanting of Blok's poem by fifty theater students. The dancers were the fifteen members of the Young Ballet, Balanchine's group of students and members of the corps de ballet of the Mariinsky who performed in what the dancer Nina Stukolkina remembers as asymmetrically moving groups with no real soloists. She describes the choreography as focusing on the general mood and metric density of the chanted text of the poem rather than its content. Instead of addressing the substance of Blok's poem literally, Balanchine apparently structured his *The Twelve* as a series of movement patterns where "at times one dancer detached from the group and performed a combination of movements, as if pronouncing a "sentence," then disappeared into the group . . . with strict musical and choreographic logic."[42] Forty years later, when Yakobson began his *The Twelve,* the same doors of formalist invention that the Revolution had opened for Balanchine in his response to Blok's work had shut in the USSR.

Hiroshima

As he worked on *The Twelve* during the period 1963–1964, Yakobson created his strongest anti-war statement, *Hiroshima*. A portrait of anguish for a cast of three men and three women who wore leotards and tights that were torn and ragged and who moved with their mouths open in silent screams, *Hiroshima* was set to the avant-garde music of Henryk Górecki. The artistic director of the Kirov canceled it once he heard the score, before it ever reached the stage. It was only in 1979, four years after Yakobson's death, that his dancers tried to restage it, but by then—according to Kirov dancer Arkadiy Ivanenko, who had seen both versions—it no longer had the ferocity of the original.[43]

Hiroshima, Choreographic Miniatures, Leningrad, 1970.
Photo: Vladimir Zenzinov.

The Land of Miracles

Makarova danced in two final Yakobson ballets before escaping to the West. In 1967 she danced the Beauty Maiden (Devitsa-krasa) character in his full-length allegory about war, *The Land of Miracles* (*Strana chudes*). Work on this ballet, the most delayed of all Yakobson's productions, actually started in 1942. A folklorist tale of the moral force of the hero in a landscape of evil, *The Land of Miracles* tells the story of the Beauty Maiden, whose beloved, Bright Falcon, danced by Valery Panov, is killed and burned in an attack by barbarians. In an interview in 2010, at the age of seventy-two, Panov spoke about this role as a pinnacle of his dancing career and an extraordinary success in the USSR. "The newspapers said that for 1967 the two most important cultural events were the artistic birth of a new genius—Mikhail Baryshnikov—and Yakobson's role for me in *The Land of Miracles*," Panov boasted, recalling how Yakobson would look for the personality of a dancer in casting and then make the choreography specifically for that dancer's abilities. "*The Land of Miracles* was an unbelievable success," Panov said.[44]

In 1944 Yakobson had begun appealing to the Kirov authorities and presenting the scenario of the ballet (also sometimes referred to as *The Wonderland*) to the Kirov administration, but he could not convince them to allow him to stage it. Then the Bolshoi expressed interest and he began to stage it for them, but the wartime privations made realizing the production impossible. Work on the ballet again halted. But Yakobson continued to work on *The Land of Miracles*. "He wrote letters to the Ministry of Culture, to political institutions, first in Leningrad then in Moscow," Irina Yakobson recounted. "The answer was always no. But all those years he continued to work on *The Land of Miracles*. He tried to improve the scenario. He worked with the composer Isaak Shvarts, he wrote a detailed plan of the performance (composition), everything was ready but he could not receive permission to stage the ballet until 1966. The premiere was in 1967, so he waited more than twenty years," she said.[45]

On its surface, the ballet was a parable about good versus evil with good exemplified by Makarova's character, the Beauty Maiden, and Valery Panov dancing as the brave handsome man, Bright Falcon. During the ballet, Bright Falcon is captured by the sinister monster, and Beauty Maiden is blinded as all positive things seem about to perish. Russian ballet photographer Nina Alovert, who saw *The Land of Miracles* at its premiere, describes the passage where the young Makarova danced as if she were blind as one of the most emotionally moving, and daring, images in the entire ballet. "As she became blind, Makarova stopped dancing on pointe and her whole body seemed to cave inward," Alovert said, demonstrating the hunkered-down form of a terrified person plunged into sudden darkness and forced to inch her way forward. Photographs of Makarova in this role show her with her toes inward and arms stretched forward; she gropes tentatively as if hoping the cavernous blackness might offer a safety railing. "In that solo Yakobson showed Makarova's possibility in another daring way even beyond Zoya in *Bedbug*," Alovert recalled of the collective response to this startling image.[46]

Hitler had indeed originally been the evil force darkening the wonderland when Yakobson first conceived the ballet as his widow attests. By early 1967, however, near the time of its premiere, there was another international conflict building, this time in the Middle East. The USSR was a distant but influential force involving increasing hostilities against Israel from its Arab neighbors Syria, Egypt, and eventually Jordan. The Soviet Union was playing what has subsequently been understood to be an incendiary role in the conflict: it deliberately misinformed the president of Egypt, Anwar Sadat, that Israel was preparing to attack Syria. On June 5, 1967, as Yakobson was rebuilding *The Land of Miracles* for its Kirov premiere, Israel made a preemptive strike against the Egyptian air force, which had begun preparations based on the Soviet misinformation, and thus began what came to be known as the Six-Day War. For six days Israel fought a four-front battle simultaneously against the four Arab countries bordering it. When the war ended less than one week later, Israel had quadrupled its area, including annexing the old city of Jerusalem. "And the implications—for Israel's place in the world, for Jewish identity, for how Jews in the Diaspora were perceived—reverberated far and wide," Gal Beckerman has written in summation about the impact of the Six-Day War on Soviet Jews, noting that it was particularly the Zionists in the Soviet Union who "felt emboldened, their lonely cause now validated" as a result of this victory.[47]

There was another forbidden subject in the ballet as well—religion. "If anyone did something with religion, for example if a dancer in the Kirov Ballet was even seen in a church, it could have resulted in being thrown

The Land of Miracles, Natalia Makarova as the Beauty Maiden,
Kirov Ballet, Leningrad. Photo: © Nina Alovert, 1962.

out of the company," Irina said. "Even so in *The Land of Miracles* Yakobson began to say something about religion," she continued, as she demonstrated an angular two-dimensional posture like an old Russian icon, a kind of artifact of religiosity that had been systematically eliminated during the Stalinist period. Irina was understandably nervous about his use of this imagery. "Ironka, do you recognize this position?" she said he would teasingly ask her as he demonstrated an icon-like posture. "Of course," she replied. "Everyone will recognize this. You can recognize it immediately—it is an icon." She explained, "He liked to tease these people, who were members of the Communist Party." "It is very dangerous," Irina said of his religious imagery in *The Land of Miracles*. "It is very interesting," he retorted.[48]

The only available performance footage of *The Land of Miracles* consists of two film fragments.[49] The first shows Makarova as the Beauty

Maiden, dancing a shimmering variation of rapidly flicking hand and foot flutters as she advances downstage framed by an ensemble of women all dressed in white transparent sparkling tunics over white leotards and tights. Their hair is tucked into little glitter-adorned caps as they tremble their upraised hands and scurry forward on pointe, their legs pressed together tightly. The effect is like watching a retinue of just hatched Lilac Fairies, so swift and wildly animated are the women's fluttering movements across their entire bodies.

The second brief film clip, which was shown in a Russian TV documentary about Yakobson broadcast in the late 1980s, is of the battalion of evil, a mass of heavily made-up male dancers with faces painted in thick black strokes and bodies covered in costumes of dense scales that, coupled with their crouched-over stabbing actions, suggest reptilian menace. The well-known ballet critic and theater director Boris Lvov-Anokhin, in a voiceover on the clip, observes, "As is often the case with Yakobson's ballets, *The Land of Miracles* combines various plastic strata, including elements of the classical dance, of the Russian folk dance, and—as you will presently see—the daring methods of radical plastic grotesque." The next image shows an animated Yakobson standing in the midst of a cluster of the male monsters, extolling them to observe and then exceed him in the originality of their wild movement choices and grimacing facial expressions. "I will execute [this] in a way that not one of you can. And what I need is for you to execute it in a way that I would not even have imagined possible," Yakobson challenges, calling forth an individual voice from the dancers that was unusual for its time.[50]

Composer Isaak Shvarts's strongly rhythmic score suggests a *Bolero*-like crescendo windup driving the monsters' actions, as they hoist their leader repeatedly into the air from a deep squat, his legs knotted around the arms of two attendants who seem to keep yanking him back to earth as if he were on an elastic cord. It's a startling image and fiercely animalistic—as if Yakobson had poured his knowledge of what distortions of terror and fear feel like into movements that seem to rip the body apart. Panov, as Bright Falcon, wearing an abbreviated costume of white armor and armed with a thick sword in each hand and a falconlike crest on his headband, attacks the head of this evil, Main Monster, by throwing himself into a roll across the floor like a log hurtling toward the evil. "The head of the evil characters was Anatoliy Sapogov," Irina said, noting that he was perfect for the role of creature-person caught between the forms of a fish, snake, and animal "because he moved as if he had no bones."[51]

The scale of the action in *The Land of Miracles* is epic, as is the set, which was an image from a miniature Palekh lacquered box that had been expanded to cover the full stage. The Kirov Theater discovered, too late to make a substitution, that a crew of folk artist masters who knew how to paint these dainty egg tempera objects had to be imported to Leningrad from their village to adapt their delicate miniature style from the lids of lacquered, papier-mâché black boxes onto an enormous wall the height of the Kirov stage. Literally thousands of eggs also had to be purchased as the basis of the paint. The effect was reportedly stunning, with the visual flavor of Old Russian icons enlarged to a massive scale. The backdrop scene depicted an idealized happy Russian village with fruit trees of huge apples—"fairy-tale apples"—and a real waterfall with a stream flowing down one side of the stage. For Yakobson finally getting the ballet on stage had been a huge effort, and once that was in place he fought to keep his vision as intact as possible.

The system of censorship and oversight that bookended every creation Yakobson made was an aspect of what was known as khudsovet (arts council). In practice this was the process by which the ruling order in the

Rehearsal of *The Land of Miracles* (1967), Valery Panov as Bright Falcon, Kirov Ballet, Leningrad. Photo: Daniil Savelyev.

USSR imposed its power over cultural production. "[*Kh*]*udsovets* consisted of members of unions of composers, writers, filmmakers, as well as party and Komsomol functionaries who had varying degrees of interest in art. [*Kh*]*udsovets* did not have permanent membership; for each separate case the makeup of a council formed separately. Any program of musical groups, theater troupes, a new film and other works of mass art was supposed to pass [the *Kh*]*udsovet's* validation."[52] Decisions made by the members of the khudsovet council were effectively orders. The members of the council made comments and suggestions to the creators that needed to be followed as part of the exercise of political, moral, and artistic censorship of artworks.

Yakobson set the lead roles for *The Land of Miracles* on two casts. Particularly for the character Bright Falcon, he had in mind someone who, in his widow's words, "could be very heroic, strong and brave with a good heart but also be very kind and sweet." He picked Panov, with Yuriy Solovyov for the second cast. The ballet was a pointed allegory, with Bright Falcon captured by Main Monster, the Beauty Maiden blinded, and the country pillaged. The ballet's resolution involves vanquishing the evil by the country's young men, resurrecting Bright Falcon, restoring Beauty Maiden's sight, and reinstating justice. "The audience, of course, understood the allegory," Yakobson's widow said. "There was no doubt about it. The Main Monster was Hitler."[53]

The acclaim for *The Land of Miracles* was widespread and had a significant effect on the dancers. The ballet became a featured part of the Kirov repertoire from its premiere in late 1967 through July 1968, when the Kirov Theater closed for three years of extensive remodeling. (The Kirov Ballet shifted the production to a House of Culture, where the stage proved less hospitable to such a big ballet.) Makarova in particular was acclaimed for her role and was named the best Soviet ballerina of the year in 1967 for her portrayal of the chaste and brave Beauty Maiden. Yakobson had drawn out of her an exemplary performance of dramatic dance, showing a facet of her that not even she had dared reveal before.

That same year Makarova danced a second role in a Yakobson ballet, the lead in *A Passing Beauty* (*Prokhodyashchaya krasotka*). This would be her last performance ever in Yakobson's choreography. Describing the ballet as a miniature that Yakobson created especially for her based on a painting, Makarova performed it only twice at the conservatory. "After the second performance, I got a telephone call from the Obkom," she recounted, referring to a Communist Party representative. "Some unknown character recommended insistently that I not dance this ballet of Yakobson's 'in consideration of my future career.'"[54] Makarova obeyed, to her subsequent regret. The dance was based on a painting by Picasso, an artist formerly forbidden in the Soviet Union, thus Yakobson did not say where he had found his initial visual inspiration. Ten years later, writing her autobiography from her new home in San Francisco, Makarova reflected on what the loss of knowledge about Yakobson's work meant for the West. "Today, having worked with [Antony] Tudor, [Jerome] Robbins, [Kenneth] MacMillan, [John] Cranko and [Glen] Tetley, I feel a sense of especial bitterness at the waste of Yakobson's potential," she wrote. "In fact, in the work of these talented Western masters, I recognized the turbulent genius of Yakobson—a genius they never saw. . . . Europe and America hardly knew him. To resurrect, even with films, Yakobson's ballets without Yakobson is impossible. But his lessons are in me, as well as his memory and my unforgettable gratitude."[55]

During this period Yakobson was also delivering his lessons in a more formal setting through a series of lectures he presented in 1964 at the Department of Choreography at the Rimsky-Korsakov State Conservatory in Leningrad. Addressing a class of dancers wishing to become choreographers, he professed his credo: "New content and contemporary themes require new forms." Remarking on the forceful resistance he kept encountering in trying to enact this belief, Yakobson confided, "We are constantly asked to create ballets on current themes. But no sooner do we begin to seek new forms, than we are at once forbidden to do so, as if in departing from an inherited language, we had violated the holy of holies."[56]

Underlining his belief that choreographic style is a choice the artist makes depending on the subject of his ballet, he mentions how in *The Land of Miracles,* the idiom of classical ballet was appropriate because this ballet, a narrative poem about World War II, is also a legend and a romantic tale. "But can we depict everyday subject matter by means of this language?" he asks rhetorically. "Do you realize that virtually all of the ballets created within the fifty-year existence of Soviet ballet employ the classical idiom? Only three ballets (and these were staged by me), have broken with the established canon and stand alone. These are *Spartacus, The Bedbug* and *The Twelve,* which are based on classical ballet techniques and on dance pantomime, on a free plastic idiom."[57] With his signature mix of candor and ego, Yakobson pushes ahead, insisting that it is not the artistic merits of these ballets he is discussing but the basic fact that in order to be expressive of its own time ballet needs a new idiom through which to speak. He concludes with as strong a diatribe against the ridiculousness of "Soviet tractor ballets" (socialist realist ballet) as was safely possible: "Form and content in ballet must not be allowed to come to that catastrophic confrontation that we have witnessed so dolefully in our own time."[58]

THE REFLECTION OF the Stakhanovite hero that was metaphorically projected onto the male dancers on the Bolshoi stage underwent a significant transformation in several of Yakobson's ballets of the postwar decades.[59] This idealized Soviet male body, which had been shaped in the visual and performing arts as if built out of a composite of "norm breaking" Stakhanovites, began to soften and fracture in Yakobson's *The Bedbug, The Twelve,* and *The Land of Miracles.* In these ballets he muted the narratives of the "extravagant virility" of the ideal Soviet man, to use historian Lilya Kaganovsky's phrase for masculinity as depicted in Soviet art.[60] Instead Yakobson rewrites the coding for maleness and power in these ballets. This shading of the model socialist male in ballet had to be doubly encrypted because social anxieties about a feminized male also always hover at the margins of the ballet stage.

In Yakobson's *Spartacus* it is possible to see this blunt image of maleness in a process of transformation. Square-jawed, tall, and commanding as he gazes off into the distance, the title character of this ballet strikes the iconic pose of the New Soviet man looking into the future, but with less certainty about his possibility of occupying it. Yakobson's choreography suggests that Spartacus is mindful and resolved to his own inevitable defeat even as he joins Phrygia in their farewell duet. Across his three major companion ballets, *The Bedbug, The Twelve,* and *Land of Miracles,* Yakobson continues rounding the edges of his heroes, portraying them as an artist, a murderous Red guardsman, a mutilated soldier, and a fairy-tale white knight. This last figure dies, his body desecrated by being burned—then, with self-conscious Christian symbolism, Yakobson resurrects him out of his bride's sorrow.

Although *Land of Miracles* was a fairy tale, by the time of its premiere in the late 1960s it had evolved from a 1940s wartime project in pride-enhancement into a daring anti-war statement. What was being contested was not just classical ballet as entertainment, but also the disciplined body emblematic of the Soviet power. The artist's duty was to instill the Communist ideal into the Soviet consciousness (and in the instance of tours abroad, that meant into the foreign consciousness as well), and to convince people of the value of that ideal, no matter what the reality. The fundamental unit here was the group, not the individual or the artist. The party was the arbiter of aesthetics and ethics on a daily basis, determining not just what toured, but even what was allowed to be realized. Yakobson was a counterpart to the complex negotiations with the Western world around who and what dance could be exported to battle Communism. His work stands as a case study of what happened to the ballet curated

Yakobson reading sports news during a rehearsal break, 1974. Photographer unknown.

internally in the USSR to rid it of the capitalist perversions of formalism, sensuality, and modernism.

Toward the end of his life Stalin had reportedly become increasingly confused in distinguishing between what Kaganovsky called "the fictions of socialist realism and Soviet reality."[61] He began requesting that convincing film stars playing criminals be arrested for illicit activities, as if art and life had finally collapsed. In his mind they had. Yakobson never abetted confusion between reality and realism in his ballets; rather he endeavored to use dance to give a magnificent aerial view of the facts. Totalitarianism had invigorated him, because it gave such force to the symbols he manipulated. By deconstructing ballet's hierarchical vocabulary he was also unraveling its narratives. These postwar ballets were displacing the circulation of power and image from the state through the artist into something much riskier: a new formulation of power from the artist against the state. In undoing the Soviet hero bit by bit in his ballets, Yakobson was working to rewrite the USSR's iconography of power.

A Company of His Own:
Privatizing Soviet Ballet

ON THE WINTRY afternoon of December 21, 1969, an exuberant Leonid
Yakobson stood on the stage of Leningrad's Dom Iskusstv (House of the
arts) on Nevsky Prospect and unveiled his plan for what would become
a new model for interactions among dance, nation, and the individual
in Soviet Russia.[1] For Yakobson the Cold War had not been a freezer, it
turned out, but an incubator.[2] Addressing an invited audience of journalists, art critics, theater associates, and, most important, fifty dancers he
had just auditioned, Yakobson introduced the project he had spent the
years since the end of World War II striving to realize: the first individual,
single-choreographer ballet company in the USSR since the 1920s.

Yakobson was endeavoring to buffer the stagnation of Soviet ballet by
creating a company that would perform his works exclusively—a haven
and a home for his creativity. That he succeeded in doing so during the

beginning of a decade-long economic and social standstill known as the era of Brezhnev stagnation only adds to his accomplishment. In a period characterized by shortages of consumer goods; corruption; the clandestine circulation of manuscripts by samizdat, sometimes with publication abroad; Jewish emigration; and multiple defections from ballet companies, including both the Kirov and Bolshoi, the success of Yakobson's new venture seems all the more remarkable.

Yakobson's attempts to found his own company were part of his escalating struggle to expand the role of independent artists in the USSR. When he began, this was a quest that seemed so improbable it might have been a dream. But he came remarkably close to realizing it. Had he lived longer he doubtless would have encountered more obstacles. Yet those he did encounter often had the effect of stimulating him as he theorized his way around them. Already he was discovering that dance modernism needed a certain institutional autonomy to make possible freer invention in the inner sanctum of the dance studio. What this building of his repertory company demanded was an appreciation for how *inter*dependent artistic freedom and organizational self-governance were. Art revealed to him how insidious and deep social structures are, and with the founding of his own company he seemed finally to be moving toward the outer edges of official surveillance, or so it appeared.

A ballet photographer who was in the audience that afternoon, Nina Alovert, remembers the anticipation as Yakobson spoke to this unprecedented assembly to introduce his new ballet company, Choreographic Miniatures (Khoreograficheskie miniatyurï). In expansive and typically self-confident terms, he described their future. "Working with you, I will create the best ballet company," he began, noting the historic occasion and the momentousness of his quest. "I will make several new ballets, we will tour to the West. I will show you the world. We will become famous," he promised, as he described the evenings of new dance he would create drawing from his already composed ballet miniatures, and many others still to be realized. Standing in the Soviet House of the Arts, he described his own house of dance, an organization that would be as close as possible to a privatized ballet as the Soviet officials could tolerate.[3]

Declaiming a new future from a site associated with ballet had strong precedents in Soviet Russia. Beginning in 1917, during the early years of the Bolshevik Revolution, Vladimir Lenin began to use the balcony of

an art nouveau mansion in Saint Petersburg owned by Imperial Ballet ballerina Mathilde Kschessinskaya as a podium for some of his most famous
speeches. In 1920, too, from the stage of the Bolshoi Theater, Lenin had
declaimed his plan to bring electrical power to all of the Soviet Union (the
GOELRO Plan). During that speech Lenin had declared to an assembly of
delegates to the Eighth All-Russia Congress of Soviets from across the
damaged country, "Communism is Soviet power plus the electrification
of the whole country," as the ragged and hungry delegates sat in the chilly,
dimly illuminated theater—feeling acutely, one imagines, how electrical
power, yoked to a political system, could change their experience in that
theater, in that moment.[4] Now, a half-century later, Yakobson too was
promising to conjure something magical to fill a void in the Russian ballet
theater. He wanted to jolt and electrify the USSR with dances that would,
in the words of ballet critic Valeriy Zvezdochkin, "undermine the existing
notions of choreography and its possibilities."[5] Zvezdochkin continued,
contextualizing Yakobson's achievement: "For the first time in the history
of Soviet Ballet a choreographic theatre is established with its own original repertory and aesthetic agenda."[6]

Yakobson's "illumination" would be powered by a radical innovation—
the first independent ballet company in the USSR since the 1920s, a troupe
centered on key elements of dance modernism yet showing its roots
in classical dance. The focus would be on individual experience, self-
definition, and a reworking of dance language to hold new meanings,
while unexamined tradition and spectacle would be avoided. His platform would be the Soviets' inaugural single-choreographer-led ballet troupe,
a company that, like Balanchine's in the United States, would eschew internal hierarchies of principals, soloists, and corps de ballet, instead distributing lead roles among all ranks of dancers depending on who seemed
most promising in the part.[7] Yakobson considered every dancer in his company a soloist.

The sixty-five-year-old Yakobson had spent twenty years petitioning
and arguing for this company, plying officials with requests since he had
first arrived at the Kirov Theater in the late 1920s. He had quickly come to
the conclusion that having his own company was the only way to possibly
lessen the layers of oversight of party committees, agencies, and Ministry
of Culture officials who stifled or prohibited so many of his productions.
So instead of accommodation he pushed toward separation.

With the whole Soviet cultural climate slowing into stagnation during the 1960s, he turned inertia into momentum. Finally in 1967, the Leningrad district party committee gave him permission to establish a ballet troupe under the auspices of Lenkontsert. He swiftly moved into action, auditioning and hiring dancers and beginning to think about repertory. Then, a few weeks later, the officials pivoted again, suddenly announcing to Yakobson that the decision had been revoked. "Probably those who had initially yielded to Yakobson's assault had had second thoughts. Or maybe Moscow intervened, reminding local party functionaries of the limits of their jurisdiction. During the Brezhnev era, it would have been inconceivable to put a Jew—and moreover not a party member—in any position of authority," Irina said, recalling her husband's disappointment and anger. "L. V. felt this rupture acutely but tried not to show it. He went about his own business: wrote librettos, contemplated, read."[8] He also found some comfort with the results of the 1967 Arab-Israeli war, taking pleasure in the dramatic Israeli victory over the hostile neighboring countries whom the Soviets were supporting.

To assume Yakobson's place after they had reneged on allowing him the company, the officials named a surprised Pyotr Andreyevich Gusev as the artistic director of this new chamber ballet company. "To Yakobson's great consternation, Gusev accepted," Irina said. Gusev, a former dancer with the Kirov and Bolshoi ballets, and when he was young, a member of Balanchine's Young Ballet, was an experienced teacher and choreographer, and known as a dance diplomat. But he was not a choreographer of original works, much less an aspirant to have his own company. "They greeted each other [in the street] as usual," Yakobson's widow said of Gusev and her husband, who had been friends, "but the rapport had been destroyed." Artistically the substitution was disastrous as well. Within two years the company had lost such a substantial sum of money due to poor attendance at its undistinguished concerts that members of Lenkontsert, the government's arts presenting organization, added their voices to the chorus asking the Ministry of Culture and the party to hand the troupe back to Yakobson so that they could earn rather than lose money.[9]

Like a chess player, Yakobson had been waiting for this moment. More than a year earlier, just a few weeks into Gusev's tenure as artistic director, Gusev had come to the Yakobsons' apartment at 11 Vosstaniya Street, in a fashionable part of Leningrad just off Nevsky Prospect, with a request, Irina recalled. "One day, shortly after the establishment of the troupe, which, under Gusev, was called the Chamber Ballet, Pyotr Andreyevich came to L. V.'s home and offered him the opportunity to stage the opening program, and to include in it anything he fancied. I was present during their conversation, in the hope of persuading L. V. to accept Gusev's proposal. So I said to L. V.: 'You have always dreamt of having your own troupe, and here Pyotr Andreyevich is giving you a carte blanche to produce anything you wish. It will be easier for the two of you to work together, because you are so talented and P. A. is so clever!' Gusev immediately retorted: 'Irochka, are you trying to say that I have no talent and he is a fool?' My attempts at persuasion came to no avail. My husband stood firm: 'You undertook [the management of] the troupe, so now you must stage the program.' This was the end of the conversation. I had never seen Pyotr Andreyevich so downcast. But what happened next was even worse: While P. A. was in the room [with Yakobson], our German shepherd got a hold of his leather briefcase, filled with documents pertaining to the troupe, and tore apart half of its contents. It was obvious that the visit had turned sour."[10]

In refusing to ghostwrite Gusev's directorship of the troupe, Yakobson was confirming his view of himself as part of the historical episodes of ballet history, even if he lacked the luxury of a well-established, long-term position from which to implement his vision. Yakobson had learned by necessity that a hit-and-run pacing was not only more likely to succeed with Soviet officials, but the best for which he could hope. His signature genre of a tale swiftly told through the choreographic miniature was a brilliant example of that strategy in action. He worked feverishly in the studio—often running rehearsals for three different ballets simultaneously as he rotated through three studios in the initial period of assembling his repertory. Irina, a prized protégée of Agrippina Vaganova and a preeminent pedagogue of her system of training for clarity and virtuosity, provided the technical anchoring of daily company class to ensure that when the dancers entered Yakobson's rehearsals, they were physically prepared for his idiosyncratic disassembly and torquing of the classical movement vocabulary. In Yakobson's presentation on December 21, 1969, in which he outlined his vision for his company, he specified his goal of creating a unified modern body in his dancers. "In the Kirov theatre ballet artists have magnificently developed feet and legs, but that is only half of the person needed to perform classical ballet. To do modern works they modernize only the top part of the artist, the torso, hands and arms. This sometimes would enrage me. How can you allow the feet of the artist to do classical while the top is doing something else?" he asked rhetorically.[11]

Yakobson had initially held open auditions a year earlier, in December 1969, from which he chose his company. He created what he called a *kollektiv truppï* (collective troupe) with a nucleus of dancers drawn primarily from the Leningrad and Perm ballet conservatories, academies known for their strong but also very traditional training. In January those who had been accepted were notified, and in February they began arriving. Tatyana Kvasova, who had originally been a member of Gusev's company, recalled the resentment she initially felt when she learned Yakobson would become the company's new director. "At first we did not like it because we finished the ballet school and wanted to dance classical ballet. We knew Yakobson by his miniatures—*Snow Maiden, Troika, The Gossips*—but I wanted to dance the classics," she said. Kvasova was so determined that she went up to his office and announced she was going to leave because of the repertoire.[12] Yakobson responded, she recalled, by saying, "If you want the classics, you are going to get classics like no one has ever danced before." The following day Yakobson began choreographing *Mozart Pas de Deux.* "He put together such a thing that no one has been able to dance it since I did," laughed Kvasova, who became one of the company's star performers. "He used to tell us: 'What are you doing? There is music playing in your feet!'"[13]

The company began rehearsing in March of 1970. For the first three months they could only rehearse in the evenings because of difficulties finding rehearsal space. The final six months of preparation prior to the company's opening were tense, with the compressed work and the necessity of getting approval and affirmation from the khudsovet oversight committees regulating culture for the USSR. Yakobson's widow recounted the succession of roadblocks put in his way as the project of assembling his own company inched forward and officials began to fear that they would not have enough control over the result. Having opened a small aperture of freedom, they were unprepared for where that would lead. Their efforts to close it became increasingly aggressive the more they realized the scope of Yakobson's influence and the scale of his ambition. Irina detailed how he played cat and mouse games with their efforts at control:

> He secured permission to select new dancers and asked for some time to prepare. The authorities granted both requests, but required Yakobson to submit his agenda for a review, and to this end they called innumerable meetings.
>
> They demanded to be told in minute detail what L. V. was planning to produce—a full account of each and every miniature. L. V. tried to joke his way out, saying: "The ballet cannot be told; it can only be shown." If the score of a miniature was by a non-Russian composer, and especially one who was uncongenial to the Soviet musical tradition, such as Alban Berg or Anton von Webern, the issue was raised: why them and not others? Shostakovich, too, was in disfavor. Yakobson was constantly reprimanded. However, he could generally win anyone over to his side and make him submit— since in questions of art he was not ready for any compromise, nor did he ever give up any of his artistic agendas. He had to fight for almost all his programs, invariably he came out the winner. It is no wonder that the authorities disliked him. They realized that he was not afraid of them. He never deferred or pandered to them—he was a free man in the full sense of this word, [a position] that was not typical for those times, as is well known.[14]

On the eve of beginning his company, however, Yakobson expressed unusual patience with these inevitable layers of oversight. "We have had three viewings," he recounted in his December 1970 talk to LOVTO, the Leningrad branch of the All-Russia Theater Association. "The first was before we were able to begin work and the last one was a week ago. I fully understand and approve of these viewings. It is necessary to check up on what I am doing because there is a lot of money every year being spent on this company—400,000 rubles—almost half a million, and our program is allocated 200,000 rubles so naturally the managers will be worried about what will be shown."[15] He then also realistically acknowledged that there were other motivations for these viewings. "I would not be objective if I did not say there are people who do not want our group to exist. Some from jealousy, others from mistrust, others from misunderstanding. During the duration of my theatre life I have gotten used to having other things that got in the way," he confided. "Sometimes it prevents you from getting positive results, but we just take the sticks out of the spokes and keep on rolling. We work with love and give every bit of ourselves."[16]

In his own work, Yakobson's quest was to reach steadily toward the individual voice with determination and love, intuitively linking his work to the imperatives of modernism that at this time were playing out with increasing velocity in dance in the West. For three decades he had been testing the limits of representation in the Soviet system through his choreography, and now he had at last broken through to the next layer, the organizational structure of a ballet company itself. Soviet authorities had toyed with Yakobson cruelly before finally giving him his company. Over the next five years the harassment would continue, now masked as proliferating rules and limitations on what he could and could not do with his company. But he had achieved what no dance artist before him in the USSR had even attempted. "I was accused of not recognizing classical dance and shoving it away," he said. "I did not shove it away, I was putting it in its rightful place where it should be. That principle was the basis on which I built the program," he said, explaining the rationale behind dividing the Choreographic Miniatures programs into separate sections, each of which highlighted specific styles of ballet from romantic and classical pas de deux, to small Russian genre ballets, to his Rodin miniatures. His goal was to create fifty miniatures, which he could then combine into seventy different programs.[17]

One prominent person who did express early on an eagerness to see a performance of Choreographic Miniatures was Sol Hurok, who once again happened to be in the USSR in search of troupes to take back to the United States. "Hurok, however, was preempted by Soviet functionaries whose job it was to instruct [Yakobson] what he could and couldn't show," recalled Irina, who was present at the meeting. "They forbade him to show The Swan; authorized only the first three sculptures from the Rodin suite—but not 'naked' as they put it, but dressed in skirts. L. V. nodded his head and agreed to everything—but at the end showed his entire repertoire." No immediate personal sanctions against Yakobson followed, but Hurok was never permitted to bring the troupe to the United States.[18]

The Yakobson supporter from Novosibirsk who would bring Yakobson and his company to the Siberian city of Akademgorodok, Novosibirsk, in the spring of 1973 to perform *Jewish Wedding* understood immediately the significance of Yakobson's project. He appreciated how being artistic director of Choreographic Miniatures was as close to private ownership of a ballet company as anyone in the Soviet Union had ever dared venture:

> For a lot of people it was like receiving new energy: the understanding of what freedom means, what does it mean to have freedom inside a human being? What does it mean to be really independent and to continue to work and to remember about your self-esteem and your dignity? Leonid Yakobson demonstrated it.
>
> It was psychological and it was a wonderful message to the people in the former Soviet Union: What does a human life mean? Is it possible to be in the society without the ideological priorities? It was a very strong message: it's wonderful just to be a human being, to remember about your inner freedom, to save your vision of what life means.
>
> It's not necessary to touch bureaucracy; it's not necessary to play games with bureaucracy. You have to be very strong. It's not necessary to go to prison to fight for your human rights. But you have to demonstrate sometime. To be soft, to be strong. And he found a very good balance, because he finally sent a message to us.[19]

The supporter's description of the symbolic importance of Yakobson's company for Soviet citizens is remarkable in how rapidly it moves to the grand concepts of freedom, dignity, and self-esteem as being embedded in the very foundation of his company. This man, who had admired Yakobson's work long before the formation of Choreographic Miniatures, acknowledged that Yakobson's ballets were transparent challenges to the bureaucracy as well as statements of strength that audiences understood. Yakobson's choice of *Jewish Wedding,* the riskiest dance he would ever make, as the first ballet he built for his new company, was unequivocal in demonstrating the degree of autonomy he wanted. Each of his ballets was about its announced narrative subject, but the very fact of its presence and performance by a company of his own dancers was also a salute to what the supporter called "human rights" and the wonder of one's humanity and inner freedom. The more that Yakobson was tested and challenged, the sharper his actions demonstrating his resistance through ballet and the existence of his company.

Joseph Brodsky once designated the Russian people "logocentric" because of their love of talking, speculating, arguing, and pondering.[20] For Brodsky this reflected the sage-like elevated stature of the poet in Russia, but it can also explain the pleasure that Yakobson seemed to derive from butting heads rhetorically with Soviet authorities as he refuted their restrictions and prohibitions on his work, meeting by meeting and dance by dance. The Russian poet Katia Kapovich similarly observed that in a repressive totalitarian regime like Soviet Russia, the poet is forced to distill everything until each word "spent" has a precious economy (in contrast to the verbosity of official Soviet rhetoric). This awareness of the pleasures of linguistic repartee coupled with the preciousness of expression appears in Yakobson's ballets as his miniaturization of narrative—a quality the title of his company celebrates.

Choreographic Miniatures: The Company

Yakobson may have been progressive in advocating for his own ballet company, but once he achieved it, his style in the rehearsal room was sharply authoritarian. In fact, his rules for his dancers were stricter than those imposed on dancers in the Kirov or Bolshoi companies, and many chafed under his directives. Some of his demands were practical, such as having all the dancers learn all the roles, but others seemed to achieve little more than a reassertion of his authority. One of the oddest demands in this regard concerned how each member of the company was instructed to formally greet Yakobson. Irina recounted being on tour with the company at a resort on the Black Sea, where the company was performing at the resort theater. While strolling along the beach, she and Yakobson passed two dancers from the troupe. Irina watched with surprise as the young woman promptly curtseyed to Yakobson while the man made a crisp bow; then both continued walking on past them as if their bodily obedience was as routine as saying hello. Indeed this physical salutation was part of the required discipline of being in Yakobson's ballet company. "Discipline is the way you walk, stand, lie down—it is your culture," he used to instruct the young people. "It is inconceivable that, on entering a room, I should find you lounging and relaxing all over the place, or that you should rush past me with a cursory 'Hi!' To you, I am (Marius) Petipa!" he used to tell them.[21]

"Yakobson was not generous with praise," recalled Lyudmila Seryozhnikova, an original member of Choreographic Miniatures. She recounted an episode where, during a performance of Yakobson's fiendishly difficult *The Brilliant Divertissement* (*Blestyashchiy Divertisment*, 1973), one of the other women, Kvasova, sprained her ankle and Seryozhnikova had to dance both her own part and Kvasova's. "No one seemed to notice that it was the same ballerina who appeared now from the right, now from the left wing," she said. "The following day, at a meeting, Leonid Veniaminovich—for the first time!—commended me on my performance: 'Well done! You managed to find a way out! We didn't have to stop the music and avoided an empty stage.'" Yakobson regarded his dancers as instruments for delivering his performances; accordingly, his praise showed that his ballets' well-being always took priority over that of the individuals performing them.[22]

Elena Selivanova, also a member of the company, described how this emphasis on the dancers serving the choreography played out in rehearsals with an even greater intensity. "Our training was incredibly rigorous. Leonid Veniaminovich didn't allow us to cut corners, and if he noticed that anyone had slackened down, he immediately started screaming. At the end of a rehearsal, every one of us could be tested. Thus, for example, Kvasova, who was not cast as a prostitute in *The City*, nevertheless had to not only learn but also rehearse the full role along with me, who was given the role. Woe to any dancer who protested or refused to execute a required pas," Selivanova said. "He would be given a strident dressing down and then kicked out of the room. When Yakobson was staging the episode involving a prostitute and her client with me, I told him that it was unnatural to ask a 19-year-old girl to impersonate a depraved woman. He yelled at me: 'Idiot! Get out of the hall!' The following day he made me try this scene again. I managed to overcome myself and followed his instructions. And suddenly he complimented me: 'Well, I never! The seduction gesture came out convincing!'"[23] Yakobson invented ballet with brutal concision—he sought out the most emotionally compact foundations on which to erect complex narrative structures through movement. Then inside of those narrative structures he pushed his dancers to learn how malleable character and social roles can be.

The dancers' timidity about portraying the characters in *The City* (*Gorod*, 1972) aligned with the party's negative reaction to the bleak and decidedly non-Soviet image of urban life depicted in that ballet. Yakobson's inspiration had been the Belgian artist Frans Masereel's raw 1925 novel *The City* (*Die Stadt*). Considered the first prototype for the genre of graphic novels, Masereel's book was a series of black and white woodcuts portraying the ugly realities of life in an unnamed metropolis between the wars. Darkly expressionistic, *The City* was subjected to a series of censorship viewings. Its cast of characters, including students, prostitutes, a gentleman with a call girl, pickpockets prowling by night, a lynching scene—all were clearly rendered and problematic. "The numerous commissions [assigned to view the piece] . . . were dissatisfied with everything." Irina said. "The composer, Carl Maria von Weber, was German not Soviet; the initial title— *The Pandemonium of Passion*—which Yakobson had come across in some literary work and thought very suitable—was utterly wrong; the personages, who came from the bottom of urban society, were deemed 'foreign' to the Soviet audience," she explained. The company's literary manager, Vladimir Zaydelson, persuaded Yakobson to change the title to *The City*. This, however, was not enough to appease the authorities: "No, the title should be more specific: 'A Capitalist City,'" Irina recounts they instructed him. "At this point, L. V. lost his equanimity and stated that there was nothing capitalist in the ballet and that [the portrayed episodes] could take place in any city."[24] In the end *The City*'s title was allowed to remain.

Arts organizations are always social constructions and this is particularly true of ballet companies, which are like little kingdoms—sequestered worlds where obedience and authority are bent to one individual's aesthetic ends. Yakobson's vision may have been progressive but his methods were not, according to those in the rehearsal room with him. He was, in quick rotation, demanding, impatient, authoritarian, temperamental, and paternalistic—imposing a monarchical power structure rather than an egalitarian one on his dancers as he instructed, persuaded, pushed, and imposed his style and aesthetic on them. Valentina Klimova, one of his strongest and most devoted dancers, explained how these various facets of Yakobson fit together:

> Leonid Veniaminovich was two different people at once. In private
> life he was gentle, never raised his voice, and was chivalrous to

women. In the rehearsal hall a completely different picture emerged: he acted like an extremely severe person. He would not let us lean against the barre, believing that this would make us slack. Neither did he encourage eating in the middle of a rehearsal: "When you eat, your blood flow is directed towards your stomach, and this makes you sluggish. You should be ravenous, like a wolf. A wolf is lean—it has stamina and can run long distances." I am sure, however, that had he not been so demanding, the theater would not have got off the ground. In terms of discipline our troupe was regarded as a model for emulation. At meetings, discipline was his favorite topic. He never tired of repeating that discipline is at the root of everything else.[25]

This air of control even extended to his wife, attested to by a letter he wrote to Irina in October 1971, when he was traveling a few months after the premiere of his company: "Ironka!" he writes, while he is en route to attend an International Music Congress in Armenia, using an affectionate Russian diminutive for Irina. He urges her to leave her position at the Vaganova Ballet Academy (Leningrad Choreographic Institute) to assist him with his company. "You must quit the school. The classes are worthless for you, they hold no interest for you and offer no prospects. As to my company—everything lies in the future. The work is promising. Step by step from pedagogy to rehearsals, and then to head of the rehearsal section, then to deputy artistic director. *You need only one thing: to know that I am the main person whose authority is indisputable, and then everything will run smoothly.* Within a short time you will be my deputy. This is the best of all situations. But the first step for you is to leave Shelkov [the director of the Vaganova School]."[26]

A few days later Yakobson wrote to his wife again, the scale of his assurance about the bright future of his company having grown even larger, and his impatience for her to quit the Vaganova School and effectively enter his employment more urgent as well:

Ironka! I sense that you have already decided to quit the school and I think that you have made the proper decision. My theater has more prospects. You can advance accordingly: at this time you are a teacher and something of a coach. Then you are in charge of the

Irina Yakobson teaching in the Vaganova Ballet Academy, 1960s. Central
State Archive of Cinema, Photographic and Phonographic Documents
in Saint Petersburg.

coaching section and a coach; then deputy to the artistic director,
and then artistic director. When I get on in age, I shall attempt to
help you with the artistic direction. As regards directing, after myself, I cannot trust anyone but you. Prepare for your new functions
in appointed stages. Kolka [their son] will design sets for all of the
productions and pieces and will be the main person in charge of
artistic lighting. I will stage thirty-seven ballets and then I shall retire on a pension because of my age. Until then we must do everything possible to create our theater. As a future director, it would
be useful for Kolka to look closely at things.[27]

It's remarkable how autocratic Yakobson's tone toward his family is in
these two letters, and how firm are his confidence and insistence on having unequivocal command of his new troupe. He is looking forward to a
bright future and a stellar legacy for himself with an assurance that is
amazing for someone only four months into the life of his company. He
describes an enterprise whose destiny sounds secure for decades. Per-

sonal correspondence with a spouse is usually where one expresses secret doubts or worries, but none of that is evident here. He even maps a
future for his son, [Kolka, the diminutive for Nicholas], who had turned
eighteen just the previous month. Nicholas is to begin with an apprentice-
ship with the company before succeeding his parents decades hence as the
artistic director. What is outlined here is not so much a family enterprise
as a dynasty whose enterprise is Yakobson's Choreographic Miniatures.
Both the dreams of succession that Yakobson describes in these letters are
about sustaining his repertoire and legacy to the exclusion of others' personal ambitions and about trusting only his family with the enterprise of
his art.

An aura of anxiousness as well as bravado filled his enterprise. In some
ways Yakobson was replicating through his own managerial style the rig-
idly controlled power hierarchy of the USSR systems in which he had
grown up. In other ways he was challenging it, aggressively carving out
a safe space to make his audacious dances. There was an edgy passive-
aggressive moodiness to his treatment of his dancers—how else to explain his cruelty inside the studio and rehearsal room and great kindness
and generosity to his dancers afterward?

Auditioning for Individuality

In some respects Yakobson was engaged in a version of warfare and the
dancers in the Choreographic Miniatures company became the initial soldiers in his crusade to carve out a place for subjective experience in the
Soviet state. This fight began with the way he structured the auditions he
held for entry into the company. Rather than asking for a demonstration
of technical mastery and virtuosity, Yakobson focused on each dancer's
capacity to tell a counter-narrative through his or her classically trained
body. Well over one hundred dancers from all over the Soviet Union
turned out to audition for his new company. Yakobson created a committee comprised of a director from another company, principal dancers
from the Kirov, teachers from the Vaganova School, and Irina to help decide who would be offered contracts. But in the end, Irina confided, he
took whom he wanted. Yakobson explained that for years as he watched
the few foreign dance companies he was allowed to see, he often thought
about what kind of a group he would have if he had the chance to create

one. "I imagined that it would be one that would show all genres, all styles, all kinds of world choreography," he said of his large-scale ambitions. "It should create dancers who are able to participate in the real classical works of the past. At the same time they should be able to transform themselves and move well on the stage, be musical enough and possess a face and body that can create choreographic plastique images. In short, these dancers in my company should be educated like no other artist in any other theater."[28]

One member of the troupe, Stepin, recalled how idiosyncratic Yakobson's criteria for selecting dancers appeared. "In choosing dancers [for Choreographic Miniatures] Yakobson followed his own, rather than conventional, criteria. He was looking for people with high energy levels, charged from within, as it were. Whether the energy was positive or negative was not important, as long as the dancer was a persona, an individual. Sometimes an artist had no idea that he possessed a certain quality, but Yakobson perceived it with a sixth sense. He often accepted dancers who looked homely or even bizarre but had a certain appeal, in order to cast them in grotesque roles in the future. Some were hired for a rainy day, but Yakobson was so busy that he never found the time to work with them."[29] It is possible to read a certain anxiety in Yakobson's leadership style as well. How does one get obedience from twenty-five individuals if the systems of control under which they developed are all suddenly changed? What if the motivator is engagement rather than fear, or at least a different balance between the two?

The key quality that Yakobson valued in dancers, according to his widow, was "individuality." He tested for it through rehearsal exercises that invoked subjectivity: he would ask each dancer to respond with movement and expression to a variety of situations. The dancer would have to improvise on the spot, suddenly switching emotional registers as he changed the prompt. "You are alone, in a dark, scary forest and feeling frightened," began one directive. "Show me what this looks like." As soon as the dancer transformed his or her body to reflect these emotions in gestures and posture, Yakobson would offer a new challenge. "Now you have suddenly found a cuddly little bunny which you pick up and hug so that it feels safe and warm. Show me this."[30] The task for the dancer was to reveal an extreme range of emotions prompted by these scenarios. Sometimes he took dancers no one else saw anything in. He was fond of saying that a dancer could be trained in technique, but character and individuality could not be trained and it was these qualities—along with the capacity to step away from the comfort of being a classically trained body—that Yakobson's unusual audition prompts were trying to reveal.

"Individuality," a core interest of modernism, was also an important quality for Yakobson's company because over the next five years he would challenge the Soviet model of social uniformity and collectivity with more than thirty new ballets. Many of Yakobson's mostly miniature works reflect a transgressive desire for ideals beyond the Soviet standard and so suggest a modernist agenda. He wanted his dancers and then his audiences to reflect and question the conditions of modern life, including urbanization, and its human costs. But it was the lure of individuality and his articulation through gesture and choreography of distinctive personalities that set Yakobson's work for Choreographic Miniatures apart from any other ballet being created in the USSR.

Yakobson was attempting to rewrite the state from its core—scattering the vestiges of the classical, unified ballet army, with its militaristically drilled corps de ballet, into what was effectively a rebel group of resistance fighters. The price was huge—it meant giving up the dancers of the Kirov and occasionally Bolshoi for a group of dancers from different ballet training programs throughout the USSR. Their unifying experience would happen in Yakobson's rehearsal room. To ensure the necessary cohesive quality of a unified ensemble, Yakobson's disciplinary methods, demands, and rehearsal idiosyncrasies intensified. One of his rules was that everyone in a ballet had to be present for all rehearsals and learn all the other dancers' parts. Dancers were often cast in roles whose demands and styles seemed at odds with their conception of the kind of dancers they were. Ironically there was something both Soviet and anti-Soviet in how Yakobson worked; he forged an innovative ballet ensemble out of differently trained dancers by actively pushing them beyond their customary pace and comfort. It was like a massive electrification project imposed on the company (his nation), where the dancers' bodies claimed liberation through obedience to authoritarian pressures.

"One cannot deny that I am a difficult person to work with," Yakobson once confessed. "I do not capitalize on the dancer's previous knowledge. I try to uncover in him new possibilities. I want him to accomplish what he never expected he could do. What counts is the dancer's individuality, both as a person and an actor. Whenever I saw that a person had individuality, I was willing to disregard many other flaws."[31] Despite this disclaimer Yakobson could be temperamental and sharp when the dancers failed to deliver what he requested. Within the safety and privacy of the ballet studio, Yakobson was approaching topics, like the prostitute and her customer in *The City,* that were still risky territory for ballet given that government leaders in the Soviet Union had denied the existence of prostitution in the country and hence saw no need to make any laws against it. In his urgency to explore social situations choreographically, Yakobson propelled his dancers into areas that were socially risky, particularly given the preceding climate of socialist realist art, when depictions were seen as being closely linked with desired realities.

Valeriy Sergeyev, one of Yakobson's most devoted dancers and a regisseur of his choreography after his death, suggested the logic behind Yakobson's temperamental outbursts but also the truth of their cruelty. "In describing Yakobson, smoothing out or idealizing his image would be a wrong thing to do," Sergeyev said. "As a company director, he was rather cruel. To him we were first and foremost raw material. He would say, 'If you find it difficult to work with me by all means quit—everyone can leave. I will find others and teach them. I do not need you.'"[32]

In addition to his unorthodox rehearsal manner, during the initial three months after he founded his company Yakobson's group was itinerant, a situation that added to the initial attrition in the company. Yakobson's wife estimates that in the first few weeks as many as ten dancers left the company, unhappy with the style of the repertoire and wanting to dance classical ballet, or preferring to be with an established company like the Kirov, or simply because they were not up to the physical, and emotional, demands of Yakobson and his work. "He used to say it was possible to teach a person to dance, but it was impossible to make someone an individual," she said.[33] Yakobson's rehearsal process was physically and emotionally demanding because he saw this as a means of producing individuality and versatility in his dancers.

Early in the company's existence they had to borrow space at the Leningrad Choreographic Institute, which was available only from 8:00 p.m. to 1:00 a.m. nightly, after the institute's regular classes had concluded. The director of the institute, Valentin Ivanovich Shelkov, who knew Yakobson from his having staged several works for the students, had offered to help by giving him use of the school's studios in these after hours. The very late rehearsals in borrowed space distressed his dancers as well as an anonymous party who complained to the authorities that it was not proper for an outside person to use the school facilities—even though technically Yakobson was not an outsider since he remained a salaried company choreographer for the Kirov during this time and until his death.

So Yakobson vacated the school studios and accepted an offer from Ilya Rakhlin, who ran the Leningrad Music Hall, a leading state musical revue theater, to use the hall for one month in the summer while Rakhlin's troupe was on vacation. By the time Rakhlin had returned, the Leningrad Choreographic Institute had identified two very small studios used for their youngest students preparing for the first level of training, which they agreed to allow Yakobson to use. These studios near the main building of the school on Rossi Street became the temporary home of Choreographic Miniatures until 1972, when the company finally moved to 15 Mayakovsky Street. There, with an entrance in a courtyard behind a facade of apartments, the company made its permanent home in a string of ground-floor rooms. These were part of a complex of buildings dating back to the time of Catherine the Great, when the odd central circular building in their midst, historically protected, had been used for horse auctions. As the rehearsal situation smoothed out and the dancers saw that they really would have a permanent home and that the company was headed for success with its repertoire, the departures from the company eased.

Two events finally secured the stability of the Choreographic Miniatures dancers. One was the arrival of two leading dancers with the Kirov, the celebrated Alla Osipenko and her partner John (Dzhon) Markovsky. They relinquished their star positions with the Kirov to dance with Choreographic Miniatures. In a letter to Irina dated July 8–9, 1972, written from Leningrad to Lvov (now Lviv) in Ukraine, where she was taking a rest cure at a spa, Yakobson explains how he measured the dancers' comfort with his work by watching how the newly arrived Osipenko and Markovsky adjusted. "Yes, Ironka, the extent to which our system is good can be seen in the following: Osipenko and Markovsky earlier rebelled against *Exercise XX* but yesterday we persuaded them to dance it." An earlier turning point—the other event that convinced the dancers to remain—was the spectacular audience reception for the first performance of Choreographic Miniatures, when the company was greeted with wild standing ovations and cheers for its first all-Yakobson program on June 7, 1971 at the Maly Theater of Opera and Ballet in Leningrad.[34] "After that opening, everyone wanted to stay," Irina said of the dancers. Osipenko recalled with affection the rare bonding that happened among the dancers in Yakobson's company. "Sometimes the dancers were twenty years younger than I, but friendship is too trivial a word to describe what was between us—we loved each other. We really rooted for the success of the troupe and that's why. I was already a People's Artist but Leonid would yell at me not to lean on anything during rehearsal just as he did the others and I supported that."[35]

Even those past their dancing careers, like Lopukhov's wife, Klara Lopukhova, eagerly applied to work as regisseurs with the new company. It was an experiment many people wanted to join. A letter Lopukhov wrote to Yakobson in October 1970 expresses his impatience that Klara was not yet hired to assist Yakobson. "I don't like this delay with Klara," Lopukhov begins his letter bluntly. "Either you need her or not. As far as my recommendation of her—she has what is needed for you and for other choreographers. She has an amazing memory of what choreographers stage and at the same time she does not change what has been staged by others," Lopukhov writes, referencing his inside familiarity with Yakobson's ballets and working process from watching Yakobson's rehearsals over many years. "This is a much needed quality exactly for your kind of staging where the smallest deviation would kill your style," he advises. Within a short while Yakobson did indeed engage Klara and she stayed with the company through the remainder of Yakobson's life.[36]

Lyudmila Putinova, who joined Choreographic Miniatures after much of the repertoire had already been created, recalled how Yakobson's penchant for control extended even to the audience's reception of his ballets and their applause in relation to bows and curtain calls. "He anticipated with unfailing accuracy at which point the public would applaud," Putinova said. "He would say, 'Here is a culmination, and here will be an ovation' as he rehearsed the ballet. He carefully planned all entrances and exits, as well as the manner in which they were to be executed. He believed that a dancer should emerge and exit unexpectedly and swiftly. A pas-de-deux was normally designed as one whole and was not meant to be interrupted by bows, so that the viewer could watch it in one breath; a pause between the duet and variations was supposed to last "ten-counts." Only at the end of a *pas-de-deux* did we get an opportunity to enjoy applause."[37]

Aspiring to the appearance of humility, Yakobson even choreographed his own acknowledgment of applause at the end of an evening. Putinova recounts that during a performance, Yakobson positioned himself in the wings to the left of the audience. His presence served as a reminder to the dancers that they were dancing for him as much as the audience. Then, at the conclusion of each program, the dancers were instructed to invite him onto the stage to join in the bows, and he warned them in advance that he would make a great show of demurring and trying to slip back into the wings. "It was a ritual that he made light of but in fact took very seriously," Putinova said. "'I will resist and try to escape,' he used to say, 'but you mustn't let me—keep dragging me there anyway.'" Yet "when he finally appeared before the audience—gray-haired and trim—the effect was striking," she reminisced. "People had no idea that the dances they had just seen, so vigorous, buoyant and animated, had actually been created by an elderly man. Time was powerless to age his soul: it was young and daring like that of a mischievous teenager. In essence, he was younger than any of us."[38]

The Dancers

Yakobson's creation of his own company was novel in so many respects— not the least of which was his having scaled back, at the age of sixty-five, his own secure position as a resident choreographer in the prestigious Kirov Theater in favor of these unknowns with a new troupe of young dancers with differing skills. Maya Plisetskaya noted this penchant Yakobson had for going against the tide when she remarked after the company's initial performances: "Yakobson is an extremely impetuous and daring master who rejects even the least conspicuous clichés in art. The performances of Choreographic Miniatures are dazzling, stirring and joyous."[39]

Yakobson's closest artistic compatriots during this time were artists outside of dance. For those Soviet artists working in the visual arts and poetry, the early 1970s were a time of blooming artistic samizdat, particularly among the underground artistic elite in Moscow and Leningrad.

Unlike Yakobson, these painters and poets only needed some wall space in their apartment, student club, or hostel on which to display their deliberately "unofficial" paintings. Poets could similarly recite their poetry in tiny rooms to one or two trusted friends. In contrast, Yakobson had to encounter the publicness of dance at every turn. In order to share his ideas with the public with as little official intrusion as possible, first the dancers needed to be won over to the effort and then the various necessities of live art secured.

So while the breathless pace of producing new ballets that Yakobson began in 1970 anticipated public viewing as its endpoint, he also had to negotiate the nature of the unique community he had constructed to disperse his ideas to the Soviet public. "Yakobson was an ardent debater," Lvov-Anokhin observed. "In art as well as in theoretical discussions he was neither calm nor reasonable, quite the contrary. He was intolerant and impulsive. When it came to polemics, no hyperbole seemed excessive to him. . . . He was often told something was forbidden, or impossible or that it could not be done. But he stood firm and ultimately asserted his right to take risks and experiment. For him art was a form of polemical thought."[40]

So many epithets attach to Yakobson. Askold Makarov called him "a stubborn visionary," typifying him as being "woven out of contradictions— kind and intolerant—an opponent of classical dance [yet] an artist who outshines many other classical choreographers who combine ready-made forms. He is radical in all his agendas. But how his working style takes getting used to!" Similarly the dancer and choreographer Nikita Dolgushin eulogized him as a man who "believed ballet is omnipotent." Dolgushin, who toured the United States in 1995 with a program of several Yakobson miniatures, is one of the few contemporaries to suggest the logic between Yakobson's domineering style inside the ballet studio and his struggle to gain autonomy outside as reflecting the displaced tensions of omnipotence and impotence that he lived his artistic life suspended between. "While in regard to government functionaries Yakobson may have been extremely vulnerable, in the ballet studio he was an omnipotent deity. Zeus-like he banged his fists and stomped his feet," Dolgushin recounted. "He demanded total understanding. He called for an immediate grasp and acceptance of everything."[41] As much as he abhorred totalitarianism, there are aspects of Yakobson's own manner in the studio that suggest he borrowed some of its emotional aroma.

Until the end of his life various authorities of the Ministry of Culture and commissions from the Communist Party made repeated attempts to dismantle Choreographic Miniatures. Selivanova suggests how this ever-present threat of censorship took an emotional toll on the dancers. "We were constantly threatened with closure, tormented by committees, and accosted with demands to make changes [in the repertoire]. But Yakobson announced once and for all: 'I would rather sacrifice a ballet than make any changes in it.' Often we finished showing a piece [to a commission] and then waited around while they discussed it—only to find out that some party functionaries had been reviling Yakobson's masterpieces. Our director [Leonid] Sorochan adored Yakobson and always stood up for him. When, during one of the official discussions of *The Bedbug,* Yakobson was thrown out of the room, Sorochan threatened to forfeit his Communist party membership, yelling at the top of his voice: 'What do you think you are doing? What impudence! To kick out the man who has created all this!' "[42]

On one level Yakobson seemed to regard disputation with censorious officials as a category of sport. Sergeyev recalled that following one such particularly frustrating showing of ballets that Yakobson wanted to include on a Choreographic Miniatures program, he turned to Yakobson and asked: "Leonid Veniaminovich, what will you do if they close us down?" Yakobson replied: "If the theatre is closed down, I will be left without a job. But no, not really. I will open up a booth at 11 Vosstaniya [Rebellion] Street and mend shoes. And I will put up a sign, which will say, 'Here works Leonid Veniaminovich Yakobson. Choreographer. Stalin Prize laureate. Genius. Jew.' "[43]

For Yakobson all four of these categories were problematic yet true. The distinction of the Stalin Prize and Honored Arts Worker of the Russian Soviet Federative Socialist Republic prizes attested to his gifts, but it was also because he was a choreographer and a Jew that so much was done to limit his resources to express that prodigious creativity. His scenario of an alternate career mending shoes while advertising the traces of his identities turns the humiliation back on the authorities and suggests the equal emptiness of their prizes and opprobrium. Yakobson's fantasy shoemaker booth also affords him the ultimate job of a Jewish outsider, that of a village tradesman, a cobbler, the archetypal shtetl Jew.

Yakobson's unnamed supporter who helped bring *Jewish Wedding* to out-of-town audiences had once referred to Yakobson's miniatures as being a "Jewish type of work" because they involved creating a lot of small pieces to show in a big performance. "He sent a secret message to the people and people immediately started to spot Leonid Yakobson," he said. "And it was a very peaceful message—'please remember, I am here, this is my work.'" Yakobson regarded his use of the genre of the miniature as a dive directly into the heart of dance content. "I have an inexplicable love for the miniature as a dance form," he once said. "Spacious yet laconic, mobile, with a clear shapeliness of contour, yet dramatically polished, it is a genre with which I feel a genuine affinity. As a small artistic genre, it has the possibility to disclose the music to the utmost, to maximally express a dancer's potential, to communicate within a circumscribed time frame, more than can a full-length ballet. Finally," he said, "it focuses the spectator's attention."[44] Artistically Yakobson saw himself as a pedagogue. He forged his ballets with a muscular, vigorous approach and he wanted people to pay attention to them, to care as much as he did about the social force of a dance image. The dance miniature was also a form of autobiographical self-portraiture for him, a terse medium in which to test his observations like notes written in movement.

The Repertoire

If Yakobson had drafted a motto it likely would have been "He wanted to choreograph everything—he disdained repeats. He found his choreography in the music." Indeed he believed that each score offered an important opportunity for invention. Stylistically and thematically his rehearsals were laboratory experiments that tested the raw physical possibility of a dancer's body as much as his or her emotional capacity to push past fear and injury. Lyudmila Seryozhnikova recounted how when Yakobson was staging a new ballet—such as in 1974 when he staged the *Donizetti Pas de Deux* to a segment of Donizetti's *The Elixir of Love* as part of his *Six Pas de Deux* cycle—he would call together the entire troupe. At seventy he was too old to demonstrate how the men lifted the women, Seryozhnikova said; nonetheless he continued at high velocity to invent the choreography without first testing out if it was possible.[45]

Seryozhnikova remembered one lift in the pas de deux where she was supposed to be thrown up in the air by her partner, corkscrew in midair, and descend in a free fall past him, grasping onto him only at the last moment. Yakobson insisted that she could only reach for her partner after she was nearly at the ground. As she repeatedly tried the move she kept missing and smacking into the floor face first. "I can't remember now how many times I crashed—on my face, knees, hands! But Yakobson demanded the lift to be performed exactly so and no other way: to grab onto the partner only after flying past him. . . . When the *Donizetti Pas de Deux* was being reconstructed some years later, this stunt had to be eliminated: it proved too difficult for any other dancer to do," Seryozhnikova said, clearly regretful that such a rare, if bruising, work was unrecoverable. "This is how [aspects of Yakobson's ballets] become irretrievably lost," she lamented. "His ballets were full of such nuances, which complicated the choreography but also rendered it highly original. They formed the essence of his works: however difficult and unusual these movements may be, without them a ballet would be missing Yakobson's signature."[46] With his own company Yakobson could finally go to the physical extremes that had been impossible to attempt with the Kirov and Bolshoi dancers and staff.

The members of Choreographic Miniatures trusted him wherever he took them, regardless of the physical risk. Still devoted to his work, these retired dancers suggest that its irretrievability now is the fault of contemporary dancers who won't persevere through the technical demands and physical risks. Seryozhnikova recounts how when she and other former Yakobson dancers, including Kvasova, taught some of Yakobson's works to a younger generation of dancers in the Maly Kirov Theater troupe that Yakobson's widow and son briefly founded in 1991, "the performers put up fierce resistance and every movement involved a fight: the position of fingers or arms, the accents," Seryozhnikova said.[47] "The spectator today is not aware that he is being robbed of the full impact of Yakobson's choreography. We [the professionals], however, see how, with each new production, it becomes increasingly impoverished," she said. "Let us take, for example, the positioning of the torso during a fall. Yakobson insisted that it should be different than in the classical ballet—say, turned sideways. Yakobson's choreography is so expressive that, if a dancer recreates it in every nuance, the result will be excellent even if deep feeling is missing," she said echoing the total trust his dancers developed for him.[48]

These stories suggest the grand ambition that Yakobson had for his company, and how urgently he felt the need to move rapidly into movement invention—to push his dancers to the physical limits of their bodies and, in the early days, to break out of the movement conformity he saw around him. The dancers who stayed with Yakobson speak of surviving these near impossible choreographic demands as if doing so gained one admission to a secret society of fortitude. Inside the drab rehearsal studios at 15 Mayakovsky Street, dancers would reach into new worlds of movement and return, like cosmonauts, to report back what they had glimpsed. Having his own company afforded Yakobson a way of probing subjectivity through both the dancers' experiences and his own.

If there was any doubt about what his company was—a Jewish village in the USSR—he announced it with the first ballet he created for them, *Jewish Wedding*. This was the work he used to fuse them into a company. While he was attempting to get *Jewish Wedding* onstage, the first few of the most vocal Soviet Zionist Jews were finally being permitted to leave the USSR, and Yakobson was asked why he didn't just go to Israel if he wanted to make ballets on Jewish themes. Irina, who was with him at the time, said he responded curtly, "I want Jewish people to have the right to do their work here."[49] *Jewish Wedding*, performed by his own company, put that belief into action. Vladimir Zenzinov, a dancer who had been with the company when Gusev directed and who became one of the inaugural members of Choreographic Miniatures under Yakobson, watched as Yakobson refused to cancel this Jewish ballet until the day of the premiere, when it was unequivocally clear it could not be performed. "Six hours before the concert began the dancers came together and saw the ticket takers busy crossing out the ballet's listing from each program: 'Who made the announcement?'" he asked rhetorically. "I cannot say exactly but it was the management. So it was a shock. I can only imagine that he did not have permission but at the last minute he hoped he could do something."[50]

Rodin, Eros, and Totalitarian Corporeality

One of the most frequently realized subjects of Yakobson's ballets for his own company in the 1971–1975 period was the sensuality of the body and its images in visual culture. While Yakobson carefully distinguished his aesthetic from erotica, the moralistic Soviet prohibitions on representations of the body and corporeality in Soviet art after the 1920s more often collapsed the differences. Starting in the 1930s, the early Stalinist years, the concept of "totalitarian corporeality" had emerged as a way to describe the body deployed in the service of Stalinist political goals.[51] Within this frame, images of nude or semiclad males and females could be depicted as powerful, yet sexless forms of Greek statuary, sportsmen, or workers, but only if they were devoid of any eroticism. It is an established convention in the visual arts that bodies in the midst of physical exertion, or poised with muscles ready as if about to perform an action, are more resistant to objectification and less inviting as seductively passive objects about which spectators can fantasize.[52] This offers some understanding of the kinds of nudity that would have been permitted and sanctioned as de-eroticized in the Soviet formulation. As Soviet society became more regressive and puritanical, however, exhibiting nudity in any form in art came to be repressed by Soviet authorities. Intimacy, when depicted in the visual arts in important paintings like Viktor Popkov's *A Couple* (*Dvoe*, 1966), or his *Summer. July* (*Leto. Iyul*, 1969), presented physical intimacy in the chaste, rehabilitated "Thaw" style of socialist realism romance. Languorous and weighted forms, they resist the spectator's attempts to sensualize their curving musculatures or to read any individuality, difference, or weakness into their bodies, which seem never to have known the warmth of touch, let alone intimate physical contact.[53] In Popkov's *A Couple* a man and a woman lie in a field of green, separated by a distance so great they might be in two separate paintings except for their similar state of partial undress. The woman wears a dresslike white slip as she reclines partially twisted to one side on her back and the man lies face down, shirtless and wearing jeans. There is the hint that there might have been a brief encounter between the two of them earlier, but the clues are so tenuous it is a struggle to build a narrative weaving them together and a viewer is left feeling foolish for trying.

In 1954 Arkady Plastov, a leading realist painter and member of the USSR Academy of the Arts, had pushed the boundaries of socialist sexuality forward with his 1954 work *Spring* (*Vesna*, 1954), a representational painting of a nude young woman crouching in a Russian bathhouse, presenting her expansive white flesh to the viewer while wrapping a cloak around her little child to keep her warm. "*Spring* created a genuine sensation when it first appeared in the all-union art exhibition that opened at the Tretyakov Gallery in January 1955," noted Alexander Borovsky. It was criticized because it "depicted nudity in the absence of an ideological context such as sport or bathing after a day at work."[54] This necessity of metaphorically anchoring the body to Soviet ideology to effectively weigh it down would prove particularly burdensome to attempts to represent the lightly clad and sensual body in dance.

In 1958 Yakobson inserted ballet into these artistic provocations with the premiere of his triptych *Rodin* at the Kirov Ballet. Through *Rodin* Yakobson was privatizing classical ballet, taking something grand and turning it into an intimate confession and revelation about the particular. The body inside that obedient classical Soviet ballet dancer, he suggested, was shimmering with sensuality and a hunger for carnal awakening. In *Rodin* Yakobson discards the traditional pas de deux attire—instead of toe shoes, tights, and tutus for the women and a cavalier jacket, tights, and shoes for the man, Yakobson costumed his dancers daringly in flesh-hued unitards and bare feet, which was as close as he could come to emulating the nudity of the sculptures. Like *Jewish Wedding,* which Yakobson also made in 1970–1971, *Rodin* symbolically claimed a public space for a dissident body and nonconformist corporeality. In *Spartacus* Yakobson had looked to antiquity to address enslavement, and now he referenced art history again—this time to consider eroticism.

Like Vaslav Nijinsky's 1912 ballet portraying sexual awakening and onanism, *The Afternoon of a Faun* (*L'après-midi d'un faune*), the sensuality in *Rodin* is presented as a narrative of self-discovery. Set to *Claire de lune* by the Impressionist composer Claude Debussy, whose music is also the accompaniment for *Faun,* Yakobson, like Nijinsky, slows down the movements in the second of the five *Rodin* miniatures, *The Kiss* (*Potseluy*), as if the weight of desire thickened the very air that the lovers move through.[55] The more languorous the dancers, the more they allow emotion to saturate their actions. Each of the dances in *Rodin* tugs at conventions of the classical pas de deux beginning with the first Rodin miniature, *The Eternal Spring* (*Vechnaya vesna*). The premise of classical partnering, with the man revealing and displaying the woman to the audience, is replaced with movements that show the man and woman focusing on each other.

In *Rodin,* a series of studies about couples, the spare economy of the stage, the color-washed scrim, and the simple attire for the dancers direct our attention all the more intensely inward to the choreography as the

The Kiss from *Rodin,* Valentina Klimova and
N. Pïkhachev, Choreographic Miniatures,
Leningrad, 1971. Photographer unknown.

only source of understanding about who the characters are and what they mean to each other.[56] The result is that Yakobson's choreography emerges as a critique of the constraints against the sensual in Soviet ballet. By going as far as he could in 1950s Soviet Russia to uncover his dancers in *Rodin,* practically as well as emotionally, Yakobson delivers a ballet miniature with an intimacy scaled to what Soviet citizens were revealing in their private photographs of one another taken at home.

Rodin, like *Jewish Wedding,* was a ballet about claiming a public space for the dissident body in which sex, love, pleasure, and improvisation commingled dangerously. The party authorities who demanded that Yakobson cover his dancers in *Rodin* with a Grecian-styled tricot over their costumes to make them "decent" for public viewing deeply offended Yakobson, but he complied so that *Rodin* could get onstage. Fuming about these priggish conditions, he said the effect was like putting clothes on a statue.

In a parallel development in 1960s Soviet visual arts, interest in the corporeal was also reemerging in a genre known as "artistic photography," in which the nude was double coded as classical and pictorial.[57] From the 1950s through to the 1960s, Soviet officials inadvertently stimulated public interest in the production of images of personal intimacy through their tolerance of amateur photography and emphasis on home life as one of the few places where photographs could be taken freely. Russian art historian Ekaterina Dyogot has noted how "life under Soviet postwar socialism was so centered on cheap self-expression—gardening, knitting, poetry writing, and photography—that even among personal anonymous photographs of the Soviet era one comes across impressive artifacts focused on exalted symbols of the private: sex, eroticism, friendship, intimacy. Into these spheres the Soviet system channeled all the interests not only of amateur photographers but of Soviet citizens as a whole."[58] Yakobson's own turn toward intimacy in dance unfolded during this same period.

Using the aesthetic and strategic schema of three different Auguste Rodin sculptures come to life, Yakobson created an intimate portrait of nontotalitarian corporeality. His choice of the sculptures of Rodin was strategic, for Rodin was broadly synonymous with both modern sculpture and sex. The Soviet mandate that the Rodin sculptures in the Hermitage be kept hidden from public view only increased the erotic charge around these works. When Yakobson unveiled his first three miniatures based on Rodin's *The Kiss*, *The Eternal Spring*, and *Eternal Idol* (*Vechnïy idol*), respectively, for the Kirov Ballet's 1958 season in Leningrad, it was like peeking behind a locked door and witnessing another one of his choreographic "bombs" being detonated. Several in the audience had heard the story of his having gained personal access to see the originals of these forbidden works in the locked rooms of the Hermitage Museum's basement. This visit had occurred thanks to the same sympathetic curator who had privately ushered Yakobson in to see the Pergamon Altar when *Spartacus* had been in preparation two years earlier. Yakobson used the medium of choreography to convey what he saw in those rooms—extending Rodin's momentary torsion of the body into an attenuated history of the paths of male and female bodies through space and passion.

"It was very sexy, just like Rodin's sculptures," said Ida Eidelman, a foreign language teacher and audience member who saw Yakobson's full eight *Rodin* miniatures in Leningrad in 1971 (when he revived the original triptych and created five additional new ones for his Choreographic Miniatures company). "Yakobson came along and he developed this new mode of choreography. He brought eroticism and sexuality to the Kirov stage."⁵⁹ Sofiya Bresler, another spectator of Yakobson's ballets in Leningrad, agreed. "It was such untraditional choreography for us because it stood between classical and modern," Bresler said. "That did not exist before in the art of dance in Russia."⁶⁰ At the time Yakobson made his *Rodin* miniatures, sex also reputedly did not exist, to paraphrase the infamous comment made during the Cold War by a young Russian woman, Lyudmila Ivanova. In July 1986, on an episode of the perestroika-era TV show *U.S.-Soviet Space Bridge* co-hosted by Vladimir Pozner and Phil Donahue, Ivanova proudly answered an American's question about sex with "There is no sex in the USSR . . . there is love," but the last three words were cut off when it was broadcast.⁶¹

In Yakobson's *Rodin*, there is sex—and love. He navigates both emotional currents by displaying the muscular actions below the surface of Rodin's sculptures. As if documenting the physical exchanges that both precede and follow the moment of arrested action that the sculptures capture, Yakobson begins and ends each *Rodin* miniature with the dancers posing as if they themselves were Rodin's sculptural subjects. For example, in *The Kiss* their bare feet are held in a high relevé prance with their bodies angled in sculptural profile. The whole premise works because Rodin's still sculptures are far from static; they are replete with their own stories. As cultural historian Debora Silverman has argued about Rodin's art, this complex surface of his cast bronze and carved sculptures "capture[s] on the surface of the flesh the signs of the internal activity of the nervous system." Historicizing Rodin, Silverman finds correspondences between Rodin's visual representation of the surface of the sculpted bodies and the contemporaneous discoveries of medical anatomy: his "conception of the correspondence between internal pressure and external tension was informed by Charcot's neuropsychiatry."⁶² In *Rodin*, Yakobson demonstrates an intuitive faith in the capacity of his dancers' bodies to convey emotions through subtle muscular shifts even as they pose to approximate Rodin's sculptures—performing what Silverman would call signs of the internal activity of the nervous system.

Art historian David Getsy, in his recent scholarship on the artist Rodin, argues that Rodin "deployed sexual desire as a conduit for expressivity and for registration of the personal and the subjective just at the point when his mature career began."⁶³ Both art historians' comments point toward Yakobson's use of Rodin as a means of stealthily exploring issues embedded in sexuality. There is a clear evolutionary progression to the sequencing of Yakobson's *Rodin* miniatures, which begin with the sexual flirtation of *The Eternal Spring,* progress to the lingering sensual explora-tion of the tentativeness of a first kiss in *The Kiss,* and continue to the pain of unrequited adoration as love deepens in *The Eternal Idol.* Zvezdochkin compared this sequence with "the morning," "the noon of feeling," and "the night," respectively.[64] When Yakobson revisits the Rodin theme in 1971, thirteen years after his first cycle of 1958, he does so as a sixty-seven-year-old man. Now it is the sorrow of love he narrates though the whirl-wind of the second circle of hell battering *Paolo and Francesca,* to the wild emotions propelling the brutality of forcible possession in the desperate tussling of *Minotaur and Nymph.*[65]

A black and white film titled "Choreographic Miniatures," directed by Yakobson and Apollinariy Dudko, assisted by M. Sheynin, made by Len-film, and viewable on YouTube, contains one of the few filmed sequences of Alla Osipenko in Yakobson's choreography, the remarkable Kirov prin-cipal on whom Yakobson created *The Kiss* section of his *Rodin.* In the 1960 film she dances his dreamy duet *Meditation (Razmïshlenie)* with Anatoliy Nisnevich. Set to *Claire de lune* by Claude Debussy, a composer whose im-pressionist compositions were dismissed as "degenerate and sterile" by some Soviet critics, *The Kiss* opens with the couple arrested in the iconic pose of that kiss in Rodin's bronze sculpture.[66] Yakobson's choreography shares Debussy's penchant for seemingly improvisatory flow and easy spontaneity. Literally falling out of their embrace, the striking Osipenko, with her slender, long legs and strong arms, swoons backward, her body seeming to echo the rhythm of her pulse as she stands in a high relevé in her bare feet. She doesn't force her presence as she swiftly caresses Nis-nevich's face with fluttering hands and then dashes away. At one instant Nisnevich catches her as she allows her body to melt backward, the small of her back catching against his arm as her chest, neck, and arms continue to arc backward like a magnificent wave breaking over him.

The high relevé placement of the dancers' bare feet and the emphasis on two-dimensional anglings of their postures in *The Kiss* are reminiscent of the love duet between Spartacus and Phrygia in *Spartacus,* but are scaled here instead to a quiet and chaste intimacy. The entire *Kiss* is built on a series of embraces and receding separations, as if literalizing how one's wishes and fears keep trading places with each other in the moment of beginning a new love. Osipenko fits effortlessly into the torqued poses that display her slender beauty and easy technical mastery of his choreography, which unfolds as a cascade of motion. It is hard to hold onto any specific steps of *The Kiss* in one's memory; rather it is the sweep of feeling and the quality of a relationship being revealed through the smallest of gestures that one remembers.

The bodies of the two dancers in *The Kiss* unfurl and rewind in bursts of passion softened by tiny drams of calm. She's like a playful adolescent girl, stroking and then fleeing from her partner who gently pursues her for the wild intimacy of resting his face briefly in the curve of her neck. They are both restless and hungry, not so much to embrace as simply to touch. They run their hands lightly over the length of one another's body as if, to paraphrase Romeo Montague, not only hands can do what lips do, but eyes as well.

Viewed from a temporal distance of more than fifty years the sensuality here feels modest and the actual physical entanglement tame, but the quality of the dancers' pressing into uncharted emotions is evident. It is not the steps but rather the momentum of invention that makes the strongest impression in all the *Rodin* miniatures. In *The Eternal Idol,* danced on another film from the 1960s with the dancers Alla Shelest and Igor Chernïshov, the easy flirtation of *The Kiss* yields to the tension of an adoring man and a coolly reserved woman who deflects his advances as if dispassionately returning a missed serve on the tennis court. The dancers suggest so much personal history as *The Eternal Idol* begins that we are pulled into their drama immediately. Shelest, a delicate dancer of effortless classical technique and easy musicality, remains always slightly removed from Chernïshov as he lifts her and carries her backward atop his body, her torso pressed against the length of his as her arms reach past him even as their bodies rest together.

Natalya Bolshakova and Vadim Gulyaev were filmed by Evgeniya Popova in a film she made in 1971 called *Ballet in Miniatures (Balet v miniatyurah)* that shows them dancing *The Eternal Spring* on a sandy Saint Petersburg beach at sunset on a freezing day in October. Bolshakova emanates a frisky joy and warmth as she dashes away from Gulyaev, inviting him to chase and embrace her, again and again. Bolshakova, like Shelest, is delicate but high-spirited and has a beautiful classical line. In bare feet and dressed in abbreviated sheer tunics over their dancer's undergarments, they spiral into the sand, stretching out their legs before quickly springing up and reaching their arms upward and out in an open gesture of wonder and trust. Popova recalled that the weather was freezing and the dancers had to go into the icy water to wash off the sand when they had finished. Bolshakova ended up with pneumonia as a result—but none of that discomfort comes through in the film, so complete is their devotion to the choreography.

In late July 1972 a young Mikhail Baryshnikov arrived to work with Yakobson's company, having requested and received special permission from the Kirov Theater to work with both troupes at the same time. The only record remaining of that short collaboration is a brief color film of Baryshnikov and Elena Evteyeva performing *The Eternal Spring* in a lush outdoor garden filled with massive pillars and classical statues. The affect that Baryshnikov and Evteyeva bring to this miniature is closer to the acted stylization of a traditional pas de deux than the more experimental and less consciously acted style of Yakobson's mood of passionate abandon. Baryshnikov in particular acts with his face, conveying delight and joy while his body flickers through poses rather than sinking into the choreography. It is useful, however, as a marker of not only how quiet and intimate the artistry of *Rodin* was compared to the Russian classics, but also how necessary Yakobson's deep coaching was for drawing out successful performances from the dancers.

These first three *Rodin* studies were labeled pornography by party members, who mandated that not just tunics but Grecian sandals as well be added to the dancer's costumes, both to dispel any suggestion of nudity and to render the source clearly Greek and not decadent impressionism. In 1961, three years after Yakobson's *Rodin* triptych premiered at the Kirov, Yury Grigorovich premiered his version of a sanctioned Soviet love story at the Bolshoi, *Legend of Love* (*Legenda o lyubvi*)—a three-act, three-hour ballet on the theme of honoring duty over love and self-sacrifice over individuality. It was staged to music that Azerbaijani composer Arif Melikov had composed to Turkish writer Nâzim Hikmet's libretto, based on Hikmet's play *Ferkhad and Shirin*. The play itself was derived from the old Persian legend of Hosrov and Shirin and subsequently inspired at least eight other choreographers to make ballets on the same subject. But the ballet that proved particularly significant for the next generation of Russian choreographers in terms of expressing a new sensuality was Yakobson's *Rodin*.

Zvezdochkin, in writing about the influence of Yakobson's ballets from this late 1950s to early 1960s period, singles out *Rodin*. "The sensuality expressed by the characters of *Rodin* or the Harmodius and Aegina duet from *Spartacus* was labeled pornography," he noted. "But Yakobson was the champion of the love motif in dance. He expended huge effort to prevail over the hypocritical arrogance of ballet aficionados and to abolish the humiliating taboos prohibiting erotic themes in ballet. [Yakobson] did this by leading the way for modern choreographers to explore the complex and dramatic world of male/female relationships."[67] Before these works, Goleizovsky had used minimal costumes and eroticism in his *Salome* and *Faune*, both of which premiered in the early 1920s and influenced Balanchine's early work, like *Enigma*. While Yakobson did not speak of Goleizovsky as a direct influence on his work, the links are there, and so too for Balanchine's creations. Goleizovsky's *Salome,* for example, had the dancer costumed in a tulle leotard with a transparent bra, which Alexandra Danilova recalled as giving the impression she was completely naked—the effect Yakobson also wanted for his *Rodin* miniatures.[68]

Yakobson did not stop with these initial three essays on youthful love. Twelve years later, in 1971–1972, he returned with his own company to the portraits of love he had begun in his initial 1958 *Rodin* triptych. He added five miniatures based on Rodin sculptures: *Paolo and Francesca (Paolo i Francheska), Minotaur and Nymph (Minotavr i nimfa),* and *Ecstasy (Ekstaz),* staged to the music of Prokofiev; as well as *Despair (Otchayanie)* and *The Crumpled Lily (Izmyataya liliya),* staged to the music of Anton von Webern.[69] In the *Paolo and Francesca* and *Minotaur and Nymph* duets, the man's passion verges on desperation as he yearns for intimacy with his partner but is propelled away—by the winds of nature in one dance and the revulsion of the Nymph in the other. This is the aged Yakobson looking on love and bringing back to the stage, as a searing coda, the despair of where all that early joy leads. Alla Osipenko reminisced about how Yakobson had cast her and Dzhon Markovsky in this duet with an eye toward it being a commentary on the combative nature of their personal relationship. "As the Minotaur and the Nymph we had to dance this fierce struggle," Osipenko said. "I was protecting my private life but it was bad at home and worse at work. Yakobson seemed to know and that's why that Rodin miniature and all those dances I did [for him] acquired this additional quality," she said.[70]

Yakobson continued to make these miniatures—like domestic choreographic snapshots—as he shaped the final two sections of *Rodin*. Working swiftly he assembled a repertoire essentially from scratch for his new company. He attached the portraits of the grotesque from earlier in his career into the lushness of his most enduring reflections on the frightening side of Eros. Rodin had made his sculptures by taking movement and presenting it as stasis, and now Yakobson did the inverse. He conjured choreography out of the frozen bronze and marble stillness, inventing ballets that were compact emotional exposés that moved from pose to animation. In these later miniatures, including *Paolo and Francesca* and *Minotaur and Nymph,* the sophistication of Yakobson's treatment of the subject of erotic conflict and pain reflects a considerable evolution from the gentler images of ardor presented by his first three miniatures. His vocabulary is much more fluent and comfortable with invention, and the digressions from classicism are bolder in these two later works. Yakobson's choreography now flows much more freely than in the original three *Rodin* miniatures, as the sophisticated compositional groupings between the two dancers in *Paolo* and *Minotaur* keep disclosing nuances of their emotional lives. Lyudmila Putinova, who danced Francesca in *Paolo and Francesca* with Yakobson's company, recalled how he explained the rationale behind every movement and every posture: "'You are being driven by the wind: the wind draws you apart and propels you toward each other,'" she quotes him as saying. "This imaginary picture produced sensations which were then rendered visible in the form of positions and lifts. He demanded—and achieved—a precise execution of his choreographic vision, which in this miniature was centered around the theme of flight."[71]

The choreography in both *Paolo* and *Minotaur* could easily pass for modern dance as it radiates an anxious energy through movements that barely resemble classical ballet. *Paolo and Francesca,* the two adulterers from Dante's Inferno condemned to be thrown against the rocks by stormy seas for their sins, keep hurtling into and past each other as they futilely try to grasp hands and anchor themselves to one another. It's a Dantean vision of eternal exile, with lovers joined yet hopelessly adrift. A recording in Irina's possession of a reconstruction of *Paolo and Francesca* made in 1998, when several of Yakobson's miniatures were reconstructed for a short-lived new Maly Kirov Company, reveals this miniature as a tiny digest of the moods of desperation. Alban Berg's thumping percussive score is the perfect companion for the choreography's emotional frenzy as cruelty and eroticism blend in the lovers' suffering. At last, costumed in the flesh-colored unitards that Yakobson originally intended, this Paolo and Francesca feel contemporary, as if they were cousins of the anxious souls who inhabit Anna Sokolow's modern dance masterpiece *Rooms* (1955).

The *Minotaur and Nymph* miniature churns through the violence of an impending rape, shown in the spectacular struggle between the hunkered-down man-bull figure of the Minotaur and the slight and desperate Nymph. Yakobson captures the emotional energy of this erotic subject by showing us their desperate conflict through tightly coordinated partnering that looks like combat and passion at the same time. The Nymph is trapped in a shrinking cycle of escape and capture like a mouse being toyed with by a cat. The Minotaur wraps her around his waist as if she were a belt and later yanks her onto his shoulders as she reaches im-

Yakobson and dancers Vera Solovyova and Nikolay Levitsky rehearsing
Minotaur and Nymph (1971) from *Rodin*. Photographer unknown.

ploringly into space, growing more exhausted with each encounter. Yakobson's choreography discloses the eroticism of this predatory cruelty.

With the 1974 premiere of the full series of *Rodin* miniatures performed by his company, Yakobson began the practice of opening and closing the entire suite of eight studies as a momentarily frozen tableau with the opening pose of each one caught in a separate pool of light on the stage. This technique makes the arc from innocence to abuse all the more dramatic in Yakobson's playbook on Eros, these *Rodin* miniatures. These postures in Rodin's sculptures hold secrets about the sexes, he is saying, and dance has the key to unlock them. According to colleagues, Yakobson was always a connoisseur of beautiful and sexy women onstage as well as in his private life, and they report that in his later years he had an ongoing relationship with a dancer in the Kirov.

"The *Rodin* miniatures demonstrate that the miniatures did not exist in isolation," Yakobson's widow said of their significance. "They showed that a group of miniatures could express human emotion through the stages of its development and also in their most sensitive nuances. They revealed the various moments of love, beginning with the original, most naïve emotion up to the brutality of total devotion."[72] *Despair* and *The Crumpled Lily,* the final two *Rodin* miniatures, are both solos, mini portraits of

Rodin (1971), the lighted tableau that opens and closes the *Rodin* suite, Choreographic Miniatures, Leningrad. Photographer unknown.

the private emotional toll of a shattered love affair. These *Rodin* pieces were among Yakobson's favorite miniatures. He once spoke of loving them and having the music ready to choreograph another seven so that he would eventually have a complete suite of fifteen.[73] But he never completed those final seven.

AS WITH MUCH of Yakobson's choreography, it is impossible to separate the dance from its cultural achievement. His sensual miniatures like *Rodin* had their genesis in the period of the Thaw. Even though they were caught in the conservative retreat of Brezhnev's stagnation that followed, the absolute repression of the Stalinist period was in the past—the Thaw had let the erotic genie out of the bottle.

By all accounts of those who were there, Yakobson helped bring down the prohibitions on eroticism and sexuality on the ballet stage with *Rodin*. He used the erotic force of stillness as an important element in his arsenal. By beginning his dances with a frozen tableau, he slowed time, heightening the eroticism and rendering the dance more aesthetically captivating, sensual, and exposed. The whole idea of opening with stillness was novel for Soviet ballet because it took a step away from the puritanical realism that art was supposed to present. Yakobson's choreography revealed dance as an invention, but one that made reality more vivid. Performance theorist André Lepecki has written about this symbolic quality of stillness as a way of what he calls "undoing the fantasy of the dancing subject" and allowing us to see the role of dance as primal impulse.[74] Yakobson's use of stillness offered his audiences a tacit reminder that sex, too, is a primal impulse—a fact that all the Soviet policing of this ballet's content could not erase.

EIGHT

Totalitarianism, Uncertainty, and Ballet

> It is often said that Yakobson destroyed tradition, in that he rejected classical
> ballet on principle. However, this is entirely untrue. . . . Yakobson had a
> perfect and profound knowledge of the classical dance and all its rules,
> and this knowledge gave him the tools and the right to experiment.
> —Tatyana Kvasova, interview with Vladimir Golubin, 1990

AS HE WORKED to shatter the traditional configuration and narrative of
the pas de deux in *Rodin* (1958–1962), creating an aperture to the sexual
tension within, Yakobson was simultaneously crafting his most bracing
investigations of the form's classical structure. Pas de deux studies spilled
out of him—*Rossini, Mozart, Donizetti, Lehár,* each is a stylistic tribute in a
different musical vernacular and a witty prod as to the type of emotional
games a courtly ordering of sexual behavior can play. Having dissected

the stories the pas de deux tells, he turned next to anatomizing its structures. Although it was impossible for Yakobson to use improvisation directly, his approach to choreography increasingly began with testing what
the dancers' bodies could do that was beyond the known movements and
gestures in ballet.

In his *Mozart Pas de Deux,* made in 1970–1971, Yakobson stripped back
the pas de deux to the bare frame of an entrée for a man and woman, an
adagio, solo variations, and a coda. He discarded the predictability and
balanced symmetry that customarily unfold within this structure containing a couple dance, and replaced it with the very *un*-Soviet aesthetic
of uncertainty and chance. *Mozart Pas de Deux* is not an improvisation,
but it does record the traces of how it was created—in a rush of free-form
questioning—a series of "what-if" encounters among Yakobson, the Mozart score, and his dancers' physical abilities. This marks it as the record of
an incursion into free experimentation. At one point the male dancer
partners the woman from a semi-reclining position on the ground, and he
later assists her in a turn by guiding her from her elbow. Every phrase in
this brief work is unique. There is not a standard ballet step at any point
where a dancer could simply cruise along—each moment is a surprise.

It is danced to the first few sections of Mozart's *Twelve Variations in C
Major,* or "Ah, vous dirai-je, Maman," also known as "Twinkle, Twinkle,
Little Star": the lilt to the music begins with deceptive simplicity, then its
tempo accelerates to a breathlessly fast speed as the notes and steps cluster
more densely. A 1960 film recording of this work as part of a Lenfilm
broadcast about Yakobson's miniatures captures Tatyana Kvasova and
Igor Kuzmin in a sparkling performance of the adagio and coda. Entering
with a courtly air, she is in a tutu resembling an abbreviated baroque ball
gown and he in a black velvet courtier's jacket over white tights; their feet
perform little skipping steps that offer a rhythmic intertext with Mozart's
score. At times they slide quick little flourishes of the feet into the movement phrases so that their actions seem like visual music that is as logical
a part of the score as the actual notes. Soon the woman is being spun in
rapid supported turns on pointe, which she executes with deliberately soft
bent legs while angling her head, arms, torso, and hands in gentle side-to-
side twists that add a flair of baroque ornamentation. He lifts and carries
her, momentarily wrapping her across his back without breaking the momentum of their partnering. The more difficult it becomes—she rotates

in finger turns from a squat so deep she seems nearly to be sitting on the floor—the more confident and relaxed are both dancers' smiles. From her squat she keeps her feet fully stretched on pointe and walks forward flicking her toes as he steers her by her upraised arms as if he were driving a miniature horse and cart. Now she tosses herself to him and he catches her, allowing her to recline against his arm. They seem to be dancing inside the music, so tight is their coordination with its rhythms, yet so inventive their movements, which look as if they might be almost classical in nature but instead swerve away to the modern at the last instant.

Virtually everything that Kvasova and Kuzmin do in the *Mozart Pas de Deux* is fresh and surprising. For example, instead of a vertical supported turn where she would ordinarily stand straight and tall, they complete a full turn, he slowly revolving her as she tilts to the side and bends her standing leg just slightly. Their conclusion is all subtlety and nuance as she scampers up his leg, onto his back, and off—then ends with the offer of her toe-shoe-clad foot, which he kisses as if it were a gloved hand. Finally, posing with a flourish that suggests they might be settling at last into a fish dive (poisson pose), they suddenly change, ending with a quirky virtuoso finish: Kvasova walks up and over Kuzmin's extended leg, pausing as he grasps her with her legs extended in a split jump as if he had simply grabbed her out of the air in mid-leap. Their ease suggests that the unexpected gives them endless pleasure. In dispensing with the traditional big-drum-roll notification that they are about to perform a special feat, Kvasova and Kuzmin showcase the felicity of the continually unexpected. Louis Pasteur's dictum "Chance favors only the prepared mind" was always on display in Yakobson's working process as he invested enormous amounts of time immersing himself in the music, as well as researching and drafting a libretto, long before he arrived in the studio. This intensive preparation freed him to improvise his way into the choreography.

Beginning in 1970, with the securing of his own company, Yakobson's ballets extol the freedom of the dance studio as a sacred space. He was fashioning art by inviting the unexpected, an act that carried with it an implicit critique of rigid structures—such as a totalitarian political system that denied even the existence of uncertainty. (By contrast, chance as an artistic and political strategy was strongly associated with the West and Westerners' belief in individual agency and democratic freedom.) Yakob-

Mozart Pas de Deux (1971), Tatyana Kvasova and Igor Kuzmin, Choreographic Miniatures, Leningrad. Photo: Vladimir Zenzinov.

son's use of chance as a compositional device reflected his embrace of artistic freedom and a non-totalitarian view of the future from within the privacy of his studio. While his finished ballets never left anything to chance in performance, his method of building dance was filled with discovery. Valentina Klimova recalled the atmosphere in the initial rehearsals of Yakobson's company and the way in which freedom, contained by strict behavioral discipline, infused his choreographic inventions:

The entire troupe took part in the staging of a ballet. For example, when he staged a *pas-de-deux*, several pairs of dancers would be trying out a sequence of movements at the same time in the middle of the room. If one of them managed to execute a lift successfully, Yakobson—who may not have even known at the outset what that movement would look like, but now liked what he saw—immediately adopted it. We prompted his decisions through our movements and our plastic rendering [of the music].

Before every rehearsal I always felt very nervous. Yakobson created choreography extremely quickly, and in discrete small fragments. He would listen to an extremely short musical passage and immediately, while the sound still resounded in our ears, show us the movement. In order to grasp, memorize and perform it, one had to maintain absolute concentration. One had to attune oneself to the pace of his fantasy, which was as swift as lightning—if we failed to register a movement there and then Yakobson, who was constitutionally unable to visualize the same pas twice, changed it in some way. This is why he always pleaded with us: "Faster, faster—all of you, please, memorize; I won't be able to repeat this for you, but [what you just saw] was right: this is how it should be done." [The movements,] born spontaneously and instantaneously in his imagination, vanished as rapidly—and this was the only weakness of his improvisation method. His choreography was impossible to get used to—it was always full of surprises. Neither could one tell how he would begin or end a piece.[1]

For the subjects of this system, the process of working with Yakobson was by all accounts wrenching. Lyudmila Seryozhnikova shared Klimova's sense of the anxiety in the room as she recalled how the *Mozart Pas de Deux* was being created and how physically and emotionally frightening this venture into uncertainty felt:

The unusual choreography of *Mozart Pas de Deux* demands special skills and agility. The entire piece is danced on pointes, but with the legs slightly bent, so the arch is not stretched to the maximum—an unusual position that calls for a major adjustment on the part of the dancer. There are also movements on the pointes executed in *grand plié*, practically squatting down. These required a lot of practice at rehearsals, and afterwards my muscles were so sore that I couldn't go up or down the stairs. . . .

I had a very hard time [preparing] the Mozart number. I cried a lot and questioned my decision to join the troupe in the first place.

Yakobson, for his part, acted as if he had forgotten about the time: he did not ask any questions and did not rush me in any way. Once, late at night, when we were the only ones left in the entire building, having stayed there to rehearse the [*Mozart Pas de Deux*], he suddenly appeared and announced: "Show me what you've done so far. Use the tape recorder." My heart jumped into my mouth. We had not had a chance to dance the whole number, but had only practiced separate fragments to the piano accompaniment, taking breaks in between. . . . [In this pas de deux] the dancer doesn't have a moment's respite . . . which makes it extremely difficult to breathe. When we finished dancing, I was suffocating and thought that I was dying: I had turned blue in the face and my lips were livid—I must have looked like a corpse. My partner Norik Megrabyan, formerly a dancer with the Erevan Opera and Ballet Theater, did not look much better either. Yakobson, however, was satisfied: "Well, keep working—in a week's time you'll go on stage."

I have no recollection of my first performance of the Mozart number: I must have been delirious. At the end of the performance, I was so exhausted and emotionally depleted that I did not have enough energy left to drag myself off the stage. After that, every time I performed the Mozart pas de deux I vomited because of all the strain and asphyxiation. The only thing that saved my partner and me was that, in the finale, all the lights went out.[2]

Yakobson had a particular interest in duets—both on the stage and off—and the implicit chance of connection, rapport, or conflict that bringing a man and a woman together entails. Indeed, in his studio the dancers recount how he enjoyed playing matchmaker, first in rehearsal and then in the life outside the studio, setting up a male and a female dancer he thought would be a good couple by casting them in one of his virtuoso pas de deux to get things going. Former Yakobson dance Aleksandr Stepin recalled how "Yakobson was always interested in interactions among the members of his troupe, [and especially] romances and intrigues. Nothing escaped him. From [emotionally charged situations] he drew energy, which was particularly important when he was under the weather. If he felt the need to perk up, he would select some meek individual and start picking on her, often driving his victim to tears—whereupon, with a sat-isfied air, he would rub his hands and announce: 'Well, let us proceed.' However, we, the dancers, could hold our own against him very well and often parodied him at our evening gatherings." All of the dancers in Yakob-son's company speak about him with great affection, even while re-counting stories of his seemingly gratuitous cruelty in the rehearsal studio. They are quick to report that this was counterbalanced by his gen-erosity and solicitousness after hours. "In private life, Yakobson was ex-tremely affable and invariably generous," Stepin noted, pointing out that "for March 8 [International Women's Day] he always contributed a sub-stantial sum for presents for the girls."[3]

The actual movements of Yakobson's choreography gave off an aura of invention. A film fragment in Irina's possession of his *Rossini Pas de Trois*, one of the pieces in the cycle *Classicism—Romanticism* (a cycle that in-cluded *Medieval Dances with Kisses, Bellini Pas de Quatre, Cachucha, Mozart Pas de Deux,* and *Taglioni's Flight*) and choreographed in this flood of new dances made in 1970–1971, documents ballet so daring that forty years later it would still be a significant challenge for dancers. *Rossini* opens qui-etly with the ballerina in a short white skirt with a wide black belt accent-ing her waist. Slowly she turns in an off-balance pose, one leg extended high overhead as her partner pivots her from a stance that is also deliber-ately off-center and unstable. As the music and the dancing accelerate, she walks up his leg and rolls across his back, accenting her descent with a swift flutter kick of her legs. The man's variation is also accented with crisp movement flourishes, all happening so quickly that nothing is high-lighted as a big dance "event." The challenges multiply as the dancers tuck in more surprises—a whipping turn for the man that ends with a tricky landing on one foot rather than two, a zipping series of piqué turns for the woman that send her in one direction while she snaps her head and fo-cuses the other way. Often the dancer's body suggests a counterpoint of forces within a single individual as the arms and torso move with an ease while the feet and legs race through a thicket of steps, each one delivered with pithy neatness.

A contemporary American ballet dancer with training in Balanchine's style who viewed a tape of some of his classical miniatures marveled at the physical sensation of difference that just viewing Yakobson's *Rossini Pas de Trois* evoked in her. "I realized how many choreographers working today under the banner of contemporary ballet, or under the influence of Balanchine since his passing, are going in the direction of making movements bigger (higher legs, more pirouettes, more suggestive hips, more off-balance, more daring partner work) and perhaps faster," she said. "Yakobson's work looked to me to have innovated from the inside: more detail, more complexity, more influences and ideas per step, and altogether denser with difficulty. Also, it looks more successfully faster. Watching it felt a little like reading text in single-spaced, ten-point font: a lot can be communicated, and it doesn't blur on the page."[4]

Yakobson's embrace of changeability (and this ten-point-font clarity) extended to the range of styles in which he choreographed, from the lyricism of romanticism to the formality of classicism and the edgy pulse of the modern. While he was reimagining classicism through the pas de deux, he looked back toward its predecessor, romanticism, and created two small masterworks. Finding new freedoms in his own company, he was revisiting ballet history as he reached for the sublime. *Taglioni's Flight* (*Polyot Taloni*) is a sly miniature tribute to the illusionistic flight of the great romantic ballerina Marie Taglioni. A sextet for a ballerina, her partner, and four unseen attendants in all black, *Taglioni's Flight* allows the ballerina to continually dance in a floating state of ease as unseen men rush her about the stage, her billowing tulle skirt and upraised chest and arms in her white romantic tutu suggesting the bow of a ship cutting through the froth of a dark sea. "The soaring kept going and going and hypnotized the audience with the effect of the ballerina's weightlessness," V. A. Zvezdochkin wrote of the performance.[5] An old video recording in Irina's collection with Alla Osipenko and Dzhon Markovsky dancing this work shows Osipenko's regal calm. With her upper body held in a windblown curve as the tips of her feet curve backward peeking out from beneath her tulle skirt, she is transported around the stage with the profile of a woman who does seem to be airborne. We see the illusion and its making at the same time but strangely this enhances rather than detracts from the pleasure of the vision. Yakobson seems to be paying tribute on multiple levels to historic ballerinas in *Taglioni's Flight*. A more ghostly presence than Taglioni is that of Anna Pavlova, a muted memory in the USSR because of her departure from the Mariinsky to dance with Diaghilev and her subsequent decision to remain in the West from 1912 onward. One of the few historic dance film fragments that exists of Pavlova curiously depicts the

Taglioni's Flight (1971), rehearsal, Vera Solovyova
(Taglioni). Photographer unknown.

ballerina in a Duncan-like Greek tunic, striking improbably long poses in a setup far clumsier than Yakobson's, while an unseen partner in black supports her by awkwardly anchoring her leg to the ground as she balances in arabesque. She too is ferried around the dark stage by unseen male dancers in black.[6]

Valentina Klimova, who danced in *Taglioni's Flight* after the original dancer on whom Yakobson made the ballet, Alla Osipenko, left, noted how Osipenko's soft legs and strong arms are still evident in the ballet's emphasis on port de bras that are like forceful wingstrokes. Klimova recalled the rehearsal process as one in which Yakobson continually tested the impossible.

> Yakobson relayed [the text of the ballet] and then started explaining how I was to be handled. "You," he said, pointing at one of my partners, "grab her leg, but let go of it as soon as she completes a *rond,* and the next one will take over." In this way he proceeded

to instruct each of the male dancers in turn. While he was thus giving orders, my partners held me aloft attempting to adjust their grasp so that their hands wouldn't feel like manacles. Yakobson devised all these lifts, during which I was passed from one pair of hands to another, so ingenuously that, when I danced this number later on, I felt as if I were walking on clouds. . . . During the rehearsals, however, we had to repeat them so many times that the skin on my hands and legs became all chafed. So I told the coaches: "I've no skin left," and showed them the places on my upper arms that my partners had had to grasp especially firmly, since following Yakobson's instructions they had to lift, carry, and put me down in slow motion. The coaches were appalled: "Oh dear, you must show this to Leonid Veniaminovich!" I was in tears: "How could I?" Then they took the initiative: "Look, L. V., all the skin has come off." He immediately conceded to a compromise: "Well, today we will take it easy, we'll be careful." However, as soon as he immersed himself in work all the promises were forgotten, and we practiced all the lifts as usual.[7]

Yakobson's capacity for working in several different stylistic strains at once was legendary among the dancers in his company. While creating two of his most contemporary ballets, *The Ebony Concerto* (*Negrityanskiy Kontsert*) and *Distraught Dictator* (*Obezumevshiy diktator*), he created *Taglioni's Flight* as well as his other exalted tribute to romanticism, *Pas de Quatre*.[8] Set to the cantilena musical line from Vincenzo Bellini's lyric opera *Norma,* Yakobson's *Pas de Quatre* strips away all the laboring romantic ballerina poses and thinly masked ambition of Anton Dolin's conjectural reconstruction of Jules Perrot's lost 1845 original. Instead Yakobson captures an air of sweet sisterhood among the four romantic ballerinas (Lucile Grahn, Carlotta Grisi, Fanny Cerrito, and Marie Taglioni). Discarding Cesare Pugni's light score from the original, Yakobson instead uses the melodious score for the "Casta diva" aria from *Norma,* lending a flowing bel canto beauty to the four dancers' evocation of ballet romanticism as Elysian bliss.

The effect is dreamlike as the four women rise from the opening pose of the ballet, taken directly from the lithograph documenting Perrot's ballet, and softly complete the circle of that pose by joining hands. Streaming first to one corner of the stage and then another, they move their bodies with the fluency of a single body. Heads rotate in soft unison and all four dancers sweep forward, arms gently linked as a dancer in front stretches her leg forward and the one behind extends her leg back to suggest a single attenuated leaping form. Dancing with a freedom and ease that belie the difficulty of executing everything while anchored to three other people, the ballerinas in Yakobson's *Pas de Quatre* fold into and under one another's arms, never breaking the handhold and never ceasing their restless motion of upward, out, and away. Even the handholds are consciously designed with an easy grip that allows the women to slide through the movements without losing contact. The effect is that of an airborne flock of sylphs, their layered white romantic tutus pressing together as they tuck themselves under and through one another's clasped hands, stretching to lead and then dropping back to follow. Like so much of Yakobson's choreography, it is a witty and wise commentary on its subject, in this instance the women of romantic ballet. The use of Bellini's score is a brilliant stroke since it too dates from 1831, just at the very beginning of the romantic era in ballet, so the same seamless, floating line one hears in the opera has a visual counterpart in the choreography. It is also possible that Yakobson intended a sly aside here as well, since Cesare Pugni, composer of the original *Pas de Quatre,* wanted to compose for opera.

After a brief opening greeting where the *Pas de Quatre* ballerinas greet the audience, the choreography launches into lush dancing as the circle of ballerinas, moving like a living wreath, wind and unwind as they navigate the stage in a fluid and constantly shifting unit. When they finally separate to dance their variations, they are similarly succinct. Each ballerina dances a deft miniature study of floating steps and sparkling footwork, adorned with softly folded arms, flicking hand gestures, or a gently curving neck that define her character. The performance ends with the dancers settling back into the original pose, their bodies still emanating the pulse of their journey through the quick tempi of Bellini's score. The choreography in Yakobson's *Pas de Quatre* references romanticism in flavor but it is imbued with contemporary emotion and personality suited to each role. The ballet has Yakobson's signature musicality; animated by natural-looking invention, it reintroduces us to these romantic ballerinas as a quartet of terrific dancers, not just ossified nineteenth-century divas.

Pas de Quatre (1971), Choreographic Miniatures, Leningrad.
Photographer unknown.

In the initial months of building his new company's repertoire, Yakob-son worked in three studios simultaneously, switching not just steps but entire genres of dance from one room to the next. It was a strategy with a particular political resonance during the Cold War years in the USSR, for his improvisatory quickness and capacity for fluid invention was seen as a decidedly Western and bourgeois aesthetic. It also had a curious, mer-curial stylistic variability that suggested a rootlessness in regard to his choreographic style. Yakobson's aesthetic home was deliberately not clas-sicism nor neo-classicism nor modernism, but a fluid circulation through these styles. That early lesson of finding one's place in the midst of mate-rial homelessness—which he had learned by necessity as a child of the Petrograd Children's Colony—had stayed with him his entire life.

These ballets premiered as part of the opening performances of the Choreographic Miniatures company on June 7, 1971, which were received as a revelation. Natalie Zundelevich was a student working as an English translator for a visiting American chemist that summer when through his hotel the chemist secured three precious tickets to these opening performances. Zundelevich recounted that as soon as Yakobson's name appeared on Leningrad billboards in the summer of 1971 it caused

an immediate sensation. "Since its performances took place in the inti-
mately small building of the Maly Opera and Ballet Theatre, tickets were
scarce, not nearly enough to accommodate hordes of ballet buffs storming it every night. Scalpers got wild and a police patrol was installed to
protect peace and order," she said.[9] Zundelevich got lucky when the
American brought her along to the performance. She was unprepared for
what she saw; decades later she still recalled the sexual tension that hov-
ered over the concert that evening, which included her awe at seeing an
early version of what would become *Sextet* (*Sekstet*, 1974) danced to an excerpt from Mozart's Piano Concerto No. 21. Like the plot of Shakespeare's
A Midsummer Night's Dream, but without the happy resolution, *Sextet*
turned missed connections into a ballet geometry of isolation where three
pairs of men and three women each seek the one they cannot have while
dancing half-heartedly with the one who wants them. For the young Zundelevich this was a metaphysical revelation through choreography—and
the complex philosophical meanings that these three couples presented
jolted her as "a futile attempt to unite . . . Plato's kindred halves, a longing
of the human soul for fulfillment."[10]

Her recollection was that *Rodin* was the next work and she recounted
that as the lights dimmed for *Rodin*, the entire audience gasped. "In the
moments before it began, I sensed the audience getting electrically charged,"
she said. "To everybody's stunned eyes appeared a tableau of famous Rodin marble . . . I remember the shudder sent down my spine at the sight of
a man and a woman yielding with such abandon to their passion. I became acutely aware of the presence of the two men at my sides—it felt as
if at that moment all three of us, educated civilized human beings, were
swept by the same primordial call. . . . The first thought that crossed my
mind when it became active again," the dazzled Zundelevich said, "was
How? How on earth could he have gotten away with that? Whoever in
those ideology committees that have to sanction every theater program
could have sanctioned that?"[11]

Yakobson had carefully shaped the debut program of the Choreographic Miniatures company as a succinct essay in ballet history—beginning
with a section on classicism-romanticism that included seven miniatures
choreographed in these two styles (*Rossini Pas de Trois, Medieval Dance
with Kisses, Cachucha, Bellini Pas de Quatre, Taglioni's Flight, Mozart Pas de*

Deux, and *The Swan*); then a section of the five Rodin miniatures; next a set of five Russian miniatures, consisting of the genre scenes *Troika, Russian Souvenir,* and *The Village Don Juan;* followed by his miniatures on fairy-tale themes, *Dead Tsarevna, Firebird, Snow Maiden,* and *Baba Yaga;* and concluding with *The Genre Triptych,* comprising *The Ebony Concerto, Wedding Cortège* (or *Jewish Wedding*), and *Vagabond Circus.* Here was the arc of ballet history, ending with Yakobson's iconoclastic individual voice. Immodest perhaps, but revelatory of the scale of his vision for ballet in the USSR. It was a not-so-subtle reminder that history would judge his efforts independently from the fallowness of the current situation in Soviet ballet.

In a 1971 interview with a pair of young journalists from *Yunost* (Youth), a literary magazine for the young, Yakobson called contemporary Soviet choreography sick—saying it was suffering from "ailing thematics." He said the fault resided with classical ballet, whose possibilities were limited to the realm of the fairy tale and to romantic subjects. "But if we speak about contemporary actuality, about the thoughts and passions of a man or woman today, about the complexity and contradictions of his or her inner world, or of any kind of social issue, then the language of classical dance, with its ossified canon, its conventions, its abstractness, is simply a contradiction in terms," he said laying out what was essentially his credo for change. "The theatre is not a museum," he continued. "There are masterpieces such as *The Sleeping Beauty,* for example, or *Giselle* that hardly can be surpassed. But do you not agree, that in the language of *Giselle* one cannot find the solution to contemporary ballet?" he concluded rhetorically.[12]

What is noteworthy in the work of Yakobson in the context of Soviet ballet is that his point of departure into dance invention was the danse d'école. In the West, innovative choreographers searching during this same period for a new means to express the complexities of the inner world that Yakobson mentions invented their new physical vocabularies by working out the movements themselves, with their own bodies. In contrast, by the time he got his company Yakobson was working against the clock—of age, health, and the still-present official roadblocks to his efforts to get his ballets before the public. So the cries about his harshness in the rehearsal room were the echoes of his frustration at having to do this process by proxy on often ambivalent bodies.

Hours before Yakobson's company was scheduled to give that opening performance in June 1971, with programs all printed, lights set, timings rehearsed, costumes made, and tickets sold, Soviet officials stopped by for one last check. Grabbing the already printed programs for the debut concert, they instructed the ushers to draw a large "X" through *Wedding Cortège*. With that it was removed from the program, joining *The Ebony Concerto,* which had been forbidden a few weeks earlier. That Yakobson's individual dances were censored was nothing new, but to have an entire company subjected to such an eleventh-hour decision was brutal. "We thought they might cancel everything and we would all be out of a job," Tatyana Kvasova confided years later about the dancers' fears as they learned backstage of the last-minute censoring of *Wedding Cortège*.[13] Yakobson's robust ego would sustain him, but the dancers were new to this kind of capricious silencing. "You should not be modest because modesty gets in the way of reaching a goal," Yakobson once revealed of his own outlook. "I became convinced of that by experience. Second, modesty is a great value only when there are no other features to talk about. And third, modesty does not always help achieve the best in what you are trying to do."[14] Yakobson saw modesty as a hindrance to success in a climate of aggressive censorship. His pride in his own immodesty reveals the degree to which he had to continually rewrite the rules of behavior in order for his work to continue.

Within three months of the premiere of Choreographic Miniatures, Yakobson again found his activities monitored with increasing intensity. There were requests for innumerable viewings of the repertoire by various khudsovet commissions, and each time he wanted to stage a new work he had to battle for permission to do so. In autumn 1971, there was a closed-door viewing for a high-ranking commission from Moscow, comprised of twelve members and headed by Vasiliy Kukharsky, second in command to Minister of Culture Yekaterina Furtseva. It included Zaven Vardanyan, the head of administration of music institutions within the USSR's Ministry of Culture; Yury Grigorovich, representing the Bolshoi; a representative of the Stanislavski and Nemirovich-Danchenko Moscow Academic Music Theater; and Sofia Golovkina, director of the Moscow Academic Choreographic Institute. Irina, who was present, recalled about that afternoon:

> The viewing took place in the Maly Opera Theater in the middle of the day, to ensure that the hall was empty of people. Nevertheless,

the word had spread and all kinds of people had forced their way inside—employees of drama theaters, musicians, and artists. At the end of the performance, all the spectators gave Yakobson an ovation. They wouldn't let him go off the stage, and the commission had to wait for "all these unseemly disturbances" to end. Then Yakobson, alone, was ushered into a black Volga and taken to the party committee headquarters. There he was subjected to a barrage of accusations: his collective lacks the Soviet [spirit]; his art is bourgeois; his works are devoid of even a vestige of socialist realism; his art is abominable, harmful, etc.

All this enraged Yakobson to such a degree that he began to snap back. To Golovkina's confession that during the Rodin suite she was so embarrassed that she had to shut her eyes, Yakobson retorted: "And now shut your mouth. If you didn't see anything, how can you judge?" Then Vardanyan said, "I can't understand: was it a Soviet or a capitalist performance? If you divest the performers of their costumes and consider only the dancing, you wouldn't know they are Soviet artists." To this L. V. replied, "Well, why don't you consider your paunch. If you took off your coat, you would also look like a bourgeois rather than a Soviet citizen."

In short, Yakobson behaved disgracefully. However, he found an unexpected champion in the person of a certain Vasilyev, who, as it later turned out, represented the Lenin Prize committee. "I can only repeat the words of Chatsky [the protagonist of the 1825 play *Woe from Wit* by Aleksandr Griboyedov]," he said. "'Forgive me, but I'm in the dark: I can hear [the words being spoken] but their meaning escapes me.' What I saw this afternoon is by far the best of what is worthy of a Lenin Prize." The atmosphere became tense. The head of the commission, Kukharsky, pretending not to have heard Vasilyev's remark, stated that the troupe should be dismantled. This, however, kindled patriotic feelings in the secretary of the Leningrad district Party Committee, who politely put the Muscovite [Kukharsky] in his place: "We deeply respect our visitors and are honored by the attention shown to our troupe. However, this troupe was established through our initiative and we will decide when to shut it down. I suggest that we wait for the next program. We must understand that the author [sic] is very nervous and forgive his not-altogether-appropriate conduct; naturally, he will take your criticism into account and include some Soviet items into his next program." On his part, Kukharsky passed a death sentence on the troupe, albeit through another strategy: "All right," he said, "let the troupe exist until the next program, but it must on no account leave Leningrad."

Kukharsky's verdict essentially meant that the troupe would have to stage fifteen performances each month. By the end of the year, all Leningrad residents would have seen every one of them, and the troupe would be completely deprived of income. This, in turn, entailed that there would be no venues for performances, and the troupe would be compelled to close down. The upshot of all this was that, from now on, in addition to fighting for the right to stage performances [Yakobson] would have to fight for the permission to tour as well.[15]

Yakobson understood that with Choreographic Miniatures effectively under city arrest, forbidden to tour outside the limits of Leningrad, the company had been given a slow death sentence. Like the Lilac Fairy in *Sleeping Beauty* who softens the evil fairy Carabosse's curse of death into a hundred years' sleep for the little princess Aurora, the secretary of the Leningrad district party committee had muted the demand for the immediate closure of the company into a restriction of performing only within the city. Yakobson followed up this decree by boldly insisting on a meeting with the minister of culture herself, Yekaterina Furtseva. Securing an appointment, he went to Moscow to plead with her to see the company for herself to decide if the embargo could be lifted. She refused.

Although there is no record of Yakobson ever commenting on Furtseva's animus toward him as being fueled by anti-Semitism, it was acknowledged in the USSR that she was active in a number of anti-Jewish activities, which included making secret lists of Jews to be deported, actively influencing the planned deportation of Soviet Jews to Spitsbergen Island in the Norwegian archipelago, and decreasing the quota of Jewish students allowed into universities in the USSR. Reports are that in 1969 she was also behind a "secret order" to "oust Jews and the Jewish idiom from Soviet music."[16]

While Yakobson was master of the new world he was building inside the rehearsal halls, Communist Party officials intensified their restrictions against him in the world outside that safe haven. The toll on him was emotional but increasingly also physical as he fought capricious restrictions designed to bring his new company to its knees financially so that it would be forced to disband. A series of personal letters he wrote to his wife in July 1972, while she was recouping from overwork at a spa in the Ukrainian city of Lvov and he was in Leningrad working with the company, attest to the psychological strain of the intimidation tactics that the officials were using on him. "At our premiere of *The City* and *The Symphony of Eternity* [*Simfoniya bessmertiya*, 1972] not a single Party boss appeared," he wrote. "And there has been no interest in the birth of the great Soviet heroic epics and the overthrow of the Capitalist way of life in Masereel's *The City*," Yakobson continued, referring sarcastically to the disinterest of high party officials in even viewing the works whose themes should have pleased them but which their subordinates wanted banned.

The little dance company that the Soviets had allowed to begin was making waves with both the daring of its repertoire and its strong popularity with audiences. Yakobson wrote Irina enthusiastically about Choreographic Miniatures' big audiences, warm receptions, increasingly strong ticket sales for future programs, revenue coming in, and invitations to perform in the city's prestigious White Nights Festival. But there are hints of approaching trouble around the edges of this pleasing picture. Until this point Yakobson had not risked crossing the line into political protest. His was the generation that had survived the worst of Stalin's purges and he knew the dangers of engaging with the Soviet system. Now, however, he chose to risk speaking out for the survival of his company. In the final months of 1972 Yakobson wrote a letter "to The General Secretary of the Central Committee of The Communist Party: Comrade L. I. Brezhnev." He begins, "Dear Leonid Ilyich, Extraordinary circumstances compel me to address you," then in the unprecedented act of writing a letter to the supreme leader of the Soviet Union he explains not only his achievements as a choreographer but also the feverish efforts to oppose him and silence the work of his company, which he calls "genuinely Soviet art."

Clearly a campaign is under way to artificially compromise us: our antagonists accuse us of an unspecified modernism, Westernism, and eroticism, all of which are the evil fabrications of those hostile to our enterprise. We are creating a genuinely Soviet art. The accusations against us, now in their second year, are pure slander. I should like to bring to your attention two persons, in particular, who it seems to me have been especially active in agitating against us: they are T. A. Petrova, deputy director of the culture section of the City Committee of the Communist Party (Leningrad); and V. F. Kukharsky, deputy minister of culture of the USSR (Moscow). . . . I have head that your intervention saved the Taganka Theater and that is a plus for Soviet art. Leonid Ilyich, please help us as well! I assure you, and stand behind my work, that in the very near future, we shall be the glory of Soviet art! I beseech you to normalize the conditions surrounding us.[17]

Yakobson never received a reply to this letter to Brezhnev, perhaps his supposition that it might get "lost" was prophetic and reflected the impossibility of being heard by those in power when they chose not to listen. Although Yakobson names Petrova and Kukharsky as being particularly aggressive in agitating against the company, the real force behind the prohibitions and the absolute target of his ire is Yekaterina Furtseva, the minister of culture herself. Furtseva, a former worker in a textile factory, became the first woman admitted into the Politburo of the Central Committee of the Communist Party of the Soviet Union in 1957. Soon after, she was secretly recorded by the KGB in a telephone call to a friend denouncing Khrushchev's policies. She was removed from the Politburo in part as a result of that revelation and on May 4, 1960, was appointed to the honorable, but powerless, position of the fourth Soviet minister of culture.[18] For the next fourteen years, remembered with painful irony as the "Age of Furtseva," she exerted an immense, and destructive, influence on Soviet culture.[19] Prominent actors and directors tried to secure her friendship to further their own careers, but with Yakobson she had a decidedly antagonistic relationship, censoring his work and company repeatedly yet refusing his entreaties to ever view his work for herself. Yakobson, however, was not shy about visiting her, despite how time-consuming it was to schedule an appointment and travel to Moscow for a brief audience. On three separate occasions Yakobson made appointments with her in Moscow, and in person renewed his plea for her to view his company herself and then decide if the prohibitions imposed on it were justified. Furtseva refused. She committed suicide on October 25, 1974, never having seen Yakobson's work. Irina recounted that in April 1973 Yakobson had the following exchange with Furtseva in an attempt to have the touring embargo lifted:

> He used the expression "my art," provoking the following exchange:
> [L. V.]—I want the entire Soviet Union to be exposed to my art.
> [F]—There is no such thing as your art. Everything we have is our Soviet art.
> [L. V.]—Well then, why not see for yourself? Maybe this Soviet art will be to your liking.[20]

Furtseva, however, was reluctant to take on the responsibility for assessing the troupe's performance and once again sent an emissary. Fortunately this time she chose Igor Moiseyev, himself a brilliant choreographer who at the time was in Leningrad with his ensemble. After viewing a performance by the Choreographic Miniatures at the October Hall, Moiseyev approached Yakobson and said, "Lyonya, you are a genius." Later he repeated these words to Furtseva as well, and finally Yakobson's company was allowed to travel to Moscow. With Moiseyev's pronouncement of his approval of Yakobson's work formally recorded, the travel restrictions on the company were finally, and permanently, lifted.

AS HAS BEEN suggested, by encouraging the unexpected while constructing his dances, Yakobson was rehearsing a deeper sense of freedom. Certainly Yakobson was always emboldened as an artist, but his persistence at radical invention in the face of the increased scrutiny and the prohibitions that his having his own company generated seemed to have invigorated him to greater openness rather than more caution. While Yakobson set with minute precision every action down to the gestures of the fingers that his dancers were supposed to do, it was his process of discovering that movement through a freeform outpouring of ideas that was deeply radical and free. He did not recombine steps from the existing vocabulary of ballet; he churned out new ones. The practice of accelerated, imaginative negotiation within the physical constraints of what the body can do is ideal training for finding one's way quickly in a field of open possibility.

Yakobson helped to make resistance to rules a legible aesthetic and then a social practice. Not since the imposition of the socialist realist agenda in the 1930s had anyone experimented with the ballet vocabulary as irreverently and succeeded in such a sustained way in bringing that work before the public as did Yakobson. No one had pushed back against the decrees of Furtseva and her office with such determination and eventually prevailed. Perhaps boldest of all, no Soviet choreographer had advanced so deeply, and steadily, into modernism, experimenting with self-referentiality; formalism; and a questioning of the conditions of modern life, including urbanization.

In late 1972 Yakobson took one of the defining characteristics of modernism, an emphasis on personality and individuality over broad categories of morality and community, and stepped across the threshold into creating what were essentially the first major abstract ballets of the later Soviet period—*Contrasts (Kontrastï)*, set to music by Igor Stravinsky, and *Exercise XX (Ekzersis-XX)*, set to the Swingle Singers' jazz vocalizations of J. S. Bach's *The Well-Tempered Clavier*. In *Exercise XX* there is no discernable narrative, character, or message; just a group of dancers in leotards and tights on stage performing a sequence of actions drawn from the ordering of the ballet dancer's daily catechism of pliés, beats, and fast footwork. These are actions whose meaning is located in the language of dance itself. Perhaps to help ease the ballet past the censors, the props of several ballet barres and the descriptive title *Exercise XX* were added, suggesting a ballet class. The music is as risky as the lack of discernable narrative—forbidden jazz, here riding in on the soothing harmonics of the eight voices of the Paris-based Swingle Singers who take Bach and make him swing to their syncopated a cappella rhythms. The content, however, is pure and plotless movement invention. Formalism.

As if revealing to his audience how he tweaks classicism into modernism, Yakobson begins by gently splicing in little tilts off-center in the pliés that the first group of three dancers performs at the barre. Soon percussive bounces flicker through the rond de jambe à terre foot warm-ups that a quartet of women perform. Then feet are glimpsed flexing in the grand battement leg swings, and toes rotate inward as the dancers close their feet into the hyper-crossed inverted fifth position of Yakobson's invention—his "sixth position" to augment the traditional five. (Although Yakobson and his dancers credit him with this invention, Goleizovsky had used the same toes to heels position of the feet, calling it the sixth position, decades earlier.)[21]

In a careful analysis of Yakobson's work and aesthetic, written by Lopukhov in the 1970s but never published because of what he deemed the risks, Lopukhov offers a context for understanding *Exercise XX*'s radicalisms of inward-rotated foot positions. Next to his own schematic drawing of the five cardinal turned-out foot positions he has drawn Yakobson's five additional foot positions, each one with the legs torqued so that toes are pointing inward in an inversion of Pierre Beauchamps's original seventeenth-century codification. "I believe I did enough to prepare the readers for understanding *Exercise XX* choreographed by Yakobson," Lopukhov writes:

> I will proceed to its analysis now, but before I begin I suggest we take a look at the sketches of the five old positions, which are based on the turn-out of the toes, and the five new positions—on the basis of the turn-in of the toes and the turn-out of the heels. It goes without saying, my sketches are somewhat comical—a draughtsman will do that better. But what is clear from them is turning of the toes to the side and turning them inwards. These inward rotating positions do not mean that placing movements upon them is obligatory. What's at issue here is the development of new ligaments and muscles, which are needed to prevent dancers from injuries that occur with random movements during the inward motion.[22]

Lopukhov's explanation that the body's musculature simply needs to be retrained to accommodate these injurious-looking new positions did not match well the experience of the dancers performing them. Osipenko, who was thirty-nine when she left her position as a principal dancer at the Kirov to join Yakobson's company, confided that she delegated those ligament-twisting positions to the younger dancers. "I said, 'I am saving my knees.' But the younger girls—Klimova and Kvasova—they would do it right away," she recalled.[23]

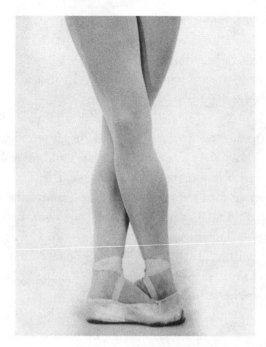

Exercise XX (1971), sixth position, Tatyana
Kvasova, Choreographic Miniatures,
Leningrad. Photo: Vladimir Zenzinov.

A scene from *Exercise XX* (1971), Yakobson's twisting
of the classical ballet vocabulary, Choreographic
Miniatures, Leningrad. Photographer unknown.

In a memorial tribute to Yakobson in 2004 on what would have been his hundredth birthday, dozens of his former dancers and associates gathered together to visit his grave and to acknowledge him with a special tribute drawn from *Exercise XX*, but that omitted this sixth position.[24] An unedited video of the tribute given to Irina shows the former Yakobson dancers traveling to the cemetery and then back into a studio where, still dressed in their street clothing, they rehearse the final polonaise from *Exercise* in preparation for a farewell coda to the evening's remembrance ceremony. The men do their best to support the women in the final series of whipping pirouettes and the women do their best to turn. Aged bodies struggle to keep up with the mind's demands, which itself is an apt tribute to the kind of art Yakobson made. "I remember as we performed the polonaise on the Mariinsky stage the audience all rose to their feet and began applauding," said Kvasova, who performed in this tribute. "And we, the dancers, just stood there crying."[25]

Only portions of a few of the ballets Yakobson made with Choreographic Miniatures were ever filmed.[26] He asked Lenfilm if they wanted to make a film about him receiving the Golden Nymph Award in 1961 and another about his company—but he died six months later, before the project could begin. The film had only progressed to the point where the libretto was drafted.

Irina recalled how adamant the Ministry of Culture authorities were about not releasing *Exercise XX*, on the grounds that it was a parody of classical ballet. "They did not understand that it not only had unusual choreographic humor but was it was a sign of ballet of the future. Today in the West everyone dances this way—with the feet turned in and the legs tied in a knot," Irina said. "Yakobson, however, who was completely cut off from contemporary Western choreography, had invented all this independently. He kept saying that it is necessary to introduce innovation into our traditional ballet class, so that it would open possibilities for the dancers. The legs should be able to move in any imaginable way: not only in the customary fifth position but in reverse as well [the toes pointing inward]," she said. "He was very proud of this sixth position." The local committees, however, did not like *Exercise XX*. Irina recalled, "The situation was saved by Fyodor Vasilyevich Lopukhov, who fervently defended Yakobson. . . . The fact that this ballet was allowed onto the stage was entirely Lopukhov's doing."[27] The competing stylistic insertions in *Exercise*

XX, however, are pure Yakobson. He both quotes classicism and departs from it. "It seems to me that choreographers who take up the contemporary theme are taking a wrong tack. They prefer the classical dance. I, of course, give the classical legacy its due. It is the basis, the school, the foundation on which one can erect diverse choreographic structures. But all the same, its possibilities are limited. The realm of the classical ballet is one of the fairy tale, of romantic subjects. These are the elements of the ballet classic—its natural milieu. But if we speak about contemporary actuality, about the thoughts and passions of a man or woman today, about the complexity and contrarieties of his or her inner world, or of any kind of social issue, then the language of the classical dance with its ossified canon, its conventions, its abstractness simply is a contradiction in terms."[28]

The subject in *Exercise XX* is movement itself. Yakobson did have one remarkable after-the-fact model for successfully navigating ballet choreography without narrative—George Balanchine. Balanchine made his second and final visit to the USSR with his New York City Ballet in the autumn of 1972. Yakobson had made his *Contrasts* and *Exercise XX* the previous year, in 1971, and he and his full company of fifty dancers attended the New York City Ballet concerts in Leningrad at the Lensovet Theater. All the Balanchine works that the New York City Ballet brought to Leningrad from September 27 to October 1, 1972, on their second trip to the USSR—*Serenade, Stravinsky Violin Concerto, Who Cares?, Jewels, Tchaikovsky Suite No. 3,* and *Symphony in C,* as well as Jerome Robbins's *The Goldberg Variations* and *Scherzo Fantastique*—present dance as an independent, unadorned language that draws its inspiration from its musical score.

Viewing these ballets by Balanchine must have been in equal measure validating, inspiring, and frustrating for Yakobson. There is no record of what Yakobson thought about this repertoire, but both Yakobson and his dancers carried themselves with an air of friendly competitive pride. The members of Choreographic Miniatures proudly attended the New York City Ballet performances as a group. Like the home team sizing up the visitors, they watched Balanchine's company as an American analogue to their own independent ballet troupe shaped under one choreographer's vision. Yakobson, for his part, also wore his satisfaction with his achievement publicly. Nina Alovert recalled how during intermission, after Jerome Robbins's *Scherzo Fantastique* had been performed to Stravinsky's *Scherzo Fantastique,* op. 3, Yakobson, whose *Traveling Circus* used selections from Stravinsky's *Suite No. 2 for Small Orchestra,* was seen sauntering down the aisles of the Lensovet Theater, gesturing and declaiming loudly, "Mine is better." "He had a big ego and was convinced he was a genius. No compromise," she said. "Without doubt he was a genius."[29]

Traveling Circus, made in 1971, was the third of six ballets that Yakobson created to a Stravinsky score.[30] Using music by Stravinsky was in itself still comparatively daring even though increased tolerance of the composer and greater availability of his music had begun after his October 1962 trip to the USSR.[31] Around this time, too, Yakobson may well have experienced a certain defensiveness about the work of the choreographer Robbins, who worked with Balanchine's company in the United States. The musicologist Peter Schmelz, in writing about the influence of Western avant-garde artists on those locked in the Soviet Union, notes how powerful a sliver of exposure could be in the following statement by Estonian composer Arvo Pärt about John Cage's long-distance influence on him:

> It's very possible that I was influenced by Cage, but it didn't come from his music, but from things that were, perhaps, completely unknown to me. I may have heard a word, or seen a face or a picture, or something by someone connected with Cage. When people are hungry they are sensitive to every hint of food. It's the same with ideas, particularly at that time in the Soviet Union. The hunger for information was so great that at times it was enough to hear just one or two chords and a whole new world was opened up.[32]

Yakobson rarely spoke about the influence of other contemporary choreographers on his work, but this second opportunity to view Balanchine's work, and much more of it than the company had brought on the 1962 tour, must have been a particularly poignant reference point now that he had his own company and was in the midst of a battle to get his works before the public. Yakobson, like Balanchine, shaped each ballet as a marvel of choreographic ingenuity, where the inspiration seems to flow from within propelled by a blend of innocence and inevitability. *Contrasts,* completed soon after *Exercise XX* in 1971, takes these lessons of the academy indexed in *Exercise XX* and shows us their potential while focusing on the architectural properties of dancing bodies. Yakobson reconsiders classicism as Balanchine does. The only two old film documents from the 1970s of both these Yakobson ballets are compelling examples of how steadily Yakobson was redefining the movement of bodies, letting his dancers pass through positions and appear alternately spontaneous and then tightly linear as they negotiated their collaboration with the music.

Yakobson in the USSR, somewhat as Balanchine had done much more freely in America, was moving toward the rich narratives that are inherent in simply watching a body move. Russian dance scholar Galina Dobrovolskaya said appreciatively of these final ballets by Yakobson that they were "compositions the subject matter of which could only be guessed." This way of describing Yakobson's plotless dances as compositions whose subject matter was strangely absent suggests just how novel abstraction in ballet appeared. "In the 1970s Yakobson again found himself in the forefront of Soviet ballet," Dobrovolskaya writes, noting that this time he was "anticipating its subsequent interest in the abstract presentation of humankind's spiritual and moral aspects."[33]

The pride of independence that Yakobson and his dancers experienced through their association with Choreographic Miniatures seems to have blossomed into a different sense of themselves as individuals in the world. "I got a theater of my own too late. But I will prove to them that it is still possible to succeed," Yakobson had proclaimed at the founding of his company, suggesting the air of urgency that fueled his race to build his repertoire and get it out to the public. "It was unbelievable," a government employee and former major supporter of Yakobson and his work said of Yakobson's feat of actually starting his own ballet company. He spoke on conditions of anonymity because of fears for his present job security if this earlier activist support of Yakobson in the 1970s were to be widely known. He said of Yakobson's achievement, "It was like going to the moon, to have organized an independent dance theater and to demonstrate his kind of creativity."[34]

Soon Soviet officials found themselves responding to outside requests for the company and Yakobson to tour and work abroad. As mentioned earlier, Sol Hurok visited the USSR in the initial months after the Choreographic Miniatures debut in search of performances to take back to the United States. Hurok was reportedly delighted by the company, remarking to the dancers backstage after the showing that he was going to bring them to the United States to prove that, contrary to everyone's assumptions that there was nothing new in Soviet ballet, here was a repertory of all new ballets.

The West was also hungry for another image of Russian ballet, and engaging Yakobson and his group would have been a way to support budding opposition to Soviet cultural authority. He was not registering artistic dissent; rather he was following his fate as a choreographer in the field of ballet modernism that had effectively been frozen by totalitarian opposition. But again, Hurok's proposed tour of Choreographic Miniatures never happened.

Yakobson Abroad

The year 1975 began propitiously for Yakobson. His projects for his company were thriving, film projects at Lenfilm and Mosfilm were being discussed, and invitations from abroad were finally making their way through the government filters. The most international of these projects was a new opera to premiere at La Scala in Milan, composed by Luigi Nono and staged by Yuri Petrovich Lyubimov, the respected Soviet director and founder of the Taganka Theater in Moscow. Lyubimov forwarded a request from Enrico Berlinguer, general secretary of the Italian Communist Party, that Yakobson be the choreographer. The project was to be modernist in style and bound up in layers of political agendas and messages, but for Yakobson it was the opportunity to work with Lyubimov and in a setting outside of the grasp of Soviet oversight that seems to have been most appealing to him.

Nono was a member of the Italian Communist Party, having joined in 1952. Italy's Communist Party was the most active in Europe and Nono was an enthusiastic member, going to demonstrations and talking with workers as he looked for ways to incorporate Communist ideology in his art. He had tailored his compositions to be inclusive of what was referred to as the "new listener," the workers. Nono was striving for ways to make connections between new society and new sounds. To this end he had written scores like *The Enlightened Factory* (*La fabbrica illuminata*) in 1960, a composition that included factory noises and the yells between workers as part of its soundscape. His score for the Lyubimov-Yakobson collaboration, *Under the Hot Sun of Love* (*Al gran sole carico d'amore*), had been composed in the same politicized spirit, in this instance celebrating "the sirens of the revolution," specifically Rosa Luxemburg and contemporary female workers and revolutionaries.[35] Filled with dissonance, it was a revolutionary opera on a sonic and ideological level, and its presence in what Lyubimov once referred to as the "citadel of holy rules about opera," La Scala Opera House in Milan, guaranteed its reception would be complicated. Compounding this was the fact that Nono had gathered about him a trio of independent-minded Soviet artists—Lyubimov, Yakobson, and the scenic designer David Borovskiy from Lyubimov's Taganka Theater in Moscow. The conductor would be the rising young Italian musician Claudio Abbado. In the mid-1970s Radiotelevisione Italiana, the Italian public-service broadcaster that operates several television stations, broadcast a performance of the production that Nono himself adapted and edited. This survives as the only documentation of the original production.

The impetus for this assembling of talent was political. After the Soviets had invaded Hungry in 1956 and then Czechoslovakia in 1968, there was the threat of a dissolution within the Eastern Bloc. The Central Committee turned to the Cold War formula of cultural diplomacy as a way to restore relationships.[36] "It was a very strange thing for us," Lyubimov said of the project, "because it started with negotiations between the chairman of the Communist Party of Italy and Leonid Brezhnev. They asked Brezhnev to allow me to come and Brezhnev said 'we will send you a good one [director], not a bad one.'" This lasted for one year, with the Italians insisting on Lyubimov and finally in 1972, with a glacial pace of change, they gave Nono a visa and he arrived in Moscow with a file filled with music sheets the size of a table to begin discussing the project with Lyubimov.[37] Nono had been to the USSR once before, in 1962 or 1963, when had he met with young Soviet composers and shared Western influences with them. They, like Yakobson, eventually found Nono's enthusiasm for Communism naive and disillusioning.[38]

Lyubimov said that in an unprecedented arrangement, the director of La Scala, Paolo Grassi, an entrenched leftist, was pushing for Nono's opera to be produced and Moscow was communicating with Grassi himself. When the contract for Lyubimov to direct *Under the Hot Sun of Love* was finally negotiated, in a dramatic first he signed it directly with La Scala rather than using the minister of culture as his proxy. In the summer of 1974 La Scala presented a season in Moscow and conversations about the Nono opera continued to move forward. Once Lyubimov was solidly confirmed as the director, he made clear that Leonid Yakobson needed to be approved to do the choreography. "But Yakobson was a choreographer whom the Soviets did not want to send abroad," Lyubimov said.[39]

He explained that once it had been decided that the stagings for the ballet would be in a modernist plastique form, Lyubimov honored the request of Enrico Berlinguer, the leader of the Italian Communist Party, to hire Yakobson to do the choreographic staging. At that time there was only a draft of a finished libretto and part of the opera with a multitude of diagrams that had to do with using new electronic technology in this music. Nono was an experimenter and one of the first to synthesize live and electronic sound. Part of the orchestra used live electronic sound that would transform the voices of the singers in any combination; the soundscape was very unusual. Having relayed the Italian's request, Lyubimov, who had never directed an opera before and was anxious about the outcome, refused to participate unless Yakobson was permitted to go. The back and forth with the Soviet authorities dragged on for weeks, with their adamantly refusing to let Yakobson participate. Then suddenly, late one evening, Lyubimov's telephone at home rang. The voice on the other end was curt and abrupt. There was no salutation: "Okay, take the Jew and go!" hissed Yekaterina Furtseva. The minister of culture had conceded.[40]

Once rehearsals began in Milan in January 1975, Yakobson quickly settled into a schedule of rehearsing with the dancers of La Scala Theater for two and a half hours in the morning and two hours in the evening. From the start he disliked Nono's experimental score. "I do not know what I have staged and to what," he lamented in a letter to Irina in Leningrad from Milan on January 26, 1975. "Because there is no music (there is, but it would be better if there were not . . .). The score simply extends a noise and that is all. It has neither meter nor rhythm nor figurativeness. I like it in and of itself, but it absolutely is not choreographic, and to be sure, was not written for dance. But I'll stage it since I have to stage something. Luigi Nono and Lyubimov sense my judgment of this music. . . . I am rehearsing La Scala ballet! Thirty dancers, six males, a typical corps de ballet. I'll try very hard."[41]

Without the scaffold of metric and danceable music, Yakobson turned toward images to generate his choreography. Nono's score employed complex and layered sonic sources ranging from electronic tape to a large orchestra, a large and a small choir, and several vocal soloists who declaimed lines from famous political tracts to create the soundscape of revolution for the opera. The performers sang texts drawn from the political, philosophical, and poetic writings of Arthur Rimbaud, Bertolt Brecht, Maxim Gorky, Karl Marx, Vladimir Lenin, Fidel Castro, and Che Guevara, among others. The opera was structured as a series of pivotal enactments in the history of class struggle, beginning with the Paris Commune of 1871 and extending across the Russian revolutions of 1905 and 1917 to contemporary conflicts in Vietnam and Latin America. Nono and Lyubimov also contributed to the libretto, which featured women revolutionaries as the protagonists of historic liberation movements. At one point, Lyubimov assembled the 120-person chorus and had them walk deliberately toward the orchestra pit in a line while singing lines from the *Communist Manifesto,* set to music. Judging by the Italian television's broadcast recording of the opera, Lyubimov's staging was so spectacularly dramatic it verged on the choreographic itself. For much of the first act of the two-act opera, the stage is filled with the theatrical image of the defenders of the Paris Commune who hover high above the audience attached to massive moving walls. This image suggests people defending the ramparts when they are vertical and bodies in a morgue when they tip horizontally—the arc of the brief, violent life of the commune fighters. The first act also contains the two longest dance sequences by Yakobson. The first is a large group section for the corps, who begin by advancing toward the audience shaking their upraised fists and pounding their feet on the stage. The movement looks deliberately shaped but each dancer behaves like a wild individual as they disperse and reassemble like a restless mob in the streets.

Their attire is dancers' rehearsal clothing—leotards and tights with knitted leg warmers, baggy shirts, sweaters knotted about their waists, and a few old sweatpants complete an image of the dancers as workers in the labor of ballet. These costumes, together with the dancers' naturalistic movements, suggest that Yakobson was reaching for movement that would be as anti-lyrical as he found Nono's music, yet like Nono's opera the choreography also shows the tradition against which it was rebelling. Toward the end of the act, in the second main dance interlude, a ballerina wearing a practice tutu is partnered by four men in all black who transport her around the stage in echoes of *Taglioni's Flight,* while the opera chorus thunders behind them. The ballerina dances with an air of extreme irony, flexing her feet as her partners lift her, knotting her legs as she pivots under their arms and snapping off supported turns from a slight squatting position with a flexed foot angularity suggesting her insouciance toward ballet's history and the French monarchy. Compared to Nono's avant-garde music radicalisms, Yakobson's choreography for the opera is much less extreme, but measured against what kind of movements and costumes would have been possible in the USSR, its lively irreverence for the traditions of ballet is a reminder that this is the only work in his lifetime Yakobson would ever make for dancers outside of the USSR and beyond the reach of its censors.

Yakobson took his inspiration for this choreography from the magnificent Renaissance sculptures he was enjoying as a tourist in Italy on his time off. He used the images from these antiquities to shape his stage picture for Nono's opera, as he had used antique bas-relief as inspiration for *Spartacus*. There was beauty in the use of these forms as the genesis for the opera's choreography, but no Communist politics. "The Italians expected something ultra modern and very new," Lyubimov said, explaining the dancers' initial reactions of incredulity. "The Italians started to speak up, 'Why do we need these pictures on the stage since we have seen them since we were very little?' "[42] Yakobson was curt, telling the Italians that they didn't understand anything.

Early in the rehearsal process the La Scala dancers also went on strike to protest the demands of Yakobson's choreography and work process. They demanded additional money, explaining that they had to work harder to learn his nonclassical movements. The strike lasted three days, during which time Yakobson, after being assured that they were not protesting working with him, only the challenge of his choreography, enjoyed touring the Italian region outside of Milan. His letters to Irina are filled with euphoric descriptions of the landscape, colors, and the surprising beauty of ordinary objects and their display. He takes pleasure in the aesthetic arrangement of objects for consumption—and compares it to the visual and emotional grayness of life in the Soviet Union and the effect of that drab existence on one's inner life. "I went down to Como, the famous lake and Italian resort, where the whole world gathers. It's 40 kilometers long. What views, what mountains, architecture, snowy Alps!!!" he wrote.[43] "Here, in general, there's a miracle at every footstep. Each store is like a fairytale. The wealth is boundless, the taste enormous, the variety astonishing—a real aesthetic," he wrote Irina. "Each store literally is like that. For example, next to us are tiny cheese stores. In their 4 steps by 4 steps space they sell 270 varieties of cheese. And the packaging! And the cleanliness! And the service, the politeness, the attention given to each customer cannot be described. We live in a hotel that is also beyond description. It consists not of rooms but of apartments."[44] This aura of childlike delight with which Yakobson greeted Italian commercialism, however, did not extend to his working environment at La Scala.

One day early in the rehearsal process, Yakobson approached Nono and told him he needed more music for the dancing in the opera he wanted to stage. Lyubimov was aghast. "In this particular situation I took the composer's side," he recalled. "How can you say to a composer go write me some more music. I need several more steps here?" he asked rhetorically. Nono was enraged. "*Who* is this?," Nono reportedly asked Lyubimov. "I spent a year composing and this crazy man wants another piece of the ballet? I have to break up the complex harmony just to give someone a chance for one more turn?"[45] Yakobson, who in this instance seems to have regarded the composer as a less independent artist than himself, was told that nothing would be added and that he would have to come up with choreography exactly for the duration of the music and not a second more. He complied, finishing the choreography in late January, going home, and then returning several weeks later to Milan for the premiere.

The various creative conflicts did not affect the show. The April 4, 1975, premiere at the La Scala, conducted by Claudio Abbado, which included thirty dance numbers by Yakobson, was a popular success. The names for the dance sequences echoed the revolutionary theme of the opera—such as *Freedom* and *The Paris Insurrection,* but Yakobson's choreographic inspiration remained based on visual artifacts from antiquity. "At the premiere I saw Yakobson the way I had never seen him before," Lyubimov said, remembering how watching that curtain call he discovered how much Yakobson enjoyed taking bows before an audience. "He did it beautifully," Lyubimov said, explaining how Yakobson would walk directly toward the audience smiling as he warmly acknowledged the applause. Reflecting back on the project thirty-eight years later, Lyubimov confided that he did not think Yakobson's contribution to the project was very interesting or inspirational.[46] Yakobson's ballet numbers paralleled the vocal parts of the opera, and this arrangement appealed greatly to both the audience and the critics. The premiere went without a hitch. Usually at La Scala a show runs six times, but Nono's opera had eighteen performances. It is not surprising, therefore, that Yakobson returned to Leningrad elated.

Upon his return to Leningrad, Yakobson also had a final round of conflicts with the Soviet authorities. It was understood that Soviet artists touring abroad were required to always bring 70 percent of whatever they had been paid and turn it over to Goskontsert, the state presenting organization, since according to the government the private artist had no right to these funds him- or herself. But when Yakobson returned from Milan he brought back no Italian money because he had spent it all. "Of course when he came back Goskontsert started asking for the money the Italians had given him," Yakobson's widow said. "He said, 'What do you mean? I staged it. I spent it. It was my money.' "[47] Yakobson had continuing troubles with the government over this simple act of private ownership, which the Soviet officials interpreted as defiance.

Irina recalled how the officials insisted that Yakobson should have known that the money was not all his to spend. " 'I don't know anything,' he replied. 'The Italians gave it to me and so I spent it.' " The minister of culture's office insisted that he repay them the 70 percent of the foreign fees. After his death they pursued Irina as well, but she told them honestly she did not have the money and that it had, after all, been given to Yakobson.[48] She suggested, sardonically, they send her abroad as the only way for her to earn the money to repay them. Eventually they gave up. Yakobson had this quality that was in equal parts remarkable and frustrating— the capacity to behave both like a child and as a fully independent man. His artistic and intellectual emancipation with the arrival of his company had empowered him to rebel. Selected to stage the Nono choreography as an exemplar of the Communist aesthetic, he had instead created a fresh, modern work based on his reading of Italian culture through antiquity. The Communist politics were far more dear to Nono than to Yakobson. Nono may have lived and worked in a totalitarian state, but his mind and art were free. Consequently he may not have appreciated the paradoxical state he enjoyed—that of being an enthusiastic and voluntary member of the Communist Party as well as an avant-garde composer who worked in an experimental Western-influenced style that would have been impossible in the USSR.

The other high-profile international project that Yakobson participated in during this period was *The Blue Bird,* the first film jointly produced by Soviet and American artists. Directed by the distinguished American director George Cukor, the film was shot at Lenfilm in Leningrad and featured Ava Gardner, Jane Fonda, and Elizabeth Taylor. The film was based on a play with the same title by the Belgian symbolist writer Maurice Maeterlinck, and it is about a young brother and sister who seek happiness, personified as a blue bird. A parable about death and the meaning of life, Maeterlinck's play enjoyed great popularity in Russia, where it had inspired a staging by Konstantin Stanislavski in 1908.

After Yakobson signed with Cukor to be the choreographer for the film, Irina remembers long delays, then, when the filming finally started, the work was rushed because there was little time remaining in the shooting schedule. Cukor had invited Yakobson to stage the dances prior to the start of the Nono project in Italy, but the delays in filming meant that Yakobson had to leave for Milan before the filming ever began. Instead Igor Belsky, a leading Kirov dancer, choreographer, and protégé of Lopukhov, was invited after Yakobson left to take over much of the choreography. Another dancer who studied at the Leningrad Choreographic Institute and was on the faculty there, Sergey Savkov, also helped stage some portions, which Irina rehearsed with members of Yakobson's company who had remained to work with her for the months that Yakobson was in Italy. Prior to leaving for Italy, Yakobson had begun choreographing the various dance sequences in *The Blue Bird,* offering a Russian ballet counterpart to Cukor's cast of American stars by casting the Bolshoi stars Maya Plisetskaya and Alexander Godunov in a pas de deux between Water (Plisetskaya) and Fire (Godunov). People who saw this duet described it as richly inventive and personalized to each dancer's particular qualities. Plisetskaya's variation focused on her famous hands and arms as she moved like water, trying to douse Godunov's bounding and agitated fire.

Yakobson tried to monitor the project from afar, writing to Irina in a letter from Milan in February 1975, "Ironka! Please give my greetings to Cukor, Jane Fonda, Elizabeth Taylor and please tell the director to postpone the shooting of Nadya Pavlova in *The Bird,* and of Plisetskaya with

Godunov in the hut." But once Yakobson departed for Italy to work on the Nono opera, Igor Belsky took over and this variation disappeared; Plisetskaya and Godunov also fell away from the project.[49] One of the remaining dance sequences that did make it into the final film shows Taylor as a fairy godmother figure who animates Fire (Yevgeniy Shcherbakov), Water (Valentina Shcherbakova), Milk (Margarita Terekhova), and Sugar (Georgiy Vitsin), who each enact a brief variation of food coming to life to the delight of the two children. The movement bears no trace of Yakobson's invention other than a vestigial reference to Plisetskaya's rippling arm movements in the variation for Water, and Irina does not even consider the dance as an example of his work. What is significant about *The Blue Bird* film in regard to Yakobson is how once he had achieved his own company his international reputation as a choreographer blossomed. *The Blue Bird* opened in 1976 to mixed reviews, the disorder surrounding its filming shadowing the finished film.

Endings

From the moment he finally received his own company, Yakobson choreographed with the urgency of someone on a desperate deadline. Part of this was certainly the enormous amount of pent-up energy he had to create ballets for his own dancers without the continual roadblocks of censorship. But there was also the quality of a finite horizon shadowing his work. Throughout his time in Italy, Yakobson wrote to Irina frequently, and along with describing the splendor of the Italian scenery and merchandise, his letters also mentioned various regimens of eating only certain fruits and vegetables, or drinking certain juices, in an effort to address some persistent but unspecified ailment. "My husband was endowed with an immense intuitive power," Irina said in regard to his continuing health concerns the last few years of his life. "He sensed that something was wrong and every year went for a stomach X-ray," she continued. "He looked healthy, but something perturbed him. Everyone was deceived by his energy and believed that getting an X-ray on a regular basis was merely another of his whims. The physician who examined the X-rays invariably wrote in his report that everything was within the normal range. Before he left for Italy, he again went for a comprehensive set of tests, but nothing unusual was found."[50]

By the time Yakobson returned from Milan for the last time, in mid-April 1975, after the premiere of *Under the Hot Sun of Love,* Irina could see that something was seriously wrong. Yakobson had lost a great deal of weight and he was pale and moving without his customary energetic briskness. He made the round of doctors, as he had been doing for years, to have tests and check-ups, and again they reassured him that he was fine after taking more abdominal X-rays, which they pronounced normal. This time, however, Yakobson's doctor suggested that the Yakobsons use their connections to find a more qualified X-ray specialist, just in case one in the clinic might have missed something. The wife of Yakobson's brother worked as a roentgenologist (radiologist) in the regional clinic, but since the X-rays had never shown any abnormality, it had never occurred to the Yakobsons to ask her to view them. Now the Yakobsons went to see her. She was shocked. She explained to Irina privately that the X-rays showed advanced stomach cancer, which had metastasized throughout Yakobson's body. She recommended that they show their years of past X-rays to Ryurik Aleksandrovich Melnikov, a famous oncologist, for a second opinion.[51]

Professor Melnikov received the Yakobsons in his home. He had just returned from a symposium in the United States and so he and Yakobson began by comparing their impressions of Italy and America. According to Irina, Yakobson—a skilled impersonator of the most subtle gestures and voices—demonstrated how Italians interact and how their gestures were different from Jews' gesticulations when they talked. Then Irina's sister, Anna, spoke confidentially with the doctor while Irina and Yakobson were in the next room and asked his candid assessment of the X-rays. On one of the X-rays, taken five years earlier, the year Yakobson had begun working so feverishly with his company, a tumor the size of a hazelnut was visible. At that stage, it could have been easily removed and his chances for survival would have been good. Now it was a different story. Yakobson, who had been a two-pack-a-day smoker for years (until quitting when he was given his company), was indeed beyond the point of remedy or treatment. "The professor said that, based on the latest X-rays, L. V. should have already been dead, that he should have neither energy nor muscle tissue left, and that he shouldn't be able to do anything but lie on the bed with his eyes closed," Irina recounted. "It can happen any time: an hour or a week from now," he told her sister who later told Irina. To Yakobson he said reassuringly, "There is nothing wrong with you. There is no need to see me again. You are simply tired and need rest."[52]

Yakobson did go on holiday to Komarovo, an artists' resort on the Gulf of Finland. He returned weaker than when he left, but he continued to work. Soon even walking the few blocks between their family apartment at 11 Vosstaniya Street to the studios at 15 Mayakovsky Street exhausted him, but he would tell Irina to walk faster as they approached the studios so that his dancers would not think he was sick (he did not realize that they already knew he was seriously ill). Just as they were finally beginning to settle into a good rapport with his choreographic style, he was dying.

A brief memo that Yakobson wrote to himself on April 28, 1975, includes a list of his objectives, both immediate and distant, and there is nothing diminished about the scale of his ambitions for his company. They include: "Get mayor of Leningrad to come see us; Make the company as important as classical ballet." They also include month-by-month plans for touring the Choreographic Miniatures company to Finland and Central Asia. He even lists five new ballets he plans to make, including *Prometheus*, a revised *Spartacus* for the Kirov, and *The Barber of Seville*. That spring he also found time to premiere his last ballet for the Kirov, *The Cowboys* (*Kovboi*, 1975), a pas de deux preserved in a film fragment and described in a libretto by Yakobson as a romance between John and Mary, two cowboys who have a comically rough courtship. His libretto explains that the ballet ends with Mary lassoing John around the neck and leading him meekly on his horse behind her like a captured trophy.[53] The gender inversion it plays with is daring, as is its obviously American theme—that he succeeded in seeing it through to the premiere indicates both the new possibilities that were opening up thematically in ballet, and that Yakobson sustained his drive to pursue them to the end.

Upon his return from Italy, Yakobson had faced one last entanglement with government officials beyond the request that he give them his guest choreographer's fee from La Scala. During the five years that the Choreographic Miniatures had been in existence, he had staged new programs incessantly, one after another—a result of both his creative exuberance and his determination to ensure the future of the theater by developing a large repertoire. It now transpired that his productivity worried both the regional and city authorities because they were obligated to pay the production costs for each ballet. Consequently, they suggested that the

Lenkontsert administration put an end to this. The Lenkontsert solution was to sue Yakobson, demanding that the court forbid him to stage so many new dances. The judicial system responded by stipulating a legally permitted norm: only one new dance production could be created each year. This meant that Lenkontsert would finance only one performance per year and Yakobson was effectively forbidden to do any more since he was prohibited from working without pay. In spite of his deteriorating health, Yakobson had to be present at the hearings about this matter, which he described to Irina as "wanton delinquency."[54]

In one of the many curious overlaps in the work of Yakobson and Balanchine, Yakobson's last major ballet was titled *Mozartiana,* as was Balanchine's. Choreographed in late 1974 for his own company as his valedictory to his continual reinvention of choreography in response to music, Yakobson's *Mozartiana* was comprised of five miniatures, the first set to an excerpt of Haydn's *Surprise Symphony* and the rest using excerpts from different Mozart concerti. The full choreography, which has been lost and was never filmed or videoed, was reportedly among Yakobson's most difficult; only the five most advanced women in his company could perform the *Female Variations*—a series of five solo variations, one by each of the five dancers, that appeared in the third section. The other sections were called *Surprise, Sextet, Male Variations, Minuet,* and *Mozart Pas de Deux.* Irina recalls that, as with the majority of Yakobson's work, it was simply the pleasure of Mozart's music that inspired him to begin stringing these little beads of beautifully formed dance miniatures together in *Mozartiana.*[55] The ballet also marks a gesture toward the baroque origins of the form, an ideal foil against which he could measure just how far he had pulled ballet into modernism through dancing that responds to the musical precision and calm phrasing of Mozart's music.

Possibilities were opening elsewhere for Yakobson as well. Furtseva had committed suicide in October 1974, and her successor was Pyotr Nilovich Demichev, a cultured man who was interested in what Yakobson was doing. After his return from Italy, Yakobson met with Demichev to discuss the possibility of an overseas tour for the company. At their meeting, Demichev was courteous and promised to come and see a performance of Choreographic Miniatures. When the company made its debut in Moscow on September 1, 1975, Demichev was indeed in the official box of the Russian Theater Hall to watch them. It was the first time that a USSR minister of culture had ever seen Yakobson's choreography, after decades of censorship. Less than a month earlier Yakobson had been shaken by the death of Dmitriy Shostakovich on August 9, and it was then that Irina saw Yakobson weep for the first time. Forty-five years earlier Yakobson and Shostakovich had launched their respective careers with *The Golden Age*, into an era that was anything but golden for such advanced and gifted artists, and now they were both closing out their lives with so many ambitions still unrealized.

Before the Choreographic Miniatures program began, with Demichev in attendance, Yakobson asked the director of the theater backstage to be taken to Demichev's box when he arrived. The director of the theater dismissed Yakobson's request, telling him disdainfully that no one could visit the minister in his special box at the theater. An hour later, at the first intermission, the director came running backstage searching for Yakobson to tell him that Demichev was asking for him. So Yakobson and his twenty-two-year-old son Nicholas watched the rest of the Choreographic Miniatures concert from the minister of culture's box, sharing the perspective of the center of Soviet cultural oversight with the minister—an intimacy that had been unthinkable for all of Yakobson's professional life. Demichev was enthusiastic about Yakobson's work, remarking on its originality and brilliance. "I have never seen anything like it," he said appreciatively. Yakobson later reported to Irina that Demichev said that from that point forward he would be the only censor of Yakobson's ballets—a promise that, despite its apparent suggestion that there could be continuing censorship, was comforting.

Like a great drama winding its way inexorably toward a tragic climax, the long-awaited rise in Yakobson's professional fortunes and recognition from the Soviet state occurred in direct proportion to his deteriorating physical condition. On September 10, the final day of the company's Moscow season, Yakobson and Irina arrived for a scheduled appointment with Demichev at the Moscow building that housed his office. Yakobson had not been feeling well so he had delayed the appointment, requested by Demichev, until the final day of the company's Moscow engagement. Upon entering the lobby of the building, Yakobson faltered and collapsed, unconscious, onto the floor. Demichev was alerted and called for Yakobson to be taken by ambulance to the Kremlin Hospital, the elite healthcare facility for the Soviet Union's top leadership. That evening Demichev attended the closing night of Choreographic Miniatures, unaware of the gravity of Yakobson's illness as he witnessed the standing ovation that greeted the final work on the program, *Jewish Wedding* (which was listed in the program as *Wedding Cortège,* as stipulated by Soviet authorities who would still not allow the word "Jewish" in the program). For ten minutes the entire hall was on its feet applauding this work that was emblematic in so many ways of Yakobson's artistic vision and personal fortitude. The title may have been modified, but the content was not. The ballet that had been eliminated by authorities when it was scheduled on the opening program of Choreographic Miniatures four years earlier now closed the troupe's triumphant homecoming in its first official season in the Soviet capitol.

Boris Ruchkan, the company' manager, sent the following letter to Yakobson on September 11, 1975, to tell him of the unprecedented success of his company on that final night of their Moscow season. Irina read it to him in his hospital room.

Dear Leonid Veniaminovich,

Just a couple of words about yesterday's Sept. 10 performance. I'll begin by saying we did not forget about Afanasyev: he was there with his wife and son and he witnessed an unbelievable success yesterday after *Wedding Cortège.* The applause continued even after the curtain fell; the audience did not leave. Everything went very well. There were no mis-timings, conflicts or mistakes. The company danced quickly, intermissions did not drag and the performance ended at 10:05 p.m. Before the start, Elena Lutskaya [a famous Russian dance critic] ran up to me beaming and related the conversation between Demichev and Māris Liepa which took place yesterday during the day. Liepa called them immediately and told them that Pyotr Nilovich suddenly, for no reason, started talking about you. He said that Yakobson's ballet made a huge impression on him and that this is the best of what Soviet choreography can be proud of today. That your work is the art of tomorrow.

I cannot but help but write down for you from the [guest book in the lobby] a note by Lilya Brik [Mayakovsky's muse] "first of all—about *Bedbug.* It's a strikingly talented work. Most of all I was touched by the way you showed the torments of Mayakovsky's feelings with his heroes. You captured the real Mayakovsky far better than anyone." Other audience comments included praise and appreciation. "You have wonderful theatre. Yakobson is a genius. Thank you for the joy."

The critic Vadim Gayevsky wrote "Time passes but Yakobson's place in our ballet does not change. Eternal avant-gardist. Eternal free thinker. The sharpest poet with the best sense of humor and the poet of sharp humor. Spiritual colleague of Rodin, Chagall and Shostakovich. Who else can boast of titles like that?"

I have probably tired you out. I, the troupe and all your thankful members of the audience wish you to gather strength, rest and get well. We are taking care of everything before you get back. I will try to keep you informed about all the most important things.

With much love and respect,

Boris Ruchkan

P.S. I am including the newspaper with the review.[56]

Demichev had been delighted with what he saw of Choreographic Miniatures as well, and he assured Yakobson that he could freely show whatever of his work he wished. Soon after, on September 28, the entire troupe set out for its first tour outside the USSR—a short tour of Hungary and East Germany, where they performed as part of the Berlin Festival—but without Yakobson. He would never leave the Kremlin Hospital. Irina remained by his side through the five final weeks of his life. Initially they forced her to leave in the evenings, but Demichev intervened at Irina's request and she was allowed to stay by her husband's bedside around the clock.

Even in the hospital Yakobson continued his habit of reading, working his way through novels by Maxim Gorky from the hospital's library. Once, when he closed his eyes while reading, Irina thought he had fallen asleep. After a few minutes, he opened them again, and she said it was good he had managed to nap. "I wasn't asleep," he told her. "I have just made up a new ballet." On October 17, 1975, Choreographic Miniatures returned from its triumphant first foreign tour, and Yakobson, waiting in the Kremlin Hospital for news, was informed of their success. The following day, Leonid V. Yakobson died at the age of seventy-one.

Yakobson's death was widely mourned, but in keeping with the life-long tension between the popular and the official response to him and his work, no formal obituary was ever published in the Soviet newspapers. On October 20, *Vecherniy Leningrad* (Evening Leningrad) published an abbreviated, unsigned, tribute and summary of his career highlights, signed simply "A Group of Friends." It read as follows:

Soviet art has suffered a heavy loss: Leonid Veniaminovich Yakobson—one of the most prominent Soviet choreographers, recipient of the USSR State Prize, Honored Worker of Arts of the Russian Federation, passed away at the age of 71.

L. V. Yakobson's extensive artistic career began half a century ago. After graduating from the Leningrad Choreographic Institute, he joined the troupe of the State Kirov Theater of Opera and Ballet, and from that time on, all his creative work was connected with it. He started out as a member of the corps de ballet and then became a soloist, creating an array of grotesque characters. Subsequently, Leonid Veniaminovich worked as a choreographer, staging numerous short and full-scale productions. Even his first choreographic project was outstanding—the staging of the ballet *The Golden Age* to Shostakovich's score, in collaboration with V. Vainonen and V. Chesnakov.

The production of F. Yarullin's *Shurale* by the Kirov Theater in 1950 was an important event in the cultural life of the country. Both the ballet and its stage directors [sic] received the USSR State Award.

One of L. V. Yakobson's most significant productions is A. Khachaturian's *Spartacus*. L. V. Yakobson went down in the history of the Soviet choreography as a surprising and inimitable master of choreographic miniatures—each a complete short ballet in its own right, with distinct dramaturgy, expressive characters and a plot.

L. V. Yakobson's innovative approach and his constant quest for new expressive means are manifested in his pieces *Bedbug* (1962), *Twelve* (1964), and *The Land of Miracles* (1967).

In 1970, he founded a Leningrad-based company named Choreographic Miniatures, which gained popularity over a very short time. While with this company, Leonid Veniaminovich stage[d] interesting ballet performances of variegated genres, including single-act ballets and cycles of choreographic miniatures.

[We are mourning] the death of a great artist, a man of immense talent and inexhaustible energy, who has bequeathed us numerous matchless creations that will enliven the theater stage for many years to come.[57]

Yakobson's life was in equal measure tragic and heroic. Tragic in how much force he had to expend against Soviet structures in order to get his work seen, and heroic for his persistence in expending that force, day after day, ballet by ballet. His dances changed people, changed the way they thought about their lives in the wasted cultural climate of Stalinist and Soviet Russia. Certainly he had many opportunities taken from him, but the friction from arbitrary and often absurd Soviet limitations also pushed him personally and creatively.

Jewishness bracketed his life as well as that of his work. The final ballet he was working on at the time of his death was the story of King Solomon, a Jewish theme. His company's life had begun with the censoring of *Jewish Wedding* and closed with its triumph. This triumph was a testament to Yakobson's larger achievement and passion in keeping Jewishness as a subject and identity before the Soviet public. "He would have liked to prove that Jewish people have the right to do anything other people do," Irina said of his larger vision. "That was not political—it was the Jewish Question in the country." In preparation for the full-length King Solomon ballet he planned to make, Yakobson had already gone to the Choral Synagogue in Moscow to listen to the Jewish prayers. He didn't have a yarmulke, so he knotted the ends of a handkerchief from his pocket and put it on his head as he listened and watched.[58]

The day after Yakobson died there was a huge, stately funeral cortege in Leningrad preceding his burial. It began at 15 Mayakovsky Street, where his dancers, the staff of his company, and their families said an intimate farewell to him as he lay in an open casket. From there private cars and chartered buses carrying scores of mourners moved through the streets to the Kirov Theater. There his body lay in state in the ornate second-floor gallery known as the White Hall, where famous and respected members of the Kirov Theater were paid tribute when they died.[59]

Hundreds of people, including the artists, administration, and staff of the Kirov, filled the theater to say a final farewell. For hours Yakobson's body remained there and the Kirov orchestra played the music that he had used for his miniatures, especially scores from his ballets that had tragic themes, including the final farewell scene from *Spartacus*. The funeral cortege then moved on, filling Architect Rossi Street, also known as Theater Street—the famous street on which the Vaganova School is located near the former Alexandrinsky Theater and across which aspiring youths progress from ballet students into ballet artists. The cortege of cars and buses paused in front of the Vaganova School, and the faculty and students streamed out to say their final farewells. The mournful caravan then moved on to the cemetery, having traced, in reverse, his progress as an artist from the school to the Kirov and finally to his own company at 15 Mayakovsky.

Valeriy Zvezdochkin, who was there, recounted how the official speakers called Yakobson "their pride," naming the ballets he had produced on the stage of the Kirov Theater. "No one mentioned the ballets and miniatures that had been forbidden from reaching the stage, many by people who were present at the funeral," he lamented, mentioning the final seven years of Yakobson's life when the Kirov Theater administration had rejected almost every proposal for a new ballet that Yakobson had brought them.[60] These never-realized plans for his new ballets included a ballet about the high-spirited World War II Soviet soldier Vasiliy Tyorkin with Yuriy Solovyov in the leading part, a *Figaro* with Baryshnikov, and a *Prometheus* and *Hamlet*, among others. Only two of his ballets were approved to be produced at the Kirov during these years; the official excuse for prohibiting the rest was that they "did not fit the theatre's prospective repertoire."[61]

Yakobson was buried not at the elite Serafimovskoye Cemetery, as Irina had wished, and as Demichev had promised her, but in the more modest Bogoslovskoe Cemetery on the outskirts of Leningrad.[62] When Irina had asked Demichev for permission to have Yakobson buried in Serafimovskoye, he had agreed and sent her to an office down the hall for assistance in arranging for a plot there. The clerk on duty began to question Irina about why she wanted Yakobson buried in Serafimovskoye, informing her curtly that only artists who have attained the special distinction of having received official medals, like being designated People's

Yakobson's tombstone at Bogoslovskoe
Cemetery in Saint Petersburg.
Photographer unknown.

Artist, were eligible. Irina explained that he should be buried there because Yakobson had done so much for the art of ballet in the USSR. "Yes,
he did," the woman replied curtly. "But he didn't think to make himself
a people's artist. He cannot be buried there."[63] Indeed Yakobson did not
think to make himself a People's Artist; rather he worked as an artist for
the people.

Yakobson was laid to rest in the wooded setting of the Bogoslovskoe
Cemetery, a very old cemetery in Saint Petersburg that has since become
more prestigious over time. One year later Irina added a final silent and
intimate tribute, a kind of performance coda. She commissioned a sculpture for the gravesite—inspired by the final pas de deux in *Spartacus*. It is
a sculpted stone image of Spartacus and his devoted mate, Phrygia, at his

knees. The sculptor saw the ballet and then Irina gave him, for inspiration, a photo of the moment in the pas de deux before Spartacus goes to battle. Her intent was to represent Yakobson as Spartacus and herself as Phrygia. Irina had chosen an image from *Spartacus* because of the resemblance she saw between this epic and her and Yakobson's own life narrative. Yakobson himself never voiced a personal identification with Spartacus, nor had he said anything about perhaps someday putting this image on his grave. Yet today, sitting atop his grave is a stone portrait of Spartacus standing defiant with his devoted Phrygia folded at his feet in deep sorrow, knowing he will soon leave for his final, fateful battle.

EPILOGUE

AFTER LEONID YAKOBSON's death, Irina, his widow, was appointed director of Choreographic Miniatures, where she served for eight months as she searched for a permanent replacement. The minister of culture, Pyotr Demichev, advised her not to rush the process, but she was concerned that her presence as director might make it easier for the authorities to eliminate the company completely. "Of course they could not promise that they would keep me as director," she said. "I was not a choreographer and I was Jewish." She persuaded Demichev to give the troupe to Askold Makarov, whose celebrity as a Kirov dancer owed much to his performances in Yakobson's ballets. Although Demichev advised against appointing Makarov, Irina insisted. "I thought Makarov was a very energetic young man; he had important connections and I hoped that he would use them to preserve Yakobson's heritage," she said.[1]

After Makarov became director, however, he began to edge Irina out. "He started pushing Irina out after about six months," recalled Vladimir Zenzinov, a former dancer with the company and now a part-time archivist of Yakobson memorabilia in the building that houses the current incarnation of his company.[2] First the casting, then the programming and frequency of performances of Yakobson's ballets, began to shift from Irina's control to Makarov's. Finally, when Irina was away in Moscow for several months assisting Maya Plisetskaya, who was staging her *Seagull* (*Chayka,* 1980) for the Bolshoi Ballet, Makarov quietly replaced her altogether, making his wife the new assistant director of Yakobson's company. "When I returned I found out from the secretary that I had been fired," Irina recalled. "Next my husband's name disappeared from the programs, other choreographers' works were mixed in with the miniatures and I realized that Makarov could not understand anything. I could not help the company so I decided it was better to leave the USSR."[3] Feeling that her options to preserve Yakobson's work in the USSR were fading, in August 1980 Irina, her son, and her mother applied to emigrate to Israel, hoping to bring Yakobson's work to the West. The Jackson-Vanik Amendment, passed in the United States in 1974, which linked U.S.-Soviet trade to Jewish emigration from the USSR, had made it possible to leave the Soviet Union—but only if one claimed a desire to go to Israel. As Yuri Slezkine has noted, this "late twentieth-century exodus [of Jews from Russia] was similar to the early twentieth-century one in that the overwhelming majority of émigrés preferred America to Palestine; the main difference was that the only way to go to America (or anywhere else) was by applying to go to Palestine."[4] So this is what the Yakobsons did, knowing that San Francisco was their true desired destination.

The process of developing an independent single-choreographer company that Yakobson had begun now began to unravel more quickly. The troupe, which Zvezdochkin eulogized as redefining existing notions of choreography and its possibilities in the USSR, was too young to have a plan of succession in place, and represented too new a model to guarantee its survival beyond its founder and choreographer. Choreographic Miniatures passed through three directors beginning with Makarov, each one trying to find the right mixture of classical staples, new ballets, and Yakobson repertory works that would enable the company to survive. Makarov continued to direct until his death in 2000, when Yuriy Petukhov began

Yakobson taking a curtain call with dancers of Choreographic
Miniatures, ca. 1975. Photographer unknown.

his eleven-year tenure as director. In 2011 Andrian Fadeyev, a former principal dancer at the Mariinsky, replaced Petukhov.

In 1975, prior to this devolution of Yakobson's company, Evgeniya Popova, the respected TV director at Lenfilm, a division of the Russian film
industry, and a longtime friend and admirer of Yakobson, decided to make
a film about Yakobson's troupe. "He did not participate in it, although we
started shooting it while he was still alive," she recalled. "All of the studios
at Lenfilm were overloaded with work so we only filmed at night from 11
p.m. to 6 a.m. when everything was empty." The filming continued on a
tight time and financial schedule after Yakobson's death. "We could not
do more than three takes of any dance we were filming. My goal was to
save as much as possible of his achievement," said Popova in 2012 from her
apartment in Saint Petersburg. In her eighties, she had known Yakobson
since the late 1950s when she was studying dance. "I wanted to give an idea
of his work," she explained. "Yakobson was disliked quite a bit as an artist,
and as a private person he was constantly reprimanded."[5]

Popova filmed *Contrasts* out of commitment to his work, not knowing
if Soviet Central Television would broadcast it or if she would even be
paid. "We selected the dances to be filmed, then after I edited the footage
I would let the editors see our completed work and then the administration at Moscow. Each time we did this something was taken out," she recalled. "For example, *The Village Don Juan* (*Derevenskiy Don Zhuan*, 1971)

was excluded because the officials said it was mocking the Soviet people. Then there was *The Twelve*. They asked why the red was shown through the rags—was that an affront to the Communist Party?"[6] With each criticism Popova had to sit down and re-edit the film and its soundtrack, excising the offending bits and moving everything around again and again to try and retain some visual and audio coherence to the film. "We had to cut each piece of the take and the sound separately," she said. "We would clean out the film with a razor and use the acetone to glue the new ends together. Each time we had to cut the film we saved every bit that was cut."[7]

Stripped of decor and the formal setting of a theater and stage, Popova's *Contrasts* (*Kontrastï*, 1976) stands as a remarkable document of the modernist purity of Yakobson's choreography, even if today only a fragment of it exists. She shot the film in the hallways and interior balconies of the Palace of Culture in Leningrad. During one midnight session it began to snow heavily as they were filming, delivering a stunning backdrop. The falling white snowflakes seen through the illuminated windows and the black of the shadows around the dancers accentuate the black and white film so that the dancers become pure silhouettes. The austere formalism of the building vividly offsets the simplicity of Yakobson's modernist choreography for *Exercise XX*. Nothing about this performance of *Exercise XX* suggests Soviet-era ballet—it looks abstract and edgy enough to be an experimental dance film from the twenty-first-century West.

A belated official embracing of Yakobson's work began in 2000 as part of Russia's efforts to rehabilitate its lost heritage. Symbolically the return to Yakobson's ballets also became an act of recovering one who had resisted, who had exhibited rare intellectual and emotional defenses against a system that had crushed so many others. In some ways this new interpretation is also a burden for Yakobson's art—because his primary goal in making his ballets was to assign himself interesting problems to solve, and this effort often lay where the blockades between his aesthetic ambitions and official limits were at that moment. That is, Yakobson's work was made according to this private agenda rather than being deliberately confrontational, but this distinction was lost when, in the early twenty-first century, the cultural officials of the "new" Russia embraced his choreographic legacy as a prototype of modernism and daring. While the choreographer is somewhat more fortunate than a dancer whose career unfolds in a sequestered nation and whose work ends when he or she stops performing, Yakobson's work was never notated nor adequately filmed or documented, so every reconstruction is also in part a re-invention and a dilution.

Russian officials, too, deliberately re-engaged with Yakobson's choreography as part of the Russian nationalism project, but this time in the interest of bringing the state to his art rather than his art to the state. Perhaps in belated recognition of the role of performance in transmitting social knowledge and memory, Russian officials at the Mariinsky (Kirov) and Bolshoi ballets began staging revivals of his three major full-length ballets: the Mariinsky Theater remounted Yakobson's *Bedbug* in 2001; *Shurale* was presented by the Bolshoi in 2008, 2009, 2013, and 2014; and *Spartacus* was performed, also by the Bolshoi, in 2010 and 2012.

Russians' long-held practice of considering Yakobson as the representative choreographer for performance modernism during the era of the USSR has been remarked on by Russian theater historian Olga Levitan, who recalled watching his performances in Leningrad when she was a young theater critic in the early 1970s: "I remember it was very important to see Yakobson's ballets," she said. "He was Petersburgian as an artist and for an artist to be Petersburgian means that he also contributed to the cultural tradition, bringing new ideas."[8]

The private communities that Yakobson had spent so many years imagining in the rehearsal room, and when he was fortunate, onstage, were suddenly of value retrospectively because they conjured memories of an original voice that had emanated from deep inside the Soviet years. In a conversation in 2000 at a ballet conference in New Orleans, Louisiana, the Russian dancer and choreographer Nikita Dolgushin suggested that this shift reflected how cultural officials were trying to reclaim their lost past, which included Yakobson.

What Dolgushin described is a process of belated recognition among officials that the Soviets had degraded their collective cultural remembrances, in a process that scholar Diana Taylor would likely explain as corrupting the archives of the embodied practices and knowledge that performance produces.[9] Taylor's paradigm is a useful frame for considering how this belated recognition in the former Soviet Union has reversed the ways in which political manipulation shrank Russia's cultural archive and why efforts to reinstate Yakobson's work are so complicated. These

revivals also open questions about the transmission of culturally trau-
matic memories and about how the Soviet period narrowed and stalled
the learning, storing, and transmitting of knowledge and truth for so
many years.

Thus nearly two decades after his death, the mechanisms of power
that had worked against Yakobson so strenuously in his lifetime finally
turned to courting his memory. With the demise of the Soviet Union at
the end of 1991, the nation's artistic life was in chaos. As historian W. Bruce
Lincoln has noted of the shifting cultural climate, the cultural changes of
this era tumbled together "not as a result of being deprived of the firm
precepts that had guided it during the Soviet era, but precisely because so
many long-separated currents were flowing together."[10] In literature the
result was a lot of artistic output tinged with regret and resentment: "Parodies of Stalinism, satires of Soviet life, and bitter remembrances of lives
spoiled and talents destroyed by men who placed ideology ahead of humanity all poured forth, as people finally had their say after lifetimes
spent in silence."[11] Thus a redefinition of what it meant to be Russian after
the dissolution of the Soviet Union in December 1991 played out differently across the various art forms.

Once the Soviet experiment, with its chilling prohibitions on artistic
production, began to falter, Russia's cultural heritage started to be reshaped. In literature this transformation proceeded more swiftly than in
the performing arts as samizdat came out from underground: there is no
"choreographing for the drawer" as there is in writing book manuscripts,
musical scores, or plays. While this is a severe constraint on a choreographer, it also affords a unique immediacy to the work that *does* get produced because it represents the choreographer's vision in tandem with the
conditions to which he or she is responding.

For the dance historian trying to retrieve these occasions the effect is
like attempting to capture a long-vanished insect, together with the plant
on which it fed, fossilized in amber. The nation and its arts revealed what
it meant to be Russian after three-quarters of a century as "Soviet." "There
is no escaping the fact that our country has cruelly forfeited the entire
twentieth century," was how the writer Aleksandr Solzhenitsyn phrased
the state of Russia shortly before Mikhail Gorbachev received the Nobel
Peace Prize in 1990. "Our much-trumpeted achievements all have turned

out to be illusory. From a flourishing condition we have been hurled back to a state of semi-barbarity, and we sit amid the wreckage."[12]

In the world of Russian ballet, having the doors suddenly opened to the long suppressed repertoire from the West led to the hasty acquisition of works by outside choreographers, especially ballets by Balanchine. For artists whose works had been known in the Soviet Union only through glimpses of occasional touring companies, there was also no dance equivalent of this kind of foreign samizdat. In the new openness of glasnost in 1989, Kirov director Oleg Vinogradov acquired Balanchine's *Theme and Variations* and *Scotch Symphony* for the company and former New York City Ballet dancers Francia Russell and Suzanne Farrell came to Saint Petersburg to set these ballets on the Kirov dancers. These became the first two ballets by Balanchine to be performed by a Soviet company since he had left the newly formed USSR in 1924. Works by William Forsythe and others flowed into the Kirov's repertoire as well. Initially the physical speed and novel styling of the Western choreography posed challenges for the Kirov dancers. Yakobson's widow suggested that Russian audiences also lacked a context for the works.[13]

A curiosity about those ballets in Russia that preceded the creation of these works led directly to the dances of Yakobson, which moved from circumscribed and marginal to being viewed as central to the state's new mission of self-definition and reconnection with a severed cultural past. In 1988, Valeriy Sergeyev, previously a leading dancer in Yakobson's ballets and a teacher in his company, was hired by Konstantin Sergeyev, artistic director and choreographer for the Kirov Ballet. Valeriy Sergeyev was asked to take over Konstantin Sergeyev's class and to teach the students in classes six, seven, and eight the Yakobson repertoire, to give them the skills for how to act onstage—an arrangement that was still on going in 2014. Valeriy Sergeyev, like other former Yakobson dancers now teaching the next generation of Russian dancers, considers Yakobson's work priceless as a teaching tool. For them there is nothing like his character-saturated miniatures—*Baba Yaga*, *The Snow Maiden*, *Jewish Wedding*, *The Gossips*, *Troika*. These are the Yakobson works regularly taught to Mariinsky Ballet students in preparation for their exams. They are taught the classics as repertoire they need to know and Yakobson's repertoire, which hones their dramatic skills as dancers.[14]

Then in 2006, on the occasion of a festival in London celebrating the centenary of Dmitriy Shostakovich's birth, the Mariinsky restaged Yakobson's Shostakovich-scored *Bedbug* to mixed and puzzled foreign reviews.[15] These revivals of Yakobson's ballets, along with his wife's 2001 Russian-language publication in the United States of his long-suppressed book detailing his choreographic credo, *Letters to Noverre*, were heralded as significant but belatedly rediscovered treasures of Russian culture. Russian ballet scholar Valeriy Zvezdochkin wrote in 1989 in his introduction to the Yakobson manuscript, "If Yakobson's book had appeared a quarter century ago (when it should have seen the light), it undoubtedly would have produced the effect of a bomb exploding. How much emotional debate would have surrounded it!" Zvezdochkin mourned that Yakobson's theories were suppressed from the public for so long.[16] He laments that their influence was muted by time while still acknowledging them as foundational in the development of mid-twentieth-century Russian ballet. "One thing is certain: without thoroughly investigating and understanding Yakobson's thought processes, without correlating his theories and practices (provided the master's work is preserved in its original form) with the issues that we face today—it is impossible to comprehend the essence of what is taking place in choreography at the end of the twentieth century," he wrote in his foreword to this Yakobson choreographic treatise, *Letters to Noverre*.[17]

Indeed Yakobson seemed to put forth his ideas simultaneously in the multiple formats of dancing and writing, making new ballets as often as he was given access to dancers and studios and writing on his own in the evenings. When he was barred from the studio, he listened repeatedly to audio recordings of possible music for future ballets. He also drafted dance libretti in his head while scripting a philosophy of dance modernism that framed it all. These libretti did not describe choreography but rather displayed his evolving ideas about characters or themes that he was exploring in the reading and research he often did prior to going into the studio. His belief was both simple yet radical: he saw Russian ballet stagnating and falling behind the kind of innovation displayed in the other arts. He worried that it was too tethered to the movement vocabulary of danse d'école and too inflexible to adapt its vocabulary to new contemporary expression. "Yakobson said when all the other arts were changing ballet stayed at the same level," Irina recalled. "On stage he saw other choreographers using all the same movements of legs and arms that existed in ballet class and old ballets. Even when the costumes, staging, décor and music were new the movements remained unchanged."[18] His credo was to accelerate the expressivity and inventiveness in ballet to the same level of imagination and novelty that existed in music.

Despite the flurry of revivals in the early twenty-first century, no company has consistently performed Yakobson's works in Russia. With fitting irony his repertoire today lives most vividly in the Vaganova Russian Ballet Academy (known as the Vaganova Leningrad Choreographic Institute until 1991), where several of his miniatures continue to be the heart of the character classes taught to the young conservatory students. Yakobson's dances are used to train these students into Russian dancers and to show them how to express character and individuality. Here is the Yakobson legacy perhaps in its most potent form.

In 2012 even Yakobson's former company, Choreographic Miniatures, found it financially impossible to perform Yakobson's works exclusively, and fill the theaters, despite new artistic director Fadeyev's interest in Yakobson's legacy. Fadeyev, who gave up his career as a leading dancer with the Mariinsky Ballet to direct Yakobson's company, renamed the troupe "Leonid Yakobson Saint Petersburg State Academic Ballet Theater." A generation too young to have known Yakobson personally, Fadeyev was introduced to his ballets when he was a student in the Vaganova School. "Yakobson's heritage is a pearl of Saint Petersburg that needs to be preserved," he says. "When I was still at the Vaganova School we studied the miniatures of Yakobson—we studied and performed them and we also performed them for the stage examinations," he said. Asked how he and the other students regarded this work then, Fadeyev replied, "It was very interesting, colorful and full of character. It was something you were allowed to be free doing and to have a lot of fun. For me it was more interesting to do a ballet like *Spartacus* than *Giselle* because everyone had a well-defined role and stood out."[19] In terms of the challenges of reviving Yakobson's work today, Fadeyev cites the fact that Yakobson created his choreography for specific artists, "so that not only is it impossible to hide behind technique, but you need a personality that stands out for each role. He would teach ten dancers a part and only one or two would eventually dance it," Fadeyev said, underscoring the kind of individuality necessary to perform Yakobson's choreography.[20]

In the summer of 2012 the Mariinsky Ballet included a revival of Yakobson's *Spartacus* as part of its repertory for the White Nights Festival, and two of the young dancers performing leading roles reflected on the unique challenges of the choreography. Aleksandr Sergeyev, whose parents, Klimova and Sergeyev, were leading dancers in Yakobson's company, performed the role of Harmodius, while the younger Seregeyev's wife, Darya Pavlenko, also a Mariinsky dancer, danced the role of the temptress, Aegina. "There is no senseless movement or empty pose in Yakobson's *Spartacus*," Pavlenko says. "When I dance Aegina, I cannot turn myself off, that's part of Yakobson and the audience sees it right away. Even if you feel like an idiot you have to feel the aroma of the choreography all the time. It is stupid to think that if you are not on pointe it's easy. It is not easy choreography at all." Pavlenko is also mindful of the political weight of the ballet historically. "There is not a single pirouette in the ballet," she noted. "And the male dancers touch the women in a way that is very different from how you touch a dancer normally."[21] Sergeyev also spoke of the psychological difficulty of the work as being as challenging as the physical demands. "You have to use your legs, arms, shoulders, everything. Because you are expressing human emotion. It was such a revolutionary ballet," he said.[22]

Leaving

For two years after she submitted her request to immigrate to Israel, Irina was forced into unemployment. She was barred from doing any teaching or coaching at the Kirov Theater. One reason she was told she could not leave the USSR was that officials were concerned she would take the Kirov repertoire with her (through her memory of the choreography of its classical ballets) and teach it to the West, as if choreography were as precious a state secret as insider knowledge of nuclear physics. Irina's name and her identity as "the widow of a famous choreographer" surfaced soon afterward on lists of "refuseniks" (Soviet Jews refused permission to leave for Israel) being circulated in the United States by activists for Soviet Jewry. Finally Maya Plisetskaya and her husband, Rodion Shchedrin, a composer and pianist, spoke with an influential person they knew, and Irina, her twenty-eight-year-old son, and her mother were suddenly informed they could leave. This official notification came with a curt two weeks' notice; a list of the few personal items they could take; and an accounting of everything that they would have to leave behind, including all of Yakobson's personal archives and library, the entire contents of their apartment, and their Russian passports.[23] Irina begged the authorities to prolong their departure by ten days to give her a little more time to get his archives into museums and secure all the required permissions from the utility companies and government agencies proving that no money was owed to any of them. The official granted them just seven additional days.

Fortunately Irina had sold their dacha two years before they applied to emigrate, and with the cash she had cleverly purchased a huge—seven- or eight-carat—diamond ring. Since it was impossible to take the money out of Russia—all that was allowed for Jews leaving was 100 rubles (about $96 dollars at that time) per person, she gave the ring to her sister Anna's husband for safekeeping, eventually selling it and dividing the proceeds among Yakobson's surviving siblings.

On September 26, 1982, the Yakobsons boarded a plane bound for Vienna and arrived at the immigration center there. Known informally as a "notorious loophole," the Israelis would eventually close this option after 1988, "when the overall proportion of those going to America [rather than Israel from Vienna] reached 89 percent." The U.S. government supported this change, later agreeing "to significantly decrease the immigration quotas for Soviet Jews."[24] As soon as the Yakobsons arrived in Vienna, they announced their decision to go to America rather than Israel. Consequently they were sent to Italy for three weeks to wait through their health quarantine. Nicholas, who had been to art school, painted little Russian landscapes that he sold in a crafts market to help bring in additional money since the three hundred dollars they had arrived with was soon gone. Irina had chosen the United States as their destination because of its strong ballet companies, and she knew there was no professional ballet in Israel. "Everybody in the Soviet Union knew what was going on abroad, what companies were touring." she said. Initially Makarova and Baryshnikov suggested to Irina that she stay in New York, explaining that it was much easier to find dance work in New York than in other cities.

Once they reached New York City, Irina asked to watch a class at New York City Ballet, and although Balanchine was not there, it proved fortuitous. In the hallway of the State Theater she ran into Rudi van Dantzig, director of the Dutch National Ballet, who recognized her. He approached her and after confirming she was indeed Madame Yakobson, he said how much he admired Yakobson's work. "He had tears in his eyes as he spoke about my husband," Irina recalled. Van Dantzig invited Irina to work with him in Amsterdam with the Dutch National Ballet. Needing the work, she accepted gladly. Makarova was especially helpful—lending Irina her assistant, Dina Makarova, to go with her as a translator and assistant. Later, when Hamburg Ballet Director John Neumeier expressed an interest in meeting Irina, Makarova sent the cash-strapped Irina a plane ticket so she could come to New York for the meeting.

Now that she was separated from the Yakobson repertoire, Irina's gifts as a masterful teacher and coach of classical ballet assumed a new prominence—and marketability in the international ballet world. Very soon she had competing offers to become a permanent member of the teaching staff at the Dutch National Ballet, the Royal Ballet in London, and eventually the San Francisco Ballet. Helgi Tomasson, who had arrived in 1985 as the new director of the San Francisco Ballet, immediately recognized Irina's skill as a teacher and hired her to teach in the school and company. "She's a wonderful teacher, she's really sought after," Tomasson said. "When I was able to convince her to stay with us, I was very happy."[25] In the initial years of her teaching at the San Francisco Ballet, Makarova often met with Irina for private coaching as well. "Irina has the talent to teach, the eye, the conception, the taste, so much," she explained. "Anybody who finished the Vaganova School is special, but Irina was Vaganova's own pupil. She finished with Vaganova herself. There are not so many left now."[26]

In 1987 Irina became a member of the dance faculty at the San Francisco Ballet, where she remained for thirteen years before relocating to Israel with her sister, Anna, in 2000. Throughout her time in San Francisco and subsequently in Hamburg, where she coached Neumeier's Hamburg Ballet, Irina taught her signature classes. She continued teaching several months every year at the Hamburg Ballet as a guest faculty member and coach until soon after she turned eighty-seven, in 2011, when she retired due to declining health. Her dream of finding a home for Yakobson's repertory in the West never materialized—the gap between the conditions of its creation and the new world of its reception in the West was simply too large to surmount. Then a strange thing happened: the same nation that had made Yakobson's existence as an artist so burdensome began to embrace him as the author of a vital lost part of its history. In a curious way, then, those decades of socialist controls on art making have indeed embedded themselves in Yakobson's ballets. Decades into the post-Soviet era, they have become a vivid reminder of a time when to make art was a radical and dangerous act and when choreography could be a medium of political and social resistance.

In early 1975, several months before he died, Leonid Yakobson wrote his final reflection on ballet. Titled simply *Choreography—A Complex Art,* and published only in 2001, it is a remarkable document, his valedictory to the art form in which, and through which, he lived his life. The tone is not congratulatory or summative, but forward-looking and coldly realistic about the massive amount of work still needed to be done to shepherd ballet out of what he calls "the dead end in which choreography finds itself worldwide." This essay has echoes of one of the first works that Yakobson ever published, his 1929 "For a New Generation in Choreography!" essay for *Rabochiy i teatr,* where he argued for the obsolescence of ballet.[27] Now he is back at the battlements but he has fine-tuned his target. He is revisiting his beginnings at the end of his life, awakening to what T. S. Eliot once called the realization that "We shall not cease from exploration / And the end of all our exploring / Will be to arrive where we started / And know the place for the first time."[28]

Yakobson is not sparing in describing the end of ballet, but he finally knows how to fix it: "Ballet is exhausted and cannot renew itself. It is impossible for the classical dance to say anything relevant today: representation is beyond its grasp," he writes. "The ballet master who endeavors to treat contemporary subjects in the style of the classical ballet is like a fool attempting to sound wise."[29]

For Yakobson the lesson learned from the scores of miniatures and several longer ballets he has made is simple: if one saves the training but radicalizes the choreography, refreshed content will follow. "A revolution must take place in choreography. From the school of the classical dance, the entire universal system of professional training and movement development that leads to the career of a ballet artist must remain. But the style in which this system is imprisoned must be discarded. Then a new art will be born."[30] He asks rhetorically, How can one portray revolutionary topics *en pointe* without changing the classical language? Yakobson is describing a process that is both radical and supremely simple—this is the premise of dance modernism. He is struggling to put Russian ballet back

A contemplative moment for Yakobson, sitting
in the audience at the Maly Opera Theater,
Leningrad. Photographer unknown.

on the track from which it was derailed back in the 1930s—just as his own
career as a dance maker began. He shaped ballet into a medium through
which those on society's margins could speak to the center, and in doing so revealed ballet's capacity to give shape to cultural displacement.
Through his choreography he was effectively offering new insights about
the idea of homeland.

Yakobson's Choreography in Israel

Leonid Yakobson never visited Israel, but his ability to bring out the
ephemeral and the individual in the performances of the micro-narratives
he created are now part of the fabric of Russian ballet history—a cultural

history that many of the one million Jews from the former Soviet Union who migrated to Israel in the 1970s to 1990s have imported with them. In 2000 Yakobson's widow, Irina, and her sister, Anna Klimentenko, made their second, and final, migration—this time to Haifa, Israel, to be near relatives. Once Irina arrived in Israel, news of her presence spread quickly through the emigré dance community, and she received several requests from Israeli ballet schools and companies wanting to stage Yakobson's ballets. The demands of most of his choreography preclude all but the most technically accomplished dancers from performing the work. But she did agree to a request from the former Bolshoi ballerina Nina Timofeyeva.

Although Valery Panov's arrival in Israel in 1974 was the most heavily documented of that of any Jewish artist from the Soviet Union, in the decades following his emigration other ballet artists who were primarily interested in teaching continued to arrive, and Nina Timofeyeva, a graduate of the Vaganova School, was one of the most prominent of these. Her daughter, Nadya, who now directs the Jerusalem Ballet and its school of a hundred students, explained that when they first arrived in Israel in 1991, along with Nadya's Jewish grandmother, they intended to teach at Israel's leading arts conservatory, the Jerusalem Academy of Music and Dance, and to found a ballet company. They were very surprised at how sparse the ballet activity was. "It was really another planet," the younger Timofeyeva said, describing their shock at the absence of professional ballet training and companies.[31] For two years after they arrived, Nadya, who is a strong and captivating dancer, performed as a guest artist with the Panov Ballet Company. She voices her respect for the efforts of Panov—and of Berta Yampolsky, who also teaches and directs a ballet company in Israel—to bring ballet to Israel.

Nina Timofeyeva, Nadya's mother, had danced Aegina in Yakobson's Bolshoi production of *Spartacus* as a principal dancer for the company and she had great respect for his work. She was among the first to contact Irina Yakobson when news of her arrival in Israel circulated through the network of former Russian dancers living there. In 2009, Timofeyeva approached Irina and asked her if she would stage Yakobson's *Pas de Quatre* on the four most advanced dancers in her company.

Irina, cautious, taught the dancers a trial class to see their technical level. Afterward she gave her consent to their learning and performing one Yakobson ballet. Yakobson's *Pas de Quatre* was subsequently performed by the Jerusalem Ballet Company in its 2010 season to an enthusiastic reception. Preserved in photographs on the company's website, the performance is their link to diasporic ballet flows and the only one by an Israeli ballet company of a Yakobson dance. Timofeyeva regards Yakobson's work in general, and *Pas de Quatre* in particular, as "still very modern" because of "the fresh vision" of the body it offers. "Even if the technique of the dancers performing is not always strong," she says, knowingly, "the *Pas de Quatre* gives beauty and enjoyment because of how he built it. We need more of that here in Israel."[32]

The Soviet Jews who immigrated to Israel and brought ballet with them also transported an understanding of pluralisms through the accommodations they made to adapt yet retain a separate cultural sphere. Those like Panov and Timofeyeva, with major dancing careers in the USSR, immigrated believing that there might be a place for ballet in Israel. They wanted to use dance to open a new network of these diasporic dance traces in the Middle East, influenced by those vistas of Jewish content and modernism that Yakobson's work had once opened for them in Soviet ballet long ago.

There is no happy ending to Yakobson's life and work. He died too young, and too much of his choreography has been lost. Yet he kept the vitality of the art form of ballet alive by showing its capacity to stand against authority during the decades of the twentieth century when darkness closed around so much else in the USSR. That history is over. But before it ended he carried modern ballet to safety and became one of its greatest defenders. He protected ballet by claiming that it was innocuous while sharpening it into a vital and dangerous art, an emblem of opposition, beauty, and faith. Under Yakobson, ballet became the afterlife of one era and a rehearsal for the global modernity of the coming one.

Works by Leonid Yakobson

Year of First Performance	English Title	Original Russian Title	Type of Work
1925	*Waltz*	Вальс	miniature
1925	*I Love You*	Люблю тебя	miniature
1926–1931	*Dolls*	Пупсы	miniature
1926–1931	*Fantasy*	Фантазия	miniature
1926–1931	*Norwegian Dance*	Норвежский танец	miniature
1926–1931	*Turkish March*	Турецкий марш	miniature
1926–1931	*Little Priests*	Попики	miniature
1926–1931	*They About Us*	Они о нас	miniature
1926–1931	*Butterfly*	Бабочка	miniature
1926–1931	*Sport Étude*	Физкультурный этюд	miniature
1926–1931	*Waltz*	Вальс	miniature
1926–1931	*Brazilian Dances*	Бразильские танцы	miniature
1926–1931	*Spring*	Весна	miniature
1926–1931	*Waltz*	Вальс	miniature
1926–1931	*Waltz*	Вальс	miniature
1926–1931	*Impromptu*	Экспромт	miniature
1926–1931	*The Sea Suite*	Морская сюита	miniature
1926–1931	*Skriabiniana*	Скрябиниана	miniature
1927	*Physical Étude*	Физкультурная зарядка	miniature
10/26/1930	*The Golden Age*	Золотой век	ballet
1931	*Sports March*	Физкультурный марш	miniature
1932	*Adagio*	Адажио	miniature
1932	*Oriental Dance*	Восточний танец	miniature
1932	*Prelude*	Прелюд	miniature
1932	*May March*	Май – марш	miniature
1932	*Chaplin*	Чаплин	miniature
1932	*Disarmament Conference*	Конференция по разоружению	miniature
1932	*Chavdarcho (The Young Pioneers)*	Чавдарчо (Пионерия)	ballet (musical pantomime)

Ballet Company	Composer	Performers and Designers
LCS	Frédéric Chopin	V. Kaminskaya, L. Yakobson
LCS	Edvard Grieg	V. Kaminskaya, L. Yakobson
LCS	Riccardo Drigo	T. Vecheslova, L. Yakobson
LCS	Frédéric Chopin	
LCS	Edvard Grieg	
LCS	Ludwig van Beethoven	
LCS		
LCS	no music	
LCS	Edvard Grieg	N. Dudinskaya
LCS	Edvard Grieg	T. Kokhanovich, V. Fidler
LCS	Ilya Sats	F. Balabina, K. Sergeyev
KB	Darius Milhaud	
LCS	Edvard Grieg	L. Brodskaya, A. Pisarev
LCS	Franz Liszt	
LCS	Moritz Moszkowski	L. Traktina and others
LCS	Anton Arensky	
KFFE	folk music	
ESHA	Alexander Scriabin	
LCS	Dmitriy Shostakovich	
KB	Dmitriy Shostakovich	G. Ulanova, O. Mungalova, O. Iordan, V. Chabukiani, K. Sergeyev, L. Lavrovskiy, S. Kaplan, L. Yakobson, M. Mikhaylov, and others. Set design: N. Ivanovsky. Costumes: V. Khodasevich
LCS	Grigoriy Lobachyov	N. Dudinskaya, V. Fidler
LCS	Edvard Grieg	G. Ananova, V. Preobrazhensky
LCS	Lev Shvarts	N. Streltsova, R. Gerbek
LCS	Anton Arensky	
LCS	Valentin Voloshinov	
LCS	Victor Herbert	E. Kursin, V. Rïndina, V. Varkovitskiy, B. Fenster, K. Boyarsky, and others
LCS	Mikhail Glinka	
LCS	Valentin Voloshinov and Mikhail Chulaki	T. Kokhanovich, G. Kirillova, V. Varkovitskiy, N. Zheleznova, V. Bogdanov, Z. Machan, and others. Set design: A. Brushteyn. Costumes: B. Zon

(continued)

Year of First Performance	English Title	Original Russian Title	Type of Work
5/18/1933	Till Eulenspiegel	Тиль Эйленшпигель	ballet (dance pantomime)
1934	The First Polka		miniature
1934–1936	Waltz	Вальс	miniature
1934–1936	The Cock, the Hen, and the Chicken	Петух, курица и цыплята	miniature
1934–1936	Kittens	Котята	miniature
1934–1936	Eight Girls and Me Alone	Восемь девок, один я	miniature
1934–1936	Three Bears	Три медведа	miniature
1934–1936	Three Little Pigs	Три поросенка	miniature
1934–1936	Russian Dolls	Матрёшки	miniature
1934–1936	Max and Moritz	Макс и Мориц	miniature
1934–1936	Russian Dance	Русская	miniature
1934–1936	Quartet	Квартет	miniature
1934–1936	Soviet Toys	Советские игрушки	miniature
1934–1936	Skipping Rope	Скакалка	miniature
1934–1936	Pioneers' March	Пионерский марш	miniature
1934–1936	Jota	Хота	miniature
1936	Lost Illusions	Утраченные иллюзии	ballet
1938	Russian Pioneer's Dance	Русская пионерская	miniature
1938	Waltz	Вальс	miniature
1938	Waltz	Вальс	miniature
1938	Impromptu (The Nymph and the Two Satyrs)	Экспромт (Нимфа и два сатира)	miniature
1938	Meditations	Размышление	miniature
1938	Dream	Сновидение	miniature
1938	Princess-Frog	Царевна-лягушка	miniature
1939	Russian Folk Games and Dances	Русские народные игры и пляски	miniature
1939	Yurochka	Юрочка	miniature
1939	Nanai Dances	Игры нанайцев	miniature
1939	Two Naughty Boys	Два шалуна	miniature
1939	Foreigner	Иностранка	miniature

Ballet Company	Composer	Performers and Designers
LCS	Richard Strauss	V. Fidler, I. Kaplan, G. Kirillova, B. Fenster, K. Boyarsky, V. Varkovitskiy, and others. Set design: Y. Mravinsky. Costumes: N. Nikiforov
MCS	Mikhail Glinka	
MCS	Lev Shvarts	O. Lepeshinskaya and others
SCS	Modest Mussorgsky	
SCS	Pyotr Ilyich Tchaikovsky	
SCS	Alexander Dargomyzhsky	
SCS	Dmitriy Shostakovich	
SCS		
SCS	Alfredo Casella	
SCS		
SCS	Cesare Pugni	
SCS	Lev Shvarts	
SCS		
SCS	Alfredo Casella	
SCS		
MCS		
STOB	Boris Asafyev	Set design: V. Dmitriyev
MCS	folk music	
MCS	Maurice Ravel	
MCS	Claude Debussy	
MCS	Pyotr Ilyich Tchaikovsky	M. Plisetskaya, E. Evdokimov, and A. Shvachkin
MCS	Pyotr Ilyich Tchaikovsky	
MCS	Edvard Grieg	
MMH		
BB	folk music	
BB	folk music	
BB	no music	
MCS		
MCS		

(continued)

Year of First Performance	English Title	Original Russian Title	Type of Work
1939	Baba-Yaga	Баба-яга	miniature
1939	Monument	Памятник	miniature
1940	Gypsies	Цыганы	miniature
1940	The Bird and the Hunter	Птица и охотник	miniature
1940	Turkmen Djigites Dances	Танцы туркменских джигитов	miniature
1940	Ak-Shikly	Ак-шикли	miniature
1941	Shurale	Шурале	ballet
1941	The Concert of Political Cartoons: 1. Twins; 2. Back and Forth; 3. World Class Football Players; 4. Friendship Hitler Style; 5. Four Gs; 6. Two Napoleons	Концертное отделение политических шаржей: 1. Двойники; 2. Туда и обратно; 3. Футболист мирового класса; 4. Дружба по-гитлеровски; 5. Четыре "Г"; 6. Два Наполеона.	miniature
1941	Clown Dances	Клоунада	miniature
1941	Seven Cavaliers Serenade	Серенада семи кавалеров	miniature
1941	The Blind Girl	Слепая	miniature
1941	Spanish Dance	Испанский танец	miniature
1941	Navarra	Наварра	miniature
1942	Waltz	Вальс	miniature
1942	Creole Dance	Креольский танец	miniature
1942	Choreographic Étude	Хореографический этюд	miniature
1943	Devil's Dance	Бесовская пляска	miniature
1943	Poem of Ecstasy	Поэма экстаза	miniature
1943	Barcarole	Баркаролла	miniature
1943	Russian Farcical Dance	Русская шуточная	miniature

Ballet Company	Composer	Performers and Designers
ATG		
ATG		
BB	Sergei Rachmaninoff	O. Lepeshinskaya, P. Gusev, M. Gabovich
MCS	Edvard Grieg	R. Struchkova
AT	folk music	
AT	folk music	
DT	Farid Yarullin	N. Baltacheyeva, A. Kumïsnikov, K. Rïlova, B. Aktyamov, T. Baltacheyev. Designers: L. Yakobson and A. Fayzi
BB	Alexander Mosolov (*Twins*), E. Petunin (*Back and Forth*), Vladimir Enke (*World Class Football Players*), Vladimir Enke (*Friendship Hitler Style*), E. Petunin (*Four Gs*)	G. Farmanyants (*World Class Football Players*), O. Lepeshinskaya, A. Shvachkin, P. Gusev, A. Radunsky (*Four Gs*), I. Stetsky, N. Simachev (*Two Napoleons*)
MCS		V. Ryabtsev and students of Moscow Choreographic School
BB	Vladimir Enke	
BB	Lily Pons – Jascha Heifetz	O. Lepeshinksaya and P. Gusev
BB	Isaac Albéniz	Y. Sangovich, B. Borisov
BB	Isaac Albéniz	A. Bank, S. Koren, and others
KB	Johann Strauss	L. Voyshnis, B. Bruskin, V. Bogdanov
KB	Enrique Granados	I. Pevzner and I. Belsky
KB	Maurice Ravel	
KB	Farid Yarullin	T. Vecheslova, N. Zubkovsky and others
KB	Alexander Scriabin	T. Vecheslova, N. Zubkovsky, S. Kaplan
KB		A. Shelest, and others
LCS		

(continued)

Year of First Performance	English Title	Original Russian Title	Type of Work
12/7/1944	Romeo and Juliet	Ромео и Джульетта	ballet
1944	Spanish Capriccio	Испанское каприччио	ballet
1944	Hungarian Gypsy Dance	Венгеро-цыганский танец	miniature
1944	Creole Dance	Креольский танец	miniature
1944	Polo	Поло	miniature
1945	Waltz	Вальс	miniature
6/26/1946	The Stone Guest	Каменный гость	ballet
1946	Little Spanish Boys	Маленькие испанцы	miniature
1946	Alborada	Альборада	miniature
1946	Sea Suite	Морская сюита	miniature
1946	Antique Legend	Античная легенда	miniature
1/5/1946	The Orleans Virgin	Орлеанская дева	dances in opera
11/24/1946	In Winter Night	В зимнюю ночь	dances in operetta
1947	The Dragon Fly	Стрекоза	ballet
1947	Pulcinella	Полишинель	miniature
1947	Sentimental Waltz	Сентиментальный вальс	miniature
1947	Fantasia	Фантазия	miniature
1947	A Shoe	Туфелька	miniature
1947	Zoya	Зоя	miniature
1948	Waltz	Вальс	miniature
1948	Sports Suite	Спортивная сюита	miniature
1948	Heroic Deed	Подвиг	miniature
1948	Diamond Waltz	Вальс "Бриллиант"	miniature
1948	Étude	Этюд	miniature
1948	Khorumi	Хоруми	miniature
1948	The Pioneer Dance	Пионерская	miniature
1948	Polonaise and Mazurka	Полонез и мазурка	miniature
1948	Youth	Юность	miniature
1949	Mazurka	Мазурка	miniature

Ballet Company	Composer	Performers and Designers
LCS	Pyotr Ilyich Tchaikovsky	N. Petrova, V. Ukhov, Y. Druzhinin, M. Kamaletdinov. Designer: T. Bruni
LCS	Nikolai Rimsky-Korsakov	I Utretskaya, T. Baltacheyev, Y. Druzhinin, M. Kamaletdinov, E. Mikhasev, L. Kaplunov. Designer: T. Bruni
KB	Johannes Brahms	I. Pevzner and I. Belsky
KB	Manuel de Falla	I. Pevzner and I. Belsky
KB	Manuel de Falla	S. Padve and A. Shelepov
KB	Johann Strauss	F. Balabina and K. Sergeyev
LCS	Mikhail Glinka – Boris Asafyev	Kh. Mustayev, Y. Myachin, A. Miretsky, E. Petrova, V. Panova, I. Gensler. Designer: V. Boriskovitch
LCS	O. Zabotkina, L. Kaplunov, E. Mikhasev	
KB	Maurice Ravel	N. Dudinskaya, I. Belsky, and others
LR		
BB	Franz Liszt	
KT	Pyotr Ilyich Tchaikovsky	Designer: V. Dmitriyev
LMCT	Ivan Dzerzhinsky	Designer: V. Rïndin
LCS	Yuriy Efimov	O. Zabotkina, E. Mikhasev, Y. Umrikhin
KB	Sergei Rachmaninoff	K. Sergeyev
KB	Pyotr Ilyich Tchaikovsky	N. Dudinskaya and K. Sergeyev
BB	Sergei Taneyev	O. Lepeshinskaya and V. Preobrazhensky
BB	Krzysztof Penderecki	O. Lepeshinskaya and V. Preobrazhensky
IDS		Elena Terentyeva
MCS	Pyotr Ilyich Tchaikovsky	
MCS		
IDS	Frédéric Chopin	E. Terentyeva, Vashentsova, M. Mïsovskaya
IDS	Frédéric Chopin	
IDS	Alexander Scriabin	
LCS	folk music	
LCS		
LR		
LCS	Pyotr Ilyich Tchaikovsky	
MCS	Frédéric Chopin	E. Kosterina and A. Zaytsev

(continued)

Year of First Performance	English Title	Original Russian Title	Type of Work
1949	Joke	Шутка	miniature
1949	The Gossips	Кумушки	miniature
1949/1958	Jewish Dance	Еврейский танец	miniature
1949	Wedding Dance	Лагодна (Свадебная)	miniature
1950	Two Spanish Girls	Две испанки	miniature
1950	Bacchanalia	Вакханалия	miniature
1950	Youth Suite	Молодежная сюита	miniature
12/31/1950	Jack Frost	Морозко	dances in opera
5/30/1950	Ali-Batïr (later: Shurale)	Шурале (Али-Батыр)	ballet
1951	Dream	Мечта	miniature
1951	Krakowiak	Краковяк	miniature
9/4/1951	Mediterranean Sea Is Whirring	Шумит Средиземное море	dances in operetta
1951	Czardas	Чардаш	miniature
2/26/1952	Spanish Capriccio	Испанское каприччио	ballet
12/25/1952	Solveig	Сольвейг	ballet
1953	Sports Suite	Спортивная сюита	miniature
1953	Mexican Dance	Мексиканский танец	miniature
1953	Russian Dance Suite	Русская танцевальная сюита	miniature
1954	Vienna Waltz	Венский вальс	miniature
1955	Vagrant	Бродяжка	miniature
1/29/1955	Shurale	Шурале	ballet
12/27/1956	Spartacus	Спартак	ballet
1957	Rickshaw	Рикша	miniature
1957	The Dying Gaul	Умирающий галл	miniature

Ballet Company	Composer	Performers and Designers
MCS	Pyotr Ilyich Tchaikovsky	M. Girvyanenko and M. Borisov
KDE	Shiko Aranov	L. Panfili, G. Samusenko, V. Rïzhikova, E. Romanova, E. Shibinskaya
KDE	folk music	
KDE	folk music	
KB	Maurice Ravel	I. Pevzner and L. Voyshnis
LCO	Franz Liszt	
LR	Pyotr Ilyich Tchaikovsky	
MTOB	Mikhail Krasev	Designers: I. and L. Korotkov
KB	Farid Yarullin	N. Dudinskaya, A. Shelest, A. Makarov, K. Sergeyev, B. Bregvadze, I. Belsky, R. Gerbek. Designers: A. Ptushko and L. Milchin
LCS	Franz Liszt	I. Kolpakova and Yu. Maltsev
LR	Polish folk music	
LMCT	Oskar Feltsman	Designer: A. Tïshler
LR	Johannes Brahms	
MTOB	Nikolai Rimsky-Korsakov	Set design: N. Akimov. Costumes: T. Bruni
MTOB	Edvard Grieg – Boris Asafyev—Evgeniy Kornblit	V. Stankevich, M. Darovskaya, N. Morozov. Designers: V. Khodasevich, P. Shterich, V. Kuper
LCS	Andrey Petrov	
LCO		A. Kim and Sh. Lauri
LR		
KB	Richard Strauss	N. Kurgapkina and B. Bregvadze
KB	Claude Debussy	I. Pevzner
BB	Farid Yarullin	M. Plisetskaya, Y. Kondratov, Y. Gofman, M. Kondratyeva, V. Levashev, V. Meshkovsky. Designer: L. Milchin
KB	Aram Khachaturian	A. Makarov, A. Shelest, B. Bregvadze, O. Moiseyeva, N. Petrova, I. Zubkovskaya, B. Shavrov, I. Belsky, A. Sapogov, M. Mikhaylov, and others. Designers: N. Volkov and V. Khodasevich
KB	no music	Y. Druzhinin
KB	no music	Yu. Maltsev

(continued)

Year of First Performance	English Title	Original Russian Title	Type of Work
1957	Two Comrades	Два товарища	miniature
1958	Choreographic Miniatures (programme) 1. Last Song; 2. Skaters; 3. Troika; 4. Encounter; 5. Stronger than Death; 6. Snow Maiden; 7. Prometheus; 8. Mother; 9. Toady; 10., 11., 12. Rodin Triptych: Eternal Spring; The Kiss; Eternal Idol.	Хореографические миниатюры: 1. Последняя песнь; 2. Конькобежцы; 3. Тройка; 4. Встреча; 5. Сильнее смерти; 6. Снегурочка; 7. Прометей; 8. Мать; 9. Подхалим; 10., 11., 12. Триптих на темы Родена : Вечная весна; Поцелуй; Вечный идол.	miniature
1958	Acrobatic Étude	Акробатический этюд	miniature
1959	The Absinthe Lover	Любительница абсента	miniature

Ballet Company	Composer	Performers and Designers
KB	Vladimir Tsïtovich	E. Mikhasev and V. Umrikhin
KB	1. Maurice Ravel (*Last Song*); 2. Boris Kravchenko (*Skaters*); 3. Igor Stravinsky (*Troika*); 4. Boris Kravchenko (*Encounter*); 5. Isaak Shvarts (*Stronger than Death*); 6. Sergei Prokofiev (*Snow Maiden*); 7. Vladimir Tsïtovich (*Prometheus*); 8. Alexander Scriabin (*Mother*); 9. Vladimir Tsïtovich (*Toady*); 10., 11., 12. Claude Debussy (*Rodin Triptych: Eternal Spring; The Kiss; Eternal Idol*).	1. Ninel Petrova (*Last Song*); 2. Lyubov Voyshnis, Igor Chernïshov, Gennadiy Selyutsky, later Ninel Kurgapkina, Nonna Yastrebova, Yuri Solovyov, Sergey Vikulov (*Skaters*); 3. Irina Gensler, Iraida Utreskaya, Olga Zabotkina and Anatoliy Gridin, later Viktoriya Potyomkina, Igor Belsky (*Troika*); 4. Lyubov Voyshnis and Yuri Maltsev, later Kaleriya Fedicheva, Nonna Zvonaryova (*Encounter*); 5. Anatoliy Gridin, Yuri Maltsev, and Igor Chernïshov, later Igor Belsky, Anatoliy Sapogov, Yuri Egupov, Aleksandr Gribov (*Stronger than Death*); 6. Irina Kolpakova, later Emma Minchonok, Galina Kekisheva, Alla Sizova (*Snow Maiden*); 7. Alla Osipenko and Askold Makarov, later Igor Chernïshov (*Prometheus*); 8. Olga Moiseyeva, later Lyubov Voyshnis, Galina Ivanova (*Mother*); 9. Konstantin Rassadin (*Toady*); 10., 11., 12. Ninel Petrova and Anatoliy Nisnevich, later Irina Kolpakova, Nonna Yastrebova, Natalya Bolshakova, Elena Evteyeva, Konstantin Shatilov, Sergey Vikulov, Mikhail Baryshnikov (*Rodin Triptych: The Eternal Spring*); Alla Osipenko and Vsevolod Ukhov, later Alla Shelest, Natalia Makarova, Anatoliy Nisnevich, Aleksandr Gribov, Nikita Dolgushin (*The Kiss*); Alla Shelest and Igor Chernïshov, later Inna Zubkovskaya, Olga Moiseyeva, Margarita Alfimova, Svyatoslav Kuznetsov, Igor Uksusnikov (*Eternal Idol*). Designers: Simon Virsaladze and Tatyana Bruni
LCO		V. Skvortsova and N. Sïray
KB	Dmitriy Shostakovich	N. Dudinskaya

(continued)

Year of First Performance	English Title	Original Russian Title	Type of Work
1959	Vagabonds	Бродяжки	miniature
1960	The Flying Waltz	Полетный вальс	miniature
4/4/1962	Spartacus (new version)	Спартак	ballet
6/24/1962	The Bedbug	Клоп	ballet
7/12/1963	Love Novellas (Ravel's Waltzes)	Новеллы любви («Вальсы Равеля»)	miniature (programme)
12/31/1964	The Twelve	Двенадцать	ballet
1964	Choreographic Picture on the Motives of the Bidstrup Cartoons	Хореографическая картинка по мотивам карикатур Бидструпа	miniature
1964	Firebird	Жар-птица	miniature
1964	Jester and Merchant	Шут и купец	miniature
1964	Minotaur	Минотавр	miniature
1964	Despair	Отчаяние	miniature
1965	Baba-Yaga	Баба-яга	miniature
1965	The Carters' Dance	Танец ломовых	miniature
1965	Matryoshkas	Матрёшки	miniature
1965	Naughty Women	Озорные бабы	miniature
1967	The Land of Miracles	Страна чудес	ballet
1967	The Passing Beauty	Проходящая красотка	miniature
1967	Confessing Magdalene	Кающаяся Магдалина	miniature
1969	The Snow Queen	Снежная королева	miniature
1969	The Village Don Juan	Деревенский Дон Жуан	miniature
1969	Vestris	Вестрис	miniature
7/7/1971	Exercise XX	Экзерсис XX века	miniature

Ballet Company	Composer	Performers and Designers
KB	Oleg Karavaychuk	I. Pevzner and A. Mironov
KB	Dmitriy Shostakovich	A. Sizova and R. Nureyev
BB	Aram Khachaturian	D. Begak, M. Plisetskaya, A. Radunsky, N. Rïzhenko. Designers: V. Rïndin and V. Klementyev
KB	Oleg Karavaychuk (under the pseudonym F. Otkazov) and Georgiy Firtich	A. Makarov, K. Rassadin, N. Makarova, N. Zvonareva. Designers: A. Goncharov, F. Zbarsky, B. Messerer, T. Selvinskaya
KB	Maurice Ravel	
KB	Boris Tishchenko	I. Chernïshov, N. Zvonareva, I. Uksusnikov. Designer: E. Stenberg
LCS	Sergei Banevich	
LCO	Igor Stravinsky	
KB	Sergei Prokofiev	A. Livshits and V. Voynov
KB	Sergei Slonimsky	E. Minchenok and Yu. Maltsev
KB	Sergei Prokofiev	A. Kashirina, I. Bazhenova, E. Shcherbakov
KB	Modest Mussorgsky	A. Livshits
KB	Dmitriy Shostakovich	Yu. Maltsev and V. Voynov
KB	Alexander Dargomyzhsky	
KB	Rodion Shchedrin	I. Gensler and others
KB	Isaak Shvarts	
KB	Sergei Slonimsky	N. Makarova, V. Lopukhov, and V. Ponomaryov
KB	Alexander Knayfel	K. Fedicheva and V. Ponomaryov
KB	Edvard Grieg	
KB	Yuriy Zaritskiy	
KB	Gennadiy Banshchikov	Mikhail Baryshnikov
CM	Johann Sebastian Bach (The Swingle Singers)	Alla Osipenko (Adagio, Duet, Tango)

(continued)

Year of First Performance	English Title	Original Russian Title	Type of Work
1971	Contrasts	Контрасты	miniature
1971	Travelling Circus	Бродячий цирк	miniature
1971	Jewish Wedding (Wedding Cortège)	Еврейская свадьба (Свадебный кортеж)	miniature
1971	Ebony Concerto	Негритянский концерт	miniature
1971	Rodin Sculptures: 1. Eternal Spring (1958); 2. Kiss (1958); 3. Eternal Idol (1958); 4. Despair (1962); 5. Paolo and Francesca; 6. Minotaur and Nymph (1962); 7. Extase; 8. The Crumpled Lily	Скульптуры Родена - 1. Вечная весна (1958); 2. Поцелуй (1958); 3. Вечный идол (1958); 4. Отчаяние (1962); 5. Паоло и Франческа; 6. Минотавр и нимфа (1962); 7. Экстаз; 8. Измятая лилия.	miniature (programme)
1971	Classicism-Romanticism: 1. Pas de Trois; 2. Medieval Dance with Kisses; 3. The Swan; 4. Pas de Quatre; 5. Cachucha; 6. Pas de Deux; 7. Taglioni's Flight	Классицизм – романтизм: 1. Па-де-труа; 2. Средневековый танец с поцелуями; 3. Умирающий лебедь; 4. Па-де-катр; 5. Качуча; 6. Па-де-де; 7. Полёт Тальони.	miniature (programme)
1971	Russian Miniatures: 1. The Dead Princess; 2. Firebird; 3. Troika; 4. The Snow Maiden; 5. Baba-Yaga	Русские миниатюры: 1. Мертвая царевна; 2. Жар-птица; 3. Тройка; 4. Снегурочка; 5. Баба-яга.	miniature (programme)

Ballet Company	Composer	Performers and Designers
CM	Igor Stravinsky	
CM	Igor Stravinsky	
CM	Dmitriy Shostakovich	Designer: Valery Levental
CM	Igor Stravinsky	
CM	1. Claude Debussy (*Eternal Spring*); 2. Claude Debussy (*Kiss*); 3. Claude Debussy (*Eternal Idol*); 4. Sergei Prokofiev (*Despair*); 5. Alban Berg (*Paolo and Francesca*); 6. Alban Berg (*Minotaur and Nymph*); 7. Sergei Prokofiev (*Extase*); 8. Anton Webern (*The Crumpled Lily*).	Alla Osipenko (*Minotaur and Nymph*)
CM	1. Gioachino Rossini (*Pas de Trois*); 2. Sergei Prokofiev (*Medieval Dance with Kisses*); 3. Camille Saint-Saëns (*The Swan*); 4. Vincenzo Bellini (*Pas de Quatre*); 5. Pablo de Sarasate (*Cachucha*); 6. Wolfgang Amadeus Mozart (*Pas de Deux*); 7. Wolfgang Amadeus Mozart (*Taglioni's Flight*)	
CM	1. Igor Stravinsky (*The Dead Princess*); 2. Igor Stravinsky (*Firebird*); 3. Igor Stravinsky (*Troika*); 4. Sergei Prokofiev (*The Snow Maiden*); 5. Modest Mussorgsky (*Baba-Yaga*)	Alla Osipenko (*Firebird*)

(*continued*)

Year of First Performance	English Title	Original Russian Title	Type of Work
1972	The City	Город	miniature
1972	Symphony of Eternity	Симфония бессмертия	miniature
1973	Brilliant Divertissement	Блестящий дивертисмент	miniature
?	Menuet	Менуэт	miniature
?	Sextet	Секстет	miniature
?	Female Variations	Женские вариации	miniature
?	Male Variations	Мужские вариации	miniature
1973	Mozartiana	Моцартиана	miniature
1973	Six Pas de Deux	Шесть па-де-де	miniature (programme)
1974	The Bedbug	Клоп	ballet
1974	Surprise	Сюрприз	miniature
1975	Ecstasy	Экстаз	miniature
1975	The Cowboys	Ковбои	miniature
1979 (staged 1963/64)	Hiroshima	Хиросима	miniature
1985 (staged 1971/72)	Distraught Dictator	Обезумевший диктатор	miniature

Note: The following abbreviations have been used for ballet companies: AT: Ashkhabad Theater, Ashkhabad; ATG: Artek Theater, Gurzuf (Crimea); BB: Bolshoi Ballet, Moscow; CM: Choreographic Miniatures, Leningrad; DT: Dzhalil Theater (Tatar Academic State Theater for Opera and Ballet), Kazan; EHSA: Experimental Studio of the House of Arts, Leningrad; IDS: Isadora Duncan Studio, Moscow; KB: Kirov Ballet, Leningrad; KDE: Kishinev Dance Ensemble; KFFE: Kronstadt Fleet Folk Ensemble; KT: Kirov Theater, Leningrad; LCO: Leningrad Concert Organization; LCS: Leningrad Choreographic School/Institute; LMCT: Leningrad Musical Comedy Theater; LR: Vocal and Dance Ensemble of the Leningrad Municipal Administration of Labor Reserves; MCS: Moscow Choreographic School; MMH: Moscow Music Hall; MTOB: Maly Theater for Opera and Ballet, Leningrad; SCS: Sverdlovsk Choreographic School; STOB: Sverdlovsk Theater for Opera and Ballet. *Vestris* was performed at the International Ballet Competition in Moscow.

Ballet Company	Composer	Performers and Designers
CM	Anton Webern	
CM	Boris Tishchenko	
CM	Mikhail Glinka (based on Vincenzo Bellini's opera *La sonnambula*)	Alla Osipenko
CM	Wolfgang Amadeus Mozart	
CM	Wolfgang Amadeus Mozart	
CM	Wolfgang Amadeus Mozart	
CM	Wolfgang Amadeus Mozart	
CM	Wolfgang Amadeus Mozart	
CM	Gioachino Rossini, Gaetano Donizetti, Franz Lehár, Benjamin Britten, Arthur Honegger, and Frédéric Chopin	
CM	Dmitriy Shostakovich	
CM	Joseph Haydn	
CM	Sergei Prokofiev	
KB	Timur Kogan	Gabriela Komleva, Konstantin Zaklinskiy
CM	Henryk Górecki	
CM	Dmitriy Shostakovich	

Notes

Introduction

1. Ralph Parker, "At the Bolshoi," *S. Hurok Presents the Bolshoi Ballet* (New York: Hurok Concerts, 1962), n.p.
2. Simon Shuster, "Raising the Barre: Moscow's Bolshoi Theatre Gets a $700 Million Makeover," *Time,* October 29, 2011.
3. *Danse d'école* refers to the pure academic style of classical ballet founded on the principles laid down by Beauchamps, Blasis, and subsequent teachers.

Chapter One. Ballet and Power

Epigraph: Boris Lvov-Anokhin, *O balete* (On ballet), TV documentary, Central Television of the USSR, 1962, Yakobson Collection, Special Collections and University Archives, Stanford University.

1. According to Irina Yakobson, the choreographer's widow, it was common for correspondents to freely enter dancers' dressing rooms prior to their appearances onstage

and also customary for Yakobson to be backstage doing a final brush-up with Baryshnikov. Irina Yakobson, interview with Janice Ross, November 4, 2011, Haifa, Israel, unpublished data in author's possession.

2. Yuri Slezkine, *The Jewish Century* (Princeton, N.J.: Princeton University Press, 2004), 286.

3. Mikhail Baryshnikov, interview with Janice Ross, February 1, 2014, Berkeley, CA, unpublished data in author's possession.

4. See Julie Kavanagh, *Nureyev: The Life* (New York: Pantheon, 2007), 417.

5. Joan Acocella, *Twenty-Eight Artists and Two Saints: Essays* (New York: Pantheon, 2007), 275.

6. "Baryshnikov's short stature, clear full musculature, and boyish features gave evidence that he would become a demi caractère dancer, yet his exceptional technical prowess and unwavering control gave strong promise of the elegance and serenity that mark the danseur noble." See Robert Greskovic in Selma Jeanne Cohen, *International Encyclopedia of Dance,* vol. 1 (New York: Oxford University Press, 2004), 371.

7. "Dancers are sorted by physique, style, and temperament into certain kinds of roles and remain there for the rest of their careers." Acocella, *Twenty-Eight Artists,* 275.

8. Irina Yakobson, interview with Janice Ross, May 14, 1999, San Francisco, CA, unpublished data in author's possession.

9. M. Baryshnikov, interview with Janice Ross, February 1, 2014, Berkeley, CA, unpublished data in author's possession.

10. Jean Georges Noverre, *Letters on Dancing and Ballets,* trans. Cyril W. Beaumont (Brooklyn, NY: Dance Horizons, 1966), 78, 98.

11. Tatyana Bruni's costume sketches for *Vestris* are in the A. A. Bakhrushin State Central Theatre Museum, Moscow.

12. Helgi Tomasson, interview with Janice Ross, May 11, 1999, San Francisco, CA, unpublished data in author's possession.

13. Natalia Makarova, *A Dance Autobiography* (New York: Knopf, 1979), 56.

14. Baryshnikov interview, February 1, 2014.

15. Irina Yakobson, interview with Janice Ross, November 1, 2011, Haifa, Israel, unpublished data in author's possession.

16. Quoted in Louis Rapoport, *Stalin's War against the Jews: The Doctors' Plot and the Soviet Solution* (New York: Free Press, 1990), 253.

17. Ibid., 87.

18. Susan Tumarkin Goodman, *Chagall and the Artists of the Russian Jewish Theater* (New York: Jewish Museum, 2008), 170.

19. In his 1976 book *Baryshnikov at Work,* Baryshnikov reported that Yakobson was engaged in response to the dancer's own "insistence" on Yakobson. Baryshnikov, *Baryshnikov at Work: Mikhail Baryshnikov Discusses His Roles* (New York: Knopf,

1976), 111. Yakobson's widow, however, disputes this, saying it was the Kirov authorities who approached Yakobson on their own and that given Baryshnikov's stature as a new member of the Kirov he would not have likely had the authority to specify Yakobson (I. Yakobson, phone interview with Janice Ross, April 6, 2014, unpublished data in author's possession). Indeed in 1984, Nina Alovert quoted Baryshnikov as saying, "It was a wonderful opportunity for me that the theater management invited Leonid Veniaminovich Yakobson to stage the contemporary short ballet required for the competition, because he is famous for working in this genre." Nina Alovert, *Baryshnikov in Russia* (New York: Holt, Rinehart, and Winston, 1984), 200.

20. I. Yakobson interview, November 1, 2011.

21. Irina Yakobson, interview with Janice Ross, May 5, 1993, San Francisco, CA, unpublished data in author's possession. She reported that the party commissioners complained the ballet was not classical, not traditional, and it had a part about an old man who dies. It was also considered very erotic and thus they pronounced it not appropriate for the Kirov.

22. Christina Ezrahi, *Swans of the Kremlin: Ballet and Power in Soviet Russia* (Pittsburgh: University of Pittsburgh Press, 2012), 30.

23. Miklós Haraszti, *The Velvet Prison: Artists under State Socialism* (New York: Basic Books, 1987), 40.

24. Ibid., 68, 78.

25. Ibid., 102.

26. Leonid Yakobson, handwritten planning notes for *Vestris,* 1967, Yakobson collection, file 87-1-174, p. 6, Central State Archive for Literature and the Arts, Saint Petersburg.

27. This shift away from religion to art as a moral teacher in Russia actually extends back three centuries earlier to Peter the Great (1672–1725), who was criticized for subordinating the church to the state and for the shift toward the secularization of Russia's cultural life. This gives a historical context to Lenin's "art for the people" decree where the arts function deliberately as a replacement for religion. Lenin wanted this not because of a desire to render Russia more European, as had been one of Peter's motivations, but pragmatically because he viewed the arts as a propagandistic means. This suggests why Lenin's formulation of the arts as a means of propaganda also opened the door for them to be turned against themselves and used as a protest medium by artists. The Soviet state had previously designated the arts as a leading channel of information in Soviet life, so for Yakobson his medium was already politically charged before he ever entered the studio to begin work. For Sorokin's comment, see Vladimir Sorokin, "Ilya Kabakov and Vladimir Sorokin—A Conceptual Dialogue," panel discussion on Russian dissident art convened by Nariman Skakov, Stanford Humanities Center, Stanford University, October 26, 2011.

28. Ibid. From notes in author's possession.

29. Kavanagh, *Nureyev*, 417.

30. *Cultural Policy in the Russian Federation* (Strasbourg: Council of Europe Publishing, 1997), 40.

31. Jennifer Homans, *Apollo's Angels: A History of Ballet* (New York: Random House, 2010), 122.

32. When he retired and became a ballet master, Auguste Vestris used to coach dancers to deliver his all-out approach to ballet performance with the following encouragement about going to dramatic extremes: "Be coquettish, give to your every movement the greatest liberty possible. Before and after each pas, you must inspire love; everyone in the parterre and the orchestra must want you in his bed." Mindy Aloff, *Dance Anecdotes: Stories from the Worlds of Ballet, Broadway, the Ballroom, and Modern Dance* (New York: Oxford University Press, 2006), 1. This is an injunction to dramatic intensity and seduction of the viewer, one that Yakobson's own shaping of Baryshnikov's portrayal in the dressing room coaching session reproduces.

33. Baryshnikov, *Baryshnikov at Work*, 112.

34. Matthew Cullerne Bown, *Art under Stalin* (New York: Holmes & Meier, 1991), 91.

35. Dmitri Shostakovich, *Testimony: The Memoirs of Dmitri Shostakovich as Related to and Edited by Solomon Volkov*, trans. Antonina W. Bouis (New York: Limelight Editions, 1984), xiv. (Note that the accuracy of Volkov's text has been a matter of dispute among some musicologists.)

36. Alexander Bratersky, "Yeltsin Ally Saw 'Swan Lake' as Call to Arms," *Moscow Times*, August 19, 2011, http://www.themoscowtimes.com/news/article/yeltsin-ally-saw-swan-lake-as-call-to-arms/442318.html (accessed November 25, 2013); Lt. General Brent Scowcroft, interview with Svetlana Babaeva, "How the United States Slept While the Soviet Union Crashed," *RIA Novosti*, August, 19, 2011, http://en.ria.ru/analysis/20110819/165923872.html (accessed November 25, 2013); Natalya Bubnova, "Feting a Failed Coup and Those Who Resisted," *Moscow Times*, August 18, 2011, http://www.themoscowtimes.com/opinion/article/feting-a-failed-coup-and-those-who-resisted/442242.html (accessed November 25, 2013); Gideon Weinbaum, interview with Estelle Winters, "Two Decades On It's Just a Great Place to Be!," *Voice of Russia*, August, 19, 2011, http://voiceofrussia.com/radio_broadcast/2249329/54885454/ (accessed November 25, 2013).

37. Jim Heintz, "Soviet Coup Anniversary Quietly Marked in Russia," *Yahoo! News*, August 19, 2011, http://news.yahoo.com/soviet-coup-anniversary-quietly-marked-russia-115037134.html (accessed November 25, 2013).

38. "Russia: Mir i Druzhba," *Time*, August 10, 1959.

39. Homans, *Apollo's Angels*, 342.

40. Faubion Bowers, *Broadway, U.S.S.R. Ballet, Theatre and Entertainment in Russia Today* (New York: Thomas Nelson & Sons, 1959), 32–33.

41. Sergei Filatov, in Bratersky, "Yeltsin Ally Saw 'Swan Lake' as Call to Arms."

42. J. Michael Lyons, "Baltics Mark Moscow Coup Anniversary," *Baltic Times,* August 23, 2001, http://www.baltictimes.com/news/articles/5350/#.Ux3lKV5kJe4 (accessed November 25, 2013).

43. Solomon Volkov, *Balanchine's Tchaikovsky: Interviews with George Balanchine,* trans. Antonina W. Bouis (New York: Simon and Schuster, 1985), 12.

44. Benedict Anderson, "Cultural Roots," *Imagined Communities: Reflections on the Origin and Spread of Nationalism* (London: Verso, 2006), 9–36.

45. Roland John Wiley, *Tchaikovsky's Ballets: Swan Lake, Sleeping Beauty, Nutcracker* (Oxford, Eng.: Clarendon Press, 1985), 64.

46. Ibid., 213. Taken by themselves, the individual steps for the corps in *Swan Lake* are simple. Wiley similarly describes the ensemble choreography in another dance passage for the corps that Ivanov choreographed to Tchaikovsky—the *Waltz of the Snowflakes* in *The Nutcracker.*

47. Deborah Jowitt, *Time and the Dancing Image* (New York: W. Morrow, 1988), 242–243.

48. Tim Scholl, *Sleeping Beauty: A Legend in Progress* (New Haven: Yale University Press, 2004), 68.

49. Quoted in Wiley, *Tchaikovsky's Ballets,* 80.

50. Laurie Nussdorfer, review of *Dance as Text: Ideologies of the Baroque Body,* by Mark Franko, *Dance Research Journal* 27, no. 1 (Spring 1995): 41–43. Note that Franko calls the dances of 1580–1660 baroque instead of periodizing it 1660–1750 as dance historians have traditionally done. The practice of spelling out words, for example, in the textual French Valois court dances stretches back into the 1500s.

51. The theatrical spaces in which opera and ballet were performed during the reigns of Louis XIV and Louis XV, and before that in the equestrian ballets of Louis XIII, suggest that this unison movement of the corps—whereby a quasi-militaristic discipline is used to deliver a gracefully intricate stage picture—evolved to meet both practical and aesthetic needs. Music historian Barbara Coeyman posits that because it was initially the courtiers rather than professionals who performed in the danced ensembles of the prologues of court productions, their movements were likely less technical than those of the soloists and thus required less room per dancer—fitting into the limited available space. See Barbara Coeyman, "Theatres for Opera and Ballet during the Reigns of Louis XIV and Louis XV," *Early Music* 18, no. 1 (February 1990): 31. Coeyman's supposition might be expanded to include the idea that these restrictions could have led to simple actions, repeated in unison or even cascading canonical sequence, by these many performers of limited technical training, which then eventually became the corps de ballet's role. Multiple bodies thus could be a figurative vehicle for the experience of sovereignty (or nation) and their rhythmic uniformity a somatic reflection of ideology.

52. Other scholars, including Kate van Orden, have traced music's importance in promoting the absolutism that the French monarchy would fully embrace under Louis XIV, arguing that pressure on French noblemen to take up the life of the warrior gave rise to a genre of bellicose art forms such as sword dances and equestrian ballets. Far from being construed as effeminizing, such combinations of music and the martial arts were at once refined and masculine—a perfect way to display military prowess. The influence also flowed the other way and the incursion of music into riding schools and infantry drills contributed materially to disciplinary order, enabling the larger and more effective armies of the seventeenth century because of the practical and imaginative training provided by the movement arts. Kate van Orden, *Music, Discipline and Arms in Early Modern France* (Chicago: University of Chicago Press, 2005). This body and its maneuvering through carefully designed geometric and rhythmic group patterns minimized the lack of variety in the actual steps. André Levinson's critical dance writing from Paris in the 1920s traces how a design aesthetic evolved into a musical and choreographic one in baroque dance when he writes about a show of Jean Bérain's theatrical designs and observes that Bérain's theatrical costume design for Louis XIV "expresses the conventions of the court through the conventions of the theatre." See André Levinson, "Bérain and the French Costume Tradition," in Joan Acocella and Lynn Garafola, *André Levinson on Dance: Writings from Paris in the Twenties* (Hanover, NH: University Press of New England, 1991), 57. This theater, Levinson continues, was "aloof, abstract, removed to an heroic plane but splendidly human. Its dramatic style was marked by symmetry, rhythm, a musical and majestic prosody" (60). This idea of the heroic but splendidly human is the corps in its essence. We always see the individual and the mass simultaneously, just as with an orchestra one hears individual instruments and their blending.

53. Stephanie Schroedter, "The Practice of Dance at the Crossroad between Pragmatic Documentation, Artistic Creativity and Political Reflection: Sources of the Theatrical Dance of the Early Nineteenth Century," in Ann Cooper Albright, Dena Davida, and Sarah Davies Cordova, *Repenser pratique et théorie,* Proceedings, 30th Annual Conference of the Society of Dance History Scholars (Birmingham, AL: Society of Dance History Scholars, 2007), 508–514.

54. Arthur Saint-Léon, "Organisation des corps de ballet" [Organization of the ballet corps], in *De l'état actuel de la danse* [On the present state of dance] (Lisbon: Progresso, 1856), n.p.

55. William H. McNeill, *Keeping Together in Time: Dance and Drill in Human History* (Cambridge, MA: Harvard University Press, 1995), 116.

56. The evocation of the opposite of this harmony of the mass—the cacophony of the mob—has also been exemplified in early twentieth-century dance by a tight union of music and group choreography. One of the most vivid examples is the 1913 premiere of *Le Sacre du printemps* (*Vesna svyashchennaya*), where Vaslav Nijin-

sky's choreography for primal and percussive bodies pounding into the ground evoked, hand in hand with Igor Stravinsky's score, the alternately numbed and frenzied mass of civilization and its discontents. The chaos of the modern era, on the cusp of World War I, was signaled alternatively by the discord and the physical and emotional rigidity of the corps de ballet in tandem with Stravinsky's score—the effect was an inverse acoustic and visual image of social and civic disharmony. From a dance historical perspective *Sacre* is often cited as completing the rupture with classicism that Michel Fokine had initiated. It destroyed the equilibrium of his masses and what Lincoln Kirstein has called "the magic of gracious acrobatics in self-impelled movement." See Lincoln Kirstein, *Nijinsky Dancing* (New York: Knopf, 1975), 145. Ballets Russes scholar Lynn Garafola has noted of Nijinsky's choreography for *Sacre*, "Nijinsky created a biologic order that designed the body into both an instrument and object of mass oppression." Lynn Garafola, *Diaghilev's Ballets Russes* (New York: Oxford University Press, 1989), 69. This body is ordered yet pitiless—a killing machine without the softening grace of romantic music to take down its edges as Adolphe Adam's score does for the Wilis in act 2 of *Giselle,* muting their murdering rage. The roar of the corps in *Sacre* marked a turning point—a sustained image of the masses as a representation of chaos and *dis*equilibrium.

57. McNeill, *Keeping Together in Time,* 2.
58. Arlene Croce, *Afterimages* (New York: Knopf, 1977), 71.
59. Ibid.
60. Ibid.
61. Valery Panov and George Feifer, *To Dance* (New York: Knopf, 1978), 271.
62. Maya Plisetskaya, *I, Maya Plisetskaya,* trans. Antonina W. Bouis (New Haven: Yale University Press, 2001), 229.
63. *Cultural Policy in the Russian Federation,* 39.
64. Homans, *Apollo's Angels,* 248–249.
65. Vance Kepley, Jr., "Soviet Cinema and State Control: Lenin's Nationalization Decree Reconsidered," *Journal of Film and Video* 42, no. 2 (Summer 1990): 3.
66. Nikolay Aleksandrovich Lebedev, *Lenin, Stalin, partiia o kino* [Lenin, Stalin, the party on the cinema], 7, quoted in Kepley, "Soviet Cinema and State Control," *Journal of Film and Video* 42, no. 2 (Summer 1990): 6.
67. W. Bruce Lincoln, *Between Heaven and Hell: The Story of a Thousand Years of Artistic Life in Russia* (New York: Viking, 1998), 326.
68. Orlando Figes, *Natasha's Dance: A Cultural History of Russia* (London: Allen Lane, 2002), 450–451.
69. Ibid., 451.
70. Ironically Lenin himself became the personal subject of visual "saturation" when after his death the Committee for the Immortalization of Lenin's Memory oversaw plans for a proliferation of Lenin images, including his picture on ciga-

461

rette packages and toys. In 1926–1927 on a visit to Moscow, the German critic Walter Benjamin noticed these mass-produced images of Lenin next to newly made icons still for sale at street markets. Reading these side-by-side marketed images, Benjamin concluded presciently that Lenin might one day acquire the significance of a religious figure.

71. Mary Grace Swift, *The Art of the Dance in the USSR* (Notre Dame, IN: University of Notre Dame Press, 1968), 32.

72. Ibid., 37–38.

73. Ibid., 34.

74. Donald W. Treadgold, *The West in Russia and China: Religious and Secular Thought in Modern Times, 1582–1949* (Cambridge, Eng.: Cambridge University Press, 1973).

75. Elizabeth Souritz, *Soviet Choreographers in the 1920s,* trans. Lynn Visson (Durham, NC: Duke University Press, 1990), 319.

76. Ibid., 319.

77. Ibid., 320.

78. Robert Conquest, *The Great Terror: A Reassessment* (London: Pimlico, 2008), 447.

79. Nikita Sergeyevich Khrushchev, *Khrushchev Remembers,* trans. and ed. Strobe Talbott (Boston: Little, Brown, 1970), 497.

80. Figes, *Natasha's Dance,* 452.

81. Charles France, phone interview with Janice Ross, May 7, 1999, unpublished data in author's possession.

82. Ibid.

83. Baryshnikov, interview with Janice Ross, February 1, 2014, Berkeley, CA, unpublished data in author's possession.

84. Alovert, *Baryshnikov in Russia,* 9.

85. Vladislav Krasnov, *Soviet Defectors: The KGB Wanted List* (Stanford, CA: Hoover Institution Press, 1986), 158.

86. David Caute, *The Dancer Defects: The Struggle for Cultural Supremacy during the Cold War* (Oxford, Eng.: Oxford University Press, 2003), 5.

87. Henri Lefebvre, *Everyday Life in the Modern World,* trans. Sacha Rabinovitch (New York: Harper & Row, 1971), xi.

88. Natalia Makarova's *A Dance Autobiography* was published in 1979, and *Baryshnikov: From Russia to the West,* written by Gennady Smakov, was published in 1981.

89. Alovert, *Baryshnikov in Russia,* 7.

90. "At the museum on the first floor of the 250-year-old Vaganova Academy . . . a small corner of the museum has recently been allocated to photographs of Soviet émigrés and defectors, and alongside many images of Natalia Makarova, Mikhail Baryshnikov and Rudolph Nureyev is a single portrait of a young, pensive Balanchine." Toni Bentley, "Dancer to Dancer: First Encounters with Balanchine," *New York Times,* July 2, 1989, http://www.nytimes.com/1989/07/02/arts/dancer

-to-dancer-first-encounters-with-balanchine.html?pagewanted=all&src=pm (accessed November 26, 2013). "[Vinogradov] lamented, for example, that until this February, his dancers had never seen Natalia Makarova dance. Miss Makarova was a 30-year-old Kirov star when she defected to the West during a 1970 company tour in London." Esther B. Fein, "The Kirov Enters the World of Glasnost," *New York Times*, July 2, 1989, http://www.nytimes.com/1989/07/02/arts/the-kirov-enters-the-world-of-glasnost.html?pagewanted=all&src=pm (accessed November 26, 2013).

91. Susan Manning, *Modern Dance, Negro Dance: Race in Motion* (Minneapolis: University of Minnesota Press, 2004), xix.

92. Michael Rouland, "A Nation on Stage: Music and the 1936 Festival of Kazak Arts," in Neil Edmunds, *Soviet Music and Society under Lenin and Stalin: The Baton and Sickle* (London: RoutledgeCurzon, 2004), 181–200.

93. Ibid., 190–191.

94. Ibid., 188.

95. I. Yakobson interview, May 14, 1999.

96. Olga Levitan, interview with Janice Ross, November 30, 2010, Jerusalem, unpublished data in author's possession.

97. Quoted in Panov and Feifer, *To Dance*, 291.

98. Lincoln, *Between Heaven and Hell*, 420.

99. Irina Yakobson, interview with Janice Ross, October 30, 2010, Haifa, Israel, unpublished data in author's possession.

100. Askold Makarov, "Pervïe vstrechi s narodnïm geroem" [First meetings with the hero of the people], in Pyotr Andreyevich Gusev, *Muzïka i khoreografiya sovremennogo baleta* [The music and choreography of the contemporary ballet], vol. 1 (Leningrad: Muzïka, 1974), 220–221.

101. Sorokin, "Ilya Kabakov & Vladimir Sorokin—A Conceptual Dialogue." Novelist Vladimir Sorokin and conceptual visual artist Ilya Kabakov have both said that they believed at the time that the repression would never change.

102. Irina Yakobson, "Zhizn i sudba" [Life and fate], in Nataliya Zozulina, *Teatr Leonida Yakobsona: Stati Vospominaniya Fotomaterialï* [The theater of Leonid Yakobson: Articles, reminiscences, photographs] (Saint Petersburg: Liki Rossii, 2010), 15.

103. Quoted in Boris Lvov-Anokhin, "O Leonide Yakobsone" [On Leonid Yakobson], *Teatralnaya zhizn* 9, no. 738 (May 1989): 18.

104. Oleg Vinogradov, *Tribute to Leonid Yakobson*, Russian TV broadcast, 1991, Irina Yakobson Archives, Special Collections and University Archives, Stanford University.

105. Valeriy Zvezdochkin, "Provozvestnik novogo" [The harbinger of the new], n.d., http://www.russianballet.ru/dissertacii/dissertac4-5_09.html (accessed March 12, 2014).

106. Tatyana Kvasova, interview with Vladimir Golubin, "Vospominaniya o budushchem" [Recollections of the future], *Muzïkalnaya zhizn* 16, no. 786 (August 1990): 6.

107. Keith Money, *Anna Pavlova, Her Life and Art* (New York: Knopf, 1982), 71.

108. Homans, *Apollo's Angels*, 295.

109. Keith Money reports that "the exact provenance of *The Swan* is intriguingly uncertain," and notes the suggestion by (Bronislava) Nijinska that had he not become ill, Vaslav Nijinsky would have performed a pas de deux from *Swan Lake* at the gala and that the substitution of the Saint-Saëns piece was a last-minute necessity. Money, *Anna Pavlova*, 71.

110. Igor Kuzmin, interview with Vladimir Golubin, in "Vospominaniya o budushchem," 6.

111. Valentina Klimova, "Maksimalizm kak osoznannaya neobhodimost" [Maximalism as conscious necessity], in Zozulina, *Teatr Leonida Yakobsona*, 135.

112. Kuzmin interview in "Vospominaniya o budushchem," 6.

113. I. Yakobson interview, October 30, 2010.

114. John Chapman, "Auguste Vestris and the Expansion of Technique," *Dance Research Journal* 19, no. 1 (Summer 1987): 12.

115. Judith Butler, "Violence, Mourning, Politics," *Studies in Gender and Sexuality* 4, no. 1 (2003): 11.

Chapter Two. Beginnings

Epigraph: Boris Pasternak, *Doctor Zhivago*, trans. Max Hayward and Manya Harari (New York: Pantheon, 1957), 146.

1. League of Red Cross Societies, *Help Us to Restore These Children to Their Parents* (Geneva, 1920), 150–152; Zvi Gitelman, *Jewish Life after the USSR* (Bloomington: Indiana University Press, 2003).

2. Irina Yakobson, interview with Janice Ross, December 17, 2011, Hamburg, Germany, unpublished data in author's possession.

3. Ibid.

4. The name of the city changed three times, and I will refer to it by its proper title for the time period being referenced. From 1703 to 1914, Saint Petersburg; from 1914 to 1924, Petrograd; from 1924 to 1991, Leningrad; at present, Saint Petersburg.

5. I. Yakobson, "Zhizn i sudba" [Life and fate], in Nataliya Zozulina, *Teatr Leonida Yakobsona: Stati vospominaniya fotomateriali* [The theatre of Leonid Yakobson: Articles, reminiscences, photographs] (Saint Petersburg: Liki Rossii, 2010), 23.

6. The term "rootless cosmopolitan" (*bezrodniy kosmopolit*) referred mostly, but not explicitly, to Jewish intellectuals, as an accusation concerning their lack of patriotism, i.e., lack of full allegiance to the Soviet Union. The expression was first coined by Russian literary critic Vissarion Belinsky to describe writers who lacked (Russian) national character.

7. Christina Ezrahi, *Swans of the Kremlin: Ballet and Power in Soviet Russia* (Pittsburgh: University of Pittsburgh Press, 2012), 177.

8. Irina Yakobson, interview with Janice Ross, November 11, 2010, Haifa, Israel, unpublished data in author's possession.

9. Ibid.

10. Musya Glants, "Jewish Artists in Russian Art: Painting and Sculpture in the Soviet and Post-Soviet Eras," in Gitelman, *Jewish Life after the USSR,* 226.

11. Steven Zipperstein, *Imagining Russian Jewry: Memory, History, Identity* (Seattle: University of Washington Press, 1999), 82. Gitelman; introduction to *Jewish Life after the USSR,* 4.

12. Ibid., 3.

13. Orlando Figes, *Natasha's Dance: A Cultural History of Russia* (London: Allen Lane, 2002), 438.

14. Ibid., 439.

15. Jane Swan, "The Odyssey of the Lost Children," *Swarthmore College Bulletin* (May 1988): 10.

16. James Loeffler, *The Most Musical Nation: Jews and Culture in the Late Russian Empire* (New Haven: Yale University Press, 2010), 32.

17. The American Red Cross, *Report of the Department of Civilian Relief (Eastern Division)* (1919?), 2, Hoover Institution Library and Archives, Stanford University.

18. Ibid., 2.

19. Jane Swan, the second wife of Alfred Swan, who was a young teacher in Russia and also helped save the children, has written about her husband's role in *The Lost Children: A Russian Odyssey* (Carlisle, Pa.: South Mountain Press, 1989).

20. American Red Cross, *Report of the Department of Civilian Relief,* 3.

21. Floyd Miller, *The Wild Children of the Urals* (New York: Dutton, 1965), 83.

22. Ibid., 99–100.

23. Ibid., 101.

24. Ibid.

25. Ibid., 102.

26. Leonid Yakobson, notebooks, 1920, A. A. Bakhrushin State Central Theatre Museum, Moscow.

27. The American Red Cross, Sister Kourgouzoff, letter to Dr. Davison, June 21, 1920, 1 , 3, Hoover Institution Library and Archives, Stanford University.

28. Ibid., 3. Emphasis in the original.

29. Irina Yakobson, interview with Janice Ross, June 27, 2007, Hamburg, Germany, unpublished data in author's possession.

30. Swan, *Lost Children,* 148.

31. Leonid Yakobson, notebooks, 1920.

32. Swan, *Lost Children,* 134.

33. Irina Yakobson, interview with Janice Ross, November 8, 2010, Haifa, Israel, unpublished data in author's possession.

34. V. Bolshakov, "Zavershenie Odissei" [The end of the odyssey], *Pravda*, August 16, 1973, 6.
35. Miller, *The Wild Children*, 194–195, 212.
36. McKay Coulter, "The Odyssey of 1,000 Children," *American Medicine* 27 (April 1921): 198.
37. Swan, "The Odyssey," 15.
38. Galina Stolyarova, "New Book Recounts Children's Forgotten Civil War Odyssey," *St. Petersburg Times*, November 29, 2005, http://www.sptimes.ru/index.php?action_id=2&story_id=16221 (accessed December 3, 2013).
39. Ibid.
40. "City Children's Civil War Odyssey Rediscovered," *St. Petersburg Times*, December 28, 2004, http://sptimes.ru/index.php?action_id=2&story_id=2455 (accessed December 3, 2013).
41. *The Children's Ark by Vladimir Lipovetsky*, catalogue (Seefeld, Ger.: Nibbe & Wiedling Literary Agency, 2004), 11, http://www.nibbe-wiedling.de/docs/childrens_ark.pdf (accessed March 10, 2014).
42. Stolyarova, "New Book."
43. Yakobson, "Avtobiografiya" [Autobiography], September 17, 1953, Irina Yakobson's personal collection, unpublished data in author's possession.
44. V. Bolshakov, "Prodolzhenie odissei" [The odyssey continued], *Pravda*, April 1, 1973, 4; Bolshakov, "Zavershenie odissei," 6.
45. I. Yakobson interview, June 27, 2007.
46. "The Reunion of The Children's Colony in Leningrad," reminiscence from Burle Bramhall's visit to Leningrad [1976?], unpublished material, Burle Bramhall Collection, Hoover Institution Archives, Stanford, CA.
47. Yakobson, interview with N. Kuzmichev and N. Plekhanova, "Moya bitva za novuyu khoreografiyu" [My battle for a new choreography], *Yunost* 12 (1971): 98.
48. I. Yakobson, interview with Janice Ross, June 28, 2005, Hamburg, Germany, unpublished data in author's possession.
49. Elizabeth Souritz, *Soviet Choreographers in the 1920s*, trans. Lynn Visson (Durham, NC: Duke University Press, 1990), 65.
50. Fedor Lopukhov, *Writings on Ballet and Music*, trans. Dorinda Offord (Madison: University of Wisconsin Press, 2002), 128–129.
51. Asaf Messerer, *Classes in Classical Ballet* (Garden City, NY: Doubleday, 1975), 21.
52. Ibid.
53. Maya Plisetskaya, *I, Maya Plisetskaya*, trans. Antonina W. Bouis (New Haven: Yale University Press, 2001), 231.
54. Galina Ulanova, quoted in Zozulina, *Teatr Leonida Yakobsona*, 2.
55. Askold Makarov, "Neistovïy Yakobson" [The tempestuous Yakobson], in Galina Dmitrievna Kremshevskaya, *Muzïka i khoreografiya sovremennogo baleta* [The music and choreography of the contemporary ballet], vol. 2 (Leningrad: Muzïka, 1977), 168.

56. Nataliya Zozulina, interview with Janice Ross, November 14, 2011, Saint Petersburg, unpublished data in author's possession.

Chapter Three. What Is to Be Done with Ballet?

Epigraph: Leonid Yakobson, "Assotsiatsiya novovo baleta" [The new ballet association], *Zhizn iskusstva* 43 (1928): n.p.

1. *What Is to Be Done?* is the title of Vladimir Lenin's famous treatise in which he argues that the working class will not spontaneously become political simply by fighting economic battles with employers over wages, working hours, and the like. To convert the working class to Marxism, Lenin argues that Marxists should form a political party, or "vanguard," of dedicated revolutionaries to spread Marxist political ideas among the workers. The parallel was strong for dance.

2. Robert Conquest, *The Great Terror: A Reassessment* (London: Pimlico, 2008), 447.

3. Christina Ezrahi, *Swans of the Kremlin: Ballet and Power in Soviet Russia* (Pittsburgh: University of Pittsburgh Press, 2012).

4. GATOB stands for Gosudarstvennïy akademicheskiy teatr operï i baleta, or State Academic Theater for Opera and Ballet. It was the name given to Saint Petersburg's Mariinsky Theater, home of the Kirov Ballet, between 1920 and 1935.

5. From July 1921 to January 1928 the full official name of the school was the State Theater Ballet School of the RSFSR's National Education Kommissariat's Governance of Academic Theaters (Gosudarstvennoe teatralnoe baletnoe uchilishche Upravleniya akademicheskih teatrov Narodnogo komissariata prosveshcheniya RSFSR). This was the first time "academic" was used in any of the school's names.

6. Yakobson, "Assotsiatsiya novovo baleta," n.p.

7. Tim Scholl, *Sleeping Beauty: A Legend in Progress* (New Haven: Yale University Press, 2004), 74.

8. Sollertinsky was a close friend of the composer Dmitriy Shostakovich, and his death in 1944 at the age of forty-two under mysterious circumstances left Shostakovich bereaved. In memoriam he composed his *Third Piano Trio* to Sollertinsky's memory, the same score that Yakobson would use as accompaniment for one of his late major works, *Jewish Wedding* (1970).

9. Ivan Sollertinsky, quoted in Mary Grace Swift, *The Art of the Dance in the USSR* (Notre Dame, IN: University of Notre Dame Press, 1968), 81.

10. Elizabeth Kattner-Ulrich, "The Early Life and Works of George Balanchine (1913–1928)," Ph.D. diss, Freie Universität, Berlin, 2008, 213–214.

11. Scholl, *Sleeping Beauty*, 72.

12. Swift, *Art of the Dance in the USSR*, 62; Ezrahi, *Swans of the Kremlin;* Elizabeth Souritz, *Soviet Choreographers in the 1920s*, trans. Lynn Visson (Durham, NC: Duke University Press, 1990).

13. Swift, *Art of the Dance in the USSR*, 73.

14. Natalia Roslavleva, *Era of the Russian Ballet* (New York: Dutton, 1966), 217.

15. Galina Ulanova, in S. M. Volfson, *Leonid Yakobson: Tvorcheskiy put baletmeystera, ego baletï, miniatyurï, ispolniteli* [Leonid Yakobson: The creative way of the choreographer, his ballets, miniatures and the performers] (Leningrad; Moscow: Iskusstvo, 1965), 12.

16. Ibid.

17. Swift, *Art of the Dance in the USSR*, 68; Ezrahi, *Swans of the Kremlin;* Souritz, *Soviet Choreographers in the 1920s.*

18. Swift, *Art of the Dance in the USSR*, 68; Souritz, *Soviet Choreographers in the 1920s*, 212.

19. James Loeffler, *The Most Musical Nation: Jews and Culture in the Late Russian Empire* (New Haven: Yale University Press, 2010), 189.

20. Ulanova, in Volfson, *Leonid Yakobson*, 12.

21. Katerina Clark, *Petersburg: Crucible of Cultural Revolution* (Cambridge, MA: Harvard University Press, 1995), 186.

22. Loeffler, *Most Musical Nation*, 205; Sheila Fitzpatrick, "Cultural Revolution in Russia, 1928–32," *Journal of Contemporary History* 9, no. 1 (January 1974): 33.

23. Souritz, *Soviet Choreographers in the 1920s*, 260; Lynn Garafola, foreword to Vera Krasovskaya, *Vaganova: A Dance Journey from Petersburg to Leningrad*, trans. Vera Siegel (Gainesville: University Press of Florida, 2005), xxiv.

24. Krasovskaya, *Vaganova*, 148.

25. Souritz, *Soviet Choreographers in the 1920s*, 260.

26. Swift, *Art of the Dance in the USSR*, 66; Souritz, *Soviet Choreographers in the 1920s*, 212.

27. J. Arch Getty, "*Samokritika* Rituals in the Stalinist Central Committee, 1933–38," *Russian Review* 58, no. 1 (1999): 49, 53.

28. Swift, *Art of the Dance in the USSR*, 66–67; Ezrahi, *Swans of the Kremlin;* Souritz, *Soviet Choreographers in the 1920s.*

29. Garafola, foreword to Krasovskaya, *Vaganova*, xxviii.

30. Souritz, *Soviet Choreographers in the 1920s*, 318.

31. Fedor Lopukhov, *Writings on Ballet and Music*, trans. Dorinda Offord (Madison: University of Wisconsin Press, 2002), 7.

32. Referenced in Swift, *Art of the Dance in the USSR*, 110–111; see also Ezrahi, *Swans of the Kremlin;* Souritz, *Soviet Choreographers in the 1920s.*

33. Stephanie Jordan, ed., *Fedor Lopukhov: Writings on Ballet and Music* (Madison: University of Wisconsin Press, 2002).

34. Sheila Fitzpatrick, *The Cultural Front: Power and Culture in Revolutionary Russia* (Ithaca, NY: Cornell University Press, 1992), 239.

35. Getty, "*Samokritika* Rituals," 68.

36. Elizabeth Kendall, *Balanchine and the Lost Muse: Revolution and the Making of a Choreographer* (New York: Oxford University Press, 2013), 229.

37. Juliet Bellow, "Balanchine and the Deconstruction of Classicism," in Marion Kant, *The Cambridge Companion to Ballet* (Cambridge, Eng.: Cambridge University Press, 2007), 239.
38. The Russian Wikipedia entry "List of Kasyan Goleizovsky's ballets" (http://ru .wikipedia.org/wiki/Список_балетов_Касьяна_Голейзовского) lists at least six of his later Bolshoi productions: *Polovetskie plyaski* (1934), *Don Quixote* (1942), *Vecher khoreograficheskih miniatyur* (1959), *Skryabiniana* (1962), *Leyli i Medzhnun* (1964), and *Mimolyotnosti* (1968).
39. Souritz, *Soviet Choreographers in the 1920s*, 215.
40. In 1928 the school became the Leningrad State Choreographic Technicum, and in 1937 it was renamed the Leningrad State Choreographic Institute (Lenigradskoe gosudarstvennoe khoreograficheskoe uchilishche). In 1957 it assumed its present title, the A. Ya. Vaganova Academy.
41. Kasyan Goleizovsky and Bronislava Nijinska often referred to their short works like these as dance "études," adapting the musical term for brief musical studies to dance. See Lynn Garafola, "An Amazon of the Avant-Garde: Bronislava Nijinska in Revolutionary Russia," *Dance Research* 29, no. 2 (November 2011): 147.
42. "Ulitsa zodchego Rossi" [The architect Rossi street], http://www.dancesport.by /content/ulitsa-zodchego-rossi (in Russian, accessed December 18, 2013).
43. Clark, *Petersburg*, 186.
44. Akim Volïnskiy [Volynsky], *Kniga likovaniy: Azbuka klassicheskoga tantsa* [The book of exaltations: ABC's of classical ballet] (Leningrad: Khoreograficheskiy tekhnikum, 1925).
45. Yakobson, "Za baletmeysterskuyu smenu!" [For a new generation in choreography!], *Rabochiy i teatr* 39 (April 29, 1929): 2.
46. Irina Yakobson, interview with Janice Ross, September 30, 2004, Haifa, Israel, unpublished data in author's possession.
47. Quoted in Clark, *Petersburg*, 186.
48. Yakobson, "Za baletmeysterskuyu smenu!" 2.
49. Yuriy Brodersen, "Otvet tov. L. Yakobsonu" [Reply to Comrade L. Yakobson], *Rabochiy i teatr* 26 (1931): 9.
50. Garafola, foreword to Krasovskaya, *Vaganova*, xxiv.
51. Quoted in Swift, *The Art of the Dance in the USSR*, 85–87; Ezrahi, *Swans of the Kremlin*; Souritz, *Soviet Choreographers in the 1920s*.
52. Garafola, "Amazon of the Avant-Garde," 147.
53. "Dinamo" is also the name of a real, still-operating soccer team founded in Leningrad in 1922.
54. Swift, *Art of the Dance in the USSR*, 88; Ezrahi, *Swans of the Kremlin*; Souritz, *Soviet Choreographers in the 1920s*.
55. Sofia Moshevich, *Dmitri Shostakovich, Pianist* (Montreal: McGill-Queen's University Press, 2004), 65.

56. Harlow Robinson, "Bolshoi Gold: Revised Shostakovich Ballet Comes to L.A.," *Los Angeles Times,* August 2, 1987, http://articles.latimes.com/1987-08-02/entertainment/ca-494_1_golden-age (accessed December 18, 2013).

57. Derek C. Hulme, *Dmitri Shostakovich Catalogue: The First Hundred Years and Beyond* (Lanham, MD: Scarecrow Press, 2010), 52–56.

58. Robinson, "Bolshoi Gold."

59. Quoted ibid.

60. Manashir Yakubov, *"The Golden Age:* The True Story of the Première," in David Fanning, *Shostakovich Studies* (Cambridge, Eng.: Cambridge University Press, 1995), 192.

61. This larger theme of music with symphonic intensity and dramatic development was also important for another score that Shostakovich had already begun as he was working on *The Golden Age:* his remarkable and controversial opera *Lady Macbeth of the Mtsensk District (Ledi Makbet Mtsenskovo uezda),* which premiered in early 1934, less than four years after *The Golden Age.*

62. This quality of Shostakovich's score is one of the features that drew Russian choreographers Yury Grigorovich and Alexei Ratmansky to stage their own versions of *The Golden Age.* Grigorovich premiered his in 1982 and Ratmansky has made re-creations of all three Shostakovich ballets in the twenty-first century.

63. Fitzpatrick, *Cultural Front,* 195.

64. Ibid.

65. The October 26, 1930, premiere at the Mariinsky Theater had the following cast: Galina Ulanova (Komsomolka), Olga Iordan (Diva), Olga Mungalova (Western Komsomolka), Boris Shavrov (Fascist), and Alla Shelest (Angel of Peace).

66. There is a video recording of the 1982 Yury Grigorovich choreography at the Bolshoi with Natalia Bessmertnova and Irek Mukhamedov in the leading parts (Irina Yakobson Archives, Special Collections and University Archives, Stanford University). The conductor was Yuriy Simonov.

67. Lopukhov's plotless dance symphony *The Magnificence of the Universe* (1923) and Goleizovsky's *The Faun* or *Joseph the Beautiful* are earlier plotless modernist works.

68. DSCH publishing house is the Moscow publishing house that published the 150-part *New Collected Works of Dmitri Shostakovich* in 2005.

69. Yakubov, *"The Golden Age,"* 197.

70. Laurel E. Fay, *Shostakovich: A Life* (Oxford, Eng.: Oxford University Press, 2000), 61.

71. Konstantin Rudnitsky, *Russian and Soviet Theater, 1905–1932* (New York: Harry N. Abrams, 1988), 191.

72. Natalya Sheremetyevskaya, *Dlinnïe teni: o vremeni, o tantse, o sebe* [Long shadows: On time, dance, myself] (Moscow: Redaktsiya zhurnala "Balet," 2007), 41.

73. Galina Ulanova, "Pamyati Leonida Yakobsona" [In memory of Leonid Yakobson], in Galina Dmitrievna Kremshevskaya, *Muzïka i khoreografiya sovremennogo baleta* [The music and choreography of the contemporary ballet], vol. 2 (Leningrad: Muzïka, 1977), 164–165.

74. Robert Gottlieb, *George Balanchine: The Ballet Maker* (New York: HarperCollins/ Atlas Books, 2004), 18.

75. Askold Makarov, "Neistovïy Yakobson" [The tempestuous Yakobson], in Kremshevskaya, *Muzïka i khoreografiya sovremennogo baleta,* 166.

76. Nancy Van Norman Baer, *Theatre in Revolution: Russian Avant-Garde Stage Design, 1913–1935* (New York: Thames and Hudson, 1991), 69–71.

77. Alla Rosenfeld, *Defining Russian Graphic Arts: From Diaghilev to Stalin, 1898–1934* (New Brunswick, NJ: Rutgers University Press, 1999), 62.

78. "Proletarskiy muzïkant" was published by the Russian Association of Proletarian Musicians (1923–1932) according to the Russian Wikipedia entry (http://ru .wikipedia.org/wiki/Российская_ассоциация_пролетарских_музыкантов; accessed March 10, 2014), and it operated in the spirit of "bolshevization" of music culture. It was an organ of "tchekist" control and viewed many forms of classical music and jazz as ideologically alien to the proletariat. The entries on "Rabochiy i teatr" in Bolshaya Rossiyskaya Entsiklopediya, 1992 (http://dic.academic.ru/dic.nsf/enc_sp/2183/Рабочий; accessed March 10, 2014) and Bolshaya Sovetskaya Entsiklopediya, 1969–78 (http://dic.academic.ru/dic.nsf/bse /125543/Рабочий; accessed March 10, 2014) do not state any relation to Communist activities. A. V. Lunacharsky was one of the contributors to the journal.

79. Swift, *Art of the Dance in the USSR,* 88; Ezrahi, *Swans of the Kremlin;* Souritz, *Soviet Choreographers in the 1920s.*

80. Yuriy Brodersen, "Legalizatsiya prisposoblenchestva" [The legalization of time-serving], *Rabochiy i teatr* 60, no. 1 (1930): 8–9, quoted in Yakubov, "The Golden Age," 200.

81. Ibid.

82. Aleksandr Gauk, "Tvorcheskiye vstrechi: D. D. Shostakovich" [Artistic encounters: D. D. Shostakovich], in Gauk, *Memuari, izbrannïe stati, vospominaniya sovremennikov* [Memoirs, selected articles, recollections of my contemporaries], 125, quoted in Yakubov, "The Golden Age," 195.

83. Boris Lvov-Anokhin, "About the Choreographer," in *S. Hurok Presents the Bolshoi Ballet* (N.p.: 1962).

84. Dmitriy Shostakovich to Zakhar Lyubinskiy, October 28, 1930, Lyubinskiy Archive, A. A. Bakhrushin State Central Theatre Museum, Moscow, quoted in Yakubov, "The Golden Age," 197.

85. Shostakovich, "Nashi tvorcheskiye vstrechi s Leonidom Yakobsonom" [My artistic association with Leonid Yakobson], in Volfson, *Leonid Yakobson,* 11.

86. What stands out in these accounts of Yakobson's work in *The Golden Age* is the fluency with which he speaks in different registers through his choreography. He can play for the enchantment of spectacle by giving the audience an easy to grasp visual of the Capitalist character that spirals into a Pioneer, presumably through a shift in his bodily attitude as well as his costume. But Yakobson can just as quickly raise the demands up a notch, and sample how in a young art form like film, spectatorship changes so that tricks of cinema return us to the world with new perceptions about time and motion. The capacity of art to make the familiar strange, which Viktor Shklovsky theorized as "defamiliarization," unfolds in these dance passages where the familiar becomes unfamiliar and a deeper aesthetic dimension to sports is made possible, one that extends beyond simply sprinkling athletic moves throughout a classical dance. Finally what sealed the fate of *The Golden Age* was the progressing of the period of the Great Break, the ending of a short spell of semiprivate economic policy and the beginning of the deadly period of forced collectivization and industrialization and tightening of control over Soviet culture that Stalin proclaimed in 1929. Two decades earlier, in his 1902 pamphlet *What Is to Be Done? (Chto delat?)*, Lenin had argued that the working class will not spontaneously become political simply by fighting economic battles with employers over wages, working hours, and the like. To convert the working class to Marxism, Lenin contended that Marxists should form a political party, or "vanguard," of dedicated revolutionaries to spread Marxist political ideas among the workers. Yakobson had placed himself in that vanguard. Even after it became far too dangerous for that vanguard among artists to continue publicly, he persisted privately through his dances, taking the success, and failures, from *The Golden Age* forward.
87. Barbara Makanowitzky, "Music to Serve the State," *Russian Review* 24, no. 3 (1965): 269, 273.
88. Fitzpatrick, *Cultural Front*, 198.
89. Yakobson, "Puti sovetskoy khoreografii" [The paths of Soviet choreography], *Rabochiy i teatr* 26 (October 1931): 6.
90. Ibid.
91. In 1931, the school was still called "institute" (*uchilishche*). The name "academy" would be given to the school only in 1991, although the adjective "academic" has intermittently been a part of the official names of the school since 1921.
92. Yakobson, "Puti sovetskoy khoreografii," 7.
93. Ibid.
94. Ezrahi, *Swans of the Kremlin*, 30–31.
95. Ibid., 32.
96. Ibid., 65.
97. Scholl, *Sleeping Beauty*, 65.

98. Anatoly Vasilyevich Lunacharsky, "Novïe puti operï i baleta" [New paths for opera and ballet], *Proletarskiy muzïkant* 5 (1930): 4–5.

99. Souritz, *Soviet Choreographers in the 1920s*, 174.

100. Others—Nijinska, Balanchine, Nijinsky—took what influence of this impulse they wanted to the West. Yakobson, by necessity, explored what was possible locked within the site of its birth, which had now become a totalitarian state.

101. Sheremetyevskaya, *Dlinnïe teni*, 34.

102. Ibid., 36.

103. Ibid., 37.

104. Ibid., 39.

105. Ibid., 40.

106. Ibid., 36.

107. Ibid., 41–42.

108. Ibid., 42.

109. Ibid., 43.

110. Yakobson, "Avtobiografiya" [Autobiography], September 17, 1953, Irina Yakobson's private collection (unpublished material).

111. Fay, *Shostakovich*, 84–85.

112. The Maly Opera Theater production had its Leningrad premiere in 1933 and its Moscow premiere (under the title *Katerina Izmaylova*) in 1934. In two years it was performed in these two cities approximately two hundred times. The Bolshoi Theater production was first performed on December 26, 1935. (In 1935, the opera was performed in the United States as well as in seven other countries.) A very informative article published on the Bolshoi theater site http://www.bolshoi.ru/performances/68/details/ (accessed March 10, 2014) states that the Soviet leadership saw the Bolshoi (and not the Maly) production one month after the premiere.

113. For a full listing of the titles and dates of these ballets please consult the Appendix.

114. I. Yakobson, phone interview with Janice Ross, December 7, 2010, unpublished data in author's possession.

115. In 1920 the State Moscow Choreographic Technicum became affiliated with the Bolshoi Theater and was renamed the State Ballet School. In 1931 its name was changed to the Ballet Technicum. In 1937 the technicum was renamed the Moscow Choreographic School.

116. Maya Plisetskaya, *I, Maya Plisetskaya*, trans. Antonina W. Bouis (New Haven: Yale University Press, 2001), 27.

117. Ibid., 50.

118. Ibid., 51.

119. Francine Hirsch, *Empire of Nations: Ethnographic Knowledge and the Making of the Soviet Union* (Ithaca, NY: Cornell University Press, 2005), 216–217.

120. Ibid., 280.

121. Irina Yakobson, interview with Janice Ross, September 9, 2004, Haifa, Israel, unpublished data in author's possession. In 1989 the Moiseyev Company toured to Israel. It was soon after its return that Russia and Israel established diplomatic relations.

122. Elizabeth Souritz defines "drambalet" as the harmonious, dramatically tight genre of ballet that dominated the 1930s and 1940s. The archetype of this genre was *The Fountain of Bakhchisarai* (1934).

123. Michael Rouland, "A Nation on Stage: Music and the 1936 Festival of Kazak Arts," in Neil Edmunds, *Soviet Music and Society under Lenin and Stalin: The Baton and Sickle* (London: RoutledgeCurzon, 2004), 197.

124. Ibid.

125. Ashkhabad was the capital and cultural center of the former Turkmenia or Turkmen Soviet Socialist Republic, now the independent country Turkmenistan.

126. Elizabeth Souritz, "Moscow's Island of Dance, 1934–1941," *Dance Chronicle* 17, no. 1 (1994): 76.

127. This analysis is based upon studying an archival video recording of the full ballet from the Mariinsky Ballet's 2009 revival, courtesy of Irina Yakobson.

128. The Golem was a cultural reference taken from *Golem: How He Came into the World* (*Der Golem, wie er in die Welt kam*), the celebrated 1920 German silent horror film by Paul Wegener about the looming stone and wood mythic defender of the Jews of sixteenth-century Prague who blends in with his gray urban habitat just as the green fur- and vine-covered Shurale melts into his dark woods.

129. Yakobson, "Baletmeyster: Shurale" [The choreographer: Shurale], 1941, Irina Yakobson's private collection (unpublished manuscript). Emphasis added.

130. Boris Lvov-Anokhin, "O Leonide Yakobsone" [On Leonid Yakobson], in Volfson, *Leonid Yakobson*, 7.

131. I. Yakobson interview, September 30, 2004.

132. Ibid.

133. Roslavleva, *Era of the Russian Ballet*, 282.

134. Hélène Bellew, *Ballet in Moscow Today* (Greenwich, CT: New York Graphic Society, 1956), 8.

135. Yakobson, "Director's Exposition for *Shurale,* Ballet in Three Acts, to the Board of Art Affairs," February 15, 1941, Kazan, Irina Yakobson's private collection (unpublished material).

136. Makarov, "Pervïe vstrechi s narodnïm geroem" [First meetings with the hero of the people], in Pyotr Andreyevich Gusev, *Muzïka i khoreografiya sovremennogo baleta* [The music and choreography of the contemporary ballet], vol. 1 (Leningrad: Muzïka, 1974), 222.

137. Ibid., 226.

138. Ibid., 228.

139. Quoted in Souritz, "Moscow's Island of Dance, 1934–1941," 78. Souritz is in fact quoting from a letter sent to her from Nora Nemchenko dated March 17, 1989.
140. Ibid.
141. Makarov, "Neistovïy Yakobson," 167.
142. Krasovskaya, "Lirika i drama v baletnom spektakle" [Lyricism and drama in a ballet performance], in *Stati o balete* [Essays on ballet] (Leningrad: Iskusstvo, 1967), 33.
143. Makarov, "Pervïe vstrechi s narodnïm geroem," 223.
144. Ibid., 223–224.
145. Ibid., 224.
146. C. Brooks Peters, "Hitler Begins War on Russia," *New York Times,* June 22, 1941, 2.
147. W. Bruce Lincoln, *Sunlight at Midnight: Saint Petersburg and the Rise of Modern Russia* (New York: Basic Books, 2000), 9.
148. Jennifer Homans, *Apollo's Angels: A History of Ballet* (New York: Random House, 2010), 361.
149. Irina Yakobson, interview with Janice Ross, March 3, 2003, Hamburg, Germany, unpublished data in author's possession.
150. Makarov, "Pervïe vstrechi s narodnïm geroem," 221.
151. I. Yakobson interview, September 30, 2004.
152. The poem, translated by Anna Klimentenko, is from Irina Yakobson's private collection (unpublished material).
153. John Martin, "Bolshoi's Ballet Does Tatar Work," *New York Times,* June 7, 1956, 20.
154. Ibid.
155. I. Yakobson interview, September 30, 2004.
156. F. V. Lopukhov, *Shestdesyat let v balete* (Moscow: Iskusstvo, 1966), n.p.
157. Fitzpatrick, *Everyday Stalinism: Ordinary Lives in Extraordinary Times: Soviet Russia in the 1930s* (New York: Oxford University Press, 1999), 10.
158. Valeriy Zvezdochkin, "Sudba novatora" [The innovator's lot], *Teatralnaya zhizn* 9, no. 738 (May 1989): 19.
159. For this notice, see the Tatar website http://gabdullatukay.ru/eng/index.php?option=com_content&task=view&id=125&Itemid=59 (accessed December 19, 2013).
160. Irina Yakobson, interview with Janice Ross, April 2, 2000, San Francisco, unpublished data in author's possession.
161. Ibid.
162. Yakobson, Contract with Pevzner Family, November 7, 1943, Molotov, USSR, storage unit 144, A. A. Bakhrushin State Central Theatre Museum, Moscow.
163. Joseph Roach, *Cities of the Dead: Circum-Atlantic Performance* (New York: Columbia University Press, 1996), 5.

164. Benedict Anderson, *Imagined Communities: Reflections on the Origin and Spread of Nationalism* (London: Verso, 2006), 88.

Chapter Four. Chilling and Thawing

Epigraph: Abram Tertz [Andrei Sinyavsky], *"The Trial Begins" and "On Socialist Realism"* (1960, 1959; Berkeley: University of California Press, 1982), 147.

1. Jeffrey Veidlinger, *The Moscow State Yiddish Theatre: Jewish Culture on the Soviet Stage* (Bloomington: Indiana University Press, 2000), 252.

2. Ibid., 257.

3. Yuri Slezkine, *The Jewish Century* (Princeton, NJ: Princeton University Press, 2004), 298.

4. Ibid., 299.

5. Fedor Lopukhov, *Shestdesyat let v balete: Vospominaniya i zapiski baletmeystera* [Sixty years in the ballet: Memoirs and notes of a choreographer] (Moscow: Iskusstvo, 1966), 322.

6. Artur Romanenko, quoted in Viktor Snitkovsky, "25 let bez Yakobsona" [Twenty-five years without Yakobson], http://www.berkovich-zametki.com/Snitko16.htm (accessed January 5, 2014).

7. Irina Yakobson, interview with Janice Ross, September 30, 2004, Haifa, Israel, unpublished data in author's possession.

8. Henri Hamburger, *The Function of the Predicate in the Fables of Krylov: A Text-Grammatical Study* (Amsterdam: Rodopi, 1981), 348–349.

9. Lev Semenovich Vygotsky, *Educational Psychology* (Boca Raton, FL: Saint Lucie Press, 1997), 243.

10. The premiere of the opera took place on September 28, 1947, at the Opera Theater of the city Stalin (today Donetsk in Ukraine).

11. Krzysztof Meyer, *Shostakovich. Zhizn. Tvorchestvo. Vremya* [Shostakovich. Life, work, time], trans. E. Gulyayeva (Saint Petersburg: DSCH/Kompozitor, 1998), 280.

12. Ibid.

13. Slezkine, *Jewish Century,* 297.

14. Veidlinger, *Moscow State Yiddish Theatre,* 260.

15. Ibid., 263.

16. Natalia Roslavleva, "Prechistenka 20: The Isadora Duncan School in Moscow," *Dance Perspectives* 64 (1975): 8.

17. Isadora Duncan, "Iskusstvo i kultura—Iskusstvo dlya mass" [Art and culture—Art for the masses], *Izvestia,* November 23, 1921.

18. Barbara O'Connor, *Barefoot Dancer: The Story of Isadora Duncan* (Minneapolis: Carolrhoda Books, 1994), 75.

19. I. Yakobson interview, September 30, 2004.

20. Roslavleva, "Prechistenka 20," 42.

21. Ibid.

22. Veidlinger, *Moscow State Yiddish Theatre*, 267.

23. Slezkine, *Jewish Century*, 297.

24. Veidlinger, *Moscow State Yiddish Theatre*, 268.

25. Ibid., 267.

26. Ann Daly, *Done into Dance: Isadora Duncan in America* (Bloomington: Indiana University Press, 1995), 6.

27. Fredrika Blair, *Isadora: Portrait of the Artist as a Woman* (New York: McGraw-Hill, 1986), 406.

28. Daly, *Done into Dance*, 79.

29. Lopukhov, *Shestdesyat let v balete*, 321.

30. Ibid., 322.

31. S. Levin and M. Irshai, "Shurale Getting Ready for Socialist Competition" [in Russian], *Sovetskoye iskusstvo* 6 (1950): 3.

32. According to the East View database (http://online.eastview.com, accessed August 10, 2011), the only article published in *Pravda* in which Yakobson is mentioned in his lifetime is "Zavershenie Odissei" [The end of odyssey, published on August 16, 1973], about a visit by the American who ran the orphaned children's ship on which Yakobson sailed as a child. *Izvestia* contains no references to Yakobson in his lifetime.

33. Mikhail Dolgopolov, "Tatarskiy balet 'Shurale'" [Tatarian ballet "Shurale"], *Izvestia*, March, 11, 1955, Moscow.

34. Kirov Ballet Party meeting minutes, April 1, 1949, and April 11, 1950, folder 87, catalogue no. 1/166, Leonid Yakobson personal files, Central State Archive for Literature and the Arts, Saint Petersburg.

35. The recipients of the prizes for the year 1950 were announced in the March 17, 1951, edition of *Pravda*.

36. Irina Yakobson, interview with Janice Ross, September 30, 2004, Haifa, Israel, unpublished data in author's possession.

37. N. L. Badkhan, "Annihilate Completely Bourgeoisie Cosmopolitism" [in Russian], *Sovetskoe iskusstvo*, March 31, 1949.

38. Robert Conquest, *The Great Terror: A Reassessment* (London: Pimlico, 2008), 462.

39. James Loeffler, *The Most Musical Nation: Jews and Culture in the Late Russian Empire* (New Haven: Yale University Press, 2010), 207.

40. Conquest, *The Great Terror*, 476.

41. Irina Yakobson, interview with Janice Ross, December 11, 2006, Haifa, Israel, unpublished data in author's possession.

42. Aleksandr Solzhenitsyn, quoted in Shimon Markish, "The Role of Officially Published Russian Literature in the Reawakening of Jewish National Consciousness (1953–1970)," in Yaacov Ro'i and Avi Beker, *Jewish Culture and Identity in the Soviet Union* (New York: New York University Press, 1991), 214.

43. Nikolay Petrovich Ivanovsky, *Balnïy tanets XVI-XIX vekov* [Ballroom dance from the sixteenth century through the nineteenth century] (Moscow; Leningrad: Iskusstvo, 1948).

44. Juri Jelagin, *Taming of the Arts*, trans. Nicholas Wreden (New York: Dutton, 1951), 238.

45. Nancy Reynolds, *Repertory in Review: 40 Years of the New York City Ballet* (New York: Dial Press, 1977), 118.

46. Ann Pellegrini, *Performance Anxieties: Staging Psychoanalysis, Staging Race* (New York: Routledge, 1997), 18.

47. Matthew Cullerne Bown, *Art under Stalin* (New York: Holmes & Meier, 1991), 114.

48. Pellegrini, *Performance Anxieties*, 20, 21.

49. Ibid., 22, 23.

50. Ramsay Burt, *The Male Dancer: Bodies, Spectacle, Sexualities* (London: Routledge, 1995).

51. Catriona Kelly, *Petrushka: The Russian Carnival Puppet Theatre* (Cambridge, Eng.: Cambridge University Press, 1990), 66.

52. Deborah Jowitt, *Jerome Robbins: His Life, His Theater, His Dance* (New York: Simon & Schuster, 2004), 20.

53. Nicholas Fox Weber, "From Stravinsky to the Sharks," *New York Times*, August 1, 2004.

54. Quoted in Eric Herschthal, "Ballet Values, Jewish Values," *Jewish Week*, January 25, 2011.

55. Andrea Most, *Making Americans: Jews and the Broadway Musical* (Cambridge, MA: Harvard University Press, 2004), 1.

56. Ibid., 3, 7.

57. Ibid., 13, 10.

58. Ibid., 15.

59. Thomas DeFrantz, "Donald Byrd: Re/making 'Beauty,'" in Susanne Franco and Marina Nordera, *Dance Discourses: Keywords in Dance Research* (London: Routledge, 2007), 223.

60. Brenda Dixon Gottschild, *Digging the Africanist Presence in American Performance* (Westport: Greenwood Press, 1996), 64.

61. The force of exclusion could at times be enough to make black dancers in the United States actually switch dance genres, as happened with Joan Myers Brown. A leading contemporary dancer who began her training in ballet with British choreographer Antony Tudor in the 1940s, Brown recalled being cast with another black female dancer in a production of *Les Sylphides* in the forerunner to Pennsylvania Ballet, the Ballet Guild. In a review in the local paper the morning after her debut, the writer noted, "The ballet would have been fine except for the two flies in the buttermilk." Myers Brown recalled being so devastated that the critic only saw skin tone rather than dancing skill that it "was my last escapade as a ballet dancer . . . I never fit in. I never did. I always felt that I was outside of ev-

erything." These efforts at stretching ballet in the United States to embrace black performers suggest an initial emphasis on body proportions and skin color—the surface signifiers of difference. Much later in the twentieth century, in the mid-1990s, choreographer Donald Byrd explored the implicit racial limits of both romantic and classical ballet by working from the inside, attacking their technique and choreographic strategies through his own versions of *Giselle* and *The Nutcracker*. In his analysis of Byrd's choreography in these two works, DeFrantz traces how "Byrd's choreography consistently engages a recognizably black identity in its fierce deployment of Africanist principles throughout." These principles are kinesthetic in dimension and are displayed in the quality of the dancers' attack, phrasing, antiphonal gestural responses, and spatial alignments—what De-Frantz identifies as compositional strategies that align with the aesthetic of the cool as defined by Robert Farris Thompson. DeFrantz, "Donald Byrd," 221–235.

62. I. Yakobson interview, September 30, 2004.
63. Vladimir Zenzinov, interview with Janice Ross, July 7, 2012, Saint Petersburg, unpublished data in author's possession.
64. Alvin Ailey to Leonid Yakobson, October 30, 1970, Anatoly Pronin's private collection (unpublished material).
65. Susan Leigh Foster, *Choreographing Empathy: Kinesthesia in Performance* (London: Routledge, 2011), 5.
66. Maya Plisetskaya, *I, Maya Plisetskaya* (New Haven: Yale University Press, 2001), 234.
67. I. Yakobson interview, September 30, 2004.
68. What the French sociologist Pierre Bourdieu describes as the embodied form of cultural capital exists in the form of long-lasting dispositions of the mind and body. Bourdieu argues that fundamentally cultural capital is linked to the body and presupposes embodiment, a process that involves "a labor of inculcation" which, like acquiring a muscular physique or suntan "cannot be done second hand." In Bourdieu's formulation cultural capital can also be acquired to some extent unconsciously, with markers that reflect the region, class, or other conditions of its acquisition, but this cultural capital "declines and dies with its bearer" and the passing of his memory. Pierre Bourdieu, "The Forms of Capital," in John G. Richardson, *Handbook of Theory and Research for the Sociology of Education* (Westport, CT: Greenwood Press, 1986), 244, 245.
69. Michael Gardiner, "Bakhtin's Carnival: Utopia as Critique," in David Shepherd, *Bakhtin: Carnival and Other Subjects* (Amsterdam: Rodopi, 1993).
70. Irina Yakobson, interview with Janice Ross, May 14, 1999, San Francisco, CA, unpublished data in author's possession.
71. Ibid.
72. Ibid.
73. Irina Yakobson, interview with Janice Ross, December 17, 2011, Hamburg, Germany, unpublished data in author's possession.

74. Ibid.

75. I. Yakobson interview, May 14, 1999.

76. Markish, "Role of Officially Published Russian Literature," 213.

77. Ibid.

78. Shmuel Ettinger, "The Position of Jews in Soviet Culture: A Historical Survey," in Jack Miller, *Jews in Soviet Culture* (New Brunswick, NJ: Transaction Books, 1984), 5.

79. Debora Silverman, *Van Gogh and Gauguin: The Search for Sacred Art* (New York: Farrar, Straus and Giroux, 2000), 107.

80. Igor Golomstock, "Jews in Soviet Art," in Miller, *Jews in Soviet Culture*, 42.

81. I. Yakobson interview, December 17, 2011.

82. Loeffler, *The Most Musical Nation*, 211.

83. Orlando Figes, *Natasha's Dance: A Cultural History of Russia* (London: Allen Lane, 2002), 492.

84. Evgenija Petrova, "Chagall in Russia after 1922," in Susan Tumarkin Goodman, *Marc Chagall: Early Works from Russian Collections* (New York: The Jewish Museum, 2001), 89.

85. Irina Yakobson, "Zhizn i sudba" [Life and fate], in Nataliya Zozulina, *Teatr Leonida Yakobsona: Stati Vospominaniya Fotomateriali* [The theater of Leonid Yakobson: Articles, reminiscences, photographs] (Saint Petersburg: Liki Rossii, 2010), 19.

86. I. Yakobson interview, September 30, 2004.

87. Lopukhov, "Analiticheskiy otchet=razbor khoreograficheskikh miniatyur L. Yakobsona, Yu. Vzorova, G. Aleesidze, N. Markaryantsa, Mayorova, K. Boyarskovo, Zamuelya, Eyfmana, Elizarova i dr. sikh ispolnitelyami" [Analysis: Report about Leonid Yakobson's Choreographic Miniatures, his performers and serious issues], 1971, A. A. Bakhrushin State Central Theatre Museum, Moscow, 55–59 (unpublished data).

88. Ibid., 63.

89. Sidney Alexander, *Marc Chagall: A Biography* (New York: Putnam, 1978), 17.

90. Richard Taylor, " 'But Eastward, Look, the Land Is Brighter': Toward a Topography of Utopia in the Stalinist Musical," in Evgeny Dobrenko and Eric Naiman, eds., *The Landscape of Stalinism: The Art and Ideology of Soviet Space* (Seattle: University of Washington Press, 2003), 203.

91. Eric Naiman, introduction to Dobrenko and Naiman, *The Landscape of Stalinism*, xiii.

92. Harriet Murav, *Music from a Speeding Train: Jewish Literature in Post-Revolution Russia* (Stanford, CA: Stanford University Press, 2011), 73.

93. Aleksandr Kamensky, *Chagall: The Russian Years, 1907–22* (New York: Rizzoli, 1989), 25, 259.

94. Yakobson, "Zhizn i sudba," 21–22.

95. Ibid., 25-26.
96. Carrie Noland, *Agency and Embodiment: Performing Gestures/Producing Culture* (Cambridge, MA: Harvard University Press, 2009), 2-3.
97. Ibid., 212, 206, and 2.
98. Ibid., 19.
99. Ibid., 29.
100. Ibid., 13.
101. Sander L. Gilman, *Difference and Pathology: Stereotypes of Sexuality, Race, and Madness* (Ithaca, NY: Cornell University Press, 1985), 32.
102. Mary Douglas, *Purity and Danger: An Analysis of Concepts of Pollution and Taboo* (New York: Praeger, 1966), 124.
103. The author took Irina Pevzner Yakobson (the choreographer's widow) to see Oakland Ballet's production of Bronislava Nijinska's *Les Noces* in the late 1980s, and this was the first time she had ever seen this ballet. Her husband never saw it.
104. Valeriy Zvezdochkin, "Sudba novatora" [The innovator's lot], *Teatralnaya zhizn* 9, no. 738 (May 1989): 20.
105. Zvi Gitelman, "The Evolution of Jewish Culture and Identity in the Soviet Union," in Ro'i and Beker, *Jewish Culture and Identity in the Soviet Union*, 5.
106. Simon Morrison has detailed how even for a highly celebrated and accommodating Soviet artist like the composer Sergei Prokofiev, the layers of censorship imposed by the Soviet cultural establishment on each new score or ballet could have a chilling effect on artistic creation. "Artistic creation as Prokofiev understood it had been eradicated: rather than evolving from a private process into a public exchange, it began and ended in a bureaucratic tangle. . . . The reigning Soviet aesthetic stupefied composers and audiences alike by emphasizing ideological obviousness. The impulse to demand one set of changes after another . . . debased what the bureaucrats claimed to honor." Simon Morrison, *The People's Artist: Prokofiev's Soviet Years* (Oxford, Eng.: Oxford University Press, 2009), 369.
107. Esti Sheinberg, *Irony, Satire, Parody and the Grotesque in the Music of Shostakovich: A Theory of Musical Incongruities* (Aldershot, Eng.: Ashgate, 2000), 313.
108. Gitelman, "The Evolution of Jewish Culture and Identity in the Soviet Union," 8.
109. Leonid Yakobson, interview with N. Kuzmichev and N. Plekhanova, "Moya bitva za novuyu khoreografiyu" [My battle for a new choreography], *Yunost* 12 (1971): 98.
110. See anonymous interview subject with Janice Ross, July 18, 2003, Saint Petersburg, unpublished data in author's possession, for the quotations in this and the following paragraphs.
111. There is no record of what other ballets the program included.

112. Igor Kuzmin, interview with Vladimir Golubin, "Vospominaniya o budush-chem" [Recollections of the future], *Muzikalnaya zhizn* 16, no. 786 (August 1990): 7.

113. Most, *Making Americans*.

114. Howard Reich, "The Rebel Soviet 'Fiddler,'" *Chicago Tribune*, November 10, 1988.

115. Leonid Yakobson to Irina Yakobson, January 26, 1975, Irina Yakobson's private collection.

116. Maya Plisetskaya, title unknown, *Soviet Culture* (May 1971): 1.

117. Natalya Sheremetyevskaya, *Dlinnïe teni: O vremeni, o tantse, o sebe* [Long shadows: On time, dance, myself] (Moscow: Redaktsiya zhurnala "Balet," 2007), n.p.

118. Hague Convention on the Protection of Cultural Property in the Event of Armed Conflict, May 14, 1954, 249, in United Nations Treaty Series 240.

119. Michael F. Brown, "Heritage Trouble: Recent Work on the Protection of Intangible Cultural Property," *International Journal of Cultural Property* 12 (2005): 42.

120. Foster, *Choreographing Empathy*, 1.

121. Ibid., 2.

122. Jonathan Lear, quoted in Alice Karekezi, "What Happened to Irony?," *Salon*, November 3, 2011, http://www.salon.com/2011/11/04/what_happened_to_irony/ (accessed January 23, 2014).

123. Olga Levitan, interview with Janice Ross, November 11, 2010, Jerusalem, unpublished data in author's possession.

124. Dwight Conquergood, quoted in Henry Bial, *Acting Jewish: Negotiating Ethnicity on the American Stage and Screen* (Ann Arbor: University of Michigan Press, 2005), 3.

125. In March 2008 Choreographic Miniatures under the direction of Yuri Petukhov toured to New York and performed three Rodin miniatures, *Jewish Wedding*, and *Pas de Quatre*, all by Yakobson.

Chapter Five. *Spartacus*

Epigraph: Vsevolod Meyerhold, *Stati pisma rechi besedï, chast vtoraya, 1917–1939* [Articles, letters, speeches, interviews, vol. 2, 1917–1939] (Moscow: Iskusstvo, 1968), 147.

1. Valeriy Zvezdochkin, "Sudba novatora" [The innovator's lot], *Teatralnaya zhizn* 9, no. 738 (May 1989): 19. It could be argued that Yury Grigorovich's *Stone Flower* (1957) or *Legend of Love* (1959), both ballets choreographed for the Kirov, also opened a new era in Soviet ballet. Certainly the post-Soviet glasnost period of the 1990s was one of many changes, including the reunification with works of the Russian choreographers Michel Fokine and George Balanchine.

2. Aram Khachaturian, "Kak sozdavalsya balet 'Spartak'" [How the *Spartacus* ballet was made], *Moskovskiy komsomolets*, March 29, 1958, in Khachaturian, *Stati i*

vospominaniya [Essays and memoirs] (Moscow: Sovetski kompozitor, 1980), 133, 134.

3. Harlow Robinson, "The Caucasian Connection: National Identity in the Ballets of Aram Khachaturian," *Nationalities Papers: The Journal of Nationalism and Ethnicity* 35, no. 3 (2007): 436.

4. Martin M. Winkler, *Spartacus: Film and History* (Malden: Blackwell, 2007), 77–78.

5. Karl Marx and Vladimir Ilyich Lenin, quoted in Robinson, "Caucasian Connection," 436.

6. Winkler, *Spartacus*, 78.

7. Geoffrey Wheatcroft, review of *Arthur Koestler: The Homeless Mind*, by David Cesarani, *New Statesman*, November 20, 1998, http://www.newstatesman.com/darkness-noon-arthur-koestler-was-his-heart-yet-his-early-work-inspired-his-disillusionment-communis (accessed January 29, 2014).

8. According to a letter in the Yakobson archives of the Bakhrushin Museum in Moscow, Aram Khachaturian wrote a letter dated May 19, 1946, that makes clear the idea to do a ballet about Spartacus originated with Yakobson. Khachaturian got the idea from Yakobson and then went to Volkov for the libretto. But Yakobson rewrote the libretto—this also was never credited to him. In 1955–1956 Volkov invited Chabukiani and he asked Moiseyev to choreograph it and he said he couldn't (for Mariinsky). The third one who was asked was Yakobson.

9. Khachaturian to Leonid V. Yakobson, May 19, 1946, A. A. Bakhrushin State Central Theatre Museum, Moscow.

10. Robinson, "Caucasian Connection," 436. (The main body of Robinson's text lists 1951 as the year of the publication of the *Sovetskoe iskusstvo* article, though his endnote gives the year as 1953.)

11. Khachaturian, quoted ibid.

12. Leonid Yakobson, *Pisma Noverru* [Letters to Noverre] (Tenafly, NJ: Hermitage, 2001), 97–290.

13. Ibid., 217.

14. Fedor Lopukhov, *Shestdesyat let v balete: vospominaniya i zapiski baletmeystera* [Sixty Years in the Ballet: Memoirs and Notes of a Choreographer] (Moscow: Iskusstvo, 1966), 319.

15. Yakobson, *Pisma Noverru*, 102.

16. Tatyana Legat, quoted in Viktor Snitkovsky, "25 let bez Yakobsona" [25 years without Yakobson], http://www.berkovich-zametki.com/Snitko16.htm (accessed January 29, 2014).

17. Lopukhov's ballet *Ledyanaya Deva* ("Ice Maiden"), also known as *Solveig*, was staged to Edvard Grieg's music and premiered at the Kirov on April 24, 1927.

18. Lopukhov, *Shestdesyat let v balete*, 320. Leonid Lavrovsky's Leningrad premiere of *Romeo and Juliet* to Prokofiev's score took place in 1940 and Fyodor's brother, Andrey Lopukhov, danced the part of Mercutio in this production.

19. Ibid., 321.

20. Ibid., 325.

21. Ibid., 326.

22. Yakobson, *Pisma Noverru*, 124.

23. Krasovskaya was unaware of modern dance works such as Doris Humphrey's *New Dance* trilogy and Martha Graham's *Clytemnestra,* full-evening works danced in bare feet. Many Fokine works and Nijinsky's *Rite of Spring* were danced in footwear other than pointe shoes. These, of course, were not full-evening productions.

24. Yakobson, *Pisma Noverru*, 180–181.

25. Ibid., 183.

26. Boris Lvov-Anokhin, *O balete* [On ballet], TV documentary, Central Television of the USSR, 1962, Yakobson Collection, Special Collections and University Archives, Stanford University.

27. Maya Plisetskaya, quoted in Lvov-Anokhin, "The Magic of an Art," in Galina Kapterova, *Maya Plisetskaya,* trans. Kathleen Cook (Moscow: Progress Publishers, 1976), 120.

28. Lvov-Anokhin, *O balete.*

29. Robinson, "Caucasian Connection," 429.

30. Lopukhov, *Shestdesyat let v balete,* 325.

31. Irina Yakobson, interview with Janice Ross, January 5, 2000, San Francisco, CA, unpublished data in author's possession; Yakobson, *Pisma Noverru.*

32. The quotation is from Postanovlenie Politbyuro TSK VKP(b) Ob opere "Velikaya druzhba" [The resolution of the Politburo of the Central Committee of the Communist Party of the Soviet Union on the opera *The Big Friendship*], *Pravda,* February 11, 1948.

33. Robinson, "Caucasian Connection," 437.

34. Fast stated that in October 1956 (after he had left the U.S. Communist Party) he received a letter from the Soviet embassy informing him that "in Moscow *Spartacus* was published in 300,000 copies. He also wrote that he never received the promised fee from Russian publication of *Spartacus,* probably because in February 1957 it became clear from a *New York Times* article that he had left the Communist Party. Henceforth, his books ceased being published in Russia until the time of Perestroika. In the early 1950s Fast was one of the most widely published American authors in the USSR and in 1953 he was awarded the International Stalin Peace prize (the award jury was presided over by Louis Aragon).

35. Yakobson, *Pisma Noverru*, 120.

36. Ibid., 121.

37. Ibid.

38. Viktoriya Teryoshkina, in *Spartak* [Spartacus], video clip, Mariinsky Media, 2010, http://mariinsky.tv/n/274 (accessed January 30, 2014).

39. Legat, quoted in Snitkovsky, "25 let bez Yakobsona."
40. Janice Ross, "Irina Jakobson Comes to San Francisco: A Survivor's Story," *Dancemagazine* 62 (April 1988): 78.
41. Yakobson, *Pisma Noverru*, 124.
42. Irina Yakobson, interview with Janice Ross, October 31, 2010, Haifa, Israel, unpublished data in author's possession.
43. Zvezdochkin, "Sudba novatora," 19.
44. Yakobson, *Pisma Noverru*, 127, 128.
45. Mikhail Bresler, interview with Vera Eidelman, June 18, 2004, Boston (unpublished data).
46. Ibid.
47. Ibid.
48. A Russian Wikipedia article on *Petrushka* (http://ru.wikipedia.org/wiki/Петрушка _(балет)) states that the ballet was shown in the Mariinsky (then the Petrograd Theater of Opera and Ballet) in 1920 (choreography Leontyev, based on Fokine's choreography), in the Bolshoi in Moscow (renewal of Fokine's choreography), and in the Leningrad Maly Theater (choreography Boyarsky, based on Fokine's choreography) in 1961, as well as again in the Bolshoi in 1964 (choreography Boyarsky, based on Fokine's choreography).
49. Julie Kavanagh, *Nureyev: The Life* (New York: Pantheon, 2007), 53.
50. Ibid.
51. Robert Conquest, *The Great Terror: A Reassessment* (London: Pimlico, 2008), 476.
52. Lorraine Nicholas, "Fellow Travellers: Dance and British Cold War Politics in the Early 1950s," *Dance Research* 19, no. 2 (Winter 2001): 83.
53. The Bolshoi star Galina Ulanova's memoirs *Ya ne khotela tantsevat* [I didn't want to dance] (Moscow: AST-Press SKD, 2005; excerpts: http://vk.com/topic-8348403 _23262428; accessed January 30, 2014) and the Kirov dancer Khashim Mustaef's memoirs *Dalekoe i blizkoe: Albom vospominaniya* [Far and close] (Dubna: OOO "Polipak," 2012; excerpts: http://www.hmustaev.ru/?part_id=403,418,474; accessed January 30, 2014).
54. Milton Bracker, "Russian Dancers Cheered at 'Met'; 3,600 Jam Opera House to See Moiseyev Troupe—Line forms at 10 a.m.," *New York Times,* April 15, 1958.
55. Peter Carlson, "Nikita in Hollywood," *Smithsonian* 40, no. 4 (July 2009): 50.
56. Irina Yakobson, interview with Janice Ross, December 17, 2010, Hamburg, Germany, unpublished data in author's possession.
57. Peter Jelavich, *Berlin Cabaret* (Cambridge, MA: Harvard University Press, 1993), 34.
58. Ibid., 33.
59. Ibid., 34.
60. Associated Press, "Shoplifting Ballerina Moscow Bound," *Miami News,* July 1, 1958.

61. P. Abolimov, report, April 14, 1959, file 87-1-154, Yakobson Collection, the Central State Archive of Literature and the Arts, Saint Petersburg.

62. *Rodin Triptych,* poster, Poster Collection, A. A. Bakhrushin State Central Theatre Museum, Moscow.

63. Nina Alovert, *Baryshnikov in Russia* (New York: Holt, Rinehart, and Winston, 1984), 68.

64. Vladimir Vasiliev, quoted in "Galina Ulanova: A Russian Ballet Icon Remembered," londondance.com, May 11, 2011, http://londondance.com/articles/features/galina-ulanova-a-russian-ballet-icon-remembered (accessed January 30, 2014).

65. Natalya Arkina, "Schastliviy duet" [A happy pair], *Kultura i zhizn* [Culture and life] 3 (1974): 18.

66. Vasiliev, quoted in Vadim Kiselev and Leonid Yakobson, ". . . Ya delayu to, chto slïshu v muzïke" [. . . I do what I hear in music], *Sovetskaya muzïka* 9 (September 1989): 111–112.

67. "Druzheskiy sharzh—L. Yakobsonu" [A friendly cartoon—for L. Yakobson], drawing by Aleksandr Radunskiy, *Newspaper of the Bolshoi Theatre,* 1962, Irina Yakobson's private collection.

68. Maya Plisetskaya, *I, Maya Plisetskaya,* trans. Antonina W. Bouis (New Haven: Yale University Press, 2001), 232.

69. "Bolshoi to Give New Works Here: Hurok, in Moscow, Lists 3 September Premieres," *New York Times,* June 5, 1962.

70. "The Bolshoi Returns," *Time* 80, no. 11 (September 14, 1962): 74.

71. Ralph Parker, "At the Bolshoi," in *S. Hurok Presents the Bolshoi Ballet* (New York: Hurok Concerts, Inc., 1962), n.p.

72. Seymour Topping, "Bolshoi Dancers Give 'Spartacus,'" *New York Times,* April 6, 1962.

73. British dance historian Lorraine Nicholas has written about the first tour of Soviet dancers to the United Kingdom, concluding in a comment that "it became a fixed belief amongst critics that choreographic invention in the Soviet Union had stagnated because it was denied the influence of Diaghilev's choreographers." Nicholas, "Fellow Travellers," 87–88.

74. Boris Lvov-Anokhin, "About the Choreographer," in *S. Hurok Presents the Bolshoi Ballet.*

75. Ibid.

76. Natalia Makarova, *A Dance Autobiography* (New York: Knopf, 1979), 56.

77. Rosemary Novellino-Mearns, "Ah . . . Spar-tac-ous: Performing in the Bolshoi's *Spartacus,*" November 29, 2011, http://readwhatrosiewrote.blogspot.com/2011_11_01_archive.html (accessed January 30, 2014).

78. Wendy Perron, interview with Janice Ross, March 29, 2012, New York City, unpublished data in author's possession.

79. Ibid.

80. Allen Hughes, "Ballet: Bolshoi Stages U.S. Premiere of 'Spartacus': Much-Heralded Work Is Mainly a Pageant," *New York Times*, September 13, 1962.

81. Walter Terry, *I Was There: Selected Dance Reviews and Articles, 1936–1976* (New York: M. Dekker, 1978), 431, 432.

82. Ibid., 432.

83. Edwin Denby, *Dancers, Buildings and People in the Streets* (New York: Horizon Press, 1965), 132.

84. Ibid., 139.

85. Ibid., 140–141.

86. Martin J. Medhurst, *Cold War Rhetoric: Strategy, Metaphor, and Ideology* (New York: Greenwood Press, 1990), xiv.

87. Hughes, "About *Spartacus*: Can It Be Understood Though Disliked?," *New York Times*, September 23, 1962.

88. Ibid.

89. James Waring, "Spartacus Praised," *New York Times*, September 23, 1962.

90. "Bolshoi, in Shift, Cancels 3 'Spartacus' Showings," *New York Times*, September 18, 1962.

91. "*Spartacus* Taken Out of Ballet Repertoire," *Los Angeles Times*, September 24, 1962, C12.

92. Harlow Robinson, *The Last Impresario: The Life, Times, and Legacy of Sol Hurok* (New York: Viking, 1994), 401.

93. Plisetskaya, *I, Maya Plisetskaya*, 233, 234.

94. Ibid.

95. John Martin, "City Ballet Ends Leningrad Stand: New Yorkers Won Ovations after Each Performance," *New York Times*, November 9, 1962.

96. Ibid.

97. Gay Morris, *A Game for Dancers: Performing Modernism in the Postwar Years, 1945–1960* (Middletown, CT: Wesleyan University Press, 2006), 73.

98. Irina Yakobson, interview with Janice Ross, February 20, 1999, San Francisco, unpublished data in author's possession.

99. Quoted in Winkler, *Spartacus*, 8.

100. Naima Prevots, *Dance for Export: Cultural Diplomacy and the Cold War* (Middletown, CT: Wesleyan University Press, 1998), 81.

101. John Martin, "Ballet: Visit to Bolshoi: New York City Troupe Opens 8-Week Soviet Tour at Moscow Theater," *New York Times*, October 10, 1962.

102. Elizabeth Souritz, "Balanchine in Russia," *Ballet Review* 39, no. 1 (2011): 53.

103. Aram Khachaturian, "Vstrecha s amerikanskim baletom—Pervoe vpechatlenie" [Meeting with American ballet: First impression], *Izvestia*, October 11, 1962.

104. Souritz, "Balanchine in Russia," 53.

105. George Balanchine, in "Shock Waves in Moscow," *Time,* October 19, 1962, 63, quoted in Mary Grace Swift, *The Art of the Dance in the USSR* (Notre Dame, IN: University of Notre Dame Press, 1968), 271.

106. Prevots, *Dance for Export,* 84.

107. "U.S. Girl for Bolshoi," *Life,* September 12, 1960, 30.

108. "Edmund Stevens, 81, a Reporter In Moscow for 40 Years, Is Dead," obituary, *The New York Times,* May 27, 1992.

109. Perron interview, March 29, 2012.

Chapter Six. Dismantling the Hero

Epigraph: Lilya Kaganovsky, *How the Soviet Man Was Unmade: Cultural Fantasy and Male Subjectivity under Stalin* (Pittsburgh: University of Pittsburgh Press, 2008), 3.

1. Ibid., 228.

2. See Vladimir Mayakovsky, *Klop* [The bedbug, 1928], staged by Vsevolod Meyerhold, 1929, at the Meyerhold Theater, Leningrad. *Dvenadtsat* [The twelve, 1918] is a long narrative poem written by the great lyric poet Aleksandr Blok (1880–1921) as his reaction to the 1917 Revolution.

3. Mayakovsky's play *The Bedbug,* directed by Vsevolod Meyerhold, tells the story of a lapsed party member, Prisïpkin, who marries the daughter of a petit-bourgeois hairdresser. He disappears in a fire during his drunken wedding orgy. In the second part Prisïpkin is brought back to life by a future generation living "ten Five-Year Plans" later. The vulgar Prisïpkin is out of place in the world of the hygienic clinical workers of the future and he is seen as a source of physical and moral infection. In this satire Mayakovsky was criticizing the betrayal of revolutionary ideals by the partial revival of bourgeois values in the early post-revolutionary period.

4. Leonid Yakobson, interview with Esfir Markovna Brusilovskaya, "L. V. Yakobson," in Pyotr Andreyevich Gusev, *Muzïka i khoreografiya sovremennogo baleta* [The music and choreography of the contemporary ballet], vol. 1 (Leningrad: Muzïka, 1974), 104.

5. Ibid., 100.

6. Ibid., 102.

7. Shostakovich once recalled that Mayakovsky asked him to write a score for *The Bedbug,* shaping it as something suitable for a "local fireman's band." Although this was not exactly in Shostakovich's line, he did his best. On hearing the music for the first time Mayakovsky merely remarked: "Well, in general it will do."

8. Yakobson interview with Brusilovskaya, 101.

9. Boris Lvov-Anokhin, *O balete* (On ballet), TV documentary, Central Television of the USSR, 1962, Yakobson Collection, Special Collections and University Archives, Stanford University.

10. Irina Yakobson, interview with Janice Ross, December 12, 2012, Haifa, Israel, unpublished data in author's possession.

11. Yuriy Gromov, "On videl mir tantsuyushchim" [He saw the world as dancing], in Valeriy Zvezdochkin, *Tvorchestvo Leonida Yakobsona* [Creative work of Leonid Yakobson] (Saint Petersburg: Sankt-Peterburgskiy gumanitarnïy universitet profsoyuzov, 2007), 8.

12. Viktor Vanslov, *Stati o balete* [Essays on ballet] (Moscow: Muzïka, 1980), n.p.

13. Editorial in Pravda on January 28, 1936, "Sumbur vmesto muzïki" [Muddle instead of music], reputedly written by Andrei Zhdanov, quoted in David Caute, *The Dancer Defects: The Struggle for Cultural Supremacy during the Cold War* (Oxford, Eng.: Oxford University Press, 2003), 416–417.

14. Natalia Makarova, *A Dance Autobiography* (New York: Knopf, 1979), 56, 57, 60.

15. Yakobson interview with Brusilovskaya, 105.

16. Makarova, *A Dance Autobiography*, 61.

17. This movement description of *The Bedbug* is based on viewing documentary footage of a performance by Yakobson's own company in 1974. The video is from a personal collection of Irina Yakobson now in Yakobson Collection, Special Collections and University Archives, Stanford University.

18. Makarova, *A Dance Autobiography*, 61.

19. Ibid., 60.

20. Galina Dobrovolskaya, "Yakobson, Leonid," in Selma Jeanne Cohen, *International Encyclopedia of Dance*, vol. 1 (New York: Oxford University Press, 1998), 412.

21. Gromov, "On videl mir tantsuyushchim," 8.

22. Leonid Arnoldovich Entelis, *100 baletnïkh libretto* [100 ballet libretti] (Leningrad: Muzïka, 1966), 301.

23. Yakobson interview with Brusilovskaya, 108.

24. Ibid., 101.

25. Leon Aron, "The Cunningly-Inventive Aleksandr Solzhenitsyn," *Commentary* 132, no. 5 (December 2011): 67.

26. I. Yakobson, "Zhizn i sudba" [Life and fate], in Nataliya Zozulina, *Teatr Leonida Yakobsona: Stati Vospominaniya Fotomaterialï* [The theater of Leonid Yakobson: Articles, reminiscences, photographs] (Saint Petersburg: Liki Rossii, 2010), 19–20.

27. Ibid.

28. Irina Yakobson, interview with Janice Ross, April 11, 1999, San Francisco, unpublished data in author's possession.

29. Ibid.

30. The House of Writers' Creation was a hotel in Komarovo (26 miles from Leningrad), on the shore of the Gulf of Finland, where many renowned Soviet and Russian artists lived.

31. I. Yakobson interview, April 11, 1999.

32. In Russian, the abbreviation "com" is used for "committee," and the authorities are sometimes derisively referred to as "coms."

33. Yakobson, "Zhizn i sudba," 21.

34. Sergei Hackel, *The Poet and the Revolution: Aleksandr Blok's "The Twelve"* (Oxford, Eng.: Clarendon Press, 1975), n.p. The quotation can be found in the entry on Aleksandr Aleksandrovich Blok in *Merriam Webster's Encyclopedia of Literature* (Springfield, MA: Merriam-Webster, 1995), 149.

35. Lvov-Anokhin, *O balete*.

36. Tatyana Bruni's costume sketches for *The Twelve* are in the collection of the A. A. Bakhrushin State Central Theatre Museum, Moscow.

37. Kaganovsky, *How the Soviet Man Was Unmade*, 143. The quotation can also be found at http://russiandinosaur.blogspot.de/2011_06_01_archive.html (accessed May 18, 2014).

38. Blok's *The Twelve* is set in the streets of the city during a blizzard at night. Twelve revolutionaries march through the almost deserted streets, chanting and yelling revolutionary slogans. They are rowdies, mistreating the bystanders, robbing and burning homes. Blok emphasizes their proletarian background by having them wear convict attire. They are looked upon with fear, suspicion, and hatred by their traditional enemies on the sidewalks—an old lady, a bourgeois, a writer, a priest, and two fur-coated ladies—all representing the old world that is crumbling in that winter night. The observers stand, as if nailed to the ground, while the revolutionaries move ahead, signaling progress. The poem reaches a climax by having an apparition of Jesus Christ appear in front of the twelve—symbols of Christ's twelve Apostles. *The Twelve* remains artistically one of the best-known literary works about the Bolshevik Revolution.

39. Makarova, *Dance Autobiography*, 64.

40. Ibid.

41. Ibid., 64, 65.

42. Quoted in Elizabeth Kattner-Ulrich, "The Early Life and Works of George Balanchine (1913–1928)," Ph.D. diss., Freie Universität, Berlin, 2008, 76.

43. Arkadiy Ivanenko, interview with Janice Ross, July 4, 2012, Saint Petersburg, unpublished data in author's possession.

44. Valery Panov, interview with Janice Ross, November 12, 2010, Ashdod, Israel, unpublished data in author's possession.

45. I. Yakobson interview, April 11, 1999.

46. Nina Alovert, interview with Janice Ross, April 19, 2012, New York City, unpublished data in author's possession.

47. Gal Beckerman, *When They Come for Us, We'll Be Gone: The Epic Struggle to Save Soviet Jewry* (Boston: Houghton Mifflin Harcourt, 2010), 100.

48. The choreography began with Mary Magdalene as if being pushed on from the wings upstage, so that for the audience the impression was that she was here—then

gone—then there in another wing—then gone. Then suddenly, as if magically, Christ appeared in the center of the stage in a pool of light. And because everyone's attention had been on her he had entered unseen. Irina was watching from the wings and she froze with fear when the dancer portraying Christ knelt down to Mary's feet. "The audience exploded with applause," she said at this sign that no one is without sin. Backstage, however, the director of the Philharmony Theater handed Yakobson a note warning him that if he ever dared to show such a thing without permission again he would be fired.

49. These film fragments are in the Irina Yakobson Archives, Special Collections and University Archives, Stanford University.

50. Lvov-Anokhin, *O balete.*

51. I. Yakobson interview, April 11, 1999.

52. Russian Wikipedia article on khudsovet, ru.wikipedia.org/wiki/Художественный_совет (accessed February 01, 2014).

53. I. Yakobson interview, April 11, 1999.

54. Makarova, *A Dance Autobiography,* 65.

55. Ibid., 68.

56. Yakobson, "Beseda vtoraya—Problema Khoreograficheskovo yazïka" [Second conversation: The problem of choreographic language], in *Pisma Noverru* [Letters to Noverre] (Tenafly, NJ: Hermitage, 2001), 298.

57. Ibid., 302.

58. Ibid., 303.

59. The term Stakhanovism denotes a worker in the Soviet Union who dramatically surpassed his production quota. The Stakhanovite movement was named after Aleksei Stakhanov, who had mined 102 tons of coal in less than six hours (fourteen times his quota).

60. Kaganovsky, *How the Soviet Man Was Unmade,* 7.

61. Ibid., n.p.

Chapter Seven. A Company of His Own

1. This cultural institution served as a meeting point for writers, painters, and other artists but was never really used as a theater proper.

2. This is a reference to Elizabeth Pond's remark about the Cold War; see Elizabeth Pond, "Europe in the 21st Century," *American Diplomacy,* April 2000, http://www.unc.edu/depts/diplomat/AD_Issues/amdipl_15/pond_15.html (accessed February 3, 2014).

3. Nina Alovert, interview with Janice Ross, April 19, 2012, New York City, unpublished data in author's possession.

4. Vladimir Ilyich Lenin, "Our Foreign and Domestic Position and Party Tasks," speech delivered to the Moscow Gubernia Conference of the R. C. P. (B.),

November 21, 1920, in *Collected Works,* vol. 31 (Moscow: Progress Publishers, 1965), 419.

5. Valeriy Zvezdochkin, "Sudba novatora" [The innovator's lot], *Teatralnaya zhizn* 9, no. 738 (May 1989): 19.

6. Ibid., 20.

7. Igor Moiseyev, of course, directed his folk ballet company but his repertoire was almost exclusively his theatricalized restagings of international folk dances.

8. Irina Yakobson, "Zhizn i sudba" [Life and fate], in Nataliya Zozulina, *Teatr Leonida Yakobsona: Stati Vospominaniya Fotomateriali* [The theater of Leonid Yakobson: Articles, reminiscences, photographs] (Saint Petersburg: Liki Rossii, 2010), 13, 14.

9. Irina Yakobson, interview with Janice Ross, April 26, 2012, Haifa, Israel, unpublished data in author's possession.

10. Yakobson, "Zhizn i sudba," 14.

11. Leonid Yakobson, "Beseda v LOVTO" [Talk at the meeting of LOVTO—Leningrad Branch of All-Russian Theatrical Association], December 21, 1970, Irina Yakobson's private collection (unpublished material).

12. Tatyana Kvasova, interview with Janice Ross, July 7, 2012, Saint Petersburg, unpublished data in author's possession.

13. Ibid.

14. Yakobson, "Zhizn i sudba," 15.

15. Yakobson, "Beseda v LOVTO."

16. Ibid.

17. Ibid.

18. Yakobson, "Zhizn i sudba," 17.

19. A supporter who wished to remain anonymous, interview with Janice Ross, July 8, 2003, Saint Petersburg, unpublished data in author's possession.

20. Ian Frazier, "Letter from Saint Petersburg: Invented City," *New Yorker* 79, no. 20 (July 28, 2003): 41.

21. Irina Yakobson, interview with Janice Ross, September 30, 2004, Haifa, Israel, unpublished data in author's possession.

22. Lyudmila Seryozhnikova, " 'Trebuetsya malenkaya solistka . . .' " [A small soloist needed . . .], in Zozulina, *Teatr Leonida Yakobsona,* 114.

23. Elena Selivanova, " 'Nu i stupay k svoemu Yakobsonu!' " ["Then go to your Yakobson!"], in Zozulina, *Teatr Leonida Yakobsona,* 122–123.

24. Yakobson, "Zhizn i sudba," 18.

25. Valentina Klimova, "Maksimalizm kak osoznannaya neobhodimost" [Maximalism as calculated necessity], in Zozulina, *Teatr Leonida Yakobsona,* 136.

26. Leonid Yakobson to Irina Yakobson, October 7, 1971, Irina Yakobson's private collection (unpublished material). Emphasis added.

27. Yakobson to Irina Yakobson, n.d. (1971), Irina Yakobson's private collection (unpublished material).

28. Yakobson, "Beseda v LOVTO."

29. Aleksandr Stepin, "Tochno atomnïy reactor . . ." [A nuclear reactor precisely . . .], in Zozulina, *Teatr Leonida Yakobsona*, 128.

30. Irina Yakobson, interview with Janice Ross, October 30, 2010, Haifa, Israel, unpublished data in author's possession.

31. Yakobson, quoted in Zozulina, *Teatr Leonida Yakobsona*, 87.

32. Valeriy Sergeyev, "Baletmeyster, geniy, evrey . . ." [Choreographer, genius, Jew . . .], in Zozulina, *Teatr Leonida Yakobsona*, 95.

33. I. Yakobson interview, April 26, 2012.

34. Since 2007 this has been known as the Mikhaylovsky Theater.

35. I. Yakobson, telephone interview with Janice Ross, October 30, 2010, unpublished data in author's possession; Alla Osipenko, interview with Janice Ross, July 7, 2012, Saint Petersburg, unpublished data in author's possession.

36. Fedor Lopukhov to Leonid Yakobson, October 14, 1970, Irina Yakobson's private collection (unpublished material).

37. Lyudmila Putinova, "Perst sudbï" [The finger of destiny], in Zozulina, *Teatr Leonida Yakobsona,* 144–145.

38. Ibid., 145.

39. Maya Plisetskaya, in Boris Lvov-Anokhin, *O balete* [On ballet], television program on videotape, Central Television of the USSR, n.d, Yakobson Collection, Special Collections and University Archives, Stanford University.

40. Lvov-Anokhin, *O balete.*

41. A. Makarov, *Leonid Veniaminoch Jacobson,* trans. Nina Luskin, n.d., unpublished data in author's possession; Nikita Dolgushin, interview with Janice Ross, June 8, 2000, New Orleans, unpublished data in author's possession.

42. Selivanova, "'Nu i stupay k svoemu Yakobsonu!,'" 123.

43. Sergeyev, "'Baletmeyster, geniy, evrey . . . ,'" 99.

44. Yakobson, interview with N. Kuzmichev and N. Plekhanova, "Moya bitva za novuyu khoreografiyu" [My battle for a new choreography], *Yunost* 12 (1971): 98.

45. Seryozhnikova, "Trebuetsya malenkaya solistka . . . ," 113.

46. Ibid.

47. This troupe, which ceased operating after a couple of years, was separate and independent from the Leonid Yakobson Saint Petersburg State Academic Theater.

48. Seryozhnikova, "'Trebuetsya malenkaya solistka . . . ,'" 114.

49. I. Yakobson interview, September 30, 2004.

50. Vladimir Zenzinov, interview with Janice Ross, July 6, 2012, Saint Petersburg, unpublished data in author's possession.

51. Alexander Borovsky, "Closer to the Body," in Diane Neumaier, *Beyond Memory: Soviet Nonconformist Photography and Photo-Related Works of Art* (New Brunswick, NJ: Jane Voorhees Zimmerli Art Museum, 2004), 78.

52. Ramsay Burt, *The Male Dancer: Bodies, Spectacle, Sexualities* (London: Routledge, 1995), 53.

53. Borovsky, "Closer to the Body," 80.

54. Ibid.

55. When mentioned in Russian sources (including Zvezdochkin's book), this piece usually appears as the second in the 1958 series of the first three Rodin pieces. In Irina's list it is third (after *Despair* and *The Eternal Spring*).

56. Stylistically this also aligns Yakobson's later *Rodin* miniatures with the unembellished simplicity of the austere style a painter like Popkov was using in works such as *A Couple*.

57. Borovsky, "Closer to the Body," 82.

58. Ekaterina Degot (Dyogot), "The Copy Is the Crime: Unofficial Art and the Appropriation of Official Photography," in Neumaier, *Beyond Memory*, 113.

59. Ida Eidelman, interview with Vera Eidelman, July 2004, Boston (unpublished data).

60. Sofiya Bresler, interview with Vera Eidelman, July 2004, Boston (unpublished data).

61. A broadcast of the episode is available at http://ru.wikipedia.org/wiki/B_CCCP _секса_нет (accessed February 12, 2014).

62. Debora L. Silverman, *Art Nouveau in Fin-de-Siècle France* (Berkeley: University of California Press, 1989), 252.

63. David Getsy, *Rodin: Sex and the Making of Modern Sculpture* (New Haven: Yale University Press, 2010), 26.

64. Valeriy Zvezdochkin, *Tvorchestvo Leonida Yakobsona* [Creative work of Leonid Yakobson] (Saint Petersburg: Sankt-Peterburgskiy gumanitarnïy universitet profsoyuzov, 2007), 155, 157.

65. The Sovetskaya encyclopaedia entry on the Choreographic Miniatures company (http://www.ballet-enc.ru/html/h/horeografi4eskie-miniat7r3.html) gives the following years for the Rodin pieces: *The Eternal Spring, The Kiss, The Eternal Idol* (all in 1958), *Despair* (1964), *Paolo and Francesca, Minotaur and Nymph* (both in 1971), and *Ecstasy* (1972).

66. The music of Debussy and Ravel had been made acceptable briefly on the Soviet stage during the Thaw under Khrushchev from the mid-1950s to the mid-1960s; censorship, especially of music in the USSR, eased and previously concealed musical scores by composers like Debussy, Ravel, and Schoenberg became available.

67. Zvezdochkin, "Sudba novatora," 19.

68. Alexandra Danilova, *Choura: The Memoirs of Alexandra Danilova* (New York: Knopf, 1986), 58.

69. Zvezdochkin, *Tvorchestvo Leonida Yakobsona*, 155; the Sovetskaya encyclopedia 1981 article on Choreographic miniatures (http://www.ballet-enc.ru/html/h/horeo grafi4eskie-miniat7r3.html, accessed February 03, 2014).

70. Osipenko interview, July 7, 2012.

71. Putinova, "Perst sudbï," 147.

72. I. Yakobson interview, September 30, 2004.

73. Yakobson, "Beseda v LOVTO."

74. André Lepecki, "Undoing the Fantasy of the (Dancing) Subject: 'Still Acts' in Jérôme Bel's *The Last Performance*," in Steven de Belder and Koen Tachelet, *The Salt of the Earth: On Dance, Politics and Reality* (Brussels: Vlaams Theater Instituut, 2001).

Chapter Eight. Totalitarianism, Uncertainty, and Ballet

Epigraph: Tatyana Kvasova, interview with Vladimir Golubin, "Vospominaniya o budu-shchem" [Recollections of the future], *Muzikalnaya zhin* 16, no. 786 (August 1990): 6.

1. Valentina Klimova, "Maksimalizm kak osoznannaya neobhodimost" [Maximalism as calculated necessity], in Nataliya Zozulina, *Teatr Leonida Yakobsona: Stati vospominaniya fotomateriali* [The theater of Leonid Yakobson: Articles, reminiscences, photographs] (Saint Petersburg: Liki Rossii, 2010), 133.

2. Lyudmila Seryozhnikova, "Trebuetsya malenkaya solistka . . ." [A small soloist needed . . .], in Zozulina, *Teatr Leonida Yakobsona,* 110–111.

3. Aleksandr Stepin, "Tochno atomnïy reactor . . ." [A nuclear reactor precisely . . .], in Zozulina, *Teatr Leonida Yakobsona,* 129, 130.

4. Emily Hite, interview with Janice Ross, May 13, 2012, Stanford, CA, unpublished data in author's possession.

5. Valeriy Zvezdochkin, *Tvorchestvo Leonida Yakobsona* [The creative work of Leonid Yakobson] (Saint Petersburg: Sankt-Peterburgskiy gumanitarnïy universitet profsoyuzov, 2007), 185.

6. PBS *Dance in America* special broadcast, "Trailblazers of Modern Dance," directed by Merrill Brockway and Judy Kinberg, produced by WNET New York, 1977.

7. Klimova, "Maksimalizm kak osoznannaya neobhodimost," 132.

8. The 1997 encyclopaedia *Russian Ballet* in its article on Yakobson (http://www.pro-ballet.ru/html/8/8kobson.html, accessed February 07, 2014) states that in 1971–1972 Yakobson staged *Distraught Dictator* to a fragment of Shostakovich's *Ninth Symphony,* that it was subsequently named *Distraught Dictator,* and that it was shown publicly only in 1985.

9. Natalie Zundelevich, "Revival of the Dissidents of Dance," *San Francisco Chronicle,* December 24, 1989, "Image" section, 18.

10. Ibid., 18–19.

11. Ibid., 19.

12. Leonid Yakobson, interview with N. Kuzmichev and N. Plekhanova, "Moya bitva za novuyu khoreografiyu" [My battle for a new choreography], *Yunost* 12 (1971): 98, 99.

13. Tatyana Kvasova, interview with Janice Ross, July 7, 2012, Saint Petersburg, unpublished data in author's possession.

14. Yakobson, "Beseda v LOVTO" [Talk at the meeting of LOVTO—Leningrad branch of the All-Russian Theatrical Association], December 21, 1970, Irina Yakobson's private collection (unpublished material).

15. I. Yakobson, "Zhizn i sudba" [Life and fate], in Zozulina, *Teatr Leonida Yakobsona,* 15–16.

16. Jack Miller, *Jews in Soviet Culture* (New Brunswick, NJ: Transaction Books, 1984), 89.

17. Yakobson to Comrade L. I. Brezhnev, 1972, Irina Yakobson's private collection (unpublished material).

18. This may have been only one reason for the demotion. It is also said that Khrushchev was easily fascinated with people but also easily disappointed in them. He is also said not to have wanted to have in the Central Committee the members who had ever (and especially in 1957) helped him stay in power (Furtseva included), because that's how they were to a certain degree in control of him.

19. The Russian Wikipedia article on Furtseva (http://ru.wikipedia.org/wiki /Фурцева,_Екатерина_Алексеевна, accessed February 7, 2014) states that she served as the member of the Politburo until October 17, 1961, that is, more than a year after she had become the minister of culture. Some other Russian sites say she was simultaneously demoted from the Politburo and appointed minister of culture (on May 4, 1960).

20. Ekaterina Furtseva and Yakobson, in I. Yakobson, "Zhizn i sudba," 17.

21. Sally Banes, "Goleizovsky's Ballet Manifestos," *Ballet Review* 11, no. 3 (Fall 1983): 73.

22. Fyodor Lopukhov, "Analiticheskiy otchet=razbor khoreograficheskikh miniatyur L. Yakobsona, Yu. Vzorova, G. Aleesidze, N. Markaryantsa, Mayorova, K. Boyarskovo, Zamuelya, Eyfmana, Elizarova i dr. sikh ispolnitelyami" (Analysis: Report about Leonid Yakobson's Choreographic Miniatures, his performers and serious issues, Yu. Vzorova, G. Aleesidze, N. Markaryantsa, Mayorova, K. Boyarskovo, Zamuelya, Eyfmana, Elizarova, and others), 1971, A. A. Bakhrushin State Central Theatre Museum, Moscow (unpublished material).

23. Alla Osipenko, interview with Janice Ross, July 7, 2012, Saint Petersburg, unpublished data in author's possession.

24. An article in the *Peterburgian Theater Journal* (http://ptj.spb.ru/archive/35/music -theatre-35/yakobson/, accessed February 7, 2014) recounts that the "historic date of the Yakobson anniversary gathered together all his former comrades-in-arms and they were given the opportunity to speak about the Master: from January 19 to 20, 2004, at the House of Actors [Dom aktyora] the conference 'Leonid Yakobson—artist, choreographer, thinker' took place. In the Karelian Living Room [Karelskaya Gostinaya] of the House of Actors of the Union of Theater

Workers [Dom aktyora STD] in Saint Petersburg convened those who knew Yakobson personally and collaborated with him."

25. Kvasova interview, July 7, 2012.

26. This article on the film from the 2004 Lenfilm catalogue (http://lenfilm.aca
demic.ru/1261/ХОРЕОГРАФИЧЕСКИЕ_МИНИАТЮРЫ, accessed February
7, 2014) states that the film was awarded both The Golden Nymph award at the
Monte-Carlo Television Festival (1961) and the Honorary award at the Montreux
Television Festival (1961).

27. I. Yakobson, "Zhizn i sudba," 18–19.

28. Leonid Yakobson, interview with N. Kuzmichev and N. Plekhanova, "Moya
bitva za novuyu khoreografiyu" [My battle for a new choreography], *Yunost* 12
(1971): n.p.

29. Nina Alovert, interview with Janice Ross, April 19, 2012, New York City, unpublished data in author's possession.

30. The six ballets are *Contrasts, Ebony Concert, Troika, Fire-Bird, Dead Tsarevna,* and
Traveling Circus.

31. Peter J. Schmelz, *Such Freedom, if Only Musical: Unofficial Soviet Music during the
Thaw* (New York: Oxford University Press, 2009), 59–60.

32. Arvo Pärt, interview with Jamie McCarthy, quoted in ibid., 65.

33. Galina Dobrovolskaya, "Yakobson, Leonid," in Selma Jeanne Cohen, *International Encyclopedia of Dance,* vol. 1 (New York: Oxford University Press, 1998),
412.

34. Anonymous supporter, interview with Janice Ross, July 8, 2003, Saint Petersburg, unpublished data in author's possession.

35. The title comes from a poem by Arthur Rimbaud.

36. Yuri Lyubimov, in Leyla Guchmazova, "Poyushchie vmeste" [Singing together],
Itogi 51, no. 810 (December, 12, 2011).

37. Ibid.

38. Schmelz, *Such Freedom, if Only Musical,* 63.

39. Lyubimov, in Guchmazova, "Poyushchie vmeste."

40. Lyubimov, interview with Anna Veligzhanina, "Yuri Lyubimov: 'Ona bïla ne na
svoem meste. No ochen staralas'" [Yuri Lyubimov: "She was out of place. But
she cared a lot"], *Komsomolskaya pravda,* November 17, 2011.

41. Leonid Yakobson to Irina Yakobson, January 26, 1975, Irina Yakobson's private
collection (unpublished material).

42. Ibid.

43. Ibid.

44. Ibid.

45. Lyubimov, in Guchmazova, "Poyushchie vmeste."

46. Lyubimov, e-mail interview with Janice Ross via Sergey Lavrentyev, January 5,
2014, Moscow, unpublished data in author's possession.

47. Irina Yakobson, interview with Janice Ross, January 5, 2000, San Francisco, unpublished data in author's possession.

48. Ibid.

49. Igor Belsky graduated from the Leningrad Choreographic Institute and had a career both in the Kirov and as the pedagogue (and later as the artistic director).

50. Irina Yakobson, interview with Janice Ross, October 31, 2010, Haifa, Israel, unpublished data in author's possession.

51. I. Yakobson interview, January 5, 2000.

52. I. Yakobson interview, October 31, 2010.

53. Yakobson, libretto for *The Cowboys,* 1974, A. A. Bakhrushin State Central Theatre Museum, Moscow (unpublished material).

54. Irina Yakobson, interview with Janice Ross, April 2, 2000, San Francisco, unpublished data in author's possession.

55. I. Yakobson interview, October 31, 2010.

56. Boris Ruchkan to Leonid Yakobson, Leonid Yakobson collection, A. A. Bakhrushin State Central Theatre Museum, Moscow (unpublished material).

57. Gruppa tovarishchey (A group of friends), "L. V. Yakobson," *Vecherniy Leningrad* (Evening Leningrad), October 20, 1975.

58. I. Yakobson interview, October 31, 2010.

59. Arkadiy Ivanenko, interview with Janice Ross, July 4, 2012, Saint Petersburg, unpublished data in author's possession.

60. Zvezdochkin, *Tvorchestvo Leonida Yakobsona,* 5.

61. Valeriy Zvezdochkin, "Tvorchestvo Leonida Yakobsona" [The theater scene], *Issue* 9, no. 738 (May 1989): 5.

62. Ibid., 6.

63. Irina Yakobson, interview with Janice Ross, April 2, 2000, San Francisco, unpublished data in author's possession.

Epilogue

1. Irina Yakobson, interview with Janice Ross, December 7, 2010, Hamburg, Germany, unpublished data in author's possession.

2. Vladimir Zenzinov, interview with Janice Ross, July 6, 2012, Saint Petersburg, unpublished data in author's possession.

3. Irina Yakobson, interview with Janice Ross, September 30, 2004, Haifa, Israel, unpublished data in author's possession.

4. Yuri Slezkine, *The Jewish Century* (Princeton, NJ: Princeton University Press, 2004), 357.

5. Evgeniya Popova, interview with Janice Ross, July 7, 2012, Saint Petersburg, unpublished data in author's possession.

6. Ibid.

7. Ibid.

8. Olga Levitan, interview with Janice Ross, November 11, 2010, Jerusalem, unpublished data in author's possession.

9. Diana Taylor, *The Archive and the Repertoire: Performing Cultural Memory in the Americas* (Durham, NC: Duke University Press, 2003), 1–52.

10. W. Bruce Lincoln, *Between Heaven and Hell: The Story of a Thousand Years of Artistic Life in Russia* (New York: Viking, 1998), 448.

11. Ibid., 449.

12. Aleksandr Solzhenitsyn, quoted in ibid., 450.

13. Irina Yakobson, interview with Janice Ross, October 30, 2010, Haifa, Israel, unpublished data in author's possession.

14. Valeriy Sergeyev, interview with Janice Ross, December 15, 2013, Saint Petersburg, unpublished data in author's possession.

15. "This brief dance outing for Shostakovich is, I feel, mistaken. Whatever the merits of the scores, the ballets (even with Leningrad Symphony as focus) are choreographic revenants rather than flesh-and-blood dance." Clement Crisp, "Shostakovich Majors on Nostalgia," review of Mariinsky Theater's *Leningrad Symphony, The Lady and the Hooligan,* and *The Bedbug, Financial Times,* July 28, 2006.

16. Valeriy Zvezdochkin, "Tvorets" [The creator], introduction to Leonid Yakobson, *Pisma Noverru* [Letters to Noverre] (Tenafly, NJ: Hermitage, 2001), 8.

17. Ibid., 31.

18. Irina Yakobson, interview with Janice Ross, December 11, 2006, Haifa, Israel, unpublished data in author's possession.

19. Andrian Fadeyev, interview with Janice Ross, July 6, 2012, Saint Petersburg, unpublished data in author's possession.

20. Ibid.

21. Darya Pavlenko, interview with Janice Ross, July 4, 2012, Saint Petersburg, unpublished data in author's possession.

22. Aleksandr Sergeyev, interview with Janice Ross, July 4, 2012, Saint Petersburg, unpublished data in author's possession.

23. The largest holdings of Yakobson's materials are in the Bakhrushin Museum in Moscow. The items that Irina Yakobson brought with her to the West have been divided between the New York Public Library and Janice Ross, who donated them to the San Francisco Museum of Performance and Design and the Stanford University Libraries.

24. Slezkine, *Jewish Century,* 358.

25. Helgi Tomasson, in Janice Ross, "Irina Jakobson Comes to San Francisco: A Survivor's Story," *Dancemagazine* 62 (April 1988): 78.

26. Natalia Makarova, in Ross, "Irina Jakobson Comes to San Francisco," 78.

27. Yakobson, "Za baletmeysterskuyu smenu!" [For a new generation in choreography!], *Rabochiy i teatr* 39 (April 29, 1929): 2.

NOTES TO PAGES 431-434

28. T. S. Eliot, *Four Quartets* (New York: Harcourt, Brace, 1943), 39.
29. Yakobson, "Khoreografiya—Iskusstvo slozhnoye" [Choreography—A complex art], in Yakobson, *Pisma Noverru*, 366, 367.
30. Ibid.
31. Nadya Timofeyeva, interview with Janice Ross, December 14, 2010, Jerusalem, unpublished data in author's possession.
32. Ibid.

Acknowledgments

My first thanks must go to Irina Yakobson, Leonid Yakobson's widow, who opened her memories, friendships, archives, and rehearsals to me, generously sharing everything she brought to the West from her late husband's personal archives. This included videos of his dances, unpublished and published writings, letters, photographs, programs, and clippings. She participated generously in countless interviews, lunches, and telephone conversations during the more than fifteen years I worked on this project. She permitted me to film her as she restaged Yakobson's *Vestris* and *Pas de Quatre* and to observe her teaching and coaching the dancers of San Francisco Ballet and Hamburg Ballet. Her sister, Anna Klimentenko, a former professor in the Academy of Sciences in Moscow, generously translated documents and, as Irina aged and her preferred language reverted to Russian, Anna generously and tirelessly translated for us.

I owe an enormous debt of gratitude to Lynn Garafola for her insightful criticisms on earlier drafts of the manuscript and for her generous foreword. Tim Scholl,

Marion Kant, Mindy Aloff, and two anonymous readers also offered discerning comments. I am especially thankful to Ann Daly, who offered essential encouragement at many critical moments in the life of this project. I am very grateful to the many individuals whose work and lives intersected with Yakobson and his remarkable choreography and who generously shared their memories with me. These individuals include Nina Alovert, Mikhail Baryshnikov, Mikhail Bresler, Sofiya Bresler, Nikita Dolgushin, Ida Eidelman, Boris Eifman, Andrian Fadeyev, Charles France, Tatyana Kvasova, Greta Levert, Olga Levitan, Yuri Lyubimov, Natalia Makarova, Alla Osipenko, Valery Panov, Galina Panova, Darya Pavlenko, Wendy Perron, Yuri Petukhov, Maya Plisetskaya, Evgeniya Popova, Anatoly Pronin, Aleksandr Sergeyev, Valeriy Sergeyev, Elizabeth Souritz, Nadya Timofeyeva, Helgi Tomasson, Vladimir Zenzinov, and Nataliya Zozulina. I also thank the photographers who allowed me to use their work: Nina Alovert, V. Nikitin, Anatoly Pronin, Tatyana Ribakova, and Vladimir Zenzinov. I extend appreciation as well to the remarkable translators and researchers who assisted me—Marina Brodskaya, Sergey Lavrentyev, Nina Luskin, Ruth Rischin, and Evgeniya Rodina.

I owe a very special thanks to Ljubisa Matic for his meticulous and tireless research, translations, and fact-checking over the final years of this project, and to Emily Hite for her assistance with myriad details including manuscript and photograph preparation. I am very thankful to the director and archivists of the A. A. Bakhrushin State Central Theatre Museum in Moscow, the St. Petersburg Museum of Theatrical and Musical Art, the Russian State Archive of Literature and Art, the archives of the Mariinsky Theater, the library of the Bolshoi Theater, the archives of the Saint Petersburg State Academic Ballet Theater of Leonid Yakobson, as well as the Jerome Robbins Dance Division of the New York Public Library and the San Francisco Museum of Performance and Design, for giving me access to their archives. Glen Worthey, digital humanities librarian at the Stanford University Libraries, was helpful in arranging for the transfer of Yakobson's fragile VHS tapes into DVDs and the scanning of Yakobson's photographs. Thanks also to Warren Hellman and the Memorial Foundation for Jewish Culture, both of whom generously supported my early research on Yakobson.

I would like to give profound thanks to the Stanford Humanities Center and particularly its director, Aron Rodrigue, for a fellowship during the 2012–2013 academic year that allowed me time to research and to test out ideas among a remarkable community of scholars. A Fulbright fellowship to Israel in 2010–2011 was also critical to my completion of this project, enabling me to conduct a final round of interviews with Irina Yakobson, her sister, Anna Klimentenko, and Jews from the former Soviet Union, now living in Israel, who remembered Yakobson vividly.

I cannot conclude without expressing my gratitude to my editors at Yale University Press, foremost among them Steve Wasserman, for his faith in the merit of the project, Susan Laity, Julie Carlson, for her masterful editing, and Erica Hanson, for shepherding the manuscript and photographs. My gratitude and love to my daughter, Maya, my late son, Josh, and my husband, Keith, who succumbed to cancer just as this manuscript was being edited. I extend to them my final and eternal thanks for their love and support over the years.

Index

Page numbers in *italics* indicate illustrations.